# Management Science
## An Introduction

## Note to the Student

Dear Student,

If you winced when you learned the price of this textbook, you are experiencing what is known as "sticker shock" in today's economy. Yes, textbooks are expensive, and we don't like it anymore than you do. Many of us here at Kent have sons and daughters of our own attending college, or we are attending school part time ourselves. However, the prices of our books are dictated by the cost factors involved in producing them. The costs of paper, designing the book, setting it in type, printing it, and binding it have risen significantly each year along with everything else in our economy. You might find the following table to be of some interest.

| Item | 1967 Price | 1984 Price | The Price Increase |
|------|-----------|-----------|--------------------|
| Monthly Housing Expense | $114.31 | $686.46 | 6.0 times |
| Monthly Automobile Expense | 82.69 | 339.42 | 4.1 times |
| Loaf of Bread | .22 | 1.00 | 4.6 times |
| Pound of Hamburger | .39 | 1.48 | 3.8 times |
| Pound of Coffee | .59 | 2.45 | 4.2 times |
| Candy Bar | .10 | .35 | 3.5 times |
| Gasoline | .35 | 1.20 | 3.4 times |
| Men's Dress Shirt | 5.00 | 25.00 | 5.0 times |
| Postage | .05 | .22 | 4.4 times |
| Resident College Tuition | 294.00 | 1,581.00 | 5.4 times |

Today's prices of college textbooks have increased only about 2.8 times 1967 prices. Compare your texts sometime to a general trade book, i.e., a novel or nonfiction book, and you will easily see significant differences in the internal design, quality of paper, and binding. These features of college textbooks cost money.

Textbooks should not be looked on only as an expense. Other than your professors, your textbooks are your most important source for what you hope to learn in college. What's more, the textbooks you keep can be valuable resources in your future career and life. They are the foundation of your professional library. Like your education, your textbooks are one of your most important investments.

We are concerned, and we care. Please write to us at the address below with your comments. We want to be responsive to your suggestions, to give you quality textbooks, and to do everything in our power to keep their prices under control.

*Wayne Barcomb*

Wayne A. Barcomb
President

Kent Publishing Company
20 Park Plaza
Boston, MA 02116

# Management Science

## An Introduction

**K. Roscoe Davis**
University of Georgia

**Patrick G. McKeown**
University of Georgia

**Terry R. Rakes**
University of South Carolina

**Kent Publishing Company**
**A Division of Wadsworth, Inc.**
**Boston, Massachusetts**

Senior Editor: John B. McHugh
Production Editor: Linda A. Belamarich
Production Coordinator: Marcia A. Stanczyk
Interior Design: Jean Hammond
Cover Design: Steve Snider

Kent Publishing Company
20 Park Plaza, Boston, MA 02116
A Divison of Wadsworth, Inc.

Printed in the United States of America

1 2 3 4 5 6 7 8 9—89 88 87 86

**Library of Congress Cataloging in Publication Data**

Davis, K. Roscoe, 1940–
  Management science.

  Includes index.
  1.  Industrial management—Mathematical models.
2.  Operations research.  I. McKeown, Patrick G.,
1943–      II. Rakes, Terry R.  III. Title.
HD30.25.D37    1985    658.4'034    85-23867
ISBN 0-534-06006-4

To

Halaine, Kevin, and Kimberly
K.R.D.

Carolyn, Ashley, and Christopher
P.G.M.

Gale, Amanda, and Stephanie
T.R.R.

# About the Authors

**K. Roscoe Davis** is Professor and Head of Management Sciences at the University of Georgia. He earned his B.S. and M.S. degrees at Louisiana Polytechnic Institute, and his Ph.D. at North Texas State University. He has published extensively in journals such as *Management Science; OMEGA: The International Journal of Management Sciences; Decision Sciences; Interfaces; Computers and Operations Research.* In addition to this text, he is the author of *Quantitative Models for Management,* (Kent Publishing Company, 1984); and *Accounting Information Systems* (Prentice-Hall, 1983). He is a fellow in the American Institute for Decision Sciences and is currently a vice president of that organization. In addition, he is past president of the Southeast American Institute for Decision Sciences, the past president of the southeastern chapter of The Institute of Management Sciences (TIMS), and is active in several other professional organizations, including the American Production and Inventory Control Society (APICS). He has more than ten years of industrial experience in the electronics field with Texas Instruments, Inc., and Honeywell, Inc. He has also served as a consultant to several organizations, including Radio Corporation of America (RCA), Texas Instruments, Inc., and International Business Machines Corporation (IBM).

**Patrick G. McKeown** is Professor of Management Science at the University of Georgia. He earned his B.A.E. and M.S.I.M. degrees from the Georgia Institute of Technology and his Ph.D. in Business Administration from the University of North Carolina at Chapel Hill. He was a faculty member at the State University of New York at Albany and at New York University. He has worked for Lockheed-Georgia Company, Marietta, Georgia, and Systems Planning Associates of Durham, North Carolina, and has served as a consultant to various organizations such as Oak Ridge National Laboratories, F.S. James Company, Little Rock Land Company, and the U.S. Census Bureau. He is the author of four other textbooks, including *Living with Computers* and *Structured Programming Using FORTRAN 77* (Harcourt Brace Jovanovich, 1984) and *Quantitative Models for Management* (Kent Publishing Company, 1984). He has presented papers at numerous conferences, and his work has appeared in a variety of professional journals including *Management Science; Operations Research; Mathematical Programming; Interfaces; Naval Research Logistics Quarterly; Computers and Operations Research; Journal of Risk and Insurance; Journal of the American Real Estate and Urban Economics Association;* and the SIAM *Journal of Scientific and Statistical Computing.*

**Terry R. Rakes** is an Associate Professor of Management Science at the University of South Carolina. He earned his B.S., M.B.A., and Ph.D. at Virginia Polytechnic Institute and State University. He has published extensively in journals such as *Management Science; Operations Research Letters; Computers & Operations Research; Information & Management; OMEGA: The International Journal of*

*Management Science; International Journal of Production Research; Socio-Economic Planning Sciences.* He is currently the program chairperson for the southeastern chapter of the American Institute for Decision Sciences, and is a past president of the southeastern chapter of The Institute of Management Sciences (TIMS). He has close to ten years of experience in teaching management science methods, and has won several teaching awards. He is also active in continuing education, and has worked as a consultant to several organizations.

# Preface

Since the emergence of management science/operations research (MS/OR) as a discipline in the 1940s, the application of these techniques has spread to encompass almost every facet of modern business management and decision making. The inevitable impact of this on business education is that management science has become an integral part of business curricula, and a host of textbooks dealing with the subject have been written.

We wrote this text because we felt that we could, in many respects, improve upon what has been written in the past. Three major pedagogical issues that have influenced the writing of this text are: (1) the role of the computer in teaching management science, (2) the matching of presentation style to the audience of the text, and (3) the necessary content to accommodate a variety of instructor styles and syllabi.

Every instructor who has ever taught an introductory course on management science has been asked, Why are we spending time to learn about management science when the computer can do all of this for us? How well the instructor fields this question may determine whether the class becomes a motivated learning group or a disinterested mass. The answer to this question lies in the fact that every decision problem involves three stages of effort: (1) problem formulation (or model development), (2) solution of the problem, and (3) interpretation and testing of the solution results. While current computer software and computer-based decision support systems are very useful for mathematical computation and problem solution, few are able to provide much assistance in either the formulation of the problem or the interpretation of the results. The computer generates solutions for a wide variety of input parameters, but lacks interpretive judgment about these solutions. In effect, the computer still plays the same role as a calculator or a paper and pencil; it is a tool in the decision-making cycle. We are not trying to downplay the importance of the computer, since most contemporary management science problems could not be solved without one. However, we do not think that the role of the trained decision-maker should be downplayed, since his or her role is just as crucial. The bottom line is that an individual who is well-trained in management science techniques can very quickly adapt to user-friendly management-science computer software, while the best software available cannot help a decision-maker who does not understand these techniques.

Given this belief, there are two approaches that could be taken. The first is to use computer output liberally in the text and attempt to integrate the presentation of formulation and interpretation with commercial computer codes for solving the problems. The problem here is that there is little standardization of computer hardware and software at colleges and universities. This makes this approach completely useful only at those schools that have hardware that can run the code used in the text. The other approach is to concentrate in the text on the management-science issues and defer the computer integration to the instructor, who can choose computer software that is compatible with available hardware and with syllabus design. We have chosen the latter approach.

The second issue of presentation style and audience is highly related to the first issue of the role of the computer. Since the computer will continue to be the prime method of problem solution, it is our belief that the vast majority of future managers and engineers will be involved in the formulation and interpretation stages, with the solution stage left to the computer and individuals who have specialized in MS/OR. Since this is an introductory text that will be used by business students in general, we have stressed the formulaic and interpretive aspects, and have used small cases at the beginning of all chapters except the review chapters to help illustrate these aspects.

Our emphasis on formulation and interpretation does not mean that we have ignored the problem-solution stage. If the text is to be used in an upper-level course involving those students majoring in MS/OR, the solution methodologies will be an important part of the coverage. We have attempted to provide the maximum flexibility by presenting the solution methodologies in such a way that the instructor may, if he or she so chooses, exclude them without detracting from the presentation of the other two decision stages.

The third issue is that of content. In an effort to make the text useful to as wide an audience as possible, we have included chapters on most topics normally considered to fall within the area of MS/OR. In order to keep the presentation simple and make the text readable, we have tried to keep the chapters short and make the presentation concise. Consequently, the text should be appropriate for a variety of different syllabi.

In terms of organization, the book begins with an introduction to management science, and then illustrates the concept of modeling using chapters on breakeven analysis and forecasting. While a college algebra course and a probability course would be the expected prerequisites for a course using this text, we have included a review chapter on mathematics early in the text, and review chapters on probability and calculus in later chapters, in order to help those who did not retain all that they should from those courses, and to make the text a single-source reference for those students.

Chapters 5 through 8 introduce the foundations of deterministic models through the topics of linear programming formulation, the simplex solution method, and sensitivity and duality. Chapters 9 through 14 explore other deterministic models, and include PERT/CPM, transportation and assignment models, other network models, goal programming, integer programming, and inventory models. Chapters 15 through 19 deal with probability models and, after a review of probability, cover the areas of decision analysis, Markov processes, and game theory. Chapters 20 and 21 discuss additional probabilistic models, and present queueing theory and simulation. Chapters 22 through 24 discuss more advanced models in terms of mathematical and computational complexity, and consist of dynamic programming, a calculus review, and a discussion of nonlinear models. The final chapter concerns model utilization, and deals with implementation issues and cautions.

In terms of order of coverage, it would be possible to cover either deterministic models or probabilistic models first. However, Chapters 5 through 8 must come before Chapters 9 through 14, Chapters 15 through 19 must come before Chapters 20 and 21, and the final chapters should be covered last. Because of the possible combinations of chapter coverage, the text could be used at several levels. While the text has been designed for the introductory undergraduate course (or two-course sequence), the inclusion of advanced concepts at the discretion of the instructor would also make the text appropriate for a course for management science majors, and possibly for the introductory MBA course as well.

This text could not have been completed without the assistance of a great many people. We wish to thank Kathy Fitzpatrick, David Pentico, Ray Souder who reviewed earlier drafts of the manuscript and made many useful suggestions. We also want to thank our Senior Editor at Kent Publishing Company, Jack McHugh, who kept us moving along, and Linda Belamarich, our Production Editor. Finally, we want to thank our families who endured many lost weekends and provided unending support during the writing of this book.

# Contents

# 3   Breakeven Analysis   52

# 4   Forecasting   72

# 5 Introduction to Linear Programming 98

# 6 Linear Programming: Model Formulations 128

# 7  LP Simplex Method  182

# 8  Sensitivity Analysis and Duality  228

# 9  PERT/CPM  258

## 10    Transportation and Assignment Models    298

## 11    Other Network Models    336

## 12    Goal Programming    360

## 13    Integer Programming    406

## 14   Inventory Models   438

# 15  Probability Review    482

# 16  Decision Models I    518

# 17  Decision Models II   546

# 18  Markov Processes   568

# 19  Game Theory   586

## 20   Queuing Analysis: Waiting Line Problems   610

# 21   Simulation   644

# 22   Dynamic Programming   684

# Appendixes    778

# Management Science
## An Introduction

1

# Introduction to Management Science

## Introduction

During the past ten years management practice has been strongly affected by management science and computer technology. Consider, for example, the following:[1]

1. The Fuels Management and Flight Control Department of National Airlines employs a fuel management and allocation model which, over a four-year period, has resulted in a multimillion-dollar saving. The model specifies the best fueling station and vendor for each flight, on the basis of prices, availability, fuel burn, flight data, and cost of tankerage. The model also uses extensive sensitivity analysis techniques to alert management as to when a new policy may be required.

2. Cahill May Roberts, a large pharmaceutical company (over $35 million in annual sales), employs a facilities and resource planning system that has achieved savings in delivery and transport cost of 23.3% and 20%, respectively, and has increased customer service levels by 60%. The planning system is used to evaluate alternative management strategies in the face of fluctuating costs and population movements. Apart from defining unique territories for the company's distribution centers and optimal customer servicing schedules within those territories, the system can be used to evaluate alternative locations for distribution centers under the twin uncertainties of cost and demand.

3. Planners of Du Page County, Wheaton, Illinois, report the use of a land use planning model for preparing a comprehensive land use plan that considers several objectives simultaneously and also satisfies constraints on desired growth patterns. The land use plan recommended by the model has resulted in a 50% reduction in the use of high-cost acreage required by alternative land use plans. The model minimizes the conflict between adjacent land uses, minimizes travel time, minimizes tax costs, minimizes adverse environmental impact, and minimizes costs of community facilities. The model can also be used to evaluate the impact of population growth and changing employment levels.

[1]These cases are actual real-world applications that were reported in *Interfaces*, Vol. 9, No. 2, Pt. 2, February 1979. Case 1: "Fuel Management and Allocation Model," D. Wayne Darnell and Carolyn Loffin, pp. 64–65; Case 2: "A Planning System for Facilities and Resources in Distribution Networks," H. Harrison, pp. 6–22; Case 3: "Development of a Comprehensive Land Use Plan by Means of a Multiple Objective Mathematical Programming Model," Deepak Bammi and Dalip Bammi, pp. 50–63.

These cases are only a few of many possible cases that illustrate the impact management science can have and has had on management and decision making. Broadly defined, *management science* is the application of scientific procedures, techniques, and tools to operating, strategic, and policy problems in order to develop and help evaluate solutions. As a discipline, management science includes all rational approaches to management decision making that are based on an application of scientific methodology.

Management science builds upon the philosophy that a large portion of decision making consists of (1) identifying and analyzing problems that can be quantified, (2) understanding relationships among interacting factors, and (3) isolating factors over which the decision maker has control. The objective of management science is to provide procedures and processes that will aid in problem solving.

Since management science is a broad subject, attention will be restricted to major aspects of the subject so that an overall understanding of general concepts can be developed. In this text we will present fundamental theoretical developments of the tools of management science; however, the emphasis will be on *problem formulation, interpretation of model* (algorithm) *output*, and *implementation*.

The basic developments in and framework of management science are presented in this chapter. Specifically, the chapter examines: (1) the *evolution of management science*, (2) the *role of model building*, (3) the *process of problem solving*, and finally (4) the *computer and management sciences*. Obviously historical factors play a role in the development of any field; this also is true of management science. However, our key objective in the chapter is not to belabor historical developments, but rather to give the reader a basic understanding of how the area evolved. The substantive matter of the chapter is included in the latter sections.

## ■ Evolution of management science

Management science is still a new term to many people even though the field had its beginnings during World War II, and the first issue of the journal entitled *Management Science* was published in October 1954.

During the early part of the twentieth century, researchers were beginning to use scientific procedures to investigate problems outside the pure sciences, but it was not until the outbreak of World War II that these efforts were brought together to work toward a common objective. In 1937, in Great Britain, a team of natural scientists, mathematicians, and engineers was assembled to study the strategic and tactical problems associated with the defense of the country. The team's objective was to determine the most effective utilization of limited military resources. The activities of this group, which was organized under the *Operational Staff* of Britain's military organization, were not referred to as management science, but rather as **operational research,** because the team was dealing with research on (military) operations.

*operational research*

The successes of the British operational research teams in many of their research efforts motivated the United States to develop similar activities. Successful activities of the United States teams included the study of complex logistical problems, the development of aircraft flight patterns, the planning of sea maneuvers, and the effective utilization of military resources.

After the war, many of those associated with operational research during the war realized that many of the same approaches and techniques applied to the military problems could be applied to industrial problems. However, it was not until computers were developed and made commercially available in the 1950s that these concepts and ideas began to appear in industry. Initially, many of the industrial problems studied, such as inventory control and transportation systems, paralleled military problems. But today one can easily find numerous cases where operational research/management science concepts have been applied to purchasing, marketing, accounting, financial planning, and other areas.

Although Great Britain is credited with initiation of operational research as a discipline, researchers in the United States have made significant contributions to its development. One of the most widely accepted mathematical techniques, the simplex method of linear programming, was developed in 1947 by an American, George B. Dantzig. This particular technique has had broad applications to many operational problems and is the basis for many other mathematical techniques, such as integer and goal programming.

In Britain, the terms *operations research* and *operational research* were used in describing developments in the field. In the United States, traditionally the terms operations research (OR) and *management science* (MS) have been used. The term management science received its initial impetus with the establishment of **The Institute of Management Sciences (TIMS)** in 1953.[2]

*The Institute of Management Sciences (TIMS)*

Although numerous applications of management science occurred in the 1950s, it was not until the early 1960s that academic programs emphasizing the field were established, and the mid-1960s arrived before individuals formally trained in management science began to emerge. Consequently formal operations research/management science staff groups did not begin to appear in industrial organizations and governmental operations until the late 1960s.

The development of formal MS/OR staff groups did not, however, lead to successful usage of management science techniques. On the contrary, many management science specialists were accused of being more interested in manipulating problems to fit techniques than in working with management to analyze problems, develop suitable solutions approaches, and develop and implement workable systems to provide the defined solutions. In retrospect, during the growth of the academic programs in management science, the focus was on the development of techniques and tools of management science rather than on applications and strategies for implementing the techniques. And while the state of the art advanced in areas associated with techniques and mathematical models, MS/OR experienced limited success with the application of techniques in its formative years.

Management science has now matured, and a great many of the implementation problems that appeared in the late 1960s and early 1970s have been overcome,

---

[2]Numerous attempts have been made to distinguish between MS and OR, but it is difficult to make any clear-cut distinction. In this text we will use the terms MS and OR interchangeably.

thanks to developments in computer technology and changing academic curriculums. Improved technique and model development, stress on implementation and application, and the availability of computers have greatly expanded the range and size of problems that can be analyzed. The development of time-sharing computer systems and microcomputers has aided in the implementation area by making it possible for decision makers to interact directly with management science models. This has resulted in reducing the need for a management science expert to interface between the manager and the management science model and has allowed the manager to explore "what if" questions in order better to understand and appreciate the potential of the model. Time-sharing systems and microcomputers have also made the power of computers available to a large number of firms, thus broadening the potential application of management science techniques.

One can gain some appreciation of the range and power of MS/OR, as well as some of its limitations, by examining both successful and unsuccessful applications. However, to appreciate fully the different aspects of MS/OR, it is necessary first to develop a basic understanding of the techniques and then to determine how they can or cannot be used in various circumstances. But before we examine some of the techniques, it is first necessary to understand the general concepts of *modeling* and *model development* better and how these relate to the field of management science.

## ■ Model building and management science

Whether it is in the private sector or the public sector, a major function of a manager is problem solving—that is, managers are problem solvers. Whether the manager realizes it or not, he or she addresses the task of problem solving primarily through model building, or modeling. Model building provides a means by which a manager can analyze and study problems and examine different alternatives.

Model building is not a new idea; the process is used daily, often unconsciously, in basic problem situations. Consider the problem of a hostess who wishes to rearrange the furniture in her living room. The objective is to have a suitable arrangement that is attractive but also functional for the bridge group that is scheduled for the evening. One approach to the problem is to visualize different arrangements of the furniture and evaluate each alternative; that is, the hostess can employ a **mental model** of the problem. A second approach would be for the hostess to ask her husband to move the furniture around the room until the arrangement suited her. This approach would likely be more suitable for several reasons: the mental model just was not manipulative enough, there were too many items to maintain mentally, or the hostess could not visualize how each arrangement would appear. One could move more toward a management science approach to the problem by developing a scale model of the room and examining different arrangements. This last approach can be used only if the hostess accepts the scale model as a valid representation of the problem.

Consider now the problem faced by a manager in charge of plant layout at a major manufacturing firm. Similar to the furniture arrangement problem, the problem of plant arrangement is difficult to solve *mentally:* the manager's image of the plant is

*mental model*

too vague, there are too many restrictions on where certain equipment and items must be located, etc. There is one difference between the two problems. The plant manager cannot afford to solve the problem by having a group of employees try four or five different arrangements, running production on each arrangement, and observing how each works. However, the manager might rely on a **scale model,** as suggested for the hostess problem. The manager also has the option of employing a mathematical model, particularly if aware that a general plant layout model (CRAFT) exists.[3] A mathematical modeling approach to the manager's problem would likely be a more economical means for evaluating different alternatives.

*scale model*

Obviously model building has existed for many years, particularly in the form of mental and scale models, but **mathematical models** are relatively new, particularly in relation to management decision making. Most management science analyses are conducted by using mathematical models. Such models are developed by using mathematical symbols to represent different components of the problem.

*mathematical models*

Not all mathematical models are complex. For example, we can develop a mathematical model to determine the pay of a salesperson who receives a commission of $20 on each sale. More specifically, assume we are given the following data that describe the relationship between the salesperson's commission and the number of sales.

| number of sales | | 0 | 1 | 2 | 3 | 4 | 5 ... |
|---|---|---|---|---|---|---|---|
| dollars of commission income | | 0 | 20 | 40 | 60 | 80 | 100 ... |

Rather than use the table as a descriptive model of the problem, we can develop a more symbolic mathematical model by developing a *functional* relationship between the number of sales and commission income. If we let $x$ represent the number of sales, whatever it may be, and $y$ represent the dollars of income, then the mathematical function between sales and income is expressed:

$$y = 20x \tag{1.1}$$

This functional relationship can be viewed mentally as representing a *processing operation*, much in the same manner as we would visualize a data processing operation. The various values of $x$ (0, 1, 2, 3, ... ) can be thought of as inputs, with the corresponding values of $y$ (0, 20, 40, 60, ... ) being outputs. The inputs and outputs are commonly called *variables*. A variable is merely a representation of something that can take on varying numerical values.

Using conventional mathematical terminology, the *input* variable is referred to as the *independent variable* and the *output* variable as the *dependent variable*. Thus, in equation (1.1) $x$ is the independent variable and $y$ is the dependent variable. The numerical value 20 is referred to by several labels: *constant, coefficient,* and *parameter*. If, in the functional relationship, the amount paid per sale were

---

[3]CRAFT is an acronym for Computerized Relative Allocation of Facilities Technique.

designated as "*a* dollars per sale" instead of "$20 per sale," the function would be expressed:

$$y = ax \qquad (1.2)$$

where *a* is referred to as the model parameter.

In mathematical modeling it is sometimes useful to express the functional relationship in general terms. In our particular model if we say that *y* is an unspecified function of the number of sales *x*, then the symbolic representation is expressed:

$$y = f(x) \qquad (1.3)$$

This notation does not mean that *y* is equal to *f* times *x*. Rather, it says that the *variable y* has its numerical value determined by a *function* (or "processing rule") *f* and by the numerical value of the variable *x*.

Obviously, modeling in management science involves more than developing abstract or functional relationships between variables. In the next subsection we look at different models in management science and the solution processes used to identify solutions to these models.

## ■ Mathematical modeling and management science

### *Normative versus descriptive models*

*descriptive models*
*normative models*

Within mathematical modeling, two key types of models exist—**descriptive models** and **normative models.** A descriptive model is one that represents a relationship but does not indicate any course of action. A normative model, sometimes referred to as an optimization model, is prescriptive in that it prescribes the course of action that the manager (decision maker) should take to achieve a defined objective. Descriptive models are useful in predicting the behavior of systems but have no capability to identify the "best" course of action that should be taken. The model we developed in the sales commission example [equation (1.1)] could be labeled a descriptive model. It describes, or can be used to predict, commission from sales, given that the number of sales is specified. Many statistical models are descriptive. For example, a regression model indicates the relationship between a dependent variable and one or more independent variables; such models do not indicate what values to select for the independent variables. The waiting-line models discussed in Chapter 20 are descriptive in that they allow the decision maker to predict various characteristics of waiting-line situations, given certain knowledge of the independent variables.

A normative model may contain descriptive submodels, but it differs from the descriptive model in that it is possible to determine an optimal or best course of action. This implies that an objective is incorporated in the model and that it is possible to identify the effects of different courses of action on the objective. Since many management science models fall under the classification of normative models, it is appropriate to identify the key characteristics of such models. Most normative models are made up of three basic sets of elements: (1) *decision variables and parameters*, (2) *constraints*, and (3) *one or more objective functions*.

**1. Decision variables and parameters.**     The unknown quantities to be determined in the solution to the model are the decision variables. An example of a **decision variable** would be the quantity of a given product to be produced in a production operation where multiproducts could be produced from the same basic resource. *Parameters* are those values that describe the relationship between the decision variables. Parameters remain constant for each problem but change for different problems. An example would be the hours of labor required in the production of one unit of a given product.

*decision variable*

**2. Constraints.**     To account for physical limitations occurring in the problem being modeled, the model must include any constraints that limit the decision variables to permissible (feasible) values. **Constraints** are usually expressed in the form of mathematical functions (descriptive submodels). For example, let us assume that $x_1$ and $x_2$ (decision variables) represent the number of units of two products being considered for production, and let $a_1$ and $a_2$ (parameters) be the respective per unit raw material requirements for producing the products. If we are told the total available amount of raw material is $b$, the corresponding constraint function could be expressed by $a_1x_1 + a_2x_2 \leq b$.

*constraints*

**3. Objective function.**     The effectiveness of the model as a function of the decision variables is defined by the **objective function.** As an example, if the objective is to maximize total profits, the objective function must then describe profit in terms of the decision variables. Mathematically the function $Z = 4x_1 + 5x_2$ describes profits in terms of decision variables, given it is known that a \$4.00 profit accrues from each $x_1$ and \$5.00 accrues from each $x_2$. In general, the optimal solution to the model results when the values of the decision variables yield the best value of the objective function while satisfying all constraints.

*objective function*

The relationship between descriptive and normative models can be explained further by taking a specific example. Assume that we have a production process in which three separate and distinctive products can be produced. The only limited resource in our operation is labor; 400 man-hours of labor are available weekly. From prior experience we know that product #1 requires 8 hours of labor per unit of product output, product #2 requires 4 hours per unit of output, and product #3 requires 2 hours per unit of output. If we assumed for a moment that an unlimited amount of labor exists and if we let $x_1$ represent the number of units of product #1 to be produced, $x_2$ represent the number of units of product #2 to be produced, and $x_3$ the number of units of product #3 to be produced, then the following would be a descriptive model of total labor requirements:

$$L = 8x_1 + 4x_2 + 2x_3 \qquad (1.4)$$

But we already know that only 400 man-hours of labor are available; therefore, our functional relationship is, in reality,

$$8x_1 + 4x_2 + 2x_3 \leq 400 \tag{1.5}$$

With either model, we can make some statement about the problem; however, we have no way of determining the best course of action. In the first case, equation (1.4), if we assume certain values of $x_1$, $x_2$, and $x_3$, then we can predict the total labor required. In the second case, equation (1.5), we can easily compute the maximum number of units of each product that can be produced (50, 100, 200), assuming that no units of the two remaining products are produced.

Assume that, in addition to the initial data we were given, we are told that product #1 contributes \$12 per unit to profits, product #2 contributes \$10 per unit, and product #3 contributes \$8 per unit. From these data we can develop a descriptive model for total profits Z; this is expressed as follows:

$$Z = 12x_1 + 10x_2 + 8x_3 \tag{1.6}$$

As was the case with model (1.4), this model can be used to predict profits only if certain values of $x_1$, $x_2$, and $x_3$ are given. But if we combine models (1.5) and (1.6), and assume our objective is to maximize profits, then we will have a normative model. This model would appear thus:

MAXIMIZE:      $Z = 12x_1 + 10x_2 + 8x_3$

SUBJECT TO:      $8x_1 + \quad 4x_2 + 2x_3 \leq 400$      (1.7)

Our task at this point is to solve the model for values of $x_1$, $x_2$, and $x_3$ that would result in the largest value for Z. We will discuss this point in detail shortly; however, before moving to that material some additional comments are in order regarding mathematical models and management science.

## Classification of models

In addition to the descriptive/normative classification discussed above, several other model classifications are often mentioned in management science literature: *deterministic* versus *stochastic*, *linear* versus *nonlinear*, *static* versus *dynamic*, and finally *simulation models*. One could argue that these are different model classifications. But in actuality, these are subclassifications of normative and descriptive models, and a particular model can be classified by applying one or several of these terms. An examination of each of the terms will clarify this point.

*deterministic model*

In a **deterministic model,** the functional relationships, that is, the model parameters, are known with certainty. Model (1.6) could be referred to as a deterministic model since the parameters (the contribution coefficients—\$12, \$10,

$8$) are known with certainty. Model (1.5) likewise could be labeled a deterministic model.

If in model (1.5) we did not know for certain that 8 hours of labor were required in the production of one unit of product #1 (for example, assume there is a .60 probability that 10 hours of labor will be required), then we would develop a **stochastic model** to incorporate the uncertainty. A stochastic model may have some functional relationships that are both deterministic and stochastic or all relationships may be stochastic. Such models, if they are structured in the form of a normative model, are such that solutions can be derived that provide the best *expected* results; that is, the objective function is optimized for maximum or minimum expected results.

*stochastic model*

Another subclassification of modeling is that of linear and nonlinear models. A **linear model** is one in which all the functional relationships are such that the dependent varible is proportional to the independent variables. (The concept of linearity will be discussed in some depth in Chapter 5.) **Nonlinear models,** on the other hand, employ curvilinear or nonproportional equations. As is the case with stochastic models, it is not necessary that all functional relationships in the model be nonlinear to classify the model as nonlinear. If one or more relationships are nonlinear, the model is classified as a nonlinear model. The solution processes—the algorithms required to solve nonlinear models—are much more complex than those required for a linear model. In this text we will emphasize the use of *linear models* in management decision making.

*linear model*

*nonlinear model*

A third subclassification of models is static versus dynamic models. **Static models** are defined at a fixed point in time and assume that the conditions of the model do not change for that particular time period in the solution process for the model. An optimal decision or course of action is determined without regard to the course of action taken in prior or future time periods. A **dynamic model** differs from a static model in that the optimal or best course of action is determined by examining multiple time periods. Dynamic models are employed in situations where the optimal course of action over a multiple number of periods cannot be determined without considering the action taken in each period collectively. Chapter 22 involves dynamic models, their characteristics, and an associated solution process for determining the optimal actions for such models.

*static model*

*dynamic model*

The final subclassification of modeling we will note is *simulation*. Simulation is a modeling/experimentation process used to describe and/or analyze a given problem or problem area. We used the term modeling/experimentation process because simulation can be used for both purposes. From the data and descriptive characteristics given for our production problem we were able to formulate a normative model, that is, model (1.7). However, often the complexity or nature of the problem may be such that it may be impossible to develop a mathematical formulation that adequately fits the problem. Under such circumstances it may be possible to simulate the problem in order to analyze different courses of action. Because simulation models do not require closed-form mathematical functions to relate variables, it is possible to simulate complex systems that cannot be modeled mathematically.

## *Solution processes*

Three solution processes or approaches can be used to arrive at optimal or near optimal solutions to management-science–based problems: (1) algorithms, (2) heuristics, and (3) simulation. Since the algorithmic approach is the most commonly used solution process, a detailed explanation is warranted; but before exploring this area, a few comments are in order regarding the use of simulation and heuristics.

When we departed from the discussion of model (1.7), we noted that the next step in the process was to solve the model. In a few moments we will demonstrate that an analytical solution to the model can be derived; however, this may not be true in many cases. In some problem situations it may be impossible to solve the model analytically—that is, mathematically. In such cases we can employ simulation to analyze the problem, but the solution that results from a simulation process will not necessarily be the optimal solution. A simulation model "simulates" the behavior of the problem for a defined set of input conditions. To determine the "best course of action" one must analyze the model behavior under varying inputs and select the course of action that provides the desired level of results.

Sometimes the mathematical formulation of a problem may be so complex that an analytical solution is nearly impossible, and evaluation via simulation is impractical *heuristics* because of excessive processing time. In these cases, **heuristics** can be used to develop good approximate solutions. The heuristic solution process relies on intuitive or empirical rules, which, when applied to the model, provide one or more solutions. Heuristics are search procedures that try to move from one solution point to another in such a manner that the model objective is improved with each successive move. When no further improvements in the model objective can be found using the search rule employed, the attained solution is labeled an *approximate* solution. In this text we will minimize the discussion of heuristic solution processes since they usually depend strongly on the particular problem being solved, are generally used for particularly complex problems, and often *rely* on algorithms to solve parts of the problem. We will concentrate on the use of algorithms.

*algorithm* An **algorithm** is simply a set of procedures or rules which, when followed in a step-by-step manner, will provide the best solution to a given model. Since an algorithm is developed for a defined or given model, it is applicable only in solving a problem that adheres to the specific characteristics of the model. Although it may be possible to alter an algorithm to meet the requirements of specialized problems, this most likely would become a cumbersome task since it would probably necessitate altering the computer codes that exist for the algorithms.

The concept of an algorithm can be illustrated by using our previously formulated model of the production process [model (1.7)]. Recall that the model was expressed thus:

MAXIMIZE:     $Z = 12x_1 + 10x_2 + 8x_3$

SUBJECT TO:     $8x_1 + 4x_2 + 2x_3 \leq 400$

Recall also that 12, 10, and 8 were the respective contributions to profit from the sale of the products #1, #2, and #3, and the 8, 4, and 2 were the labor hours per unit required in the production of the respective products. In examining the model we can note that product #1 contributes $12 to profits as opposed to $10 and $8 for the other two products; thus we might conclude that we should produce as much of product #1 as our resources would allow. But, if we examine the labor cost associated with the first product (8 hours/unit), we quickly see that it has the highest per unit labor requirement. Our decision to produce as much of product #1 as possible may not be a wise decision. Since both the contribution coefficients and the per unit labor coefficients affect the decision regarding the number of units of products #1, #2, and #3 to produce, we need a means by which we can examine both coefficients simultaneously. We can accomplish this by developing a ratio of the two coefficients. These ratios would be thus:

$$\#1: \quad \frac{\$12/\text{unit}}{8 \text{ hours/unit}} = 1.50 \text{ dollars/hour}$$

$$\#2: \quad \frac{\$10/\text{unit}}{4 \text{ hours/unit}} = 2.50 \text{ dollars/hour}$$

$$\#3: \quad \frac{\$8/\text{unit}}{2 \text{ hours/unit}} = 4.00 \text{ dollars/hour}$$

These ratios give us the "contribution dollars per hour of labor expended" in the production of the respective products. From examining these ratios we can conclude that the proper decision would be to produce as much of product #3 as our labor resource will allow.

To determine the actual number of units of product #3 to produce we divide the labor requirements for the product (2 hours/unit) into the total labor hours available (400 hours). The "best course of action" is then to produce 0 units of product #1 ($x_1 = 0$), 0 units of product #2 ($x_2 = 0$), and 200 units of product #3 ($x_3 = 200$). The resulting profit in this case would be

$$Z = 12(0) + 10(0) + 8(200)$$

$$= \$1600$$

The loosely defined algorithm for model (1.7) would be expressed thus:

Compute a ratio for each product by dividing the per unit labor coefficient into the respective contribution to profit coefficient.

The largest ratio denotes the "product to be produced."

Determine the "quantity to produce" by dividing the labor coefficient of the product to be produced into total labor hours available.

Since this algorithm is loosely defined, that is, it does not take into account the possibility of negative coefficients or negative ratios, and is so closely tied to this specific problem, we need to develop a more mathematically structured algorithm that would fit a *general model* that could be used for this problem as well as other problems.

We can begin by developing a *general model* of model (1.7). If we let $c_j$ represent the contribution per unit from product $j$, $a_j$ represent the labor requirement per unit for the production of product $j$, and $b$ represent the total labor available, then the model could be expressed as follows:

MAXIMIZE:
$$Z = c_1 x_1 + c_2 x_2 + c_3 x_3$$

SUBJECT TO:
$$a_1 x_1 + a_2 x_2 + a_3 x_3 \leq b$$

Since we are trying to develop a *general model,* we need to take into consideration that more than three products can be produced. We will assume that $n$ products can be produced. To be realistic we also need to note that all our decision variables ($x_1$, $x_2$, and $x_3$) are zero or larger. The model thus would be

MAXIMIZE:
$$Z = c_1 x_1 + c_2 x_2 + c_3 x_3 + \cdots + c_n x_n$$

SUBJECT TO:
$$a_1 x_1 + a_2 x_2 + a_3 x_3 + \cdots + a_n x_n \leq b \tag{1.8}$$

$$x_1, x_2, x_3, \cdots, x_n \geq 0$$

Expressed in a more compact mathematical form the general model is as follows:

MAXIMIZE:
$$Z = \sum_{j=1}^{n} c_j x_j$$

SUBJECT TO:
$$\sum_{j=1}^{n} a_j x_j \leq b \tag{1.9}$$

and
$$x_j \geq 0 \quad \text{for all } j$$

This model is a more general model than model (1.7), but like model (1.7) it fully models the production problem.

The algorithm for this general model would be:

Compute the ratio $c_j/a_j$, for all variables where $a_j > 0$.

Note the largest ratio, and label the associated decision variable as $\hat{x}_j$. (If several ratios of equal value exist, this denotes that the production of the associated products will yield the same level of profits.)

If the noted largest ratio is equal to or less than zero, then produce nothing—the optimal course of action is to produce no units. If the largest ratio is greater than zero, then continue.

Compute the optimal quantity to produce with the relationship $\tilde{x}_j = b/\tilde{a}_j$, where $\tilde{a}_j$ is the labor coefficient associated with the largest ratio noted earlier. (If ratio ties exist, then alternative optimal policies exist.)

Obviously this algorithm is not complex since model (1.8) is not a very complex model; however, it demonstrates very well the concept of algorithm development.

## ■ The MS/OR problem-solving process

We indicated earlier in the chapter that our objective in the text is not to develop or extend the theory of solution algorithms, but rather to examine and study the structure of the problem to which a given algorithm can be applied. We will examine certain algorithms only as an aid in better understanding the structure of the problems to which they apply. Our objective is much broader. Solving a problem, or, in more specific terms, using MS/OR models to aid in problem solving, involves more than finding an algorithm that fits a given problem.

There are certain steps that must be employed in any MS/OR study; these begin with recognition of the problem and carry through to a final implementation and evaluation of the system designed to solve the problem. These steps should be adhered to if one is to expect any degree of success in the modeling process. We will label these steps the **problem-solving process.**

*problem-solving process*

The MS/OR problem-solving process can be described in a six-step framework as follows:

1. problem recognition, observation, and formulation
2. model construction
3. solution generation
4. testing and evaluation of solution
5. implementation
6. evaluation

A more detailed and practical representation of the process is shown in Figure 1-1. The six steps of the process are identified by the dashed boxes labeled 1–6.

Step 1 begins when the decision maker observes reality and notes that a desired or perceived result is not forthcoming under the existing operations. The second phase of the step involves the model builder and the decision maker. Here the problem is observed in order to identify key variables and relationships in the problem. Problem observation can be performed collectively or separately. A unified approach, however, must evolve; thus strong interaction between the decision maker and model builder must occur. The final phase of step 1 is to describe the problem verbally. The verbal problem is a narrative description of the variables, constraints, and the objective, and a general suggestion as to model relationships. The verbal description of the problem is an extremely important phase of step 1 since it is the basis upon which the mathematical model will be formulated.

FIGURE 1-1.
The MS/OR Problem-Solving Process (Adapted from Ronald V. Hartley, *Operations Research: A Managerial Emphasis,* Goodyear Publishing Co., 1976, p. 10)

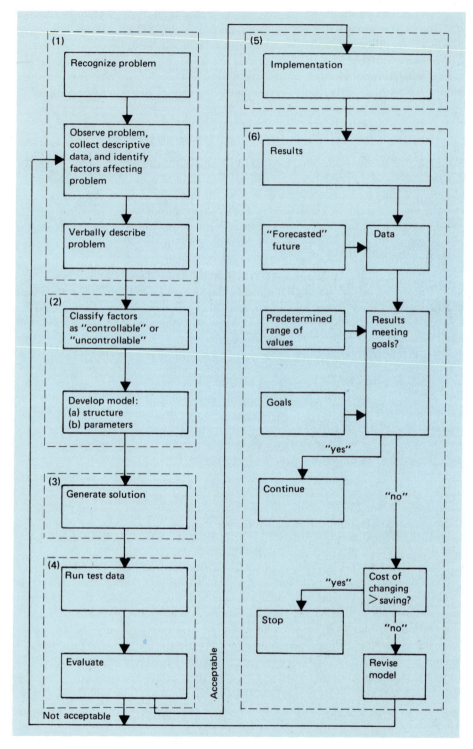

Step 2 of the problem-solving process involves model development, but before structuring the problem mathematically the factors identified in step 1 must be examined to differentiate between the controllable and uncontrollable variables. Controllable variables can be manipulated or changed by the decision maker; the uncontrollable variables cannot be changed. To aid in formulating the mathematical model the decision maker should identify the significant controllable variables. On the basis of these key variables and the relationships identified and documented in the verbal model, the model builder pulls together a model that mathematically describes the defined and documented problem. It may be necessary to make some assumptions that will place boundaries on the real problem so that it is solvable. Quite often it is necessary to test an initial formulation of the model in order to determine what assumptions must be made.

The algorithm development or selection process occurs in step 3. In actual practice, there is some degree of feedback between steps 2 and 3 since one must be certain that the problem formulated in step 2 satisfies all the conditions or assumptions of the algorithm employed in step 3. Actually we should be careful in our usage of the term algorithm at this point, because a solution process is not limited to algorithms. Recall that we noted that heuristics as well as simulation can be employed to solve given problems. We have elected to emphasize the algorithm solution process at this point since the majority of the problems addressed in the text can be solved by employing an algorithm.

The model adopted or developed in step 3 is evaluated and tested in step 4 to determine if it yields useful results for the original problem. Several procedures can be used to test the model. First, the decision maker can simply examine the results and make some judgment as to *reasonableness* of the results. Second, a testing procedure can be adopted in which a prior historical situation is used as a base model. That is, the information from a prior decision can be input to the model and the results compared with what actually occurred. Regardless of whether one, or both, or other test processes are used to evaluate the model, it must be revised if it does not satisfy the needs of the decision maker. Quite often the revision process involves adding and deleting variables, but it could involve returning to the originally observed problem. (This is shown in Figure 1-1 as the return loop to step 1.)

Step 5 in the MS/OR problem-solving process is implementation of the validated model. Unfortunately most management scientists fail to realize that implementation begins on the first day of the project, not when the model is developed and running. Management must be involved in the MS/OR project throughout its duration. Implementation does not mean that the running model is simply delivered to management and that the model builder is thereby divorced from the project. The model builder must: (1) work with the decision maker to identify the problem properly (step 1), (2) get feedback from the decision maker regarding validity of the model (step 4), and (3) work with the decision maker in implementing and using the model.

Chapter 25 examines the area of implementation in detail. An implementation-gaming model is identified in the chapter and several studies related to implementation problems are presented. In this chapter we have noted that implementation is a key step in the problem-solving process and, unless management is involved throughout the project and fully supports the project objective, odds are that the model will be judged only as a provocative exercise for the model builder.

The last step of the problem-solving process (step 6) is evaluation/revision of the model. Since it is not uncommon for an MS/OR model to be used repeatedly in the analysis of decision problems, the model must continually be evaluated to determine whether parameter values have changed and/or whether the model still meets the goals of the decision maker. If characteristics of the problem change or if the goals of the decision maker are not being met, then a revision of the model should be *considered*. We use the term "considered" because the cost of changing the model must be compared with the saving to be gained by the revision. If the cost of revision outweighs projected saving, then the project should be discontinued. Again, this is where management can have a poor experience with MS/OR modeling. If management fails to recognize when a project exceeds its usefulness, poor results during later usage of the model can overshadow prior performance when the model truly addresses the problem.

## ■ Management science and the computer

One of the key factors that has aided in the growth, as well as the development, of management science is the advent of the computer. Without the computer, the use of management science techniques would be severely limited. From the discussion on "Mathematical Modeling and Management Science," it is obvious that the solution processes employed in management science can become quite cumbersome and, in some cases, complex. Fortunately, much of the mathematical complexity and the computational burden of employing different solution techniques can be reduced by utilizing the computer. This does not say that we can ignore the "MS/OR Problem-Solving Process." On the contrary, it simply says that the task is reduced significantly by the computation power and speed of the computer.

Though the emphasis of this text is on *applying* solution techniques and examining the development of some techniques, we recognize that the computer is an integral part of the problem-solving process. Throughout the text we will emphasize the interpretation of model output, and in the majority of cases we will provide a manual output report (table). We have not included computer output, but we urge users to employ such in their study of the techniques. It is hoped that this approach will encourage the use of computerized procedures, but not at the expense of totally excluding examination of the solution process employed.

## ■ Constraints in the MS/OR field

Management science, like any other field, has certain constraints and limitations. One limitation is the necessity for making assumptions in structuring or formulating the problem being addressed. Quite often simplifications are necessary because the original problem is so complex it is difficult to model and/or solve. To solve the problem, then, simplifications are made in the form of assumptions about certain variables. This simplification process yields a simplified problem or model that can be manipulated in order to arrive at an initial solution to the problem. An example from economics is the study of the marketplace. This very complex situation is greatly simplified by assuming that perfect competition exists. This is a broad assumption; yet, with it, a basic economics model can be developed that is useful in studying the effects that various forces have on the marketplace. Since models are simplified representations of reality, the question often arises as to whether a model captures the essence of the original, more complex, problem. It is indeed possible to make so many assumptions in simplifying the original problem that the resulting model is no longer useful. It is important therefore that the model builder ascertain from the decision maker the assumptions that would result in the model being valid. The model builder can then attempt to solve a more complex version of the model that will be useful to the decision maker. This process is shown graphically in Figure 1-2.

In this figure, the model builder begins at time $t_0$ with the complex problem. Assumptions are then made that simplify the problem so that a solution is reached at time $t_1$. Then, one by one, assumptions are relaxed and the model moves back toward reality, using what was learned in the simple model solution to solve the increasingly complex versions of the problem.

A second limitation of management science is that most models consider only one objective function. In the discussion of the formulation of normative models, only single-objective functions were noted. Management science techniques such as linear

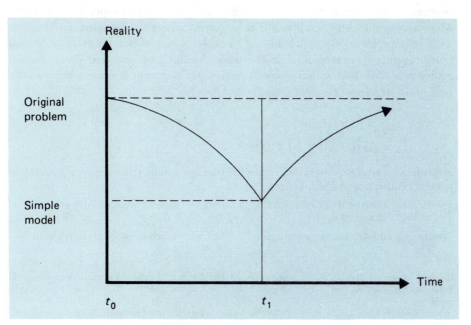

**FIGURE 1-2.
Model Simplification Versus Reality**

programming, integer programming, and transportation models consider only a single objective.

In practice, single-objective models can be a key problem since decision makers often have objectives other than maximizing profit or minimizing costs. One technique, goal programming (Chapter 12), does provide the capability to handle multiple objectives. A number of researchers are currently involved in developing other multicriteria decision models.

Another problem area in management science is the size of the system of equations (that is, the constraints within the problem area) that exists in a practical problem. Many problems in industry, government, and the public sector contain a large number of constraints. This presents two problems in the MS/OR modeling process. First, in academia there is a tendency to examine small, unique problems in order to demonstrate the model or concept. The modeler or decision maker may develop a very naive view of practical problems. It should be recognized that many problems in practice may contain several hundred constraints.[4]

The second problem is the computational burden. The algorithms that we will describe in the text are directly suitable for small basic problems. When a large set of equations results, computationally efficient algorithms must be employed, otherwise the cost of the modeling process may be excessive.[5] Quite often, solutions to large problems can be approximated by applying the simplification process we noted.

A final problem area that should be noted is that of cost versus benefit. This question must be addressed before a management science project is undertaken. One can easily get involved in MS/OR modeling to the point that the computerized problem-solving capabilities of management science are adopted without examining the potential benefit that will accrue. In many situations the cost of developing and implementing a model may outweigh the saving gained by employing the model. Many decision-making problems can be solved without employing sophisticated models. A problem often encountered by both the model builder and the decision maker is to get so involved with the model building process that every decision problem is addressed with a decision model. Management science, like any other field, must be employed and applied with logical reason.

## ■ Glossary of terms

**algorithm:**   a set of procedures that, when followed in a step-by-step manner, will provide an optimal solution to a problem.

**constraint:**   a mathematical function that describes or places a feasible limit on the model and/or decision variables.

**decision variables:**   the unknown quantities to be determined in the solution to a model.

---

[4]In this text we will present, as our counterparts have in the past, basic problems that demonstrate the *nature* of the problem that can be addressed. It is beyond our objective to examine large complex problems.
[5]A number of computationally efficient algorithms exist in practice; these are available through computer manufacturers and/or software houses.

**descriptive model:** a mathematical model that represents a functional relationship but does not indicate a course of action.

**deterministic model:** a model in which the model parameters are known with certainty.

**dynamic model:** a model whose characteristics change from period to period. To determine the optimal course of action requires the examination of multiple time periods.

**heuristic:** a solution process that relies on intuitive or empirical rules to provide an approximate solution to a problem.

**linear model:** a model in which all the functional relationships are such that the dependent variable is proportional to the sum of the independent variables. Such models will also have the characteristic that for any change in one independent variable, while all others are held fixed, the change in the dependent variable is directly proportional.

**mathematical model:** an abstract symbolic representation of a problem.

**mental model:** a mental image of the structure that describes a problem.

**nonlinear model:** a model in which nonproportional equations or functions exist. Such models will have variables raised to a power other than one and/or will have products of two or more variables.

**normative model:** a mathematical model that describes a functional relationship and prescribes a course of action for achieving the defined objective included in the model.

**objective function:** a mathematical function that defines the effectiveness of the model as a function of the decision variables.

**operational research:** the label used to describe the management science/operations research activities of the British military operational staff during World War II.

**ORSA:** Operations Research Society of America; parent group given credit for development of operations research in the United States.

**problem-solving process:** the steps (framework) involved in developing and implementing an OR/MS model.

**scale model:** a physical structure, reduced in size, that represents the life-size problem.

**static model:** a model defined at a fixed point in time.

**stochastic model:** a model in which the model parameters are not known with certainty, i.e., the probability of occurrence of different model parameters exists.

**TIMS:** The Institute of Management Sciences; organization founded in 1953 in the United States to emphasize applied research in management science/operations research.

## ■ Review questions

1. Briefly discuss the evolution of the MS/OR field.

2. How is model building related to management science?

3. Differentiate between a descriptive and a normative model. Give examples of each.

4. What basic set of elements exists in any normative model? Comment on each of these elements.

5. What are the subclassifications of normative and descriptive models?

6. Differentiate between a deterministic model and a stochastic model.

7. Differentiate between a linear and a nonlinear model.

8. Differentiate between a static and a dynamic model.

9. When are simulation models employed in management science?

10. What solution processes exist in the MS/OR field? Briefly explain or comment on each.

11. Is it necessary to develop an algorithm for every problem that is addressed in an MS/OR study? (Assume that an algorithm is the appropriate technique to employ as compared with a heuristic or a simulation solution approach.)

12. Identify the general steps that should be taken in any MS/OR study. Comment on each step.

13. Identify some of the limitations or problems that exist in the field of management science.

14. Can multiobjective problems be handled with an existing MS/OR technique?

15. Comment on the cost versus benefit problem as related to an MS/OR project.

## ■ True/false questions

1. The term management science received its initial impetus with the establishment of The Institute of Management Sciences (TIMS) in 1953.

2. A scale model is created by visualizing different arrangements and evaluating each alternative.

3. A descriptive model represents a relationship and indicates a proper course of action.

4. A normative model may never contain descriptive submodels.

5. The effectiveness of the model as a function of the decision variables is defined by the objective function.

6. Given qualities in a model that enable the user to make decisions are referred to as decision variables.

7. A linear model is one in which all the functional relationships are such that the dependent variable is proportional to the independent variables.

8. An algorithm is a set of procedures or rules that, when followed in a step-by-step manner, will provide the best solution to a given model.

9. A heuristic solution process relies on intuitive or empirical rules to provide an optimal solution to a problem.

10. A dynamic model is defined at a fixed point in time.

**2**

# Mathematical Review

## ■ Introduction

In Chapter 1 the foundation and structure of the modeling process were presented, as were the basic steps involved in the development and use of management science techniques. We also noted the importance of functional relationships among problem elements. In this chapter we will review the mathematics necessary to represent functional relationships and to solve systems or sets of these functions. The objective of this chapter is not to provide a complete review of mathematics, as some areas would not be particularly relevant to management science applications and many are better left to explanation within the context of the problem being solved. Instead the objective is to review a few fundamental concepts that represent the foundation of many of the techniques presented in later chapters, especially those dealing with linear programming.

## ■ Linear equations and inequalities

As we saw in the previous chapter, many decision problems revolve around the idea of describing equality relationships between expressions. The mathematical statement of this equality is known as an **equation.** Some examples of equations are        *equation*

$$2x + 3 = 45 \tag{2.1}$$

$$6k - 8 = 90 \tag{2.2}$$

$$5p = 21 \tag{2.3}$$

Each of the equations above has only one unknown quantity or **variable.** Equations        *variable*
may have many variables, such as the following:

$$2x + 5y + 7z + 21 = 100 \tag{2.4}$$

Whether an equation has one variable or many variables, it is a **linear equation** if it        *linear*
is of the form $a_1x_1 + a_2x_2 + a_3x_3 + \ldots + b = c$ and if $a_1, a_2, \ldots, a_n, b,$ and $c$ are real        *equation*
numbers and at least one of the $a_i$ is nonzero. An equation is **nonlinear** if any of the        *nonlinear*
variables have an exponent other than 1, if any variables are used in cross products, if an absolute value operation is employed on a variable, or if some other evaluation such as $e^x$ or $\ln(x)$ is used.

## *Graphical representation*

Equations with two variables (and maybe three if you are a good artist) can be displayed graphically. Concentrating on linear equations for a moment, if we construct a two-variable linear equation such as

$$2x_1 + 4x_2 = 16 \qquad (2.5)$$

the graphical plot of this equation would be Figure 2-1. Note that the equation plots as a straight line, and that every point on the line (pair of values for $x_1$ and $x_2$) satisfies the equation.

In order to plot an equation such as the one in Figure 2-1, we must be able to identify two things related to the equation. If we can identify any two points that lie on the line, we can plot the line simply by connecting those two points. Or if we can identify any one point and the slope of the equation (where slope is the steepness of a line defined as the change in the vertical variable for each unit change in the horizontal variable, as illustrated in Figure 2-1), we can plot it by beginning at the point and extending outward in the direction specified by the slope. To illustrate this idea, let us look at equation (2.5). Suppose that we decide to plot this equation by identifying two points on the line. The easiest two points to identify are the

**FIGURE 2-1.
Graphical Illustra-
tion of Equation
(2.5)**

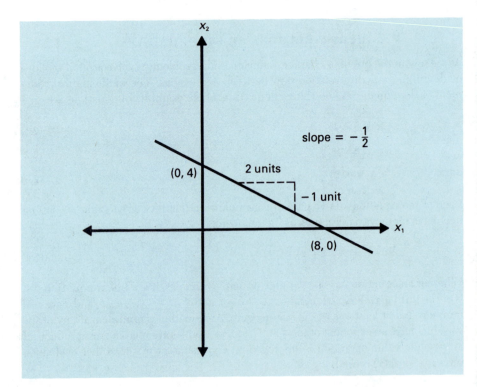

**intercepts,** the points where the equation crosses the $x_1$ and $x_2$ axes. At the point where the equation crosses the $x_1$ axis, $x_2$ will have a value of zero because the $x_2$ value represents movement away from the $x_1$ axis in the $x_2$ direction. Letting $x_2$ equal zero in equation (2.5) yields

$$2x_1 + 4(0) = 16$$

$$2x_1 + 0 = 16$$

$$2x_1 = 16$$

$$x_1 = \frac{16}{2}$$

$$x_1 = 8$$

Therefore, the $x_1$ intercept for equation (2.5) is 8, and we have found one of our two necessary points for plotting. From this point on, the solutions will be referred to by the notation $(x_1, x_2)$; that is, the point we just found is (8, 0). Using the same logic to find the $x_2$ intercept, when $x_1$ equals zero, $x_2$ equals 4, and our second point for equation (2.5) is (0, 4). By locating these two points on our graph and connecting them, we arrive at the plot illustrated in Figure 2-1.

## Slope-intercept form

As was indicated earlier, we could also plot the line by finding one point and the slope of the equation. A handy approach for finding the slope is to put the equation into **slope-intercept form.** If we can express our equation in the form

$$y = mx + b \tag{2.6}$$

where $y$ is the variable on the vertical axis ($x_2$ in Figure 2-1) and $x$ is the variable on the horizontal axis ($x_1$ in Figure 2-1), then $m$ will be the slope of the equation and $b$ will be the vertical intercept. To put equation (2.5) into slope-intercept form, we must isolate the $x_2$ variable on the left side of the equation by solving as follows:

$$2x_1 + 4x_2 = 16$$

$$4x_2 = 16 - 2x_1$$

$$x_2 = \frac{16 - 2x_1}{4}$$

$$x_2 = \left(\frac{-2}{4}\right)x_1 + \frac{16}{4}$$

Thus, the slope of equation (2.5) is $-\frac{2}{4}$ or $-\frac{1}{2}$, and the $x_2$ intercept is 4. By starting at the point (0, 4) and moving down one unit for every two units we move in the $x_1$

FIGURE 2-2.
Graph of a Rela-
tion That Is Not a
Function

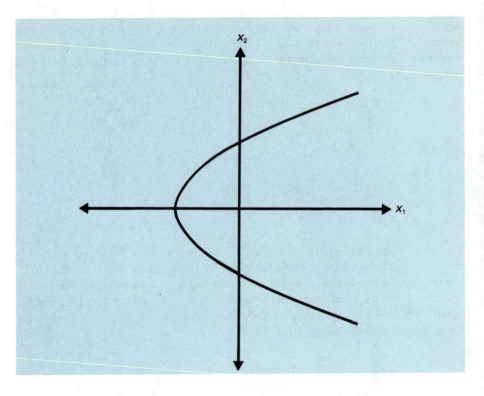

FIGURE 2-2.
Graph of a Relation That Is Not a Function

direction, we once again trace the line in Figure 2-1. These concepts of slope, intercept, and graph of a linear equation will be used extensively in our discussion of linear programming a little later on.

Let us take this opportunity to introduce some other terms used extensively in discussing equations and graphs such as the ones we have been working with. Any rule that produces sets of ordered pairs such as our $(x_1, x_2)$ points is called a **relation,** since it defines the relationship between two different variables. A relation is also a **function** if, for each value of the horizontal or $x_1$ variable, there is one and only one value for the vertical or $x_2$ variable. We refer to the variable on the vertical axis of a function as the **dependent variable** and the variable on the horizontal axis as the **independent variable.** Figure 2-2 is an example of a relation that is *not* a function. Because of their very nature, all linear equations are functions except for the equation that plots as a vertical line.

We said earlier that equations are used to express equality relationships between the left-hand side and the right-hand side of expressions. In some instances we are required to express relationships where the left-hand side is either greater than, greater than or equal to, less than, or less than or equal to the right-hand side of the expression. This kind of statement is called an **inequality.** Statements (2.7) through (2.10) are examples of these four types of expressions.

*relation*

*function*

*dependent variable*

*independent variable*

*inequality*

$$4x_1 + 5x_2 > 22 \tag{2.7}$$

$$6x_1 + 2x_2 \geq 15 \tag{2.8}$$

$$3x_1 + x_2 < 60 \tag{2.9}$$

$$x_1 + x_2 \leq 50 \tag{2.10}$$

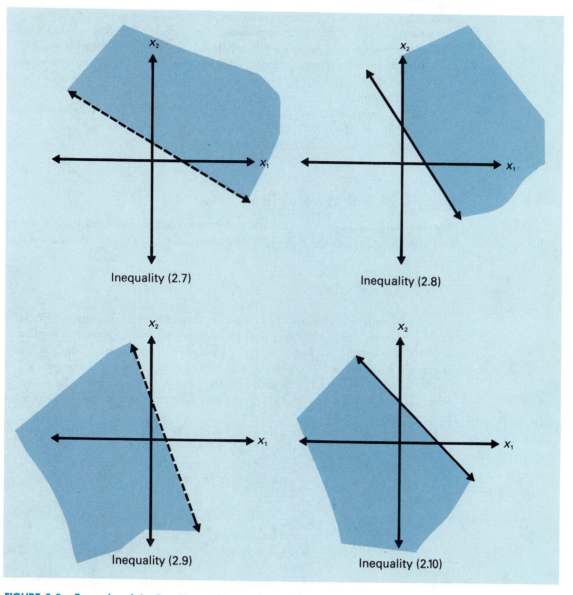

Inequality (2.7)

Inequality (2.8)

Inequality (2.9)

Inequality (2.10)

**FIGURE 2-3.  Examples of the Four Types of Inequality Statements**

These expressions are used when it is necessary to place a limit on the value of the left-hand side. For example, if 500 tons of steel were available to build cars on a certain day, the amount of steel we may plan to use, call it $x$, could be 500 tons or it could be something less than 500 tons. This would be an example of a less than or equal to situation.

The graph of an inequality is constructed in exactly the same way as an equality. The difference arises in representing the points that actually satisfy the relationship. Where the solution to an equality was restricted to only those points actually lying on the equation line, the solution to an inequality includes those points in the half space above or below the line, depending on whether it is a greater than or less than type. The shaded areas in Figure 2-3 illustrate the regions that satisfy the various types of inequalities. The dotted line on two of the graphs indicate that the line is not part of the shaded region.

Note that inequalities are relations but they are not functions, since for some values of the independent variable there will be more than one value for the dependent variable that will satisfy the relation.

### ■ Polynomial functions

*polynomial*

Another important class of equations and/or inequalities, in contrast to the linear form discussed previously, is the **polynomial** equation. A polynomial equation is of the form

$$c_n x^n + c_{n-1} x^{n-1} + \ldots + c_1 x_1 + c_0 = 0 \tag{2.11}$$

where $c$ represents a constant. This constant may be zero in any given term, and consequently the polynomial may not contain every decreasing term as is implied in (2.11). While linear equations are actually a subset of the polynomial family wherein the largest exponent is $n = 1$, polynomial equations are a subset of the larger class of nonlinear equations referred to earlier in the chapter. We will defer discussion of other nonlinear forms until later chapters where they may be discussed in the context of the problem at hand.

If, in our presentation of the polynomial expression, we are relating the expression to some dependent variable, then we call it a polynomial function in the case of an equality and a polynomial relation in the case of an inequality. Equations (2.12) and (2.12a) are examples of a simple polynomial function and a polynomial relation, respectively:

$$4x^3 - 2x^2 - 6x + 8 = y \tag{2.12}$$

$$5x^4 + 3x^2 - 4x - 3 \le y \tag{2.12a}$$

It is often possible to simplify polynomial equations. Since polynomial expressions involve exponents, we are well able to simplify them so long as we remember the simple rules for working with exponents. In order to add or subtract terms, they must be like terms (the variable must have the same exponent in both terms). The terms are then added or subtracted by combining the constants in the specified manner. For example, $5x^2 + 6x^2 = 11x^2$ and $9x^3 - 7x^3 = 2x^3$. In order to multiply or divide terms, the base (variable) must be the same. We multiply terms by adding exponents and divide by subtracting exponents and by performing the indicated operation on any preceding constants. For example, $2x^2 \times 5x^3 = 10x^5$, and $8x^6/2x^2 = 4x^4$. By remembering these simple rules, and realizing that they can also be used in reverse to "factor" or break down an expression, it is usually possible to simplify polynomials. Returning to equation (2.12), suppose that we collect terms and rewrite it as

$$4x^3 - 2x^2 - 6x = y - 8$$

If we divide both sides by $2x$, we get

$$2x^2 - x - 3 = \frac{y - 8}{2x}$$

$$2x(2x^2 - x - 3) = y - 8$$

We can simplify further by factoring the polynomial in parentheses. This term can be factored by breaking $2x^2$ into $2x \times x$, and by finding a pair of constants that have a product of $-3$ and that sum to $-1$ when weighted by 2 and 1, the two coefficients on $x$ in the prior step. The resulting factorization is

$$2x(2x - 3)(x + 1) = y - 8$$

This polynomial cannot be simplified further, but it is now in a more workable form than was equation (2.12). Admittedly, much of factorization is trial and error, and some polynomials cannot be factored to any great degree.

The purpose of factorization really depends on whether we are faced with a polynomial equation or a polynomial function. If we are working with an equation with only one variable, the purpose is to help us solve the equation. If it is a function with a dependent variable, there is not "a solution" but an infinite set of solutions as the dependent variable takes on the value specified by the expression. In that case, factorization might make it easier to evaluate the expression in order to calculate the dependent variable value.

## Quadratic functions

For one particular type of polynomial equation, the **quadratic** equation, where the largest exponent on any variable is $n = 2$ such that $ax^2 + bx + c = 0$ with $a$ not equal to zero, we may solve it either through factorization or by using the quadratic formula:

*quadratic*

$$x = \frac{-b \pm \sqrt{b^2 - 4ac}}{2a} \qquad\qquad (2.13)$$

To illustrate the solution of a quadratic equation, let us approach the same expression both by factorization and by the quadratic formula.

Suppose that we have the quadratic

$$x^2 + 2x - 8 = 0$$

The factorization, by finding two constants whose sum is $+2$ and whose product is $-8$, is $(x - 2)(x + 4) = 0$. If the product of these two factors is zero, then one of the two terms that are multiplied together must be zero. Consequently, this factored equation would be satisfied if $(x - 2) = 0$ or if $(x + 4) = 0$. In the first case, where $x - 2 = 0$, $x$ must equal 2. In the second case, $x$ must equal $-4$. Therefore, there are two solutions to the quadratic equation: $x = 2$ and $x = -4$.

Using the quadratic equation to solve the same quadratic, we see that $a = 1$, $b = 2$, and $c = -8$. This gives $x = (-2 \pm \sqrt{2^2 - 4(1)(-8)})/2(1)$. This yields $(-2 \pm \sqrt{36})/2$, which is $(-2 \pm 6)/2$. When we add the terms in parentheses, $(-2 + 6)/2$ is 2; and when we subtract, $(-2 - 6)/2$ is $-4$. These are the same two solutions we arrived at by factorization. Again, these two methods are useful when we need to solve a quadratic equation. When we need to evaluate a quadratic function in order to find the value of the dependent variable, we simply plug in the value of $x$ that we are concerned with and calculate the resulting value.

## ■ Vectors and matrices

In our discussion thus far, we have concerned ourselves with the situation where one equation, inequality, or function is used to describe a relationship. In many cases, if not most, there actually will be several relationships that must hold true to describe the situation. As an example, consider a manufacturing situation where two products are to be produced and each requires time in two different assembly lines. Let us assume that product 1 requires 1 hour in assembly line 1, product 2 requires 2 hours in assembly line 1, and assembly line 1 has 8 hours available in a given day. Likewise, product 1 requires 2 hours in assembly line 2, product 2 requires 1 hour in assembly line 2, and line 2 has only 7 hours of available operating time. Assuming that all of the hours in each line must be used, the *system of linear equations* that represents this situation is the pair of equations

$$x_1 + 2x_2 = 8$$

$$2x_1 + x_2 = 7$$

assuming that $x_1$ and $x_2$ represent the numbers of units of product 1 and 2, respectively, that are to be made. Because these are equalities and are not parallel (do not have the same slope), there will be at most one combination of $x_1$ and $x_2$ that will satisfy the system of equations. Figure 2-4 identifies that point (the point of intersection of the two lines). We see that the only possible solution to this situation is to make 2 units of product 1 and 3 units of product 2. In addition to this graphical solution approach, it is also possible to solve sets of equations by the method of

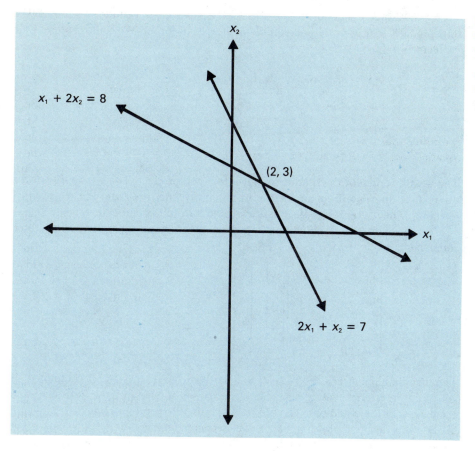

FIGURE 2-4.
Graphical Solution
of a System of
Two Equations
with Two Variables

$x_1 + 2x_2 = 8$

(2, 3)

$2x_1 + x_2 = 7$

substitution, where one equation is solved in terms of the first variable and the resulting expression is inserted for that same variable in the second equation. The result is an equation with only one variable that can be solved by simple algebraic rearrangement.

## Representing systems of equations as a matrix

While this process of describing and solving simultaneous equations graphically, or by substitution, is fine when we have very small systems of equations, it is not so fine when we are faced with large systems of equations for analysis. Suppose we have the same type of manufacturing problem that we just solved, except that we now have four products to be produced on four assembly lines. We obviously cannot graph such a problem, and substitution would be a formidable task. To aid in the analysis of such systems of equations, we would normally resort to a shorthand notation known as *matrix notation*, and a set of manipulating procedures known as *matrix algebra*. A **matrix** is nothing but a table (collection of rows and columns) that allows us to represent equations more compactly.

*matrix*

To illustrate the notion of a matrix, let us look at a generic version of the four-product, four-assembly-line problem referred to earlier. We could represent the problem as follows:

$$a_{11}x_1 + a_{12}x_2 + a_{13}x_3 + a_{14}x_4 = b_1$$

$$a_{21}x_1 + a_{22}x_2 + a_{23}x_3 + a_{24}x_4 = b_2$$

$$a_{31}x_1 + a_{32}x_2 + a_{33}x_3 + a_{34}x_4 = b_3$$

$$a_{41}x_1 + a_{42}x_2 + a_{43}x_3 + a_{44}x_4 = b_4$$

The $x$'s still represent the production level for each product. The $a_{ij}$'s represent the production time requirement for the $i$th assembly line (row) and the $j$th product (column). The $b_i$'s represent the hours available for each assembly line.

We write this set of equations in matrix notation by separating these three components as

$$\begin{bmatrix} a_{11} & a_{12} & a_{13} & a_{14} \\ a_{21} & a_{22} & a_{23} & a_{24} \\ a_{31} & a_{32} & a_{33} & a_{34} \\ a_{41} & a_{42} & a_{43} & a_{44} \end{bmatrix} \begin{bmatrix} x_1 \\ x_2 \\ x_3 \\ x_4 \end{bmatrix} = \begin{bmatrix} b_1 \\ b_2 \\ b_3 \\ b_4 \end{bmatrix}$$

The first component is a $4 \times 4$ matrix. That is, it has 4 rows and 4 columns. It is generally referred to as a coefficient matrix, as it contains the left-hand-side coefficients of the equations. The symbol [A] is used to represent this matrix, where the brackets denote that it is a matrix. The second component is a $4 \times 1$ matrix that contains the equation variables, but it will be referred to after this as the *vector* of variables, a **vector** simply being a single row or column collection. The symbol $x$ will be used to denote this vector (vector identifiers do not have brackets around them). The third component is the right-hand-side vector, and it will be referred to as $b$.

*vector*

Thus, we have established a simple notational form for representing systems of equations or, for that matter, anything consisting of a collection of rows and columns. We will also be able to manipulate this form in order to arrive at a solution to the system of equations. First, however, we need to review the basics of manipulating vectors and matrices known as matrix algebra.

## ■ Matrix algebra

### *Matrix addition*

Probably the simplest operation involving matrices or vectors is matrix addition. In order to add two matrices, we create a third matrix whose elements are the sums of the elements in the same position in the first two matrices. This means that in order to add two matrices, they must each have the same number of rows and they must each have the same number of columns so that there will be a position in the second matrix corresponding to each position in the first matrix. In matrix terminology, we refer to the number of rows and columns a matrix has as its **dimensions**. A matrix with an equal number of rows and columns is called a **square matrix**. If its dimensions are not equal, it is called a **rectangular matrix**. If a matrix has $m$ rows and $n$ columns, we say that its dimensions are $m \times n$ (read $m$ by $n$), or that it is an $m \times n$ matrix ($m = 4$ and $n = 4$ for our coefficient matrix on the previous page). Consequently, the only matrix that can be added to an $m \times n$ matrix is another $m \times n$ matrix.

As an example, suppose that we want to find the sum of the two matrices

$$\begin{bmatrix} 2 & 7 & 5 \\ 15 & 3 & 5 \\ 4 & 6 & 2 \end{bmatrix} \text{ and } \begin{bmatrix} 6 & 1 & 13 \\ 4 & 2 & 6 \\ 12 & 4 & 9 \end{bmatrix}$$

The sum would be found by adding the respective elements as follows:

$$\begin{bmatrix} 2 & 7 & 5 \\ 15 & 3 & 5 \\ 4 & 6 & 2 \end{bmatrix} + \begin{bmatrix} 6 & 1 & 13 \\ 4 & 2 & 6 \\ 12 & 4 & 9 \end{bmatrix} = \begin{bmatrix} 2+6 & 7+1 & 5+13 \\ 15+4 & 3+2 & 5+6 \\ 4+12 & 6+4 & 2+9 \end{bmatrix} = \begin{bmatrix} 8 & 8 & 18 \\ 19 & 5 & 11 \\ 16 & 10 & 11 \end{bmatrix}$$

Another point worth mentioning is that in matrix addition, the order of addition does not matter. In matrix addition $[A] + [B] = [B] + [A]$. This is a property we recognize from regular nonmatrix or **scalar** addition.

## Matrix subtraction

Since subtraction is nothing more than negative addition, we can subtract two matrices in the same manner as above. For our same two matrices, the difference is

$$\begin{bmatrix} 2 & 7 & 5 \\ 15 & 3 & 5 \\ 4 & 6 & 2 \end{bmatrix} - \begin{bmatrix} 6 & 1 & 13 \\ 4 & 2 & 6 \\ 12 & 4 & 9 \end{bmatrix} = \begin{bmatrix} 2-6 & 7-1 & 5-13 \\ 15-4 & 3-2 & 5-6 \\ 4-12 & 6-4 & 2-9 \end{bmatrix} = \begin{bmatrix} -4 & 6 & -8 \\ 11 & 1 & -1 \\ -8 & 2 & -7 \end{bmatrix}$$

Of course, order does make a difference here. The difference $[A] - [B]$ does not equal $[B] - [A]$ but $-([B] - [A])$. This is again analogous to the way subtraction works for scalar numbers.

## Matrix multiplication

The next operation we can define on matrices is multiplication. The simpliest form of multiplication involving a matrix is the multiplication of a matrix by a single number or scalar. To accomplish this, we multiply the scalar times each individual element of the matrix, and the dimensions of the matrix can be anything. An example is

$$2\begin{bmatrix} 6 & 2 & 5 & -9 \\ 3 & 11 & 1 & 12 \\ 1 & 4 & 7 & 7 \end{bmatrix} = \begin{bmatrix} 12 & 4 & 10 & -18 \\ 6 & 22 & 2 & 24 \\ 2 & 8 & 14 & 14 \end{bmatrix}$$

It is more complicated to multiply two matrices. The procedure involves multiplying the elements of a row of the first matrix times the elements in the comparable positions of a column of the second matrix and summing the resulting products to get just one element of the product matrix. This procedure is then repeated for each row–column combination of the first and second matrices. Because of this, matrices can be multiplied only if the number of columns in the first matrix equals the number of rows in the second matrix. That is, an $m \times k$ matrix can be multiplied by a $k \times n$ matrix. The result will be an $m \times n$ matrix. As a generic example, suppose that we have the matrices

$$[A] = \begin{bmatrix} a_{11} & a_{12} \\ a_{21} & a_{22} \end{bmatrix} \qquad [B] = \begin{bmatrix} b_{11} & b_{12} & b_{13} \\ b_{21} & b_{22} & b_{23} \end{bmatrix}$$

The product $[A] \times [B]$ is

$$\begin{bmatrix} a_{11}b_{11} + a_{12}b_{21} & a_{11}b_{12} + a_{12}b_{22} & a_{11}b_{13} + a_{12}b_{23} \\ a_{21}b_{11} + a_{22}b_{21} & a_{21}b_{12} + a_{22}b_{22} & a_{21}b_{13} + a_{22}b_{23} \end{bmatrix}$$

Suppose that we now put in numbers and define $[A]$ and $[B]$ as

$$[A] = \begin{bmatrix} 2 & 3 \\ 1 & 4 \end{bmatrix} \qquad [B] = \begin{bmatrix} 7 & 9 & 8 \\ 10 & 5 & 6 \end{bmatrix}$$

The product $[A] \times [B]$ is

$$\begin{bmatrix} 2 \times 7 + 3 \times 10 & 2 \times 9 + 3 \times 5 & 2 \times 8 + 3 \times 6 \\ 1 \times 7 + 4 \times 10 & 1 \times 9 + 4 \times 5 & 1 \times 8 + 4 \times 6 \end{bmatrix} = \begin{bmatrix} 44 & 33 & 34 \\ 47 & 29 & 32 \end{bmatrix}$$

It is important to note here that order is important in matrix multiplication. $[A] \times [B]$ does not necessarily equal $[B] \times [A]$. Multiplication in the reverse direction may not even be possible, as is the case in our example. While it is possible to multiply a $2 \times 2$ matrix by a $2 \times 3$ matrix, it is not possible to multiple a $2 \times 3$ by a $2 \times 2$ matrix.

## Matrix inversion and the Gauss-Jordan method

The next logical matrix operation to be discussed is division. However, division is not defined for matrices. Instead, for matrices we employ the concept of the **multiplicative inverse.** In simple scalar algebra, remember that the inverse of a number $x$ is $1/x$, and that multiplying by the inverse is the same as dividing by the number. If we can define an analogous inverse concept for a matrix, then division can be accomplished through multiplication by this inverse.

    To explain the approach for finding a matrix inverse, let us return again to scalar math for a moment. In scalar math, if we divide a number by itself, the result is the number 1. In matrix algebra, if we "divide" a matrix by itself by multiplying by its inverse, we get an **identity matrix.** An identity matrix is a square matrix whose diagonal elements are all 1's and whose off-diagonal elements are all 0's. For example, the $3 \times 3$ identity matrix is

*multiplicative inverse*

*identity matrix*

$$[I] = \begin{bmatrix} 1 & 0 & 0 \\ 0 & 1 & 0 \\ 0 & 0 & 1 \end{bmatrix}$$

The notation $[I]$ will always refer to a matrix with this structure but with varying dimensions.

    Because of this identity property of matrices and their inverses, we can write the mathematical statement for a matrix $[A]$ and its inverse $[A^{-1}]$:

$$[A \times A^{-1}] = [I]$$

We can also note another interesting fact here. For a matrix and its inverse, order of multiplication does not make any difference. That is, $[A^{-1} \times A]$ is also equal to $[I]$. In order for this to be true, it is obvious that $[A]$ must be a square matrix, since only for square matrices is multiplication defined in both directions. Consequently, the whole process of finding a matrix inverse is valid only for a square matrix.

    Now that we understand the concept of the matrix inverse, how do we find it? While there are several methods available for finding the inverse, we will discuss just one: the **Gauss-Jordan elimination method.** To begin the Gauss-Jordan procedure, we take the square matrix to be inverted $[A]$ and **augment** it by drawing a vertical line and adding on an identity matrix $[I]$ of the same dimensions as $[A]$. The resulting augmented matrix is then of the form

*Gauss-Jordan elimination method*

*augment*

$$[A \mid I]$$

The Gauss-Jordan method then proceeds through the application of **row operations** such that the matrix on the left side of the vertical line is transformed into an identity matrix, and what is left on the right side is the matrix inverse. To see this, look at

*row operations*

what would happen if we already knew the inverse and multiplied it times both sides of the augmented matrix. We would get

$$[A \times A^{-1} \mid I \times A^{-1}] = [I \mid A^{-1}]$$

because of the identity property discussed earlier and the fact that any matrix multiplied by an identity matrix is unchanged (just as multiplication by 1 does not affect a number). Although we do not yet know what $[A^{-1}]$ looks like, we do know that if we can create an identity matrix on the left side, we will have its inverse on the right.

What, then, are the row operations that will allow us to do this? There are three allowable operations:

1. Any two rows of a matrix may be interchanged.

2. Any matrix row may be multiplied by a nonzero constant.

3. Any multiple of a row may be added to (or subtracted from) any other row of the matrix.

To illustrate the application of the Gauss-Jordan elimination method, let us look at a numerical example. Suppose that we want to find the inverse of the matrix

$$[A] = \begin{bmatrix} 6 & 1 \\ 3 & -2 \end{bmatrix}$$

Our first step is to form the augmented matrix

$$[A/I] = \left[ \begin{array}{cc|cc} 6 & 1 & 1 & 0 \\ 3 & -2 & 0 & 1 \end{array} \right]$$

Now, in order to move the identity matrix to the left side of the vertical line, we need to create a 1 in the upper left-hand corner where the 6 is currently located. To do this, we will use a row operation and multiply the first row by 1/6, yielding

$$\left[ \begin{array}{cc|cc} 1 & \frac{1}{6} & \frac{1}{6} & 0 \\ 3 & -2 & 0 & 1 \end{array} \right]$$

Next, we need a 0 underneath the 1 we just created so that we will have completed an identity vector for the first column. That is, we need a 0 where we currently have a 3. To create the 0, we will multiply the new row 1 that we just created by $-3$ and add the result to row 2. The resulting augmented matrix will be

$$\left[ \begin{array}{cc|cc} 1 & \frac{1}{6} & \frac{1}{6} & 0 \\ 0 & -\frac{5}{2} & -\frac{1}{2} & 1 \end{array} \right]$$

Now, we need to work on the identity vector for the second column by creating a 1 at the bottom of the second column where the $-\frac{5}{2}$ is currently. To do this, we will multiply row 2 by $-\frac{2}{5}$, giving

$$\left[\begin{array}{cc|cc} 1 & \frac{1}{6} & \frac{1}{6} & 0 \\ 0 & 1 & \frac{1}{5} & -\frac{2}{5} \end{array}\right]$$

If we can change the $\frac{1}{6}$ at the top of column 2 to a 0, we will have moved the identity matrix to the left side of the vertical line. Multiplying the new second row by $-\frac{1}{6}$ and adding to the first row, we get

$$\left[\begin{array}{cc|cc} 1 & 0 & \frac{2}{15} & \frac{1}{15} \\ 0 & 1 & \frac{1}{5} & -\frac{2}{5} \end{array}\right]$$

and our inverse matrix is

$$[A^{-1}] = \left[\begin{array}{cc} \frac{2}{15} & \frac{1}{15} \\ \frac{1}{5} & -\frac{2}{5} \end{array}\right]$$

We can verify that this is the inverse matrix by multiplying $[A] \times [A^{-1}]$, and noting that the result is the $2 \times 2$ identity matrix $[I]$.

It is also important to note at this point that not all square matrices have an inverse. Suppose that we have the matrix

$$\left[\begin{array}{cc|cc} 3 & 6 & 1 & 0 \\ 1 & 2 & 0 & 1 \end{array}\right]$$

Multiplying row 1 by $\frac{1}{3}$ will give

$$\left[\begin{array}{cc|cc} 1 & 2 & \frac{1}{3} & 0 \\ 1 & 2 & 0 & 1 \end{array}\right]$$

Multiplying new row 1 by $-1$ and adding to row 2 yields

$$\left[\begin{array}{cc|cc} 1 & 2 & \frac{1}{3} & 0 \\ 0 & 0 & -\frac{1}{3} & 1 \end{array}\right]$$

and we have an identity vector in the first column. The problem arises in now trying to create a 1 at the bottom of the second column for the second column's identity vector. No matter what we multiply times 0, we cannot make it into a 1. And if we add a multiple of the first row in order to get the 1 at the bottom of the second column, we will destroy the 0 that we just created at the bottom of the first column. In other words, there is no way to move the identity matrix to the left side of the vertical line, and consequently the matrix does not have an inverse.

## ■ Solving systems of linear equations

We have reviewed the basic matrix algebra operations of addition, subtraction, multiplication, and construction of the inverse. Now let us return to our discussion of solving systems of equations using matrix procedures. Remember that earlier we represented the set of equations

$$a_{11}x_1 + a_{12}x_2 + a_{13}x_3 + a_{14}x_4 = b_1$$

$$a_{21}x_1 + a_{22}x_2 + a_{23}x_3 + a_{24}x_4 = b_2$$

$$a_{31}x_1 + a_{32}x_2 + a_{33}x_3 + a_{34}x_4 = b_3$$

$$a_{41}x_1 + a_{42}x_2 + a_{43}x_3 + a_{44}x_4 = b_4$$

in matrix form as

$$
\begin{bmatrix}
a_{11} & a_{12} & a_{13} & a_{14} \\
a_{21} & a_{22} & a_{23} & a_{24} \\
a_{31} & a_{32} & a_{33} & a_{34} \\
a_{41} & a_{42} & a_{43} & a_{44}
\end{bmatrix}
\begin{bmatrix}
x_1 \\ x_2 \\ x_3 \\ x_4
\end{bmatrix}
=
\begin{bmatrix}
b_1 \\ b_2 \\ b_3 \\ b_4
\end{bmatrix}
$$

or more simply as

$$[A] \times x = b$$

The Gauss-Jordan elimination method presented in the last section can also be used to find the solution to a matrix equation representing a system of individual equations like the one above. Suppose that we know the inverse of [A] and multiply this inverse by both sides of the matrix equation. We get

$$[A^{-1} \times A] \times x = [A^{-1}] \times b$$

This gives

$$[I] \times x = [A^{-1}] \times b$$

or just

$$x = [A^{-1}] \times b$$

Therefore, if we find the inverse of $[A]$ and multiply it by $b$, we will have the solution to the system of equations. In fact, we can find the inverse and multiply by $b$ all in one step. Suppose that we take the $[A]$ matrix and augment it using the $b$ vector, giving $[A \mid b]$. If we multiply both sides of this augmented matrix by $[A^{-1}]$, we get

$$[A^{-1} \times A \mid A^{-1} \times b] = [I \mid A^{-1} \times b]$$

Thus, by forming a slightly different type of augmented matrix than the one we used previously and by using our Gauss-Jordan method (row operations) once again to create an identity matrix to the left of the vertical line, we come up with the $[A^{-1} \times b]$ term that we have already shown is the solution to the system of equations.

It is time again for a numerical example. Suppose that we have to solve the system of equations

$$2x_1 - 2x_2 + 4x_3 = 10$$

$$x_1 + 2x_2 + x_3 = 6$$

$$4x_1 - 4x_2 - x_3 = 2$$

We set up the augmented matrix as

$$\begin{bmatrix} 2 & -2 & 4 & 10 \\ 1 & 2 & 1 & 6 \\ 4 & -4 & -1 & 2 \end{bmatrix}$$

To create an identity matrix on the left side of the line, we first multiply row 1 by $\frac{1}{2}$, giving

$$\begin{bmatrix} 1 & -1 & 2 & 5 \\ 1 & 2 & 1 & 6 \\ 4 & -4 & -1 & 2 \end{bmatrix}$$

Now we subtract 1 times the new row 1 from row 2 and 4 times the new row 1 from row 3:

$$\begin{bmatrix} 1 & -1 & 2 & 5 \\ 0 & 3 & -1 & 1 \\ 0 & 0 & -9 & -18 \end{bmatrix}$$

Next, we multiply row 2 by $\frac{1}{3}$:

$$\begin{bmatrix} 1 & -1 & 2 & 5 \\ 0 & 1 & -\frac{1}{3} & \frac{1}{3} \\ 0 & 0 & -9 & -18 \end{bmatrix}$$

We add 1 times the new row 2 to row 1:

$$\begin{bmatrix} 1 & 0 & \frac{5}{3} & \Big| & \frac{16}{3} \\ 0 & 1 & -\frac{1}{3} & \Big| & \frac{1}{3} \\ 0 & 0 & -9 & \Big| & -18 \end{bmatrix}$$

And multiply row 3 by $-\frac{1}{9}$:

$$\begin{bmatrix} 1 & 0 & \frac{5}{3} & \Big| & \frac{16}{3} \\ 0 & 1 & -\frac{1}{3} & \Big| & \frac{1}{3} \\ 0 & 0 & 1 & \Big| & 2 \end{bmatrix}$$

Now we subtract $-\frac{1}{3}$ times new row 3 from row 2 and $\frac{5}{3}$ times new row 3 from row 1:

$$\begin{bmatrix} 1 & 0 & 0 & \Big| & 2 \\ 0 & 1 & 0 & \Big| & 1 \\ 0 & 0 & 1 & \Big| & 2 \end{bmatrix}$$

Therefore

$$\begin{bmatrix} x_1 \\ x_2 \\ x_3 \end{bmatrix} = \begin{bmatrix} 2 \\ 1 \\ 2 \end{bmatrix}$$

Thus, we have shown how the Gauss-Jordan elimination method can be used to solve a system of equations where the $[A]$ matrix is square. The next obvious question is: What do we do if we have a system of equations to be solved that do not result in a square matrix? The next section describes the method for handling systems of $m$ equations with $n$ variables when $m$ and $n$ may not be equal (i.e., the matrix may not be square).

## ■ Solving $M \times N$ systems of equations

A system of $m$ equations with $n$ variables may have no solution. For example, if two linear equations with two variables are parallel, the system of equations has no solution, because the two lines never intersect. When a system of equations has no *inconsistent*   solution, the system is said to the **inconsistent.**
*consistent*    Systems of equations that have a solution are said to be **consistent.** It is possible for

a consistent system of equations to have one unique solution or to have an infinite number of solutions. The *rank* of a matrix, or of a system of equations, can be used to determine if a system is consistent and whether it has one or an infinite number of solutions.

## Rank of a matrix

The **rank** of a matrix (an augmented matrix if we are solving a system of equations) is defined as the number of linearly independent rows or columns in the matrix. A row is linearly dependent if it can be calculated as a linear combination of other rows in the matrix. In the matrix

$$\begin{bmatrix} 1 & 4 & 6 & | & 3 \\ 2 & 8 & 12 & | & 6 \\ 3 & 12 & 18 & | & 9 \end{bmatrix}$$

it is obvious that row 2 is twice row 1, and row 3 is three times row 1. Both rows 2 and 3 are linearly dependent on row 1, and the rank of this augmented matrix is just 1. When a matrix is less than *full rank* (when its rank is less than the number of rows in the matrix), as we do row operations we will arrive at a point where the dependent row will become all 0's. This condition will signal that the matrix is less than full rank.

In order for a system of equations to be consistent (have a solution), the rank of the augmented matrix must be the same as the rank of the coefficient or [A] matrix. If the ranks of the two matrices are different, there will not be a solution to the system of equations.

Rank is also used to determine whether a consistent system has one or an infinite number of solutions. If the rank of the coefficient matrix for the system is the same as the number of variables in the system, there will be a unique solution to the system of equations. Otherwise, there will be an infinite number of solutions.

## Basic solutions

How do we deal with the situation where there are more variables than equations, since certainly the rank of the matrix, even if it is full rank, must be less than the number of variables? How do we solve a system of equations that has an infinite number of solutions? Obviously, the best we can do is to calculate one of the solutions, then another and another until we are satisfied that we have identified enough solutions to suit our purposes. We do this through the concept of a basic solution.

If we take a system of $m$ equations (rank of $m$) with $n$ variables and set $n - m$ of the variables equal to zero, the solution of the system in terms of the remaining variables is called a **basic solution.** If we have a system with three equations and six variables, by arbitrarily setting three of the variables equal to zero we get a square matrix that can be solved for the other three variables. The key here is that for every different combination of three variables that could be set to zero, a different solution of three other variables will result. This procedure generates a subset of the infinite number of possible solutions.

As a numerical example, consider the system of equations

$$5x_1 + x_2 + 0x_3 = 15$$

$$2x_1 + 0x_2 + x_3 = 10$$

If we arbitrarily set $x_1 = 0$, then the solution clearly is $x_2 = 15$ and $x_3 = 10$. If we set $x_2 = 0$, then from the first equation $x_1 = 3$ and plugging into the second equation gives $x_3 = 4$. If $x_3 = 0$, then $x_1 = 5$ and $x_2 = -10$. Thus, our three basic solutions to this system of equations are

| | |
|---|---|
| basic solution 1: | $x_1 = 0, x_2 = 15, x_3 = 10$ |
| basic solution 2: | $x_1 = 3, x_2 = 0, x_3 = 4$ |
| basic solution 3: | $x_1 = 5, x_2 = -10, x_3 = 0$ |

## Feasibility and degeneracy

*basic feasible solution*

Before we conclude our discussion of basic solutions, we shall introduce two terms that will be helpful later on in the application of these concepts to linear programming. When all of the $m$ variables that have a value for a particular basic solution (the so-called basic variables) are nonnegative, it is said to be a **basic feasible solution.** If one or more of the variables is negative, it is a nonfeasible solution. In our example, two of the three solutions are basic feasible solutions. The term feasibility has to do with the fact that in later applications where we will be trying to determine how many products to make, how many people to hire, and so on, it does not make sense to allow negative values for the variables.

*degenerate basic solution*

The second term we wish to present is degeneracy. If one or more of the $m$ basic variables that we did not set equal to zero turns out to be zero anyway, we call that basic solution a **degenerate basic solution,** as the size of the basis or variable collection has degenerated below the normal size. In our numerical example, none of the basic solutions was degenerate.

## ■ Summary

In this chapter we have reviewed the basics of mathematics and linear and matrix algebra that are necessary for a thorough understanding of many of the remaining chapters in the text. We have examined the concepts of linear and nonlinear equations, how to represent systems of equations using matrices, and how to manipulate matrices in order to arrive at a solution to a system of equations regardless of its structure. Still, we have only scratched the surface. While a few other related concepts may be introduced in context in later chapters, many of the more advanced aspects of the subject have been purposefully omitted. The interested student can find additional material in more advanced texts.

## ■ Glossary of terms

**basic feasible solution:**   a basic solution where none of the variables have negative values.

**basic solution:**   a solution to a set of $m$ equations with $n$ variables where $n - m$ of the variables are set to zero.

**consistent:**   the condition where a system of equations has one or more solutions.

**degenerate basic solution:**   a basic solution with one or more of the basic variables equal to zero.

**dependent variable:**   the variable in a function that depends on the rest of the expression.

**equation:**   a mathematical statement of equality.

**function:**   a relation where the dependent variable can take on only one value for each value of the independent variable.

**Gauss-Jordan elimination method:**   a matrix method for solving systems of linear equations.

**identity matrix:**   a matrix with all 1's down the diagonal and all 0's for the off-diagonal elements.

**inconsistent:**   when a system of equations has no solution.

**independent variable:**   the variable or variables in a function that do not depend on the values of any other variables.

**inequality:**   a mathematical expression where the left-hand side of the expression is either less than, greater than, less than or equal to, or greater than or equal to the right-hand side.

**intercept:**   the point on a graph at which a line crosses an axis.

**inverse:**   a matrix such that multiplying the inverse of a matrix is analogous to dividing by the original matrix.

**linear equation:**   an equation that plots as a straight line.

**matrix:**   a tabular (row and column) arrangement of data and/or variables.

**nonlinear:**   plotting in a curvilinear fashion.

**polynomial:**   a class of nonlinear statements with exponents greater than 1 on variables, but with no cross product, root, or absolute value terms.

**quadratic:**   a polynomial with a largest exponent of 2.

**rank:**   the number of linearly independent rows or columns in a matrix.

**relation:**   any rule that produces ordered pairs of variable values.

**scalar:**   a constant.

**system of equations:**   a collection of equations subject to simultaneous solution.

**variable:**   a symbol representing an unknown quantity.

**vector:**   a matrix with only one row or one column.

# ■ Review questions

1. Describe the two methods for plotting a straight line. Use a two-dimensional graph to help develop your explanation.

2. What is the difference between a relation and a function? Are linear equations functions or relations?

3. Discuss the two methods described in the chapter for simplifying quadratic equations. Which of these two methods might also be applicable to simplifying polynomials in general?

4. Discuss at least four business applications where matrices or vectors could be used to represent data compactly. Do not use the production line example from the chapter as one of the four.

5. Why do only square matrices have inverses?

6. Name the three allowable row operations that can be performed on any matrix.

7. What is an augmented matrix?

8. Describe the steps of the Gauss-Jordan elimination method for solving simultaneous equations.

9. Discuss the concept of basic solutions for solving an $m \times n$ system of equations. What is a basic feasible solution? What is a degenerate solution?

# ■ True/false questions

1. An equation is nonlinear if one of the terms contains the square root of one of the variables.

2. An intercept is the point where two equations cross on a graph.

3. In order to write an equation in slope-intercept form, we isolate the horizontal variable on the left side of the equation.

4. All inequalities are relations, but they can never be functions.

5. Polynomial equations are special cases of the larger class of linear equations.

6. All polynomial equations may be factored.

7. It is always possible to add two rectangular matrices.

8. It is always possible to subtract two square matrices.

9. An identity matrix is a square matrix whose diagonal elements are all 1's and whose off-diagonal elements are all 0's.

10. The inverse of a matrix is equal to the matrix of inverses of all the scalars within the matrix.

11. Not all matrices have inverse, but all square matrices do.

12. An inconsistent system of equations is a system with no solution.

13. In a system of equations, if the coefficient matrix is of full rank, there will be a unique solution to the system of equations.

14. The method of basic solutions generates all possible solutions to a system of equations.

15. A basic feasible solution is a basic solution where all of the variable values in the solution are nonnegative.

# ▪ Problems

1. Plot the following linear equations by identifying both intercepts:

   **a.** $6x + 3y = 36$
   **b.** $4p + 5q = 32$
   **c.** $2z - 3w = 21$
   **d.** $-a + 7b = -9$

2. Write each of the equations in Problem 1 in slope-intercept form and graph each using the slope method.

3. Graph the function $f(x) = 4x - 2$. Is this any different than graphing the equation $4x - y = 2$?

4. Given the graph in Figure P2-4, determine the function that this graph represents.

5. Godwinn Roofing charges a flat rate of $800 for the labor involved in installing a new roof. Shingles are currently selling for $7.80 per bundle. Write a function that will yield the cost of a new roof given the number of bundles of shingles required to cover the roof.

6. Columbia Antenna produces antennas for CB radios and marine radios. The production cost of a CB antenna is $4.35, and the production cost of a marine antenna is $5.13. Because of production efficiencies, once the production level reaches 500 units of each antenna, the production cost for each type drops by $0.04 for every unit beyond 500. Construct a cost equation that will yield total production cost assuming that the quantity produced of each type of antenna is some variable level beyond 500 units.

**FIGURE P2-4.**

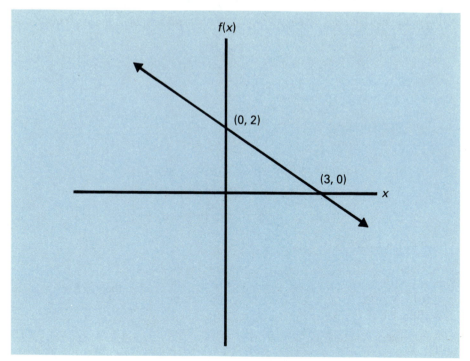

7. Graph the following inequalities on the same graph:

$$2x_1 - 4x_2 \geq 16$$

$$3x_1 + 9x_2 \leq 27$$

Shade in the area on the graph such that the points in that area will satisfy both of the inequalities at the same time.

8. Graph the following polynomials:
   a. $f(x) = 2x^3 - x^2 + 2x + 5$
   b. $f(x) = (2x - 1)/(3x + 2)$
   c. $f(x) = 4x^2 + 9x - 3$

9. Solve each of the following quadratic equations using both the quadratic formula and factoring
   a. $4x^2 - 7x + 3 = 0$
   b. $2x^2 + 4.2x = 5.1$
   c. $6x^2 - 2x = -3.1$

   What can we say about part (c)?

10. The average nightly cost of a hotel room at Miracle Beach is $75 during the prime season and $35 in the off-season. A condo costs $95 per night in season and $55 in the off-season. A beach house is $100 during the season and $40 in the off-season. Express this situation by constructing an "accommodation cost matrix" for Miracle Beach.

11. Represent the following system of equations in matrix notation as a combination of matrices and vectors:

$$2x_1 + 6x_2 - 3x_3 = 21$$

$$5x_1 - 4x_2 - 3x_3 = 55$$

$$4x_1 + 9x_2 + 8x_3 = 37$$

12. Given the two matrices,

$$[A] = \begin{bmatrix} 2.5 & 6.0 & 3.2 \\ 8.0 & 4.7 & 1.2 \\ 4.2 & 3.3 & 0.9 \end{bmatrix} \qquad [B] = \begin{bmatrix} 5.5 & 3.6 & 2.9 \\ 2.9 & 7.5 & 3.9 \\ 6.7 & 6.6 & 5.8 \end{bmatrix}$$

find the following:
   a. $2 \times [A]$
   b. $[A] + [B]$
   c. $[A] - 3 \times [B]$
   d. $[B] - 1.5 \times [A] + 4$

13. For the matrices in Problem 12, find $[A] \times [B]$.

**14.** For the matrices,

$$[A] = \begin{bmatrix} 2 & 5 & 9 \\ 4 & 7 & 1 \end{bmatrix} \quad [B] = \begin{bmatrix} 1 & 6 \\ 4 & 9 \\ 3 & 5 \end{bmatrix} \quad [C] = \begin{bmatrix} 4 & 3 & 9 \\ 0 & 4 & 5 \\ 8 & 8 & 6 \end{bmatrix}$$

find:

**a.** $[B] \times [A]$ (Is multiplication in the other direction possible in this case?)
**b.** $[B] \times [A] \times [C]$
**c.** $[A] \times [C]$

**15.** Using the Gauss-Jordan method, find the inverse of the following matrix:

$$\begin{bmatrix} 4 & 3 \\ 2 & 5 \end{bmatrix}$$

**16.** Find the inverse of the following matrix using the Gauss-Jordan method:

$$\begin{bmatrix} 2 & 7 & 4 \\ 3 & -2 & -1 \\ -2 & 3 & 7 \end{bmatrix}$$

**17.** Find the inverse of the following matrix:

$$\begin{bmatrix} 4 & 6 & 7 \\ 8 & 12 & 14 \end{bmatrix}$$

What is the problem with attempting to find an inverse for this matrix?

**18.** Solve the following system of equations using the matrix inverse (Gauss-Jordan) method:

$$4x_1 + 3x_2 = 22$$
$$2x_1 - 6x_2 = 24$$

**19.** Use the matrix inverse method to solve the following system of equations:

$$x_1 - 2x_2 + 6x_3 = 20$$
$$2x_1 + 3x_2 + 2x_3 = 30$$
$$2x_1 - x_2 + 4x_3 = 40$$

**20.** Given the two matrices:

$$[A] = \begin{bmatrix} 4 & 1 & 2 \\ 3 & 2 & 5 \\ 6 & 1 & 8 \end{bmatrix} \qquad [B] = \begin{bmatrix} 5 & 8 & 7 & 4 \\ 10 & 4 & 3 & 5 \\ 10 & 16 & 14 & 8 \end{bmatrix}$$

What is the rank of $[A]$? What is the rank of $[B]$?

**21.** For the system of equations:

$$4x_1 + 3x_2 + 8x_3 = 5$$

$$-2x_1 - 1x_2 + 6x_3 = 3$$

$$8x_1 + 6x_2 + 16x_3 = 9$$

What is the rank of the coefficient matrix? What is the rank of the augmented matrix? Is there a solution to this system of equations? Why or why not?

**22.** Suppose that the right-hand side of the third equation in Problem 21 were 10 instead of 9. Would this revised system of equations have a solution? Why or why not? If the system of equations has a solution, is it a unique solution?

**23.** Identify all of the basic solutions for the following system of equations:

$$3x_1 + 0x_2 + 2x_3 = 18$$

$$6x_1 + 5x_2 + 0x_3 = 30$$

Are any of the basic solutions infeasible?

**24.** For the system of equations:

$$2x_1 + 1x_2 + 5x_3 + 0x_4 = 20$$

$$1x_1 + 1x_2 + 0x_3 + 2x_4 = 10$$

Find all basic solutions. Are any of the basic solutions infeasible? Are any of the solutions degenerate?

# Breakeven Analysis

## ■ Introduction

The first two chapters presented the fundamental ideas of modeling as a tool for quantitative analysis and reviewed some basic mathematics needed in modeling and model solution. This chapter introduces our first application of quantitative modeling, to be followed by many more through the course of the text. This first application area is known by the broad title, *Breakeven Analysis*.

Many decision problems faced by management scientists and other decision makers involve a determination of the minimum volume or quantity of a good or service that must be produced or provided in order for revenues to cover the cost of the product or service. At this point where revenues equal costs, the firm will just break even on the product or service. At volumes beyond the breakeven point, the firm will realize a profit. Consequently, this area of decision making is often referred to either as cost–volume–profit analysis or **breakeven analysis.** While the basic *breakeven* concept of breakeven analysis is quite simple, there are complications to be handled *analysis* that arise in most real breakeven applications. For instance, the relationship between cost and volume or revenue and volume may not be a simple linear relationship. The aforementioned relationships may not be continuous, but may have volume levels at which costs or revenue jump by some increment. There may be constraints on the volume that can be provided or that the market will absorb. Or we may have to make breakeven decisions about multiple products simultaneously. We will discuss these and other related concepts in this chapter.

To aid in the discussion and development of breakeven models, this chapter, as well as many of the subsequent chapters, will build upon a case example. The case in this chapter is simplistic, but it contains many of the same aspects as real problems that exist in practice.

### ■ Case
# The Smartdisk Software Company

Smartdisk Software develops and markets a full line of business application software, concentrating on the areas of quantitative models for decision support. Their current line of software, available for both microcomputers and large mainframe computers, includes packages for statistical decision making; accounting; financial and portfolio management; inventory management; and production planning, scheduling, and control. Thus far, the company has stayed away from the areas of word processing and basic database models because of the tremendous competition in those areas.

Hal Berkely, the manager for marketing and distribution for Smartdisk, recently attended a conference of business computer users where the main topic of conversation was the need for better and less expensive integrated softwares for microcomputers. Integrated softwares are those that can communicate with each other and pass information back and forth to perform multiple tasks, such as retrieving information from a database, doing a financial analysis on the data, and then passing it to a word processor for report generation. Based on the market direction indicated by the conference participants, Hal is convinced that Smartdisk must develop and market an integrated microcomputer package so that users will perceive that Smartdisk offers a full product line.

In preparation for presenting his idea to the other company executives at the next monthly planning meeting, Hal has begun to gather some data concerning the implementation of his idea. Because the company does not have any experience in development in the database and word processing areas, both necessary for an integrated system, Hal estimates that it would take approximately one year for development. During this time,

a staff of programmers would have to be assigned full time to the tasks of programming, testing, and writing documentation, causing the company to incur a substantial salary cost for development. Also, there would be costs related to equipment and supplies. In total, Hal estimates that the development costs would be in the neighborhood of $700,000. Once development is complete, the cost of a marketing campaign of sufficient strength to penetrate an established market of this nature would be about $150,000. It would also be necessary to establish a new marketing outlet for this product, as it is so different from the company's current line. The initial cost of dealer training and establishing the market network would be about $125,000.

Additional costs would be incurred as the software is distributed. Assuming that the software would require about four diskettes, the cost of the distribution medium would be about $1.50 per diskette or $6.00 per copy of the total software. The printing and reproduction cost of the documentation manuals to accompany the software would be about $40.00 per copy. Finally, the cost to pack the diskettes and manuals and ship the package to distributors would average about $5.00 per copy.

On the revenue side, Hal feels that the market would not accept a price in excess of $395 for the package, and that the company's price to the distributors could not, therefore, be any more than about $300. He is sure that such a pricing scheme would ensure the company of selling at least 5000 copies of the software within the time that the company normally allows for recovery of expenses on new products.

All this leaves Mr. Berkely with many questions to answer before the next planning meeting. Can the company make a profit on this new product? What is the likely level of this profit? Is this pricing/quantity scheme the most logical one?

# ■ Linear breakeven analysis

We can use linear breakeven analysis to answer many of Mr. Berkely's questions, but first we must discuss some of the details of breakeven analysis. Breakeven models deal with the relationship between *total revenue* and *total cost* at any given volume of operation. It is useful to break total cost down into *fixed costs* and *variable costs* for the purpose of breakeven analysis. While the makeup of these components is rather intuitive to those with a business background, we will review them briefly for those who are just beginning their business education.

**Total revenue** for a product is the sum of all incomes directly attributable to the particular product. Usually, total revenue is found by multiplying the selling price of one unit of the product times the number of units we expect to sell. Notice that we said the volume we expect to sell, since breakeven analysis is rarely of benefit after marketing and/or production decisions have already been made. These expected volumes may be the result of a sales forecast or a combination of forecasts and promised future orders for the product.      *total revenue*

**Fixed costs** are those costs that must be incurred whether we sell one unit or a million units of the product. While these costs are sometimes incurred up front in the production process, they do not necessarily have to be up-front costs to be fixed. For example, rent is generally a fixed cost at least over a certain range of volume (if the volume gets too large, we might have to rent a bigger facility), and rent may be paid in installments. Still, it is a fixed cost because we must have a facility whether we produce one unit or many units. Some other examples of fixed costs are depreciation on capital equipment, certain salaries, lump-sum advertising expenses, insurance and property taxes, and research and development expenditures.      *fixed costs*

**Variable costs** are the expenses of doing business that can be attributed directly to the creation of an individual unit of product. Examples of this type of cost would be raw materials, direct labor expenses, packaging and shipping costs, sales commissions, and operating expenses (electricity, water, etc.) that vary with the volume produced. Because these costs can be summed to find the total variable cost per unit, we need only multiply this variable cost per unit times the volume in units to arrive at total variable cost.      *variable costs*

Figure 3-1 illustrates the relationship of the cost components. By adding in the revenue component, Figure 3-2 illustrates the total relationship and the breakeven point.

Note that the breakeven volume or quantity occurs where the total revenue exactly equals the total cost. At any volume below the breakeven point, the firm will experience a loss. At any volume above the breakeven point, the firm will make a profit. Because of the difference in slopes of the cost line and the revenue line, the farther we move in either direction from the breakeven point, the greater our loss or profit.

While a graphical representation is useful for visualizing the cost/profit relationship, it is probably not the most efficient approach for finding the breakeven quantity. An equation-based model that can be solved to indicate breakeven quantity directly would be more efficient. In order to develop such a model, let us

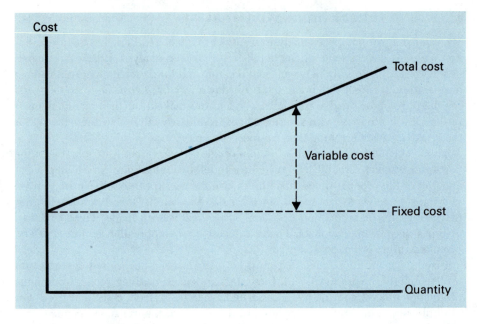

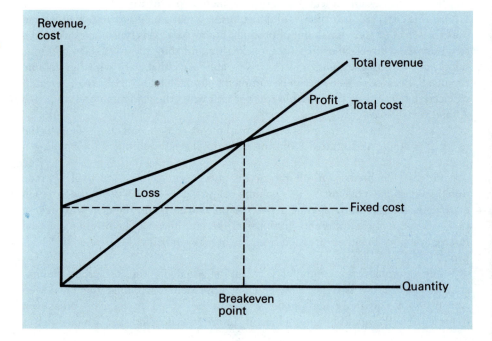

define the variables and parameters that would be contained in such a model. Suppose that we let:

$Q$ = the breakeven quantity or volume

$Z$ = profit

$P$ = price per unit

$C_f$ = fixed cost

$C_v$ = variable cost per unit

$TR$ = total revenue

$TC$ = total cost

There are several things that we know from our discussion and the development of the breakeven graph. First, we know that total revenue may be computed as the product of the variable quantity $Q$ and the fixed price $P$. Therefore:

$$TR = P \times Q$$

Also we know that total cost is the sum of fixed and variable cost:

$$TC = C_f + (Q \times C_v)$$

Finally, we know that profit is equal to the excess of revenue beyond expenses:

$$Z = TR - TC$$
$$= (P \times Q) - C_f - (Q \times C_v)$$

Since breakeven occurs where profit is zero, we must set $Z = 0$ and collect terms:

$$0 = (P \times Q) - C_f - (Q \times C_v)$$
$$= Q(P - C_v) - C_f$$
$$Q(P - C_v) = C_f$$
$$Q = \frac{C_f}{P - C_v}$$

Therefore, to find the breakeven quantity all we have to do is divide the total fixed cost by the difference between price and unit variable cost. If we think carefully about what this equation is saying, it makes perfect sense. The denominator, price minus unit variable cost, represents how much revenue above variable cost is left over for each unit sold to help cover fixed cost and, ultimately, to contribute to profit. If we divide total fixed cost by the contribution from each unit sold, this ratio will be exactly the number of units that must be sold to cover fixed cost, that is, breakeven.

For any quantity above this level, the excess contribution will accrue to profits, since fixed costs have been covered.

Now we are ready to return to the Smartdisk case and see what Hal Berkely's breakeven quantity would be. Three of the costs Hal identified are not related to volume and should be considered fixed costs. These were the development cost, marketing campaign cost, and dealer training cost. Therefore, the fixed cost would be

$$C_f = \$700,000 + \$150,000 + \$125,000 = \$975,000$$

The variable costs are the diskette expense, cost of documentation manuals, and the packing and shipping cost:

$$C_v = \$6.00 + \$40.00 + \$5.00 = \$51.00$$

The price the company could get for each unit is $P = \$300$. Therefore the breakeven quantity is

$$
\begin{aligned}
Q &= \frac{\$975,000}{\$300 - \$51} \\[2mm]
&= \frac{\$975,000}{\$249} \\[2mm]
&= 3915.66
\end{aligned}
$$

Hal Berkely feels that the company can sell at least 5,000 units at the given price, so it would appear that the new software package would be profitable since all units after the 3916th unit contribute to company profits (actually, the 3916th unit contributes a little to profit, as the breakeven is not a whole number). As to how much profit they would make, we would have to assume a total sales figure to calculate this. Using Hal's estimate of 5000 units to be conservative and returning to our earlier profit function:

$$
\begin{aligned}
Z &= (P \times Q) - C_f - (Q \times C_v) \\[2mm]
&= (\$300 \times 5,000) - \$975,000 - (5,000 \times \$51) \\[2mm]
&= \$1,500,000 - \$975,000 - \$255,000 \\[2mm]
&= \$270,000
\end{aligned}
$$

This profit level would occur at the quantity 5000, as shown on Figure 3-3. If Hal is wrong about the volume, the profit will obviously be more or less than $270,000. For each extra unit sold above the 5000 mark (in fact, above the 3916 mark), the company will make another $249 in profit. It is clear that forecasting the sales is an extremely important factor in such an analysis. That forecasting task will be the subject of a later chapter.

**FIGURE 3-3.**
**Breakeven Graph**
**for Smartdisk**

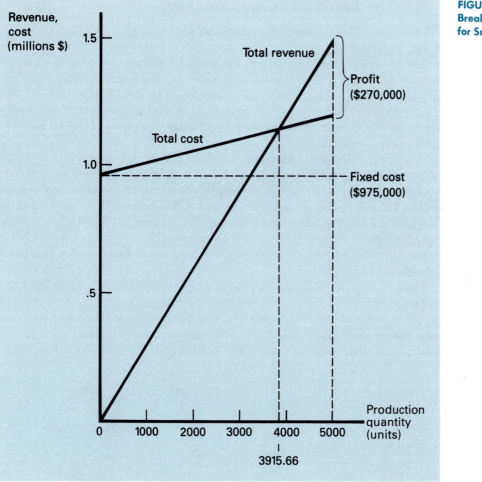

Mr. Berkely also wondered about his pricing scheme and whether better alternatives exist. In order to answer that question, we would need more information than was presented in the case. Specifically, we would need forecasts of sales at different price levels. Certainly, if the company charges a higher price for the software, they will break even at a lower volume. However, the number of units that the market will accept at this higher price might not be above the new breakeven point, or even if profit can be made it might be lower than the potential at the current price because of the lower number of units that can be sold. We will not construct other scenarios, as the analysis would be done in exactly the same way as our prior analysis. We just want to point out that in most real situations multiple options will face the decision maker and will probably necessitate repeated application of the methodology we have been using.

# ■ Investment in fixed assets

Another type of breakeven analysis that is not appropriate for the Smartdisk case but that is useful in situations where fixed assets such as machinery are used to produce a product will be presented in this section. To illustrate this idea, consider the following example. American Valve produces a high-pressure water valve on a machine that the company has owned long enough for it to be depreciated down to its salvage value. The company's fixed cost on the valve, arising from fixed operating costs, pro-rata share of salaries, and so on, is $10,000 per month. The variable cost of production per valve is $300.

American Valve is considering replacing the old machine with a newer one with improved technology. The new machine will cost $600,000. Assuming a five-year straight-line depreciation period, the monthly depreciation cost of the new machine will be $10,000, doubling fixed cost allocated to this product. However, because this machine will result in less scrappage and waste of raw materials and will require less operator time to produce a valve, it will reduce variable cost of the valves to $235 per valve. Above what volume of production will the new machine be better than the old machine?

Figure 3-4 illustrates this problem by having the two total cost curves, $TC_1$ for the old machine and $TC_2$ for the new machine, superimposed on the same graph. While the fixed cost is higher for the new machine, the increase in total cost is at a lower rate because of the lower variable cost with the new machine. This is indicated on the graph by a flatter slope for curve $TC_2$. At the breakeven point, we are indifferent

**FIGURE 3-4.**
**Breakeven Point for Investment in Fixed Assets**

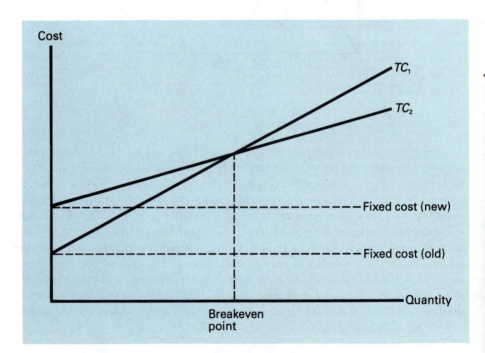

between the two machines. Above the breakeven quantity, the new machine is superior because of the lower total cost.

We can solve numerically for the breakeven quantity by constructing a simple equation. At this point, $TC_1$ and $TC_2$ are equal. Since each total cost is a sum of fixed and variable costs, we can construct the following equality:

$$\$10,000 + (Q \times \$300) = \$20,000 + (Q \times \$235)$$

By collecting terms:

$$Q(\$300 - \$235) = \$20,000 - \$10,000$$

$$Q(\$65) = \$10,000$$

$$Q = 153.8$$

Thus, if the company plans to produce 154 valves or more during the month, the new machine will be superior. At volumes below 154, the old machine is more cost efficient.

This type of analysis is quite useful for capital equipment decisions or other fixed asset acquisitions. In the next sections, we will look at changes in cost that are related directly to volume.

## ▪ Volume-related cost changes

In the previous section we examined the effect of a change in fixed cost resulting because of a capital acquisition. This cost change was across the board and was not related to volume. In some cases, however, changes in costs are volume related. Such changes do not really affect the way we perform breakeven analysis, but they are worth mentioning.

First let us look at volume-related changes in fixed cost. Suppose that we use a machine to produce a product, and that machine is the best available so we are not concerned about replacing it. However, the machine has a limited production capacity such that we will have to upgrade it if planned production volume goes beyond its capacity. This is a fixed cost change that is volume dependent. Figure 3-5 illustrates the relationship between revenue and total cost in this situation. If we wish to use our previous breakeven equation, we can do so. Because the breakeven point is beyond the step increase in fixed cost, we would use the higher fixed cost to solve the equation. Even if the graph had not been constructed, we could start off by using the lower fixed cost to solve the equation. If the breakeven point that results is greater than the volume at which fixed costs increase, we would solve the equation again using the higher fixed cost. This same trial-and-error approach could be used even if we have numerous step increases in fixed cost. In our little example here, the increase in fixed cost came from the need for greater machine production capacity. The same kind of situation might arise when increased volume demands more office or storage space, salaried personnel, and so on.

**FIGURE 3-5.
Breakeven Graph
with an Increase
in Fixed Cost
(Volume Related)**

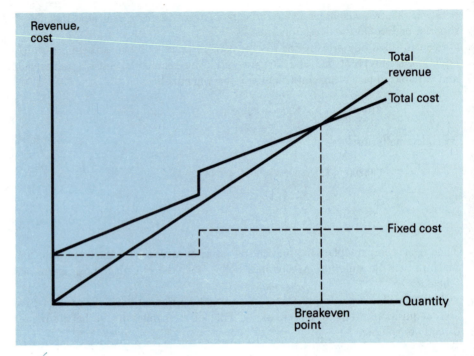

**FIGURE 3-6.
Breakeven Point
for a Change in
Variable Cost
(Volume Related)**

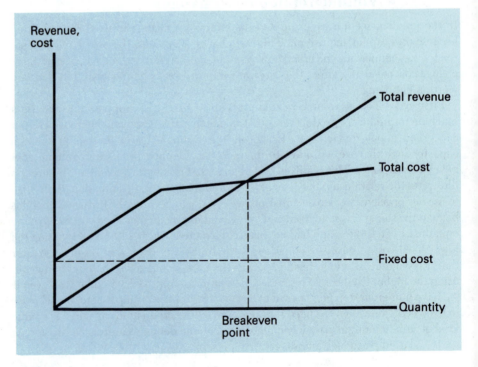

The situation where variable cost changes is illustrated in Figure 3-6. Changes in variable cost usually result from economies of scale, such as quantity discounts on the purchase of raw materials and decreasing sales commission for larger sales volumes. Once again, our prior equation could be applied starting with the initial variable cost level, and reapplied if the resulting breakeven point is above the volume at which variable costs decrease.

## ■ Nonlinear breakeven analysis

In all of our previous examples, we assumed that the total revenue and total cost "curves" are linear, the result of multiplying a uniform price times quantity and a uniform variable cost times quantity. As you might have guessed, this assumption is not always valid. Price may not be stable but may have to be continuously lowered with higher volumes as the market becomes saturated. Variable costs may increase or decrease not in step fashion but continuously with increasing volume. In this section we will look at the effect of nonlinear relationships and so-called *nonlinear breakeven analysis*.

We must realize at the beginning that there are almost unlimited variations in the way revenue and cost can behave in a nonlinear setting. Figure 3-7 illustrates a situation where variable cost decreases as economies of scale are realized and then increases as production capacity is neared and scrap and other factors become more important, and where total revenue increases at a decreasing rate as price breaks

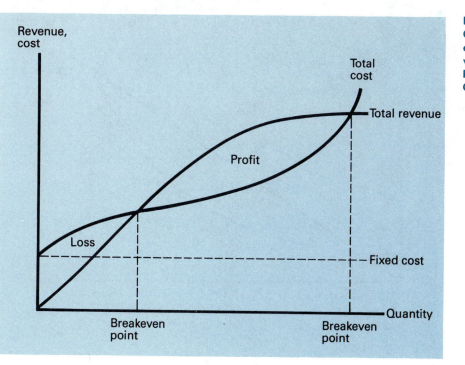

**FIGURE 3-7.
Graph of a Breakeven Situation with Nonlinear Revenues and Cost**

must be given when volume nears the market potential. In such cases where both revenue and cost are complex and the curves have several inflection points (points at which the direction of the curve change), about the only option available to the decision maker is to plot the curves as accurately as possible and estimate breakeven points from the graph (notice that there are two breakeven points in Figure 3-7 with a region of profit between them and regions of loss in both directions outward from the points).

If the nature of the curves is less complex, it may be possible to represent the revenue/cost relationship mathematically and solve for the exact breakeven and profit values. Consider the following example.

American Industrial Ceramics (AIC) produces a ceramic insulator that sells for $359, and this price is firm regardless of the volume they produce [that is, $TR = $359(Q)$]. Cost of production, however, varies with production according to the formula $TC = 2Q^2 - Q + 6400$, where $Q$ once again is the production quantity. Figure 3-8 illustrates AIC's profit situation and the fact that this product has two breakeven points. Because the nature of the revenue and cost curves is not overly complex, it is possible to calculate these two points exactly rather than estimate them from the graph. We know that these two points will both occur where $TR = TC$, or

$$359(Q) = 2Q^2 - (Q) + 6400$$

FIGURE 3-8.
Revenue/Cost
Graph for the
American Indus-
trial Ceramics
Example

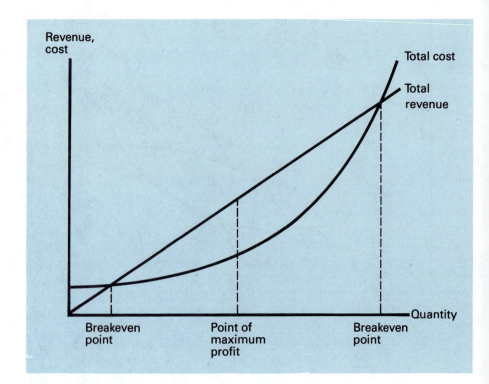

Collecting like terms, this can be written as

$$2Q^2 - 360(Q) + 6400 = 0$$

In this form, we recognize this equation to be a quadratic as we discussed in Chapter 2. Thus we may be able to solve it either by factoring or by the quadratic formula. This equation will factor as

$$(2Q - 40)(Q - 160) = 0$$

Setting each term equal to zero, we get:

$$2Q - 40 = 0 \quad \text{and} \quad Q - 160 = 0$$
$$Q = 20 \qquad\qquad Q = 160$$

Thus the company will make a profit if it produces between 20 and 160 ceramic insulators.

Where would the largest profit occur? Because of the nature of the cost curve as a quadratic, in this particular situation the cost curve moves away from the revenue curve, reaches an inflection point, and curves back toward the revenue curve in a symmetric fashion. The largest profit (largest gap between the revenue and cost curve) will occur halfway between the breakeven points, at a quantity of 90 units. This certainly will not always be the case. The methods of Chapters 23 and 24 illustrate the use of calculus to solve similar problems; where calculus cannot be used, trial-and-error calculation of profit is always a possibility.

## ■ Breakeven analysis for multiple products

In our discussion of breakeven analysis thus far, it has been possible to look at individual products and perform a unit breakeven analysis on those products. This is due to the assumption that we can identify exactly what portion of the firm's total fixed costs should be allocated to each product in our product line. In many situations, this is a very difficult task. An alternative to trying to assign a portion of fixed costs and do individual product analyses is to perform an overall breakeven analysis based on the firm's entire product line (or some subset that logically shares fixed costs). When this is done, breakeven is usually expressed as a dollar sales or production volume.

It is simple to express our single product breakeven equation in terms of dollars. In units, the equation is

$$Q = \frac{C_f}{P - C_v}$$

If we multiply both sides of the equation by $P$, the left-side term with price times quantity is the dollar equivalent of the breakeven point:

$$P \times Q = P \times \left( \frac{C_f}{P - C_v} \right)$$

$$= \frac{C_f}{1 - C_v/P}$$

On the right-hand side of the new equation, the denominator represents the percentage of each revenue dollar that is left over after variable costs to go toward covering fixed costs. When this percentage is divided into the dollar level of fixed costs, the result is the dollar sales necessary to cover fixed costs and break even. If we could somehow come up with a term similar to the denominator of this expression that represents the average percentage of each sales dollar that goes toward fixed cost and profit across all products, then breakeven dollar sales would be simple to calculate.

Let us return to our earlier example of the American Valve Company. Suppose that their entire product line consists of the water valve we discussed earlier, a gas valve, and an oxygen valve. The water valve sells for $429 and has $300 in associated variable costs. The $129 contribution of the water valve, when divided by the selling price of $429, indicates that for each dollar of sales of water valves, 30% of that dollar is left over for fixed costs and profit. The gas valve sells for $500 and has variable costs of $410 for a percentage contribution per dollar of sales of 18%. The oxygen valve sells for $538, has $430 in variable costs, and has a contribution percentage of 20%. Data pertaining to the three products is summarized in Table 3-1.

Also, we have discovered that 40% of the company's sales volume comes from the water valves, 30% from the gas valves, and 30% from the oxygen valves. The company's annual fixed costs are $360,000, and the plant's annual production capacity in sales dollars is $2.9 million.

Our next step is to take a weighted average of the percentage contributions by multiplying each product's percentage contribution by the percentage of sales represented by that product. By taking

$$.4(30\%) + .3(18\%) + .3(20\%) = 23.4\%$$

**TABLE 3-1.**
**Product Data for**
**American Valve**

| Product | Selling Price | Variable Cost per Unit | Contribution | Percentage Contribution |
|---------|---------------|------------------------|--------------|-------------------------|
| Water valve | $429 | $300 | $129 | 30% |
| Gas valve | 500 | 410 | 90 | 18% |
| Oxygen valve | 538 | 430 | 108 | 20% |

we see that across all products, for every dollar of sales the company achieves, 23.4% of the average dollar is left to cover fixed costs and finally to contribute to profit. Therefore, our breakeven point is

$$P \times Q = \frac{\$360,000}{.234}$$

$$= \$1,538,461.50$$

The company must generate slightly over $1.5 million in sales to break even, which represents $1,538,461.50/$2,900,000 or 53.05% of the firm's capacity. At any lower utilization of capacity, the firm will not break even.

While this example is rather simplistic, it nonetheless illustrates how the logic we have used for single products could be extended to multiple products. Even for cases where prices and/or cost are nonlinear, the use of average prices and average cost weighted across products can provide useful insights to the decision maker.

## ■ Summary

This chapter has outlined the basics of cost–volume–profit analysis or breakeven analysis. We have looked at the most basic case involving linearly increasing cost and revenue. We have looked at the effects of changes in fixed cost from investment in assets and changes in both fixed and variable costs that are volume-related changes. The treatment of nonlinear cost and/or revenue was discussed, and our basic model was extended to allow computation of the firm's dollar breakeven point across an entire product line. While the actual scenarios that a decision maker might encounter are obviously more complex than most of our examples, and while we have not discussed every form of analysis a firm might wish to undertake, our discussion at least indicates the logic and structure of thought necessary to tackle breakeven problems.

## ■ Glossary of terms

**breakeven analysis:**   the identification of output volume such that total costs are covered by total revenue.

**contribution:**   the portion of the revenue from a unit of product above and beyond variable cost that is left to cover fixed cost or contribute to profit.

**fixed cost:**   those costs that must be incurred whether one unit or many units are produced.

**total cost:**   the sum of fixed and variable costs.

**total revenue:**   the dollar revenue expected to occur for a given quantity of production.

**variable cost:**   the direct costs of production that can be attributed to individual units of product.

## ■ Review questions

1. List at least five different categories of fixed costs that a company might incur.
2. Name at least five examples of variable costs.
3. "The breakeven quantity may be found by dividing total fixed cost by the difference between price and unit variable cost." Discuss this statement. Are there any circumstances where this statement would not be true?
4. Explain the steps in the trial-and-error (nongraphical) approach to finding breakeven with volume-related cost changes.
5. What is the most common approach for finding breakeven quantities when either revenue or costs or both follow a nonlinear pattern as quantity increases?
6. Discuss the extension of single-product breakeven analysis to analysis with multiple products. Name at least one example where fixed costs could not be allocated to individual products and would have to be handled in aggregate.

## ■ True/false questions

1. Advertising expenses are typically treated as variable costs.
2. The breakeven quantity occurs at the point where the total fixed cost exactly equals the total variable cost.
3. Breakeven quantity may be found by dividing total fixed cost by the unit contribution to profit.
4. If a company charges a higher price for their product, they will always break even at a lower production quantity.
5. The only possible way to determine the breakeven quantity when fixed or variable costs change by step increases is to draw a graph and estimate the quantity from the graph.
6. With nonlinear revenue or cost behavior, it is possible for higher production volumes to result in lower total profits.
7. When working with multiple products, breakeven is usually expressed in terms of total dollar sales.

## ■ Problems

1. Find the breakeven quantity given the following:
   a. Price per unit = $4.75
      Total fixed costs = $5000
      Variable cost per unit = $2.11
   b. Price per unit = $9.67
      Total fixed costs = $3422
      Variable cost per unit = $4.95

2. Spanky's Hot Dogs derives almost all of its revenues from its sales of regular hot dogs. A hot dog sells for $1.25, and the ingredients necessary to make the hot dog costs $0.65.

Spanky's overhead (rent, taxes, salaries, etc.) total about $500 per week. How many hot dogs does Spanky have to sell each week before he begins to make a profit?

3. Bob's Motel has 20 rental units. Each month, Bob incurs about $12,200 in fixed costs for items such as payments on the motel, taxes and insurance, and salaries. Also, for each night that each room is rented, Bob has to pay out $10 for maid service, linen service, soap, and other incidentals. Bob is currently renting rooms in his motel for $30 per night. How many rental nights does Bob need in a month to break even? Assuming a 30-day month, does Bob have a problem? Suppose that Bob raised his rates to $45 per night. What would be the new breakeven point? How much profit would Bob make at this higher rate if the motel had no vacancies for the entire month?

4. Columbia Retread has the equipment to put new tread onto worn tires, and then it sells these tires on a retail basis. Columbia Retread's monthly fixed costs are $6000. They spend approximately $12 recapping each tire by the time they purchase a worn carcass, supply new rubber, and pay for the other supplies attributable directly to the tire. They would like to break even by the time they reach monthly sales of 275 tires. What price should Columbia Retread charge for its tires?

5. Apex Fiberglass Products (AFP) produces a fiberglass awning for home patios. The company's fixed costs on the facility that produces the awning are $15,000 per month. The current variable cost per awning produced is $130. A new fiberglass molding machine has just come on the market that would reduce the labor required to produce an awning and reduce the variable cost per unit to $106. However, the monthly lease price of this new machine would be $2800. What production quantity would be needed to make it advisable for AFP to lease the new machine?

6. For a certain manufactured part, the variable cost to produce the part is $2.00 and we sell the part for $4.50. As long as we produce 1000 units or less, our fixed cost is $3000. However, in order to produce beyond 1000 units, we will have to add additional machine capacity which will increase our fixed costs to $4200. What is the breakeven production quantity for this situation?

7. Suppose that in Problem 6 there are also certain economies of scale that are realized such that the variable cost per unit decreases to $1.85 for all units above 1100. Taking into account this step change in variable cost and the fixed cost levels described in Problem 6, what is the breakeven quantity? (You might want to graph this one before you begin your calculations.)

8. American Electronics manufactures computer chips that sell for $18.00 each. The daily cost of producing these chips varies with production quantity according to the formula $TC = 2Q^2 - 182Q + 2000$, where $Q$ is the production quantity. Draw a graph of this situation. Over what range of production quantities would manufacture of the chip be profitable (use the quadratic formula to derive exact answers)? What would be the most profitable level of production?

9. Southern Office Furniture manufactures and sells office chairs. The selling price is $100 per chair. The monthly production cost of chairs is $TC = -2Q^2 + 400Q + 1000$. Graph this situation. Above what production quantity will Southern begin to make a profit? Once again, exploit the quadratic structure of the cost formula to find the exact quantity.

10. Consolidated Heating produces three different sizes of industrial furnaces. Information

about these furnaces is given below:

| Furnace Size | Selling Price per Furnace | Average Cost to Produce | Percentage of Total Dollar Sales |
|---|---|---|---|
| Small | $1085 | $ 725 | 25 |
| Medium | 1995 | 1105 | 40 |
| Large | 2595 | 1850 | 35 |

Assuming that the company has annual fixed costs of $2 million, what is the breakeven point in terms of dollar sales? If the company has an annual production capacity in sales dollars of $9 million, at what capacity must they operate to break even? If the plant ran at full capacity for the year, what would total profit be?

4

# Forecasting

## ■ Introduction

In the previous chapter we learned the fundamentals of breakeven analysis where price and quantity are related to one another for the purpose of identifying breakeven production quantities. In looking at the case in that chapter, as well as the other example problems, a very important assumption was made. We assumed that demand for the product could be estimated, for without some estimate of product demand we would not know whether or not the breakeven level is attainable. When decision makers are forced to estimate future outcomes such as product demand, they are said to be **forecasting** these outcomes.

*forecasting*

Product demand is not the only thing that business decision makers are forced to forecast. They must routinely forecast interest rates, investment returns, labor availability, market prices, and a myriad of other variables. Because so many decisions depend on these estimates of the future, forecasting is undeniably one of the most important activities undertaken by most companies. In this chapter we will learn the basics of forecasting.

■ **Case**

## Sierra Industries

Sierra Industries is a firm that produces and markets outdoor recreational equipment, including fishing, hunting, camping, and backpacking gear. One of Sierra's products is a new graphite fishing rod that has only been on the market for one year. John Phillips, the Vice President of Marketing for Sierra, is concerned about the lack of knowledge the company has as to month-by-month demand for this product. The following data represents sales in thousands of the graphite fishing rod since its introduction one year ago:

| Month | Sales (in thousands) |
|-------|----------------------|
| Jan   | 23 |
| Feb   | 25 |
| Mar   | 31 |
| Apr   | 27 |
| May   | 35 |
| Jun   | 33 |
| Jul   | 52 |
| Aug   | 45 |
| Sep   | 40 |
| Oct   | 46 |
| Nov   | 41 |
| Dec   | 45 |

John suspects that the market demand for this type of product is complex in that there may be some seasonal variation in demand, some long-term growth in demand as the product gains acceptance and a greater market share, and obviously significant random buying behavior that cannot be explained. As he begins a new year, he would like to have more information about likely period-by-period demand in the form of market forecasts. The problem is that John knows very little about forecasting, leaving him with many questions to be answered. What are the different techniques that could be used to forecast demand for the fishing rods? Which of the methods is best? How far into the future can accurate demands be developed?

## ■ Forecasting typologies

Forecasting activities can be categorized according to two major factors. The first is how far into the future we are required to forecast, and the second is the methodology by which we estimate the future outcomes. In relation to the time frame of the forecast, forecasts are generally classified as either short-range, medium-range, or long-range forecasts. Short-range forecasts normally involve forecasting one or two periods into the future. Day-to-day operational business decisions such as determination of product demand and availability of raw material would probably require short-range forecasts to support these decisions. Medium-range forecasts are those that require estimates of what will happen beyond one to two time periods up to perhaps a year into the future. This category would include forecasting to support tactical business decisions involving such factors as market prices and labor availability. Anything beyond one to two years is generally considered a long-range forecast. Such long-range projections are commonly necessary for strategic planning and decision making, and might involve such items as forecasting interest rates, market trends, or general economic growth.

The further removed a forecast is into the future, the more difficult it is to forecast with any degree of accuracy. Long-range forecasts, and in many cases medium-range forecasts, tend to rely more on subjective assessment and expert opinion than on any sort of a quantitative foundation. These subjective methods might include the **Delphi method** (which is based on soliciting expert opinion), market research, panel consensus, or historical analogy. While these are certainly important forecasting topics, we will not cover these more subjective methods but instead focus our attention on short- to medium-range forecasting techniques that have a quantitative foundation more in line with the purpose of this text. Therefore all of the forecasting techniques we will discuss in this chapter are designed primarily for short- to medium-range forecasting.

*Delphi method*

The second factor we mentioned for categorizing forecasting activities was the methodology for predicting the future outcomes. Methodologies for forecasting tend to be of one of two types. The first type is called projective techniques. **Projective techniques** depend on past behavior of the variable to be forecast, and attempt to isolate the behavior of the variable so that this behavior can be projected forward into the future and used as a forecast. The second type is **causal models,** which attempt to forecast by relating the behavior of the variable of interest to the behavior of one or more other variables that we believe to have a cause-and-effect relationship with it.

*projective techniques*

*causal models*

In the next section we will look at a set of techniques known as time series methods, which are purely projective techniques. A little later in the chapter we will look at some models that can be applied both as a projective technique or for modeling causal relationships.

## ■ Time series techniques

A **time series** is a historical record or list of the behavior of a variable over time. The 12-month history of demands for graphite fishing rods in the Sierra Industries case is an example of a time series. In line with our definition of a projective technique, if we can isolate the behavior of a variable over the recent past and project that behavior forward, it should suffice as a short-range forecast provided that environmental factors do not interfere and alter the historical behavior of the variable. It is not always easy, however, to isolate the behavior of a variable because of the many patterns of behavior that may be present in a time series. There are four major elements that are typically present in a time series:

*time series*

1. secular trend pattern
2. cyclic pattern
3. seasonal pattern
4. random variation

*secular trend*

Secular trend, or simply trend for short, is the smooth underlying component that represents the general long-term sweep or movement of the data values. A cyclic pattern consists of wavelike patterns similar to a sine wave with duration longer than one year. These patterns tend to be related to general business cycles. Seasonal patterns also consist of this wavelike variation, but the duration of a seasonal cycle, as the name implies, is one year or less. Random variation is not a pattern but is the "noise" around one or more of the other three patterns, and is caused by outside factors that are generally not predictable.

*cyclic pattern*
*seasonal*
*patterns*
*random*
*variation*

Obviously, in using a projective technique we need to determine what the trend, cycle, and seasonal patterns are, since these are the behaviors that must be projected in order to obtain a forecast. In order for these patterns to be evident, it is necessary to remove or smooth out the random variation (it may also be necessary to smooth out a cyclic or seasonal pattern before we can discern the secular trend). Time series techniques that are used to remove this random variation (or even the wavelike patterns) are called smoothing techniques. We will discuss several such smoothing techniques in the following sections.

*smoothing*
*techniques*

## Simple moving average

The simple moving average is perhaps one of the easiest of the smoothing methods to use and understand. Simple moving average consists of dividing the time series into segments or windows of length $n$, such that the first window consists of observations $Y_1, Y_2, \ldots, Y_n$, where $Y_i$ represents the $i$th observation in the time series. The next window consists of observations $Y_2, Y_3, \ldots, Y_{n+1}$, and so on. In order to compute the moving average, we calculate the arithmetic average of the observations within each segment or window. The arithmetic average of each window is then considered to be the forecast for the period just beyond that window. In other words, the forecast for any period $t$ is the average of the values in the window that ends with period $t - 1$. Using $F_t$ to represent a forecast for any period $t$, we can use the following formula to compute moving average forecasts:

$$F_t = \frac{Y_{t-1} + Y_{t-2} + \cdots + Y_{t-n}}{n}$$

Table 4-1 lists the forecasts for Sierra Industries utilizing moving averages of both three months and five months. The first three-month forecast is computed as

$$F_4 = \frac{F_1 + F_2 + F_3}{3}$$

$$= \frac{23 + 25 + 31}{3}$$

$$= 26.333$$

Each forecast in the table is computed using the same logic.

| Month | $Y_t$ (sales) | $F_t$ (three-month) | $F_t$ (five-month) |
|-------|---------------|--------------------|--------------------|
| Jan | 23 | — | — |
| Feb | 25 | | |
| Mar | 31 | — | — |
| Apr | 27 | 26.33 | |
| May | 35 | 27.66 | — |
| Jun | 33 | 31 | 28.2 |
| Jul | 52 | 31.66 | 30.2 |
| Aug | 45 | 40 | 35.6 |
| Sep | 40. | 43.33 | 38.4 |
| Oct | 46 | 45.66 | 41 |
| Nov | 41 | 43.66 | 43.2 |
| Dec | 45 | 42.33 | 44.8 |
| — | — | 44 | 43.4 |

**TABLE 4-1.
Moving Average
Forecasts for the
Sierra Industries
Data**

Obviously, when using a three-month moving average, no forecasts are generated for the first three months in the series. Likewise, using a five-month moving average, no forecasts are generated for the first five months in the series. You may wonder why we bother to calculate forecasts for any months other than the coming month, since the actual values for those periods are already known. The reason for calculating these forecasts of demands that have already occurred is to assess how well the forecasting technique extracts the trends of the time series (how well it works). We will look at some methods a little later on for assessing just how well any given technique is able to forecast actual values, and these methods will require that we have matched pairs of forecasts and actual values. For now, we can look at a graph of the actual demands for fishing rods versus three-month and five-month moving average forecasts. Figure 4-1 is a graph of demands and forecasts superimposed so that we may see the relative patterns of each. The actual demands are connected by solid lines, the three month moving average forecasts are connected by dashed lines, and the five-month moving average forecasts are connected by dotted lines.

Note that the three-month moving average forecasts are much smoother than the actual demands. Also note that as we move to a five-month moving average forecast, even more of the variation has been smoothed out. This is to be expected, as averaging observations over a broader window tends to spread random variation more evenly over each observation. The longer the moving average, the more likely we are to see the underlying long-term trend. This is because as we move to a long moving average base, we tend to smooth out cycles and seasonal patterns as well as random variation. If we specifically desire to smooth out a seasonal effect, one common method for doing this is to choose a moving average equal to the length of one seasonal cycle. That is, for monthly data, use a moving average of length 12. For quarterly data, use a moving average of length 4. If we do not desire to smooth out the seasonal effect, we must choose a shorter length for the moving average to prevent this oversmoothing.

**FIGURE 4-1.
Graph of De-
mands and Fore-
casts for the Sierra
Industries Case**

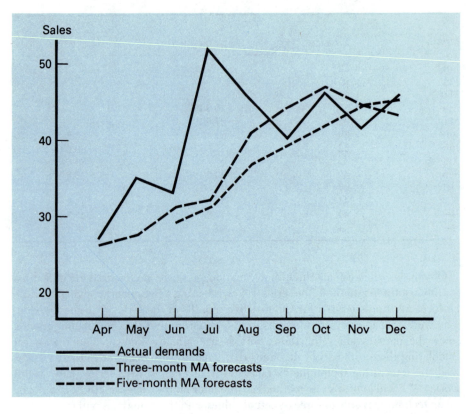

Obviously, if we make the moving average too long, we will even smooth out the long-term trend (if the moving average is the same length as the time series, we will smooth everything into one static average value). The bottom line is that through proper choice of the moving average length, we can adequately remove random variation from our forecasts while controlling the degree to which other components are smoothed.

## *Weighted moving average*

One of the problems with simple moving average is that it is often sluggish to respond to meaningful changes in a series such as those related to seasonal or cyclic patterns. The weighted moving average is a slight modification of the simple moving average that allows for more responsiveness to current observations. By weighting each observation within a window by a different amount, with greater weight normally put on the later observations, the arithmetic average is biased toward the more recent observations. Letting $w_1, w_2, \ldots, w_n$ be the weights applied to the $n$ values within a window, the moving average formula can be restated as:

$$F_t = \frac{w_1 Y_{t-1} + w_2 Y_{t-2} + \cdots + w_n Y_{t-n}}{w_1 + w_2 + \cdots + w_n}$$

Note that we are now dividing the weighted sum of the data values in a particular window by the sum of the weights utilized.

For the Sierra data, suppose that we want to calculate a three-month weighted moving average using weights of 4, 3, and 2. Our first forecast would be

$$F_4 = \frac{2(23) + 3(25) + 4(31)}{9}$$

$$= \frac{245}{9}$$

$$= 27.222$$

This value is closer to the actual value for period 4 than was our simple forecast using equal weights that we developed earlier. Table 4-2 lists all of the weighted forecasts calculated using the 4, 3, 2 weights so that you may check yourself on calculating these weighted forecasts. In this example, the choice of weights of 4, 3, and 2 was rather arbitrary. By trying different combinations of weights and comparing the resulting moving average forecasts to the actual time series values, a forecaster may eventually arrive at a set of weights that appears to be "optimal" for that particular time series.

## Simple exponential smoothing

Exponential smoothing is another form of weighted forecasting technique. In order to calculate a forecast for some period $t + 1$, we weight the observation in period $t$ and the forecast in period $t$ and add these together. Letting $\alpha$ and $(1 - \alpha)$ represent our weights, where $\alpha$ is between 0 and 1.0, the formula for exponential smoothing forecasts is

$$F_{t+1} = \alpha Y_t + (1 - \alpha)F_t$$

| Month | $Y_t$ (Sales) | $F_t$ (4-3-2 weighted) |
|---|---|---|
| Jan | 23 | — |
| Feb | 25 | — |
| Mar | 31 | — |
| Apr | 27 | 27.22 |
| May | 35 | 27.88 |
| Jun | 33 | 31.44 |
| Jul | 52 | 32.33 |
| Aug | 45 | 41.88 |
| Sep | 40 | 44.66 |
| Oct | 46 | 44.33 |
| Nov | 41 | 43.77 |
| Dec | 45 | 42.44 |
| — | — | 43.88 |

TABLE 4-2.
Weighted Moving Average Forecasts for the Sierra Industries Data

We begin in period 1 by letting $F_1 = Y_1$ and then we apply the formula for each subsequent period. As an example, suppose that $\alpha = .2$ and $(1 - \alpha) = .8$. For the Sierra data for period 1 we have

$$F_1 = Y_1 = 23$$

For period 2 we get

$$F_2 = .2(Y_1) + .8(F_1)$$
$$= .2(23) + .8(23)$$
$$= 23$$

For period 3 we get

$$F_3 = .2(Y_2) + .8(F_2)$$
$$= .2(25) + .8(23)$$
$$= 5 + 18.4$$
$$= 23.4$$

For period 4 we get

$$F_4 = .2(Y_3) + .8(F_3)$$
$$= .2(31) + .8(23.4)$$
$$= 6.2 + 18.72$$
$$= 24.92$$

**TABLE 4-3.**
**Exponentially Smoothed Forecasts for the Sierra Industries Data Using $\alpha = .2$ and $(1 - \alpha) = .8$**

| Month | Sales | $F_t$ |
|-------|-------|-------|
| Jan | 23 | — |
| Feb | 25 | 23.00 |
| Mar | 31 | 23.40 |
| Apr | 27 | 24.92 |
| May | 35 | 25.34 |
| Jun | 33 | 27.27 |
| Jul | 52 | 28.42 |
| Aug | 45 | 33.14 |
| Sep | 40 | 35.51 |
| Oct | 46 | 36.41 |
| Nov | 41 | 38.33 |
| Dec | 45 | 38.86 |
| — | — | 40.10 |

And so on. Table 4-3 lists the rest of the exponential smoothing forecasts for Sierra Industries so that you may check your ability to apply the formula. Once again, while the last forecast (the one for the period yet to come) is the important one, the other forecasts will allow us to determine how good the exponentially smoothed forecasts are.

If you thought carefully about what we were doing in the example computations above, you already know why this method is called exponential smoothing. Whereas the moving average used only windows of data to form a forecast, the exponential smoothing model uses all prior data, but as we move farther into the future, past data is reflected at an exponentially decreasing rate. To see this, let us write the first few terms of an exponentially smoothed series totally in terms of the observations. Remembering that $F_1 = Y_1$ and therefore:

$$F_2 = \alpha Y_1 + (1 - \alpha)F_1$$
$$= \alpha Y_1 + (1 - \alpha)Y_1$$
$$= Y_1$$

Next:

$$F_3 = \alpha Y_2 + (1 - \alpha)F_2$$
$$= \alpha Y_2 + (1 - \alpha)Y_1$$

Then:

$$F_4 = \alpha Y_3 + (1 - \alpha)F_3$$
$$= \alpha Y_3 + (1 - \alpha)[\alpha Y_2 + (1 - \alpha)Y_1]$$
$$= \alpha Y_3 + \alpha(1 - \alpha)Y_2 + (1 - \alpha)^2 Y_1$$

We have taken the series far enough to see the pattern. The forecast for period 4 is still reflecting the observation in period 1, but the effect of that observation is diminishing exponentially. If $\alpha$ were .2 again and $(1 - \alpha)$ were .8, whereas $Y_1$ was weighted with .8 to get $F_3$, $Y_1$ is only weighted by $.8(.8) = .64$ in calculating $F_4$. The influence of $Y_1$ will continue to decrease exponentially as we move ahead.

We have not really said much about the choice of $\alpha$ in these models. It should be obvious that the extremes of $\alpha = 0$ and $\alpha = 1.0$ represent total smoothing and no smoothing, respectively. If $\alpha = 0$, every forecast would be equal to the first observation in the time series and would smooth the series down to a flat line. If $\alpha = 1.0$, every forecast would be equal to the observation in the previous period, and the series would not be smoothed at all but would lag the forecasts one period behind the actual values.

In practice, we never choose these extremes but experiment with values of $\alpha$ until we find one that is satisfactory. Figure 4-2 shows the original Sierra data along with our forecasts from Table 4-3 where $\alpha = .2$, and forecasts that would result using

FIGURE 4-2.
Graph of De-
mands and Fore-
casts for the Sierra
Industries Case

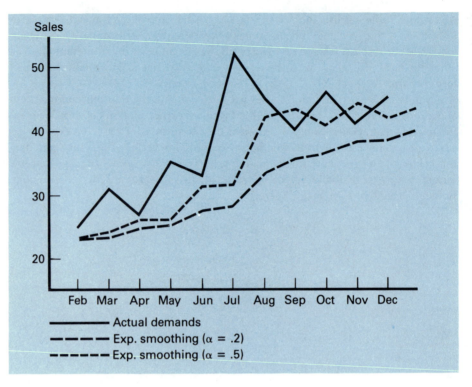

α = .5. Computer support is very useful for quickly experimenting with numerous values of α where the series is long.

## Double exponential smoothing

The simple exponential smoothing forecasting model that we presented in the last section is particularly appropriate when a time series is constant or stable over time. If a series is linear over time (has a linear trend underlying the series), a doubly smoothed forecast (sometimes referred to as a second-order exponential smoothing forecast) is probably more appropriate. If we plan to forecast more than one period ahead—say, to some period $t + T$, where $t$ is the current period—it is essential that we reflect the trend of the series.

Letting $FD_{t+T}$ be the forecast for some period $t + T$ computed through double exponential smoothing, the formula is

$$FD_{t+T} = \left(2 + \frac{\alpha T}{1 - \alpha}\right) F_{t+1} - \left(1 + \frac{\alpha T}{1 - \alpha}\right) F_{t+1}(2)$$

where $F_{t+1}(2) = \alpha F_{t+1} + (1 - \alpha)F_t(2)$ and $F_{t+1}$ is our simple exponential smoothing forecast.

To illustrate double smoothing, let $F_1(2) = Y_1$ just as we did with $F_1$ earlier to get the process started, and assume that we will still use $\alpha = .2$ so that we can use the $F_{t+1}$ values from Table 4-3 and do not have to recalculate them. For period 2:

$$F_2(2) = \alpha F_2 + (1 - \alpha)F_1(2)$$

$$= .2(23) + .8(23)$$

$$= 23$$

and

$$FD_2 = \left[2 + \frac{\alpha(1)}{1 - \alpha}\right]F_2 - \left[1 + \frac{\alpha(1)}{1 - \alpha}\right]F_2(2)$$

$$= \left(2 + \frac{.2}{.8}\right)(23) - \left(1 + \frac{.2}{.8}\right)(23)$$

$$= 23$$

The doubly smoothed forecast is the same as the simple forecast for period 2 because we let $F_1$ and $F_1(2)$ both be 23 to get the process started. Now let us look at period 3:

$$F_3(2) = .2F_3 + .8F_2(2)$$

$$= .2(23.4) + .8(23)$$

$$= 23.08$$

and

$$FD_3 = \left(2 + \frac{.2}{.8}\right)F_3 - \left(1 + \frac{.2}{.8}\right)F_3(2)$$

$$= (2.25)(23.4) - (1.25)(23.08)$$

$$= 52.65 - 28.85$$

$$= 23.8$$

Thus, for each period we already have a simple exponentially smoothed forecast, and now we are computing a double-smoothing adjustment for each period and using them to modify the period forecasts. Table 4-4 details the rest of the adjusted forecasts for the Sierra data.

We have seen how to calculate a simple and a double exponential forecast. It is also possible to calculate a triple exponential forecast, or even higher order than triple, in

**TABLE 4-4.**
**Double**
**Exponential**
**Smoothing**
**Forecasts for the**
**Sierra Industries**
**Case Using** $\alpha = .2$

| Month | Sales | $F_t$ | $F_t(2)$ | $FD_t$ |
|-------|-------|-------|----------|--------|
| Jan | 23 | — | — | — |
| Feb | 25 | 23.00 | 23.00 | 23.00 |
| Mar | 31 | 23.40 | 23.08 | 23.80 |
| Apr | 27 | 24.92 | 23.45 | 26.76 |
| May | 35 | 25.34 | 23.83 | 27.23 |
| Jun | 33 | 27.27 | 24.52 | 30.71 |
| Jul | 52 | 28.42 | 25.30 | 32.32 |
| Aug | 45 | 33.14 | 26.87 | 40.98 |
| Sep | 40 | 35.51 | 28.60 | 44.15 |
| Oct | 46 | 36.41 | 30.16 | 44.22 |
| Nov | 41 | 38.33 | 31.79 | 46.51 |
| Dec | 45 | 38.86 | 33.20 | 45.94 |
| — | — | 40.10 | 34.58 | 47.00 |

order to reflect seasonal or cyclic trends better. As the order of the model gets higher, computational requirements increase rapidly. We will not look at any models of order higher than the double-smoothing model, and suggest that the reader interested in those more complex models consult a specialized text dedicated to forecasting.

## ■ Judging the accuracy of forecasting models

Before we look at any more forecasting, we had better discuss some method for deciding which model performs best for forecasting any particular time series. Eyeballing a graph as we did a little earlier in the chapter is a method, but it is not very precise as it is open to differences in perception. What we need is a method or methods that provide a relative numerical measure of the performance of any given forecasting technique.

*residuals*
The most common approach to a numerical measure of forecast accuracy is to work with some function of the forecast errors or **residuals.** For any period $t$ for which we have both an actual value and a forecast, the error or residual is the difference of the two. That is:

$$e_t = Y_t - F_t$$

For our earlier moving average example, the forecast errors are shown in Table 4-5. Just by looking at the forecast errors in columns 4 and 6 of the table, it is still difficult to say which method is more accurate. Two measures or functions of the forecast errors that may make this task a little easier are the mean square error and the mean absolute deviation.

*mean square*
*error*
As the name **mean square error** (MSE) implies, if we look at the average of the squared error terms, this should provide some indication of the relative goodness of

| Month | $Y_t$ | $F_t$ (three-month) | $Y_t - F_t$ | $F_t'$ (five-month) | $Y_t - F_t'$ |
|-------|-------|---------------------|-------------|---------------------|--------------|
| Jan | 23 | — | — | — | — |
| Feb | 25 | — | — | — | — |
| Mar | 31 | — | — | — | — |
| Apr | 27 | 26.33 | 0.67 | — | — |
| May | 35 | 27.66 | 7.34 | — | — |
| Jun | 33 | 31.00 | 2.00 | 28.2 | 4.8 |
| Jul | 52 | 31.66 | 20.34 | 30.2 | 21.8 |
| Aug | 45 | 40.00 | 5.00 | 35.6 | 9.4 |
| Sep | 40 | 43.33 | −3.33 | 38.4 | 1.6 |
| Oct | 46 | 45.66 | 0.34 | 41.0 | 5.0 |
| Nov | 41 | 43.66 | −2.66 | 43.2 | −2.2 |
| Dec | 45 | 42.33 | 2.67 | 44.8 | 0.2 |
| — | — | 44.00 | — | 43.4 | — |

**TABLE 4-5.**
**Forecast Errors for the Three- and Five-Month Moving Average Models**

two or more methods. Notice that we say relative goodness, because the actual value of MSE may not mean much to us. Is a MSE of 500 good or bad? We do not know. If the actual values and forecasts are small numbers, 500 may represent a large average squared error. But if the observations are themselves in the hundreds, 500 may represent a very small average squared deviation. However, we can be sure that an average deviation of 500 for one method is larger than, say, an average deviation of 250 for another method (another possibility is to express the MSEs as a percentage of the average scale of the observations in order to alleviate the scale problem). Using the formula

$$\text{MSE} = \sum_t \frac{(Y_t - F_t)^2}{n}$$

where $n$ is the number of error terms or residuals available, we would get a MSE of 58.05 for the three-month moving average forecasts and a MSE of 88.44 for the five-month moving average forecasts, indicating that the three-month windows seem to be more appropriate.

The other measure mentioned was the **mean absolute deviation** (MAD). In the MAD, instead of squaring each error we take the absolute value of each. Consequently, the MAD does not penalize large deviations to the same degree as the MSE. The formula for the MAD is

*mean absolute deviation*

$$\text{MAD} = \sum_t \frac{|Y_t - F_t|}{n}$$

For the forecast errors in Table 4-5, the MAD would be 4.93 for the three-month moving average forecasts and 6.43 for the five-month moving average forecasts. Again, the three-month moving average seems better.

There are other measures of forecast accuracy that we will not discuss in this chapter, and it may often happen that two measures will give conflicting signals as to which forecasting method is better. It is for this reason that we sometimes say that forecasting is as much an art as it is a science, and encourage anyone engaged in forecasting to explore many alternatives before settling on a particular technique. Having discussed the concept of forecast accuracy, let us finish this chapter with a discussion of the other category of forecasting models: regression-based models.

## ■ Regression-based techniques

### Simple regression

*regression*

Simple **regression** is a method for fitting a linear equation to a set of data points. The equation will be of the form

$$y = a + bx$$

where $a$ is the intercept of the fitted equation and $b$ is the slope. $Y$ is referred to as the dependent variable and $x$ as the independent variable, as we hope to forecast $y$ based on $x$. The usual criteria is to choose the intercept and slope such that the sum of the squared differences between the data points and the equation is at a minimum, and is referred to as the **least-squares** criteria (it is basically the same as choosing a model such that the numerator of our MSE measure in the last section, the total sum squared error, would be at a minimum).

*least-squares*

As the derivation of formulas for choosing the intercept and slope such that the total sum squared error is minimized involves the use of calculus, which we will not cover until Chapter 23, we will not attempt to derive these formulas but instead will present them without proof:

$$a = \bar{y} - b\bar{x}$$

$$b = \frac{\Sigma\, xy - n\bar{x}\bar{y})}{(\Sigma\, x^2 - n\bar{x}^2)}$$

In these formulas, $n$ represents the number of pairs of $x$ and $y$ values available in the data set, and $\bar{x}$ and $\bar{y}$ represent the means of $x$ and $y$, respectively.

We stated earlier in the chapter that regression-based methods could be used either as projective or causal models. Let us first look at a case where regression is used as a projection technique.

### The autoregressive model

Observations in a time series may be closely related with one another over time. This phenomenon is known as serial correlation. If this time-phased relationship is strong enough, it can be used as the basis for a regression model. For instance, if every observation in a time series were strongly correlated with the immediately preceding observation, we could let each observation be a value of the dependent variable $y$ and pair with it the immediately preceding observation as a value of the independent variable $x$. We could then fit a regression model of the form

$$y = a + bx$$

or

$$y_t = a + by_{t-1}$$

This form of model is referred to as a first-order autoregressive model, because it uses lags of one period as the basis of the model.

Suppose that we apply a first-order autoregressive model to the Sierra Industries data. The necessary calculations to support our formulas for $a$ and $b$ are shown below:

| Month | $y = Y_t$ | $x = Y_{t-1}$ | $xy$ | $x^2$ |
|-------|-----------|---------------|------|-------|
| 1 = Jan | 23 | — | — | — |
| 2 | 25 | 23 | 575 | 529 |
| 3 | 31 | 25 | 775 | 625 |
| 4 | 27 | 31 | 837 | 961 |
| 5 | 35 | 27 | 945 | 729 |
| 6 | 33 | 35 | 1,155 | 1,225 |
| 7 | 52 | 33 | 1,716 | 1,089 |
| 8 | 45 | 52 | 2,340 | 2,704 |
| 9 | 40 | 45 | 1,800 | 2,025 |
| 10 | 46 | 40 | 1,840 | 1,600 |
| 11 | 41 | 46 | 1,886 | 2,116 |
| 12 | 45 | 41 | 1,845 | 1,681 |
| Total | 420 | 398 | 15,714 | 15,284 |

Note that month 1 was not included in our calculations because there is not a value for $x$ in month 1.

$$\bar{x} = \frac{398}{11} = 36.182$$

$$\bar{y} = \frac{420}{11} = 38.182$$

Therefore:

$$b = \frac{15,714 - (11)(36.182)(38.182)}{15,284 - (11)(36.182)^2}$$

$$= \frac{15,714 - 15,196.512}{15,284 - 14,400.508}$$

$$= \frac{517.488}{883.492}$$

$$= .586$$

and

$$a = 38.182 - (.586)(36.182)$$

$$= 38.182 - 21.203$$

$$= 16.979$$

Thus, our autoregressive forecasting equation is

$$y_t = 16.979 + .586y_{t-1}$$

To forecast the demand for fishing rods for January, the coming month, we would use December's demand as $y_{t-1}$ and get

$$y_{13} = 16.979 + .586(45)$$

$$= 43.349$$

How do we know how good this forecast is? Again, we could calculate the residuals or forecast errors and examine them. In addition, in regression we often look at a measure known as the **coefficient of determination**:

*coefficient of determination*

$$r^2 = \left\{ \frac{n \, \Sigma \, xy - \Sigma \, x \, \Sigma \, y}{\sqrt{[n \, \Sigma \, x^2 - (\Sigma \, x)^2][n \, \Sigma \, y^2 - (\Sigma \, y)^2]}} \right\}^2$$

This measure tells us the percentage of variability in the time series that is accounted for by our regression model, with $r^2 = 1.0$ representing 100%. For the autoregressive model we just developed, the coefficient of determination is

$$r^2 = \left\{ \frac{11(15,714) - (398)(420)}{\sqrt{[11(15,284) - 398^2][11(16,780) - 420^2]}} \right\}^2$$

$$= (.6386)^2$$

$$= .408$$

On the basis of this information, it appears that the autoregressive model we developed would be of little benefit for forecasting the demand for Sierra's fishing rod. If the model is only able to explain 40.8% of the variability in the time series, we certainly would not have much confidence in its ability to forecast the future.

Why was the $r^2$ so low for this time series? Obviously, the relationship between adjacent observations is not strong enough to form a basis for forecasting. What could we do to improve it? We could include more terms in the autoregressive model (although we will not discuss it here, a graph called a correlogram can help us determine where a strong relationship exists: consult most any statistics text for information on correlograms). If we include $p$ terms in our regression model, it would be called a $p$th-order autoregressive model, and would be of the form:

$$y_t = a + b_1 y_{t-1} + b_2 y_{t-2} + \cdots + b_p y_{t-p}$$

where each of the terms could be included or left out. The only difficulty we would encounter in applying such a $p$th-order model to our Sierra data is that our simple regression formulas could not be used. Instead, we would need to resort to multiple regression analysis where many simultaneous slopes for the many independent variables could be determined. Such techniques are found in every general statistics text and computer software for multiple regression is abundant.

The availability of the multiple regression technique would also make it possible to project nonlinear trends. A multi-term autoregressive model that could be used to fit a quadratic trend would be:

$$v_t = a + b_1 y_{t-1} + b_2 y_{t-1}^2$$

It is also possible to fit models to and project forecasts from data with sinusoidal trends and many other wave-like patterns.

We have gone about as far as we can with autoregressive models within the format of an introductory text. Let us now look at regression-based forecasting applied in a different manner.

## Causal models

In each of the models thus far, our independent variables have been observations or functions of the observations of a time series. This is due to the fact that we had restricted our attention to models that project from historic data. There is another very important class of forecasting models called causal models that attempts to relate the dependent variable to some independent variable or variables that have a cause-and-effect relationship with the dependent variable. These models are generally based on the regression concepts we presented earlier.

As an example of causal modeling, suppose that we asked John Phillips back at Sierra Industries to give us data on how many advertising dollars were spent in each of the months preceding the demands that we already know. Let us assume that the advertising expenditures in thousands of dollars are as follows:

| Month | Sales (thousands) | Prior Advertising (dollars in thousands) |
|-------|-------------------|------------------------------------------|
| Jan   | 23                | 10                                       |
| Feb   | 25                | 10.5                                     |
| Mar   | 31                | 11                                       |
| Apr   | 27                | 11                                       |
| May   | 35                | 12                                       |
| Jun   | 33                | 12                                       |
| Jul   | 52                | 13                                       |
| Aug   | 45                | 13                                       |
| Sep   | 40                | 12                                       |
| Oct   | 46                | 13                                       |
| Nov   | 41                | 12                                       |
| Dec   | 45                | 13                                       |

Let us treat sales as $y$ and advertising as $x$ and see what the regression model would look like:

| Month | $x$   | $y$ | $xy$    | $x^2$    |
|-------|-------|-----|---------|----------|
| 1     | 10    | 23  | 230     | 100      |
| 2     | 10.5  | 25  | 262.5   | 110.25   |
| 3     | 11    | 31  | 341     | 121      |
| 4     | 11    | 27  | 297     | 121      |
| 5     | 12    | 35  | 420     | 144      |
| 6     | 12    | 33  | 396     | 144      |
| 7     | 13    | 52  | 676     | 169      |
| 8     | 13    | 45  | 585     | 169      |
| 9     | 12    | 40  | 480     | 144      |
| 10    | 13    | 46  | 598     | 169      |
| 11    | 12    | 41  | 492     | 144      |
| 12    | 13    | 45  | 585     | 169      |
| Total | 142.5 | 443 | 5,362.5 | 1,704.25 |

$$\bar{x} = \frac{142.5}{12} = 11.875$$

$$\bar{y} = \frac{443}{12} = 36.917$$

$$b = \frac{5,362.5 - (12)(11.875)(36.917)}{1,704.25 - (12)(11.875)^2}$$

$$= \frac{101.83}{12.063}$$

$$= 8.44$$

$$a = 36.917 - (8.44)(11.875)$$

$$= -63.308$$

Thus, the causal model for forecasting sales based on advertising expenses is:

$$y_t = -63.308 + 8.44x_t$$

where $x_t$ is the amount spent on advertising in the prior period. All we have to do to forecast next month's sales is plug in for $x$ the amount we plan to spend this month on advertising. The $r^2$ for this regression model on the Sierra data is .90 (verify this for yourself), indicating that the model is very appropriate for forecasting.

This is but one example of causal modeling. We could have a model with many causal variables, or even a mixture of causal and autoregressive terms if we find it to be appropriate. The name of the game for forecasting is try and try again until you find a model that works.

## ■ Summary

In this chapter we have discovered that there are two basic techniques that may be used for forecasting: projection and causal modeling. We looked at moving average, weighted moving average, exponential smoothing, double exponential smoothing, and autoregressive models as methods of projection. For causal modeling, we noted that regression is the underlying concept, and we saw an example of its application.

We also looked at residuals, mean square error, mean absolute deviation, and coefficient of determination as measures of the goodness of a certain model for forecasting a certain variable. In later chapters we will assume that valid forecasts can be developed, as many of the topics in those later chapters will depend on forecasted data.

## ■ Glossary of terms

**causal models:**   models that attempt to forecast by relating the behavior of a variable of interest to the behavior of one or more other variables.

**coefficient of determination:**   a measure that indicates the percentage of variability in a set of data that is accounted for by a regression model.

**cyclic pattern:**   a wavelike pattern with a duration longer than one year in a time series.

**Delphi method:**   a subjective forecasting method based on the solicitation of expert opinion.

**forecasting:**   the act of estimating future outcomes.

**mean absolute deviation:**   a measure of forecast accuracy based on the average absolute values of forecast residuals.

**mean square error:**   a measure of forecast accuracy based on average squared forecast residuals.

**projective techniques:**   forecasting techniques that rely on the projection of historical trends.

**random variation:**   the variability in a time series that cannot be accounted for through trends or cycles.

**regression:**   a procedure for fitting a trend line to a set of data.

**residuals:**   the difference between an actual value and the forecasted value for that same period.

**seasonal pattern:**   a time series cycle of less than one year's duration.

**secular trend:**   the smooth underlying component that represents the general long-term movement of a time series.

**smoothing techniques:**   techniques used to remove random variation or selected cycles or trends from a time series.

**time series:**   a historical record or list of the behavior of a variable over time.

## ■ Review questions

1. Discuss the forecasting typologies presented in the chapter. Is it always clear which type of forecasting activity is appropriate for a given situation?

2. Name the four patterns of behavior that may be present in any time series. Briefly describe each of these patterns.

3. How do we determine how many periods to include in a moving average forecast?

4. Discuss the two techniques for weighted forecasting. How do these methods differ?

5. Explain what happens to the degree of smoothing in an exponential smoothing model as the smoothing coefficient varies from 0 to 1. How do we normally go about choosing this constant?

6. When is a doubly smoothed forecast appropriate?

7. Differentiate between MSE and MAD as measures of forecast accuracy. Discuss the scale problem inherent in such measures.

8. Explain the concept of an autoregressive forecasting model. Name at least one situation where serial correlation would be present such that autoregression would be appropriate.

9. Could MSE or MAD be used to assess the adequacy of a regression forecasting model? If so, why might the coefficient of determination be a more appealing measure?

10. Name at least three situations where causal modeling might be appropriate as a forecasting methodology.

## ■ True/false questions

1. The Delphi method would typically be used to forecast short to medium-range activities.

2. Because of the difference in approaches, it is not possible to mix projective and causal techniques in one forecasting model.

3. A cyclic pattern generally tends to be related to long-term business cycles.

4. Random variation is not really a pattern, but is the unexplainable absence of a pattern.

5. If we want to use a moving average to smooth out a seasonal pattern, we should always use 12 periods in our window.

6. A weighted moving average is more responsive to current observations than is a simple moving average.

7. An exponential smoothing model utilizes all prior data in forming a forecast.

8. If the smoothing constant is equal to 0 in an exponential smoothing model, every forecast will be equal to the observation in the previous period, and no smoothing will occur.

9. A doubly smoothed forecast will always result in a better forecast than a simple exponential smoothing model.

10. It is possible for MSE and MAD to give conflicting signals as to the relative accuracy of different forecasting methods.

11. Regression may be used as either a projective or a causal technique.

12. The coefficient of determination can be an indicator of the degree of serial correlation in a time series.

## ■ Problems

1. Using the accompanying sales data, compute a three-month moving average forecast for periods 4 through 11. Plot the original time series and your forecasts on the same graph. How accurate do the forecasts appear to be?

| Month | Sales |
|-------|-------|
| 1 | 52 |
| 2 | 54 |
| 3 | 63 |
| 4 | 58 |
| 5 | 62 |
| 6 | 61 |
| 7 | 68 |
| 8 | 65 |
| 9 | 70 |
| 10 | 74 |

2. For the data in Problem 1, compute forecasts using a five-month moving average. Does the three-month or five-month smoothed forecast seem to be more accurate?

3. Barker Wholesale keeps its sales records on a quarterly basis. The following time series represents Barker's sales by quarter for the last three years:

| Year | Quarter | Sales (×$10,000) |
|------|---------|------------------|
| 1983 | 1 | 28 |
|      | 2 | 32 |
|      | 3 | 37 |
|      | 4 | 35 |
| 1984 | 1 | 30 |
|      | 2 | 33 |
|      | 3 | 40 |
|      | 4 | 38 |
| 1985 | 1 | 35 |
|      | 2 | 39 |
|      | 3 | 44 |
|      | 4 | 41 |

Suppose that we would like to smooth out any seasonal pattern in the series in order to reveal any long-term trends.

a.   Choose the appropriate length moving average and develop the forecasts for Barker Wholesale.

b.   Plot the original series and the forecasts. Was there a seasonal component in the original series? Did smoothing adequately remove that component? Is there an underlying trend in Barker's sales?

4. Delgado's Marine sells boats and other recreational supplies. As they do not always have a particular boat in stock when a customer asks for it, they prefer to do their planning based on past demands rather than past sales. This allows them to plan to fill demands as they occur rather than to react to past sales that lagged demand. The following series represents demand for boats over the last nine months:

| Month | Demand |
| --- | --- |
| 1 | 18 |
| 2 | 23 |
| 3 | 24 |
| 4 | 20 |
| 5 | 29 |
| 6 | 32 |
| 7 | 21 |
| 8 | 23 |
| 9 | 26 |

a.   Compute a three-month moving average forecast for periods 4 through 10.

b.   Compute a weighted three-month moving average forecast for periods 4 through 10. Use weights of 3, 2, and 1, with the larger weight on the most recent observation.

c.   Plot the original series and both forecast series. Which forecasting method seems to perform best?

5. For the data in Problem 4, compute weighted moving average forecasts using weights of 6, 4, and 2. Do the weights seem to have a significant effect on the accuracy of the forecasts? Which set of weights appears to be better?

6. For the data in Problem 4, develop exponential smoothing forecasts using $\alpha = .2$. Compare these forecasts to the three month moving average forecasts from part (a) of that problem.

7. Computer Maintenance, Inc., wants to forecast its weekly service calls so that better personnel scheduling may be accomplished. The calls for service over the last ten weeks

have been as follows:

| Week | Calls |
|------|-------|
| 1 | 44 |
| 2 | 40 |
| 3 | 36 |
| 4 | 43 |
| 5 | 41 |
| 6 | 47 |
| 7 | 45 |
| 8 | 42 |
| 9 | 44 |
| 10 | 48 |

a. Compute exponential smoothing forecasts for periods 2 through 11 using $\alpha = .2$.
b. Compute exponential smoothing forecasts using $\alpha = .4$.
c. Plot the original series and the two exponentially smoothed series. Which value of $\alpha$ seems to be most appropriate?

8. Compute forecasts for Computer Maintenance, Inc. (Problem 7), using double exponential smoothing with $\alpha = .2$. Does the doubly smoothed series appear to be any better than the simple exponential smoothing forecasts developed in Problem 7?

9. Using the data for Barker Wholesale from Problem 3, compute forecasts using simple exponential smoothing and double exponential smoothing with $\alpha = .3$. Plot these two series against the original data. Which method seems to best forecast the underlying trend?

10. Problem 2 asks you to assess relative forecast accuracy based on visual perception. Use mean square error for each of the two forecasting methods and reassess their relative accuracies.

11. Calculate both the mean square error and the mean absolute deviation for the three-month moving average forecasts and the weighted three-month forecasts for Delgado Marine in Problem 4. Which of the two forecasting methods seems to be best?

12. For the Computer Maintenance data in Problem 7, assess the relative accuracies of the two exponential smoothing forecasts using both MAD and MSE. Which $\alpha$ level seems to be best?

13. Construct two sets of residuals, each containing at least two observations, such that MAD and MSE would give conflicting signals as to relative forecast accuracy. Can this happen in a real data set?

14. For the sales data in Problem 1, develop an autoregressive forecasting model based on a one-period lag. Calculate $r^2$ for this model. Does the autoregressive model appear to be appropriate for this situation?

15. Demand for rental cars at Hurts Rent-a-Dream has been as follows for the past ten months:

| Month | Demand |
|-------|--------|
| 1 | 72 |
| 2 | 87 |
| 3 | 75 |
| 4 | 90 |
| 5 | 76 |
| 6 | 89 |
| 7 | 77 |
| 8 | 95 |
| 9 | 80 |
| 10 | 98 |

   a. Develop a second-order autoregressive forecasting model with the first-order term omitted for Hurts (i.e., use a lag of two periods between observations for values of the independent and dependent variables).
   b. Calculate $r^2$ for the model. Is this autoregressive model able to explain much of the variability in demand for rental cars?
   c. Use the model to develop a forecast for month 11.

16. John Carrey, Manager of Quality Control at ABCON Industries, believes that the number of defective parts produced on any given line in the plant is related to the average experience level of the employees working on that line. John has collected some data on the number of defective parts and the average experience (years with the company) as follows:

| Years | Defective Parts |
|-------|-----------------|
| 2.4 | 155 |
| 5.3 | 110 |
| 6.6 | 108 |
| 4.3 | 131 |
| 5.0 | 111 |
| 1.1 | 162 |

   a. Use regression to develop a model that predicts the number of defective parts based on the average experience of the workers.
   b. How many defective parts would you predict on a line with an average experience of 3.8 years?
   c. Calculate $r^2$ for this model. Is the relationship between defective parts and experience a strong one?

17. The following data represents the grades that students received on a management science exam and the number of hours they had spent studying for the exam:

| Study Hours | Exam Grade |
|-------------|------------|
| 6 | 77 |
| 4 | 63 |
| 7 | 85 |
| 7 | 89 |
| 5 | 83 |
| 8 | 90 |
| 10 | 95 |

a. Develop a model to forecast the exam grade a student will receive based on how long he or she studies.

b. What is the expected score of a student who studies for 7.5 hours?

c. Calculate $r^2$. How strong is the relationship between study time and exam score?

**5**

# Introduction to Linear Programming

## ■ Introduction

In Chapter 1 the foundation and structure of the modeling process were presented, as were the basic steps involved in the development and use of management science techniques. We also noted that linear models have broad applications in management science. In this chapter we will develop the foundations for basic linear models. Specifically, we will

1. present an overview of the formulation of a linear model

2. outline a graphical procedure for solving the basic model

3. discuss some limitations of the graphical solution process

4. present a tabular approach to represent the linear model

To aid in the discussion and development of linear models, this chapter, as well as those subsequent, will build upon a case example. The case in this particular chapter is simplistic, but realistically highlights a typical problem that exists in practice.

### ■ Case
## Agro-Tech Inc.

Tom Anderson, the production manager of Agro-Tech Inc., needs to plan the mixing of fertilizer for the next month and is confused as to how to go about devising such a plan. Agro-Tech is a small chemical company that manufactures, among other items, two types of fertilizer, which are produced by combining ingredients bought from outside suppliers. Each month Tom has to plan the amount of each fertilizer to produce. His plan has to take into account the cost of ingredients, the selling price of the fertilizers, any orders that have to be filled, and any restrictions on the use of the company's resources—labor, raw materials, or machine time. The planning process for this month is more difficult than normal. Agro-Tech usually produces fertilizers according to customer orders, but this month all fertilizers are going to be sold through a wholesaler. This complicates matters because Tom has to come up with a production schedule that will lead to the greatest possible profit for Agro-Tech while using only the amount of ingredients that are available for the month.

### Production considerations

The two fertilizers produced by Agro-Tech are mixtures called 5-5-10 and 5-10-5. In each case, the first value refers to the percentage of the chemical nitrate in the final product, the second value gives the percentage of phosphate in the final product, and the third value gives the percentage of potash in the final product. The balance of the fertilizer is made from a filler material such as clay. For example, the 5-5-10 is made up of 5% nitrate, 5% phosphate, 10% potash, and 80% clay. The wholesaler will buy all of both the 5-5-10 and 5-10-5 that Agro-Tech can produce. He is willing to pay $71.50 per ton for the 5-5-10 and $69 per ton for the 5-10-5. This month, raw material availability and costs are 1100 tons of nitrate at $200 a ton, 1800 tons of phosphate at $80 per ton, and 2000 tons of potash at $160 per

ton. The filler is available in unlimited quantities at a price of $10 per ton, but only those quantities noted are available for the other three ingredients. There are no restrictions on the use of labor nor are there restrictions on use of machinery for the month, but there is a $15 per ton mixing cost for the fertilizer. The question that Tom must address is: How does one use the scarce resources (nitrate, phosphate, and potash) available to Agro-Tech in a manner that will provide the greatest profit for the company?

### Characteristics of the case

There are several characteristics of the case that are important to note. First, Tom has a single objective to achieve—the maximization of profit by the production of the two fertilizers. Second, the objective is to be achieved subject to the availability and use of scarce resources—the ingredients. Third, both the profit and the use of the scarce resources are directly proportional to the amount of the two fertilizers produced, that is, the profits from the two products can be added together to arrive at total profits. Similarly, the individual product uses of resources can be summed to determine total use. Finally, it is not possible to produce a negative amount of either product.

The characteristics of this case are common to an important type of mathematical model known as **linear programming** (LP). For this reason, it is appropriate to list and discuss each characteristic in more detail. For this model, these are the **LP assumptions**.

### Characteristics of linear programming problems

**A single objective.**   For Agro-Tech, the objective is the maximization of profits. This requirement tells us that we need not worry about more than one objective at a time. This is not an unreasonable assumption for a short-term planning model such as we are considering. As we shall see later, it is also possible to consider the maximization, minimization of other quantities as single objectives. This maximization of profit when expressed mathematically is called our *objective function.*

**Restrictions.**   *The maximization (or minimization) of an objective is subject to restrictions.* For Agro-Tech, the availability of scarce resources limits production to levels that can be supported by available resources. If we were not constrained by this restriction, it would be possible to produce an unlimited amount of the products, which, of course, is totally unrealistic. Such restrictions on production levels are called *constraints.*

**Proportionality.**   *The objective function and the constraints must be proportional to the production level of each product.* This *linearity* restriction sets this model apart from other models that seek to maximize an objective function subject to a set of constraints. In Figure 5-1, we see a linear or proportional function in a as compared with two nonlinear functions in b and c. In Figure 5-1a, $Y$ is linear in $X$ because $Y = CX$ for some constant $C$. Note that $Y = 0$ if $X = 0$ and $Y$ increases in direct proportion to the increase in $X$. In Figure 5-1b, $W$ is not linear in $X$ because $W$ increases at a faster rate than does $X$. Finally, in Figure 5-1c, $V$ is not linear in $X$ because the increase in $V$ is not directly proportional to the increase in $X$. In this case, $V$ increases at a decreasing rate as $X$ increases.

While it might appear that the assumption of linearity is unreasonable, the fact remains that many practical problems are, in actuality, linear or can be modeled as a linear programming (LP) problem.

**Additivity.**   *The contributions of individual products are additive.* Expressed in other words, this simply means the whole is equal to the sum of the parts and there are no interactive effects between production levels.

**Divisibility.**   The characteristic of *divisibility* means that *fractional allocations of products are possible.* This is an important consideration where production or assignment of discrete items is concerned since linear programming solutions cannot be guaranteed to be integers.

**Nonnegativity of products.**   This is the easiest assumption to understand since we would never expect to be able to produce less than a zero amount of a product.

In addition to these requirements, it is also usually assumed that all parameters are known with certainty, that is, profits, availability of scarce resources, and relationships between levels of production and uses of resources are not subject to any uncertainty.

## Application of linear programming to Agro-Tech Inc.

Since linear programming is an abstract mathematical model of a physical problem, it is necessary to use mathematical symbols, as we noted in

**FIGURE 5-1.  Linear Versus Nonlinear Functions**

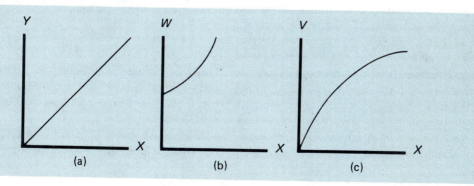

Chapter 1, to represent the physical quantities in the problem. This process is known as formulating the linear programming problem.

In our case, the physical quantities of interest (i.e., the quantities that can be varied) are the amounts of the two fertilizers that can be produced. All other physical elements will be assumed constant for now. For the Agro-Tech problem, we can let $x_1$ = (tons of 5-5-10 fertilizer produced) and $x_2$ = (tons of 5-10-5 fertilizer produced). We could have used any variable names, but to be consistent with our notation in Chapter 1, we will use $x_1$ and $x_2$. These are the **decision variables** for this problem.

The second part of modeling the physical problem as a mathematical model is to combine the decision variables defined above and the physical relationships inherent in the problem. These physical relationships will change from problem to problem, and care must be taken to insure that the mathematical model accurately portrays these relationships. In our case, the model must account for the amounts of each raw material that is utilized in each type of fertilizer. The model must also accurately describe the relationship between profit and production level of each type of fertilizer. We will discuss modeling the profit relationships first.

To determine the proper profit relationship for each level of production, we need to determine the **contribution to profit** rather than simply consider total profit. The contribution to profit is the sales revenue less all variable costs. Variable costs include direct materials, direct labor, variable manufacturing overhead, and variable selling and administrative expenses. Fixed manufacturing overhead and fixed selling and administrative expenses, by definition, do not vary with the level of production; therefore, they are not relevant for determining a product mix that maximizes profit.

In the case of Agro-Tech and the two fertilizers under consideration, the only costs that will be considered are the costs of the fertilizer ingredients—nitrate, phosphate, potash, and inert

ingredients—and the mixing costs. These mixing costs are $15 per ton of fertilizer regardless of the ingredient mixture.

For the 5-5-10 fertilizer, we have a revenue of $71.50 for each ton produced. In the final product, 5% will be nitrate, 5% will be phosphate, 10% will be potash, and 80% will be inert ingredients. We can calculate the costs of these ingredients for each ton of final product as follows:

| | |
|---|---:|
| Cost of nitrate per ton of 5-5-10 = $(.05) \times (\$200)$ | = $10.00 |
| Cost of phosphate per ton of 5-5-10 = $(.05) \times (\$80)$ | = 4.00 |
| Cost of potash per ton of 5-5-10 = $(.10) \times (\$160)$ | = 16.00 |
| Cost of inert ingredients per ton of 5-5-10 = $(.80) \times (\$10)$ | = 8.00 |
| Total cost of 5-5-10 ingredients | = $38.00 |
| Mixing cost | = 15.00 |
| Total cost | = $53.00 |

Now, since contribution to profit = revenue − variable costs, we have contribution to profit for 5-5-10 = $71.50 − $53.00 = $18.50 per ton produced.

Similarly for 5-10-5, direct costs are as follows:

| | |
|---|---:|
| Cost of nitrate per ton of 5-10-5 = $(.05) \times (\$200)$ | = $10.00 |
| Cost of phosphate per ton of 5-10-5 = $(.10) \times (\$80)$ | = 8.00 |
| Cost of potash per ton of 5-10-5 = $(.05) \times (\$160)$ | = 8.00 |
| Cost of inert ingredients per ton of 5-10-5 = $(.80) \times (\$10)$ | = 8.00 |
| Total cost of 5-10-5 ingredients | = $34.00 |
| Mixing cost | = 15.00 |
| Total cost | = $49.00 |

Now, as before, contribution to profit = revenue − variable costs, so the contribution to profit for 5-10-5 = $69 − $49 = $20.00 per ton produced.

Using these values of contributions to profit, we can write an objective function for Agro-Tech. For each ton of 5-5-10 produced, the profit is $18.50; if $x_1$ tons are produced, the total contribution to profit is $18.5x_1$. Similarly, if $x_2$ tons of 5-10-5 are produced, the total contribution to profit is $20x_2$. The total contribution from both products will be their sum, that is, $18.5x_1 + 20x_2$. So the profit function is

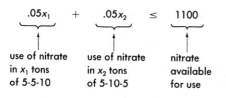

$$Z = 18.5x_1 + 20x_2$$

Now, we must consider the constraints in our problem; that is, what are the physical relationships between the production of a given fertilizer and the use of the available scarce resources? For the nitrate, we have 1100 tons available. For each ton of 5-5-10 produced, .05 ton of nitrate is used. So, if $x_1$ tons of 5-5-10 are produced, $.05x_1$ tons of nitrate will be used. Similarly, if $x_2$ tons of 5-10-5 are produced, $.05x_2$ tons of nitrate are consumed. Since only 1100 tons of nitrate are available, this could act as a restriction or constraint on the level of production of either 5-5-10 or 5-10-5. The word *could* is used since some other scarce resource may be more restrictive than the nitrate. If this were the case, our maximum-profit production mix would be such that we would end up with some nitrate left over. Since we are not forced to use all of any resource, we will write the restriction on the use of nitrate as follows:

$$.05x_1 \quad + \quad .05x_2 \quad \leq \quad 1100$$

| use of nitrate in $x_1$ tons of 5-5-10 | use of nitrate in $x_2$ tons of 5-10-5 | nitrate available for use |

This constraint simply says that the amount of nitrate used to make $x_1$ tons of 5-5-10 *plus* the nitrate used to make $x_2$ tons of 5-10-5 must be less than or equal to the amount of nitrate available.

For phosphate, if $x_1$ tons of 5-5-10 are produced, then $.05x_1$ tons of phosphate will be used.

And if $x_2$ tons of 5-10-5 are produced, $.10x_2$ tons of phosphate will be used. Since there are 1800 tons of phosphate available, the restriction on the use of phosphate can be written as follows:

$$.05x_1 \quad + \quad .10x_2 \quad \leq \quad 1800$$

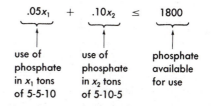

| use of phosphate in $x_1$ tons of 5-5-10 | use of phosphate in $x_2$ tons of 5-10-5 | phosphate available for use |

Finally, for potash, if $x_1$ tons of 5-5-10 are produced, $.10x_1$ tons of potash will be used up. And if $x_2$ tons of 5-10-5 are produced, $.05x_2$ tons of potash will be used up. Since there are 2000 tons of potash available for producing the two types of fertilizer, the restrictions on the use of potash can be written as follows:

$$.10x_1 + .05x_2 \leq 2000$$

In each of these restrictions, or constraints, the coefficients of the $x_1$ and $x_2$ variables are **physical rates of substitution.** That is, these coefficients give us the rate at which raw material is converted into the desired end product. Consider the potash constraint above. In this constraint, potash is converted into 5-5-10 at the rate of 10 tons of fertilizer for each ton of potash. It can also be converted into 5-10-5 at the rate of 20 tons of fertilizer for each ton of potash. So, while it appears at first glance that the two products are of about equal profitability, the efficiency of conversion of raw materials and the availability of raw materials have not been taken into account. Linear programming, however, does take the efficiency of conversion into account. Linear programming considers the unit profit on each product, the efficiency of conversion of raw materials into final products as shown by the physical rates of substitution, and the availability of the various raw materials.

To summarize, linear programming is based on six assumptions. These are:

1. a single objective function subject to constraints

2. proportionality of all relationships

3. additivity of all variables

4. divisibility of variables

5. certainty of all parameters and

6. nonnegativity of variables

## ■ The graphical method for solving LP problems

To solve small problems such as the Agro-Tech problem, that is, problems with two products or variables, we can use a graphical approach. While such a procedure is not useful for solving problems with more than two variables, it is useful for demonstrating both the solution process and the characteristics of an optimal or highest-profit solution.

### Procedural steps

There are four steps to solving a problem graphically. We will state these steps and then illustrate them using the Agro-Tech problem. The steps are:

1. State or formulate the problem mathematically.
2. Graph or plot the constraints.
3. Graph the objective function.
4. Solve for the values of variables at a highest-profit point.

**Step 1: State or formulate the problem mathematically.** Formulation of the problem involves a three-step process:

a. Define the decision variables.
b. State mathematically the profit or objective function.
c. State mathematically the resource restrictions or constraints.

For Agro-Tech, we have already defined our variables as $x_1$ = (tons of 5-5-10 produced) and $x_2$ = (tons of 5-10-5 produced).

Using the previously calculated values for contribution to profit, we may state the objective function as follows:

MAXIMIZE:        $Z = 18.5x_1 + 20x_2$                                    (5.1)

This objective function is *subject to* the resource restrictions or constraints. To state the constraints for this problem, we need to recall that each product is made up of nitrate, phosphate, potash, and inert ingredients in the proportions given on the label of the fertilizer. Recall also that we are restricted by the availability of the first three ingredients. The relationship can be stated mathematically for the use of nitrate as follows:

$$.05x_1 + .05x_2 \leq 1100 \tag{5.2}$$

This states that if $x_1$ tons of 5-5-10 and $x_2$ tons of 5-10-5 are produced, 5% of $x_1$ plus 5% of $x_2$ must be less than or equal to the amount of nitrate available, 1100 tons. For phosphate, the constraint is

$$.05x_1 + .10x_2 \leq 1800 \tag{5.3}$$

Similarly, for potash, the constraint is

$$.10x_1 + .05x_2 \leq 2000 \tag{5.4}$$

We must also remember that negative production levels are not possible, so we must include the nonnegativity restrictions,

$$x_1, x_2 \geq 0 \tag{5.5}$$

Altogether, the problem may be stated or *formulated* as follows:

MAXIMIZE: $\quad 18.5x_1 + 20x_2$ $\hspace{5cm}$ (5.1)

SUBJECT TO: $\quad .05x_1 + .05x_2 \leq 1100$ $\hspace{3.8cm}$ (5.2)

$\qquad\qquad .05x_1 + .10x_2 \leq 1800$ $\hspace{3.8cm}$ (5.3)

$\qquad\qquad .10x_1 + .05x_2 \leq 2000$ $\hspace{3.8cm}$ (5.4)

$\qquad\qquad\quad x_1, x_2 \geq 0$ $\hspace{4.5cm}$ (5.5)

**Step 2: Graph the constraints.** Since we have two variables, we need only two dimensions to graph the problem. We will let the horizontal axis measure the production of the 5-5-10 fertilizer (product $x_1$) and the vertical axis measure the production of the 5-10-5 fertilizer (product $x_2$). Using these, we can graph the inequalities above the $x_1$ axis and to the right of the $x_2$ axis.

In Figure 5-2, we see the result of graphing inequality (5.2). As with any linear relation, inequality (5.2) can be graphed by first plotting two points. In this case, the easiest way to plot the inequalities is to set $x_1 = 0$ and solve (5.2), as an equality for the value of $x_2$. In other words, if $x_1 = 0$, then

$$(.05)(0) + .05x_2 = 1100 \quad \text{or} \quad x_2 = 22,000$$

This is then reversed by setting $x_2 = 0$ and solving for $x_1$; that is, if $x_2 = 0$, then

$$.05x_1 + (.05)(0) = 1100 \quad \text{or} \quad x_1 = 22,000$$

**FIGURE 5-2.**
**Graph of Resource**
**Constraint (5.2)**

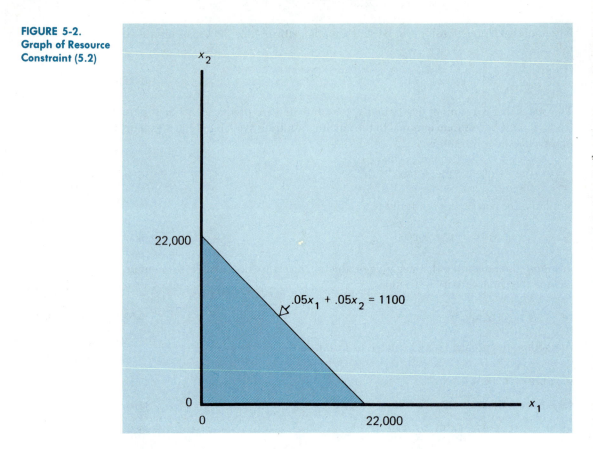

The shaded part of Figure 5-2 represents the inequality (5.2). Any solution in this shaded region satisfies the inequality. Only the **nonnegative region**—that region to the right of the $x_2$ axis and above the $x_1$ axis—is considered because only nonnegative levels of production are allowed [constraint (5.5)].

*nonnegative region*

If we graph the remaining two inequalities, (5.3) and (5.4), using the same procedure we used to graph inequality (5.2), we will arrive at Figure 5-3.

Several important things should be noted about Figure 5-3. First, note that there is a region shaded on the graph that satisfies all three inequalities simultaneously. This region is called the **feasible region.** Any point in the feasible region is a solution to the original problem. However, this is a large number of solutions to consider in looking for the one that provides the highest-profit production mix of 5-5-10 and 5-10-5. But we can reduce the number that need be considered if we look at the profits for various solutions. This can be done by plotting **iso-profit** lines on the graph of the feasible region. These are lines along which profit remains constant. The process of plotting iso-profit lines is nothing other than graphing the objective function.

*feasible region*

*iso-profit*

**Step 3: Graph the objective function.**   To graph the objective function, various levels of profit need to be considered. When the objective function is graphed for

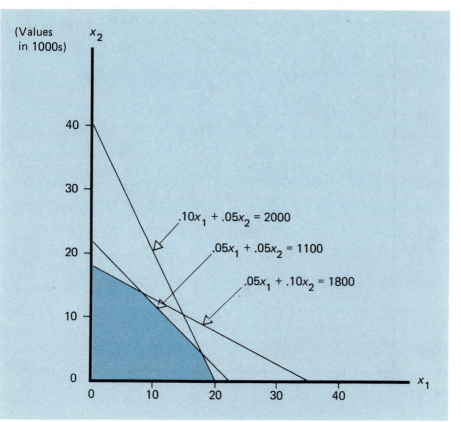

(Values in 1000s)

$.10x_1 + .05x_2 = 2000$

$.05x_1 + .05x_2 = 1100$

$.05x_1 + .10x_2 = 1800$

FIGURE 5-3.
Graph of All Re-
source Constraints

each profit level, an isoprofit line (along which the profit is the same) is formed. To maximize profits we must find the iso-profit line that is farthest from the origin but still touching the feasible region. An example of plotting an iso-profit line would be arbitrarily to select an Agro-Tech profit, say $185,000, and determine the line that has a profit of $185,000 at all points. This can be accomplished rather easily if we recall that the profit or objective function is a linear relationship expressed in the following manner:

$$P = 18.5x_1 + 20x_2 = 185,000$$

All that is required is to set $P = 185,000$ and locate any two pairs of values $(x_1, x_2)$. (A straight line is always defined by two points.) We can identify two obvious pairs of values by using the process we used to plot the constraint. That is, set $x_1$ to zero and solve for $x_2$, then set $x_2$ to zero and solve for $x_1$. One pair would be $x_1 = 0$ and $x_2 = 9,250$. Another pair is $x_1 = 10,000$ and $x_2 = 0$. This iso-profit line is shown in Figure 5-4 as line 1, along with the feasible region.

While this iso-profit line defines a group of feasible solutions, all having a profit of $185,000, it is immediately obvious from Figure 5-4 that there exist points with

**FIGURE 5-4.**
**Iso-profit Lines**

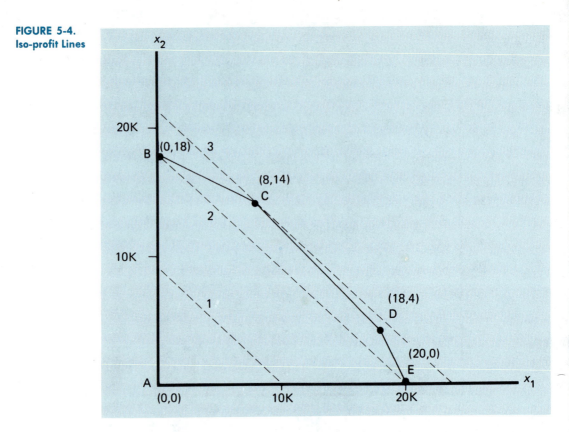

higher profit farther away from the origin. Recall that we would like to find the iso-profit line that is *farthest* removed from the origin but is feasible, that is, remains in contact with the feasible region. Another iso-profit line that we can consider is 2 in Figure 5-4. This iso-profit line has a profit of $370,000 and can be plotted by the use of the points $x_1 = 0$, $x_2 = 18,500$, and $x_1 = 20,000$, $x_2 = 0$. Note that lines 1 and 2 are parallel, with line 2 being farther removed from the origin. However, it is still possible to find an even higher iso-profit line. The iso-profit line with the largest profit that is still feasible is line 3 in Figure 5-4. By observing the graph, we note that this line touches the feasible region at only one point, $x_1 = 8,000$, $x_2 = 14,000$. If we substitute these values into the objective function, we find that the profit is equal to $428,000. Any iso-profit lines with higher profit will not contact the feasible region, and we should not consider any lines with lower profit. The highest-profit solution thus occurs at point C in Figure 5-4. This solution tells us to produce 8,000 tons of 5-5-10 and 14,000 tons of 5-10-5 for a profit of $428,000.

**Step 4: Solve for the highest-profit point.**   Several important results can be noted from this solution process. First, the only points that need be considered in our search for an optimum are those points on the **boundary** or outermost portion of the feasible region. One can reason this from the fact that for any point *in* the feasible region,

*boundary*

there will exist a higher-profit point *on* the boundary of the feasible region. Second, the *only points on the boundary that need be considered are the corner points*— those that occur at the intersection of two or more constraints. The corner points, labeled A, B, C, D, and E in Figure 5-4, are often referred to as *vertices* of the feasible region. An *optimal solution* for an LP problem always occurs at a **vertex** of the feasible region because for any other point on the boundary, there will always be a vertex that will have the same or greater profit.

*vertex*

The vertices for a two-variable problem can be found by taking pairs of constraints or nonnegativity conditions and solving them as simultaneous equations. For example, point A is found by solving

$$x_1 = 0 \quad \text{and} \quad x_2 = 0$$

Point B is found by solving

$$x_1 = 0 \quad \text{and} \quad .05x_1 + .10x_2 = 1800$$

to obtain

$$x_1 = 0, \quad x_2 = 18{,}000$$

The optimal point C is found by solving simultaneously

$$.05x_1 + .10x_2 = 1800 \quad \text{and} \quad .05x_1 + .05x_2 = 1100$$

which yields

$$x_1 = 8{,}000, \quad x_2 = 14{,}000$$

The five vertices for this problem are summarized in Table 5-1.

As discussed above, the coordinates (i.e., the $x_1$ and $x_2$ values) for points A, B, and E are easy to calculate since they occur at conditions where one or both of the production levels are zero. Point C is found by solving simultaneously inequalities (5.2) and (5.3); point D is found by solving inequalities (5.2) and (5.4). In looking at all vertices (Table 5-1), there is an important observation to be made: in having to consider only corner points or vertices, the number of solutions to consider is reduced drastically. Instead of having to look at all points in the feasible region, as shown in

**TABLE 5-1.**
**Feasible Vertices**

| Vertex | Production of $x_1$ | Production of $x_2$ | Profit |
|--------|--------------------|--------------------|---------|
| A | 0 | 0 | 0 |
| B | 0 | 18,000 | $360,000 |
| C | 8,000 | 14,000 | $428,000 |
| D | 18,000 | 4,000 | $413,000 |
| E | 20,000 | 0 | $370,000 |

Figure 5-4, or even only those on the boundary, we need consider only the five vertices. This fact is the key factor that allows us to solve large LP problems.

### Comments

If Tom Anderson uses our discussion of linear programming to solve his production planning problem, he will produce 8,000 tons of the 5-5-10 fertilizer and 14,000 tons of the 5-10-5 fertilizer. If the revenue and cost values stated previously are correct, then Agro-Tech will realize a contribution to profit of $428,000. It should be noted that in producing the fertilizers, all of the nitrate and phosphate will be used in the production process, but 500 tons of potash will be left over. It must also be remembered that in considering the use of linear programming to solve Agro-Tech's problem, the assumptions discussed earlier must hold: maximization of a single-objective function subject to availability of scarce resources; proportionality; additivity of individual contributions in the objective function and constraints; divisibility; certainty of profit values and physical rates of a substitution; and nonnegativity of variables. If any of these assumptions do not hold exactly, this does not mean linear programming should not be used. If linear programming gives useful information about the problem, the decision maker can still utilize the model. The key point is to recognize that the true situation differs from the model being used and the results should be interpreted accordingly.

## ▪ Further discussion of linear programming

An important concept noted in the previous section on graphical solutions to LP problems was that *only* vertices or corner points of the feasible region need be considered when searching for an optimal solution. We noted that each vertex occurred at the intersection of two constraints. We then solved for each vertex by simultaneously solving the set of linear equations that formed the vertex. This suggests a solution procedure based upon the simultaneous solution of sets of equations and movement from vertex to vertex until an optimal solution is reached. This is precisely how an algorithm called the *simplex method* works. At each step of the algorithm the equations that form a vertex are solved simultaneously to identify the vertex. The vertex is tested for optimality, and, if the optimum has not been reached, the algorithm moves to another vertex and repeats the process. The procedure guarantees that each vertex will be no worse than the previous vertex in terms of profit or cost.

The simplex method has the advantage over the graphical approach in that more than two variables can easily be handled. However, regardless of whether two variables, ten variables, or a large number of variables are required in a given problem, the simplex method examines only the corner points of the feasible region. To insure that this occurs, the first step of the simplex method is to convert all linear inequality constraints to linear equations.

## Conversion of inequalities to equalities

The process for converting inequalities to equalities involves adding a **slack variable**      *slack variable*
to the less-than-or-equal-to inequalities (inequalities of the form $a_{11}x_1 + a_{12}x_2 \leq b_1$)
and subtracting a **surplus variable** from the greater-than-or-equal-to inequalities      *surplus variable*
(inequalities of the form $a_{21}x_1 + a_{22}x_2 \geq b_2$). An example will illustrate the point.
Assume the following set of constraints has been defined.

$$6x_1 + 5x_2 \leq 30 \tag{5.6}$$

$$10x_1 + x_2 \geq 50 \tag{5.7}$$

The first inequality is converted to an equality by adding a slack variable, which we
call $s_1$. The resulting equation is

$$6x_1 + 5x_2 + s_1 = 30 \tag{5.8}$$

The slack variable $s_1$ is the amount by which $(6x_1 + 5x_2)$ is less than 30. If $(6x_1 + 5x_2)$
is equal to 30 (this could occur if $x_1 = 5$ and $x_2 = 0$), then $s_1 = 0$. On the other hand, if
$(6x_1 + 5x_2)$ is less than 30, then $s_1$ takes on a positive value that is the amount that
$(6x_1 + 5x_2)$ is less than 30.

The second inequality is converted to an equation by subtracting a surplus
variable, which we will call $s_2$. The resulting equation is

$$10x_1 + x_2 - s_2 = 50 \tag{5.9}$$

The surplus variable $s_2$ represents the difference between $(10x_1 + x_2)$ and 50. If
$(10x_1 + x_2)$ is equal to 50, then $s_2$ is equal to zero. But if $(10x_1 + x_2)$ is greater than
50, then $s_2$ has a positive value that is equal to the amount by which $(10x_1 + x_2)$
exceeds 50.

Let us see how this relates to the Agro-Tech Inc. problem. Recall that the problem
was stated mathematically as follows:

MAXIMIZE:     $Z = 18.5x_1 + 20x_2$                      (5.10)

SUBJECT TO:     $.05x_1 + .05x_2 \leq 1100$                      (5.11)

$.05x_1 + .10x_2 \leq 1800$                      (5.12)

$.10x_1 + .05x_2 \leq 2000$                      (5.13)

$x_1, x_2 \geq 0$                      (5.14)

where     $x_1$ = tons of 5-5-10 fertilizer produced
$x_2$ = tons of 5-10-5 fertilizer produced

Note that all of the constraints are written as inequalities. If we let $s_1$ equal the
amount (in tons) of *unused* nitrate when $x_1$ tons of 5-5-10 and $x_2$ tons of 5-10-5 are

produced, then inequality (5.11) becomes

$$.05x_1 + .05x_2 + s_1 = 1100$$

Similarly, if we let $s_2$ equal the tons of unused phosphate, inequality (5.12) can be written:

$$.05x_1 + .10x_2 + s_2 = 1800$$

Finally, if we let $s_3$ equal tons of unused potash, then inequality (5.13) becomes

$$.10x_1 + .05x_2 + s_3 = 2000$$

Using the three equalities, the revised model would be expressed thus:

MAXIMIZE:        $Z = 18.5x_1 + 20x_2 + 0s_1 + 0s_2 + 0s_3$                     (5.15)

SUBJECT TO:        $.05x_1 + .05x_2 + s_1 \qquad\qquad = 1100$                     (5.16)

$.05x_1 + .10x_2 \qquad + s_2 \qquad = 1800$                     (5.17)

$.10x_1 + .05x_2 \qquad\qquad + s_3 = 2000$                     (5.18)

$x_1, x_2, s_1, s_2, s_3 \geq 0$                     (5.19)

By adding slack variables to each of the inequality constraints we have a revised model that contains all equalities; that is, we have a system of equations. Note that in the revised model, weights of zero are used in the objective function for each slack variable; these weights are employed because slack resources contribute nothing to profits.

An additional point that should be noted regarding the revised model is that all the variables in the model, including the added slack variables, are equal to or greater than zero. If any of the slack variables were allowed to be negative, then one or more of the original inequalities would be violated.

By adding slack and negative surplus variables to inequality constraints, one can convert a system of inequalities into a system of equalities. For Agro-Tech, this required the addition of three slack variables. Note that, in this revised model of the problem, we have a system of equations with more variables than equalities. This is the general structure of an LP problem. In general terms we refer to the problem as having $m$ linear equations (three in our case) with $n$ unknowns (five in our case), where $n \geq m$.

## Finding basic feasible solutions

The reason for transforming inequalities to equalities in the simplex algorithm is to provide a set of equations that can be used to identify the corner points or vertices. The next step is to identify these vertices.

Normally one can solve a system of equations when the number of equations equals the number of variables. But in the Agro-Tech problem, as in all LP problems, we have at least as many variables as we have equations, that is, we have five variables and three equations. We can resolve this conflict, however, by applying a basic theorem of linear algebra, which states that for a system of $m$ equations and $n$ variables, where $n > m$, if a solution exists, it can be found by setting $n - m$ of the variables to zero and solving the resulting set of $m$ equations with $m$ variables. For the Agro-Tech problem, this means we must select three variables to use in solving the equations and set the remaining two variables to zero. The variables that are set to zero are referred to as *nonbasic variables;* the variables used in solving the equations are referred to as *basic variables.*

A question that must be resolved at this point is which variables should be selected to be basic and, conversely, which variables should be set to zero and made nonbasic. With $m$ equations and $n$ unknowns there are

$$\frac{n!}{m! \, (n - m)!}$$

*basic solutions* [where $n! = (n)(n - 1) \cdots (2)(1)$]. With three equations and five unknowns we have $5!/(3! \times 2!)$ or ten basic solutions.

For our revised problem [equations (5.15) to (5.19)], we can easily solve the set of equations when $x_1$ and $x_2$ are set to zero. For example, if $x_1 = 0$ and $x_2 = 0$, the system of equations is

$$.05(0) + .05(0) + s_1 \qquad\qquad = 1100 \qquad\qquad\qquad (5.20)$$

$$.05(0) + .10(0) \qquad + s_2 \quad = 1800 \qquad\qquad\qquad (5.21)$$

$$.10(0) + .05(0) \qquad\qquad + s_3 = 2000 \qquad\qquad\qquad (5.22)$$

Immediately we can note $s_1 = 1100$, $s_2 = 1800$, and $s_3 = 2000$. If we substitute the value of $x_1$, $x_2$, $s_1$, $s_2$, and $s_3$ back into the objective function, the resulting profit is $0. What this says is that if neither $x_1$ nor $x_2$ is produced, we will have 1100 tons of unused nitrate, 1800 tons of unused phosphate, and 2000 tons of unused potash, with no resulting profits.

If we continue the process of setting two variables to zero and solving the resulting set of equations, we can identify the remaining nine *basic solutions* to the system of equations. These are shown in Table 5-2. Note that five of the basic solutions are labeled *not feasible.* Recall that in formulating the original problem and in the revised problem, it was stipulated that all variables must be greater than or equal to zero. In solutions 2, 4, 5, 7, and 10 (Table 5-2), at least one variable has a negative value. Such solutions are not feasible as solutions to the LP problem because negative values for variables are meaningless. For example, solution 2 indicates that 0 tons of $x_1$ would be produced and 22,000 tons of $x_2$ would be produced, with 900 tons of

**TABLE 5-2.
All the Basic
Solutions to
Agro-Tech Problem**

| | | | Variables | | | Objective |
|---|---|---|---|---|---|---|
| Solution | $x_1$ | $x_2$ | $s_1$ | $s_2$ | $s_3$ | Function Z |
| 1 | 0 | 0 | 1,100 | 1,800 | 2,000 | $0 |
| 2 | 0 | 22,000 | 0 | −400 | 900 | Not feasible |
| 3 | 0 | 18,000 | 200 | 0 | 1,100 | $360,000 |
| 4 | 0 | 40,000 | −900 | −2,200 | 0 | Not feasible |
| 5 | 36,000 | 0 | −700 | 0 | −1,600 | Not feasible |
| 6 | 20,000 | 0 | 100 | 800 | 0 | $370,000 |
| 7 | 22,000 | 0 | 0 | 900 | −200 | Not feasible |
| 8 | 8,000 | 14,000 | 0 | 0 | 500 | $428,000 |
| 9 | 18,000 | 4,000 | 0 | 500 | 0 | $413,000 |
| 10 | 14,666.6 | 10,666.6 | −166.6 | 0 | 0 | Not feasible |

potash remaining. The negative 400, however, indicates that the production of these quantities of $x_1$ and $x_2$ would require 400 tons more nitrate than is available. Such a solution, while mathematically valid, is not logical in practice. To differentiate infeasible solutions from feasible solutions, the label *basic feasible solution* is given to each basic solution in which all variables are nonnegative.

A final point that should be noted about the basic solution set shown in Table 5-2 is that the *basic feasible solutions* are the corner points or the vertices of the feasible region that describes the problem. Figure 5-5 is a graphical display of the Agro-Tech problem showing all vertices, feasible and infeasible. Vertex 1 corresponds to basic feasible solution 1, vertex 2 to solution 2, and so forth. Note that only vertices 1, 3, 6, 8, and 9 fall in (actually on) the feasible region, while the vertices corresponding to nonfeasible solutions lie outside the region.

There are five key points to be aware of at this point in our discussion of linear programming:

1. A linear programming problem is made up of an objective function and one or more constraints.

2. The optimal solution to an LP problem will occur at a vertex or corner point of the feasible region.

3. The constraints must be converted to equalities through the addition of slack variables or subtraction of surplus variables.

4. The values of the variables at the vertices may be found by solving the $m$ simultaneous equations for the $m$ basic variables with the remaining $n$ − $m$ nonbasic variables set to zero.

5. A vertex with all nonnegative variables and the highest-profit value is termed an optimal solution.

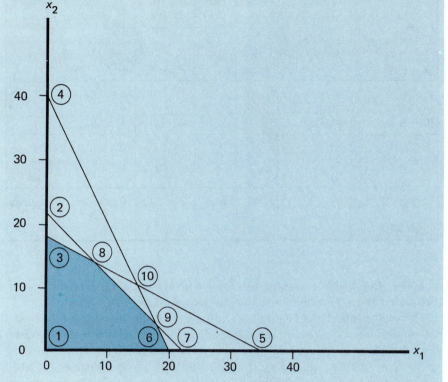

**FIGURE 5-5.**
**Graphical Plot of**
**Agro-Tech Inc.**

## A tabular approach to LP problems

*simplex tableau*

While the mechanics of the simplex method will be discussed in much detail in Chapter 7, we will briefly look at the tabular form—known as the **simplex tableau**—used in this method. Many times, tabular output actually is presented in this tableau format, so it is necessary to be able to read such a table.

The initial simplex tableau for an LP problem is simply a different form of the formulation, wherein the coefficients of the objective function and the constraints have been detached from their variables. The necessary calculations can be made easily without having to manipulate variable names. The objective function and constraint coefficients for the Agro-Tech problem [equations (5.15) through (5.19)] have been placed in a simplex tableau in Table 5-3.

The first two rows of the tableau, labeled *Contribution per Unit* and *Headings and Variables* (the shaded row), identify the coefficients of the objective function and the column headings, respectively. The coefficients are transferred directly from the objective function. The label *contribution per unit* is employed because the coefficients reflect the per unit contribution that each variable makes to the

**TABLE 5-3.**
**Initial Simplex**
**Tableau**

| $c_B$ | Variables in the Basis | Right-hand Side (Solution) | $x_1$ | $x_2$ | $s_1$ | $s_2$ | $s_3$ | |
|---|---|---|---|---|---|---|---|---|
| | $c_j$ | | 18.5 | 20.0 | 0 | 0 | 0 | Contribution per Unit |
| | Variables in the Basis | Right-hand Side (Solution) | $x_1$ | $x_2$ | $s_1$ | $s_2$ | $s_3$ | Headings and Variables |
| 0 | $s_1$ | 1100 | .05 | .05 | 1 | 0 | 0 | Coefficients |
| 0 | $s_2$ | 1800 | .05 | .10 | 0 | 1 | 0 | |
| 0 | $s_3$ | 2000 | .10 | .05 | 0 | 0 | 1 | |
| | $z_j$ | 0 | 0 | 0 | 0 | 0 | 0 | Contribution Lost per Unit Produced |
| | $c_j - z_j$ | | 18.5 | 20.0 | 0 | 0 | 0 | Net Contribution per Unit Produced |

objective. Recall that zeros are associated with the slack variables because these variables make no contribution to the objective of maximizing profits.

The coefficients of the constraints are transferred directly into the body of the tableau under the appropriate variable heading. It is not mandatory that the order of the columns be in the sequence presented. For example, one could have $s_1$, $s_2$, $s_3$ followed by columns $x_1$, and $x_2$. However, the most obvious manner for labeling columns and transferring coefficients is in the order identified in the constraint equations. The right-hand side (resource) values from the constraint equations are placed in the column labeled *Right-hand Side (Solution)*.

The second column contains descriptive row headings and *Variables in the Basis*. The term *basis* is used to refer to the set of basic variables that make up the basic feasible solution. In this particular tableau, $s_1$, $s_2$, and $s_3$ are the basic variables (point A on the graph) because they are easily found from the initial equations. If we look at the coefficients in columns, $s_1$, $s_2$, and $s_3$, we can quickly verify that these variables are the variables in the basis. The values for the basic variables, or, as they are called, the *solution* can be read directly from the solution column opposite the respective variable. In this case, the solution is $s_1 = 1100$, $s_2 = 1800$, and $s_3 = 2000$. Since $x_1$ and $x_2$ are nonbasic variables and are not in the basis, they are zero (i.e., $x_1 = 0$, $x_2 = 0$).

The column labeled $c_B$ ("contribution per unit for variables in the basis") contains the objective function coefficients of the variables in the basis. Since $s_1$, $s_2$, and $s_3$ are the variables in the basis, the $c_B$ column contains zeros. These are the same zeros as in the $c_j$ row above the $s_1$, $s_2$, and $s_3$ columns.

The next to the last row contains the $z_j$ values for each variable. These values indicate the profit that will have to be given up to increase the value of each variable.

The last row of the tableau, the $(c_j - z_j)$ row, is computed by subtracting the $z_j$

value from the $c_j$ value for each respective variable column. This is the difference between the gain $(c_j)$ and loss $(z_j)$ arising from one unit of $x_j$ being produced. Since the $z_j$ values are all zero in the initial tableau, the $(c_j - z_j)$ values are simply the $c_j$ values. This is the row that gives the *net improvement* in the objective function due to a one-unit increase in the value of each variable. On some computer outputs, the $z_j$ row will not be shown, but the $(c_j - z_j)$ row [or its negative, $(z_j - c_j)$] will always be shown. If a $(c_j - z_j)$ value is *positive* [$(z_j - c_j)$ being negative], this indicates that the profit can be increased by increasing the value of the corresponding variable. If all $(c_j - z_j)$ values are nonpositive (zero or negative), the tableau represents an optimal solution.

The Z value or the objective function value for the basic feasible solution shown in the initial tableau is zero. This implies that zero profits result from $s_1 = 1100$, $s_2 = 1800$, and $s_3 = 2000$; this is the same result that we achieved in the graphical solution. The Z value is calculated by summing the products of the $c_B$ coefficients and the solution values of the variables in the basis. For example, in this case $Z = (0)(1100) + (0)(1800) + (0)(2000) = 0$. The Z value is shown in the tableau as the bottom entry in the *Right-hand Side (Solution)* column.

In Table 5-4 we show the optimal simplex tableau for the same Agro-Tech linear programming problem. We know this tableau is optimal since all $(c_j - z_j)$ or "net contribution per unit produced" values are negative or zero. Any change in production level for the variables would reduce the profit.

The tableau in Table 5-4 may be interpreted as follows: The optimal objective value is $428,000, and this profit comes from producing 8,000 tons of type 1 (5-5-10) fertilizer and 14,000 tons of type 2 (5-10-5) fertilizer. There are 500 tons of potash left over $(s_3)$. Finally, there is no nitrate or phosphate left over since the corresponding slack variables $s_1$ and $s_2$ are nonbasic and are, consequently, equal to zero.

| $c_j$ | | | 18.5 | 20.0 | 0 | 0 | 0 | Contribution per Unit |
|---|---|---|---|---|---|---|---|---|
| $c_B$ | Variables in the Basis | Right-hand Side (Solution) | $x_1$ | $x_2$ | $s_1$ | $s_2$ | $s_3$ | Headings and Variables |
| 18.5 | $x_1$ | 8,000 | 1 | 0 | 40 | −20 | 0 | Coefficients |
| 20.0 | $x_2$ | 14,000 | 0 | 1 | −20 | 20 | 0 | |
| 0 | $s_3$ | 500 | 0 | 0 | −3 | 1 | 1 | |
| | $z_j$ | 428,000 | 18.5 | 20.0 | 340 | 30 | 0 | Contribution Lost per Unit Produced |
| | $c_j - z_j$ | | 0 | 0 | −340 | −30 | 0 | Net Contribution per Unit Produced |

**TABLE 5-4.**
**Optimal Simplex Tableau**

In Chapter 7, we will take up the mechanics of the simplex method, which would allow one to move from an initial tableau such as Table 5-3 to an optimal tableau such as Table 5-4.

# ■ Summary

In this chapter we have looked at a very important management science model, linear programming. In the terminology of Chapter 1, linear programming is a normative model that is both linear and deterministic. It is also a static model since changes of parameters over time are not allowed.

We have seen that linear programming is based on several conditions or assumptions. These are proportionality, additivity, divisibility, maximization (or minimization) of a single objective, certainty, and nonnegativity. We have also seen that for problems with two variables, solutions can be found using a graphical approach. Using that approach, we first formulated the problem using decision variables, then graphed the constraints to form a feasible region. We next graphed iso-profit lines until the highest such profit line was found that still touched the feasible region. It was noted that this would always occur at a vertex or corner point of the feasible region. We also saw that linear programming will always involve trade-offs between products to find the highest-profit solution.

# ■ Glossary of terms

**boundary:**   The outer limit of the feasible region.

**contribution to profit:**   The difference between revenue and variable or direct costs.

**decision variable:**   A symbol used to represent an unknown quantity of some item.

**feasible region:**   The region that satisfies all constraints as well as the nonnegativity conditions.

**iso-profit line:**   A line along which the objective function retains the same value.

**linear programming:**   A linear, deterministic model that is normative by nature. Often used to allocate scarce resources or to determine product mixes.

**LP assumptions:**   (1) Single objective, (2) proportionality, (3) additivity, (4) divisibility, (5) certainty, and (6) nonnegativity of variables.

**nonnegative region:**   The region where all variables are greater than or equal to zero.

**physical rates of substitution:**   The rate at which a scarce resource can be converted into a finished product.

**simplex tableau:**   A tabular presentation of the LP constraints in equality form.

**slack (surplus) variables:**   Variables that are added to (or subtracted from) inequalities to convert them to equalities.

**vertex:**   The intersection of two or more constraints to form a corner point of the feasible region.

# ■ Review questions

1. Of all the assumptions on linear programming, which one do you think could be the most unrealistic in a practical problem? Why?

2. Can you think of any situation where the nonnegativity conditions may not be necessary?

3. In the Agro-Tech case, what other objectives might Mr. Anderson have to consider besides simple maximization of profit?

4. Can linear programming always solve a problem that must have an integer solution? Why or why not?

5. Could the case occur in linear programming where a vertex would have a solution higher than all its adjacent neighbors yet not be the optimal solution?

6. What would happen in the Agro-Tech case if the profits associated with the variables changed upward by $2 on the 5-5-10 and down by $1 on the 5-10-5? Would the entire problem have to be graphed again?

7. Even though our constraints are inequalities, we solve the corner points by treating the constraints as equalities. Why can we do this?

# ■ True/false questions

1. Linear programming can be employed to solve problems with multiple objectives.

2. Limitations on the availability of resources are incorporated in the objective function.

3. The objective function must be proportional to the production level of each product whereas the constraints are inversely proportional to the production level.

4. Linear programming solutions are always integers.

5. The contributions of individual products are additive.

6. Linear programming assumes that all parameters are known with certainty.

7. LP formulations involve only one decision variable.

8. The proper profit relationship for each level of production is defined by considering the contribution to profit rather than the total profit.

9. The coefficients of the decision variables in the constraints represent the physical rates of substitution.

10. In LP, variables may be positive, negative, or zero.

11. The graphical method is useful for solving LP problems with a large number of variables.

12. The objective function is independent of the constraints.

13. Any point in the feasible region is a solution to the original problem.

14. The iso-profit line represents the line where profit is maximized.

15. To maximize profits, we must find the iso-profit line that is farthest from the origin but still touching the feasible region.

16. In the search for an optimal solution, all points on the boundary of the feasible region must be considered.

17. An optimal solution for an LP problem always occurs at a vertex of the feasible region.

# ■ Problems

1. Given the following linear programming problem:

   MAXIMIZE:    $Z = 4x_1 + 5x_2$

   SUBJECT TO:    $2x_1 + 3x_2 \leq 120$

   $2x_1 + 1.5x_2 \leq 80$

   $x_1, x_2 \geq 0$

   a. Find the optimal solution to the problem using the graphical method.
   b. How many vertices are there on your graph? Solve for the values of these vertices in order to demonstrate that your graphical solution is optimal.

2. Given the following linear programming problem:

   MAXIMIZE:    $Z = 3x_1 + 2x_2$

   SUBJECT TO:    $x_1 \leq 10$

   $x_2 \leq 10$

   $x_1 + x_2 \leq 16$

   $x_1, x_2 \geq 0$

   a. Graphically show the feasible region for the problem.
   b. What are the values for the vertices of the problem?
   c. Solve the problem for the optimal solution.
   d. If the objective function were changed to $2x_1 + 3x_2$, what would be the optimal solution?

3. Given the following programming problem:

   MAXIMIZE:    $Z = 3x_1 + 1x_2$

   SUBJECT TO:    $6x_1 + 4x_2 \leq 48$

   $3x_1 + 6x_2 \leq 42$

   $x_1, x_2 \geq 0$

   Graphically solve the problem. Using your results, demonstrate that "the optimal solution to a linear programming problem is feasible, but a feasible solution is not necessarily optimal."

4. Graph each of the following constraints and identify whether the feasible region lies "to the right," "to the left," "above," "below," or "directly on" the constraint.

   a. $6x_1 + 5x_2 \leq 10$
   b. $x_1 + 5x_2 = 30$

c. $-4x_1 + 3x_2 \geq 12$

d. $x_2 \geq 9$

e. $x_1 \leq 9$

5. Use the graphical method to show that the problem:

MAXIMIZE:     $Z = 2x_1 + 2x_2$

SUBJECT TO:         $3x_1 + 2x_2 \leq 24$

$4x_1 + 7x_2 \leq 56$

$-5x_1 + 6x_2 \leq 30$

$x_1, x_2 \geq 0$

is equivalent to the following problem:

MINIMIZE:     $Z = -2x_1 - 2x_2$

SUBJECT TO:         $3x_1 + 2x_2 \leq 24$

$4x_1 + 7x_2 \leq 56$

$-5x_1 + 6x_2 \leq 30$

$x_1, x_2 \geq 0$

6. Given the following minimization linear programming problem:

MINIMIZE:     $Z = 50x_1 + 20x_2$

SUBJECT TO:         $2x_1 - 1x_2 \geq 0$

$1x_1 + 4x_2 \geq 80$

$.9x_1 + .8x_2 \geq 40$

$x_1, x_2 \geq 0$

Solve the problem graphically.

7. Consider the following linear programming problem:

MAXIMIZE:     $Z = 1x_1 + 1x_2$

SUBJECT TO:         $2x_1 + 4x_2 \leq 12$

$3x_1 + 2x_2 \leq 12$

$x_1, x_2 \geq 0$

a. Find the optimal solution using the graphical procedure.

   **b.** If the objective function were changed to $1x_1 + 3x_2$, what would be the optimal solution?

   **c.** How many vertex points are there on your graph? What are the $x_1$ and $x_2$ values at each extreme point?

8. Graph the following constraints and indicate the area of the feasible solutions:

$$3x_1 + 3x_2 \leq 300$$

$$6x_1 + 3x_2 \leq 480$$

$$3x_1 + 3x_2 \leq 480$$

$$x_1, x_2 \geq 0$$

9. Consider the following linear programming problem:

   MAXIMIZE:      $Z = 20x_1 + 22x_2$

   SUBJECT TO:      $8x_1 + 6x_2 \leq 48$

   $$6x_1 + 8x_2 \leq 48$$

   $$7x_1 + 7x_2 = 42$$

   $$x_1, x_2 \geq 0$$

   Solve the problem graphically.

10. Consider the following linear programming problem:

    MAXIMIZE:      $Z = 80x_1 + 60x_2$

    SUBJECT TO:      $x_1 + x_2 = 200$

    $$x_1 \qquad \leq 50$$

    $$x_2 \geq 80$$

    $$x_1, x_2 \geq 0$$

    Solve the problem graphically.

11. Consider the following linear programming problem:

    MINIMIZE:      $Z = 1.5x_1 + 2x_2$

    SUBJECT TO:      $2x_1 + 2x_2 \leq 8$

    $$2x_1 + 6x_2 \geq 12$$

    $$x_1, x_2 \geq 0$$

    Solve the problem graphically.

12. Graphically solve the following linear programming problem:

MAXIMIZE:     $Z = 3x_1 + 2x_2$

SUBJECT TO:        $3x_1 + 5x_2 \leq 45$

$6x_1 + 4x_2 \leq 48$

$x_1, x_2 \geq 0$

13. Use the graphical approach to solve the following problem:

MAXIMIZE:     $Z = 2x_1 + x_2$

SUBJECT TO:           $x_2 \leq 10$

$2x_1 + 5x_2 \leq 60$

$x_1 + x_2 \leq 18$

$3x_1 + x_2 \leq 44$

$x_1, x_2 \geq 0$

a. Circle all extreme points.
b. Indicate the optimal solution.

14. The AHM Corporation has a small plant where it produces two products. For formulation purposes we will label the products $x_1$ and $x_2$. The profit contributions for the products (as determined by the accounting department) are \$10 and \$12 respectively. The products pass through three production departments at the plant. The time required in the production of each product and the total time available in the respective departments are shown in Table P5-14.

TABLE P5-14

| Department | Man-hours of Production Time per Product | | Total Man-hours Available per Month |
|---|---|---|---|
| | $x_1$ | $x_2$ | |
| 1 | 2.0 | 3.0 | 1500 |
| 2 | 3.0 | 2.0 | 1500 |
| 3 | 1.0 | 1.0 | 600 |

The management of AHM wishes to determine the production mix of products $x_1$ and $x_2$ that will maximize profits.

a. Identify the objective function and constraints for the problem.
b. Find the optimal solution to the problem using the graphical method.
c. Is there anything unusual about any of the constraints?

**15.** Given the following problem:

MAXIMIZE:     $Z = 1x_1 + 1x_2$

SUBJECT TO:     $1x_1 + 2x_2 \leq 6$

$6x_1 + 4x_2 \leq 24$

$3x_1 + 3x_2 \leq 21$

$x_1, x_2 \geq 0$

**a.** Identify the feasible region for the problem.

**b.** Does the problem have an unnecessary constraint? If so, what is it? Would the optimal solution to the problem change if the constraint were removed?

**16.** For the following constraints, the corresponding graphical representation is given. Using the constraints and the graphical representation, answer the questions below the graph in Figure P5-16.

$$2x_1 + 3x_2 \leq 12, \qquad -x_1 + x_2 \leq 2, \qquad x_1, x_2 \geq 0$$

**FIGURE P5-16.**
**Graphical Representation**

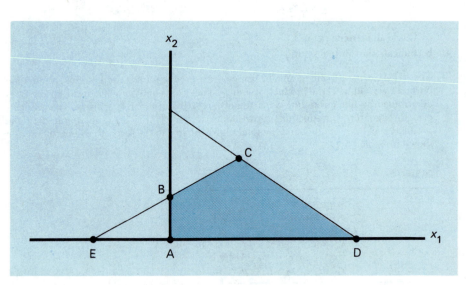

**a.** Fill in the missing values of the following table:

| Vertex | Variable | |
| --- | --- | --- |
| | $x_1$ | $x_2$ |
| A | 0 | 0 |
| B | | |
| C | | |
| D | | |

**b.** Which vertices are feasible? Have we left any out?

**c.** If the objective function is to maximize $Z = 5x_1 - 2x_2$, what are the objective values at each vertex?

A_____ B_____ C_____ D_____

**d.** Which vertex is optimal?

17. Which of the following mathematical relationships would be found in a properly structured linear programming problem? For those relationships that are improper, identify the restriction that prevents them from being acceptable.

   **a.** $2x_1 + 3x_2 = 400$

   **b.** $16.5x_1 + 10x_2 + 15x_3 \geq 80$

   **c.** $4x_1^2 + 5x_2 + x_3 \leq 20$

   **d.** $2x_1 - 8\sqrt{x_2} \geq 100$

   **e.** $4.5x_1 + x_2 = x_3$

   **f.** $100 \leq x_1 + x_2$

18. Given the following linear programming problem:

   MAXIMIZE:     $Z = 10x_1 + 5x_2$

   SUBJECT TO:     $4x_1 + 2x_2 \leq 16$

   $3x_1 + 3x_2 \geq 18$

   $1x_2 \geq 3$

   $x_1, x_2 \geq 0$

   **a.** Solve the problem graphically.

   **b.** Does the problem have more than one optimal solution? If so, identify the solutions.

19. Assume we have the following linear programming problem:

   MAXIMIZE:     $Z = 8x_1 + 10x_2$

   SUBJECT TO:     $4x_1 + 6x_2 \leq 240$

   $4x_1 + 3x_2 \leq 160$

   $1x_1 + 1x_2 \geq 120$

   $x_1, x_2 \geq 0$

   **a.** Graph the constraints and the objective function, and identify the feasible region.

   **b.** Does the problem have an optimal solution? Explain your answer.

20. Assume we have the following linear programming problem:

   MAXIMIZE:     $Z = 2x_1 + 4x_2$

   SUBJECT TO:     $-2x_1 + 2x_2 \leq 4$

   $2x_1 + 1x_2 \geq 8$

   $x_1, x_2 \geq 0$

a. Graph the objective function and constraints.
b. Identify the vertices for the feasible region.
c. Does the problem have an optimal solution? If so, identify the solution; if not, explain why no optimal solution exists if a feasible region exists.

21. The marketing manager of a diet food company is considering the promotion of a new product. The advertising budget of the company includes $60,000 for this purpose. The company can advertise the new product via television commercials and/or magazine ads. Each television commercial costs $8,000, but it has been estimated that such commercials will be seen by 50,000 people. Each magazine advertisement costs $4,500. It is estimated that these advertisements will be viewed by 25,000 people. Because the holding company of the diet food company also holds interest in several printing plants, top management has instructed the marketing manager to place at least three advertisements in magazines. The marketing manager has decided that the company should have at least as many television commercials as magazines ads. To aid his decision-making process, the marketing manager has formulated the problem as follows:

MAXIMIZE: 
$$Z = \left(\frac{x_1}{8,000}\right)50,000 + \left(\frac{x_2}{4,500}\right)25,000$$

SUBJECT TO:
$$x_1 + x_2 \leq 60,000$$

$$\frac{x_2}{4,500} \geq 3$$

$$\frac{x_1}{8,000} \geq \frac{x_2}{4,500}$$

$$x_1, x_2 \geq 0$$

where     $x_1$ = dollars to be spent on television commercials

$x_2$ = dollars to be spent on magazine advertisements

a. Explain the structure of the objective function.
b. What does the $x_1 + x_2 \leq 60,000$ constraint represent?
c. What does the $x_1/8,000$ term in the objective function represent?
d. Explain the structure of the constraint $x_1/8,000 \geq x_2/4,500$.

**6**

# Linear Programming: Model Formulations

## ■ Introduction

Now that you have been exposed to the basics of linear programming and the graphical solution procedure, we are ready to examine more realistic and more complex problems. Obviously most real-world problems are more complex than the two-variable Agro-Tech example given in Chapter 5. In this chapter we will examine a variety of problems and cases involving activities such as gasoline blending, advertising media selection, production scheduling, and investment analysis. Some examples will require a few variables; others will employ 15 or more variables.

The objective of the chapter is to expose the student to the process of formulating an LP problem and to demonstrate the variety of problem areas to which LP can be applied. The presentation of the problems is organized in a threefold fashion: (1) problems are presented in a progressive order of difficulty (that is, the first examples can be regarded as introductory exposure to the problem-formulation experience while the final problems are somewhat more complex); (2) problems are included from the private sector as well as the public sector (although no attempt is made to label the problems as such); (3) the problems are identified using traditional MS/OR labels such as blending, diet transportation, assignment, *and* capital budgeting. The reasoning behind identifying the problems with these labels is that in some cases specialized algorithms, identified with these labels, have been developed.

It is hoped that the examples in this chapter will provide a firm grounding in the formulation process and provide motivation for study of the simplex method presented in Chapter 7. Solutions are provided to reinforce and support the problem-formulation process.

## ■ Formulation framework

Before we turn to the example formulations, we need to develop a general framework for LP models. Recall that in Chapter 5 we identified some general characteristics of LP models such as (1) single-objective function, (2) maximization of an objective function subject to availability of resources, (3) proportionality of objective function and constraints to the production level of each product, etc. If we express these conditions in a slightly modified form and consider them more in the order in which they relate to the formulation of the model, then it can be stated that a problem that is amenable to solution by linear programming meets the following requirements.

1. An objective function for the problem can be stated in terms of decision variables, that is, as $x_1, x_2, \ldots, x_n$.

2. The variables of the problem must be interrelated in the generation of the "total output," that is, a quantity of one product (variable) may be foregone to produce or use more of another product (variable).

3. Constraints related to the availability or use of resources, satisfaction of requirements, or meeting of demands must be linear in form.

4. The values of the variables in the solution can be fractional but must be greater than or equal to zero.

Expressed in a general mathematical form, the basic LP model is as follows:

MAXIMIZE:

$$Z = c_1 x_1 + c_2 x_2 + \cdots + c_n x_n$$

SUBJECT TO:

$$a_{11} x_1 + a_{12} x_2 + \cdots + a_{1n} x_n [\leq, \geq, =] b_1$$

$$a_{21} x_1 + a_{22} x_2 + \cdots + a_{2n} x_n [\leq, \geq, =] b_2$$

$$a_{31} x_1 + a_{32} x_2 + \cdots + a_{3n} x_n [\leq, \geq, =] b_3$$

$$\vdots \qquad \vdots \qquad\qquad \vdots \qquad \vdots \qquad \vdots$$

$$a_{m1} x_1 + a_{m2} x_2 + \cdots + a_{mn} x_n [\leq, \geq, =] b_m$$

$$x_1, x_2, \ldots, x_n \geq 0$$

where  $x_1, x_2, \ldots, x_n$ represent the decision variables

$a_{11}, a_{12}, \ldots, a_{1n}$
$a_{21}, a_{22}, \ldots, a_{2n}$ represent the physical rate of substitution (usage) coefficients; for example, these could describe the rate of usage of raw material $i$ (where $i$ varies from 1 to $m$) in the production of variable $j$ (where $j$ varies from 1 to $n$),
$a_{m1}, a_{m2}, \ldots, a_{mn}$

$c_1, c_2, \ldots, c_n$ represent the contribution coefficients

$b_1, b_2, \ldots, b_m$ represent the available resources of raw materials

## The art of formulating

*formulation*

The ability to transform a real-world problem into a properly formulated LP model is an art. Most individuals seeking to employ operations research/management science models have more difficulty with the **formulation** process than with other aspects of the field. If the problem can be properly formulated, a standard computer code can be used to provide an answer to the problem. The art of problem formulation comes with patience, practice, and a suitable framework for addressing problems. In formulating problems, the following procedures have been found to be useful:

> First focus on identifying the overall objective. What is the end objective of the problem—maximizing profits, minimizing costs, minimizing raw materials required, maximizing manpower utilization, etc.?
>
> Second, state the problem objective *verbally*, including in the expression how the objective is related to the various factors (decision variables) over which the decision maker has control.
>
> Third, identify and verbally state each constraint.

Once the problem has been described verbally, the next step is to transform the verbal descriptions into the proper *mathematical structure*. A workable procedure to employ at this stage of the problem-formulation process is as follows:

1. Identify and define the decision variables (the $x_j$'s) associated with the problem, including in the definition the units of measure associated with each respective variable.

2. Identify the contribution coefficients (the $c_j$'s) associated with each variable, including in the definition the associated unit of measure.

3. Formulate the objective function and check for consistency of units of measure.

4. Identify the physical rate of substitution coefficients (the $a_{ij}$'s), including in the definition the associated units of measure for the respective coefficient.

5. Identify the available resources or requirements, that is, the right-hand-side coefficients (the $b_i$'s), including in the definition the units of measure associated with the resources.

6. Formulate the constraints related to each respective resource or requirement and check each constraint for consistency of units of measure.

7. Define the nonnegativity condition associated with the decision variables.

These procedural steps will be employed in formulating each of the example problems in this chapter. Employing these procedures should help to minimize errors associated with the formulation process, such as inappropriate selection of decision variables, lack of consistency in the units of measure in a defined constraint, and lack of consistency of terms in the objective function.

As a final preface to the example problems, it should be emphasized that in numerous instances there may be alternate ways of defining the decision variables, formulating constraints, and formulating the objective function. Workable formulations will be presented in the example problems; but this does not mean that alternative formulations do not exist. This is true in all formulations. Generally there are many "correct" models for a given problem. In formulating problems, an individual will become accustomed to viewing problems from a given perspective; therefore, when the formulations of two individuals are compared, they may differ. This does not mean that either formulation is in error. If the problem-formulation process has been adhered to and the general requirements for an LP model have been met, then both formulations could well be appropriate. Do not abandon your formulation simply because it is not a replica of the formulation developed by another individual. Check your formulation against the model requirements.

## Continuous versus discrete variables

One of the assumptions we made regarding the formulation of LP problems was that the values of the variables in a solution can be fractional or continuous. This assumption is not always practical in the real world. For example, if we are dealing with a problem involving the production of large-volume items such as automobiles or aircraft, or if the problem involves such matters as contracts, leases, or advertisements, discrete values for the variables are more realistic since neither fractional automobiles nor fractional aircraft can be produced and fractional leases, contracts, and advertisements do not exist. We can avoid this problem in linear programming by rounding the continuous values so they are discrete; however, this does not always result in a feasible solution. Algorithms exist that provide optimal discrete solution values, but we will delay discussing these until later chapters. In discussing the formulations, we will identify the more obvious cases where discrete solution values would be more applicable than fractional variables. Since the simplex algorithm does not guarantee the occurrence of discrete values, we will simply report the results as they occur. We will leave the rounding of the solution values, where applicable, to the reader.

## ■ Single-period problems

In Chapter 1 we defined a static model as a model used to address a problem at a fixed point or interval of time in which the conditions of the problem remain constant. The optimal decision or course of action for such a problem is determined without regard to the course of action taken or to be taken in prior or future time periods. In this section we will examine a number of *static* problems or, in more traditional terms, single-period problems.

*resource allocation problems*

The most fundamental single-period application of linear programming can be found in what can be labeled **resource allocation problems;** that is, problems where limited resources exist and maximum utilization of the resources is sought. The first three of the following examples demonstrate this concept. These examples are less complex than many practical problems; however, the difference is not in the structure of the problem but in the fact that most real-world problems require more variables and constraints.

■ **Example**

## Breeding Manufacturing Inc.

Breeding Manufacturing Inc. produces and sells two types of hydraulic pumps: (1) standard and (2) oversize. The manufacturing process associated with production of the pumps involves three activities: assembly, painting, and testing (quality control). The resource requirements for assembly, painting, and testing of the pumps are shown in Table 6-1. The profit contribution from the sale of a standard pump is $50, while the profit from an oversize pump is $75. There are 4800 hours of assembly time, 1980 hours of paint time, and 900 hours of test time available per week. Prior sales experience indicates that the company can expect to sell at least 300 standard pumps and 180 oversize pumps per week. Breeding would like to determine the quantity of each type of pump to produce weekly in order to maximize profits.

■ **Solution**

This is a fairly basic problem that deals with the *product mix* that will maximize profits. Breeding must decide on the quantity of each product to produce during any week, recognizing that there are certain resource limitations (4800 hours of assembly time, 1980 hours of painting time, and 900 hours of testing time). To meet weekly demand, Breeding must produce 300 standard pumps and 180 oversize pumps.

To formulate the problem mathematically, we can employ the following decision variables:

$x_1$ = number of units of the *standard pump* that should be produced during a given week

$x_2$ = number of units of the *oversize pump* that should be produced during a given week

Since the objective is to maximize profits, the objective function will have units of measure expressed in dollars. From previous discussion, we know that the general form of the objective function is

$$Z = c_1 x_1 + c_2 x_2$$

The $c_1 x_1$ and $c_2 x_2$ terms thus must be expressed in dollars.

| Type | Assembly Time | Painting Time | Testing Time |
|------|---------------|---------------|--------------|
| Standard | 3.6 | 1.6 | 0.6 |
| Oversize | 4.8 | 1.8 | 0.6 |

**TABLE 6-1.** Manufacturing Requirements (hours): Breeding Mfg. Inc.

The $c_1$ coefficient is the contribution to profits resulting from the sale of one unit of the standard pump, or $50; while $c_2$ is the contribution to profits resulting from the sale of each oversize pump, or $75. The $c_1x_1$ term, therefore, is

($50/unit of the standard pump) × ($x_1$ units of the standard pump)

and the $c_2x_2$ term is

($75/unit of the oversize pump) × ($x_2$ units of the oversize pump)

When the units of measure for the operations are collected, the result is expressed in dollars. The objective function for the problem, therefore, is expressed as follows:

MAXIMIZE:        $Z = 50x_1 + 75x_2$

To develop constraints for the problem, we need to identify the $a_{ij}$ coefficients and determine how they relate to the decision variables ($x_1$ and $x_2$) and the available resources. In structuring the constraints we need to keep in mind the two general rules identified in Chapter 5. To emphasize these rules, they are restated here.

1.  The units of measure on the right-hand side of a constraint (that is, on the right-hand side of the equality or inequality) *must* always equal the units of measure on the left-hand side of the constraint.

2.  It *is not* necessary that all constraints be expressed in the same units of measure (that is, one constraint may be expressed in dollars, while a second constraint may be expressed in hours and a third in pounds, square feet, or some other unit of measure).

Three production resource constraints exist for the problem. Consider first the constraint associated with the assembly operation. Since each standard pump requires 3.6 hours of assembly time and since $x_1$ is the number of units of the standard pump that is produced weekly, $3.6x_1$ is the total number of assembly hours required in the production of standard pumps. Similarly, $4.8x_2$ is the total number of assembly hours required in the production of oversize pumps. Since 4800 hours of assembly time are available, the assembly production constraint is

$3.6x_1$ hours $+ 4.8x_2$ hours $\leq$ 4800 hours

The constraint associated with painting is similar to the assembly constraint. There are $1.6x_1$ hours of painting time required to produce $x_1$ standard pumps and $1.8x_2$ hours of painting required to produce $x_2$ oversize pumps. Since 1980 hours of painting time are available weekly, the constraint is

$1.6x_1$ hours $+ 1.8x_2$ hours $\leq$ 1980 hours

Using the same procedural analysis, the constraint associated with testing is

$$0.6x_1 \text{ hours} + 0.6x_2 \text{ hours} \leq 900 \text{ hours}$$

The final two constraints are those associated with projected minimum sales levels. These are relatively easy to structure since the units of measure are balanced on each side of the constraints. These constraints are:

$$(x_1 \text{ units of the standard pump}) \geq (300 \text{ units of the standard pump})$$

$$(x_2 \text{ units of the oversize pump}) \geq (180 \text{ units of the oversize pump})$$

Collecting all constraints and adding the nonnegativity conditions ($x_1$, $x_2 \geq 0$) results in the following model:

MAXIMIZE: $\quad Z = 50x_1 + 75x_2$

SUBJECT TO: $\quad 3.6x_1 + 4.8x_2 \leq 4800$

$$1.6x_1 + 1.8x_2 \leq 1980$$

$$0.6x_1 + 0.6x_2 \leq 900$$

$$x_1 \qquad\qquad \geq 300$$

$$x_2 \geq 180$$

$$x_1, x_2 \geq 0$$

In Table 6-2 we have shown the solution to the Breeding Manufacturing Inc. problem. In this case, we have shown only the values of the objective function and the variables used in the formulation of the problem (the "structural variables"). In later chapters we will present a more detailed solution for linear programming problems, but for this chapter this abbreviated solution will be sufficient to allow you to determine the optimal solution to the problem. A solution similar to the one in Table 6-2 will be given for each problem formulated in this chapter. In this case, the solution in Table 6-2 indicates that the optimal solution to this problem is to produce 300.0 standard pumps and 775.0 oversize pumps, with a resulting profit of $73,125.01.

| The Value of the Objective Function is 73,125.01 | |
|---|---|
| Structural Variables | Values |
| $x_1$ | 300.00 |
| $x_2$ | 775.00 |

**TABLE 6-2.**
Solution for Breeding Manufacturing Inc.

### ■ Example
## *Hickory Desk Company*

The Hickory Desk Company, an office furniture manufacturer, produces two types of desks: executive desks and secretary/stenographer desks. The company has two plants at which the desks are made. Plant 1, which is an older plant, operates on a double shift of 80 hours per week. Plant 2 is a newer plant and is not running at full capacity. However, since management plans to operate the second plant on a double-shift basis similar to plant 1, operators have been employed to work two shifts. Currently each shift at plant 2 works 25 hours per week. No premium is paid to second-shift workers. Table 6-3 shows production time (in hours/unit) and standard costs (in dollars/unit) at each plant.

The company has been competitive in the past by pricing the executive desks at $350. However, it appears the company will have to drop the price on the secretary/stenographer desks to $275 in order to be competitive. The company has been experiencing cost overruns in the past eight to ten weeks; therefore, management has set a weekly budget constraint on production costs. The weekly budget for the total production of executive desks is $2000, while the budget for secretary/stenographer desks is $2200. Management would like to determine the number of each type of desk that should be produced at each plant in order to maximize profits.

### ■ Solution

In the first example a rather detailed solution process was given. This was provided to give the reader a feeling for the formulation procedure. In this and subsequent examples we will streamline the process, leaving some of the details for the reader.

### *Objective (verbal)*

The company must determine the number of executive and secretary/stenographer desks to make at plant 1 and the number of executive and secretary/stenographer desks to make at plant 2 in order to maximize profits. The profit per unit at the respective plants is the difference between the selling price and standard costs.

**TABLE 6-3.**
**Time (hours) and**
**Costs (dollars):**
**Hickory Desk Co.**

|  | Production Time (hours/unit) | | Standard Costs (dollars/unit) | |
|---|---|---|---|---|
|  | *Plant 1* | *Plant 2* | *Plant 1* | *Plant 2* |
| Executive desks | 7.0 | 6.0 | 250 | 260 |
| Sec./steno. desks | 4.0 | 5.0 | 200 | 180 |

## Constraints (verbal)

1.  No more than 80 hours are available for the combined production of desks at plant 1.

2.  No more than 50 hours are available for the combined production of desks at plant 2.

3.  Costs associated with the combined production of executive desks at the two plants must not exceed $2000.

4.  Costs associated with the combined production of secretary/stenographer desks at the two plants must not exceed $2200.

## Variables (math structure)

Since it is necessary to determine the quantity of each type of desk produced at both plant 1 and plant 2, four variables are required:

$x_1$ = number of executive desks produced at plant 1

$x_2$ = number of secretary/stenographer desks produced at plant 1

$x_3$ = number of executive desks produced at plant 2

$x_4$ = number of secretary/stenographer desks produced at plant 2

## Objective function coefficients (math structure)

The objective function will be expressed in dollars, since the objective is to maximize profits; therefore, the $c_j$ coefficients will be expressed in dollars/unit since the $x_j$'s are expressed in units. The $c_j$ coefficients are determined by taking the difference between the selling price of a given type of desk and the standard cost for production of the desk at the given plant. Thus:

$c_1 = 350 - 250 = \$100$/executive desk made at plant 1

$c_2 = 275 - 200 = \$75$/secretary/stenographer desk made at plant 1

$c_3 = 350 - 260 = \$90$/executive desk made at plant 2

$c_4 = 275 - 180 = \$95$/secretary/stenographer desk made at plant 2

## Objective function (math structure)

MAXIMIZE:      $Z = 100x_1 + 75x_2 + 90x_3 + 95x_4$

## Constraints (math structure)

The $a_{ij}$ coefficients and the right-hand-side values can be identified and checked for consistency of units of measure while developing the math structure of the constraints. Since the units of measure may differ from constraint to constraint, we will consider each constraint separately.

1. Production time limit, plant 1 (80 hours):

$$(7.0 \text{ hours/unit}) \times (x_1 \text{ units}) + (4.0 \text{ hours/unit}) \times (x_2 \text{ units}) \leq 80 \text{ hours}$$

2. Production time limit, plant 2 (50 hours):

$$(6.0 \text{ hours/unit}) \times (x_3 \text{ units}) + (5.0 \text{ hours/unit}) \times (x_4 \text{ units}) \leq 50 \text{ hours}$$

3. Cost constraint, executive desks ($2000):

$$(250 \text{ dollars/unit}) \times (x_1 \text{ units}) + (260 \text{ dollars/unit}) \times (x_3 \text{ units}) \leq \$2000$$

4. Cost constraint, secretary/stenographer desks ($2200):

$$(200 \text{ dollars/unit}) \times (x_2 \text{ units}) + (180 \text{ dollars/unit}) \times (x_4 \text{ units}) \leq \$2200$$

## Math formulation

MAXIMIZE:    $Z = 100x_1 + 75x_2 + 90x_3 + 95x_4$

SUBJECT TO:

$$7.0x_1 + 4.0x_2 \qquad\qquad\qquad \leq 80$$
$$6.0x_3 + 5.0\,x_4 \leq 50$$
$$250x_1 + \qquad 260x_3 \qquad\quad \leq 2000$$
$$200x_2 + \qquad 180x_4 \leq 2200$$
$$x_1, x_2, x_3, x_4 \geq 0$$

Note that in this particular problem two constraints are expressed in dollars and two are expressed in hours. The $x_j$ variables, however, retain the same units of measure in all constraints and in the objective function.

**TABLE 6-4.
Solution for
Hickory Desk
Company**

*The Value of the
Objective Function is
1900.00*

| Variables | Values |
| --- | --- |
| $x_1$ | 8.00 |
| $x_2$ | 2.00 |
| $x_3$ | 0.00 |
| $x_4$ | 10.00 |

Table 6-4 shows that the optimal solution is to produce 8.00 executive desks at plant 1; 2.00 secretary/stenographer desks at plant 1; 0.00 executive desks at plant 2; and 10.00 secretary/stenographer desks at plant 2, for a profit of $1900. As was the case for the first two examples, rounding is not necessary to express the output variables in discrete units.

---

### ■ Example

# *Senora General Hospital*

Ms. B. M. Haddox, the dietitian for the Senora General Hospital, is responsible for planning and managing food requirements for patients. Ms. Haddox is currently examining a case in which a patient is restricted to a special diet that consists of two food sources. The patient is not restricted in the quantity of the two foods consumed; however, the following minimum nutritional requirements must be met per day: 1000 units of nutrient A, 2000 units of nutrient B, and 1500 units of nutrient C. Each ounce of food source #1 contains 100 units of nutrient A, 400 units of nutrient B, and 200 units of nutrient C; each ounce of food source #2 contains 200 units of nutrient A, 250 units of nutrient B, and 200 units of nutrient C. Both food sources are rather expensive (food source #1 costs $6.00 per pound and food source #2 costs $8.00 per pound); therefore, Ms. Haddox desires to determine the minimal cost combination of the food sources that will meet all nutrition requirements.

### ■ Solution

## *Objective (verbal)*

The objective in this case is to determine the number of ounces of each of the two food sources that cost the least and still meet the nutrition requirements for nutrients A, B, and C. An important point to recognize is that the units of measure for the food sources are expressed in ounces while the costs of food sources are expressed in pounds.

## *Constraints (verbal)*

1. At least 1000 units of nutrient A must be consumed per day.

2. At least 2000 units of nutrient B must be consumed per day.

3. At least 1500 units of nutrient C must be consumed per day.

4. No restriction exists on the quantity of either food source consumed daily.

## Variables (math structure)

Two variables will be required since we wish to determine the quantity of the two food sources that should be consumed:

$x_1$ = number of ounces of food source #1 that should be consumed daily

$x_2$ = number of ounces of food source #2 that should be consumed daily

## Objective function (math structure)

Unlike the first three problems we examined, which involved maximizing an objective function, the objective of this problem is to minimize cost. The only adjustment to the cost coefficients that is necessary is to recognize that in outlining the problem, the costs of the respective food sources were expressed in pounds rather than ounces. Therefore, $c_1$ = \$6.00/16 = \$0.375 per ounce and $c_2$ = \$8.00/16 = \$0.50 per ounce, since 16 ounces exist in each pound of the respective food sources. The objective function thus can be expressed as follows:

MINIMIZE:      $Z = .375x_1 + .50x_2$

## Constraints (math structure)

Table 6-5 has been developed to aid in structuring the constraints, which follow.

1. Nutrient A constraint:

   [(100 units of nutrient A)/(ounce of source #1)] × ($x_1$ ounces of source #1)
   + [(200 units of nutrient A)/(ounce of source #2)] × ($x_2$ ounces of source #2)
   $\geq$ 1000 units of nutrient A

2. Nutrient B constraint:

   [(400 units of nutrient B)/(ounce of source #1)] × ($x_1$ ounces of source #1)
   + [(250 units of nutrient B)/(ounce of source #2)] × ($x_2$ ounces of source #2)
   $\geq$ 2000 units of nutrient B

3. Nutrient C constraint:

   [(200 units of nutrient C)/(ounce of source #1)] × ($x_1$ ounces of source #1)
   + [(200 units of nutrient C)/(ounce of source #2)] × ($x_2$ ounces of source #2)
   $\geq$ 1500 units of nutrient C

| Nutrient | Units Per Ounce | | Total Required Units |
|----------|-----------------|--------|----------------------|
| | Food Source #1 | Food Source #2 | |
| A | 100 | 200 | 1000 |
| B | 400 | 250 | 2000 |
| C | 200 | 200 | 1500 |

**TABLE 6-5.
Nutrient Data:
Senora General
Hospital**

## Math formulation

MINIMIZE: $Z = .375x_1 + .50x_2$

SUBJECT TO:
$$100x_1 + 200x_2 \geq 1000$$
$$400x_1 + 250x_2 \geq 2000$$
$$200x_1 + 200x_2 \geq 1500$$
$$x_1, x_2 \geq 0$$

From Table 6-6 we note that the optimal solution calls for the use of 5.00 ounces of food source #1 and 2.50 ounces of food source #2. This diet will meet all nutritional requirements of nutrients A and C and will exceed the requirements of nutrient B by 625.00 units. The cost associated with the resulting diet is $3.12.

The **diet problem** is a classic among the problems for which linear programming is used. Basically, the problem involves determining the minimal-cost food combination that will meet certain nutritional requirements. Around the mid 1970s, this type of model was extended and generalized to applications in large-scale food management.[1]

*diet problem*

Most authors classify the mixing of feeds (such as in a livestock operation) as a diet problem. However, some authors prefer the term **blending problem,** since agricultural feed-mix problems can be concerned with the blending of feeds (food) to produce a feed with minimal nutritional values. The more traditional blending problem is presented in the next section.

*blending
problem*

The Value of the
Objective Function is
3.12

| Variables | Values |
|-----------|--------|
| $x_1$ | 5.00 |
| $x_2$ | 2.50 |

**TABLE 6-6.
Solution for Senora
General Hospital**

[1]Joseph L. Balintfy, "A Mathematical Programming System for Food Management Applications," *Interfaces*, 6, no. 1 (November 1975), pp. 23–31.

### ■ Example

## *Evans Oil Distributors*

Evans Oil Distributors markets two grades of gasoline: *premium* and *regular*. Each gasoline must meet certain specifications, such as maximum allowable vapor pressure and minimum octane rating. Manufacturing requirements for the gasoline and the price per barrel are shown in Table 6-7.

Three types of raw blending gasoline are used to produce the premium and regular gasolines. Characteristics of the raw gasolines are shown in Table 6-8.

Evans has a commitment to a buyer to supply 30,000 barrels of regular gasoline per week. No commitments have been made on the premium gasoline. The company would like to determine the manufacturing plan for the two grades of gasoline that will maximize profits.

### ■ Solution

### *Objective (verbal)*

Evans would like to blend the three raw gasolines (types 1, 2, and 3) to produce premium and regular gasolines such that the total profit from the sales of the produced quantities (barrels) is maximized.

### *Constraints (verbal)*

1. The maximum weekly supply of type 1 raw gasoline is 32,000 barrels. Type 1 can be used in the production of both end products.

**TABLE 6-7.**
**Manufacturing Specifications and Per-barrel Price: Evans Oil Distributors**

| Gasoline | Minimum Octane Rating | Maximum Vapor Pressure | Selling Price (per barrel) |
|---|---|---|---|
| Regular | 80 | 9 | $21.00 |
| Premium | 100 | 6 | $24.00 |

**TABLE 6-8.**
**Characteristics of Raw Gasoline: Evans Oil Distributors**

| Raw Gasoline | Octane Rating | Vapor Pressure | Maximum Supply (barrels) | Cost (per barrel) |
|---|---|---|---|---|
| Type 1 | 108 | 4 | 32,000 | $22.00 |
| Type 2 | 90 | 10 | 20,000 | $20.00 |
| Type 3 | 73 | 5 | 38,000 | $19.00 |

2. The maximum weekly supply of type 2 raw gasoline is 20,000 barrels. Type 2 can be used in the production of both end products.

3. The maximum weekly supply of type 3 raw gasoline is 38,000 barrels. Type 3 can be used in the production of both end products.

4. The vapor pressure of the blended regular gasoline must not exceed 9 units per barrel. (Units in this case could be pounds per square inch, that is, 9 psi; however, we can simply use the term units.)

5. The octane rating of the blended regular gasoline must be at least 80 units per barrel.

6. The vapor pressure of the blended premium gasoline must not exceed 6 units per barrel.

7. The octane rating of the blended premium gasoline must be at least 100 units per barrel.

8. At least 30,000 barrels of regular gasoline must be produced in order to meet committed orders.

## Variables (math structure)

This problem will require the use of six variables, since we must determine the quantity of each of the raw gasolines that must be blended to produce the two end products. Use of so many variables may appear to be somewhat misdirected since the problem objective is to determine the quantities of the two end products to produce, but if we do not take this approach, we have no means of identifying how the end products will be produced. Therefore, let

$x_1$ = number of barrels of raw type 1 gasoline to be used to produce regular gasoline

$x_2$ = number of barrels of raw type 2 gasoline to be used to produce regular gasoline

$x_3$ = number of barrels of raw type 3 gasoline to be used to produce regular gasoline

$x_4$ = number of barrels of raw type 1 gasoline to be used to produce premium gasoline

$x_5$ = number of barrels of raw type 2 gasoline to be used to produce premium gasoline

$x_6$ = number of barrels of raw type 3 gasoline to be used to produce premium gasoline

The quantities of regular and premium gasoline required to maximize profits can be determined by adding $x_1$, $x_2$, and $x_3$, and $x_4$, $x_5$, and $x_6$, respectively, from the optimal solution to the problem.

## Objective function coefficients (math structure)

The objective function (Z) will be expressed in dollars since the objective is to maximize profits. The $c_j$ coefficients, therefore, will be expressed as dollars/barrel since the $x_j$'s are expressed in barrels. To determine contribution to profits for the respective raw gasolines, we simply take the difference between the selling price/barrel and the cost/barrel:

$$c_1 = 21.00 - 22.00 = -1.00 \text{ dollar/barrel of raw stock 1 used in regular}$$

$$c_2 = 21.00 - 20.00 = 1.00 \text{ dollar/barrel of raw stock 2 used in regular}$$

$$c_3 = 21.00 - 19.00 = 2.00 \text{ dollar/barrel of raw stock 3 used in regular}$$

$$c_4 = 24.00 - 22.00 = 2.00 \text{ dollar/barrel of raw stock 1 used in premium}$$

$$c_5 = 24.00 - 20.00 = 4.00 \text{ dollar/barrel of raw stock 2 used in premium}$$

$$c_6 = 24.00 - 19.00 = 5.00 \text{ dollar/barrel of raw stock 3 used in premium}$$

## Objective function (math structure)

MAXIMIZE:    $Z = -1.00x_1 + 1.00x_2 + 2.00x_3 + 2.00x_4 + 4.00x_5 + 5.00x_6$

## Constraints (math structure)

1.  Type 1 raw gasoline supply constraint:

    ($x_1$ barrels of raw stock 1 used in regular)
    $$+ (x_4 \text{ barrels of raw stock 1 used in premium})$$
    $$\leq 32,000 \text{ barrels of raw stock 1}$$

2.  Type 2 raw gasoline supply constraint:

    ($x_2$ barrels of raw stock 2 used in regular)
    $$+ (x_5 \text{ barrels of raw stock 2 used in premium})$$
    $$\leq 20,000 \text{ barrels of raw stock 2}$$

3.  Type 3 raw gasoline supply constraint:

    ($x_3$ barrels of raw stock 3 used in regular)
    $$+ (x_6 \text{ barrels of raw stock 3 used in premium})$$
    $$\leq 38,000 \text{ barrels of raw stock 3}$$

4.  Vapor pressure of regular gasoline:
    This constraint is structured by recognizing that the vapor pressure of the regular gasoline is determined by the proportion of the gasoline that is attributable to the respective raw stock and the vapor pressure associated with the given stocks. The proportion of raw stock in a barrel of regular gasoline is determined by dividing the quantity (barrels) of each raw stock that goes into the regular gasoline by the total number of barrels of regular gasoline. Since the sum of $x_1$, $x_2$, and $x_3$ is the total barrels of regular gasoline, the proportions are expressed as follows:

    $$\frac{x_1}{x_1 + x_2 + x_3}, \quad \frac{x_2}{x_1 + x_2 + x_3}, \quad \frac{x_3}{x_1 + x_2 + x_3}$$

If we multiply the respective proportions by the vapor pressure associated with each raw stock, the results will be the vapor pressure contributed by each raw stock in each barrel of regular gas. These vapor pressure values are expressed as follows:

$$\frac{4x_1}{x_1 + x_2 + x_3}, \quad \frac{10x_2}{x_1 + x_2 + x_3}, \quad \frac{5x_3}{x_1 + x_2 + x_3}$$

Since the vapor pressure for regular gasoline must be no greater than 9 units per barrel, the constraint is

$$\frac{4x_1}{x_1 + x_2 + x_3} + \frac{10x_2}{x_1 + x_2 + x_3} + \frac{5x_3}{x_1 + x_2 + x_3} \leq 9$$

5. Octane rating of regular gasoline:

This constraint is structured in the same manner as the vapor pressure constraint, with the exception that octane ratings are used in the place of vapor pressures.

$$\frac{108x_1}{x_1 + x_2 + x_3} + \frac{90x_2}{x_1 + x_2 + x_3} + \frac{73x_3}{x_1 + x_2 + x_3} \geq 80$$

6. Vapor pressure of premium gasoline:

$$\frac{4x_4}{x_4 + x_5 + x_6} + \frac{10x_5}{x_4 + x_5 + x_6} + \frac{5x_6}{x_4 + x_5 + x_6} \leq 6$$

7. Octane rating of premium gasoline:

$$\frac{108x_4}{x_4 + x_5 + x_6} + \frac{90x_5}{x_4 + x_5 + x_6} + \frac{73x_6}{x_4 + x_5 + x_6} \geq 100$$

The reader can check the units of measure on constraints 4, 5, 6, and 7. It can be verified quickly that the constraints balance if it is recognized that the ratios such as $x_1/(x_1 + x_2 + x_3)$ are proportions and have no units of measure.

8. Committed orders:

The total number of barrels of regular gasoline produced is the sum of $x_1$, $x_2$, and $x_3$ (that is, $x_1 + x_2 + x_3$). Since Evans has a commitment for 30,000 barrels of regular gasoline, the constraint is

$$x_1 + x_2 + x_3 \geq 30{,}000$$

Before the model can be expressed in the general LP form, constraint equations 4 through 7 must be transformed algebraically. Constraint 4 is expressed

$$\frac{4x_1 + 10x_2 + 5x_3}{x_1 + x_2 + x_3} \le 9$$

Multiplying both sides of the inequality by $x_1 + x_2 + x_3$, we have

$$4x_1 + 10x_2 + 5x_3 \le 9(x_1 + x_2 + x_3)$$

Collecting terms, constraint 4 is

$$-5x_1 + x_2 - 4x_3 \le 0$$

The constraint is now expressed in the general LP form. Similar operations can be performed on constraints 5, 6, and 7.

## Math formulation

MAXIMIZE:     $Z = -1.00x_1 + 1.00x_2 + 2.00x_3 + 2.00x_4 + 4.00x_5 + 5.00x_6$

SUBJECT TO:

$$x_1 \qquad\qquad + \quad x_4 \qquad\qquad\qquad \le 32{,}000$$
$$x_2 \qquad\qquad + \quad x_5 \qquad\qquad \le 20{,}000$$
$$x_3 \qquad\qquad + \quad x_6 \le 38{,}000$$
$$-5x_1 + \quad x_2 - \quad 4x_3 \qquad\qquad\qquad\qquad \le 0$$
$$28x_1 + \quad 10x_2 - \quad 7x_3 \qquad\qquad\qquad\qquad \ge 0$$
$$- \quad 2x_4 + \quad 4x_5 - \quad x_6 \le 0$$
$$8x_4 - \quad 10x_5 - \quad 27x_6 \ge 0$$
$$x_1 + \quad x_2 + \quad x_3 \qquad\qquad\qquad \ge 30{,}000$$
$$x_1, x_2, x_3, x_4, x_5, x_6 \ge 0$$

Table 6-9 is the solution for Evans Oil Distributors. Using these data, we will find that the optimal policy is to blend 0.0 barrels of type 1, 19,970.59 barrels of type 2,

**TABLE 6-9.**
**Solution for Evans Oil Distributors**

*The Value of the Objective Function is 188,500.03*

| Structural Variables | Values |
| --- | --- |
| $x_1$ | 0.00 |
| $x_2$ | 19,970.59 |
| $x_3$ | 28,529.41 |
| $x_4$ | 32,000.00 |
| $x_5$ | 29.42 |
| $x_6$ | 9,470.59 |

and 28,529.41 barrels of type 3 raw gasoline to produce 48,500.00 barrels of regular gasoline, and to blend 32,000.00 barrels of type 1, 29.42 barrels of type 2, and 9,470.59 barrels of type 3 raw gasoline to produce 41,500.01 barrels of premium gasoline. This results in a total profit of $188,500.03.

This small example illustrates one of the traditional applications of LP, namely, the *blending* of raw ingredients to produce refined products. Blending problems, however, need not be restricted simply to the blending of fuels; as we have noted, the problem of producing a feed mix from a given set of basic feeds can be viewed as a blending problem. Likewise, the production of different grades of alcoholic beverages from raw stock can be viewed as a blending problem. The problem of producing a portfolio from a given group of stocks could also be viewed as blending.

■ **Example**
**State Employee Retirement Fund**

Mr. F. T. Wells is a financial analyst for the State of Utah. Mr. Wells has been asked by the finance committee to prepare investment recommendations for the $2,000,000 in the State Employee Retirement Fund. The committee has suggested that investments be diversified by allocating the fund among the following: certificates of deposit, treasury notes, blue-chip stock, speculative stock, corporate bonds, and real estate. Mr. Wells has estimated the annual yield for each class of investment and, for each investment class, has developed a risk factor that indicates the probability that the actual yield of the investments in that class will be less than the expected yield. Finally, he has developed a forecast of the average number of years that the expected yield for the respective investment class will be realized. This information is given in Table 6-10.

The state finance committee has indicated it would like to have a weighted average investment period of at least five years. The committee also has indicated that the weighted average risk factor should be no greater than .20. Regulation prohibits more than 25% of the state's investments being placed in real estate and speculative stock. What recommendation should Mr. Wells make if the expected return from the $2,000,000 is to be maximized?

| Class of Investment | Expected Annual Yield (%) | Risk Factor | Average Term of Investment (years) |
|---|---|---|---|
| Certificates of deposit | 8.5 | .02 | 8 |
| Treasury notes | 9.0 | .01 | 2 |
| Blue-chip common stock | 8.5 | .38 | 5 |
| Speculative stock | 14.3 | .45 | 6 |
| Corporate bonds | 6.7 | .07 | 2 |
| Real estate | 13.0 | .35 | 4 |

**TABLE 6-10.**
**Expected Yields and Risk Factors: State Employee Retirement Fund**

# ■ Solution

## *Objective (verbal)*

The objective is to determine the fractional portion of $2,000,000 that should be invested in each of six classes of investments such that the total expected annual return is maximized. The dollar investment in each respective investment category can be determined, after solving for the optimal mix, by simply multiplying the values of the decision variables by $2,000,000.

## *Constraints (verbal)*

1. All available funds (i.e., the $2,000,000) must be invested in one or more of the investment categories.
2. The weighted average risk factor, that is, the probability that the expected earnings will not result, must be no greater than .20.
3. The weighted average investment period must be at least five years.
4. At most, 25% of the company's investment can be invested in real estate and growth stocks.

## *Variables (math structure)*

Six variables are required since we have six classes of investments:

$x_1$ = fractional part of portfolio invested in certificates of deposit

$x_2$ = fractional part of portfolio invested in treasury notes

$x_3$ = fractional part of portfolio invested in blue-chip common stock

$x_4$ = fractional part of portfolio invested in speculative stock

$x_5$ = fractional part of portfolio invested in corporate bonds

$x_6$ = fractional part of portfolio invested in real estate

## *Objective function (math structure)*

Based upon the verbal statement of the problem, one might conclude that the objective function should be expressed in dollars since the objective is to maximize expected revenue; however, this is not true. The $c_j$ coefficients for the problem are the expected yields (Table 6-10) for the respective investment classes,

$$c_1 = 8.5, \quad c_2 = 9.0, \quad c_3 = 8.5, \quad c_4 = 14.3, \quad c_5 = 6.7, \quad \text{and} \quad c_6 = 13.0.$$

Since the $x_j$ variables are fractional values, the $c_j x_j$ factor is simply a percentage. When these are summed we have a weighted percentage. If we express the objective function as follows:

MAXIMIZE:    $Z = 8.5x_1 + 9.0x_2 + 8.5x_3 + 14.3x_4 + 6.7x_5 + 13.0x_6$

then we are maximizing the *expected* yield from the investments. What this means is that regardless of the amount available for investment (in this case, $2,000,000), the model will be structured to give the optimal portfolio.

## Constraints (math structure)

1. Total investment constraint:

$$x_1 + x_2 + x_3 + x_4 + x_5 + x_6 = 1$$

   Since all funds must be invested, the fractional part must sum to 1. No units of measure exist for the $x_j$ coefficients or for the right-hand side.

2. Risk factor constraint:
   Since the $x_j$ variables are the fractional parts of the total investment in the respective class of investment, the product of the risk factor and the associated variable will give the weighted risk of the investment. The weighted risk factor of all investments is the sum of the individual weighted risk factors in Table 6-10.

$$.02x_1 + .01x_2 + .38x_3 + .45x_4 + .07x_5 + .35x_6 \le .20$$

   No units of measure exist.

3. Investment period constraint:
   Logic for this is identical to the risk factor constraint:

$$[(8 \text{ years}) \times x_1] + [(2 \text{ years}) \times x_2] + [(5 \text{ years}) \times x_3]$$
$$+ [(6 \text{ years}) \times x_4] + [(2 \text{ years}) \times 5 \ x_5] + [(4 \text{ years}) \times x_6] \ge 5 \text{ years}$$

4. Regulation constraint:

$$x_4 + x_6 \le .25$$

No units of measure exist.

## Math formulation

MAXIMIZE: $Z = 8.5x_1 + 9.0x_2 + 8.5x_3 + 14.3x_4 + 6.7x_5 + 13.0x_6$

SUBJECT TO:
$$x_1 + x_2 + x_3 + x_4 + x_5 + x_6 = 1$$
$$8x_1 + 2x_2 + 5x_3 + 6x_4 + 2x_5 + 4x_6 \ge 5$$
$$x_4 + x_6 \le .25$$
$$.02x_1 + .01x_2 + .38x_3 + .45x_4 + .07x_5 + .35x_6 \le .20$$
$$x_1, x_2, x_3, x_4, x_5, x_6 \ge 0$$

Table 6-11 shows that $x_1 = .33$, $x_2 = .42$, $x_3 = 0.0$, $x_4 = .25$, $x_5 = 0.0$, and $x_6 = 0.0$. To determine the actual dollars that should be invested in the different

**TABLE 6-11.**
**Solution for State**
**Employee**
**Retirement Fund**

| The Value of the Objective Function is 10.16 | |
| --- | --- |
| Variables | Values |
| $x_1$ | .33 |
| $x_2$ | .42 |
| $x_3$ | 0.00 |
| $x_4$ | .25 |
| $x_5$ | 0.00 |
| $x_6$ | 0.00 |

alternatives, we simply multiply the decision variable values by $2,000,000, as indicated earlier. The yield from the optimal portfolio is 10.16%.

This example case well illustrates one of the areas in which considerable use of linear programming has been made in the recent past, namely, *investment analysis*. Specifically, the problem shows how LP can be applied to portfolio selection problems. This type of problem is often encountered by managers of insurance companies, banks, and credit unions, as well as managers of mutual funds.

■ **Example**
## B & Z Brewing Company

The B & Z Brewing Company brews an extremely popular brand of beer. To preserve quality, the company produces the beer in only three plants, where spring water is available (near Boulder, Colorado; Minneapolis, Minnesota; and Olympia, Washington). From these plants the beer is shipped by truck to four distribution warehouses located in the western portion of the United States (in San Diego, California; Provo, Utah; Albuquerque, New Mexico; and Lincoln, Nebraska). Because of the increased cost of gasoline and diesel fuel, shipping cost is a major expense item. Management is initiating a study to determine whether shipping costs can be reduced. Production

**TABLE 6-12.**
**Shipping Costs ($)**
**for B & Z Brewing**
**Company**

| Source | Destination Warehouse | | | | Output (Supply) |
| --- | --- | --- | --- | --- | --- |
| | 1 | 2 | 3 | 4 | |
| Plant 1 | 464 | 513 | 654 | 867 | 75 |
| Plant 2 | 352 | 416 | 690 | 791 | 125 |
| Plant 3 | 995 | 682 | 388 | 685 | 100 |
| Allocation (demand) | 80 | 65 | 70 | 85 | 300 |

managers at each of the three plants have estimated the expected monthly output from their respective plants. A total of 300 truckloads of beer will be produced at the three plants. Management at the corporate level at B & Z has allocated the total output to the given warehouses by examining sales data from prior months. Table 6-12 gives the supply (output) and demand (allocation) information, along with the shipping costs for each supply–demand combination. It should be noted that the supply and demand units are expressed in truckloads of beer, while the cost figures in the body of the table are expressed in dollars per truckload. The problem facing B & Z management is to determine the quantity (that is, the number of truckloads) of beer that should be shipped from each plant to each warehouse so that total shipping costs are minimized.

## ■ Solution

### Objective (verbal)

Twelve plant–warehouse (i.e., supply–demand) shipping-route combinations exist. The objective is to determine the number of truckloads of beer that should be routed from the three plants to the four warehouses so that all allocations (demands) are fully met and the total shipping cost is minimized.

### Constraints (verbal)

A constraint will exist for each supply and each demand point in a transportation problem since supply locations have limited capacities and demand locations have minimum or fixed allocations.

1. No more than 75 truckloads of beer can be shipped from plant 1.
2. No more than 125 truckloads of beer can be shipped from plant 2.
3. No more than 100 truckloads of beer can be shipped from plant 3.
4. Eighty truckloads of beer must be shipped to warehouse 1; this allocation has been committed.
5. Sixty-five truckloads of beer must be shipped to warehouse 2; this allocation has been committed.
6. Seventy truckloads of beer must be shipped to warehouse 3; this allocation has been committed.
7. Eighty-five truckloads of beer must be shipped to warehouse 4; this allocation has been committed.

### Variables (math structure)

Since 12 plant–warehouse shipping routes exist, 12 decision variables will be required. For this particular problem we will modify the procedure we have employed for labeling variables. Rather than using single subscripts to identify each shipping route, we will use double subscripts. The first subscript will identify the source, that is, the plant shipped *from*, and the second subscript will identify the destination, i.e., the warehouse shipped *to*. Therefore, let

$x_{ij}$ = number of truckloads shipped from plant $i$ to warehouse $j$, where $i$ = 1, 2, 3, and $j$ = 1, 2, 3, 4.

## *Objective function (math structure)*

The $c_{ij}$ coefficients in the objective function are the shipping costs associated with the different plant–warehouse routes, that is,

$c_{11}$ = 464 dollars/truckload

$c_{12}$ = 513 dollars/truckload

.
.
.

$c_{34}$ = 685 dollars/truckload

Therefore, the objective function is expressed as follows:

MINIMIZE:    $Z =$    $464x_{11} + 513x_{12} + 654x_{13} + 867x_{14}$

$+ 352x_{21} + 416x_{22} + 690x_{23} + 791x_{24}$

$+ 995x_{31} + 682x_{32} + 388x_{33} + 685x_{34}$

## *Constraints (math structure)*

1. Plant constraints:
   Three plant constraints exist, one for each plant. These are expressed as follows:

   $\sum_{j=1}^{4} x_{ij}$ truckloads shipped from plant $i$ to warehouse $j$

   $\leq$ capacity, expressed in truckloads, at plant $i$ ($i$ = 1, 2, 3)

2. Warehouse constraints:
   Four warehouse constraints exist, one for each warehouse. These are expressed as follows:

   $\sum_{i=1}^{3} x_{ij}$ truckloads shipped from plant $i$ to warehouse $j$

   = demand, expressed in truckloads, at warehouse $j$ ( $j$ = 1, 2, 3, 4)

## Math formulation

MINIMIZE:

$$Z = 464x_{11} + 513x_{12} + 654x_{13} + 867x_{14}$$
$$+ 352x_{21} + 416x_{22} + 690x_{23} + 791x_{24}$$
$$+ 995x_{31} + 682x_{32} + 388x_{33} + 685x_{34}$$

SUBJECT TO:

$$x_{11} + x_{12} + x_{13} + x_{14} \le 75$$
$$x_{21} + x_{22} + x_{23} + x_{24} \le 125$$
$$x_{31} + x_{32} + x_{33} + x_{34} \le 100$$
$$x_{11} + x_{21} + x_{31} = 80$$
$$x_{12} + x_{22} + x_{32} = 65$$
$$x_{13} + x_{23} + x_{33} = 70$$
$$x_{14} + x_{24} + x_{34} = 85$$
$$x_{ij} \ge 0 \quad (i = 1, 2, 3; j = 1, 2, 3, 4)$$

Table 6-13 is the solution for B & Z Brewing Company. The optimal solution is to ship 20.0 truckloads from plant 1 (Boulder, Colorado) to warehouse 2 (Provo, Utah); 55.0 truckloads from plant 1 to warehouse 4 (Lincoln, Nebraska); 80.0 truckloads from plant 2 (Minneapolis, Minnesota) to warehouse 1 (San Diego, California); 45.0 truckloads from plant 2 to warehouse 2; 70.0 truckloads from plant 3 (Olympia, Washington) to warehouse 3 (Albuquerque, New Mexico); and 30.0 truckloads from plant 3 to warehouse 4. All remaining routes are unemployed (i.e., zero units are shipped along the route). As was the case with the Senora General Hospital problem, the negative sign associated with the objective function results because the problem involves minimization.

From our general knowledge that the solution results from an LP model generally take on fractional values, one would conclude that the integer (discrete) solution

**TABLE 6-13.**
**Solution for B & Z Brewing Company**

*The Value of the Objective Function is 152535.00*

| Variables | Values | Variables | Values |
|-----------|--------|-----------|--------|
| $x_{11}$ | 0.00 | $x_{23}$ | 0.00 |
| $x_{12}$ | 20.00 | $x_{24}$ | 0.00 |
| $x_{13}$ | 0.00 | $x_{31}$ | 0.00 |
| $x_{14}$ | 55.00 | $x_{32}$ | 0.00 |
| $x_{21}$ | 80.00 | $x_{33}$ | 70.00 |
| $x_{22}$ | 45.00 | $x_{34}$ | 30.00 |

*transportation problem*

values for B & Z Brewing occurred by chance. This is incorrect; the solution values for this problem will always be discrete because it is a **transportation problem.**

A transportation problem is concerned with the transportation or physical distribution of goods and services from several supply (source) locations to several demand (destination) locations. Usually there exists a fixed capacity or limited quantity of goods at each supply location and a specified order quantity or demand at each demand location.

The transportation problem is a special type of problem under the umbrella of linear programming. Certain characteristics of the problem, however, differentiate it from other problems. First, transportation problems tend to require a large number of constraints and variables so that the standard solution method for solving linear programming problems (Chapter 5) may be very expensive or computationally prohibitive. Second, most of the $a_{ij}$ coefficients in the constraints may be zeros, and the relatively few nonzero coefficients generally appear in a distinct pattern and are all equal to 1. As a result of this latter characteristic, it has been possible to develop modified, streamlined versions of the standard LP solution method. These modified solution methods result in significant computational savings by exploiting the special structure of the problem. One of these special solution methods is discussed in detail in Chapter 10.

Our purpose in introducing the transportation problem at this point is to demonstrate that the problem can be formulated as a linear programming problem. If no special-purpose algorithm exists, the problem can, in most cases, be solved with a linear programming algorithm, if one is willing to pay the price of relatively long and costly solution times.

····················································································

■ **Example**
## *Road Improvement Board, Cook County, Illinois*

The Road Improvement Board of Cook County, Illinois, has three different road construction projects, which were approved at the last monthly meeting. The Board now faces the problem of determining the contractors to work the projects. Bids for the projects were sought from area contractors, and three contractors submitted bids. Bids submitted by the respective contractors are shown in Table 6-14, where $c_1$, $c_2$,

**TABLE 6-14. Road Improvement Bids ($00,000): Cook County, Illinois**

| Contractor | Project | | |
| --- | --- | --- | --- |
| | $p_1$ | $p_2$ | $p_3$ |
| $c_1$ | 28 | 32 | 36 |
| $c_2$ | 36 | 28 | 30 |
| $c_3$ | 38 | 34 | 40 |

TABLE 6-15.
Assignment Costs:
Cook County,
Illinois

| Assignments° | Total Costs (in $10,000 units) |
|---|---|
| $c_1, c_2, c_3$ | 96 |
| $c_1, c_3, c_2$ | 92 |
| $c_2, c_3, c_1$ | 106 |
| $c_2, c_1, c_3$ | 108 |
| $c_3, c_1, c_2$ | 100 |
| $c_3, c_2, c_1$ | 102 |

°Order of assignment is to $p_1$, $p_2$, and $p_3$, respectively.

and $c_3$ denote the contractors and $p_1$, $p_2$, and $p_3$ the projects. The bid amounts are expressed in ten thousands of dollars. The problem is to determine how to assign the projects so as to minimize the total costs of all projects. It is assumed that each contractor will be assigned only one project.

## ■ Solution

Obviously, with a small problem such as this, it is possible to determine the project assignment combination that results in the lowest cost. Only a few simple calculations are required. For this problem there are only 3! (that is, $3 \times 2 \times 1$), or 6 possible ways in which the assignments can be made. These are enumerated in Table 6-15.

From these results we quickly can note that the minimum total cost is $920,000 with $p_1$ being assigned to $c_1$, $p_2$ being assigned to $c_3$, and $p_3$ being assigned to $c_2$. But with a problem involving a large number of assignments, it would be very impractical to enumerate all possible assignments. For example, if there were seven projects and seven contractors in the Cook County problem, then there would be 7! = 5040 project–contractor assignment combinations. We can avoid enumerating all the possible assignments by structuring and solving the problem in the form of a linear programming model.

### Objective (verbal)

The problem facing the Road Improvement Board of Cook County is to assign a single road to each of the three contractors in such a way that the total cost to the county is minimized.

### Constraints (verbal)

1. Contractor 1 must receive a contract, but no more than one contract.
2. Contractor 2 must receive a contract, but no more than one contract.
3. Contractor 3 must receive a contract, but no more than one contract.

4. Project 1 $(p_1)$ must be assigned to either contractor 1 $(c_1)$, contractor 2 $(c_2)$, or contractor 3 $(c_3)$.

5. Project 2 $(p_2)$ must be assigned to either contractor 1 $(c_1)$, contractor 2 $(c_2)$, or contractor 3 $(c_3)$.

6. Project 3 $(p_3)$ must be assigned to either contractor 1 $(c_1)$, contractor 2 $(c_2)$, or contractor 3 $(c_3)$.

## Variables (math structure)

This problem requires the use of double subscripts for identifying variables, in much the same manner as in the transportation problem. Nine variables are required. Therefore, let

$x_{ij}$ = variables representing contractor $i$-project $j$ relationship, where $x_{ij}$ = 0 indicates that the project *was not assigned*; $x_{ij}$ = 1 indicates that the project *was assigned*; and $i$ = 1, 2, 3; $j$ = 1, 2, 3.

## Objective function (math structure)

The $c_{ij}$ coefficients in the objective function are the bid amounts submitted by the three different contractors for the three respective projects, that is,

$$c_{11} = 280{,}000, \quad c_{12} = 320{,}000, \quad \cdots, \quad c_{33} = 400{,}000$$

Therefore, the objective function is expressed as follows:

MINIMIZE:  $Z = 28x_{11} + 32x_{12} + 36x_{13} + 36x_{21} + 28x_{22} + 30x_{23} + 38x_{31} + 34x_{32} + 40x_{33}$

where the $c_{ij}$ coefficients are expressed in ten thousands of dollars.

## Constraints (math structure)

1. Contractor 1 $(c_1)$ constraint:

$$x_{11} + x_{12} + x_{13} = 1$$

2. Contractor 2 $(c_2)$ constraint:

$$x_{21} + x_{22} + x_{23} = 1$$

3. Contractor 3 $(c_3)$ constraint:

$$x_{31} + x_{32} + x_{33} = 1$$

4.  Project 1 $(p_1)$ constraint:

$$x_{11} + x_{21} + x_{31} = 1$$

5.  Project 2 $(p_2)$ constraint:

$$x_{12} + x_{22} + x_{32} = 1$$

6.  Project 3 $(p_3)$ constraint:

$$x_{13} + x_{23} + x_{33} = 1$$

Note that no units of measure are associated with the contraints. The $x_{ij}$ variables can take on a value of 0 or 1; therefore, they are simply flags indicating the status of the respective contractor–project relationship.

## Math formulation

MINIMIZE:  $Z = 28x_{11} + 32x_{12} + 36x_{13} + 36x_{21} + 28x_{22} + 30x_{23} + 38x_{31} + 34x_{32} + 40x_{33}$
SUBJECT TO:

$$
\begin{array}{llllllllll}
x_{11} + & x_{12} + & x_{13} & & & & & & & = 1 \\
& & & x_{21} + & x_{22} + & x_{23} & & & & = 1 \\
& & & & & & x_{31} + & x_{32} + & x_{33} & = 1 \\
x_{11} + & & & x_{21} + & & & x_{31} & & & = 1 \\
& x_{12} + & & & x_{22} + & & & x_{32} & & = 1 \\
& & x_{13} + & & & x_{23} + & & & x_{33} & = 1 \\
\end{array}
$$

$$x_{ij} \geq \quad (i = 1, 2, 3; j = 1, 2, 3)$$

From Table 6-16 we can note that the optimal solution for the county is to assign contractor 1 to project 1, contractor 2 to project 3, and contractor 3 to project 2. The total road improvement project will cost $920,000.

**TABLE 6-16.**
**Solution for Road Improvement Board, Cook County, Illinois**

*The Value of the Objective Function is $-92.00$*

| Structural Variables | Values | Structural Variables | Values |
|---|---|---|---|
| $x_{11}$ | 1.00 | $x_{23}$ | 1.00 |
| $x_{12}$ | 0.00 | $x_{31}$ | 0.00 |
| $x_{13}$ | 0.00 | $x_{32}$ | 1.00 |
| $x_{21}$ | 0.00 | $x_{33}$ | 0.00 |
| $x_{22}$ | 0.00 | | |

*assignment problem*

This problem illustrates another special-case LP problem, namely, the **assignment problem.** An assignment problem is where resources are to be allocated to a fixed number of activities on a one-to-one basis. The objective is to allocate optimally $n$ resources to $n$ activities. Unlike the transportation problem, each resource or assignee (e.g., an employee, machine, or time slot) must be assigned totally or uniquely to a particular activity or assignment (e.g., task, site, or event). Examples of assignment problems include the assignment of $n$ persons or machines to $n$ different jobs, the assignment of sales personnel to sales districts, the assignment of airline crews to flights, and the assignment of social workers to welfare cases. The objective of an assignment problem may well be to maximize profits; however, other objectives are equally as likely. For example, a production job assignment objective could be to maximize production throughput; a sales personnel assignment objective could be to maximize sales effectiveness; an airline crew assignment objective could be to minimize costs; and for a social worker case, the objective could be to maximize the number of cases handled within a specified time period.

The assignment problem is not only a special type of linear programming problem, it is also a special type of transportation problem. Specifically, the resources or assignees can be interpreted as transportation problem *sources*, each having a supply of 1. The assignments similarly can be interpreted as transportation problem *destinations*, each with a demand of 1.

Similar to the transportation problem, the assignment problem has a unique structure. Because of the special structure, streamlined solution methods have been developed that have a high degree of computational efficiency. This is not to say that the algorithm for the standard linear programming solution cannot be employed to solve an assignment problem; it simply means that the algorithm for an assignment solution is more efficient in arriving at the solution.

## ■ Multiperiod problems

The problems we have considered thus far have focused on situations that involve determining an optimal solution for a fixed time period. But there are numerous situations where managment must take into consideration changes that may occur in future time periods. For example, trends in demand, and inflationary costs, as well as seasonal variations, might affect how a firm should operate in the current time period. One might argue that the multi-time-period problem that would result from considering these factors could be viewed as a series of subproblems and that each subproblem simply involves optimizing the operation of the organization during a single time period. However, if one views the problem in this manner, suboptimization may well result; that is, the sum of the optimal solutions for each subperiod will be less than the optimal solution for all periods considered collectively.

To demonstrate the formulation process associated with multiperiod problems, we will consider two examples.

*multiperiod problems*

**Multiperiod problems** are not limited to these two cases; however, these cases demonstrate the concepts and factors that must be considered in formulating such problems.

■ **Example**
## *Odessa Manufacturing*

The Odessa Manufacturing Company produces a product that has a rising and falling demand. For example, the forecasted demand for the next four months is 1800, 2200, 3400, and 2800, respectively. Because of the demand variations, management at Odessa has found that in some months excess production exists, which results in large holding/storage costs, while in other months the company is unable to meet demand. The company can produce 2400 items per month on regular shifts. By using overtime, an additional 800 items per month can be produced. Because of the higher labor costs for overtime, a $7 per item cost increase results for any item not produced during the regular shift. Management has estimated that a storage cost of $3 per month will be incurred for any item that is produced in a given month and not sold in the same month. Odessa would like to determine an optimal production schedule that minimizes the total costs of production and storage. The schedule should be such that all sales demands are met.

■ **Solution**
### *Objective (verbal)*

Odessa would like to determine the quantity of units that should be produced during the *regular shift* and the *overtime shift* for the next four months in order to minimize total costs. The company must take into consideration the unit cost of production during regular and overtime shifts, the demand for units during a given month as well as coming months, and the cost of holding (storing) units not consumed during the month in which they are produced.

### *Constraints (verbal)*

Twelve constraints exist; four constraints are related to demand and eight constraints are related to production capacity.

1. The total number of units produced on regular and overtime shifts in the first month must at least meet the demand of 1800 units.

2. The total number of units produced on regular and overtime shifts in month 2 plus any inventory from month 1 must at least meet the demand of 2200 units.

3. The total number of units produced on regular and overtime shifts in month 3 plus any inventory from month 2 must at least meet the demand of 3400 units.

4. The total number of units produced on regular and overtime shifts in month 4 plus any inventory from month 3 must meet the demand of 2800 units.

**5.–12.** The number of units produced on regular shifts in months 1, 2, 3, and 4 cannot exceed 2400—the available monthly production capacity. The number of units produced on overtime shifts in months 1, 2, 3, and 4 cannot exceed 800—the monthly production capacity in overtime.

## Variables (math structure)

Upon first examining the problem, one could conclude that eight variables would be required since the decision must be made regarding the quantity of units to produce on both regular and overtime shifts for the four months. However, the optimal operating policy may be to produce excess units in one or more months for use in future months. Therefore, three additional variables will be used, these variables will represent inventory in months 1, 2, and 3. Inventory will not be considered in month 4 since the structured problem terminates after four months. Therefore, let

$$x_j = \text{number of units to produce on regular shifts in month } j$$

$$y_j = \text{number of units to produce on overtime shift in month } j$$

$$z_j = \text{inventory at the end of month } j$$

where $j = 1, 2, 3, 4$. ($z_4$ does not exist since inventory in month 4 is not allowed.)

## Objective function (math structure)

Since regular production costs will be incurred in the production of any unit, we need not be concerned with this factor in minimizing costs. The factors that must be considered are the additional cost of production during the overtime shift and storage costs. Therefore, the objective function for the problem can be expressed as follows:

MINIMIZE:     $Z = 7y_1 + 7y_2 + 7y_3 + 7y_4 + 3z_1 + 3z_2 + 3z_3$

where 7 is the overtime cost per unit and 3 is the storage cost per unit.

## Constraints (math structure)

1. Period 1 demand constraint:

   ($x_1$ units produced on regular shift, period 1)

   + ($y_1$ units produced on overtime shift, period 1)

   = (1800 units demanded, period 1)

   + ($z_1$ units of inventory, period 1)

2. Period 2 demand constraint:

$(x_2$ units produced on regular shift, period 2)

$+ (y_2$ units produced on overtime shift, period 2)

$+ (z_1$ units of inventory, period 1)

$= (2200$ units demanded, period 2)

$+ (z_2$ units of inventory, period 2)

3. Period 3 demand constraint:

$(x_3$ units produced on regular shift, period 3)

$+ (y_3$ units produced on overtime shift, period 3)

$+ (z_2$ units of inventory, period 2)

$= (3400$ units demanded, period 3)

$+ (z_3$ units of inventory, period 3)

4. Period 4 demand constraint:

$(x_4$ units produced on regular shift, period 4)

$+ (y_4$ units produced on overtime shift, period 4)

$+ (z_3$ units of inventory, period 3)

$= 2800$ units demanded, period 4

5.–8. Regular production capacity contraints:

$x_i$ units produced during regular shift, period $i$
$\leq 2400$ units of regular production capacity, period $i$ $(i = 1, 2, 3, 4)$

9.–12. Overtime production capacity constraints:

$y_i$ units produced during overtime shift, period $i$
$\leq 800$ units of overtime production capacity, period $i$ $(i = 1, 2, 3, 4)$

## Math formulation

MINIMIZE:
SUBJECT TO:

$$Z = 0x_1 + 0x_2 + 0x_3 + 0x_4 + 7y_1 + 7y_2 + 7y_3 + 7y_4 + 3z_1 + 3z_2 + 3z_3$$

$$
\begin{aligned}
x_1 + && y_1 - && z_1 && = 1800 \\
x_2 + && y_2 + && z_1 - z_2 && = 2200 \\
x_3 + && y_3 + && z_2 - z_3 && = 3400 \\
x_4 + && y_4 + && z_3 && = 2800
\end{aligned}
$$

$$x_1 \qquad\qquad\qquad\qquad \le 2400$$

$$x_2 \qquad\qquad\qquad\qquad \le 2400$$

$$x_3 \qquad\qquad\qquad\qquad \le 2400$$

$$x_4 \qquad\qquad\qquad\qquad \le 2400$$

$$y_1 \qquad\qquad\qquad\qquad \le 800$$

$$y_2 \qquad\qquad\qquad\qquad \le 800$$

$$y_3 \qquad\qquad\qquad\qquad \le 800$$

$$y_4 \qquad\qquad\qquad\qquad \le 800$$

$$x_i \ge 0;\; y_i \ge 0;\; z_1, z_2, z_3 \ge 0 \quad (i = 1, 2, 3, 4)$$

It should be recognized that no storage limitation exists in the problem. To incorporate a maximum storage constraint into the problem, additional constraints would be required. Also, defining the inventory variables simply as $z_1$, $z_2$, and $z_3$ does not identify the period in which the inventory will be used. We could have broken these variables down further (at the variable definition step) such that our final solution would not only reflect the inventory in a given period, but would highlight the future period in which we would expect to sell the units.

From Table 6-17 we note that the optimal solution is

$$x_1 = 2400.00 \quad y_1 = \quad 0.00 \quad z_1 = 600.00$$

$$x_2 = 2400.00 \quad y_2 = \quad 0.00 \quad z_2 = 800.00$$

$$x_3 = 2400.00 \quad y_3 = 200.00 \quad z_3 = \quad 0.00$$

$$x_4 = 2400.00 \quad y_4 = 400.00$$

The cost of this production schedule is $8,400.00. But we need to remember that our objective function does not take into consideration the regular time cost of production, so the obtained objective value is an understatement of total cost.

**TABLE 6-17. Solution for Odessa Manufacturing**

*The Value of the Objective Function is* $-8400.00$

| Variables | Values | Variables | Values |
|-----------|--------|-----------|--------|
| $x_1$ | 2400.00 | $y_3$ | 200.00 |
| $x_2$ | 2400.00 | $y_4$ | 400.00 |
| $x_3$ | 2400.00 | $z_1$ | 600.00 |
| $x_4$ | 2400.00 | $z_2$ | 800.00 |
| $y_1$ | 0.00 | $z_3$ | 0.00 |
| $y_2$ | 0.00 | | |

## ■ Example

### *Brooks-Hall Investment Company*

The Brooks-Hall Investment Company, a newly formed investment brokerage house, has $600,000 to be invested in a group of investment alternatives. Investment type 1 is available in each of the next six years and is expected to yield a 28% return on every dollar invested when it matures at the end of three years. Investment type 2 is also available in each of the next six years. This investment will yield $1.16 for every dollar invested and will mature at the end of two years. Investment type 3 is available only at the begining of the second year and will yield $1.50 at the end of the fourth year for each dollar invested. Investment type 4 is available at any time after the third year and will yield a 40% return at the end of two years. The final investment opportunity, type 5, is available only once, at the beginning of year 1. This investment will return $1.45 for every dollar invested but will not mature until the beginning of year 5. When investments mature they are available for reinvestment. Brooks-Hall would like to determine the investment portfolio that will maximize the growth of the total investment over a six-year span, (i.e., to the end of the sixth year).

**TABLE 6-18. Brooks-Hall Investment Pattern**

| Investment Available | | Year 1 | Year 2 | Year 3 | Year 4 | Year 5 | Year 6 |
|---|---|---|---|---|---|---|---|
| Year 1 | Type 1 | | 28% | | | | |
| | Type 2 | | 16% | | | | |
| | Type 5 | | | 45% | | | |
| | Type 6 | 0% | | | | | |
| Year 2 | Type 2 | | | 16% | | | |
| | Type 3 | | | 50% | | | |
| | Type 6 | | 0% | | | | |
| Year 3 | Type 1 | | | | 28% | | |
| | Type 2 | | | 16% | | | |
| | Type 6 | | | 0% | | | |
| Year 4 | Type 1 | | | | | 28% | |
| | Type 4 | | | | | 40% | |
| | Type 6 | | | | 0% | | |
| Year 5 | Type 4 | | | | | 40% | |
| | Type 6 | | | | | 0% | |
| Year 6 | Type 6 | | | | | | 0% |

## ■ Solution

This problem is similar to the state employee retirement fund portfolio investment problem. In this case, however, we are specifically interested in the complete investment package being terminated at the end of six years. In formulating the problem, a pictorial diagram such as Table 6-18 is needed to show the investments available in each respective year, the year in which the investments will mature, and the associated return on the investment.

Several comments should be made about the data presented in Table 6-18. First, note that a type 6 investment has been added to the group of available investment categories. This investment category simply represents idle funds, that is, funds not invested during the year. The need for this extra category results from the fact that it may be more profitable in one or more periods to hold dollars for investment in future time periods rather than currently committing the funds to long-term investments. It should also be noted that investment type 2 has been omitted in years 4 and 5 even though it is an available alternative. Since both are two-year investments, and investment type 4 yields 40%, while investment type 2 yields 16% for a two-year period, the higher yielding investment would automatically be preferred. The same reasoning can be used to delete investment type 1 in period 2, where investment type 3 takes precedence since it has a yield of 50%.

No investment opportunity is considered beyond the begining of year 5 since none of the investments mature in one year.

### Objective (verbal)

Brooks-Hall must determine the dollars that should be invested in each of the available investment categories for the next six years. Investments should be such that maximum return on the $600,000 results at the end of the six-year investment period.

### Constraints (verbal)

The constraints associated with this problem are related to funds available for investment in a given year. Six constraints are required since we have six investment periods. The funds available for investment in any year depend upon the actions taken in previous years. For example, at the beginning of year 2 the only funds available are funds that were not invested in year 1, that is, funds that remained idle through year 1. At the beginning of year 3 the total dollars available for investment are the dollars that were idle in year 2 plus the dollars that were invested in investment type 2 at the beginning of year 1. (This investment matured at the end of the second year.) The constraints can be expressed in the following manner:

1. The total dollars invested in investment types 1, 2, 5, and 6 at the beginning of year 1 must equal $600,000.

2. The total dollars invested in investment types 2, 3, and 6 at the beginning of year 2 must equal the idle dollars in year 1.

3. The total dollars invested in investment types 1, 2, and 6 at the beginning of year 3 must equal the idle dollars in year 2 plus the yielded investment from type 2 made in year 1.

4. The total dollars invested in investment types 1, 4, and 6 at the beginning of year 4 must equal the idle dollars in year 3 plus the yielded investments from type 1 in year 1 and from type 2 in year 2.

5. The total dollars invested in investment types 4 and 6 at the beginning of year 5 must equal the idle dollars in year 4 plus the yielded investments from type 5 in year 1, type 3 in year 2, and type 2 in year 3.

6. The total dollars available at the beginning of year 6 must equal the idle dollars in year 5 plus the yielded investments from type 1 in year 3 and from type 4 in year 4.

## Variables (math structure)

If every investment category (type) were available in each of the 6 years, then 36 variables would be required. However, the problem, as stated, will require only 16 variables since many of the investments are not available in more than one year. To aid in keeping abreast of the investment type and the year in which the investment is made, we will use double subscripts, where the first subscript will identify the investment category (type) and the second subscript will identify the year in which the investment is made:

$$x_{ij} = \text{dollars invested in investment type } i \text{ in year } j$$

## Objective function (math structure)

Upon first analyzing the problem, one might conclude that the objective function would be to maximize the sum of the yields from the 16 investments. However, this would be incorrect since a large portion of the $600,000 could be *reinvested* several times; and while maximizing the sum of yielded investments would provide the optimal solution values for the decision variables $(x_{11}, x_{21}, \ldots, x_{66})$, the value of the objective function would overstate the actual value of the $600,000 invested. The overall objective is to maximize total dollars at the end of the sixth year.

Each dollar invested in investment type 1 in year 4 yields 28% at the end of year 6; the net investment is the original investment plus $.28, that is, $1.28. Each dollar invested in investment type 4 in year 5 yields 40% at the end of year 6; thus the resulting net investment is $1.40. Investment type 6 yields 0% at the end of the year for each dollar invested; so the net result is $1.00. Since these three investments are the only ones that mature in year 6, the objective functions only include these variables. The objective function is expressed as:

MAXIMIZE: $\quad Z = 1.28x_{14} + 1.40x_{45} + 1.0x_{66}$

## *Constraints (math structure)*

1. Year 1 investment constraint:

$$x_{11} + x_{21} + x_{51} + x_{61} = 600{,}000$$

2. Year 2 investment constraint:

$$x_{22} + x_{32} + x_{62} = 1.0x_{61}$$

3. Year 3 investment constraint:

$$x_{13} + x_{23} + x_{63} = 1.0x_{62} + 1.16x_{21}$$

4. Year 4 investment constraint:

$$x_{14} + x_{44} + x_{64} = 1.0x_{63} + 1.28x_{11} + 1.16x_{22}$$

5. Year 5 investment constraint:

$$x_{45} + x_{65} = 1.0x_{64} + 1.45x_{51} + 1.50x_{32} + 1.16x_{23}$$

6. Year 6 investment constraint:

$$x_{66} = 1.0x_{65} + 1.28x_{13} + 1.40x_{44}$$

The variables on the left side of each constraint are the investment alternatives available at the beginning of the respective period, and the variables on the right side of the contraints are the funds available for investment. The units of measure in all cases are expressed in dollars.

## *Math formulation*

MAXIMIZE:    $Z = 1.28x_{14} + 1.40x_{45} + 1.0x_{66}$

SUBJECT TO:

$$
\begin{array}{llllll}
x_{11} + & x_{21} + & & x_{51} + & x_{61} & = 600{,}000 \\
& x_{22} + & x_{32} - & & 1.0x_{61} + x_{62} & = 0 \\
x_{13} - & 1.16x_{21} + & x_{23} - & & 1.0x_{62} + x_{63} & = 0 \\
-1.28x_{11} + x_{14} - 1.16x_{22} + & & x_{44} - & & 1.0x_{63} + x_{64} & = 0 \\
& - 1.16x_{23} - 1.50x_{32} + & x_{45} - 1.45x_{51} - & 1.0x_{64} + x_{65} & = 0 \\
-1.28x_{13} - & & 1.40x_{44} - & & 1.0x_{65} + x_{66} & = 0
\end{array}
$$

$$x_{11}, x_{13}, x_{14}, x_{21}, x_{22}, x_{23}, x_{32}, x_{44}, x_{45}, x_{51}, x_{61}, x_{62}, x_{63}, x_{64}, x_{65}, x_{66} \geq 0$$

| The Value of the Objective Function is 1,259,999.66 | | | |
|---|---|---|---|
| Variables | Values | Variables | Values |
| $x_{11}$ | 0.00 | $x_{45}$ | 900,000.00 |
| $x_{13}$ | 0.00 | $x_{51}$ | 0.00 |
| $x_{14}$ | 0.00 | $x_{61}$ | 600,000.00 |
| $x_{21}$ | 0.00 | $x_{62}$ | 0.00 |
| $x_{22}$ | 0.00 | $x_{63}$ | 0.00 |
| $x_{23}$ | 0.00 | $x_{64}$ | 0.00 |
| $x_{32}$ | 600,000.00 | $x_{65}$ | 0.00 |
| $x_{44}$ | 0.00 | $x_{66}$ | 0.00 |

**TABLE 6-19.
Solution for
Brooks-Hall
Investment
Company**

The solution to this problem will provide the dollar values of investments that should be made each period. The resulting Z value will be the total value of the $600,000 after investments.

Table 6-19 is the solution for Brooks-Hall. The optimal solution is $x_{32} = 600,000$, $x_{45} = 900,000$, and $x_{61} = 600,000$. This means that the company should invest $600,000 in investment type 3 in year 2, $900,000 in investment type 4 in year 5, and $600,000 in investment type 6 in year 1. The total value of the investment at the end of the sixth year would be $1,259,999.66.

## ▪ Summary

The examples in this chapter were designed to demonstrate the formulation process associated with linear programming. We hope you now have a better understanding of the process.

In several of the examples it was pointed out that the linear programming solution algorithm (simplex) will not guarantee an optimal solution. We noted this specifically in the discussion of the advertising and capital budgeting problems. We should also point out that even though all these problems were formulated as LP problems, it is possible in many cases to structure the problems to fit other solution algorithms. For example, the multiperiod production scheduling problem can also be formulated as a transportation problem and the multiperiod investment problem can be formulated as a *dynamic programming* problem. Some of the problems in this chapter will be used as examples in future chapters.

It should not be concluded that the only kinds of problems amenable to solution by linear programming are those presented in this chapter. Numerous other applications exist, such as *make-or-buy problems, agriculture allocation problems, break-even analysis, trim-loss problems,* and *shrinkage problems.*

## ▪ Glossary of terms

**assignment problem:** A special type of linear programming problem where the objective is optimally to allocate $n$ resources to $n$ activities. Examples include the assignment of $n$ persons to $n$ different jobs, that is, the assignment of sales personnel to sales districts, the assignment of airline crews to flights, and the assignment of social workers to welfare cases.

**blending problems:**   Problems that can be formulated as LP models, where the objective is to blend raw ingredients to produce refined end products. Examples include blending of gasoline, production of a feed mix, and the blending of paints, chemicals, and alcoholic beverages.

**diet problem:**   A "classical" LP problem concerned with determining the minimal-cost food combination that will meet certain nutritional requirements.

**formulation:**   The art of transforming an unstructured problem into a mathematical form. For linear programming, the mathematical form is expressed as a linear objective function subject to a defined set of linear constraints.

**multiperiod problems:**   Problems that can be formulated as LP models when the formulation process spans several time periods. Examples include production scheduling and investment analysis.

**resource allocation problems:**   Problems where limited resources exist and maximum utilization of resources is sought.

**transportation problem:**   A special type of problem that can be grouped under the umbrella of linear programming. The problem is concerned with the transportation or physical distribution of goods and services *from* several supply locations *to* several demand locations.

## ■ Review questions

1. Identify the general mathematical form of the basic LP model.

2. Briefly describe the procedures/steps that should be employed in formulating a problem as an LP model.

3. Differentiate between a diet problem and a blending problem. Give examples of each.

4. What characteristic of capital budgeting problems can possibly result in an unimplementable solution, if LP is used to solve such problems?

5. What characteristic of transportation problems makes it possible to develop streamlined versions of the standard LP solution method?

6. How does a transportation problem differ from an assignment problem? Be specific in your answer. Give examples.

7. Identify the characteristics of a multiperiod problem. Is it possible to solve such problems by viewing the overall problem as a series of subproblems; that is, can we optimize each time period and add the results? Explain.

## ■ True/false questions

1. Any problem can be reduced to only one correct LP model.

2. Values of the variables in optimal LP solutions are rounded to the next higher integer.

3. Resource allocation problems are examples of multiperiod problems.

4. Resource allocation problems seek to maximize the utilization of limited resources.

5. All constraints must be expressed in the same units of measure.

6. Diet problems specifically involve determining the minimal-cost food combination that meets certain nutritional requirements.

7. The problem of producing a portfolio from a given group of stocks may be regarded as a blending problem.

8. In the case of capital budgeting problems, LP insures that the optimal solution does not contain any fractional problems.

9. Solution values for transportation problems are always discrete.

10. The problem of assigning a number of employees to a machine may be regarded as an assignment problem.

11. Assignment problems involve assignment of $n$ persons or machines to $n$ different jobs.

12. Transportation problems involve the physical distribution of goods and services from one warehouse/supply location to several demand locations.

13. Multiperiod investment problems may be formulated as dynamic programming problems.

## ▪ Problems

1. Smith Motors, Inc., sells standard automobiles and station wagons. The company makes $300 profit on each standard auto it sells and $400 on each station wagon sold. The manufacturer cannot supply more than 300 standard automobiles and 200 station wagons per month. Dealer preparation time requires 2 hours for each standard auto and 3 hours for a station wagon. The company has 900 hours of shop time available each month for new car preparation. Formulate an LP problem to determine how many standard automobiles and station wagons should be ordered so that profit is maximized.

2. The EZ Company makes three high-fashion products, which the marketing department has named Mad, Mud, and Mod. These three products are made from three ingredients, which, for security reasons, are code-named Alpha, Baker, and Charlie. The pounds of each ingredient required to make one pound of final product are shown in Table P6-2.

**TABLE P6-2.**

| Product | Ingredient | | |
|---------|-------|-------|---------|
|         | Alpha | Baker | Charlie |
| Mad     | 4     | 7     | 8       |
| Mud     | 3     | 9     | 7       |
| Mod     | 2     | 2     | 12      |

The firm has 400, 800, and 1000 pounds, respectively, on hand of the ingredients Alpha, Baker, and Charlie. Under current market conditions, the profit contributions for the products are $18 for Mad, $10 for Mud, and $12 for Mod. Formulate an LP problem to determine the amount of each high-fashion product to produce.

3. The Clear-Tube Company produces electronic parts for television sets and radios. The company has decided to produce and market AM-FM radios and tape players. It has built a plant that can operate 48 hours a week with an overhead of $10,000 per week. Production of an AM/FM radio will require 2 hours of labor and production of a tape player will require 3 hours of labor. Each radio will contribute $20 to profit while each tape player will contribute $25 to profit. The marketing department at Clear-Tube has determined that a maximum of 150 radios and 100 tape players can be sold each week. Formulate an LP problem to determine the optimum production mix that will maximize the contribution to profits.

4. Lord Manufacturing Company makes three products for the rapidly expanding micro-computer market: diskettes, tape cassettes, and disk-drive head-cleaning kits. Per-unit contribution to profit for each product is shown in Table P6-4a.

**TABLE P6-4a.**

| Product | Contribution to Profit |
|---------|------------------------|
| Diskette | $2 |
| Cassette | $1 |
| Cleaning kit | $3.50 |

Each of the products passes through three manufacturing and testing centers as a part of the production process. Times required in each center to produce one unit of each of the three products are shown in Table P6-4b.

**TABLE P6-4b.**

| Product | Hours per Unit | | |
|---------|---------|---------|---------|
| | Center 1 | Center 2 | Center 3 |
| Diskette | 3 | 2 | 1 |
| Cassette | 4 | 1 | 3 |
| Cleaning kit | 2 | 2 | 2 |

Each of the centers has time available for next week and overhead costs as shown in Table P6-4c.

**TABLE P6-4c.**

| | Time | Overhead |
|---|------|----------|
| Center 1: | 60 hours | $1000 |
| Center 2: | 40 hours | $2000 |
| Center 3: | 80 hours | $1500 |

Formulate an LP problem to schedule production in such a manner as to maximize contribution to profits.

5. Ware Farms of the Schoharie Valley near Albany, N.Y., grows broccoli and cauliflower on 500 acres of bottomland. An acre of broccoli brings a $500 contribution to profit and the contribution from an acre of cauliflower is $1000. Because of government regulations, no more than 200 acres can be planted in broccoli. During the planting season, 1200 man-hours of planting time will be available. Each acre of broccoli requires 2.5 man-hours and each acre of cauliflower 5.5 man-hours. Formulate an LP problem to determine how many acres of broccoli and how many acres of cauliflower should be planted to maximize contribution to profits.

6. The Pro-Shaft Company produces and markets three lines of tennis rackets: A, B, and C; A is a "standard" racket and B and C are "professional" rackets. The manufacturing process for the rackets is such that two production operations are required—all rackets pass through both operations. Each racket requires 3 hours of production time in operation 1. In operation 2, racket A requires 2 hours of production time; racket B requires 4 hours;

and racket C requires 5 hours. Operation 1 has 50 hours of production time per week and operation 2 has sufficient manpower to support 80 hours of production per week. The market group for Pro-Shaft has projected that the demand for the standard racket will be no more than 25 per week. Because rackets B and C are similar in quality, the combined demand for these rackets has been forecasted—the total demand is ten or more, but not more than 30 per week. The sale of racket A results in $7 profits while rackets B and C provide $8.00 and $8.50 profits respectively. How many rackets of type A, B, and C should be produced weekly if the company seeks to maximize profits? Formulate the problem as a standard LP model.

7. The Higgins Company produces a high-precision metal housing used in automobile racing engines. The housing is manufactured in a refining-forging process and requires minimum amounts of various metals. Each housing requires 40 ounces of lead, 48 ounces of copper, and 60 ounces of cast iron. Four types of ore are available for the refining–forging process. Type 1 ore contains 4 ounces of lead, 2 ounces of copper, and 2 ounces of cast iron per pound. One pound of type 2 ore contains 2 ounces of lead, 6 ounces of copper, and 6 ounces of cast iron. A pound of type 3 ore contains 1 ounce of lead, 4 ounces of copper, and 4 ounces of cast iron. Finally, type 4 ore contains ½ ounce of lead, 1 ounce of copper, and 8 ounces of cast iron per pound. The costs per pound for the four ores are $20, $30, $60, and $50 respectively. Higgins would like to mix the ores in such a way that the housing specifications are met and the cost of producing the housing is minimized. Define the decision variables and formulate the appropriate LP model.

8. The Georgia Outdoors Company makes three types of trail mix, which they then wholesale to various retail outlets. The three types are regular, special, and super, and they sell for $1.50, $2.20, and $3.50 per pound respectively. Each mix is made up of the same three ingredients: peanuts, raisins, and carobs. The costs of these ingredients are:

> Peanuts: $0.90/lb
>
> Raisins: $1.60/lb
>
> Carobs: $1.50/lb

The mixing requirements are as follows:

> Regular: at least 5% of each ingredient
>
> Special: at least 20% of each ingredient and no more than 50% of any one ingredient
>
> Super: at least 25% raisins and no more than 25% peanuts

The production facilities are such that a maximum of 1000 pounds of peanuts, 2000 pounds of raisins, and 3000 pounds of carobs are available each week. There is a $2000 overhead cost for production of the mixes. There is also a limitation that the regular mix be limited to 20% of total production. Formulate an LP to maximize profits.

9. The production supervisor of a refinery must schedule two blending processes. When process 1 is run for one hour, inputs of 100 barrels of domestic crude and 300 barrels of imported crude are consumed. Similarly, when process 2 is run for an hour, inputs of 100 barrels of domestic crude and 200 barrels of imported crude are consumed. On the output side, process 1 generates 4,000 gallons of gasoline and 1,750 gallons of kerosene per hour of operation. Process 2 generates 3,500 gallons of gasoline and 2,250 gallons of kerosene per hour. For the upcoming production run, there are 1,200 barrels of domestic crude and

1,800 barrels of imported crude available. Sales contracts require the production of 28,000 gallons of gasoline and 12,000 gallons of kerosene. Contributions to profit per hour of operation are $1,000 and $1,100 for process 1 and process 2, respectively.

**a.** Formulate a linear programming model to determine the production schedule that maximizes total contribution. Be sure to indicate the units in which the decision variables are measured and the unit in which each constraint is measured.

**b.** The U.S. Department of Energy may issue an order that limits total gasoline production to not more than twice the amount of kerosene produced. What constraint must be added to your model to implement this restriction?

10. The Carpenteria Shipping Company runs a combined passenger/cargo jet between Newark Airport and Bonn, West Germany. Because of high operational expenses, the jet will not depart until all decks are loaded with cargo. The aircraft has three decks: lower, middle, and upper. Owing to the limited deck space, the jet cannot carry more than 100 tons of cargo for each leg of the trip.

No more than 40 tons of cargo should be carried on the lower deck. For balance purposes, the middle deck must carry one-third of the load of the lower deck and the upper deck must carry two-fifths of the load of the lower deck. However, no more than 60 tons of cargo should be loaded on the middle and upper decks combined. The profit from the shipping is $8 per ton for cargo on the lower deck, $10 per ton for cargo on the middle deck, and $12 per ton for cargo in the upper deck, after all of the necessary expenses are defrayed. Formulate an LP problem to determine the highest profit loading of cargo.

11. The H. R. Russell Manufacturing Company is a major producer of stereophonic equipment. Management at Russell is currently considering adding a new product line to its existing group of stereophonic systems. The new line will include four new products. Russell has two plants in which it can manufacture the new product line. The manufacturing process in plant #1 is structured somewhat differently than in plant #2. Three process operations are required in plant #1; only two process operations are required at plant #2. Because the manufacturing operations at the two plants differ, variable costs at the plants differ; therefore, it may be more profitable to produce one product of the product line at one plant and one or more of the remaining products at the second plant. The selling price and variable costs, as well as maximum demand for the new products, are shown in Table P6-11a.

The manufacturing operations for the two plants are described in Table P6-11b (numbers in the table express hours of manufacturing time). The plant manager at plant #1 has indicated that the following hours of monthly production capacity can be devoted to the new product line: operation A, 30,000 hours: operation B, 100,000 hours; operation C, 16,000 hours. Twenty thousand hours of production time are available at each of the operations in plant #2. Russell would like to determine the quantity of each of the four types of products that should be produced monthly at the two plants, such that the contribution to profits for the company is maximized.

**TABLE P6-11a.**

| Selling Price and Demand | Product | | | |
|---|---|---|---|---|
| | #1 | #2 | #3 | #4 |
| Selling price | $200 | $300 | $250 | $280 |
| Variable cost: plant #1 | $160 | $270 | $240 | $270 |
| Variable cost: plant #2 | $220 | $300 | $200 | $220 |
| Demand (units) | 1000 | 3000 | 4000 | 6000 |

**TABLE P6-11b.**

|  | Product | | | |
|---|---|---|---|---|
|  | #1 | #2 | #3 | #4 |
| Plant #1: | | | | |
| Operation A | 6.0 | 7.2 | 4.0 | 7.0 |
| Operation B | 18.0 | 20.0 | 16.0 | 18.0 |
| Operation C | 2.0 | 2.0 | 1.0 | 1.0 |
| Plant #2: | | | | |
| Operation X | 8.0 | 8.0 | 4.0 | 8.0 |
| Operation Y | 10.0 | 16.0 | 8.0 | 6.0 |

**a.** Formulate the problem as an LP model.

**b.** Assume that top management at Russell has decided that each plant will produce 50% of the demand for each product. Formulate the two models that would represent this policy. How would you go about convincing management at Russell that this is not an optimal policy for the company?

12. The Overland Farm Company is a large farming cooperative. The company has 130 acres on which it produces three primary products: soybeans, wheat, and corn. The products produced by the cooperative are for both membership consumption and external sale. The cooperative is organized such that the demands of the membership must be met before any goods are sold externally. All excess production is sold at market price. Table P6-12 summarizes for each product, over the growing season, the projected yield per acre, the number of bushels demanded by the membership, the maximum market demand (in bushels), and the estimated profit per bushel. Formulate an LP model for the problem that would enable the cooperative to determine the number of acres that should be allocated to each crop such that total profits are maximized.

**TABLE P6-12.**

| Crop | Yield (bushels per acre) | Membership Demand (bushels) | Market Demand (bushels) | Profit ($/bushel) |
|---|---|---|---|---|
| Soybeans | 420 | 2000 | 10,000 | 1.50 |
| Wheat | 200 | 5000 | 8,000 | 1.80 |
| Corn | 70 | 1000 | 3,000 | 2.50 |

13. The Beta Corporation has just purchased an existing franchise operation for the limousine service between the DFW Airport and the downtown area. Previously, the limo service had operated a fleet of 30 station wagons; however, the volume of business is such that additional vehicles could easily be justified. In addition, most of the vehicles are very old and require heavy maintenance. Because of the small investment required in the purchase of the franchise, Beta is in a position to replace *all* existing vehicles. Three types of vehicles are under consideration: station wagons, minibuses, and large buses. The company has examined each type of vehicle and collected the data shown in Table P6-13. The board of directors at Beta has authorized $500,000 for the purchase of vehicles. Beta has projected that it can adequately employ as many vehicles as it can afford to put into the fleet; however, the service and maintenance facilities are limited. Currently, the maintenance department can handle 30 station wagons. At the present time the company does not wish

to expand the maintenance facilities. Since the new fleet may contain minibuses and large buses, the maintenance department must be able to handle these. A minibus is equivalent to 1½ station wagons and each large bus is equivalent to 3 station wagons. Formulate a linear model that will allow Beta to determine the optimum number of each type of vehicle to purchase in order to maximize expected annual profits.

**TABLE P6-13.**

| Vehicle Type | Purchase Price | Expected Annual Net Profit (per vehicle) |
|---|---|---|
| Station wagon | $ 6,500 | $2,000 |
| Minibus | 10,500 | 2,800 |
| Large bus | 29,000 | 6,500 |

14. Dixon's, Inc., is an exclusive retail outlet of men's suits and topcoats. Dixon carries three lines of wearing apparel: leisure/sports, young executive, and top-of-the-line. In general, these lines can be characterized as *medium priced, moderately expensive,* and *expensive.* The more expensive lines require more elaborate display layouts and more sales personnel time; however, higher profits are made on the more expensive lines. For planning purposes, Dixon has determined that the average profit per item in the leisure/sports line is $6.50, while the per-item profit for the young executive and top-of-the-line is $13.70 and $23.25, respectively. Profits within the lines do not differ from suits to topcoats. From prior experience Dixon has determined that 200 sq ft are required to display 1000 units of the leisure/sports line while 450 sq ft per 1000 items are required for the young executives line and 690 sq ft per 1000 items are required to display the top-of-the-line. Prior experience indicates that the man-hours of sales personnel required per 1000 items sold for the respective lines are 250, 650, and 1800.

To maintain a reasonable variety of suits and topcoats, Dixon orders at least 1000 items from each line. To reflect the fact that more suits sell than topcoats. Dixon maintains an 80/20 ratio across each line when ordering. Dixon has 65,000 sq ft of display floor space. Management has determined that the season in which the items will be marketable is approximately 16 weeks in length. Currently Dixon has a sales force of 8 people. The standard work week for all sales personnel is 48 hours. Formulate a linear programming model of the problem that can be used to determine the number of suits and topcoats in each line that Dixon's buyers should order in order to maximize profits.

15. The Clark County school district has two high schools that serve the needs of the county. High school #1 has a student capacity of 6500 while high school #2 has a capacity of 4500. The school district is subdivided into six areas. Each area is different in size (student population) and minority mix. Table P6-15a describes the six respective areas:

**TABLE P6-15a.**

| Area | Total Student Population | Number of Minority Students |
|---|---|---|
| A | 1900 | 200 |
| B | 2475 | 1600 |
| C | 1000 | 490 |
| D | 2150 | 450 |
| E | 1800 | 870 |
| F | 1400 | 590 |

A court-ordered desegregation plan has been sent to the district that specifies that each high school must have at least 32% minority enrollment. No school can have more than 45% minority enrollment. In attempting to comply with the court order, the district wishes to minimize the number of miles students must be bused. Data that indicates the distances (miles) from each of the areas to the respective schools are shown in Table P6-15b.

**TABLE P6-15b.**

| Area | High School #1 | High School #2 |
|------|----------------|----------------|
| A | 1.5 | 2.5 |
| B | 1.8 | 1.9 |
| C | 2.2 | 2.6 |
| D | 2.5 | 2.3 |
| E | 2.9 | 1.8 |
| F | 2.8 | 1.1 |

If possible, the district would like to avoid busing a student more than 2.8 miles. Formulate an LP model that will allow the district to meet the desegregation plan and the busing restriction.

16. The E. L. Griffith Company is a large shoe manufacturer, located in the Midwest region of the United States. Griffith specializes in the production of western boots. Griffith does not sell directly to the public, but instead sells through retail outlets. Owing to fluctuations in various component costs, the company has noted that the cost of production varies from month to month. Because of these cost variations (and the low cost of storage and handling, namely, $1.00 per month per pair of boots), Griffith feels it may be desirable to produce excess pairs of boots in some months for sale in future months. Management at Griffith has forecast demand and costs for the next seven months as shown in Table P6-16. The company wishes to schedule production such that total production and handling costs are minimized. Formulate an LP model for the problem. (No capacity restriction exists on production or on storage.)

**TABLE P6-16.**

| Month | Forecasted Demand | Projected Cost (per pair) |
|-------|-------------------|---------------------------|
| 1 | 150,000 | 36.00 |
| 2 | 110,000 | 42.00 |
| 3 | 180,000 | 38.00 |
| 4 | 100,000 | 40.00 |
| 5 | 200,000 | 35.00 |
| 6 | 180,000 | 39.00 |
| 7 | 110,000 | 37.00 |

17. A large farming cooperative in the southwestern United States operates four farms. The production (output) of each farm is limited by the amount of water available for irrigation and the number of acres available for farming. The data in Table P6-17a describe the farms. The cooperative normally produces three different crops, although each farm does not necessarily produce *all* crops. Because of the limitation of the availability of harvesting equipment, constraints exist on the number of acres of each crop produced on each farm.

The data in Table P6-17b reflect the maximum acres of each crop that can be produced on each farm. The water required (expressed in 1000 cubic feet per acre) for the respective crops is as follows: 6, 5, and 4. The projected profit per acre from the three crops are $500, $350, and $200, respectively.

To maintain a balanced workload among the four farms, the cooperative has adopted the policy of having an equal percentage of usable acreage planted at each farm. Formulate an LP model of the problem that will allow the cooperative to determine the quantity (acreage) of each crop that should be planted at each farm such that the total expected profit for the cooperative is maximized.

**TABLE P6-17a.**

| Farm | Water Availability (cubic feet) | Land Availability (acres) |
|---|---|---|
| 1 | 480,000 | 450 |
| 2 | 1,320,000 | 650 |
| 3 | 370,000 | 350 |
| 4 | 890,000 | 500 |

**TABLE P6-17b.**

| Crop | Farm 1 | Farm 2 | Farm 3 | Farm 4 |
|---|---|---|---|---|
| A | 200 | 300 | 100 | 250 |
| B | 150 | 200 | 150 | 100 |
| C | 200 | 350 | 200 | 300 |

18. The AJAX Fertilizer Company produces and markets a general-purpose fertilizer (10-10-10). The company produces the fertilizer at three different plants and ships the end product to four different warehouses, located at different points throughout the United States. Since some plant operations have been in existence longer than others, different production costs exist at the different plants. (The newer plants use more modern, up-to-date processes, which result in reduced production costs.) The production costs in dollars per ton and the capacity (tons) at the plants are shown in Table P6-18a.

**TABLE P6-18a.**

| Plant | Costs | Capacity |
|---|---|---|
| 1 | $38 | 650 |
| 2 | $45 | 600 |
| 3 | $30 | 600 |

The requirements (in tons) at the four warehouses are 300, 450, 500, and 600 respectively. Because each warehouse operates separately, the prices per ton at the respective warehouses differ slightly. The sales prices are $62, $63, $64, and $64. Management's objective at AJAX is to maximize the total profit for the company. Therefore, it must consider the freight cost associated with shipping from a given plant to a given warehouse. The shipping costs (expressed in dollars per ton) for the different shipping routes are shown in Table P6-18b. Formulate an LP model that will allow AJAX to meet its objective of maximizing profits.

**TABLE P6-18b.**

| Plant | Warehouse | | | |
|-------|----|----|----|----|
|       | 1  | 2  | 3  | 4  |
| 1     | 23 | 18 | 21 | 25 |
| 2     | 21 | 24 | 23 | 18 |
| 3     | 18 | 21 | 27 | 23 |

19. The H & L Manufacturing Company specializes in manufacturing parts for the automotive industry. The company currently has a capacity problem and is being forced to buy parts from a competitor company in order to meet committed demands. The problem facing the company is as follows: The company has four products; the products are made on six machines. The production times (in *hours*) required in producing the products are shown in Table P6-19. Sixty hours of time is available on each machine. H & L has a committed order of 250 units per week of each product. The costs of manufacturing the four products are $2.60, $2.25, $4.40, and $2.10. If H & L buys the parts from the outside competitor, the purchase prices are $3.15, $2.75, $4.70 and $2.30, respectively. Formulate an LP model that could be used to identify the quantities of the four products that H & L should *produce* and the quantities to *buy* in order to minimize cost.

**TABLE P6-19.**

| Product | Machine | | | | | |
|---------|------|------|------|------|------|------|
|         | #1   | #2   | #3   | #4   | #5   | #6   |
| 1       | 0.08 | 0.04 | 0.04 | 0    | 0.06 | 0.12 |
| 2       | 0    | 0.02 | 0.10 | 0.30 | 0.18 | 0.12 |
| 3       | 0.04 | 0.12 | 0    | 0.15 | 0.50 | 0.45 |
| 4       | 0.12 | 0.08 | 0.35 | 0    | 0    | 0.10 |

20. The production-line manager in an electronic firm has five jobs that must be filled. Five operators are available for assignment. The line manager has available test data that reflect a numerical productivity rating for each of the five workers on each job. These data were developed through a testing/operating exam administered by the industrial engineering department (see Table P6-20). Assuming that an operator can perform only one job, formulate a model that will provide the optimal job assignment.

**TABLE P6-20.**

| Operator Number | Job Number | | | | |
|--------|----|----|----|----|----|
|        | 1  | 2  | 3  | 4  | 5  |
| 1      | 12 | 16 | 24 | 8  | 2  |
| 2      | 6  | 8  | 20 | 14 | 6  |
| 3      | 10 | 6  | 16 | 18 | 12 |
| 4      | 2  | 4  | 2  | 24 | 20 |
| 5      | 7  | 10 | 6  | 6  | 18 |

**21.** The Reed Service Company is in the washing machine/dryer home repair business. The company services customers throughout the city. The company has five service people who live in different locations in the city. In order to save on start-of-the-day driving time and costs, the service people drive directly from their homes to the jobs. Table P6-21 indicates the distances associated with the first five jobs that must be worked. Each service person is paid for driving; therefore Reed wants to minimize the extra travel distance. Formulate the appropriate LP model.

**TABLE P6-21.**

| Service Person | Job Number | | | | |
|---|---|---|---|---|---|
| | 1 | 2 | 3 | 4 | 5 |
| 1 | 20 | 14 | 6 | 10 | 22 |
| 2 | 16 | 8 | 22 | 20 | 10 |
| 3 | 8 | 6 | 24 | 14 | 12 |
| 4 | 20 | 22 | 2 | 8 | 6 |
| 5 | 4 | 16 | 22 | 6 | 24 |

**22.** The Eat-A-Bite Fastfood Company operates a 24-hour food service. The company employs a number of individuals; each employee works 8 consecutive hours per day. Because demand varies throughout the day, the number of employees required varies throughout the day. On the basis of prior experience, the company has projected the minimum labor requirement for each 4-hour period of the day (see Table P6-22). Formulate an LP model that will indicate the minimum number of employees that will be required to staff the 24 hours of operations.

**TABLE P6-22.**

| Time | Minimum Number of Employees Required |
|---|---|
| 12:00 midnight to 4:00 A.M. | 3 |
| 4:00 A.M. to 8:00 A.M. | 5 |
| 8:00 A.M. to 12:00 noon | 10 |
| 12:00 noon to 4:00 P.M. | 6 |
| 4:00 P.M. to 8:00 P.M. | 10 |
| 8:00 P.M. to 12:00 midnight | 8 |

**23.** The Riccardo Manufacturing Company is considering expanding plant capacity over the next eight quarters. The company's objective is to have its plant capacity as large as possible at the end of two years (at the end of the eight quarters).

The company produces a single product. Raw material and other variable costs amount to $120 per unit. Each unit produced requires 1.2 units of production capacity. All costs and production requirements occur in a single period; sales occur in the immediate following period. Each unit sells for $175.

For expansion purposes (in any period) the company has two policies; either or both policies can be employed. Under policy 1, each unit of added capacity requires $24,000 at the beginning of the period; the new capacity is available for use at the beginning of the following period. Each unit of capacity added under policy 2 requires $18,000 at the beginning of the period in which the expansion is started, but the capacity is not available until the beginning of the period after the following one.

The company has $320,000 at the beginning of period 1. These dollars are to be used for financing production and plant expansion. After period 1, no additional "outside" funding is available. Both production and plant expansion, after period 1, must be financed from the material fund or sales generated funds. At the beginning of period 1, a total of 960 units of capacity are operational. All expansion must be operational by the end of period 8. Formulate an LP model that will indicate the number of assets of capacity that Riccardo should add each quarter and the construction policy(s) to employ in the expansion.

24. The BL & C Paper Company manufactures paper for sale to commercial vendors. The company produces a "standard" 120-inch width roll of paper; however, all orders are not necessarily for this width. The company frequently receives orders for narrower rolls. To satisfy these orders, the narrower rolls are cut from the standard roll. For the coming month the company has committed orders for the following number of rolls:

| Roll Width | Orders |
|---|---|
| 80 in. | 1800 |
| 70 in. | 500 |
| 60 in. | 1200 |
| 50 in. | 1400 |

BL & C would like to determine the minimum number of standard rolls that will be required to satisfy this demand. Formulate an appropriate LP model for the problem.

25. The D. M. Riddle Company is a retailer of novelty products. The company is considering adding two new products to its existing product line. The company has decided to carry the products on a two-year trial basis. Both products will be purchased from a wholesaler. The cost per unit for each product over the two-year time horizon is shown in Table P6-25. Product 1 will sell for $1.20 and product 2 will sell for $1.05. The selling price will be fixed for the two-year time period.

**TABLE P6-25.**

| Product | Cost | | Sales | |
|---|---|---|---|---|
| | Year 1 | Year 2 | Year 1 | Year 2 |
| 1 | $0.75 | $0.80 | 6 units | 7 units |
| 2 | $0.70 | $0.85 | 9 units | 12 units |

The company recognizes that sales of the new products will depend strongly on advertising. The advertising department has projected the sales over the next two years. These projections, expressed as units sold per dollar of advertising, are also shown in Table P6-25. The advertising department has also projected that in both years at least 30% but no more than 60% of the total units sold (both products) will be product type 2.

At the beginning of year 1, the company has $12,000 available for *advertising* and *purchasing*. Products may be purchased in one year and held until the following year without incurring holding costs. Advertising in any one year impacts sales only in that year. Purchasing and advertising expenses in year 2 can be funded from earnings in year 1. Riddle would like to develop a model that will reflect the dollars of advertising and purchasing that should be expended in each of the next two years in order to maximize total profit over the two-year period.

**26.** The B. H. Billings Company is a large roofing contractor. Since the price of shingles changes with the seasons of the year, the company tries to build up a stock of shingles when prices are low and store them for use at a later date. The company charges the current market price for the shingles when they are installed, regardless of when they were purchased. Table P6-26 reflects what the company has projected as the cost, price, and demand for shingles over the next four seasons. When the shingles are purchased in one season and stored for use in a later season, a handling cost of $6 per 1,000 squares is incurred as well as a storage cost of $12 per 1,000 squares for each season stored. A maximum of 220,000 squares can be stored in the warehouse; this includes material purchased for use in the same period. The company has set a policy that no materials will be held longer than four seasons. Formulate a model for the problem that will allow Billings to maximize its profits over the four-season time period.

**TABLE P6-26.**

| Season | Purchase Price ($ per square) | Market Price ($ per square) | Sales (000's of squares) |
|--------|------------------------------|-----------------------------|--------------------------|
| Summer | 21.00 | 22.00 | 100 |
| Autumn | 22.00 | 23.25 | 140 |
| Winter | 26.00 | 28.50 | 200 |
| Spring | 24.00 | 25.50 | 160 |

# LP Simplex Method

## ■ Introduction

In Chapter 5 we presented an introduction to linear programming, discussed the formulation of a linear model (i.e., the development of an objective function, constraints, and nonnegativity conditions), identified the assumptions that underlie the use of linear programming, and described the use of a graphical method for solving LP problems. We have pointed out that the graphical method is limited to solving problems with two variables, and noted that linear programming problems with numerous variables and/or constraints can be solved by using a mathematical procedure (algorithm) known as the simplex method. The objective of this chapter is to provide a detailed, step-by-step examination of the simplex method. This should provide a better understanding of linear programming and some of the special conditions that can be encountered in employing the simplex method.

## ■ Review

In Chapter 5 we used the Agro-Tech Inc. problem to present many of the basic linear programming concepts. Since many of those concepts support the conceptual base on which the simplex method builds, it is appropriate to review the Agro-Tech example.

Recall that we defined

$$x_1 = \text{tons of 5-5-10 fertilizer produced}$$

$$x_2 = \text{tons of 5-10-5 fertilizer produced}$$

We then formulated the problem as follows:

MAXIMIZE: $\quad Z = 18.5x_1 + 20x_2$ $\hfill$ (7.1)

SUBJECT TO: $\quad .05x_1 + .05x_2 \leq 1100$ $\hfill$ (7.2)

$\quad\quad\quad\quad .05x_1 + .10x_2 \leq 1800$ $\hfill$ (7.3)

$\quad\quad\quad\quad .10x_1 + .05x_2 \leq 2000$ $\hfill$ (7.4)

$\quad\quad\quad\quad x_1, x_2 \geq 0$ $\hfill$ (7.5)

By employing three slack variables, $s_1$, $s_2$, and $s_3$, we converted the inequality constraints to equalities. Recall that $s_1$ is the amount (in tons) of unused nitrate, $s_2$ is the amount (in tons) of unused phosphate, and $s_3$ is the amount (in tons) of unused potash, when $x_1$ tons of 5-5-10 and $x_2$ tons of 5-10-5 are produced. The revised model was expressed as

MAXIMIZE:
$$Z = 18.5x_1 + 20x_2 + 0s_1 + 0s_2 + 0s_3 \tag{7.6}$$

SUBJECT TO:
$$.05x_1 + .05x_2 + s_1 \qquad\qquad = 1100 \tag{7.7}$$

$$.05x_1 + .10x_2 \qquad + s_2 \qquad = 1800 \tag{7.8}$$

$$.10x_1 + .05x_2 \qquad\qquad + s_3 = 2000 \tag{7.9}$$

$$x_1, x_2, s_1, s_2, s_3 \geq 0 \tag{7.10}$$

*basic solution*

*nonbasic variables*
*basic variables*
*basic feasible solution*
*optimal solution*

Using this equation form of the model, we then developed several important concepts. First, we noted that if for a given problem (model) there are $n$ variables (5 in our case) and $m$ equations (3 in our case, since we exclude nonnegativity conditions), then a **basic solution** to the problem can be obtained by setting $n - m$ of the variables to zero and solving the resulting $m$ equations simultaneously. We defined the $(n - m)$ variables that were set to zero as **nonbasic variables,** while the $m$ variables used in the solution process were labeled **basic variables.** A key point we noted in the discussion was that if all the basic variables for a basic solution are nonnegative, then the solution is termed a **basic feasible solution** and corresponds to a vertex of the feasible region. Finally, we noted that the basic feasible solution that has the greatest objective value (in a maximization problem) is the **optimal solution.**

For the Agro-Tech case we computed all the basic solutions; recall that ten basic solutions exist. These were summarized in Table 5-2; for convenience we present these ten solutions again, as Table 7-1.

**TABLE 7-1.**
**Basic Solutions to Agro-Tech Inc. Problem**

| Solution No. | Variables | | | | | Objective Function Z |
|---|---|---|---|---|---|---|
| | $x_1$ | $x_2$ | $s_1$ | $s_2$ | $s_3$ | |
| 1 | 0 | 0 | 1,100 | 1,800 | 2,000 | $0 |
| 2 | 0 | 22,000 | 0 | −400 | 900 | Not feasible |
| 3 | 0 | 18,000 | 200 | 0 | 1,100 | $360,000 |
| 4 | 0 | 40,000 | −900 | −2,200 | 0 | Not feasible |
| 5 | 36,000 | 0 | −700 | 0 | −1,600 | Not feasible |
| 6 | 20,000 | 0 | 100 | 800 | 0 | $370,000 |
| 7 | 22,000 | 0 | 0 | 900 | −200 | Not feasible |
| 8 | 8,000 | 14,000 | 0 | 0 | 500 | $428,000 |
| 9 | 18,000 | 4,000 | 0 | 500 | 0 | $413,000 |
| 10 | 14,666.6 | 10,666.6 | −166.6 | 0 | 0 | Not feasible |

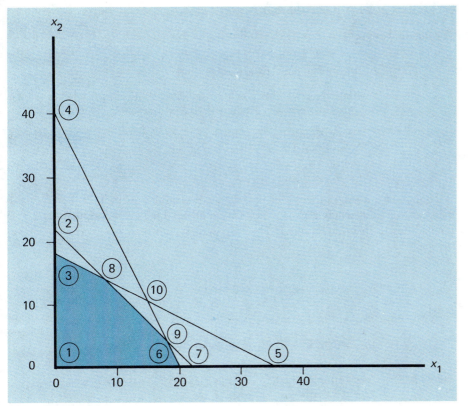

FIGURE 7-1.
Graphical Plot of
Agro-Tech Inc.
Problem

Graphically, this solution set is represented as shown in Figure 7-1. (This is a duplication of Figure 5-5.) If the objective function [equation (7.1)] is plotted on a graph, it can be verified that solution 8 is the optimal solution.

## ■ The simplex method

From the above discussion it is obvious that in searching for an optimal solution it is neither desirable nor necessary to examine all basic solutions for a given set of $m$ equations with $n$ unknowns. Since the vertices of the feasible region correspond to the basic feasible solutions, it is only necessary to examine these vertices. A desirable solution process thus would be a process that (1) moves from one vertex to another in such a way that each new vertex is an improvement over (or at least no worse than) the previous vertex and (2) stops when the optimal solution has been reached. As we indicated earlier, this is precisely how the simplex method (algorithm) works. Before we introduce the simplex method, however, we will examine an algebraic approach. The **algebraic approach** has many of the basic characteristics of the simplex method and well illustrates the workings of the algorithm.

*algebraic approach*

## An algebraic approach

The algebraic approach requires the following steps:

1.  Identify an initial basic feasible solution.

2.  Determine whether a better feasible solution exists. If a better solution exists, perform step 3; otherwise, the present solution is optimal.

3.  Move to the better feasible solution by exchanging a nonbasic variable for a basic variable, while keeping all variables nonnegative, then return to step 2.

To demonstrate the process, let us once again examine Agro-Tech Inc. We will begin at the point where slack variables have been added to the original constraint inequalities to form equations (7.7), (7.8), and (7.9), which we repeat for convenience.

$$.05x_1 + .05x_2 + s_1 \qquad\qquad = 1100 \qquad\qquad (7.7)$$

$$.05x_1 + .10x_2 \quad + s_2 \quad = 1800 \qquad\qquad (7.8)$$

$$.10x_1 + .05x_2 \qquad\quad + s_3 = 2000 \qquad\qquad (7.9)$$

An obvious initial solution is to set $x_1 = 0$, $x_2 = 0$, in which case we get

$$s_1 = 1100, \qquad s_2 = 1800, \qquad \text{and} \qquad s_3 = 2000$$

This solution corresponds to point 1 in Figure 7-1, which is a basic feasible solution since it lies on the feasible region. However, it is not a very profitable solution. In fact, the profit is zero! We would, therefore, like to look for a better solution.

First, let us rewrite equations (7.7)–(7.9) in a slightly different form as equations (7.11), (7.12), and (7.13).

$$s_1 = 1100 - .05x_1 - .05x_2 \qquad\qquad (7.11)$$

$$s_2 = 1800 - .05x_1 - .10x_2 \qquad\qquad (7.12)$$

$$s_3 = 2000 - .10x_1 - .05x_2 \qquad\qquad (7.13)$$

Now recall that the objective function was

MAXIMIZE:     $Z = 18.5x_1 + 20x_2 + 0s_1 + 0s_2 + 0s_3$

We can now substitute the expressions (7.11), (7.12), and (7.13) for $s_1$, $s_2$, and $s_3$ into this objective function. We then end up with

$$Z = 18.5x_1 + 20x_2 + 0(1100 - .05x_1 - .05x_2)$$
$$+ 0(1800 - .05x_1 - .10x_2)$$
$$+ 0(2000 - .10x_1 - .05x_2)$$
$$= 18.5x_1 + 20x_2$$

(7.14)

It would appear that we have accomplished very little from this maneuver, but be patient. We now have the equations set up, so we can consider other solutions. (This process will be repeated each time we examine a different solution.)

We already know that to find any basic solution for Agro-Tech Inc., we simply set two variables to zero and solve for the remaining three. To get another basic solution from our current solution ($s_1 = 1100$, $s_2 = 1800$, $s_3 = 2000$, $x_1 = 0$, and $x_2 = 0$), we will exchange one basic variable with one nonbasic variable. If we are to be assured that the new basic solution is a **basic feasible solution** (that is, that all variables are greater than or equal to zero), we must check this factor in our exchange process. Since $x_1$ and $x_2$ are now nonbasic variables, the question that must be answered is: *Which nonbasic variable should be chosen to be made basic?* If we examine our objective function (7.14) at this point, we note that the coefficient of $x_2$ (20.0) is larger than the coefficient of $x_1$ (18.5). This indicates that a larger per-unit increase in Z will result if we choose to make $x_2$ basic. Therefore, we will increase $x_2$ from zero, keeping $x_1$ at zero, and reduce either $s_1$, $s_2$, or $s_3$ to zero. One of these will become a nonbasic variable.

*basic feasible solution*

Once we have decided *which* variable to make basic, the questions are: *How large can we make the new basic variable?* and *Which current basic variable will become nonbasic?* Recall that a *basic feasible solution* requires that all variables have nonnegative values. If we make $x_2$ too large, then $s_1$, $s_2$, or $s_3$ may become negative. We can avoid this by examining the equation set (7.11)–(7.13) for $s_1$, $s_2$, and $s_3$. Examining equation (7.11), we note that as $x_2$ increases from zero to a positive value, $s_1$ starts to decrease since

$$s_1 = 1100 - .05x_1 - .05x_2$$

As $x_2$ becomes larger and larger, $s_1$ becomes smaller and smaller. If $x_2$ were made large enough, eventually $s_1$ would become negative. This, however, would be undesirable since, for the solution to be basic feasible, all variables, including $s_1$, must be greater than or equal to zero. Thus equation (7.11) indicates that we can make $x_2$ no larger than

$$\frac{1,100}{.05} = 22,000$$

(7.15)

If we examine equations (7.12) and (7.13) in a similar manner, we see that (7.12) constrains $x_2$ to be no larger than

$$\frac{1,800}{.10} = 18,000 \qquad (7.16)$$

and (7.13) requires $x_2$ to be less than or equal to

$$\frac{2,000}{.05} = 40,000 \qquad (7.17)$$

Note that (7.16) is the equation that limits $x_2$ most strictly, and that when $x_2$ has a value of 18,000, $s_2$ becomes zero.

We now know that $x_1$ and $s_2$ are the new nonbasic variables and the new basic variables are $x_2$, $s_1$, and $s_3$; therefore, the final step in our solution process is to solve for $x_2$, $s_1$, and $s_3$, in terms of $x_1$ and $s_2$. We begin by solving equations (7.11)–(7.14) such that $x_2$, $s_1$, and $s_3$ are expressed in terms of $x_1$ and $s_2$. To accomplish this, we can use equation (7.12) to solve for $x_2$ in terms of $x_1$ and $s_2$. Thus we have

$$.10x_2 = 1,800 - .05x_1 - s_2$$

$$x_2 = \frac{1,800 - .05x_1 - s_2}{.10} \qquad (7.18)$$

$$= 18,000 - .5x_1 - 10s_2$$

Substituting equation (7.18) into equation (7.11), we have

$$s_1 = 1,100 - .05x_1 - .05(18,000 - .5x_1 - 10s_2)$$

$$= 200 - .025x_1 + .5s_2 \qquad (7.19)$$

Substituting equation (7.18) into equation (7.13), we have

$$s_3 = 2,000 - .10x_1 - .05(18,000 - .5x_1 - 10s_2)$$

$$= 1,100 - .075x_1 + .5s_2 \qquad (7.20)$$

When we substitute equation (7.18) into the prior objective function, equation (7.14), we have

$$Z = 18.5x_1 + 20(18,000 - .5x_1 - 10s_2)$$

$$= 360,000 + 8.5x_1 - 200s_2 \qquad (7.21)$$

The new representation of our system of equations thus becomes

$$x_2 = 18,000 - .5x_1 - 10s_2 \qquad (7.18)$$

$$s_1 = 200 - .025x_1 + .5s_2 \qquad (7.19)$$

$$s_3 = 1,100 - .075x_1 + .5s_2 \tag{7.20}$$

$$Z = 360,000 + 8.5x_1 - 200s_2 \tag{7.21}$$

Setting $x_1$ and $s_2$ equal to zero, the basic feasible solution corresponding to this system of equalities is

$$x_1 = 0 \qquad x_2 = 18,000$$

$$s_1 = 200 \qquad s_2 = 0 \qquad s_3 = 1,100$$

The value of Z for this solution set is $360,000.

Referring to Figure 7-1, note that the above basic feasible solution corresponds to point 3. In our analysis of determining the values for $x_2$, had we allowed $x_2$ to equal 22,000, based on equation (7.15), the resulting solution would have been point 2 on Figure 7-1. Similarly, had we allowed $x_2$ to equal 40,000, on the basis of equation (7.17), the resulting solution would have been point 4. Both points 2 and 4 are not feasible solutions since they lie outside the feasible region. Therefore, we were correct in restricting $x_2$ to equal 18,000, on the basis of equation (7.16).

We now have a solution that will result in a profit of $360,000, but if we examine the objective function in our new set of equations, we find that profit can be increased further. In equation (7.21), $x_1$ has a positive coefficient, while $s_2$ has a negative coefficient. So, if we increase $x_1$ from zero, Z will increase $8.5 for each unit change in $x_1$; while, if we increase $s_2$ from zero, Z will decrease $200 for each unit change in $s_2$. Profit thus can be increased by making $x_1$ a basic variable. Note that no longer is there an $18.5 increase in profit for each unit increase in $x_1$; the profit increase is now $8.5. The reason for this decrease in the per-unit profit contribution can be seen by examining equation (7.18), where we can see that an increase in $x_1$ will *decrease* the production of $x_2$, thereby decreasing the total profit contribution from $x_2$. We will earn $18.5 for the ton of $x_1$ produced, but we will, at the same time, *lose* $(.5) \times (\$20) = \$10$ per ton because we are producing less $x_2$. The net increase is then $\$18.5 - \$10 = \$8.5$ per ton of $x_1$ produced.

Just as before, the task now is to determine the amount $x_1$ can be increased without forcing any other variables to become negative. Examining equations (7.18)–(7.20) and setting $s_2$ equal to zero, since this variable will remain nonbasic, we note that equation (7.19) limits $x_1$ to $200/.025 = 8,000$, equation (7.18) limits $x_1$ to $18,000/.5 = 36,000$, and equation (7.20) limits $x_1$ to $1,100/.075 = 14,666.6$. Taking the minimum of these units, we set $x_1 = 8,000$, which will cause $s_1$ to become zero and thus the new nonbasic variable. This means that we must now solve the set of equations for $x_1$, $x_2$, and $s_3$. Since equation (7.19) was used to determine the limit on $x_1$ and to identify the new nonbasic variable, we can use this equation to determine our new arrangement of the equations. When revised, equation (7.19) becomes

$$x_1 = \frac{200 - s_1 + .5s_2}{.025} \tag{7.22}$$

$$= 8,000 - 40s_1 + 20s_2$$

Substituting this equation into the remaining equations (7.18), (7.20), and (7.21), the new set of equations is

$$x_1 = 8,000 - 40s_1 + 20s_2 \tag{7.22}$$

$$x_2 = 14,000 + 20s_1 - 20s_2 \tag{7.23}$$

$$s_3 = 500 + 3s_1 - 1.0s_2 \tag{7.24}$$

$$Z = 428,000 - 340s_1 - 30s_2 \tag{7.25}$$

Setting $s_1$ and $s_2$ equal to zero, we find that the basic feasible solution for this set of equations is

$$x_1 = 8,000 \qquad s_1 = 0$$

$$x_2 = 14,000 \qquad s_2 = 0 \qquad s_3 = 500$$

The profit associated with this solution is \$428,000. This solution matches point 8 in Figure 7-1.

By examining equation (7.25), the objective function in the revised set of equations, we can determine if we should continue looking for a better solution. Observing equation (7.25), we note that the coefficients of both $s_1$ and $s_2$ are negative. This tells us that any increase in either of these nonbasic variables will result in a decrease in profits. The current basic feasible solution is, therefore, the optimal feasible solution. In examining Figure 7-1 we note that this conclusion is in agreement with the graphical solution.

## The simplex tableau

The simplex method (algorithm) uses exactly the same logic we have just employed with the algebraic approach. The only difference is that the problem being solved is written in a tabular or table format rather than in the form of equations. The advantage of the tabular format is that it is computationally easier to handle and avoids the task of continually rewriting variables and equations.

*simplex method*     The first step in applying the **simplex method** (as was the case for the algebraic method) is to transform all inequality constraints to equalities by adding slack variables and subtracting surplus variables. Using Agro-Tech Inc. as our example once again, recall that our transformed problem was expressed as follows:

MAXIMIZE:      $Z = 18.5x_1 + 20x_2 + 0s_1 + 0s_2 + 0s_3$ $\tag{7.6}$

SUBJECT TO:     $.05x_1 + .05x_2 + s_1 \qquad\qquad = 1100$ $\tag{7.7}$

$$.05x_1 + .10x_2 \qquad + s_2 \qquad = 1800 \tag{7.8}$$

$$.10x_1 + .05x_2 \qquad\qquad + s_3 = 2000 \tag{7.9}$$

$$x_1, x_2, s_1, s_2, s_3 \geq 0 \tag{7.10}$$

In order to identify the first or initial tableau, we must know which variables will be basic and which will be nonbasic. In our previous analysis of the Agro-Tech problem we selected $s_1$, $s_2$, and $s_3$ to be the initial basic variables. This selection was not by chance. These variables were selected because in setting $x_1$ and $x_2$ to zero we could immediately write the solution to the set of equations. However, identifying an initial basic feasible solution may not always be this obvious unless one employs certain procedures to identify the basic variables. The most efficient procedure for this is to look for an $m \times m$ *identity matrix* within the constraint coefficients.[1] Writing the coefficients of our constraints in a tabular form, we have

| $x_1$ | $x_2$ | $s_1$ | $s_2$ | $s_3$ |
|------|------|------|------|------|
| .05 | .05 | 1 | 0 | 0 |
| .05 | .10 | 0 | 1 | 0 |
| .10 | .05 | 0 | 0 | 1 |

Since the coefficients of $s_1$, $s_2$, and $s_3$ form a $3 \times 3$ identity matrix, we know that if these are selected to be basic variables, while $x_1$ and $x_2$ are labeled nonbasic, then we can immediately write the solution to the problem by looking at the right-hand-side values of the constraints (in this case 1100, 1800, and 2000).

This process of selecting an identity matrix will always result in an initial basic feasible solution and will always provide the first step of basic variables. However, adding slack variables and subtracting surplus variables from inequality constraints, in order to produce equality constraints, will not always produce an identity matrix within the constraint coefficients. It may be necessary to add other variables (artificial variables) in order to complete the matrix. But since our coefficient matrix does contain the appropriate identity matrix, we will delay discussing this point.

Given that we know which variables are *basic* and which are *nonbasic*, we are ready to transfer the objective function and constraint set into the simplex tableau. The initial tableau is shown in Table 7-2, which is a repeat of Table 5-3. A detailed explanation of the general structure of the tableau was given in Chapter 5; however, we will quickly review this information. Recall that the objective function coefficients are transferred directly into the $c_j$ **row** and reflect the per-unit contribution to the objective. Likewise, the coefficients of the constraints are transferred directly into the body of the tableau, under the appropriate variable heading. The right-hand-side values from the constraint equations are transferred to the column labeled *Right-hand Side (Solution)*. Recall also that the column labeled *Variables in the Basis* refers to the set of basic variables that make up the basic feasible solution. For this particular tableau, these are $s_1$, $s_2$, and $s_3$. Finally, the $c_B$ column contains the objective-function coefficients of the variables in the **basis;** and, since $s_1$, $s_2$, and $s_3$ are in the basis, these are zero.

$c_j$ *row*

*basis*

The above information is transferred directly into the initial tableau and the shaded portions of the tableau are simply row and column descriptive headings.

---

[1] An $m \times m$ identity matrix is a grouping of $m$ rows and $m$ columns, in which the elements (or numbers) along the diagonal contain 1's and the remaining elements are zero. Refer to Chapter 2.

**TABLE 7-2.**
**Initial Simplex**
**Tableau**

| $c_j \rightarrow$ | | | 18.5 | 20.0 | 0 | 0 | 0 | Contribution per Unit |
|---|---|---|---|---|---|---|---|---|
| $c_B$ | Variables in the Basis | Right-hand Side (Solution) | $x_1$ | $x_2$ | $s_1$ | $s_2$ | $s_3$ | Heading and Variables |
| 0 | $s_1$ | 1100 | .05 | .05 | 1 | 0 | 0 | |
| 0 | $s_2$ | 1800 | .05 | .10 | 0 | 1 | 0 | Coefficients |
| 0 | $s_3$ | 2000 | .10 | .05 | 0 | 0 | 1 | |
| | $z_j$ | 0 | 0 | 0 | 0 | 0 | 0 | Contribution Lost per Unit Produced |
| | $c_j - z_j$ | | 18.5 | 20.0 | 0 | 0 | 0 | Net Contribution per Unit Produced |

$z_j$ *row*

Therefore, the only portions of the initial tableau that are computed are the $z_j$ **row** and the $(c_j - z_j)$ row. The row labeled $z_j$ is computed by summing the products of the coefficients in the $c_B$ column times the coefficients in the associated variable column $(x_1, x_2, s_1, s_2, s_3)$. For example,

$$z_1 = (0)(.05) + (0)(.05) + (0)(.10) = 0$$

$$z_2 = (0)(.05) + (0)(.10) + (0)(.05) = 0$$

The values for each of the $z_j$'s are zero in this particular tableau since the objective function coefficients of the variables in the $c_B$ column are zero.

The $z_j$ values can be described as "contribution lost per unit produced," since each $z_j$ value is found by summing the cross-products of the physical rates of substitution and the profit associated with the respective basic variables. The physical rate of substitution indicates the number of units of a basic variable that must be given up to produce one unit of a nonbasic variable. By taking the product of a physical rate of substitution and the corresponding basic profit, we find the profit that will be lost on that basic variable to produce one unit of the nonbasic variable. By summing the cross-products, we find the total profit contribution that will have to be given up to produce one unit of a nonbasic variable.

The Z value, or the objective function value, for the solution is shown in the tableau as the bottom entry in the *Right-hand Side (Solution)* column. For this tableau this value is zero since zero profits result from $s_1 = 1100$, $s_2 = 1800$, and $s_3 = 2000$. Recall that the Z value is calculated by summing the products of the $c_B$ coefficients and the solution values of the variables in the basis. For example, in this case Z = 0(1100) + 0(1800) + 0(2000) = 0.

$(c_j - z_j)$ *row*

Recall also that the last row of the tableau, the $(c_j - z_j)$ **row**, is computed by subtracting the $z_j$ value from the $c_j$ value for each respective variable column. This is the difference between the gain $(c_j)$ and the loss $(z_j)$ arising from one unit of $x_j$ being produced. In essence, this row reflects the *net improvement* in the objective function for a one-unit increase in the value of each variable.

## Improving the solution

When we discussed the algebraic process, we found that it was necessary at each step of the process to test for optimality. If the existing solution was not optimal, a new basic feasible solution was generated by (1) determining which nonbasic variable would be made basic, that is, which variable should be brought into the basis; (2) determining which variable should be replaced, that is, which variable should be removed from the basis; and (3) solving the new set of equations for the new basic variables. This same solution process is employed in the simplex method, but in a slightly refined manner, which makes the computations a little easier.

The $(c_j - z_j)$ row in the tableau is used to determine if the optimal solution has been reached and, if not, which variable should be brought into the basis. The numbers in the $(c_j - z_j)$ row reflect the change in the objective function that will result from having one unit of variable $x_j$ in the basis. In the initial tableau, the $(c_j - z_j)$ row indicates that the objective function will increase \$18.5 for each ton of $x_1$ produced; \$20.0 for each ton of $x_2$ produced; 0 dollars for each ton of $s_1$; 0 dollars for each ton of $s_2$; and 0 dollars for each ton of $s_3$. (Recall that the units on the variables $x_1$, $x_2$, $s_1$, $s_2$, and $s_3$ were expressed in tons.) Since the objective is to *maximize Z*, the variable that results in the largest per-unit increase in the objective function should be selected as the **incoming variable.** In this example, $x_2$ is the incoming basic variable since the objective function will increase by \$20.0 for each ton of $x_2$ produced. If, in examining the $(c_j - z_j)$ row, all quantities in the row are either zero or negative, then the solution is optimal. Under these conditions, bringing any additional variables into the basis will not increase profits. In terms of the algebraic approach, the $(c_j - z_j)$ value for each variable is the same as the coefficient of that variable in the objective function equation at each iteration.

*incoming variable*

The procedure for determining which variable to bring into the basis can be summarized as follows:

> **Step 1.** The selection of a variable to enter the basis is based upon the values in the $(c_j - z_j)$ row of the tableau. Assuming this row has been examined for optimality and some positive value(s) exist, select the variable with the largest positive value. Label the column associated with the variable the incoming column. The selected variable is the incoming (new) variable.

In certain cases it may be such that no single $(c_j - z_j)$ value is largest, but rather two or more may have equal values. For example, if the $(c_j - z_j)$ value for $x_1$ were changed from 18.5 to 20.0, the $(c_j - z_j)$ values for $x_1$ and $x_2$ would be equal. In the case of ties, it is acceptable to select arbitrarily either of the variables for entry into the basis.

As was the case with the algebraic method, once we have decided which variable to bring into the basis, the next step is to determine which variable in the basis should

*outgoing*
*variable*

be removed. The procedure for identifying the **outgoing variable** is to divide the *Right-hand Side* column by the positive coefficients in the incoming $x_j$ column (that is, exclude negative and zero coefficients) and select the variable with the minimum ratio. If a tie results for the minimum ratio, either row may be selected as the outgoing variable.

To get a better understanding of the process for determining the outgoing variable, we can examine the coefficients in the body of the tableau. These coefficients, as indicated earlier, are *physical rates of substitution*. For example, the coefficients associated with $x_1$, namely .05, .05, and .10, indicate that to get one ton of 5-5-10 fertilizer ($x_1$), it is necessary to give up .05 ton of nitrate, .05 ton of phosphate, and .10 ton of potash. (Recall that the remaining materials in the mixture are inert ingredients that are readily available at no cost.) To produce one ton of $x_2$, one must give up .05 ton of nitrate, .10 ton of phosphate, and .05 ton of potash. Since we decided in step 1 to bring $x_2$ into the basis, these latter coefficients will be used to determine which variable will be removed from the basis.

To produce a ton of $x_2$ requires the use of nitrate, phosphate, and potash. Currently we have 1,100 tons of nitrate ($s_1 = 1,100$), 1,800 tons of phosphate ($s_2 = 1,800$), and 2,000 tons of potash ($s_3 = 2,000$). If the production of one ton of $x_2$ required only nitrate and inert ingredients, we could determine the quantity of $x_2$ to produce by simply dividing 1,100 by the physical rate of substitution of nitrate for $x_2$ (i.e., $1,100/.05 = 22,000$). But since the production of $x_2$ also requires phosphate and potash, we must also examine these ratios. The ratios for all three ingredients are summarized in Table 7-3, which indicates that a maximum of 18,000 tons of $x_2$ can be produced. Attempting to produce more than 18,000 tons will require more phosphate than is available. Producing exactly 18,000 tons of $x_2$ will consume all the phosphate, causing $s_2$ to become zero and leave the basis. Note that this is identical to choosing the variable to set to zero in the algebraic procedure.

The procedure for determining which variable will leave the basis is summarized in step 2.

**Step 2.**   The variable to leave the basis is selected by dividing the positive coefficients in the incoming variable column (that is, the positive coefficients of the variable entering the basis) into the associated quantities in (that is, those in the same row) the Right-hand Side column. Select the row with the smallest nonnegative ratio as the row to be replaced. This outgoing row is associated with the variable that will leave the basis.

**TABLE 7-3.**
**Ingredient Ratios**
**for 5-10-5**
**Fertilizer**

| Row | Right-hand Side (Solution) | $x_2$ Coefficient | Ratio |
|-----|----------------------------|-------------------|-------|
| 1 | 1,100 | .05 | 22,000 |
| 2 | 1,800 | .10 | 18,000 |
| 3 | 2,000 | .05 | 40,000 |

Having decided which variable to bring into the basis and which to remove, the next step in the simplex method is to update the coefficients in the body of the new tableau to reflect the change in the basic variables. Before beginning this process, let us reexamine the procedure used in the algebraic method. Recall that once we decided which variable was to enter the basis and which was to leave, we restructured our equations such that the basic variables were defined in terms of the nonbasic variables. At the second iteration of the solution, the equations were expressed as follows:

$$x_2 = 18,000 - \quad .5x_1 - 10s_2 \tag{7.18}$$

$$s_1 = \quad 200 - .025x_1 + .5s_2 \tag{7.19}$$

$$s_3 = \quad 1,100 - .075x_1 + .5s_2 \tag{7.20}$$

Using basic algebraic operations, we can rearrange these equations such that all variables are on the right side of the equal sign. To put the equations in the same order as they will appear in the new tableau, we will place equation (7.18) below equation (7.19). The alternate set of equations is

$$18,000 = + \quad .5x_1 + 1x_2 + 0s_1 + 10s_2 + 0s_3 \tag{7.18a}$$

$$200 = + .025x_1 + 0x_2 + 1s_1 - .5s_2 + 0s_3 \tag{7.19a}$$

$$1,100 = + .075x_1 + 0x_2 + 0s_1 - .5s_2 + 1s_3 \tag{7.20a}$$

Recall that we solved the original set of equations by setting the nonbasic variables to zero. If we set $x_1$ and $s_2$ to zero in this alternate equation set, then we immediately know that $s_1 = 200$, $x_2 = 18,000$, and $s_3 = 1,100$. The fact that allows us to write the solution to the set of equations immediately is that the coefficients associated with the basic variables form an identity matrix. (Note the coefficients associated with $s_1$, $x_2$, and $s_3$ in the alternate equation set.) This result suggests that in moving from tableau to tableau in the simplex method one should seek to transform the incoming variable so that the elements of the associated column of the identity matrix result. This is precisely what occurs in the tableau updating process.

Referring to the initial simplex tableau (Table 7-2), we note that the coefficients associated with $s_2$ in the body of the tableau make up the column vector $\begin{bmatrix} 0 \\ 1 \\ 0 \end{bmatrix}$. Since $x_2$ is the new incoming variable and $s_2$ is the outgoing variable, the coefficients for $x_2$ in the updated tableau should contain this same column vector of zeros and ones. We can achieve this by a two-step row operation.

The use of row operations to update the tableau for the new basic variables is called *pivoting*. The **pivot element** is the element at the intersection of the *incoming column* (that is, the variable entering the basis) and the *outgoing row* (that is, the variable leaving the basis). In the initial tableau, the pivot element, located at the intersection of the $x_2$ column and the $s_2$ row, is .10. The first step in pivoting is to

*pivot element*

divide the outgoing row by the pivot element. The resulting row is termed the *replacing row*. For Agro-Tech Inc., this gives

$$\frac{1,800}{.10} = 18,000; \quad \frac{.05}{.10} = .5; \quad \frac{.10}{.10} = 1, \quad \frac{0}{.10} = 0; \quad \frac{1}{.10} = 10, \quad \frac{0}{.10} = 0$$

The new row is entered in Tableau II, Table 7-4. The procedure for updating the outgoing row can be summarized as follows:

**Step 3.** Initial updating of the tableau is begun by transforming the row associated with the outgoing variable. The transformation begins by labeling the element at the intersection of the *incoming column* and the *outgoing row* as the *pivot element*. The updated row (the *replacing row*) for the new tableau is computed by dividing all coefficients and the Right-hand Side value by the pivot element.

It may not be obvious at this point, but the row operation for updating the outgoing row is identical to the process used in the algebraic method. In the algebraic method we began with equations (7.11), (7.12), and (7.13):

$$s_1 = 1100 - .05x_1 - .05x_2 \tag{7.11}$$

$$s_2 = 1800 - .05x_1 - .10x_2 \tag{7.12}$$

$$s_3 = 2000 - .10x_1 - .05x_2 \tag{7.13}$$

Having decided that $x_2$ was the new incoming basic variable and $s_2$ was the outgoing variable, we solved equation (7.12) for $x_2$. This provided equation (7.18):

$$x_2 = \frac{1800 - .05x_1 - s_2}{.10}$$

**TABLE 7-4.**
**Tableau II**

| $c_B$ | Variables in the Basis | Right-hand Side (Solution) | 18.5 $x_1$ | 20.0 $x_2$ | 0 $s_1$ | 0 $s_2$ | 0 $s_3$ |
|---|---|---|---|---|---|---|---|
| 0 | $s_1$ | 200 | .025 | 0 | 1 | −.5 | 0 |
| 20 | $x_2$ | 18,000 | .5 | 1 | 0 | 10 | 0 |
| 0 | $s_3$ | 1,100 | .075 | 0 | 0 | −.5 | 1 |
| | $z_j$ | 360,000 | 10 | 20 | 0 | 200 | 0 |
| | $c_j - z_j$ | | 8.5 | 0 | 0 | −200 | 0 |

or

$$x_2 = 18,000 - 0.5x_1 - 10s_2 \qquad (7.18)$$

Note that $x_2$ is computed by simply dividing the old equation (outgoing row) by the element associated with the incoming variable (pivot element). This is the same procedure used in the solution process. If we wish to rearrange equation (7.18) to appear identical to the second row of Tableau II (Table 7-4) we perform basic algebraic operations; thus,

$$-18,000 = -.5x_1 - x_2 - 0s_1 - 10s_2 - 0s_3$$

or

$$18,000 = .5x_1 + 1x_2 + 0s_1 + 10s_2 + 0s_3$$

The initial row operation will result in a 1 in the pivot element location of the incoming-variable column ($x_2$ in our case). The remaining row operations are made so as to have zeros in the incoming-variable column. The transformed column will then contain a vector of the identity matrix. To transform the remaining elements requires a row-by-row operation and use of both the old and the new tableau. The operation involves multiplying the *intersecting element in the old row* by the *corresponding elements in the replacing row* and then subtracting the results from the *elements in the old row*. The *intersecting element in the old row* is the element at the intersection of the row being updated and the incoming-variable column, and the *replacing row* is the row in the new tableau associated with the new variable (step 3). An example operation will demonstrate the concept. Assume we are to update $s_1$, that is, we want to compute the $s_1$ row for Tableau II. Observing the initial tableau, Table 7-2, the intersecting element for the $s_1$ row is the .05 coefficient at the intersection of the $s_1$ row and the $x_2$ column. The elements of the *replacing* row are the elements associated with the new $x_2$ row in Tableau II, Table 7-4 (18,000, .5, 1, 0, 10, and 0). The multiplication/subtraction operation, therefore, is

$$
\begin{array}{rrrrrrr}
(1,100 & .05 & .05 & 1 & 0 & 0) \\
-(.05)(18,000 & .5 & 1.00 & 0 & 10 & 0) \\
\hline
200 & .025 & 0 & 1 & -.5 & 0 \\
\end{array}
$$

The resulting numbers are entered in the $s_1$ row of Tableau II.

Using the .05 intersecting element for the $s_3$ variable (taken from the initial tableau) and the replacing row (taken from Tableau II), the new $s_3$ row in Tableau II is computed as follows:

$$
\begin{array}{rrrrrrr}
(2,000 & .10 & .05 & 0 & 0 & 1) \\
-(.05)(18,000 & .5 & 1.00 & 0 & 10 & 0) \\
\hline
1,100 & .075 & 0 & 0 & -.5 & 1 \\
\end{array}
$$

The procedure for updating all rows of the new tableau, other than the initial outgoing (replacing) row, can be summarized as follows:

**Step 4.**   All rows of the tableau other than the row associated with the outgoing variable can be transformed (updated) through use of the following formula:

New row = (elements in the old row) − (intersecting element in old row)

× (elements in the replacing row)

It should be noted at this point that the coefficients of the $s_1$, $s_3$, and $x_2$ rows in Tableau II are identical to the coefficients for equations (7.18a), (7.19a), and (7.20a). This is because the row operations for updating the tableau are nothing other than the equation manipulation procedure used in the algebraic solution process. The simplex method avoids the equation manipulation process through use of the row operations.

To see the relationship between the simplex pivoting operation and the algebraic manipulations used to exchange basic and nonbasic variables, consider the pivot used to transform the $s_1$ row in our example. This pivoting operation is shown below with the variables written above the coefficients:

| | RHS | $x_1$ | $x_2$ | $s_1$ | $s_2$ | $s_3$ |
|---|---|---|---|---|---|---|
| | $(1,100 = .05$ | | $.05$ | $1$ | $0$ | $0)$ |
| $-(.05)$ | $(18,000 = .5$ | | $1.00$ | $0$ | $10$ | $0)$ |
| | $200 = .025$ | | $0$ | $1$ | $-.5$ | $0$ |

Let us now rewrite this slightly by dropping the zero terms and rearranging:

$$
\begin{aligned}
s_1 &= \quad 1{,}100 - .05x_1 - .05x_2 \\
-(.05)(x_2 &= 18{,}000 - .5x_1 \qquad\qquad - 10s_2) \\
\hline
s_1 - .05x_2 &= \quad 200 - .025x_1 - .05x_2 + .5s_2
\end{aligned}
$$

or

$$s_1 = 200 - .025x_1 + .5s_2$$

The results are the same as equation (7.19) of the corresponding algebraic transformation. So pivoting is nothing but a mechanical way of performing the algebraic manipulations to exchange a nonbasic variable for a basic variable.

Just as we could immediately write the solution to the set of revised equations for the algebraic method, we can write the solution to the updated tableau. From Tableau II, $s_1 = 200$, $x_2 = 18,000$, and $s_3 = 1,100$. Since $x_1$ and $s_2$ are nonbasic variables, and thus not in the basis, they are equal to zero.

The final step of the simplex method is to compute the new $z_j$ and $(c_j - z_j)$ rows for the updated tableau and check for optimality. This step is also necessary in order to complete the new tableau. Before one can compute the $z_j$ values, the values for the new $c_B$ column must be determined. This simply requires the transfer of the cost (profit) coefficients associated with variables in the basis; these values are the $c_j$ values for the variables in the basis. For Tableau II, the coefficients associated with $s_1$, $x_2$, and $s_3$ are 0, 20, and 0, respectively. The $z_j$ values for the tableau are calculated by summing the products of the values in the $c_B$ column times the coefficients in the $x_j$ column; thus,

$$Z = 0(200) + 20(18,000) + 0(1,100) = 360,000$$

$$z_{x_1} = 0(.025) + 20(.5) \quad + 0(.075) \quad = 10$$

$$z_{x_2} = 0(0) \quad + 20(1) \quad + 0(0) \quad = 20$$

$$z_{s_1} = 0(1) \quad + 20(0) \quad + 0(0) \quad = 0$$

$$z_{s_2} = 0(-.5) + 20(10) \quad + 0(-.5) = 200$$

$$z_{s_3} = 0(0) \quad + 20(0) \quad + 0(1) \quad = 0$$

Recall that the $(c_j - z_j)$ values are found by subtracting the $z_j$ row from the $c_j$ row. Since the $(c_j - z_j)$ value for $x_1$ is positive $(+8.5)$, we have not reached the optimal solution.

The final step of the simplex method is summarized as follows:

**Step 5.** Compute new $z_j$ and $(c_j - z_j)$ rows and check for optimal solution. The optimal solution results when the $(c_j - z_j)$ row has no coefficients greater than zero (all zeros or negative). If an optimal solution does not exist return to step 1.

To continue our iterative process we return to simplex step 1. The variable to enter the basis is the variable with the largest positive $(c_j - z_j)$ value. From Tableau II, Table 7-4, we note that the $(c_j - z_j)$ value for $x_1$ is the only positive coefficient, therefore $x_1$ should be brought into the basis.

Using step 2 of the simplex method, we can determine the variable to be removed from the basis. The ratio of the values in the Right-hand Side column to the positive coefficients in the $x_1$ column are $200/.025 = 8,000$, $18,000/.5 = 36,000$, and $1,100/.075 = 14,666.66$. Consequently, $s_1$ should be removed from the basis and replaced by $x_1$.

The row values for the new incoming variable, $x_1$, are determined by step 3. Recall that this step simply involves dividing the outgoing row in the old tableau by the pivot element. The pivot element in this case is equal to .025 (the element is underlined in Table 7-4). The new $x_1$ row resulting from this operation is shown in Tableau III (Table 7-5).

The remaining rows of the new tableau are computed by use of the row operations in step 4. For the $x_2$ row, the intersecting element is .5. The new $x_1$ row (Tableau III) is multiplied by .5 and subtracted from the old $x_2$ row (Tableau II). The new $x_2$ row shown in Table 7-5 results. Multiplying the new $x_1$ row (Tableau III) by .075, the

**TABLE 7-5.**
**Tableau III**

| $c_B$ | Variables in the Basis | Right-hand Side (Solution) | $c_j \rightarrow$ 18.5 $x_1$ | 20.0 $x_2$ | 0 $s_1$ | 0 $s_2$ | 0 $s_3$ |
|---|---|---|---|---|---|---|---|
| 18.5 | $x_1$ | 8,000 | 1 | 0 | 40 | −20 | 0 |
| 20.0 | $x_2$ | 14,000 | 0 | 1 | −20 | 20 | 0 |
| 0 | $s_3$ | 500 | 0 | 0 | −3 | 1 | 1 |
| | $z_j$ | 428,000 | 18.5 | 20.0 | 340 | 30 | 0 |
| | $c_j - z_j$ | | 0 | 0 | −340 | −30 | 0 |

intersecting element value for row $s_3$, and subtracting the results from the old $s_2$ row (Tableau II), provides the new $s_3$ row for Tableau III. The value for the basic variables can now be read directly from the Right-hand Side column. The solution is $x_1 = 8,000$, $x_2 = 14,000$, $s_3 = 500$, $s_1 = 0$, and $s_2 = 0$. The $s_1$ and $s_2$ variables are zero because they are nonbasic variables and thus not in the basis. The Z value for this solution is

$$(18.5)(8,000) + (20)(14,000) = \$428,000$$

The $(c_j - z_j)$ values are all zero or negative; therefore, the solution in this tableau is optimal. A quick check of the algebraic and graphical solution will support this result.

Before we leave this example, it might be helpful to reexamine the three tableaus (Tables 7-2, 7-4, 7-5). Note that in each case, in the $(c_j - z_j)$ row under the columns for the variables in the basis, the values are always zero. This can be used as a computational check. If the $(c_j - z_j)$ values for the variables in the basis are not zero, it is a signal that computational errors exist in the tableau.

## Optimality and alternate optima

**Optimality.** According to step 5 of the simplex method, the solution to a linear programming problem (a maximization problem) is optimal if all values in the $(c_j - z_j)$ row are zero or negative. Let us examine the Agro-Tech Inc. problem just completed in order to better understand this rule. Examination of the $z_j$ and $(c_j - z_j)$ rows in each tableau will highlight the rule.

In the initial tableau, Table 7-2, the three slack variables are in the basis. Since the $(c_j - z_j)$ value for $x_2$ is greater than the $(c_j - z_j)$ values for the other variables, $x_2$ enters the basis. The net contribution of bringing $x_2$ into the basis and removing $s_2$ is 20.0. The $(c_j - z_j)$ value is equal to the $c_j$ value because the cost of bringing $x_2$ into the basis is zero (that is, the contribution to profit for $s_1$, $s_2$, and $s_3$ is zero). The 20.0 value of $(c_j - z_j)$ for $x_2$ means that each unit of $x_2$ will add 20.0 to the objective function. Since $x_2 = 0$ in the initial tableau (Table 7-2) and $x_2 = 18,000$ in the second tableau (Table 7-4), a total of 18,000 units of $x_2$ are included in this second iteration. The total contribution to the objective function thus is the 20.0 $(c_j - z_j)$ value multiplied by the change in $x_2$, 18,000, that is, $(18,000)(20.0) = 360,000$. In moving from the initial to the second tableau, we have to give up 900 tons of $s_1$ $(1,100 - 200)$, all 1,800 tons of $s_2$ and 900 tons of $s_3$ $(2,000 - 1,100)$. However, these resources are worth zero dollars in terms of contributions to profits; that is, in the raw form, the resources contribute nothing to profits.

The $(c_j - z_j)$ value for $x_1$ is positive in the second tableau (Table 7-4). This indicates that $x_1$ should be brought into the basis. The net contribution $(c_j - z_j)$ for bringing each unit of $x_1$ into the basis is 8.5. To bring a unit of $x_1$ into the basis, it is necessary to give up .025 unit of $s_1$, .5 unit of $x_2$, and .075 unit of $s_3$. Since each $x_2$ is worth \$20, and each unit of $s_1$ and $s_2$ is worth zero dollars, the net contribution lost per unit of $x_1$ produced is \$10 $(0.5 \times \$20 = \$10)$. The solution in Table 7-5 (the third tableau) indicates that $x_1 = 8,000$, $x_2 = 14,000$, $s_3 = 500$, and $Z = \$428,000$. The \$68,000 change in profits $(\$428,000 - \$360,000)$ results from producing 8,000 units (tons) of $x_1$ and giving up 4,000 units (tons) of $x_2$ $(8,000 \times \$18.5 - 4,000 \times \$20 = 148,000 - 80,000 = \$68,000)$.

The $(c_j - z_j)$ values in the third tableau (Table 7-5) are less than or equal to zero. This means that introducing any of the nonbasic variables (that is, $s_1$ or $s_2$) into the basis would lead to a decrease in the objective function. For example, if $s_2$ were brought into the basis, then profits would decrease by \$30 for each unit (ton) of $s_2$ in the new solution. The \$30 per unit loss would result from having to give up 20 tons of $x_2$ and making an additional 20 tons of $x_1$. That is, $[\$20 \times (-20) + \$18.5 \times 20] = -\$30.0$. We could perform a similar analysis of the $-340$ $(c_j - z_j)$ value in the $s_1$ column. The solution in the third tableau (Table 7-5), therefore, is optimal.

**Alternate optima.**    In the previous section, we discussed the optimality condition for the simplex method and demonstrated how one recognizes these conditions in a given tableau. One might conclude from that discussion that a single optimal solution exists for every problem solved via the simplex method. This is not true; a unique optimal solution does not always exist. If the objective function is parallel to one of the constraints that form the feasible region, there will exist more than one optimal solution. This condition is referred to as **alternate optimal** solutions and is portrayed graphically in Figure 7-2.

*alternate optimal*

The possible existence of multiple or alternate optimal solutions is determined in the tableau process by examining the $(c_j - z_j)$ row of the final tableau. A possible alternate optimal solution exists if the $(c_j - z_j)$ value for a nonbasic variable is zero. We use the word "possible" because, as we will note shortly, a zero in the $(c_j - z_j)$ row under a nonbasic variable does not "guarantee" that an alternate optima exists.

In discussing the third tableau (the optimal solution) for Agro-Tech Inc., we noted that the $(c_j - z_j)$ value of $-30$ for $s_2$ indicates that profits will decrease by that amount for each unit of $s_2$ brought into the basis. If the $(c_j - z_j)$ value had been zero, it would indicate that no change in profits would result if $s_3$ were brought into the

FIGURE 7-2.
Graphical Repre-
sentation of Alter-
nate Optima

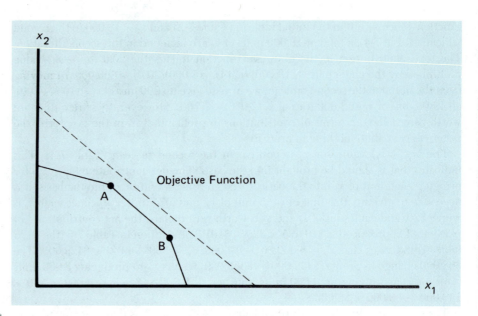

basis. A $(c_j - z_j)$ value of zero for a nonbasic variable, therefore, means that if the variable can be brought into the basis, the value of the objective function will not change. When a nonbasic variable is brought into the basis, a new set of solution values will result that will provide the same optimal Z value.

To illustrate the concept, we will modify the Agro-Tech Inc. problem slightly. Assume that the contribution to profits, $c_1$, for product $x_1$ is \$10.0 per ton as opposed to the original \$18.5 per ton. The problem is then expressed as follows:

MAXIMIZE:        $Z = 10x_1 + 20x_2$                                         (7.26)

SUBJECT TO:        $.05x_1 + .05x_2 \leq 1{,}100$                             (7.27)

$.05x_1 + .10x_1 \leq 1{,}800$                                               (7.28)

$.10x_1 + .05x_2 \leq 2{,}000$                                               (7.29)

$x_1, x_2 \geq 0$                                                           (7.30)

Solving this revised problem with the simplex method will result in the tableau shown in Table 7-6. This tableau results after one iteration of the process. Since all values in the $(c_j - z_j)$ row in the tableau are zero or negative, the solution is optimal. The solution for this revised problem is $s_1 = 200$, $x_2 = 18{,}000$, and $s_3 = 1{,}100$. The Z value for the problem is \$360,000. The maximum profit for the revised problem is less than for the original problem (Table 7-5) because the contribution to profits for product #1 is \$10.0 per ton rather than the original \$18.5 per ton.

In examining the $(c_j - z_j)$ row in Table 7-6, we note that the $(c_j - z_j)$ value for $x_1$ is zero. Since $x_1$ is a nonbasic variable, this indicates that if we can bring $x_1$ into the basis, it will have no impact on the objective-function value (that is, the \$360,000

| $c_B$ | Variables in the Basis | Right-hand Side (Solution) | $c_j \rightarrow$ |||||
|---|---|---|---|---|---|---|---|
| | | | 10 | 20 | 0 | 0 | 0 |
| | | | $x_1$ | $x_2$ | $s_1$ | $s_2$ | $s_3$ |
| 0 | $s_1$ | 200 | .025 | 0 | 1 | −.5 | 0 |
| 20 | $x_2$ | 18,000 | .50 | 1 | 0 | 10 | 0 |
| 0 | $s_3$ | 1,100 | .075 | 0 | 0 | −.5 | 1 |
| | $z_j$ | 360,000 | 10 | 20 | 0 | 200 | 0 |
| | $c_j - z_j$ | | 0 | 0 | 0 | −200 | 0 |

**TABLE 7-6.**
**Optimal Tableau for Modified Agro-Tech Inc. Problem**

profits). To determine whether $x_1$ can be brought into the basis, we check to see if any positive coefficients exist in the $x_1$ column. If a positive coefficient did not exist in the column, we would be unable to bring $x_1$ into the basis; therefore, alternate optima would not exist. In this case, all the coefficients are positive; therefore, we can proceed. To bring $x_1$ into the basis, we decide which variable to remove from the basis (step 2) and then use the row operations (steps 3–5) to update the tableau. The new tableau is shown in Table 7-7. The alternate optimal solution is $x_1 = 8{,}000$, $x_2 = 14{,}000$, and $s_3 = 500$, and a \$360,000 profit will result.

Referring to Figure 7-1, the graphical plot of the original Agro-Tech Inc. problem, it can be noted that the first optimal solution, Table 7-6, is point 3 in the graph. The alternate optimal solution, Table 7-7, is shown as point 8 on the graphical plot. If you plot the objective function for the revised problem ($Z = 10x_1 + 12x_2$) into Figure 7-1, it will quickly be noted that the new objective function parallels the constraint that connects points 3 and 8. The optimal and alternate optimal solutions for the revised problem shown in the tableaus thus conform to the optimal and alternate optimal solutions noted in the graph. Using the ($c_j - z_j$) row analysis, we thus can easily check for alternate optimal solutions.

| $c_B$ | Variables in the Basis | Right-hand Side (Solution) | $c_j \rightarrow$ |||||
|---|---|---|---|---|---|---|---|
| | | | 10 | 20 | 0 | 0 | 0 |
| | | | $x_1$ | $x_2$ | $s_1$ | $s_2$ | $s_3$ |
| 10 | $x_1$ | 8,000 | 1 | 0 | 40 | −20 | 0 |
| 20 | $x_2$ | 14,000 | 0 | 1 | −20 | 20 | 0 |
| 0 | $s_3$ | 500 | 0 | 0 | −3 | 1 | 1 |
| | $z_j$ | 360,000 | 10 | 20 | 0 | 200 | 0 |
| | $c_j - z_j$ | | 0 | 0 | 0 | −200 | 0 |

**TABLE 7-7.**
**Alternate Optimal for Modified Agro-Tech Inc. Problem**

# ■ Variations in the simplex method

The simplex method can be applied to both maximization and minimization problems (as noted in Chapter 5) and can handle conditions where there are greater-than-or-equal-to constraints as well as negative right-hand-side values. However, certain modifications and additions need to be made in the objective function and/or constraints prior to transferring the problem into the initial tableau. Let us examine some of these variations.

## *Minimization*

The simplex method can be applied to a minimization problem if one is willing to modify the procedural steps of the algorithm. Two changes are necessary. One, the optimality test (step 5), is changed such that the solution process continues until all values in the $(c_j - z_j)$ row are zero or positive. (Recall that for maximization problems the process is continued until all values are zero or negative.) Two, the rule for determining the incoming variable (step 1) is modified such that the selected variable is the one with the most negative $(c_j - z_j)$ value. [Recall that the standard procedure is to select the variable with the largest positive $(c_j - z_j)$ value.]

But there is an easier way to solve minimization problems. *One can convert the minimization problem into a maximization problem by simply multiplying the coefficients in the objective function of the minimization problem by −1.* Once the maximization problem is established, one simply continues with the standard maximization simplex procedure.

To illustrate the concept, consider the following problem:

MINIMIZE: $\qquad Z = 30x_1 + 10x_2$ $\hfill$ (7.31)

SUBJECT TO: $\qquad 2x_1 + 4x_2 \leq 80$ $\hfill$ (7.32)

$\qquad\qquad\qquad x_1 + x_2 = 25$ $\hfill$ (7.33)

$\qquad\qquad\qquad 8x_1 + 6x_2 \geq 120$ $\hfill$ (7.34)

$\qquad\qquad\qquad x_1, x_2 \geq 0$ $\hfill$ (7.35)

To apply the maximization algorithm, simply multiply equation (7.31) by −1, giving

MAXIMIZE: $\qquad Z = -30x_1 - 10x_2$ $\hfill$ (7.31a)

SUBJECT TO: $\qquad 2x_1 + 4x_2 \leq 80$ $\hfill$ (7.32a)

$\qquad\qquad\qquad x_1 + x_2 = 25$ $\hfill$ (7.33a)

$\qquad\qquad\qquad 8x_1 + 6x_2 \geq 120$ $\hfill$ (7.34a)

$\qquad\qquad\qquad x_1, x_2 \geq 0$ $\hfill$ (7.35a)

We can now apply the simplex algorithm to the revised problem. As in any linear programming problem, however, we must first convert the inequalities to equalities and we must be assured that the equations contain a basic feasible solution. Before we go through these steps, let us graphically display the problem in order to get a better overall understanding. Figure 7-3 is a pictorial representation of the problem; note that only solutions that lie on the line segment A–B will satisfy all the constraints. Point A is the minimal-cost point since it intersects the lowest iso-cost line (which is the objective function). In our solution process we thus should expect a minimum-cost-value of 450 with $x_1 = 10$ and $x_2 = 15$.

Returning now to the converted problem [equations (7.31a)–(7.35a)], we must add a slack variable to the first constraint and subtract a surplus variable from the third constraint in order to produce a set of equality constraints. This operation gives the following:

MAXIMIZE:      $Z = -30x_1 - 10x_2 + 0s_1 + 0s_2$                                      (7.36)

SUBJECT TO:         $2x_1 + 4x_2 + 1s_1 + 0s_2 = 80$                                   (7.37)

$x_1 + x_2 + 0s_1 + 0s_2 = 25$                                                         (7.38)

$8x_1 + 6x_2 + 0s_1 - 1s_2 = 120$                                                      (7.39)

$x_1, x_2, s_1, s_2 \geq 0$                                                            (7.40)

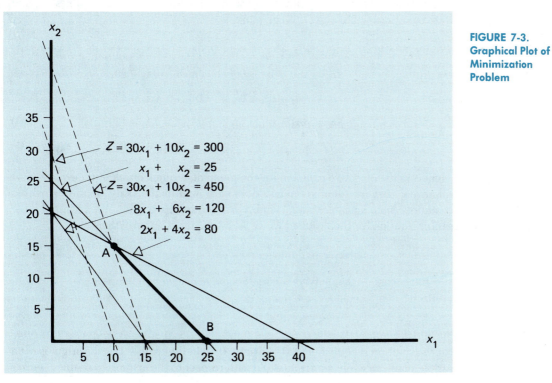

**FIGURE 7-3.**
**Graphical Plot of Minimization Problem**

Before transferring the equality constraints into the initial tableau, we must identify a basic feasible solution. This requires that an identity matrix exist within the body of the constraints. In checking equations (7.37)–(7.39), we note that only variable $s_1$ contains a vector of the matrix. Variable $s_2$ cannot be included as it was when we solved the Agro-Tech Inc. problem, since the column vector contains $-1$ rather than $+1$. Merely adding slack and surplus variables to constraints will not always produce an initial basic feasible solution. We can resolve this problem, however, by employing artificial variables.

## Artificial variables

Artificial variables are employed in the simplex method only as an aid to identifying an initial basic feasible solution to the problem. Such variables are necessary when a problem contains greater-than-or-equal-to ($\geq$) and equality ($=$) *constraints*. Artificial variables are used to complete the identity matrix and thus provide an initial solution.

The rule for employing artificial variables is to add one of these variables to each greater-than-or-equal-to and equality constraint that exists in the original problem. These variables can be added when the slack and surplus variables are added; however, since we have already added slack and surplus variables, we will add the artificial variables to our equality constraint set. Adding artificial variables ($A_1$ and $A_2$) to equations (7.38) and (7.39) gives us

MAXIMIZE:    $Z = -30x_1 - 10x_2 + 0s_1 + 0s_2 - 300A_1 - 300A_2$     (7.41)

SUBJECT TO:    $2x_1 + 4x_2 + 1s_1 + 0s_2 + 0A_1 + 0A_2 = 80$     (7.42)

$x_1 + x_2 + 0s_1 + 0s_2 + 1A_1 + 0A_2 = 25$     (7.43)

$8x_1 + 6x_2 + 0s_1 - 1s_2 + 0A_1 + 1A_2 = 120$     (7.44)

$x_1, x_2, s_1, s_2, A_1, A_2 \geq 0$     (7.45)

Ignoring the objective function for the moment, a quick check of the equation set will reveal that an identity matrix does exist within the body of the converted constraints (note variables $s_1$, $A_1$, and $A_2$). Therefore, we can write an initial basic feasible solution for the problem. If we set $x_1$, $x_2$, and $s_2$ to zero, then

$1s_1 + 0A_1 + 0A_2 = 80$

$0s_1 + 1A_1 + 0A_2 = 25$

$0s_1 + 0A_1 + 1A_2 = 120$

The initial solution, then, is $x_1 = 0$, $x_2 = 0$, $s_1 = 80$, $s_2 = 0$, $A_1 = 25$, and $A_2 = 120$. Note that this solution is equivalent to the origin $(0, 0)$ in Figure 7-3. But the origin is not a feasible point; so while we are feasible with respect to the artificial variables, we are infeasible with respect to the original variable. Therefore, our first task is to become feasible in terms of the original variable.

We are now ready to enter the equation set into the initial tableau and begin the solution process.

## The solution process with artificial variables

Artificial variables provide a convenient means for identifying the initial basic feasible solution, which is the starting point for applying the simplex method. Since such variables have no meaning in terms of the solution to the problem, a procedure must be employed to assure that the artificial variables are not in the final tableau. For the maximization problem, we can assure that artificial variables will not occur in the final solution by assigning large negative numbers to the coefficients of the artificial variables in the objective function. In equation (7.41), a value of $-300$ has been assigned to the coefficients associated with $A_1$ and $A_2$. Since we are maximizing profits, the $-300$ indicates that a $300 loss would result for each unit of $A_1$ or $A_2$ that would be included in the solution. Therefore, to maximize profits it is most desirable to have zero units of $A_1$ and $A_2$ in the final solution.

The $-300$ assigned to $A_1$ and $A_2$ for equation (7.41) is an arbitrary value. A workable rule of thumb is to employ a coefficient that is an order of magnitude larger than the absolute value of the largest coefficient in the objective function. In our case the largest coefficient was 30; therefore, we selected 300 as our coefficient. The negative sign is assigned to 300 since we are working with a maximization problem. Remember that the negative signs associated with the coefficients of $x_1$ and $x_2$ occur because we converted the problem from a minimization to a maximization problem.

Had we worked with the original minimization problem rather than the converted maximization problem, we would have assigned large positive coefficients to the artificial variables. Rather than immediately converting our initial problem to a maximization problem, we could have added slack, surplus, and artificial variables to the problem in order to form equalities. We could have then multiplied all the $c_j$ coefficients by $-1$. Had we employed this approach, the initial coefficients associated with $A_1$ and $A_2$ would have been $+300$. These would switch to $-300$ when we multiplied by $-1$ in converting to a maximization problem. Positive coefficients are used for the artificial variables only when the minimization simplex logic is used rather than converting the problem to a maximization problem.

The initial tableau for the problem represented in equations (7.41)–(7.45) is given in Table 7-8. The solution at this step is $s_1 = 80$, $A_1 = 25$, $A_2 = 120$, $x_1 = 0$, $x_2 = 0$, and $s_2 = 0$. The large coefficients associated with $A_1$ and $A_2$ result in large $(c_j - z_j)$ values for $x_1$ and $x_2$, so that variable $x_1$ enters the basis and $A_2$ leaves the basis. Note that the $Z$ value for the first tableau is $-43,500$. The magnitude of $Z_j$ has no meaning since we arbitrarily selected the artificial variable coefficients; but, as we move from tableau to tableau, this number should approach zero or become positive.

Table 7-9 contains the second tableau for the problem. Variable $A_2$ has left the

**TABLE 7-8.**
**Initial Tableau for Maximization Problem with Artificial Variables**

| $c_B$ | Variables in the Basis | Right-hand Side (Solution) | $c_j \rightarrow$ $x_1$ $-30$ | $x_2$ $-10$ | $s_1$ $0$ | $s_2$ $0$ | $A_1$ $-300$ | $A_2$ $-300$ |
|---|---|---|---|---|---|---|---|---|
| 0 | $s_1$ | 80 | 2 | 4 | 1 | 0 | 0 | 0 |
| $-300$ | $A_1$ | 25 | 1 | 1 | 0 | 0 | 1 | 0 |
| $-300$ | $A_2$ | 120 | 8 | 6 | 0 | $-1$ | 0 | 1 |
| | $z_j$ | $-43{,}500$ | $-2{,}700$ | $-2{,}100$ | 0 | 300 | $-300$ | $-300$ |
| | $c_j - z_j$ | | 2,670 | 2,090 | 0 | $-300$ | 0 | 0 |

basis and $x_1$ has entered. The new Z value is $-3450$. Since we still have positive $(c_j - z_j)$ values, we continue the solution process. Variable $x_2$ is to enter the basis and variable $s_1$ should be removed. Variable $A_1$ is not to be removed at this point, but if we are to reach optimality, $A_1$ must eventually be removed. The simplex procedure does not guarantee that all artificial variables will be removed prior to removing other variables. The process will remove all artificial variables, but not as first priority.

Removing $s_1$ and bringing $x_2$ into the basis results in the third tableau (Table 7-10). Since $A_1$ is still in the basis, we still see a large negative value for Z, but the value of Z is moving toward zero. The $(c_j - z_j)$ value for $s_2$ is still positive so we bring that variable into the basis and remove $A_1$.

Table 7-11 is a display of the optimal tableau. The solution is $x_1 = 10$, $x_2 = 15$, $s_2 = 50$, $A_1 = 0$, $A_2 = 0$, and $s_1 = 0$. A quick check of Figure 7-3, our graphical plot of the problem, will confirm that this is the optimal solution. However, Table 7-11 shows $Z = -450$ rather than $+450$. This occurs because we converted from minimization to maximization; it did not occur because artificial variables were employed. With a minimization problem, the optimal Z value will be negative if one uses the standard

**TABLE 7-9.**
**Tableau II for Maximization Problem with Artificial Variables**

| $c_B$ | Variables in the Basis | Right-hand Side (Solution) | $c_j \rightarrow$ $x_1$ $-30$ | $x_2$ $-10$ | $s_1$ $0$ | $s_2$ $0$ | $A_1$ $-300$ | $A_2$ $-300$ |
|---|---|---|---|---|---|---|---|---|
| 0 | $s_1$ | 50 | 0 | 2.5 | 1 | .25 | 0 | $-.25$ |
| $-300$ | $A_1$ | 10 | 0 | .25 | 0 | .125 | 1 | $-.125$ |
| $-30$ | $x_1$ | 15 | 1 | .75 | 0 | $-.125$ | 0 | .125 |
| | $z_j$ | $-3450$ | $-30$ | $-97.5$ | 0 | $-33.75$ | $-300$ | 33.75 |
| | $c_j - z_j$ | | 0 | 87.51 | 0 | 33.75 | 0 | $-333.75$ |

**TABLE 7-10.**
**Tableau III for Maximization Problem with Artificial Variables**

| $c_j \rightarrow$ | | | $-30$ | $-10$ | $0$ | $0$ | $-300$ | $-300$ |
|---|---|---|---|---|---|---|---|---|
| $c_B$ | Variables in the Basis | Right-hand Side (Solution) | $x_1$ | $x_2$ | $s_1$ | $s_2$ | $A_1$ | $A_2$ |
| $-10$ | $x_2$ | 20 | 0 | 1 | .40 | .10 | 0 | $-.10$ |
| $-300$ | $A_1$ | 5 | 0 | 0 | $-.10$ | .10 | 1 | $-.10$ |
| $-30$ | $x_1$ | 0 | 1 | 0 | $-.30$ | $-.20$ | 0 | .20 |
| | $z_j$ | $-1700$ | $-30$ | $-10$ | 35 | $-25$ | $-300$ | 25 |
| | $c_j - z_j$ | | 0 | 0 | $-35$ | 25 | 0 | $-325$ |

maximization simplex procedure to solve the problem and all the $c_j$ values are originally positive. The final step in the solution process, therefore, is to multiply Z by $-1$. The minimum profit associated with $x_1 = 10$, $x_2 = 15$, and $s_2 = 50$ in this example is 450.

## Negative right-hand-side values

If one examines the Right-hand Side column of any of the tableaus presented thus far in the chapter, it can be noted that nonnegative values *always* exist, even in the initial tableau. But often one may be confronted with a constraint where the right-hand value is negative. For example, consider the constraints $2x_1 - 4x_2 = -8$, $x_1 + 2 \le x_2$, and $2x_1 + 7 \ge x_2$. Rearranging terms, we could express these constraints as

$$2x_1 - 4x_2 = -8 \tag{7.46}$$

$$x_1 - x_2 \le -2 \tag{7.47}$$

$$2x_1 - x_2 \ge -7 \tag{7.48}$$

**TABLE 7-11.**
**Optimal Solution for Maximization Problem**

| $c_j \rightarrow$ | | | $-30$ | $-10$ | $0$ | $0$ | $-300$ | $-300$ |
|---|---|---|---|---|---|---|---|---|
| $c_B$ | Variables in the Basis | Right-hand Side (Solution) | $x_1$ | $x_2$ | $s_1$ | $s_2$ | $A_1$ | $A_2$ |
| $-10$ | $x_2$ | 15 | 0 | 1 | .5 | 0 | $-1$ | 0 |
| $0$ | $s_2$ | 50 | 0 | 0 | $-1$ | 1 | 10 | $-1$ |
| $-30$ | $x_1$ | 10 | 1 | 0 | $-.5$ | 0 | 2 | 0 |
| | $z_j$ | $-450$ | $-30$ | $-10$ | 10 | 0 | $-50$ | 0 |
| | $c_j - z_j$ | | 0 | 0 | $-10$ | 0 | $-250$ | $-300$ |

But these constraints will have **negative right-hand-side** values, which, before we can consider initiating the simplex procedure, must be converted to positive values. The process is simple: multiply both sides of the constraint by $-1$ and, if the constraint is an inequality, reverse the inequality sign. For the above constraints, the following would result:

$$-2x_1 + 4x_2 = 8 \qquad (7.49)$$

$$-x_1 + x_2 \geq 2 \qquad (7.50)$$

$$2x_1 - x_2 \leq 7 \qquad (7.51)$$

The constraints can now be employed in the tableau process.

## ■ Special problems

Thus far we have considered problems that have at least one optimal solution that can be found either graphically or via the simplex method. We will now consider two situations where this is not true. These are *unbounded problems* and *inconsistent problems*. We will demonstrate these problems, both graphically and through the simplex method. We will also provide computer output for each.

*degeneracy*    In addition to examining these special-case problems, we will consider a situation known as **degeneracy.** Graphical, tabular-analysis, and computerized versions of a problem will be presented.

### *Unbounded problems*

Occasionally in LP problems, an error in formulation can result in the problem having no optimal solution. For problems of this nature, it will appear that the objective function can be increased without bound, a situation that is obviously not realistic in practice. An example of this type of variation is shown diagrammatically in Figure 7-4.

An example of an unbounded problem that would appear as in Figure 7-4 is as follows:

MAXIMIZE: $\quad Z = \quad x_1 + x_2 \qquad (7.52)$

SUBJECT TO: $\qquad -x_1 + x_2 \leq 2 \qquad (7.53)$

$$+x_1 - x_2 \leq 2 \qquad (7.54)$$

$$x_1, x_2 \geq 0 \qquad (7.55)$$

Note that for this problem the objective function can become infinitely large as long as the absolute difference between $x_1$ and $x_2$ is less than 2. For example, the solution $x_1 = 101$ and $x_2 = 100$ is feasible or likewise $x_1 = 2001$, $x_2 = 2000$. The problem thus requires a revision in formulation in order to be useful to a decision maker.

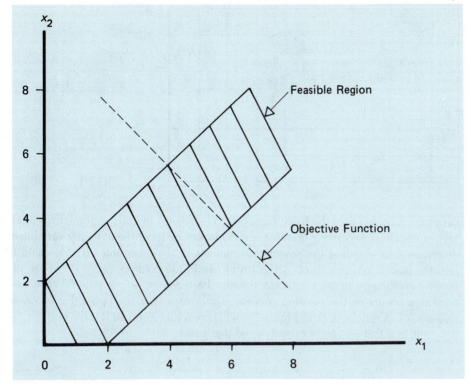

FIGURE 7-4.
Graphical Repre-
sentation of an
Unbounded
Problem

Since the feasible region for an unbounded problem is not bounded, it is impossible for the simplex method to step from vertex to vertex around the region in searching for the optimal solution. To see what happens when one attempts to solve an unbounded problem with the simplex method, let us consider the above example.

Converting to equalities, adding slack variables, and performing the solution process results in Tables 7-12 and 7-13. Tableau II (Table 7-13) indicates that

TABLE 7-12.
Initial Tableau for
Unbounded
Problem

| $c_B$ | $c_j \rightarrow$ Variables in the Basis | Right-hand Side (Solution) | 1 $x_1$ | 1 $x_2$ | 0 $s_1$ | 0 $s_2$ |
|---|---|---|---|---|---|---|
| 0 | $s_1$ | 2 | −1 | 1 | 1 | 0 |
| 0 | $s_2$ | 2 | 1 | −1 | 0 | 1 |
| | $z_j$ | 0 | 0 | 0 | 0 | 0 |
| | $c_j - z_j$ | | 1 | 1 | 0 | 0 |

**TABLE 7-13.**
**Tableau II for**
**Unbounded**
**Problem**

| $c_B$ | Variables in the Basis | $c_j \rightarrow$ Right-hand Side (Solution) | 1 $x_1$ | 1 $x_2$ | 0 $s_1$ | 0 $s_2$ |
|---|---|---|---|---|---|---|
| 0 | $s_1$ | 4 | 0 | 0 | 1 | 1 |
| 1 | $x_1$ | 2 | 1 | $-1$ | 0 | 1 |
| | $z_j$ | 2 | 1 | $-1$ | 0 | 1 |
| | $c_j - z_j$ | | 0 | 2 | 0 | $-1$ |

variable $x_2$ should enter the basis; however, the elements in the $x_2$ column are either zero or negative. According to step 2 of our simplex method, the outgoing variable is determined by dividing the *positive* coefficients in the incoming-variable column into the associated quantities in the Right-hand Side column. Since there are no positive coefficients in the $x_2$ column, the next basis cannot be computed. When this condition occurs in the solution process, it indicates that the optimal solution is *unbounded*. A quick check of Figure 7-4 will reveal that Tableau II is the vertex $x_1 = 2$, $x_2 = 0$, and that no vertex exists beyond that point.

## Inconsistent problems

Another situation that arises through errors in formulation of LP problems is that of inconsistent constraints. In this situation, there is no single feasible region because the constraints violate one another. This type of problem is diagrammed in Figure 7-5. Note that in this diagram a single feasible region does not exist. Hence it would be impossible to find a solution that would satisfy *all* constraints simultaneously.

The graphical procedure can be used to check for inconsistent constraints when the problems involve two variables. However, from the examples in Chapter 5, it should be obvious that realistic linear programming problems may have a large number of variables as well as a large number of constraints. Thus, after formulating an LP problem it is practically impossible to determine graphically whether the structured problem has a feasible solution. In such cases one must rely on the simplex method. This is illustrated in the following problem.

MAXIMIZE:        $Z = x_1 + x_2$                                                      (7.56)

SUBJECT TO:          $x_1 + x_2 \geq 2$                                                (7.57)

$x_1 + x_2 \leq 1$                                                (7.58)

$x_1, x_2 \geq 0$                                                (7.59)

Since the two constraints are mutually exclusive, the problem has no solution; that is, the constraints identify conflicting areas of feasibility. Converting to equality

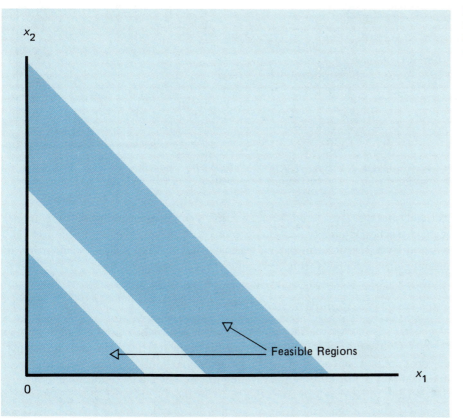

**FIGURE 7-5.**
**Graphical Repre-**
**sentation of an In-**
**consistent Problem**

Feasible Regions

constraints by adding slack and subtracting surplus variables, and adding an artificial variable to provide the initial solution, results in Table 7-14, the Initial Tableau. Performing the tableau process provides Tableau II (Table 7-15).

One can see from Tableau II that optimality has been reached, since every value in the $(c_j - z_j)$ row is zero or negative. But the solution contains an artificial variable, $A_1$.

**TABLE 7-14.**
**Initial Tableau for Inconsistent Constraint Problem**

| $c_B$ | $c_j \rightarrow$ Variables in the Basis | Right-hand Side (Solution) | 1 $x_1$ | 1 $x_2$ | 0 $s_1$ | $-100$ $A_1$ | 0 $s_2$ |
|---|---|---|---|---|---|---|---|
| $-100$ | $A_1$ | 2 | 1 | 1 | $-1$ | 1 | 0 |
| 0 | $s_2$ | 1 | 1 | 1 | 0 | 0 | 1 |
| | $z_j$ | $-200$ | $-100$ | $-100$ | 100 | $-100$ | 0 |
| | $c_j - z_j$ | | 101 | 101 | $-100$ | 0 | 0 |

**TABLE 7-15.**
**Tableau II for**
**Inconsistent**
**Constraint**
**Problem**

| $c_B$ | $c_j \rightarrow$ Variables in the Basis | Right-hand Side (Solution) | 1 $x_1$ | 1 $x_2$ | 0 $s_1$ | $-100$ $A_1$ | 0 $s_2$ |
|---|---|---|---|---|---|---|---|
| $-100$ | $A_1$ | 1 | 0 | 0 | $-1$ | 1 | $-1$ |
| 1 | $x_1$ | 1 | 1 | 1 | 0 | 0 | 1 |
|  | $z_j$ | $-99$ | 1 | 1 | 100 | $-100$ | 101 |
|  | $c_j - z_j$ |  | 0 | 0 | $-100$ | 0 | $-101$ |

This indicates that the solution is not a feasible solution to the problem. If the simplex method reaches optimality and one or more artificial variables are in the basis at a *nonzero* level, the problem has no feasible solution. The resulting solution has no meaning since it contains artificial variables.

## *Degenerate problems*

Degeneracy is another special problem that can occur when employing the simplex method. Unlike the unbounded and infeasible problems, the occurrence of degeneracy does not prevent one from reaching the optimal solution. Degeneracy can occur in the simplex method during the pivoting process when a tie results in determining the variable to be removed from the basis. In theory, this can cause *cycling* or a circular path in seeking the optimal solution. In practice, this is a rare occurrence because rules have been developed that allow for the avoidance of cycling.

When degeneracy occurs, one or more of the basic variables become not strictly positive, that is, a basic feasible solution has one or more basic variables that are equal to zero; these are degenerate variables. Geometrically, degeneracy occurs when a vertex is defined by "too many" constraints. In the simplex method, the presence of a basic variable equal to zero does not require any special action; it is necessary, of course, to be aware of the degenerate condition.

The following problem illustrates the occurrence of degeneracy in the final solution:

MINIMIZE:     $Z = x_1 + 3x_2$     (7.60)

SUBJECT TO:     $x_1 + x_2 \geq 1$     (7.61)

$2x_1 + 3x_2 \geq 2$     (7.62)

$x_1, x_2 \geq 0$     (7.63)

Solving this problem graphically, we obtain Figure 7-6, in which the optimal solution occurs at the point $x_1 = 1$, $x_2 = 0$. This vertex is said to have too many constraints because both constraints—equations (7.61) and (7.62)—and the nonnegativity

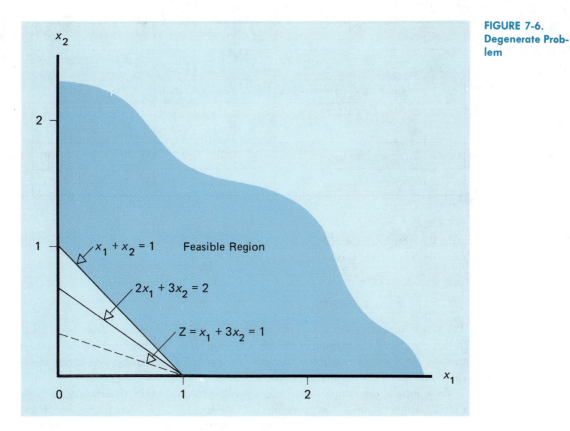

FIGURE 7-6.
Degenerate Prob-
lem

condition $x_1 \geq 0$ all intersect, but only two of the three are needed to define the vertex.

To solve this problem via the simplex method we begin with the initial tableau (Table 7-16). The optimal solution is shown in Table 7-17, where we note that $x_2 = 0$,

**TABLE 7-16. Initial Tableau for Degenerate Problem**

|  | $c_j \rightarrow$ |  | $-1$ | $-3$ | $0$ | $0$ | $-100$ | $-100$ |
|---|---|---|---|---|---|---|---|---|
| $c_B$ | Variables in the Basis | Right-hand Side (Solution) | $x_1$ | $x_2$ | $s_1$ | $s_2$ | $A_1$ | $A_2$ |
| $-100$ | $A_1$ | $1$ | $1$ | $1$ | $-1$ | $0$ | $1$ | $0$ |
| $-100$ | $A_2$ | $2$ | $2$ | $3$ | $0$ | $-1$ | $0$ | $1$ |
| | $z_j$ | $-300$ | $-300$ | $-400$ | $100$ | $100$ | $-100$ | $-100$ |
| | $c_j - z_j$ | — | $299$ | $397$ | $-100$ | $-100$ | $0$ | $0$ |

**TABLE 7-17.**
**Final Tableau for**
**Degenerate**
**Problem**

| | $c_j \rightarrow$ | | $-1$ | $-3$ | $0$ | $0$ | $-100$ | $-100$ |
|---|---|---|---|---|---|---|---|---|
| $c_B$ | Variables in the Basis | Right-hand Side (Solution) | $x_1$ | $x_2$ | $s_1$ | $s_2$ | $A_1$ | $A_2$ |
| $-1$ | $x_1$ | $1$ | $1$ | $1$ | $-1$ | $0$ | $1$ | $0$ |
| $0$ | $s_2$ | $0$ | $0$ | $-1$ | $-2$ | $1$ | $2$ | $-1$ |
| | $z_j$ | $-1$ | $-1$ | $-1$ | $1$ | $0$ | $-1$ | $0$ |
| | $c_j - z_j$ | | $0$ | $-2$ | $-1$ | $0$ | $-99$ | $-100$ |

as in the graphical solution, since it is nonbasic. Likewise, $s_2 = 0$ but $s_2$ is a basic variable. Therefore, $s_2$ is a degenerate variable.

## ■ Summary

The procedural steps employed in the simplex method (algorithm) have been given in this chapter. An algebraic approach was shown first to illustrate that the simplex method involves nothing more than solving a set of simultaneous equations and is simply a tabular representation of the algebraic process.

To highlight the simplex method, several variations other than solving a basic maximization problem were presented. These included: (1) recognizing and determining alternate optima; (2) solving a minimization problem; (3) employing artificial variables to aid in identifying an initial basic feasible solution; and (4) correcting for negative right-hand-side values.

Three special-case problems were also illustrated: unbounded problems, inconsistent problems, and degenerate problems.

The detailed procedures given in the chapter cover a broad spectrum of the simplex method. After completing this material you should be well grounded in the mechanics of the algorithm.

## ■ Glossary of terms

**algebraic approach:**  An iterative procedure allowing the substitution and solution of simultaneous equations that provides an optimal solution to an LP problem.

**alternate optima:**  An alternate solution to an LP problem; can be identified in the tableau by the presence of a zero in the $(c_j - z_j)$ row under a nonbasic variable.

**artificial variable:**  A variable used in the simplex method to aid in identifying an initial basic feasible solution.

**basic feasible solution:**  A basic solution in which all values of the solution variables are greater than or equal to zero.

**basic solution:**   A solution where the nonbasic variables are set equal to zero when solving for $m$ variables in terms of the remaining $n - m$ variables. No restriction is placed on the signs of the variables in the solution; both positive and negative values are acceptable.

**basic variable:**   One of the $m$ variables used to solve an LP problem.

**basis:**   The set of basic variables that make up a basic feasible solution.

$c_j$:   The coefficient in the objective function of the $j$th variable. Often referred to as the *contribution per unit*.

$c_j - z_j$:   The *net contribution per unit* associated with the $j$th variable. In the tableau, this reflects the net change in the objective function per unit change of $x_j$.

**degeneracy:**   A condition that occurs (1) in a simplex tableau during the pivoting process if a tie results in determining the variable to be removed from the basis and (2) in the final tableau when the basic variables are not strictly positive.

**incoming column:**   The column associated with the variable that should be brought into the basis in order to improve the solution.

**inconsistent constraints:**   A condition that occurs in the simplex tableau if optimality is reached but an artificial variable remains in the basis at a positive level.

**negative right-hand side:**   The condition that exists when negative values exist on the right-hand side of constraints associated with an LP problem. These must be converted to positive values before applying the simplex method.

**nonbasic variable:**   One of the $n - m$ variables that is set to zero in solving an LP problem.

**optimal solution:**   The basic feasible solution that has the greatest objective value (largest positive value for a maximization problem, smallest negative value for a minimization problem).

**optimality criteria:**   A condition that exists in the tableau process, associated with a maximization problem, where all the coefficients in the $(c_j - z_j)$ row are zero or negative.

**outgoing row:**   Refers to the row associated with the variable that should be removed from the basis in order to provide room for the incoming variable.

**pivot element:**   An element at the intersection of the incoming column and the outgoing row. Used in updating the tableau in the simplex method.

**simplex method:**   An iterative procedure that provides an optimal solution to an LP problem. The method employs the logic of the algebraic approach but employs a tableau structure to aid in the solution process.

**unbounded solution:**   A condition that occurs in the simplex tableau when the simplex method stops because no positive coefficients exist in the incoming column.

$z_j$:   The *contribution lost per unit* for the $j$th variable in the problem set. In the tableau, this represents that portion of the objective value of the current basic solution that must be relinquished in order to make one unit of $x_j$.

## ■ Review questions

1. Explain in a very succinct manner the simplex method. Use the concept of vertices in your answer.

2. In what form must the constraints in an LP exist before the simplex method can be applied? Why?

3. Differentiate between a *basic solution* and a *basic feasible solution*. What is the relationship between basic feasible solutions and vertices of the feasible region?

4. What is the difference between the algebraic simplex procedure and the simplex method?

5. What is the purpose of slack variables in solving an LP problem? Of surplus variables? Of artificial variables?

6. Why is it necessary to have an identity matrix exist within the body of the constraints before beginning the simplex method?

7. Identify the steps employed in the simplex method. Be precise in answering.

8. Explain how one recognizes when the optimal solution results in the solution process when solving a maximization problem. How does one recognize that an alternate optimal solution exists?

9. What type of checks can be used in the solution process to be somewhat assured that the updating process has been properly performed?

10. How does one go about solving a minimization LP problem using the simplex method?

11. If a negative right-hand-side value exists in a constraint, can the simplex method be used to solve the problem? Explain your answer.

12. How does one recognize when a problem has an unbounded solution?

13. How does one recognize when a problem has no feasible solution?

14. How does one recognize a degenerate problem?

# True/false questions

1. The algebraic approach to solving LP problems is completely different from the simplex method.

2. The first step in applying the simplex method is to transform all inequality constraints into equalities by adding slack variables and subtracting surplus variables.

3. The procedure for identifying the outgoing variable is to divide the Right-hand Side column by the positive coefficients in the incoming column and selecting the variable with the maximum ratio.

4. The coefficients in the body of the tableau are physical rates of substitution.

5. The pivot element is the element at the intersection of the incoming column and the outgoing row.

6. If the objective function is perpendicular to one of the constraints that form the feasible region, alternate optimal solutions exist.

7. To convert a minimization LP problem into a maximization problem for solution by the simplex method, $-1$ must be added to the coefficients in the objective function of the minimization problem.

8. Artificial variables are necessary when a problem contains less-than-or-equal-to constraints.

9. Negative right-hand-side values need not be converted to positive values before initiating the simplex procedure.

10. Degeneracy occurs in the simplex tableau if optimality is reached but an artificial variable remains in the basis at a positive level.

# ■ Problems

1. In Chapter 5 the following problem (Problem 1) was solved graphically:

MAXIMIZE:        $Z = 4x_1 + 5x_2$

SUBJECT TO:        $2x_1 + 3x_2 \leq 120$

$2x_1 + 1.5x_2 \leq 80$

$x_1, x_2 \geq 0$

The optimal solution computed graphically was $Z = \$213.33$, where $x_1 = 20$ and $x_2 = 26.66$.

a. Add slack variables to the problem in order to express the problem in equation form.
b. Identify all *basic solutions* for the problem.
c. Identify all *basic feasible* solutions for the problem.
d. Beginning with the basic feasible solution $x_1 = 0$, $x_2 = 0$, use the *algebraic* method to solve the problem (i.e., find the optimal solution).

2. Given the following problem:

MAXIMIZE:        $Z = 8x_1 + 6x_2$

SUBJECT TO:        $2x_1 \leq 8$

$6x_1 + 4x_2 \leq 18$

$x_1, x_2 \geq 0$

a. Convert to equalities and set up in the initial tableau of the simplex method.
b. Identify the *outgoing variable* and the *incoming variable*. *Do not solve*.

3. Use the simplex method to solve Problem 1.

a. What relationship exists between the tableau used to reach the optimal solution and the vertices in the graphical solution approach (refer to Problem 1 in Chapter 5)?
b. What relationship exists between the tableaus in the simplex method and the algebraic method [refer to part (d), Problem 1]?

4. Solve the following linear programming problem using the simplex method.

MAXIMIZE:        $Z = 10x_1 + 14x_2$

SUBJECT TO:        $4x_1 + 6x_2 \leq 24$

$2x_1 + 6x_2 \leq 20$

$x_1, x_2 \geq 0$

What are the values of the basic variables at each iteration?

5. Solve the following problem using the simplex method.

MAXIMIZE:     $Z = 2x_1 + x_2 + 3x_3$

SUBJECT TO:     $x_1 + x_2 + 2x_3 \leq 400$

$2x_1 + x_2 + x_3 \leq 500$

$x_1, x_2, x_3 \geq 0$

6. Solve the following problem using the simplex method.

MAXIMIZE:     $Z = 2x_1 + 3x_2$

SUBJECT TO:     $x_1 + x_2 \leq 6$

$x_1 \leq 3$

$x_2 \leq 2$

$x_1, x_2 \geq 0$

7. Solve the following problem using the simplex method.

MAXIMIZE:     $Z = 2x_1 + 3x_2$

SUBJECT TO:     $3x_1 + 6x_2 \leq 18$

$6x_1 + 3x_2 \leq 36$

$x_1, x_2 \geq 0$

8. Solve the following problem using the simplex method.

MAXIMIZE:     $Z = 1x_1 + 1x_2$

SUBJECT TO:     $1x_1 + 2x_2 \leq 6$

$6x_1 + 4x_2 \leq 24$

$x_1, x_2 \geq 0$

9. Solve the following problem using the simplex method.

MINIMIZE:     $Z = 3x_1 + 4x_2 + 8x_3$

SUBJECT TO:     $2x_1 + 1x_2 \geq 6$

$2x_2 + 4x_3 \geq 8$

$x_1, x_2, x_3 \geq 0$

10. For the following problem, the LP tableau is also given. Interpret the circled values in the tableau:

MAXIMIZE:  $Z = x_1 + 2x_2 + 3x_3 + 4x_4$

SUBJECT TO:  $x_1 + 2x_2 + x_3 + 2x_4 \leq 12$

$x_2 \leq 6$

$x_4 \leq 4$

$x_1, x_2, x_3, x_4 \geq 0$

| | | | 1 | 2 | 3 | 4 | | | |
|---|---|---|---|---|---|---|---|---|---|
| $c_B$ | Basis | RHS | $x_1$ | $x_2$ | $x_3$ | $x_4$ | $s_1$ | $s_2$ | $s_3$ |
| 3 | $x_3$ | ⑫ | 1 | ② | 1 | 2 | 1 | | |
| 0 | $s_2$ | ⑥ | 0 | 1 | 0 | 0 | | 1 | |
| 0 | $s_3$ | 4 | 0 | 0 | 0 | ① | | | 1 |
| | $z_j$ | 36 | 3 | 6 | 3 | 6 | ③ | 0 | 0 |
| | $c_j - z_j$ | — | ⟨-2⟩ | -4 | 0 | -2 | -3 | 0 | 0 |

a.

| Row | Column | Value | Interpretation of Value |
|---|---|---|---|
| $x_3$ | RHS | 12 | |
| $x_3$ | $x_2$ | 2 | |
| $s_2$ | RHS | 6 | |
| $s_3$ | $x_4$ | 1 | |
| $z_j$ | $s_1$ | 3 | |
| $c_j - z_j$ | $x_1$ | -2 | |

b. If you were forced to bring in $x_4$, what variable would go out?

11. Mr. Adams is the manufacturing superintendent for the Cyclone Block and Brick Company. The company manufactures both cinder blocks and bricks. The company receives a profit margin of $3.25 and $6.00 per 100 bricks and cinder blocks respectively. Currently Mr. Adams has no commitment to customers for bricks or blocks. No inventory of either bricks or blocks exists. The production of both bricks and cinder blocks requires a two-step process. They are first molded and then baked. The molding process is such that 100 bricks require 4 hours of molding time while 100 blocks can be molded in 8 hours. The baking process does not differ for bricks or blocks—8 hours are required per 100 bricks or blocks. A maximum of 80 hours per week is available for molding while the maximum time available for baking is 120 hours per week. The company has assured Mr. Adams that it can sell all the bricks and blocks he can produce since the construction industry is in a boom period.

a. Formulate a linear programming model of the problem that will allow Mr. Adams to maximize contribution to profits for the company.

b. Solve the problem using the simplex method.

c. Interpret all slack variables in the problem.

12. The Watts Manufacturing Company produces and markets AM and AM-FM radios. The production of an AM radio requires 4 hours of production time, while the production of an AM-FM radio requires 6 hours of production time. The plant is such that a total of 96 man-hours per week is available for production. Management of the company has determined that a maximum of 30 AM and 20 AM-FM radios can be sold each week. The contribution to profits from the sale of each AM radio is $6, while an AM-FM radio will contribute $12 to profits. How many of each type of radio should the company manufacture weekly, if it is to maximize its profits? Could the company increase its profits by increasing its production capacity?

13. Given the following linear programming problem:

MAXIMIZE:       $Z = 8x_1 + 12x_2 + 10x_3$

SUBJECT TO:       $2x_1 + 4x_2 + 2x_3 \leq 60$

$$9x_1 + 4x_2 + 16x_3 \leq 242$$

$$5x_1 + 4x_2 + 6x_3 \leq 125$$

$$x_1, x_2, x_3 \geq 0$$

a. Solve the problem using the simplex method.
b. Does the problem have an alternate optimum? If so, compute this alternate solution.
c. Develop a linear equation that would describe the *family of optimal solutions* that lies between the optimal solutions found in parts (a) and (b).

14. Given the initial simplex tableau for a minimization linear programming problem shown in Table P7-14:

**TABLE P7-14.  Initial Tableau for Problem 14**

| $c_B$ | Variables in Basis | Right-hand Side (Solution) | $-20$ | $-10$ | $0$ | $0$ | $-500$ | $-500$ |
|---|---|---|---|---|---|---|---|---|
| | $c_j \rightarrow$ | | $x_1$ | $x_2$ | $s_1$ | $s_2$ | $A_1$ | $A_2$ |
| $0$ | $s_1$ | $40$ | $1$ | $2$ | $1$ | $0$ | $0$ | $0$ |
| $-500$ | $A_1$ | $30$ | $3$ | $1$ | $0$ | $0$ | $1$ | $0$ |
| $-500$ | $A_2$ | $60$ | $4$ | $3$ | $0$ | $-1$ | $0$ | $1$ |
| | $z_j$ | $-45,000$ | $-3,500$ | $-2,000$ | $0$ | $500$ | $-500$ | $-500$ |
| | $c_j - z_j$ | | $3,480$ | $1,990$ | $0$ | $-500$ | $0$ | $0$ |

a. How many decision variables and constraints exist in the original problem?
b. Recognizing that the $s_1$ variable is the slack variable associated with the first constraint, $s_2$ is the surplus variable associated with the third constraint, $A_1$ is the artificial variable

associated with the second constraint, and $A_2$ is the artificial variable associated with the third constraint, reconstruct the original LP problem.

15. Set the following problems up in the initial tableau of the simplex method. *Do not solve.*

   **a.** MINIMIZE:     $Z = 18x_1 + 22x_2 + 14x_3$

      SUBJECT TO:     $4x_1 + 2x_2 + 2x_3 \geq 100$

                        $5x_1 + 3x_2 + 6x_3 \geq 153$

                        $x_1, x_2, x_3 \geq 0$

   **b.** MAXIMIZE:     $Z = 12x_1 + 8x_2 + 10x_3$

      SUBJECT TO:     $6x_1 + 3x_2 + 3x_3 \leq 60$

                        $2x_1 + 2x_2 + 2x_3 \leq 20$

                        $4x_1 + 6x_2 + 2x_3 \geq 120$

                        $x_1, x_2, x_3 \geq 0$

   **c.** MINIMIZE:     $Z = 8x_1 + 24x_2$

      SUBJECT TO:     $30x_1 + 88x_2 \leq 1320$

                        $-8x_1 + 16x_2 \leq -64$

                        $18x_1 + 30x_2 = 540$

                        $x_1, x_2 \geq 0$

   **d.** MAXIMIZE:     $Z = 10x_1 + 15x_2$

      SUBJECT TO:     $10x_1 + 8x_2 \leq 40$

                        $22x_1 = 8x_2$

                        $-8x_1 + 10x_2 \geq 20$

                        $x_1, x_2 \geq 0$

16. Assume a linear programming model has 10 decision variables ($x$'s), 5 less-than-or-equal-to ($\leq$) type of constraints, 15 greater-than-or-equal-to ($\geq$) constraints, and 5 equality ($=$) constraints.

   **a.** How many total variables exist when the problem is structured in "equation" form (i.e., after adding slack, surplus, and artificial variables)?

   **b.** How many basic solutions exist? How would you go about finding these solutions?

   **c.** Is each of the basic solutions identified in part (b) equivalent to a vertex of the feasible region? Explain.

   **d.** Explain how the simplex method avoids testing all basic feasible solutions in determining the optimal solution.

17. Consider the following constraint set and its graphical representation. The constraint set (after addition of slack, surplus and artificials) is

$$x_1 + x_2 + s_1 \qquad\qquad\qquad = 10$$

$$-2x_1 + 2x_2 \quad + s_2 \qquad\qquad = 8$$

$$x_1 \qquad\qquad + s_3 \qquad = 5$$

$$x_2 \qquad\qquad - s_4 + A_1 = 2$$

$$x_1, x_2, s_1, s_2, s_3, s_4, A_1 \geq 0$$

The graphical representation is shown in Figure P7-17. For each vertex, A–E, it is possible to compute the values of all of the variables in the constraint set. For example, for vertex A, we use the last constraint and the nonnegativity condition, $x_1 \geq 0$, to determine that $x_2 = 2$ and $x_1 = 0$. Then, substituting these values into each constraint, we arrive at the values of the remaining variables:

$$s_1 = 8, \quad s_2 = 4, \quad s_3 = 5, \quad s_4 = 0, \quad A_1 = 0$$

**FIGURE P7-17. Graphical Representation of Problem 17**

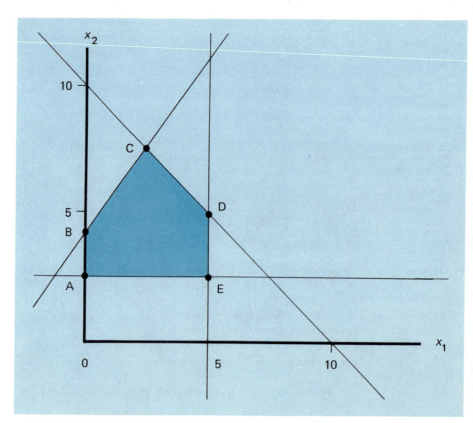

Using these values, we can reason that since $x_2$, $s_1$, $s_2$, and $s_3$ are positive, they are basic and the remaining variables are nonbasic.

**a.** The values for vertex A have been supplied in Table P7-17. Compute the values for the remaining vertices, B–E. Also, circle the *basic* variables for each vertex.

**TABLE P7-17. Values of Variables**

| Point | $x_1$ | $x_2$ | $s_1$ | $s_2$ | $s_3$ | $s_4$ | $A_1$ |
|-------|-------|-------|-------|-------|-------|-------|-------|
| A     | 0     | 2     | 8     | 4     | 5     | 0     | 0     |
| B     |       |       |       |       |       |       |       |
| C     |       |       |       |       |       |       |       |
| D     |       |       |       |       |       |       |       |
| E     |       |       |       |       |       |       |       |

**b.** For the following objective functions, determine the optimal point and its objective value:

    **i.** Maximize:     $3x_1 + 3x_2$     opt. pt. _____ Z = _____

    **ii.** Minimize:     $2x_1 - 5x_2$     opt. pt. _____ Z = _____

**c.** Did any "nonstandard" situations occur in either case? If so, what were they?

18. An air freight company wishes to maximize the revenue it receives from cargo shipped. The company has a single plane designed to transport two kinds of cargo: delicate cargo and ordinary cargo. The company does not receive a premium payment for transporting delicate cargo; however, in order to secure certain business contracts, the company has agreed to transport at least 5 tons of the delicate cargo. The delicate cargo must be carried in a pressurized cabin, while the ordinary cargo can be carried in an unpressurized mainhold. The mainhold has a capacity of 20 tons of cargo. The pressurized hold can handle no more than 10 tons of cargo. The plane has a weight restriction that permits no more than 28 tons of cargo. In order to maintain a weight balance, the pressurized cabin cargo must be equal to or less than two-thirds of the weight of the mainhold cargo plus one ton. The company receives $1000 per ton for either type of cargo shipped. Following is a linear programming formulation for the problem:

Let $x_1$ = tons of ordinary cargo transported

    $x_2$ = tons of delicate cargo transported

MAXIMIZE:      $Z = 1000x_1 + 1000x_2$

SUBJECT TO:                  $x_2 \geq 5$

               $x_1 \qquad \leq 20$

                   $x_2 \leq 10$

             $x_1 + \qquad x_2 \leq 28$

          $-\frac{2}{3}x_1 + \qquad x_2 \leq 1$

               $x_1, x_2 \geq 0$

a. Solve using the simplex method.

b. Interpret the slack variables for the problem.

c. Does the problem have an alternate optimum? Explain.

19. A contract has been given to a computer manufacturer to supply 200 microcomputers to two military bases. The manufacturer has three plants, located in different regions of the United States, in which the microcomputers are assembled. The plants and their associated monthly production capacities are as follows: Houston, Texas—50 units; Seattle, Washington—60 units; Richmond, Virginia—90 units. The requirements at the respective bases are: base 1—80 units; base 2—100 units. The per-unit shipping costs, as well as supply and demand (units), are given in the following table:

| Plant \ Base | 1 | 2 | Supply |
|---|---|---|---|
| Houston, Tx. | 75 | 110 | 50 |
| Seattle, Wa. | 100 | 85 | 60 |
| Richmond, Va. | 140 | 150 | 90 |
| Demand | 80 | 100 | 180 ⟍ 200 |

The computer manufacturer would like to develop a shipping schedule such that total shipping cost is minimized. Following is the formulated model for the problem:

Let $x_{ij}$ = number of units shipped from plant $i$ to base $j$

where $i$ = 1 (Houston, Tx.)

  = 2 (Seattle, Wa.)

  = 3 (Richmond, Va.)

  $j$ = 1, 2

MINIMIZE:   $Z = 75x_{11} + 110x_{12} + 100x_{21} + 85x_{22} + 140x_{31} + 150x_{32}$

SUBJECT TO:

$$x_{11} + x_{12} \leq 50$$
$$x_{21} + x_{22} \leq 60$$
$$x_{31} + x_{32} \leq 90$$
$$x_{11} + x_{21} + x_{31} = 80$$
$$x_{12} + x_{22} + x_{32} = 100$$

$$x_{ij} \geq 0 \text{ for all } i \text{ and } j$$

a. Add slack, surplus, and artificial variables as necessary and set up in the initial simplex tableau.

b. Solve using the simplex method. (*Note:* Because of the special structure of the problem, the solution procedure is easier than that required for a general LP problem.)

**20.** The following problems illustrate cases of problem formulations that result in *unbounded solutions* or *no feasible solutions*. Use the simplex method to identify the solution situation that exists in each of the problems. Indicate how you identify each situation.

**a.** MINIMIZE:      $Z = -4x_1 + 6x_2$

SUBJECT TO:      $18x_1 + 14x_2 \geq 126$

$10x_1 + 24x_2 \geq 60$

$x_1, x_2 \geq 0$

**b.** MAXIMIZE:      $Z = 3x_1 + 3x_2 + 3x_3$

SUBJECT TO:      $2x_1 + 10x_2 + 4x_3 \geq 500$

$2x_2 + 4x_3 \geq 100$

$x_1, x_2, x_3 \geq 0$

**c.** MAXIMIZE:      $Z = 9x_1 + 3x_2$

SUBJECT TO:      $14x_1 + 10x_2 \geq 280$

$-8x_1 + 16x_2 \leq 64$

$x_1, x_2 \geq 0$

**d.** MINIMIZE:      $Z = 5x_1 + 10x_2$

SUBJECT TO:      $-10x_1 + 6x_2 \geq 60$

$8x_1 + 15x_2 \leq 120$

$x_1, x_2 \geq 0$

# Sensitivity Analysis and Duality

## ■ Introduction

In Chapter 7 it was shown that the simplex method (algorithm) can be used to solve practical LP problems that involve large numbers of constraints and/or variables. Several variations of the standard maximization procedure (the simplex method) were also noted, such as: (1) how to handle minimization problems, (2) procedures necessary to incorporate the greater-than type of constraints, and (3) procedures for handling negative right-hand-side values. Two additional topics in linear programming, sensitivity analysis and duality, will be addressed in this chapter.

Sensitivity analysis is a method for investigating the effect of changes in different parameters on the optimal solution of an LP problem. We can change the coefficients in the objective function, the right-hand-side values of constraint equations, or the coefficients associated directly with the constraints. Quite often the coefficients of the objective function or the right-hand-side values of constraint equations are estimates, so the sensitivity of the solution to changes in these coefficients is particularly valuable. The impact of changes in the coefficients in the body of the constraints is less significant since they are derived from the technology of the problem. It is more likely that these latter coefficients are actual values as opposed to estimates. For these reasons, we will consider only changes in the objective-function coefficients and in the right-hand-side values.

Duality, or the dual formulation of the linear programming problem, provides a method for solving an alternate form of the linear programming problem. An advantage of duality is that it can reduce the computational burden of certain LP problems. These concepts and points are highlighted in this chapter. To illustrate sensitivity analysis and the concept of the dual, we will continue to use the Agro-Tech Inc. example. The case, however, will be extended to include the possible production of a third fertilizer.

*sensitivity analysis*

■ **Case**

# Agro-Tech Inc. (revised)

When we last saw Mr. Tom Anderson of Agro-Tech Inc., he was attempting to determine the most profitable production mix of 5-5-10 and 5-10-5 fertilizers, the first of which sold for $71.50 per ton; the second, for $69 per ton. In the planning process, Tom had to work within the framework of the availability of the scarce raw materials that went into production of the fertilizers. Recall that the raw materials were nitrate, phosphate, and potash. Prices of the raw materials were $200, $80, and $160 per ton, respectively; and 1100, 1800, and 2000 tons of the respective resources were available. Using this information, plus the price of $10 per ton for an unlimited quantity of filler and a price of $15 per ton for mixing, we computed the contributions to profit of $18.50/ton for the 5-5-10 and $20.00/ton for the 5-10-5. We then formulated the problem as a two-variable three-constraint linear programming problem and solved it via the simplex method. The result of this formulation and its solution was that the optimal policy would be to produce 8,000 tons of 5-5-10 and 14,000 tons of 5-10-5. The production and sale of these amounts would result in a contribution to profit of $428,000 for Agro-Tech Inc.

This month, Tom has a new problem. While the availabilities and costs of raw materials have remained the same, the company wishes to consider producing a new product, a 5-5-5 fertilizer that can be sold for $60 per ton. Tom now has three rather than two products to consider in his production decision. Since Agro-Tech does not have any back orders or committed orders that *must* be filled for any of the products, Tom wants to produce the fertilizer combination that will provide the maximum contribution to profit.

To formulate the problem, Tom had decided to let

$x_1$ = tons of 5-5-10 to be produced

$x_2$ = tons of 5-10-5 to be produced

$x_3$ = tons of 5-5-5 to be produced

Using the $60 per ton selling price and the ingredient mix (5-5-5) for the third product, the contribution to profit for the 5-5-5 fertilizer is $14.50/ton. Since no additional constraints have been added, Tom formulated the problem as follows:

MAXIMIZE:

$$Z = 18.5x_1 + 20x_2 + 14.5x_3 \qquad (8.1)$$

SUBJECT TO:

$$.05x_1 + .05x_2 + .05x_3 \leq 1100 \qquad (8.2)$$

$$.05x_1 + .10x_2 + .05x_3 \leq 1800 \qquad (8.3)$$

$$.10x_1 + .05x_2 + .05x_3 \leq 2000 \qquad (8.4)$$

$$x_1, x_2, x_3 \geq 0 \qquad (8.5)$$

Using the simplex method to solve the above problem results in the optimal tableau presented in Table 8-1. Upon examining this solution, Tom notes that the solution is exactly equal to that of the original two-product problem; that is, the company should produce 8,000 tons of the 5-5-10 fertilizer and 14,000 tons of the 5-10-5 fertilizer. The expected profits would again be $428,000. This result is somewhat puzzling to Tom since the solution means the production schedule can remain unchanged, but Tom sees no reason not to accept the solution.

However, there are some other departments within Agro-Tech that could affect Tom's decision to remain with the current production schedule. The fact that *none* of the new 5-5-5 fertilizer would be produced if the suggested LP solution were used worries Susan Jones of Agro-Tech's marketing department. Ms. Jones recognizes that the linear programming solution to the problem

| $c_B$ | Variables in the Basis | Right-hand Side (Solution) | $x_1$ | $x_2$ | $x_3$ | $s_1$ | $s_2$ | $s_3$ |
|---|---|---|---|---|---|---|---|---|
| | $c_j \rightarrow$ | | 18.5 | 20.0 | 14.5 | 0 | 0 | 0 |
| 18.5 | $x_1$ | 8,000 | 1 | 0 | 1 | 40 | $-20$ | 0 |
| 20.0 | $x_2$ | 14,000 | 0 | 1 | 0 | $-20$ | 20 | 0 |
| 0 | $s_3$ | 500 | 0 | 0 | $-.05$ | $-3$ | 1 | 1 |
| | $z_j$ | 428,000 | 18.5 | 20 | 18.5 | 340 | 30 | 0 |
| | $c_j - z_j$ | | 0 | 0 | $-4.0$ | $-340$ | $-30$ | 0 |

**TABLE 8-1.**
**Optimal Tableau for Three-Product Problem**

would yield the maximum-profit production mix, but she also knows that producing the new 5-5-5 fertilizer is important for marketing reasons. Ms. Jones cannot force the production department to sacrifice profit to produce some of the 5-5-5, but she has the power to increase the selling price of the 5-5-5 in order to make it profitable enough to be included in the optimal production mix for the upcoming month. She would like to know how much the price would have to be raised to make the production of the 5-5-5 fertilizer profitable.

At the same time that Ms. Jones is considering increasing the price of the 5-5-5, Burt Hawkins, the purchasing agent for Agro-Tech, is considering a possible change in raw materials. There is a possibility that the availability of nitrate will

decrease for the upcoming month. Mr. Hawkins is not certain what the magnitude of the decrease will be, so he cannot give Tom Anderson a value to use in planning production.

Another change being considered is a possible decrease in the price charged for the 5-5-10. Salesmen are reporting that a competing company has dropped the price on its 5-5-10. And, as a result, Agro-Tech must consider dropping the price of its 5-5-10 to meet the competition.

From an overall company point of view, Tom Anderson's decision to continue producing only two fertilizers must be reexamined in light of the points raised by the marketing and purchasing departments. Sensitivity analysis can be used to aid Tom in further study of the problem.

## ■ Sensitivity analysis

One of the assumptions we have made in our discussion of linear programming is that the values of the parameters of the problem are known with certainty. We assumed, for example, that in the extended Agro-Tech problem the objective-function coefficients were 18.5, 20, and 14.5, respectively. Similarly, we used the available resource levels of 1100, 1800, and 2000. But the values of these parameters are not always known with certainty. For example, changes in the cost of materials, cost of labor, or price of a product would cause changes in the coefficients. On the resource side, delayed shipments from suppliers, strikes, spoilage, and other factors all lead to changes in the supply of resources. Each of these changes could affect the optimal solution to the original LP problem.

Each of the price changes, material shortages, etc., in the extended Agro-Tech case is an example of what can potentially happen to one or more of the parameters in a linear programming problem. Each represents an effect that can be examined through sensitivity analysis. To understand each, it is necessary to analyze the changes separately. For example, to analyze a price increase for the 5-5-5 fertilizer, we will assume that the availability of nitrate will continue at the existing level. To examine a reduction in the availability of nitrate, we will assume the contribution to profits of the 5-5-5 fertilizer remains at the existing value, $14.50.

One means of analyzing changes in objective-function coefficients or right-hand-side values is to re-solve the linear programming problem using the new values. This is often unnecessary, however, since the changed problem may have the same optimal set of basic variables. Sensitivity analysis allows one to determine the impact of change without repeating the entire solution process.

In studying and analyzing the impact of changing a model parameter, we would like to be able to compute the limits of change in an objective-function coefficient or right-hand-side value. That is, it would be desirable to know how much a given objective-function coefficient or right-hand-side value can change without changing the current optimal solution. If a proposed parameter change falls within the allowed limits of change, then no change in the optimal solution occurs, and it is not necessary to solve the new LP problem. If the proposed change falls outside the limits, then the existing optimal solution will no longer be optimal, and a new LP optimal solution *must* be computed. The procedures of sensitivity analysis allow one to compute these limits of change.

We will use the optimal tableau of the Agro-Tech three-fertilizer problem (Table 8-1) as the vehicle for analyzing changes in both the objective-function coefficients and the right-hand-side values.

The basic analysis will be presented under three subheadings: (1) *change in the objective-function coefficient of a nonbasic variable*; (2) *change in the objective-function coefficient of a basic variable*; and (3) *change in a resource value*.

## Change in the objective-function coefficient of a nonbasic variable

We begin our analysis by considering the impact of changing the profit value (the objective-function coefficient) for one of the variables that is not currently basic (that is, for a nonbasic variable). Our example is the case regarding the new 5-5-5 fertilizer.

Recall that Ms. Jones would like to know how much to increase the price of the 5-5-5 in order to make it sufficiently profitable to be included in the optimal linear programming product mix. Recall also that a nonbasic variable is one whose net contribution to profit (that is, $c_j - z_j$) in the optimal tableau is nonpositive. The profit that would be gained by producing any quantity of a nonbasic variable is less than or equal to the profit that it would be necessary to give up in order to produce that variable. Referring to Table 8-1, we see that variables $x_3$, $s_1$, and $s_2$ are nonbasic variables.

From a graphical point of view, a change in the profit value for any variable is equivalent to a change in the slope of the iso-profit lines that are used to find the optimal solution. To see how this works, consider the hypothetical graphical solution of an LP problem shown in Figure 8-1.

In Figure 8-1, the original optimal solution occurs at point D with objective function 1. At point D, $x_1$ is basic and $x_2$ is nonbasic. However, if the profit of $x_2$ increases, the slope of the objective function changes because it takes fewer units of $x_2$ to have equal profit with a unit of $x_1$. If the profit on $x_2$ increases enough, the objective function will become the dashed line marked 2. For this objective function, the optimal solution is point C, and both $x_1$ and $x_2$ are basic.

The sensitivity of the optimal solution to changes in the coefficients of the objective function can be determined by adding an amount $\Delta_j$ to the existing objective-function coefficient, $c_j$. The new objective-function coefficient thus is

$$\bar{c}_j = \Delta_j + c_j$$

We can determine how large $\Delta_j$ can be from the optimality requirement that $(c_j - z_j)$ be zero or negative for a maximization problem. For the modified

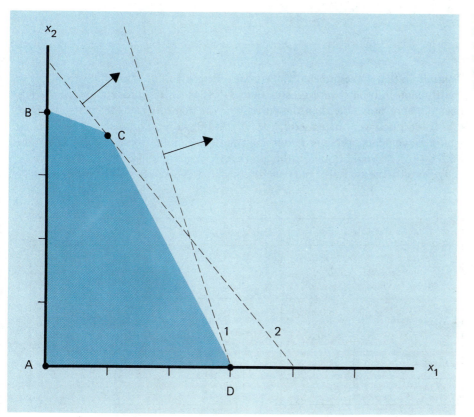

**FIGURE 8-1.**
**Graphical Change of Objective-Function Coefficient for a Two-Variable Problem**

coefficient, $\bar{c}_j$, this means that $\bar{c}_j - z_j \leq 0$. Sensitivity is measured by the value of $\Delta_j$, since it indicates the range of costs over which the existing optimal solution will remain optimal.

Considering $x_3$, recall that Ms. Jones would like to determine how much of a price increase would be required in order to produce the 5-5-5 fertilizer. We can answer this question by determining the $\Delta_3$ (and the $\bar{c}_3$) for the $x_3$ variable. We begin the process by adding a $\Delta_3$ coefficient to the $c_3$ coefficient associated with $x_3$ in the tableau.

Table 8-2 shows the modified tableau. Before $x_3$ can become basic, the $(\bar{c}_j - z_j)$ value associated with $x_3$ must become nonnegative. Expressed in terms of the actual values in the tableau, this means that

$$\Delta_3 - 4.0 \geq 0 \tag{8.6}$$

Solving for $\Delta_3$, we have $\Delta_3 \geq 4.0$. Since $\bar{c}_3 = c_3 + \Delta_3$,

$$\bar{c}_3 = 14.5 + \Delta_3$$

Substituting $\Delta_3 \geq 4.0$ yields

$$\bar{c}_3 \geq 18.5 \tag{8.7}$$

This tells us that if the price on $x_3$ were raised slightly more than \$4.00, that is, if its contribution to profits were greater than \$18.50, then the production of $x_3$ would become more profitable than the current production mix of 8,000 $x_1$'s and 14,000 $x_2$'s. If the price were increased by exactly \$4.00, we would be at a decision point where $x_3$ could be produced, but no additional profit would result. The same \$428,000 profit would result for this alternate optimal solution.

To simplify the analysis, note that equation (8.6) is taken from Table 8-2, and note

**TABLE 8-2.**
**Modified Tableau**
**for Change in $c_3$**

| $c_B$ | $c_j \rightarrow$ Variables in the Basis | Right-hand Side (Solution) | 18.5 $x_1$ | 20.0 $x_2$ | $14.5 + \Delta_3$ $x_3$ | 0 $s_1$ | 0 $s_2$ | 0 $s_3$ |
|---|---|---|---|---|---|---|---|---|
| 18.5 | $x_1$ | 8,000 | 1 | 0 | 1 | 40 | −20 | 0 |
| 20.0 | $x_2$ | 14,000 | 0 | 1 | 0 | −20 | 20 | 0 |
| 0 | $s_3$ | 500 | 0 | 0 | −.05 | −3 | 1 | 1 |
| | $z_j$ | 428,000 | 18.5 | 20 | 18.5 | 340 | 30 | 0 |
| | $\bar{c}_j - z_j$ | | 0 | 0 | $\Delta_3 - 4.0$ | −340 | −30 | 0 |

that $c_3 - z_3 = -4$ in Table 8-1. By simple algebraic substitution in equation (8.6) we have

$$\Delta_3 - 4.0 \geq 0$$

$$\Delta_3 + (c_3 - z_3) \geq 0$$

$$\Delta_3 \geq - (c_3 - z_3)$$

or

$$\Delta_3 \geq |c_3 - z_3| \qquad (8.8)$$

Therefore, rather than performing the analysis shown in Table 8-2 to determine $\Delta_3$, we could determine the upper limit on the coefficient by simply taking the absolute value of $(c_3 - z_3)$ in Table 8-1. This will be true for all nonbasic variables.

If the price of $x_3$ were reduced, that is, if $\Delta_3$ were allowed to be negative, then the resulting contribution to profits would be less than the current \$14.50 per ton of $x_3$. A quick look at Table 8-2 tells us that this would have no impact on the current optimal solution since the $(\bar{c}_3 - z_3)$ value would be more negative than $-4.0$.

To answer Ms. Jones's question regarding a price increase of product 3, it is not necessary to perform an analysis of the change in the coefficient of the other nonbasic variables, $s_1$ and $s_2$. However, one can employ the above analysis, if desired, on each of these variables.

As the above computational procedure indicates, for the case of changes in the objective-function coefficient of a nonbasic variable, sensitivity analysis is fairly simple. If the profit on the nonbasic variable decreases, there is no change in the optimal solution; or if the profit contribution increases by an amount less than the $|c_j - z_j|$ value for the variable, there will be no change in the optimal solution. *Only if the contribution to profits increases by an amount that is greater than the present value of $|c_j - z_j|$ will the optimal solution change.* Intuitively, this is what should occur. A nonbasic variable is not in the optimal solution because the profit from producing that product is less than what would be lost by producing the product. To change this relationship, it is necessary to increase the profit contribution on the product until it is equal to or greater than what would be lost by producing the product.

## Change in the objective-function coefficient of a basic variable

We have just considered a change in the profit value (objective-function coefficient) of a nonbasic variable. Now we will consider a change in the profit coefficient of a *basic* variable, that is, a variable that is basic in the optimal linear programming solution. We will use the problem being faced by Agro-Tech Inc. in regard to the

5-5-10 fertilizer to illustrate this concept. Currently, the optimal product mix contains the 5-5-10 fertilizer, but, as with the nonbasic-variable profit-coefficient case, we are interested in knowing the maximum that the basic profit coefficient can change *before* changing the remaining basic variables in the optimal solution.

From a graphical approach, this situation is equivalent to that shown in Figure 8-1 for a change in an objective-function coefficient. The change in a basic coefficient serves to change the slope of the iso-profit lines, which, in turn, can lead to a different vertex being optimal.

If the contribution to profit in a basic variable changes, then one of two results can occur. If the contribution coefficient of the basic variable decreases, then the variable could leave the basis since it may not be sufficiently profitable to keep the variable basic. On the other hand, if the contribution to profits of a basic variable increases, a greater production level for the variable under consideration may result. Unlike changes in the contribution coefficients for nonbasic variables, both increases and decreases in contribution coefficients of basic variables must be considered. And unlike the nonbasic-variable cases, changes up or down in profit-contribution coefficients for basic variables *will* in some way impact upon the existing solution.

To analyze the effect of changes in the contribution to profits for a basic variable we can, as we did in the case in the nonbasic analysis, add a $\Delta_j$ coefficient to the existing $c_j$ coefficient. We again denote the new contribution to profits as $\bar{c}_j = c_j + \Delta_j$. In the nonbasic-variable case, the addition of $\Delta_j$ affected only one column of the tableau. However, in the case of the basic variable, more than one column may be affected. So in determining the limits on $\Delta_j$, we must examine all $(c_j - z_j)$ values that are affected by the $\Delta_j$.

To illustrate the procedure for determining the sensitivity of the optimal solution to changes in objective-function coefficients of basic variables, consider the tableau shown in Table 8-3.

In this tableau, we are investigating changes in the profits for the 5-5-10 fertilizer. At this time, the profit for 5-5-10 fertilizer is \$18.50. We have added a $\Delta_1$ coefficient to use in analyzing changes in the profit for $x_1$. The $\Delta_1$ has been added in *all* places

**TABLE 8-3. Modified Tableau for Change in $c_1$**

| $\bar{c}_B$ | $\bar{c}_j \rightarrow$ | | $18.5 + \Delta_1$ | 20 | 14.5 | 0 | 0 | 0 |
|---|---|---|---|---|---|---|---|---|
| | Variables in the Basis | Right-hand Side (Solution) | $x_1$ | $x_2$ | $x_3$ | $s_1$ | $s_2$ | $s_3$ |
| $18.5 + \Delta_1$ | $x_1$ | 8,000 | 1 | 0 | 1 | 40 | $-20$ | 0 |
| 20 | $x_2$ | 14,000 | 0 | 1 | 0 | $-20$ | 20 | 0 |
| 0 | $s_3$ | 500 | 0 | 0 | $-.05$ | $-3$ | 1 | 1 |
| | $\bar{z}_j$ | 428,000 $+8,000\Delta_1$ | $18.5 + \Delta_1$ | 20 | $18.5 + \Delta_1$ | $340 + 40\Delta_1$ | $30 - 20\Delta_1$ | 0 |
| | $\bar{c}_j - \bar{z}_j$ | | 0 | 0 | $-4 - \Delta_1$ | $-340 - 40\Delta_1$ | $-30 + 20\Delta_1$ | 0 |

where $c_1$ occurs. The new $z_j$ row, $\bar{z}_j$, is then computed. For example, the $\bar{z}_j$ value for $s_1$ becomes $(340 + 40\Delta_1)$, the $\bar{z}_j$ value for $x_3$ is $(18.5 + \Delta_1)$, etc. The $(\bar{c}_j - \bar{z}_j)$ values are then computed using the revised $\bar{c}_j$ value and all revised $\bar{z}_j$ values.

For the present solution (Table 8-1) to remain optimal, we cannot have *any* $(\bar{c}_j - \bar{z}_j)$ values in Table 8-3 become positive. The question is: How much can $c_1$ change in either a positive or negative direction and maintain the optimality conditions? We can determine the magnitude of these changes, $\Delta_j$, by solving an inequality for each nonbasic $(\bar{c}_j - \bar{z}_j)$ value, that is,

$$\bar{c}_j - \bar{z}_j \le 0 \tag{8.9}$$

For example, for $x_3$, we have $-4 - \Delta_1 \le 0$, which results in $\Delta_1 \ge -4$. For $s_1$, we have $-340 - 40\Delta_1 \le 0$, which results in $\Delta_1 \ge -8.5$. Finally, for $s_2$, we have $-30 + 20\Delta_1 \le 0$, which results in $\Delta_1 \le 1.5$. In summary, we have the following conditions for a $\Delta_1$ change in the profit value $c_1$:

$$\Delta_1 \ge -4 \tag{8.10}$$

$$\Delta_1 \ge -8.5 \tag{8.11}$$

$$\Delta_1 \le 1.5 \tag{8.12}$$

Now we must select the most restrictive set of conditions. First note that we only have one less-than-or-equal-to condition that must obviously be binding. That is, $\Delta_1 \le 1.5$. There are two greater-than-or-equal-to conditions, and we pick the condition closest to zero since it will satisfy all other greater-than-or-equal-to conditions. In other words, since $-4 \ge -8.5$, if we select $\Delta_1 \ge -4$, we also satisfy the other condition.

The permissible changes in $c_1$ can be expressed as $-4 \le \Delta_1 \le 1.5$. Thus the contribution to profits on $x_1$ cannot increase by more than \$1.50 or decrease by more than \$4. From this analysis, we see that the profit on $x_1$ is limited to be between $c_1 - 4$ and $c_1 + 1.5$, or $\$14.50 \le c_1 \le \$20$.

In this problem, we had two greater-than-or-equal-to conditions and only one less-than-or-equal-to condition that existed; consequently, we found the analysis was somewhat straightforward. To aid in other problems, we may generalize our results with the following two rules.

1. If there are multiple greater-than-or-equal-to conditions of the form

$$\Delta_j \ge -g_i$$

   then the condition with the $-g_i$ value closest to zero is the one to be used in determining the appropriate range of profits.

2. If there are multiple less-than-or-equal-to conditions of the form

$$\Delta_j \le h_i$$

   then the condition with the $h_i$ value closest to zero is the one to be used in determining the appropriate range of profits.

**TABLE 8-4.**
**Revised Tableau**
**for $\Delta_1 = +6.5$**

| $\bar{c}_j \rightarrow$ | | | 25 | 20 | 14.5 | 0 | 0 | 0 |
|---|---|---|---|---|---|---|---|---|
| $\bar{c}_B$ | Variables in the Basis | Right-hand Side (Solution) | $x_1$ | $x_2$ | $x_3$ | $s_1$ | $s_2$ | $s_3$ |
| 25 | $x_1$ | 8,000 | 1 | 0 | 1 | 40 | $-20$ | 0 |
| 20 | $x_2$ | 14,000 | 0 | 1 | 0 | $-20$ | 20 | 0 |
| 0 | $s_3$ | 500 | 0 | 0 | $-.05$ | $-3$ | 1 | 1 |
| | $\bar{z}_j$ | 480,000 | 25 | 20 | 25 | 600 | $-100$ | 0 |
| | $\bar{c}_j - \bar{z}_j$ | | 0 | 0 | $-10.5$ | $-600$ | $+100$ | 0 |

If the change in the objective-function coefficient of either a nonbasic or basic variable is greater than that allowable to maintain optimality, then the tableau will have to be reoptimized. But this is generally not difficult, since one can start with the former optimal tableau and continue pivoting until optimality is achieved. For example, we have seen that $c_1$ in Table 8-3 must be above \$14.50 and below \$20 in order for the optimal product mix to remain the same. Suppose that market conditions allowed an increase in the profit for product 1 up to \$25. This is outside the above-stated limits, so the present product mix would no longer be optimal. The new $z_j$ and $(c_j - z_j)$ rows may be computed from Table 8-3 by letting $\Delta_1 = +6.5$ (i.e., \$25 − 18.5). The revised tableau is shown in Table 8-4.

We can see from Table 8-4 that the total objective value has increased by 52,000, from \$428,000 to \$480,000. The $(c_j - z_j)$ values have also changed with the $(c_j - z_j)$ value for $s_2$ becoming positive. This implies that the present product mix is no longer optimal, and that $s_2$ must be brought into the basis in order to move back to optimality.

## Change in a resource level

The sensitivity of the optimal solution to changes in the right-hand-side (resource) values of the constraint equations is often as important to a business manager as are changes in other coefficients. As was the case for changes in the objective-function coefficients, the sensitivity of the optimal solution to resource changes is measured by an upper bound and a lower bound on the resource level being changed.

Graphically, a change in a resource level serves to shift a constraint line in such a way as either to shrink or enlarge the feasible region. Consider, once again, a graphical solution for a hypothetical LP problem (see Figure 8-2).

In this problem, we assume there is either an increase, $+\Delta b_1$, or a decrease, $-\Delta b_1$, in the resource level $b_1$. If point C is the original optimal solution, then an increase in the resource level $b_1$ will shift point C to C′, but the same two variables, $x_1$ and $x_2$, are

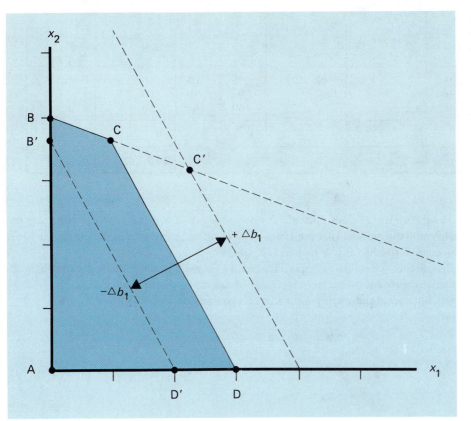

**FIGURE 8-2.**
**Graphical Change**
**in Resource Level**

still optimal. On the other hand, if there is a decrease in the resource level $b_1$, the only two feasible corner points are B' and D'. This means that the previous optimal combination of variables is no longer optimal because point C is now infeasible.

To calculate the effect of changing a resource level, we add an amount $\Delta_i$ to the resource to be changed and then go through the solution procedure once again. The initial tableau with revised resource levels for a change in the level of nitrate available is given in Table 8-5. In this case, the new resource level for nitrate is $1100 + \Delta_N$ where $\Delta_N$ is positive *or* negative to reflect possible increases or decreases in the availability of nitrate.

Now if we proceed with the normal simplex iteration and carry along the $\Delta_N$ value at each step, we arrive at the optimal tableau for this problem. Looking at the optimal tableau in Table 8-6 we see that the objective value will increase by \$340 for each additional ton of nitrate that is available for use *at the original cost*. It will also decrease by \$340 for each ton of nitrate that is no longer available for use. We may also see that the new solution values are functions of the change in the resource, $\Delta_N$.

**TABLE 8-5.**
**Initial Tableau for**
**New Resource**
**Level**

| $c_B$ | Variables in the Basis | Right-hand Side (Solution) | $x_1$ | $x_2$ | $x_3$ | $s_1$ | $s_2$ | $s_3$ |
|---|---|---|---|---|---|---|---|---|
| | $c_j \rightarrow$ | | 18.5 | 20 | 14.5 | 0 | 0 | 0 |
| 0 | $s_1$ | $1100 + \Delta_N$ | .05 | .05 | .05 | 1 | 0 | 0 |
| 0 | $s_2$ | 1800 | .05 | .10 | .05 | 0 | 1 | 0 |
| 0 | $s_3$ | 2000 | .10 | .05 | .05 | 0 | 0 | 1 |
| | $z_j$ | 0 | 0 | 0 | 0 | 0 | 0 | 0 |
| | $c_j - z_j$ | | 18.5 | 20 | 14.5 | 0 | 0 | 0 |

Since the solution values must always be nonnegative, we can use these functions to determine the amount that the availability of nitrate can increase or decrease before the current product mix is no longer optimal.

To do this, we simply set up an inequality for each function to be greater than or equal to zero and solve for the range of $\Delta_N$ that satisfies each inequality. These inequalities and the corresponding basic variables are as follows:

$$x_1: \quad 8{,}000 + 40\Delta_N \geq 0$$

$$x_2: \quad 14{,}000 - 20\Delta_N \geq 0$$

$$s_3: \quad 500 - 3\Delta_N \geq 0$$

Notice that each inequality gives a possible size for a change, $\Delta_N$. This net change must be nonnegative to maintain feasibility, hence the inequality. What we must do now is to find the most restrictive set of limits on $\Delta_N$ since these limits will also satisfy

**TABLE 8-6.**
**Optimal Tableau**
**for New Resource**
**Level**

| $c_B$ | Variables in the Basis | Right-hand Side (Solution) | $x_1$ | $x_2$ | $x_3$ | $s_1$ | $s_2$ | $s_3$ |
|---|---|---|---|---|---|---|---|---|
| | $c_j \rightarrow$ | | 18.5 | 20 | 14.5 | 0 | 0 | 0 |
| 18.5 | $x_1$ | $8{,}000 + 40\Delta_N$ | 1 | 0 | 1 | 40 | -20 | 0 |
| 20 | $x_2$ | $14{,}000 - 20\Delta_N$ | 0 | 1 | 0 | -20 | 20 | 0 |
| 0 | $s_3$ | $500 - 3\Delta_N$ | 0 | 0 | -.05 | -3 | 1 | 1 |
| | $z_j$ | $428{,}000 + 340\Delta_N$ | 18.5 | 20 | 18.5 | 340 | 30 | 0 |
| | $c_j - z_j$ | — | 0 | 0 | -4.0 | -340 | -30 | 0 |

the other inequalities. Solving for $\Delta_N$ in each inequality, we have

$$8,000 + 40\Delta_N \geq \longrightarrow \Delta_N \geq -200 \tag{8.13}$$

$$14,000 - 20\Delta_N \geq \longrightarrow \Delta_N \leq 700 \tag{8.14}$$

$$500 - 3\Delta_N \geq \longrightarrow \Delta_N \leq 166.67 \tag{8.15}$$

If $\Delta_N$ is less than 166.67, it is also less than 700, but not vice versa. So our limits on $\Delta_N$ are $-200 \leq \Delta_N \leq 166.67$. This may be interpreted to mean that the availability of nitrate may change anywhere from an increase of 166.67 tons to a decrease of 200 tons without causing the variables in the optimal solution to change. The values of the objective function and the right-hand side will change, but the present mix of variables will remain optimal.

Expressed in terms of the availability of nitrate, $b_N$, we have

$$1100 - 200 \leq b_N \leq 1100 + 166.67 \quad \text{or} \quad 900 \leq b_N \leq 1266.67$$

The present optimal solution thus will remain optimal if at least 900 tons of nitrate are available or no more than 1266.67 tons are employed.

If the actual change, $\Delta_N$, is within the limits given, we may still use the same approach to compute the new solution values and objective value. For example, if the availability of nitrate decreases by 100 tons, then $\Delta_N = -100$ (within the limits of allowable change), and we may use the functions to determine the new solution value. The new values for this case are shown in Table 8-7, from which we can see that the optimal solution would be to produce 4,000 tons of fertilizer 1 and 16,000 tons of fertilizer 2, while 800 tons of potash would remain unused. The profit in this case would drop to $394,000.

If we had to re-solve the LP problem each time there was a change in a resource level, there would be no advantage to this approach. Fortunately, it is *not* necessary to solve the problem again, because the functions of $\Delta_N$ can be computed *directly* from the current optimal tableau. Note that the coefficients of $\Delta_N$ in the optimal tableau (Table 8-6) are the *same* as the coefficients in the $s_1$ column. This should not be surprising since $s_1$ is the slack variable associated with nitrate. It will always be true that the *coefficients of the* $\Delta_i$ *variable in an optimal tableau will be the same as those for the* $s_i$ *slack variable*. For surplus variables, the signs are reversed. This then

| Basic Variable | Old Value | + | Change | = | New Value |
|---|---|---|---|---|---|
| $x_1$ | 8,000 tons | + | $(40)(-100)$ | = | 4,000 tons |
| $x_2$ | 14,000 tons | + | $(-20)(-100)$ | = | 16,000 tons |
| $s_3$ | 500 tons | + | $(-3)(-100)$ | = | 800 tons |
| $z$ | \$428,000 | + | $(340)(-100)$ | = | \$394,000 |

**TABLE 8-7.**
**Effect of Change in Resource Level**

allows us to make our calculations for the upper and lower bounds on $\Delta_i$ directly from the current optimal tableau.

Another important result that we can determine from Table 8-6 is that the $z_j$ *value for the corresponding slack gives us the value of an additional unit of that resource at the same cost.* In our example, the $z_j$ for $s_1$ was 340, so each additional unit of nitrate was worth \$340. This may also be interpreted in another way. If each additional unit of nitrate were to increase Agro-Tech's profit by \$340, then Agro-Tech would be willing to pay as much as \$340 *more* than it is now paying for nitrate. For example, if additional nitrate became available at a price of \$400/ton (\$200 more than previously charged), Agro-Tech would still buy the additional nitrate, realizing that there would then be only \$340 $-$ \$200 $=$ \$140 profit per additional ton of fertilizer.

*shadow prices*

Because the $z_j$ values for each slack indicate the value of an additional unit of the corresponding resource, these values are often referred to as **shadow prices.** The relationship between shadow prices, resources, and the objective function can be expressed as follows: *The shadow price for a given resource will reflect the impact on the objective function of a one-unit change in the resource, and this price impact will hold as long as the change in the resource is within the limits of change determined by sensitivity analysis.*

If, in the analysis above, the change had been outside the limits set by the inequalities, then we would have an infeasible solution. If $\Delta_N = 200$, for example, the new value of $s_3$ would be $500 - 3(200) = -100 < 0$. In this case, it would be necessary to re-solve the problem completely since the optimal product mix would change. Under the new solution, a different set of shadow prices would result.

As an additional exercise, let us determine the limits of change for phosphate, $\Delta_{ph}$. The pertinent information for the second slack variable, $s_2$, is given in Table 8-8.

Using the information in the table, the inequalities for the problem are expressed as follows:

$$x_1: \qquad 8{,}000 - 20\Delta_{ph} \geq 0 \rightarrow \Delta_{ph} \leq \quad 400$$

$$x_2: \qquad 14{,}000 + 20\Delta_{ph} \geq 0 \rightarrow \Delta_{ph} \geq -700$$

$$s_3: \qquad 500 + \quad \Delta_{ph} \geq 0 \rightarrow \Delta_{ph} \geq -500$$

The final limits are then $-500 \leq \Delta_{ph} \leq 400$. The change in the availability of phosphate could, therefore, be reduced by 500 tons or increased by 400 tons without forcing the present optimal variables to have an infeasible solution. Within these

**TABLE 8-8.
RHS and $s_2$
Column
from Optimal
Tableau**

| Basic Variable | Right-hand Side | $s_2$ |
| --- | --- | --- |
| $x_1$ | 8,000 | $-20$ |
| $x_2$ | 14,000 | $+20$ |
| $s_3$ | 500 | $+1$ |

limits of change we could compute the new optimal values for $x_1$, $x_2$, and $s_3$ without re-solving the entire problem.

For problems with all less-than-or-equal-to constraints, the sensitivity of the optimal solution to changes in resource levels can be generalized as follows:

1. If one has an optimal solution to a linear programming problem, the *increase* in profit resulting from an *additional* ton of the $k$th resource can be found by taking the value of the entry in the $z_j$ row for the $k$th slack variable. (This value also gives the *decrease* in profit due to a one-unit *decrease* in availability of the $k$th resource.) These values are the *shadow prices*.

2. To summarize the calculation of upper and lower limits on the availability of some scarce resource, let $b_k$ and $\Delta_k$ be the original availability of the $k$th resource and the change in the $k$th resource respectively. Also let $(rhs)_i$ and $a_{ik}$ be, respectively, the optimal right-hand side for the $i$th basic variable and the coefficient of variable $s_k$ in the $i$th row. Inequalities of the following form are then established for each of the $m$ basic variables.

$$(rhs)_i + (a_{ik})(\Delta_k) \geq 0$$

The inequalities can then be solved to determine $l$ and $\mu$, the lower and upper limits of $\Delta_k$. Then

$$l \leq \Delta_k \leq \mu$$

are the limits of change in availability of the $k$th resource in order to maintain the feasibility of the current optimal mix (optimal solution).

## Comments on the revised Agro-Tech Inc. case

Returning to the extended Agro-Tech Inc. case, we can apply the results of the chapter to the questions raised in the case. However, before going on to these questions, it is important to note that the sensitivity analysis results that we will use must be considered as mutually exclusive—the concepts of sensitivity analysis do not apply to multiple changes in profit coefficients or resource levels or both. We will consider each question separately and assume that only one of them will actually occur.

First, we had the problem of the new 5-5-5 fertilizer not being produced. Ms. Jones was interested in how much the price of this fertilizer would have to be increased before it would enter the optimal production mix. From our analysis of nonbasic objective-function coefficients, we saw that the price for the 5-5-5 would have to be increased by more than $4 before it would enter the optimal solution.

While Ms. Jones was interested in increasing the price of 5-5-5, it appeared from salesmen's reports that it might be necessary to decrease the price of the 5-5-10. From our analysis of the basic variable, we saw that the price (profit) of the 5-5-10 could increase by as much as $1.50 or decrease by as much as $4 without changing the current product mix. Since we are interested in a price decrease, we will use the latter value, $4. So we could decrease the price of 5-5-10 by $4 and not disturb the present product mix. Note that if we were to decrease the price on the product by, say, $Δ, then the total profit would decrease by $Δ × 8000 since we are producing 8000 tons of 5-5-10.

Finally, Burt Hawkins was concerned with a possible decrease in the availability of nitrate. From our analysis of changes in resource levels, we saw that the availability of nitrate could increase by as much as 166.67 tons or decrease by as much as 200 tons without causing the solution to become infeasible for the optimal variables. From this we see that Agro-Tech would continue to produce the same product mix, but in different quantities, as long as the availability of nitrate did not decrease by more than 200 tons. If the decrease in nitrate were, say, δ tons, then the total profit would decrease by $340 × δ since the shadow price for the first resource (nitrate) is $340.

## ■ Duality

Duality can be characterized with the following statement: *For every maximization linear programming problem there is an equivalent minimization problem; and conversely, for every minimization linear programming problem there is an equivalent maximization problem.*

Duality is important for two reasons. First, the dual formulation of a linear programming problem can result in a significant reduction in the computational burden of solving the problem. Second, the dual problem has an important economic link with the primal problem. Important economic information concerning the value of scarce resources employed in a firm can be provided by examining the dual problem.

### *The dual formulation*

*primal problem*
*dual problem*

The fundamental concept in duality rests on the mathematical relationship between what is referred to as the **primal problem** and the **dual problem.** The mechanics of the mathematics allow one to convert a linear maximization problem (the primal) into a related minimization problem (the dual). The original statement of the problem is referred to as the primal problem and the alternative formulation as the dual.

The general form of the duality relationship is expressed as follows. For a maximization (*primal*) problem such as

MAXIMIZE:    $$Z_p = c_1 x_1 + c_2 x_2 + c_3 x_3 \qquad (8.16)$$

SUBJECT TO:    $$a_{11} x_1 + a_{12} x_2 + a_{13} x_3 \le b_1 \qquad (8.17)$$

$$a_{21} x_1 + a_{22} x_2 + a_{23} x_3 \le b_2 \qquad (8.18)$$

$$a_{31} x_1 + a_{32} x_2 + a_{33} x_3 \le b_3 \qquad (8.19)$$

$$x_1, x_2, x_3 \ge 0 \qquad (8.20)$$

the related minimization (*dual*) problem is

MINIMIZE:       $Z_d = b_1 y_1 + b_2 y_2 + b_3 y_3$                                                 (8.21)

SUBJECT TO:     $a_{11} y_1 + a_{21} y_2 + a_{31} y_3 \geq c_1$                                    (8.22)

$a_{12} y_1 + a_{22} y_2 + a_{32} y_3 \geq c_2$                                    (8.23)

$a_{13} y_1 + a_{23} y_2 + a_{33} y_3 \geq c_3$                                    (8.24)

$y_1, y_2, y_3 \geq 0$                                    (8.25)

where $y_1$, $y_2$, and $y_3$ represent the dual variables.

The dual formulation of the primal problem is obtained in the following manner:

1.  Replace the $x_j$ variables in the primal by $y_i$ variables in the dual.

2.  Place the coefficients in the objective function of the primal as the right-hand-side values in the dual.

3.  Place the right-hand-side values of the primal as the objective-function coefficients in the dual.

4.  Transpose the primal coefficient constraint rows to column coefficients in the dual.

5.  Reverse the direction of the inequalities, that is, if the primal inequalities are greater than or equal to, the dual inequalities are less than or equal to.

Given that the dual problem has been formulated, it can be solved by use of the simplex algorithm. One important concept of the primal–dual relationship is that *if the primal problem has an optimal solution, then the related dual problem must also have an optimal solution.* It is also true that *the optimal value of the primal objective function is equal to the optimal value of the dual objective function.*

To illustrate the primal–dual relationship, let us examine Tom Anderson's original two-fertilizer problem. (We use this problem since the number of constraints does not equal the number of variables.) Recall that Tom's formulation of the maximization problem was

MAXIMIZE:       $Z_p = 18.5x_1 + 20x_2$                                                           (8.26)

SUBJECT TO:     $.05x_1 + .05x_2 \leq 1100$                                                        (8.27)

$.05x_1 + .10x_2 \leq 1800$                                                        (8.28)

$.10x_1 + .05x_2 \leq 2000$                                                        (8.29)

$x_1, x_2 \geq 0$                                    (8.30)

where $x_1$ and $x_2$ are the tons of 5-5-10 and 5-10-5 that should be produced, and 1100, 1800, and 2000 are the tons of available resources (nitrate, phosphate, and potash).

In formulating the dual, the objective is to minimize the usage of available resources in such a manner that the value of the resources used in the production of each of the respective products is equal to or greater than the profit contribution for the product. To begin the formulating we let

$y_1$ = marginal value of resource 1 (nitrate) in dollars/ton

$y_2$ = marginal value of resource 2 (phosphate) in dollars/ton

$y_3$ = marginal value of resource 3 (potash) in dollars/ton

Since resources have value to the firm (because they are used in the manufacturing of products), to maximize profits, the resources must be allocated to the most profitable combination of final products. This requires that the resources be utilized such that the marginal value of additional units of the resources is a minimum. If this were not true, additional units of resource would be of greater value than those already employed, a condition that could exist only if the input resources were not optimally employed. The objective in the dual formulation of the Agro-Tech problem thus is to allocate the resources to the production of fertilizers so that the total usage of the resources is minimized. Since there are 1100, 1800, and 2000 tons of the respective resources available, the objective function is

MINIMIZE:    $Z_d = 1100y_1 + 1800y_2 + 2000y_3$    (8.31)

Using the procedures noted earlier, the constraints in the dual formulation are expressed as follows:

$$.05y_1 + .05y_2 + .10y_3 \geq 18.5 \tag{8.32}$$

$$.05y_1 + .10y_2 + .05y_3 \geq 20.0 \tag{8.33}$$

$$y_1, y_2, y_3 \geq 0 \tag{8.34}$$

Each constraint in the dual relates to an end product (a type of fertilizer) rather than to a resource as was the case with the primal. Therefore, the rows of the dual are the same as the columns of the primal. If we check the structural arrangement of the constraints, we can examine the units of measure on each side of the inequalities. Recall that the physical rate of substitution coefficients (the $a_{ij}$'s) have units of measure in tons of resource per ton of fertilizer and the $y_j$'s are expressed in dollars per ton of resource. Using the first constraint as a sample case, we have

$$\left(.05 \frac{\text{ton of nitrate}}{\text{ton of 5-5-10}}\right) \times \left(y_1 \frac{\text{dollars}}{\text{ton of nitrate}}\right)$$

$$+ \left(.05 \frac{\text{ton of phosphate}}{\text{ton of 5-5-10}}\right) \times \left(y_2 \frac{\text{dollars}}{\text{ton of phosphate}}\right)$$

$$+ \left(.10 \frac{\text{ton of potash}}{\text{ton of 5-5-10}}\right) \times \left(y_3 \frac{\text{dollars}}{\text{ton of potash}}\right)$$

$$\geq 18.5 \frac{\text{dollars}}{\text{ton of 5-5-10}}$$

**TABLE 8-9. Comparison of Primal and Dual Formulations**

| Primal | Dual |
|---|---|
| MAXIMIZE: $\quad Z_p = 18.5x_1 + 20x_2$ | MINIMIZE: $\quad Z_d = 1100y_1 + 1800y_2 + 2000y_3$ |
| SUBJECT TO: $\quad .05x_1 + .05x_2 \leq 1100$ | SUBJECT TO: $\quad .05y_1 + .05y_2 + .10y_3 \geq 18.5$ |
| $.05x_1 + .10x_2 \leq 1800$ | $.05y_1 + .10y_2 + .05y_3 \geq 20$ |
| $.10x_1 + .05x_2 \leq 2000$ | $y_1, y_2, y_3 \geq 0$ |
| $x_1, x_2 \geq 0$ | |

Since the units of measure balance on each side of the inequality, the constraint is in proper order.

To understand fully the constraints of the dual, one must consider the quantity of resources used in the manufacturing of each product and the value of these resources. In the above example, equation (8.32),

$$.05y_1 + .05y_2 + .10y_3 \geq 18.5$$

the $.05y_1$ term is the dollar value that resource 1 (nitrate) contributes in the production of one ton of fertilizer 1; the $.05y_2$ is the dollar value contribution of resource 2 (phosphate); and the $.10y_3$ is the dollar value contribution of resource 3 (potash). The direction of the inequality guarantees that the total value of the resources consumed in the manufacture of one ton of fertilizer 1 must at least equal the contribution to profits (that is, 18.5) from the fertilizer. If the value to the firm of employing the resources to manufacture 5-5-10 fertilizer exactly equals the contribution to profits, the inequality will be strictly satisfied. If the value of the resources required to produce a ton of the 5-5-10 exceeds the contribution to profits, then the firm can more profitably employ the resources in manufacturing the other fertilizers.

The primal and dual formulations are compared in Table 8-9, and the differences between them are summarized in Table 8-10.

**TABLE 8-10. Differences Between Primal and Dual Formulations**

| | Primal | Dual |
|---|---|---|
| Variables: | units of end product produced | marginal value per ton of resource |
| Objective Function: | maximize profit = (units of product) × (profit per unit) | minimize marginal value = (marginal value per ton of resource) × (tons of resource used) |
| Constraint: | limitation on use of scarce resource | requirements on per-unit profit for each product |

In formulating the dual from the primal, the following facts should be kept in mind:

1. The number of dual variables will be equal to the number of primal constraints.

2. The number of dual constraints will be equal to the number of primal variables.

3. The objective function of the dual will be made up of the right-hand-side values of the primal.

4. The right-hand-side values of the dual will be the profit coefficients of the primal.

5. The constraint coefficients of the dual will be columns of the primal.

From this discussion, it is easy to see that if a problem has, for example, 5 decision variables and 15 constraints in the primal, it will have 15 decision variables and 5 constraints in the dual. This would probably make the dual easier to solve since it would have only 5 *basic* variables as compared with 15 *basic* variables in the primal. Therefore, if the primal has a large number of constraints and fewer decision variables, the dual problem may be easier to solve.

## ■ Summary

The problem of a change in a profit value, that is, an objective-function coefficient or a resource level, after a linear programming problem has been solved has been addressed in this chapter. This topic falls under the label *sensitivity analysis* and provides useful information about the limits of change for the linear programming parameters. The types of change considered in this chapter were a change in the profit value for a nonbasic variable, a change in the profit of a basic variable, and a change in a resource level.

In all cases, these changes should be considered on a one-at-a-time basis. Such topics as multiple changes in profit coefficients, changes in technological coefficients, and the addition of new constraints were not covered here. These topics are covered in more advanced texts.

The concept and use of duality were also discussed in this chapter.

## ■ Glossary of terms

**duality:**  The existence of a minimization LP problem that is associated with every maximization LP problem.

**dual problem:**  The minimization LP problem that is associated with a maximization LP problem.

**primal problem:**  A maximization LP problem with all less-than-or-equal-to constraints.

**sensitivity analysis:**  An investigation into the effect of a change in a parameter in an LP problem.

**shadow prices:**  The value of an additional unit of a resource; found in the $z_j$ row under the slack variable corresponding to the resource.

### ■ Review questions

1. In Chapter 5, we solved linear programming problems graphically. How does a change in profit value affect the optimal graphical solution of an LP problem?

2. How does a change in a resource level affect the optimal graphical solution of an LP problem?

3. Discuss why we never considered a downward change in the profit of a nonbasic variable.

4. Discuss why both an increase and a decrease in the profit of a basic variable were considered.

5. How can an upward change in a resource level cause the optimal solution of an LP problem to become infeasible? (*Hint:* Use the concept of physical rates of substitution.)

6. Why do we call the *dual* the mirror image of the primal problem? Can you surmise what the dual of the dual is?

7. What are shadow prices? Why are they so named?

### ■ True/false questions

1. Sensitivity analysis is a method for investigating the effect of changes in different parameters on the initial solution of an LP problem.

2. The dual formulation of the LP problem provides a method for solving an alternate form of the LP problem.

3. A change in the profit value for a basic variable is equivalent to a change in the slope of the iso-profit lines that are used to find the optimal solution.

4. The profit that would be gained by producing any quantity of a nonbasic variable is always greater than the profit that would be lost in order to produce the quantity.

5. Changes in profit-contribution coefficients for basic variables will not affect the existing solution.

6. A change in a resource level serves to shift a constraint line in such a way as either to shrink or to enlarge the feasible region.

7. The optimal value of the primal objective function is equal to the negative of the optimal value of the dual objective function.

8. There is a dual variable associated with each primal constraint and a slack variable associated with each dual constraint.

9. The value of an additional unit of a resource, found in the $z_j$ row under the artificial variable corresponding to the resource, is the shadow price for that resource.

10. The primal problem is a maximization problem with all less-than-or-equal-to constraints.

### ■ Problems

1. Consider the following linear programming problem:

MAXIMIZE:      $2x_1 + 2x_2$

SUBJECT TO:    $2x_1 + 4x_2 \leq 8$

$$3x_1 + 4x_2 \leq 12$$

$$x_1, x_2 \geq 0$$

a. Graph this problem to determine an optimal solution.

b. If the profit on $x_1$ changed from 2 to 10, what is the new optimal solution? How did changing the profit on $x_1$ change the objective function?

c. Suppose the availability on resource 1 changed from 8 to 16. Graph the new feasible region. If the profit values remain unchanged, how has the optimal solution changed?

**TABLE P8-2. Optimal Tableau for Problem 2**

| $c_B$ | Variables in the Basis | Right-hand Side (Solution) | $c_j \rightarrow$ 3 $x_1$ | 4 $x_2$ | 10 $x_3$ | 0 $s_1$ | 0 $s_2$ |
|---|---|---|---|---|---|---|---|
| 10 | $x_3$ | 10 | 1 | 1 | 1 | 1 | 0 |
| 0 | $s_2$ | 15 | 5 | 3 | 0 | 0 | 1 |
| | $z_j$ | 100 | 10 | 10 | 10 | 10 | 0 |
| | $c_j - z_j$ | | −7 | −6 | 0 | −10 | 0 |

2. For the following linear programming problem, the optimal simplex tableau is given in Table P8-2.

MAXIMIZE: $3x_1 + 4x_2 + 10x_3$

SUBJECT TO: $x_1 + x_2 + x_3 \le 10$

$5x_1 + 3x_2 \le 15$

$x_1, x_2, x_3 \ge 0$

(Assume all changes are independent of one another.)

a. For this problem, determine the increase in the profit for $x_1$ necessary for it to enter the basis.

b. Do the same for $x_2$.

c. Determine the amount the profit coefficient of $x_2$ can change before the current optimal solution would change.

d. Determine the amount that the availability of the first resource can increase or decrease before the present optimal solution would become infeasible.

e. Do the same for resource 2. Interpret your results.

3. Assume the following linear programming problem has been formulated:

MAXIMIZE: $Z = x_1 + 2x_2 + 3x_3 + 4x_4$

SUBJECT TO: $x_1 + 2x_2 + x_3 + 2x_4 \le 12$

$x_2 \qquad\qquad \le 6$

$x_4 \le 4$

$x_1, x_2, x_3, x_4 \ge 0$

The optimal solution for the problem can then be expressed as shown in Table P8-3.

**TABLE P8-3. Optimal Solution for Problem 3**

| $c_j \rightarrow$ | | | 1 | 2 | 3 | 4 | 0 | 0 | 0 |
|---|---|---|---|---|---|---|---|---|---|
| $c_B$ | Variables in the Basis | Right-hand Side (Solution) | $x_1$ | $x_2$ | $x_3$ | $x_4$ | $s_1$ | $s_2$ | $s_3$ |
| 3 | $x_3$ | 12 | 1 | 2 | 1 | 2 | 1 | 0 | 0 |
| 0 | $s_2$ | 6 | 0 | 1 | 0 | 0 | 0 | 1 | 0 |
| 0 | $s_3$ | 4 | 0 | 0 | 0 | 1 | 0 | 0 | 1 |
| | $z_j$ | 36 | 3 | 6 | 3 | 6 | 3 | 0 | 0 |
| | $c_j - z_j$ | | $-2$ | $-4$ | 0 | $-2$ | $-3$ | 0 | 0 |

a. Determine the sensitivity range on $c_1$.

b. Over what range of $b_2$ would the basic variables (not their values) remain unchanged?

c. What would be the impact on the optimal solution if $b_2 = 8$?

d. Over what range could $c_2$ vary without changing the optimal solution?

4. The Calhoun Carpet Company manufactures two types of carpeting, shag and indoor–outdoor. Both types are in popular demand, and the company can sell all the carpeting it can manufacture.

Both types go first to the dye house and then to the weaving rooms. The capacity restriction in the dye house is 320 hours per week. In shag weaving it is 400 hours per week, while in indoor–outdoor weaving it is 160 hours per week. Six products can be manufactured, four shag types and two indoor–outdoor types. Consult Table P8-4; solve this problem however you wish, and fill in the blanks below. The objective is to maximize profits.

a. *Optimal Solution*

| Product | No. Yards Produced |
|---|---|
| #1 | _____ |
| #2 | _____ |
| #3 | _____ |
| #4 | _____ |
| #5 | _____ |
| #6 | _____ |

b. Total contribution from optimal solution = $_____.

**TABLE P8-4. Required Hours of Capacity per Yard**

| | Product | | | | | |
|---|---|---|---|---|---|---|
| | #1 | #2 | #3 | #4 | #5 | #6 |
| Dye house | .5 | 1.2 | .8 | 1 | .5 | .5 |
| Shag weaving | .7 | 1.2 | .5 | 1 | 0 | 0 |
| Indoor–outdoor weaving | 0 | 0 | 0 | 0 | 1 | 1 |
| Contribution ($ per yd) | 6 | 7 | 7 | 10 | 20 | 30 |

c. How many hours of unused capacity exist in the

Dye house _____ hours

Shag weaving _____ hours

Indoor–outdoor weaving _____ hours

d. If an important customer demands 50 yards of product #2, how much contribution will be lost in filling the order?

e. If the indoor–outdoor crew stayed one extra hour, what would it do? That is, how would the optimal solution change?

f. If the dye house crew agreed to work extra hours, how many hours could it work without changing the shadow price for slack dye-house capacity?

g. How much extra contribution would be made if the indoor–outdoor crew worked 60 extra hours at a $5 per hour premium?

5. Consider the following LP problem:

MAXIMIZE: $Z = 2x_1 - x_2 + x_3$

SUBJECT TO: $3x_1 + x_2 + x_3 \leq 60$ (resource #1)

$x_1 - x_2 + 2x_3 \leq 10$ (resource #2)

$x_1 + x_2 - x_3 \leq 20$ (resource #3)

$x_1, x_2, x_3 \geq 0$

and the tableau in Table P8-5.

**TABLE P8-5. Tableau for Problem 5**

| $c_B$ | $c_j \rightarrow$ Variables in the Basis | Right-hand Side (Solution) | $x_1$ | $x_2$ | $x_3$ | $s_1$ | $s_2$ | $s_3$ |
|---|---|---|---|---|---|---|---|---|
| 0 | | 10 | 0 | 0 | 1 | 1 | −1 | −2 |
| | | 15 | 1 | 0 | .5 | 0 | .5 | .5 |
| | $x_2$ | 5 | 0 | 1 | −1.5 | 0 | −.5 | .5 |
| | $z_j$ | | | | | | | |
| | $c_j - z_j$ | | | | | | | |

a. Fill in the missing entries in Table P8-5.

b. If this tableau is optimal, answer the question below; otherwise, pivot to find the optimal tableau and then answer the questions below.

c. For the optimal solution to the linear programming problem, _____ units of $x_1$, _____ units of $x_2$, and _____ units of $x_3$ will be produced resulting in an optimal profit of Z = _____. For this solution there will be _____ units of resource #1 left over, _____ units of resource #2 left over, and _____ units of resource #3 left over.

d. Similarly, if one more unit of resource #2 were available, we would be willing to pay a premium of $_____ to obtain this resource. If one unit of resource #2 were obtained at the original (*not* premium price), the new values for $x_1$, $x_2$, $x_3$, and Z would be

$x_1$ _____         $x_3$ _____

$x_2$ _____         Z _____

e. Finally, how much would the profit on $x_3$ have to increase before we would be willing to produce it? Increase = _____. Also, how much can the availability of *resource #3* change without affecting the optimal tableau? Increase _____ and decrease _____.

6. Consider the following LP problem:

MAXIMIZE:     $Z = -x_1 + 3x_2 - 2x_3$

SUBJECT TO:       $3x_1 - x_2 + 2x_3 \leq 7$     (resource A)

$-2x_1 + 4x_2 \leq 12$     (resource B)

$-4x_1 + 3x_2 + 8x_3 \leq 10$     (resource C)

The optimal tableau for this problem is shown in Table P8-6.

**TABLE P8-6. Optimal Tableau for Problem 6**

| | $c_j \rightarrow$ | | $-1$ | $3$ | $-2$ | $0$ | $0$ | $0$ |
|---|---|---|---|---|---|---|---|---|
| $c_B$ | Variables in the Basis | Right-hand Side (Solution) | $x_1$ | $x_2$ | $x_3$ | $s_1$ | $s_2$ | $s_3$ |
| $-1$ | $x_1$ | 4 | 1 | 0 | .8 | .4 | .1 | 0 |
| 3 | $x_2$ | 5 | 0 | 1 | .4 | .2 | .3 | 0 |
| 0 | $s_3$ | 11 | 0 | 0 | 10 | 1 | $-.5$ | 1 |
| | $z_j$ | 11 | $-1$ | 3 | .4 | .2 | .8 | 0 |
| | $c_j - z_j$ | | 0 | 0 | $-1.6$ | $-2$ | $-.8$ | 0 |

a. If the amount of resource A is changed to 12, what is the effect on profit? How will the optimal solution change?

b. How much can resource B change in either direction?

c. What is the value of an additional unit of resource C?

d. How much would the profit on $x_3$ have to increase before it would be brought into the optimal basis?

7. Consider the optimal tableau shown in Table P8-7.

**TABLE P8-7. Optimal Tableau for Problem 7**

| $c_B$ | $c_j \rightarrow$ Variables in the Basis | Right-hand Side (Solution) | $x_1$ | $x_2$ | $x_3$ | $s_1$ | $s_2$ | $s_3$ |
|---|---|---|---|---|---|---|---|---|
| 4 | $x_2$ | 30 | 0 | 1 | 0 | .29 | .57 | .14 |
| 3 | $x_1$ | 1 | 0 | 0 | 1 | −.29 | .43 | −.14 |
| 4 | $x_3$ | 2 | 1 | 0 | 0 | .14 | −.29 | .14 |
| | $z_j$ | | | | | | | |
| | $c_j - z_j$ | | | | | | | |

For the following problem:

MAXIMIZE:         $4x_1 + 4x_2 + 3x_3$

SUBJECT TO:     $-7x_1 + \ x_2 - 6x_3 \leq 10$

$x_2 + \ x_3 \leq 31$

$14x_1 + \ x_2 + 8x_3 \leq 66$

$x_1, x_2, x_3 \leq 0$

a. Complete the tableau.
b. Formulate the dual.
c. If resource #2 is decreased by one unit, what will be the new objective value?
d. The original resource level for resource #3 is increased by five units. Find the resulting optimal tableau.
e. The cost of variable 1 is changed to $10. Find the resulting optimal tableau.

8. Given the following problem:

MAXIMIZE:       $Z = 2x_1 + 4x_2 + 3x_3$

SUBJECT TO:       $3x_1 + 4x_2 + 2x_3 \leq 60$

$2x_1 + \ x_2 + 2x_3 \leq 40$

$x_1 + 3x_2 + 2x_3 \leq 80$

$x_1, x_2, x_3 \geq 0$

The final (optimal) tableau is shown in Table P8-8.

**TABLE P8-8. Optimal Tableau for Problem 8**

| | $c_j \rightarrow$ | | 2 | 4 | 3 | 0 | 0 | 0 |
|---|---|---|---|---|---|---|---|---|
| $c_B$ | Variables in the Basis | Right-hand Side (Solution) | $x_1$ | $x_2$ | $x_3$ | $s_1$ | $s_2$ | $s_3$ |
| 4 | $x_2$ | $\frac{20}{3}$ | $\frac{1}{3}$ | 1 | 0 | $\frac{1}{3}$ | $-\frac{1}{3}$ | 0 |
| 3 | $x_3$ | $\frac{50}{3}$ | $\frac{5}{6}$ | 0 | 1 | $-\frac{1}{6}$ | $\frac{2}{3}$ | 0 |
| 0 | $s_3$ | $\frac{80}{3}$ | $-\frac{5}{3}$ | 0 | 0 | $-\frac{2}{3}$ | $-\frac{1}{3}$ | 1 |
| | $z_j$ | $76\frac{2}{3}$ | $3\frac{5}{6}$ | 4 | 3 | $\frac{5}{6}$ | $\frac{2}{3}$ | 0 |
| | $c_j - z_j$ | | $-1\frac{5}{6}$ | 0 | 0 | $-\frac{5}{6}$ | $-\frac{2}{3}$ | 0 |

**a.** If additional units of resource #1 were available at a premium cost (above regular cost) of $1, how many units would you purchase?

**b.** If additional units of resource #2 were available at no extra cost, how many would you purchase so as to maximize profit *without* affecting the current product mix?

**c.** How much can the profit on $x_1$ change without affecting the current solution?

**d.** How much can the profit on $x_2$ vary without changing the current product mix?

**e.** What is the range of feasibility of resource #2, that is, how much can the availability change?

**f.** Give the complete dual solution.

9. Given the following primal linear programming problem:

MAXIMIZE:    $Z = 2x_1 + 4x_2 - 6x_3$

SUBJECT TO:    $2x_1 + 4x_2 - 4x_3 \leq 16$

$$8x_1 - 2x_2 - 6x_3 \leq 14$$

$$-6x_1 + 4x_2 + 8x_3 \leq 8$$

$$x_1, x_2, x_3 \geq 0$$

Formulate the dual problem.

10. For the following formulation:

MAXIMIZE:    $Z = 12x_1 + 21x_2 + 22x_3$

SUBJECT TO:    $3.5x_1 + 2.5x_2 + 2.0x_3 \leq 1{,}200$

$$48x_1 + 43x_2 + 28x_3 \leq 13{,}560$$

$$x_1 \geq 30$$

$$x_2 \geq 55$$

$$x_3 \geq 32$$

$$x_1, x_2, x_3 \geq 0$$

Formulate the dual for the problem.

11. Given the following dual linear programming problem:

MINIMIZE:        $Z = 10y_1 + 20y_1$

SUBJECT TO:           $y_1 + 2y_2 \geq 2$

$y_1 + y_2 \geq 1$

$2y_1 + y_2 \geq 3$

$y_1, y_2 \geq 0$

Formulate the primal problem.

**9**

# PERT/CPM

## ■ Introduction

PERT (Program Evaluations and Review Technique) and CPM (Critical Path Method) are the two primary project management network techniques used today. In this chapter we will examine both, or rather subsets of both, techniques. Specifically we will demonstrate how PERT can and has been used to determine the overall expected completion date of a project, to determine the required start and completion dates for specific tasks that make up a project, and to identify the critical tasks that, if not completed as scheduled, could delay completion of the project. Using a subset of the CPM, we will demonstrate how the overall completion time of a project can be reduced, given that management is willing to allocate more resources to the project.

As has been the practice in previous chapters, we will preface the chapter presentation with a case example. This example is used later in the chapter to illustrate some of the basic computations.

## ■ Case
## The Sharp Company[1]

The Sharp Company manufactures a full line of razor products. A competitor recently introduced a new double-blade razor, which in the past 6 months has taken a significant share of a market that Sharp has held for years. Management at Sharp has decided that it must introduce a competitive product. Bill Bowen, vice president for planning and development, has identified the tasks necessary to design, develop, and market the new product, and the expected time required to complete each. (See Table 9-1.)

Bowen asked Phil Wright, his staff manager, to review the tasks and to come up with a summary report that would indicate: (1) the total time required from the beginning of the project until the new product is in the hands of the distributor, (2) the specific start and completion dates for each task, and (3) the critical tasks, that is, those tasks that must be completed on time if the project is to be completed by a specific date.

Bowen pointed out to Wright that while the completion times are expected (average) values

**TABLE 9-1. Project Tasks and Expected Completion Times**

| Task | Expected Time to Complete (weeks) |
|---|---|
| Design product | 6 |
| Design package | 2 |
| Order and receive materials for product | 3 |
| Order and receive materials for package | 3 |
| Fabricate product | 4 |
| Fabricate package | 3 |
| Package product | 1 |
| Test market product | 6 |
| Test market package | 4 |
| Distribute to dealers | 2 |

and are fairly realistic, to get a feel for the variability in the overall project it would be desirable to have some idea of worst-case and best-case times. Bowen also pointed out that the tasks were not necessarily listed in sequential order, but had been listed as they came to mind.

## ■ PERT/CPM overview

PERT/CPM can be used to aid Wright in answering some of the questions raised by Bowen. However, before we get into the details of the techniques, it is appropriate to review some of the background of PERT and CPM.

*PERT*

**PERT** was developed in the late 1950s and was used extensively in managing military research and development projects. Its first key application was in the Polaris missile project for the U.S. Navy. As a point of fact, PERT was developed by the Defense Department specifically to support the planning, scheduling, and

*activities*

control of the multitude of jobs (**activities**) associated with the project. PERT has also been applied and used by the construction industry and by industrial firms for such

[1]This case, as well as much of the exposition and also many of the problems presented in the chapter, have been adapted, with permission, from *Improved Project Management with CPM*, unpublished short course, by James M. Pruett, Industrial Engineering Department, Louisiana State University, Baton Rouge, La., 1976.

applications as the scheduling of aircraft maintenance, installation of fixed assets, plant layout, research and development program planning and management, and corporate profit planning. One of the primary features of PERT, in addition to its ability to identify required task (activity) schedules and plans, is that it can handle the uncertainties that exist in predicting the time to complete various tasks.

**CPM**, which was developed independently of PERT but is closely akin to it, is basically concerned with the trade-off between a project's cost and completion date. It focuses on shortening the duration of task or activity time by utilizing more workers and/or resources (which, in most cases, means increased costs). With CPM, the time needed to complete the various activities of the project is assumed to be known with certainty, as is the amount of resources employed.

CPM thus is not concerned with uncertain task or activity times, as in PERT, but deals with time/cost trade-offs.

Because of the differences in the basic structures of the techniques, PERT previously was applied more in research and development projects, whereas CPM was used more in projects such as construction. Today the usage distinction between PERT and CPM has largely disappeared. Most computerized versions of the techniques include options for handling uncertainty in activity times as well as time/cost trade-off analysis, and much of the current literature refers to the techniques collectively as PERT/CPM. In this chapter we will discuss both the uncertainty factor and time/cost trade-offs. However, we do not categorize either as PERT or CPM, but use the collective designation PERT/CPM.

*CPM*

## ■ PERT/CPM terminology

### *Definition of activities and predecessor relationships*

The first step in the PERT/CPM process is to identify all the tasks or activities associated with the project and their interrelationships. As an illustration of this step, consider the basic example of a motor-overhaul project, as depicted in Table 9-2.

For this example, only five activities are required; but obviously the number of activities will vary with the scope of the project. The overhauling of a motor may require only a few activities, whereas the construction of a nuclear power plant or an oil refinery might involve several thousand. The key point in either case is to have, in this planning step, an accurate and inclusive list of activities (and the correct

| Activity Code | Activity Description | Immediate Predecessors |
|---|---|---|
| A | Remove and disassemble motor | — |
| B | Clean and paint housing | A |
| C | Rewind armature | A |
| D | Replace bearings | A |
| E | Assemble and install motor in housing | B, C, D |

**TABLE 9-2.**
**Activity List and Predecessor Relationships for a Motor-Overhaul Project**

predecessor relationships for the activities), since all future computations and the final project schedules depend on these activities (and their relationships).

In addition to the project activities, Table 9-2 includes a column of information labeled "**Immediate Predecessors**" (referring to the immediate prior activity). For a given activity, all immediate predecessors must be completed before beginning that activity. In the example, activities B, C, and D cannot begin until activity A is completed; this says that before cleaning and painting the housing, before rewinding the armature, and before replacing the bearings, the motor must be removed and disassembled. The example also says that activity E cannot begin until activities B, C, and D are all complete. This also is rather obvious; before the motor can be reassembled and installed in the housing, activities B, C, and D must have been accomplished.

The identity of the predecessor relationships may often be obvious, but it is important that they be complete and accurate. The omission, as well as inclusion, of a predecessor can greatly distort the overall activity relationships.

*immediate predecessor*

## Network structure

Once a complete and accurate list of activities and their predecessors has been developed, the relationships can be depicted graphically. Prior to the development of PERT, bar charts, which were developed by H. L. Gantt and are often referred to as Gantt charts, were used to depict time duration and time relationships of activities in a project graphically. As can be seen in the bar chart of Figure 9-1 (which depicts an eight-activity project), the technique, while conceptually correct, cannot clearly show predecessor relationships. For example, do activities E and F both depend upon the completion of activities B and D? Does activity D depend upon the completion of

**FIGURE 9-1.**
**A Bar Chart Example for an Eight-Activity Project**

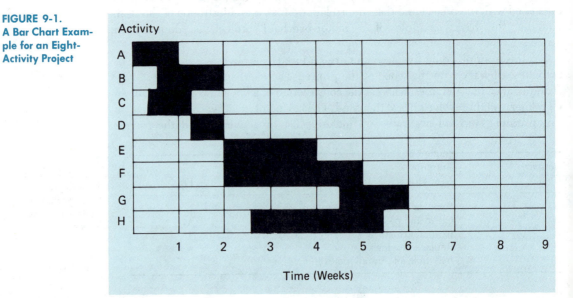

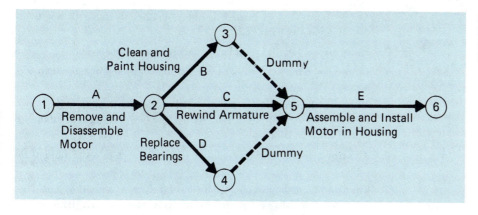

FIGURE 9-2.
Network Diagram
for Motor-Over-
haul Project

A and C, A only, C only, or none of these? It is impossible to determine these from the bar chart; a network diagram, however, can depict the proper relationship.

Figure 9-2 is a network diagram or, more traditionally, a PERT/CPM network, for our motor-overhaul example. As can be seen, the **network** consists of a number of *circles* (numbered 1 through 6) interconnected by *arrows* (labeled A, B, C, D, and E). In general network terminology, the numbered circles are referred to as **nodes,** and the interconnecting arrows are referred to as **branches** or **arcs.** In a PERT/CPM network the arrows or branches represent activities and the circles or nodes are referred to as **events.** Activities involve time and, as we shall see shortly, usually consume resources in the form of labor, material, or money. The events consume neither time nor resources, but rather serve as "project milestones" and provide the logical connecting points for linking the various activities.

*network*

*nodes*
*branches*
*arcs*
*events*

A quick comparison of Figure 9-2 with Table 9-2 will confirm that the network does indeed depict the proper predecessor relationships. Activity A precedes activities B, C, and D, and activity E cannot start before the completion of the same three activities.

Upon examining the data in Table 9-2 and the resulting network in Figure 9-2, many readers might infer that if one is given the predecessor relationships, then drawing the network diagrams is rather straightforward. This is correct; however, one should not attempt to draw the network diagram without first listing all activities, ordering the activities (in some logical fashion), and identifying, as much as possible, the predecessor relationships. When the PERT/CPM network is developed, it can be used as a visual checkpoint to verify the proper predecessor relationships.

## Developing the network

There are no secret procedures for successfully developing an accurate network; however, there are several rules that should be observed, as well as various "tips" that should ease the burden of developing the network:

1. Before an activity can begin, all preceding activities must be completed (as highlighted in several of the examples).

2. Arrows imply logical precedence only; neither their length nor their direction has any meaning.

3. Every arrow (activity) must begin and end with a node event.

4. No two nodes in the network can be directly connected by more than one arrow.

5. When numbering the nodes, it is advisable, particularly in a large network, to use multiples of tens, so that any future changes or additions can be easily incorporated.

6. All arrows in the network should be directed, more or less, from left to right.

7. The activity breakdown (i.e., the listing of the project activities) should be no more refined than is required to portray a logical, clearly defined plan of action.

One of the common errors made in network logic is to place activities into the network based on the sense of time (i.e., when they are likely to occur). Consider the sequential network example shown in part (a) of Figure 9-3. This is the time sequence of activities one is likely to visualize as occurring in the paying of a bill. Although the network might depict how the activities might be ordered, it erroneously says that "address envelopes" cannot begin until "make out checks" is complete. This, of course, is not true.

Part (b) of Figure 9-3 depicts the proper relationship of the activities. Here there is

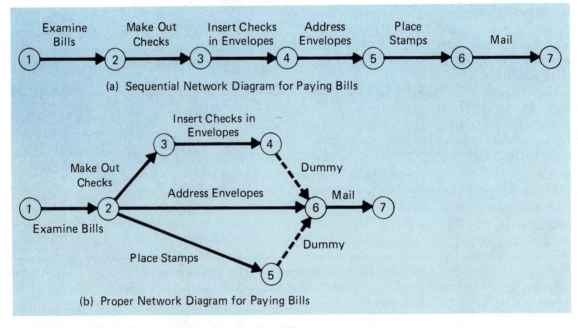

(a) Sequential Network Diagram for Paying Bills

(b) Proper Network Diagram for Paying Bills

**FIGURE 9-3. Network Diagrams Related to "Paying Bills"**

no restriction on the addressing of envelopes (or on the placing of stamps). The diagram simply says that before the letter can be mailed, the check must be in the envelope and the envelope addressed and stamped.

From this basic example, it is rather obvious that activities should not be placed in series unless absolutely necessary. Whenever two or more activities may be performed simultaneously, this possibility should be reflected in the network—even if this has not been the previous practice. Employing this procedure will result in greater flexibility in planning, and actually may shorten the project completion time.

### Dummy activities

In examining Figure 9-2, as well as Figure 9-3, we note that two activities, both of which are unlabeled, are depicted by broken arrows. These are referred to as **dummy activities** and they consume zero time and resources. Dummy activities are employed to show correct activity relationships and/or to avoid having two nodes directly connected by more than one arrow (which would violate network requirement #4). If we omitted the dummy activities from Figure 9-2, the resulting network would appear as in Figure 9-4. Obviously this figure depicts the same activity relationships as Figure 9-2, but it results in linking two nodes with multiple activities—a practice that must be avoided in building the network.

To illustrate further the need for dummy activities, consider a basic "machine installation" project. The project consists of installing a machine and training the operator. Training can begin as soon as the operator is hired and the machine is installed. Training is not dependent on machine inspection; however, inspection is required after the machine is installed.

Table 9-3 lists the activities and their predecessor relationships, and Figure 9-5 shows an improper network representation for the project and presents the correct network diagram for the project. In this example it is impossible to represent the correct activity predecessor relationships without using the dummy activity. As part (a) of Figure 9-5 illustrates, if the network is drawn as shown, the "install machine" and "hire operator" activities precede the "train operator" activity, but the "inspect machine" is shown to depend upon the completion of the same two activities—an

*dummy activities*

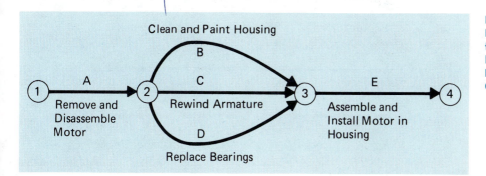

**FIGURE 9-4.** Network Diagram for Motor-Overhaul Project— Dummy Activities Omitted

Clean and Paint Housing

B

A

Remove and Disassemble Motor

C

Rewind Armature

D

Replace Bearings

E

Assemble and Install Motor in Housing

**TABLE 9-3.**
**Activity Data for**
**Machine**
**Installation Project**

| Activity Code | Activity Description | Immediate Predecessor |
|---|---|---|
| A | Install machine | — |
| B | Hire operator | — |
| C | Train operator | A, B |
| D | Inspect machine | A |

improper predecessor relationship. The problem can be corrected by employing the dummy activity as shown in part (b).

Although dummy activities may not be required for all PERT/CPM networks, large complex projects may require several dummy activities. As a matter of fact, in a large network it would be unusual if a dummy activity were not employed.

# ■ Analysis of a PERT/CPM network

Thus far we have seen what a PERT/CPM network represents and how one goes about constructing such a network. Once the network is constructed, the next task is to identify a compatible activity schedule that will permit the completion of the project in a minimum amount of time. This means that we must identify the beginning and ending times for each activity, the time relationships between activities, and the critical activities that must be completed "on schedule."

To begin the analysis, we need information on the time required to complete each activity of the network. Since our Sharp Company case includes "expected time to complete" information on each activity, we will use this as our basic example. We should point out that this analysis in essence will be deterministic since the "expected" activity times will be treated as if they were the actual durations. Later in

**FIGURE 9-5.**
**Use of Dummy**
**Activity to Depict**
**Proper Predecessor**
**Relationship**

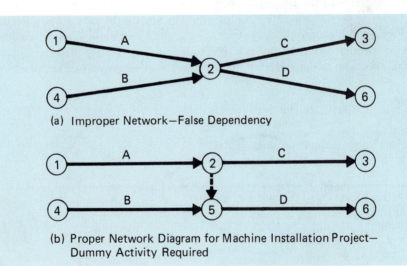

(a) Improper Network—False Dependency

(b) Proper Network Diagram for Machine Installation Project—
    Dummy Activity Required

the chapter we will show how uncertainty in activity times can be incorporated into the analysis.

## Sharp Company case

Before we can begin the analysis for the Sharp Company, we must first develop the network. In reexamining Table 9-1, we are reminded that the tasks (activities) are not in logical order and that predecessor relationships have not been identified. The first step therefore is to rework Table 9-1 to arrange the tasks (activities) in logical order and to identify the predecessor relationships.

Table 9-4 is the expanded version of activity data for Sharp. Note that the data include an activity code for each activity. These activity codes will be used in later versions of the network diagram instead of the activity descriptions.

As indicated earlier, once the predecessor relationships have been identified, the drawing of the network is rather straightforward. Figure 9-6 is the PERT/CPM network for the Sharp Company. Note that above each arrow or arc we have placed the activity code and description of the corresponding activity, and directly under the arc is the **expected time of the activity**. We have also labeled the nodes (events) from 1 to 10.

*expected time of activity*

## Basic scheduling computations

Once the PERT/CPM network is developed, attention can be focused on determining the expected completion date for the project and the activity schedule. The overall project completion date is particularly important if management is competing with another firm for the project or if management is operating on a completion-date incentive basis. The activity schedule is important since it will highlight the critical activities in the project.

If we sum all the expected activity times in Table 9-4 we have 34 weeks as the

**TABLE 9-4. Project Data for Sharp Company Case**

| Activity Code | Activity Description | Immediate Predecessors | Expected Time to Complete (weeks) |
|---|---|---|---|
| A | Design product | — | 6 |
| B | Design package | — | 2 |
| C | Order and receive material for product | A | 3 |
| D | Order and receive materials for package | B | 3 |
| E | Fabricate product | C | 4 |
| F | Fabricate package | D | 3 |
| G | Test market product | E | 6 |
| H | Test market package | F | 4 |
| I | Package product | G, H | 1 |
| J | Distribute to dealers | I | 2 |

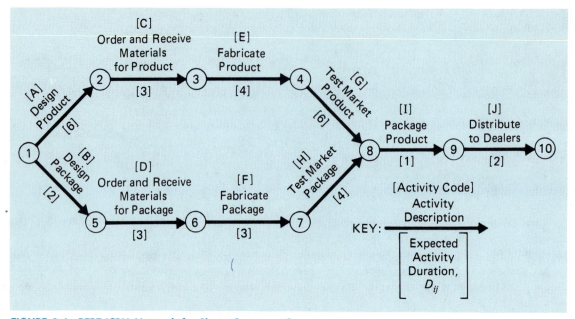

**FIGURE 9-6. PERT/CPM Network for Sharp Company Case**

project duration. From Figure 9-6, however, we know that this is not the length of time it will take to complete the project; activities A and C can be handled simultaneously, and activity C can be performed in parallel with D (depending on when activity A is completed and when activity B is completed). The true project duration may not be evident from Figure 9-6, but with a little work we should be able to compute the correct value.

*critical path*

The project duration is computed by determining the **critical path** for the network. Every network will have two or more paths, one or more of which will be critical. A *path* is defined as the sequence of activities that are traversed in moving from the starting event (node) to the ending event (node) of the network. (For the Sharp Company network, node 1 is the starting event and node 10 is the ending event.) Activities A, C, E, G, I, and J form a path that connects nodes 1, 2, 3, 4, 8, 9, and 10 in the network, while activities B, D, F, H, I, and J form a second path that connects nodes 1, 5, 6, 7, 8, 9, and 10. Since the completion of a project requires that all paths of the network be completed, the duration of the longest path in the network (the time it takes to complete) is the *critical path*. For our example, path A–C–E–G–I–J requires 22 weeks, while path B–D–F–H–I–J requires only 15 weeks. Path A–C–E–G–I–J thus is the critical path. If any activity on the critical path is delayed, the entire project will be delayed. The activities along the critical path

*critical activities*

therefore are the **critical activities.** If the total project time, 22 weeks in this case, is to be reduced, management must shorten the duration of one or more of the critical activities.

For any network one could (1) identify all the paths through the network, (2) compute the duration of each, and then (3) select the longest (critical) path. This, however, is not a very efficient way to analyze the network; also, identifying all the paths through a large network is very impractical.

A more efficient procedure is to compute time boundaries for each activity—*early start, late start, early finish,* and *late finish* times—and from these data compute the critical path. The early start and early finish time boundaries can be computed by making a **forward pass** through the network; the late start and late finish times are determined by employing a **backward pass** through the network.

*forward pass*
*backward pass*

**Forward pass—computation of early start and early finish times.** To begin the forward pass analysis, we need to define some terms and identify the notational procedure to be used. The **early start time** for an activity is the earliest possible time the activity can begin. In our calculations, we will use $ES_{ij}$ to designate the early start time, where $i$ and $j$ represent the beginning and ending nodes associated with the activity. For example, in Figure 9-6, $ES_{12}$ would denote the early start time of the "design product" activity, that is, activity A, and $ES_{15}$ would denote the early start time of the "design package" activity, that is, activity B. The **early finish time** for an activity, which we denoted by $EF_{ij}$, is its *early start time plus the duration time required to complete the activity.* For activity A in Figure 9-6, this would be $EF_{12} = ES_{12} + D_{12}$, where $D_{12} = 6$, the expected time for the activity. If the early start time of activity A is 0, that is, $ES_{12} = 0$, then $EF_{12} = 0 + 6 = 6$.

*early start time*

*early finish time*

The $ES_{ij}$ and $EF_{ij}$ calculations are not displayed directly on the network diagram; rather, the results of applying the relationships are displayed. The key used in the diagram is as follows:

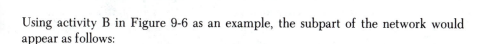

Using activity B in Figure 9-6 as an example, the subpart of the network would appear as follows:

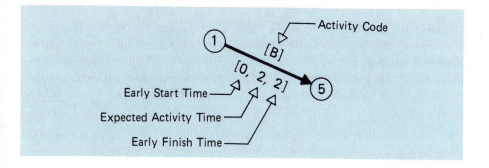

The normal procedure for analyzing a network is to start at the initial node and assume, as we have, a starting time of zero.[2] All activities are assumed to start as soon as possible, that is, as soon as all associated predecessors have been completed. Since activities A and B have no predecessors, $ES_{12} = 0$ and $ES_{15} = 0$; their corresponding finish times therefore are $EF_{12} = 0 + 6 = 6$ and $EF_{15} = 0 + 2 = 2$.

Once we have computed the early finish time for activity A we can compute the early start time for activity C—activity C cannot start until activity A is completed. Likewise, once we have the early finish time for activity B, we can proceed to the analysis of activity D. Activity C's earliest start time, $ES_{23}$ is equal to the earliest finish time for activity A, which is $E_{12} = 6$. The earliest finish time for activity C is its early start time plus its duration time, or $EF_{23} = ES_{23} + D_{23} = 6 + 3 = 9$. The early start and early finish times for activity D is as follows:

$$ES_{56} = EF_{15} = 2; \quad EF_{56} = ES_{56} + D_{56} = 2 + 3 = 5$$

Continuing this forward-pass type of analysis, we can compute the earliest start time, and then the earliest finish time, for each activity. Figure 9-7 is the completed network diagram, depicting the $ES_{ij}$ and the $EF_{ij}$ values.

Tracing through the network and making the calculations are rather straightforward for nodes that have only a single predecessor—which was the case for each of the activities examined previously. *However, where multiple activities precede an activity, the earliest start time for the activity is equal to the largest value of the earliest finish time for all predecessor activities.* For example, activity I is preceded by activities G and H; therefore, the earliest start time for activity I is 19, that is, $ES_{89} = 19$.

In examining the time calculations for Figure 9-7, we note that the earliest finish time for the final activity J is 22 weeks. This is exactly equal to the value we computed when we examined the two paths through the network.

**Backward pass—computation of latest start and latest finish times.** We can identify the total time required to complete a project by making a forward pass through the network, but we cannot answer such questions as: How much, if any, can each activity be delayed? How late can a particular activity be started and still not lengthen the project's duration? These questions can be answered, however, after making a backward pass through the network.

*latest start time*

*latest finish time*

As was the case for the forward pass, before we begin the backward pass we need to identify and define some terms, such as latest start and latest finish. The **latest start time** for an activity $LS_{ij}$ is the latest time the activity can begin without delaying the completion date of the project. The **latest finish time** for an activity $LF_{ij}$ is the latest start time plus the activity duration time $D_{ij}$. In symbolic form, these relationships are as follows: $LF_{ij} = LS_{ij} + D_{ij}$; however, for backward pass, the more useful form is $LS_{ij} = LF_{ij} - D_{ij}$.

---

[2]If calendar dates were used, then the calculations presented here would be adjusted to reflect months and days.

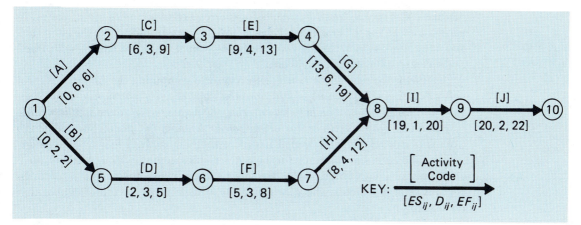

**FIGURE 9-7. Earliest Start and Earliest Finish Times for Sharp Company Case**

To begin the calculation, we start at the ending event (node 10 in our case) and set the latest finish time for the last activity equal to the total duration time computed on the forward pass, that is, $LF_{9,10} = 22$. Since it takes two days to complete activity J, the latest start time for activity J is equal to the latest finish time minus the duration time. That is, $LS_{9,10} = LF_{9,10} - D_{9,10} = 22 - 2 = 20$. For activity I, the latest finish time is 20, that is, $LF_{8,9} = 20$, which is the latest start time for activity J; while the latest start time for activity I is 19, that is, $LS_{8,9} = LF_{8,9} = 20 - 1 = 19$. At node 8, both activity G and activity H are entering the node; therefore, the latest finish time for each is 19, the latest start time for activity I—which is the only activity leaving the node.

In continuing the backward-pass analysis, we can compute the latest finish and latest start for each activity in the network. Figure 9-8 shows the resulting

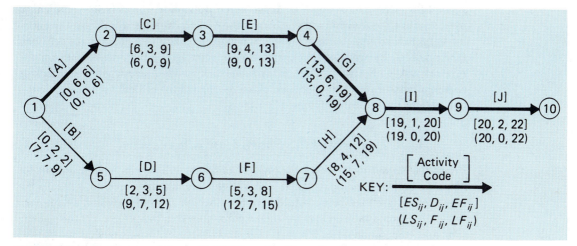

**FIGURE 9-8. Latest Start and Latest Finish Times for Sharp Company Case**

calculations. The $LS_{ij}$ and $LF_{ij}$ results for the respective activities are displayed in parentheses, below the bracketed [$ES_{ij}, D_{ij}, EF_{ij}$] values. In addition to the latest start and latest finish values, the slack or float time—which we define later—is displayed as the center value in the parentheses.

One factor that should be noted with regard to computing the $LF_{ij}$ values for a network is that *if a given node has more than one activity leaving the node, then the latest finish time for an activity entering the node is equal to the smallest value of the latest starting times for all activities leaving the node*. For the Sharp Company case, the only node that has more than one activity leaving the node is node 1. The latest starting times for the two activities leaving node 1, A and C, are 0 and 7, respectively. This says that the latest time at which the overall project can begin is time 0, which in this case would mean that activity A must begin at that point in time.

*slack time*
*float time*

**Float (slack) time.**    After the time boundaries (i.e., the start and finish times) have been completed for an entire network, the *float*, or **slack time** as it is often called, can be determined for each activity. **Float time** *is defined as the length of time an activity can be delayed without causing the duration of the overall project to exceed its scheduled completion time*. The amount of float time for an activity is computed by taking the difference between its latest start and earliest start times or its latest finish and the earliest finish times. This is expressed in equation form as: $F_{ij} = LS_{ij} - ES_{ij}$ or $F_{ij} = LF_{ij} - EF_{ij}$. In examining Figure 9-8, we can note that the float time for activity B is 7 weeks, that is, $F_{15} = LF_{15} - EF_{15} = 9 - 2 = 7$. This means that this activity can be delayed up to 7 weeks. Activity D likewise has a float time of 7 weeks, that is, $F_{56} = LF_{56} - EF_{56} = 12 - 5 = 7$; however, this does not mean that A and D can each be delayed 7 weeks. The calculations of the float for any activity assumes that the expected duration times will occur in other activities; that is, other activities will occur as scheduled.

In examining activity A in Figure 9-8, we note that the float time is zero; that is, $F_{12} = LF_{12} - EF_{12} = 6 - 6 = 0$. As we noted previously, this activity is critical; it must start at time zero and must adhere to the 6-week duration schedule if the entire project is to be completed in 22 weeks. Upon examining the float times for activities C, E, G, I, and J, we note that these also are zero. Hence the critical path for the network is A–C–E–G–I–J, which is the same path we identified when we traced the different paths through the network. We have shaded the critical path in Figure 9-8 to highlight the critical activities.

## Analysis of the Sharp Company case

Recall that in our overview of the Sharp Company, Bill Bowen, vice president for planning and development, asked Phil Wright, his staff manager, to evaluate the new product proposal being considered. Specifically, Bowen requested a summary report that would indicate: (1) the total time required in the project, (2) the specific start and completion dates for each task, and (3) the critical as well as noncritical tasks. With the completion of Figure 9-8, all this information is available. We now know that the project will take 22 weeks, and that if this scheduled time frame is to be met, activities A, C, E, G, I, and J must occur on schedule. The network analysis also tells us that 7 weeks of float (slack) time exists in that portion of the network associated with the packaging of the product. Specific start and finish times are available for all activities.

### Summary of the PERT/CPM calculations

In the next section, we will examine how uncertainty is handled in a PERT/CPM network; however, let us first summarize the basic steps used in the PERT/CPM process:

1. Identify all the tasks or activities associated with the project.

2. Identify the immediate predecessor relationships for all activities.

3. Draw the basic network for the project, showing all predecessor relationships.

4. Estimate the expected duration time for each activity.

5. Using a forward pass through the network, compute the earliest start and earliest finish times for each activity.

6. Using the expected project completion time, computed in the forward pass through the network, employ the backward pass procedures to compute the latest start and latest finish for each activity.

7. Compute the float (slack) time associated with each activity.

8. Identify the critical path for the network. The critical activities are those activities with zero float (slack) time.

## ■ Uncertainty in a PERT/CPM network

### Estimating activity times

In applying PERT/CPM to construction and maintenance projects, rather accurate estimates of activity times are possible since historical data are likely to be available and the technology employed is more or less stable. But, for the research and development type of project, where the technology is rapidly changing and products are nonstandard, accurate activity time estimates may be difficult. To provide for this type of uncertainty, the original developers of PERT enabled a user to employ three estimates of each activity time: (1) the **most probable time** $(t_m)$—the time required to complete the activity under normal conditions; (2) the **pessimistic time** $(t_p)$—the maximum time that would be required to complete the activity if significant delays were encountered throughout the project; (3) the **optimistic time** $(t_o)$—the minimum time required to complete the activity, if everything occurs in an ideal fashion. By using these three estimates, an **expected time** for an activity

*most probable time*

*pessimistic time*

*optimistic time*

*expected time*

TABLE 9-5.
Three Time
Estimates
(Optimistic, Most
Probable, and
Pessimistic) for
Activities of the
Sharp Company
Case

| Activity Code | Optimistic Time $(t_o)$ | Most Probable Time $(t_m)$ | Pessimistic Time $(t_p)$ |
|---|---|---|---|
| A | 3.0 | 5.5 | 11.0 |
| B | 1.0 | 1.5 | 5.0 |
| C | 1.5 | 3.0 | 4.5 |
| D | 1.2 | 3.2 | 4.0 |
| E | 2.0 | 3.5 | 8.0 |
| F | 1.8 | 2.8 | 5.0 |
| G | 3.0 | 6.5 | 7.0 |
| H | 2.0 | 4.2 | 5.2 |
| I | .5 | .8 | 2.3 |
| J | .8 | 2.1 | 2.8 |

duration can be calculated according to the following formula:[3]

$$t_e = \frac{t_o + 4t_m + t_p}{6} \qquad (9.1)$$

To illustrate the use of the expected time formula, assume that Bill Bowen of the Sharp Company gave three estimates of the times required to complete each of the activities for the razor project, rather than the expected values used previously in all the calculations. The specific estimates are shown in Table 9-5.

Using activity F as an example, these data indicate that Bowen estimates that the "fabricate package" activity (refer to Table 9-4 for activity description) will require from 1.8 weeks (optimistic estimate) to 5.0 weeks (pessimistic estimates), with the most likely estimate being 2.8 weeks. The value that would be likely to occur if the activity were repeated a number of times is the expected time, which in this case is

$$t_e = \frac{1.8 + 4(2.8) + 5.0}{6} = 3.0 \qquad (9.2)$$

In most PERT/CPM applications, activities are not repeated a large number of times; rather they usually occur just once. However, $t_e$ is still the best single estimate of the time required for an activity and is the one traditionally employed.

Figure 9-9 is a pictorial representation of the relationship between the optimistic $(t_o)$, most likely $(t_m)$, pessimistic $(t_p)$, and expected $(t_e)$ time estimates for an activity; data shown are for activity F, the "fabricate package" activity.

---

[3]The weights used in this formula are based on an approximation of the beta probability distribution. This particular distribution was chosen by the developers of PERT because it is unimodal (has a single peak value), has finite and nonnegative end points, and is not necessarily symmetrical. These characteristics are likely properties for the distribution of activity times.

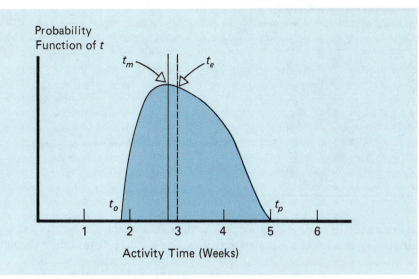

**FIGURE 9-9.**
**Probability Distri-**
**bution of Activity**
**Times for "Fabri-**
**cate Package" Ac-**
**tivity for Sharp**
**Company**

## Variability in activity times

If the $t_e$ formula is applied to the three estimates for each activity in Table 9-5, the resulting $t_e$ will be equal to the "expected time to complete" values shown in the original date for the Sharp Company (Table 9-4). One thus might ask: "What is gained from making three estimates? Why not simply estimate the expected values and make the PERT/CPM computations based on these?" The answer to these questions is that we need to know how reliable the expected time estimate is, and we can determine this if we have the three estimates. If the time required to complete an activity is highly variable—that is, if the range of the estimates is very large—then we will be less confident of the expected time than if the range were narrower. For example, if the three estimates for the "fabricate product" activity were 2, 3, and 4 rather than 1.8, 2.8, and 5.0 as we noted earlier, the average would be 3.0 days; but we would have more confidence in these revised figures since they were less variable. A wide range of estimates represents greater uncertainty, and hence less confidence in the calculated expected time. It also means, as we shall see shortly, that the probability of completing the project by a given date is reduced.

The advantage of having three time estimates is that we can calculate the dispersion of the activity times and can use this information to evaluate the uncertainty in the project being completed as scheduled. In PERT/CPM, as in other common statistical problems, the *variance* is used as a measure to describe the dispersion or variation in the activity time estimates. The actual variance formula is as follows:

$$\text{Variance of activity times} = \sigma_t^2 = \left(\frac{t_p - t_o}{6}\right)^2 \qquad (9.3)$$

**TABLE 9-6.**
**Activity Variances**
**for the Sharp**
**Company Case**

| Activity Code | Variance $(\sigma_t^2)$ |
|---|---|
| A | 1.78 |
| B | .44 |
| C | .56 |
| D | .22 |
| E | 1.00 |
| F | .28 |
| G | .44 |
| H | .28 |
| I | .09 |
| J | .11 |

By using the formula and applying it to the data in Table 9-5 we can calculate the dispersion for each of the project activities. For example, the variance for activity A is

$$\sigma_{t_A}^2 = \left(\frac{11.0 - 3.0}{6}\right)^2 = \left(\frac{8}{6}\right)^2 = 1.78 \tag{9.4}$$

Likewise for activity B, the variance is

$$\sigma_{t_B}^2 = \left(\frac{5.0 - 1.0}{6}\right)^2 = \left(\frac{4}{6}\right)^2 = .44 \tag{9.5}$$

The completed calculations for all of the activities are summarized in Table 9-6. From these data we can note that activity A has a higher degree of uncertainty than activity J, as evidenced by a variance of 1.78 as compared to a value of .11. We can verify this by examining Table 9-5; here the range on activity A is from 3.0 to 11.0, while activity J has a range from .8 to 2.8. The variance, therefore, does indeed provide a measure of the uncertainty in the activity estimates.

## Variability in project completion date

In calculating the critical path we used expected duration times for the activity times; what we obtained thus was an expected duration of the project, since each project activity is likely to be variable in length rather than fixed (as we noted in Table 9-5). The project completion time will be variable, particularly if there are large variations in the critical path activities. This does not necessarily mean that the project completion time will be extended. If variations in critical path activity times result in one or more of the times being greater than expected, then the project completion time will be greater than the computed value. But if variability in critical path activities results in shorter than expected activity times, then the completion date is likely to be earlier than the computed time. We use the term "likely" because it is also possible that variations in noncritical path activities could be such that if they were delayed long enough, they could result in a new critical path with a duration greater in length than the previous critical path.

Since the variance of an activity provides a measure of variation or uncertainty, we can use this to compute the overall variation in the expected project completion time. In computing the expected project completion time we took the sum of the expected activity times for the critical activities; to compute the variance in the project completion time ($\sigma^2$), we simply add the variances ($\sigma_t^2$'s) of the activities that make up the critical path. As with a single activity, the larger the composite variance ($\sigma^2$), the more likely it is that the actual time required to complete the project will differ from the expected completion time.

To illustrate this concept, let us examine the Sharp Company case. Recall from Figure 9-8 that the critical path included activities A, C, E, G, I, and J, with an expected completion time of 22 weeks. The variance for the project therefore is as follows:

$$\sigma^2 = \sigma_{t_A}^2 + \sigma_{t_C}^2 + \sigma_{t_E}^2 + \sigma_{t_G}^2 + \sigma_{t_I}^2 + \sigma_{t_J}^2$$

$$= 1.78 + .56 + 1.00 + .44 + .09 + .11 \qquad (9.6)$$

$$= 3.98 \text{ weeks}$$

From basic statistics we know that the standard deviation is equal to the square root of the variance; therefore, the standard deviation for the project completion is $\sigma = \sqrt{\sigma^2} = \sqrt{3.98} \approx 2$ weeks.

The fact that the variance is 3.98 weeks (and/or the standard deviation is 2 weeks) relative to the expected completion time of 22 weeks tells us something about the variability of the project. However, a great deal more could be said about the variability if we knew something about the probability distribution that describes the possible project duration times.

Recall that the developers of PERT used a beta distribution to describe the variations in the activity times. From statistics, it is known that the project completion times are not described by a beta distribution, but follow an approximately normal or bell-shaped distribution.[4] Figure 9-10 is a pictorial representation of what this means in terms of the Sharp Company case.

Since the variation in project completion time follows a normal distribution, we can use our knowledge of this distribution to make a probability statement about a specific project completion date; given a specific target completion date, we can compute the probability that the project will be completed on or before that date. To illustrate, assume that Bill Bowen, Sharp Company vice president, has indicated that it is desirable to have the project completed within 6 months (26 weeks), and would like to know the probability of this occurring. To determine this probability value,

---

[4]This result is based on the *central limit theorem*, which indicates that the sum of a large number of independent activity times will be approximately normally distributed regardless of the distribution of the individual activity times.

FIGURE 9-10.
Project Completion
Time Variation for
Sharp Company
Case—Normal
Distribution

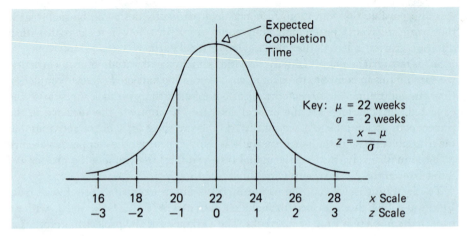

we first convert the 26-week value to a Z value. We know that the Z value is expressed by the following function:

$$Z = \frac{x - \mu}{\sigma} \tag{9.7}$$

Therefore, for $x = 26$, $\mu = 22$ (our expected completion time), and $\sigma = 2$, the Z value is

$$Z = \frac{26 - 22}{2} = 2 \tag{9.8}$$

Using $Z = 2.0$ and a table for the normal distribution, we find that the associated probability (and likewise the percentage of total area under the curve to the left of $x = 26$) is $.5000 + .4772 = .9772$. The probability that the project will be finished in 26 weeks or less is $.9772$; Mr. Bowen therefore should be fairly confident the project can be completed by this date.

## ■ Time/cost trade-offs

### *Time/cost factors*

Up to this point in the chapter, we have focused our attention on the *time* aspects of PERT/CPM and on what one should be aware of to meet a scheduled completion date. We have not discussed the cost of the resources associated with achieving a given completion date or what cost would be associated with shortening the completion time.

Many activities in a network can be shortened, but only by increasing costs. For example, in the Sharp Company network the "order and receive materials for product," activity C, and "order and receive materials for package," activity D, times probably can be reduced by spending additional dollars to expedite orders and/or being willing to pay premiums for early delivery of materials. Likewise, the fabrication activity times, E and F, and the testing activity times, G and H, can be shortened by using additional equipment and/or labor, both of which add extra cost to complete the project. Beyond some point, however, an activity time cannot be reduced, regardless of the amount of additional dollars expended. A minimum limit thus exists on the total time required to complete a project; beyond this point, the cost will simply increase, with no additional reduction in project completion time.

Figure 9-11 is a pictorial representation of the time/cost relationship in a typical project. Each point on this *time/cost trade-off curve* represents a feasible project schedule. Note that there is a *minimum time schedule* as well as a *minimum cost schedule*. Only these schedules and those lying on the curve between the two extreme points are feasible schedules.

We could develop a time/cost trade-off curve for the Sharp Company case; however, since the probability is very high (recall it was .9772) that the 26-week due date will be met, it is unlikely that management will be willing to spend extra money to reduce the project completion time. Let us, therefore, consider another example that can be used to illustrate the construction of the time/cost curve as well as other time/cost trade-off concepts. Assume that we have a project made up of eight activities. The data associated with the network, as well as the precedence relationships for the activities, are shown in Figure 9-12. The critical path calculations (noted in the network) show that activities A, B, C, and D are critical and the expected completion time is 17 days (assuming the activity times are expressed in days).

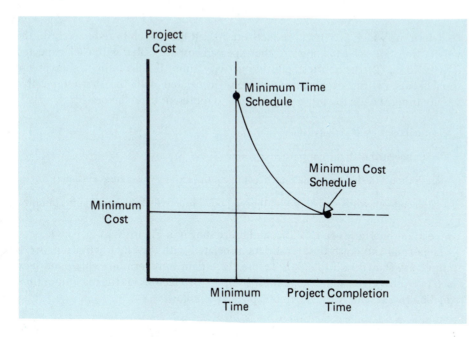

**FIGURE 9-11.
Time/Cost Trade-
off Curve**

**FIGURE 9-12.**
**Network Diagram**
**for Example**
**Project**

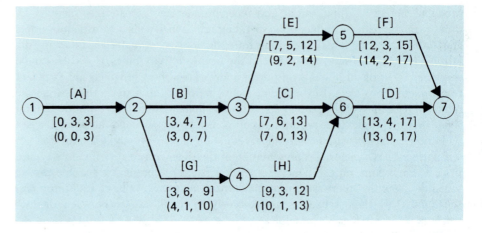

To develop a time/cost trade-off curve, we begin by assuming that the "minimum cost schedule" shown in Figure 9-11 is the 17-day schedule shown in Figure 9-12. To reduce the completion time to less than 17 days will require the shortening of some of the activity times, which, as we have noted, will require additional resources. This does not mean that all activity times should be reduced simultaneously; rather, we should sequentially reduce activities such that the maximum time reduction per dollar expended is the result. The terminology used to describe this process has been *crashing*    labeled by the PERT/CPM developers as **crashing** activity times.

## Crashing activity times

To determine which activity to reduce (crash) and how much to reduce (crash) the activity time, we need to know: (1) the expected cost associated with each expected activity time; (2) the shortest possible activity time, if maximum resources are applied; and (3) the expected activity cost associated with the shortest possible activity time. We use the following notation to represent these factors:

$t_n$ = normal (expected) activity time

$c_n$ = cost associated with the normal activity time

$t_c$ = crash time—the least possible time to complete the activity (maximum crashing)

$c_c$ = crash cost—the cost associated with the least possible activity time (maximum crashing)

The relationships between $t_n$, $c_n$, $t_c$, and $c_c$ are shown in Figure 9-13.

The normal and crash time/cost data associated with the eight-activity network example are shown in Table 9-7. To use these data to determine which and how much to crash a given activity, we must compute two factors: (1) the maximum time reduction for each activity, which is expressed as follows:

$$t_D = t_n - t_c \qquad (9.9)$$

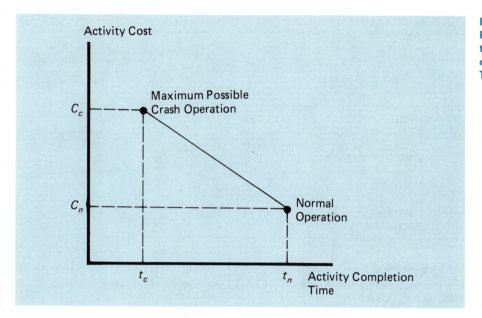

(2) the crashing cost per unit of time, which is expressed as follows:

$$S = \frac{\text{Cost}_{\text{crash}} - \text{Cost}_{\text{normal}}}{\text{Time}_{\text{normal}} - \text{Time}_{\text{crash}}} = \frac{c_c - c_n}{t_n - t_c} = \frac{c_c - c_n}{t_D} \qquad (9.10)$$

To illustrate, activity C has a normal activity time of 6 days with an associated cost of $1000 and a maximum crash time of 3 days with an associated cost of $6000. The maximum time reduction for the activity, therefore, is $t_D = t_n - t_c = 6 - 3 = 3$ days. The associated per day cost to achieve this reduction is

$$S = \frac{c_c - c_n}{t_n - t_c} = \frac{1600 - 1000}{6 - 3} = \frac{600}{3} = \$200 \text{ per day} \qquad (9.11)$$

| Activity | Normal Time $(t_n)$ | Normal Cost $(c_n)$ | Crash Time $(t_c)$ | Crash Cost $(c_c)$ |
|---|---|---|---|---|
| A | 3 | $ 300 | 2 | $ 360 |
| B | 4 | $ 500 | 2 | $ 900 |
| C | 6 | $1000 | 3 | $1600 |
| D | 4 | $ 600 | 3 | $ 650 |
| E | 5 | $1200 | 2 | $1500 |
| F | 3 | $ 500 | 3 | $ 500 |
| G | 6 | $ 800 | 5 | $1050 |
| H | 3 | $ 900 | 2 | $1200 |

TABLE 9-7.
Normal and Crash Data for Eight-Activity Example Project

**TABLE 9-8.   Maximum Crash Reduction and Crash Cost per Time Unit Data for Example Project**

| Activity | Normal Time ($t_n$) | Normal Cost ($c_n$) | Crash Time ($t_c$) | Crash Cost ($c_c$) | Maximum Crash Reduction ($t_D = t_n - t_c$) | Crash Cost per Time Unit $\left( S = \dfrac{c_c - c_n}{t_D} \right)$ |
|---|---|---|---|---|---|---|
| A | 3 | $ 300 | 2 | $ 360 | 1 | $ 60 |
| B | 4 | $ 500 | 2 | $ 900 | 2 | $200 |
| C | 6 | $1000 | 3 | $1600 | 3 | $200 |
| D | 4 | $ 600 | 3 | $ 650 | 1 | $ 50 |
| E | 5 | $1200 | 2 | $1500 | 3 | $100 |
| F | 3 | $ 500 | 3 | $ 500 | 0 | $  0 |
| G | 6 | $ 800 | 5 | $1050 | 1 | $250 |
| H | 3 | $ 900 | 2 | $1200 | 1 | $300 |
|   |   | $5800 |   | $7760 |   |   |

By performing the same operations on the remaining activities, we can determine all the maximum crash time reductions and the associated per day costs. These data are shown in Table 9-8.

Once the data in Table 9-8 have been developed, we can begin the crashing process. The procedure we will employ is to examine the critical path activities (shown in Figure 9-12) and select that activity with the least crash cost per time unit. We will reduce the activity time by one time unit, and then reevaluate the network for the critical path. If parallel critical paths appear, all critical paths must be reduced simultaneously in subsequent reduction steps. We can continue this process until all activities on any one critical path are fully crashed.

Beginning with Figure 9-12, we note that activities A, B, C, and D are all on the critical path. Since activity D has the smallest crash cost per time unit, $50, we will crash the activity by 1 day. The resulting network is shown in Figure 9-14.

Activities A, B, C, and D are still critical activities in Figure 9-14, and activity D

**FIGURE 9-14. Network After Crashing D by 1 Day**

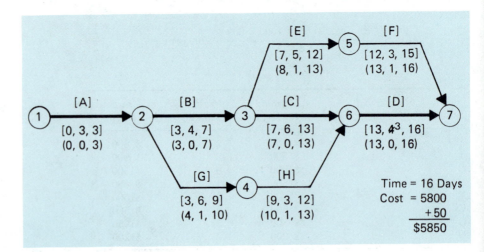

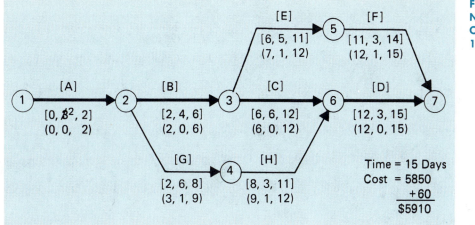

**FIGURE 9-15.**
**Network After Crashing A by 1 Day**

has been crashed the maximum possible (1 day). Since activity A has the next smallest crash cost per time unit on the critical path, we will crash this activity next. Figure 9-15 is the new network after crashing activity A by 1 day.

The critical path still includes activities A, B, C, and D, but activities A and D have been fully crashed; therefore, only activities B and C are candidates for crashing. Both of the activities have the same crash cost per time unit; however, reducing activity B will reduce the length of two paths. Thus we should crash activity B next.

From Table 9-8 we note that the maximum crash reduction for activity B is 2 days. This indicates that the activity time could be reduced by 2 days rather than 1 day; but we can make only a 1-day reduction. If a 2-day reduction were made in one step, a parallel critical path could be overlooked, which would result in an invalid network. Therefore, we will make a 1-day reduction of activity B. The resulting network for this step is shown in Figure 9-16.

By crashing B by 1 day, two critical paths are created: A–B–C–D and A–G–H–D.

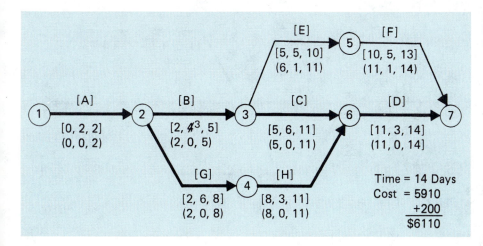

**FIGURE 9-16.**
**Network After Crashing B by 1 Day**

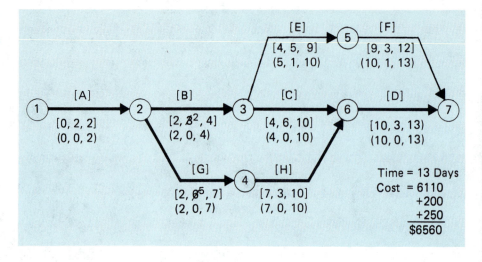

**FIGURE 9-17.**
**Network After**
**Crashing B and G**
**by 1 Day**

Both activities A and D are common to the two paths; however, these activities have been fully crashed. We therefore must simultaneously reduce (by 1 day) an activity on each of the paths. Since activity B can still be reduced by 1 day before reaching its maximum crash reduction, we can use the same reasoning as used in the previous step to select this activity for the critical path A–B–C–D. Since the crash cost per time unit for activity G is less than that for activity H (refer to Table 9-8), we should choose activity G to crash in the critical path A–G–H–D. The resulting network after crashing these activities simultaneously is shown in Figure 9-17.

Note that with each new network the cost increases. In the initial network (Figure 9-12), the cost for the 17-day schedule was $5800. The 13-day schedule shown in Figure 9-17 will result in a cost of $6560.

In Figure 9-17 the same two paths are critical that were critical in Figure 9-16, but

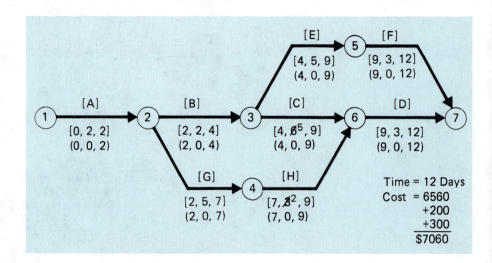

**FIGURE 9-18.**
**Fully Crashed**
**Network**

| Project Schedule No. | Project Completion Time (days) | Total Costs ($) | Last Activity Crashed | Costs per Day Saved ($) | Activities on Critical Path |
|---|---|---|---|---|---|
| 1 | 17 | $5800 | None | — | A, B, C, D |
| 2 | 16 | $5850 | [D] | $ 50 | A, B, C, D |
| 3 | 15 | $5910 | [A] | $ 60 | A, B, C, D |
| 4 | 14 | $6110 | [B] | $200 | A, B, C, D |
|   |    |       |     |       | A, G, H, D |
| 5 | 13 | $6560 | [B] | $200 | A, B, C, D |
|   |    |       | [G] | $250 | A, G, H, D |
| 6 | 12 | $7060 | [C] | $200 | A, B, C, D |
|   |    |       | [H] | $300 | A, B, E, F |

TABLE 9-9.
Summary of Crashing Process for Example Project

now both activity B and activity G are fully crashed. The only remaining activities that are candidates for crashing are activities C and H. Simultaneously crashing these activities by 1 day each and recomputing the critical paths results in the network shown in Figure 9-18.

At this point, all activities in the network are critical; therefore, if a further reduction in total project time is to be made, a reduction must be made simultaneously in all three critical paths A–B–C–D, A–G–H–D, and A–B–E–F. But all activities on path A–B–C–D have been fully crashed; the network therefore has been fully crashed.

Table 9-9 is a summary of the results of the crashing process for the project. From these data we can note that the minimum time in which the project can be completed is 12 days, at a cost of $7060. This means that for $1260 above the base cost of $5800, the project completion time can be reduced by 5 days (17 − 12 = 5).

If we plot the data from the "Project Completion Time" and "Total Costs" columns of Table 9-9 the results will be the time/cost trade-off curve for the project; this is displayed in Figure 9-19. This curve provides a comprehensive summary of possible schedules and indicates the most efficient schedule or successive reductions in project completion time. This does not say that the project should be completed in 12 days, the minimum completion time; rather, management should select the schedule that satisfies both time and cost requirements.

## ▪ Summary

In this chapter we have covered the basic concepts of a PERT/CPM network. Detailed procedures were given for developing a network, including procedures for determining the earliest start, earliest finish, latest start, and latest finish times for each activity of the network. Procedures were also given for identifying the critical path and for identifying those activities having float (slack) time.

Because the activity times associated with a project most often are estimates, the expected completion time for a project can be highly uncertain. However, if three

FIGURE 9-19.
Time/Cost Trade-
off Curve for Ex-
ample Project

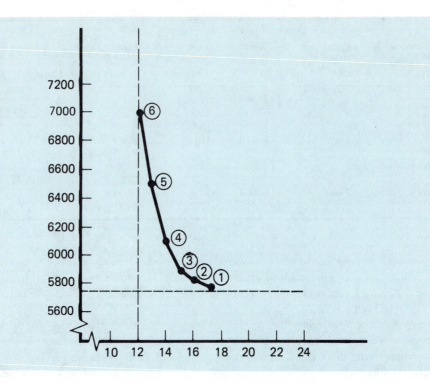

estimates are made of each activity time, these can be used to compute the probability of completing the project by a given date. A procedure and example were given to illustrate this point.

Procedures were also given for "crashing" activities of a network to reduce the completion date for a project. A detailed manual example was used to illustrate the concept.

In the last section, we developed mathematical formulations for both "finding the critical path" and "crashing activities." Example illustrations of each were given.

From the materials presented throughout the chapter, one could quickly conclude that PERT/CPM is used only to determine a project schedule—but this is incorrect. The procedures (as well as the mathematical formulations) of PERT/CPM can be used as a project progresses. Since the actual completion times of some activities may deviate from the expected values, and because the expected times of some future activities may have to be revised if new information becomes available, the PERT/CPM network may have to be revised, particularly if the changes are such that the critical path is shifted to a different set of activities in the network. Procedures exist in PERT/CPM for "revising" the network. We did not cover this material, or a number of other scheduling/control topics, simply because our objective was to provide an overview of the basic concepts and to demonstrate how such techniques can be formulated as mathematical programming problems. The interested reader is directed to the references for more detailed coverage of both PERT and CPM.

# ■ Glossary of terms

**activities:**   Specific tasks or jobs that are elements of a project. These are represented as arcs in a PERT network.

**arcs:**   See definition of *branches*.

**backward pass:**   A procedure used to determine the latest start and latest finish for each activity in a network. The procedure employs a backward movement through the network.

**branches:**   The interconnecting lines that link the nodes in a network. Also referred to as *arcs*.

**CPM (Critical Path Method):**   A project management procedure that includes the capability for crashing activities in the network.

**crashing:**   The process of reducing an activity time in a network by adding resources.

**critical activities:**   The activities that make up the critical path.

**critical path:**   The longest path in a project management (PERT/CPM) network. The duration of the project is the sum of the activity time of the critical activities.

**dummy activity:**   An activity with zero activity time, used in a PERT/CPM type of network to show dependent relationships.

**earliest finish time:**   The earliest time at which an activity may be completed.

**earliest start time:**   The earliest time at which an activity may begin.

**events:**   All activities in a network are preceded and succeeded by events. With the exception of the initial event, an event occurs when all activities preceding the event have occurred. Events are represented as nodes in a network.

**expected activity time:**   The average time required to complete an activity.

**float time:**   The length of time an activity can be delayed without causing the duration of the overall project to exceed its scheduled completion time.

**forward pass:**   A procedure used to determine the earliest start and earliest finish times for each activity in a network. The procedure employs a forward movement through the network.

**immediate predecessor activities:**   The activities that immediately precede a given activity.

**latest finish time:**   The latest time at which an activity may be completed without delaying the overall completion of the project.

**latest start time:**   The latest time at which an activity may begin without delaying the overall completion of the project.

**most probable time estimate:**   The activity time estimate (in PERT/CPM) that is most likely to occur.

**network:**   A pictorial representation of a problem, consisting of a series of nodes (circles) interconnected by arcs or branches (lines).

**nodes:**   The connection points or junctions of a network. These are used to represent the events in a PERT/CPM network.

**optimistic time estimate:**   The activity time estimate (in PERT/CPM) based on the assumption that the most favorable conditions will occur.

**PERT (Program Evaluation and Review Technique):**   A network-based project management procedure.

**pessimistic time estimate:** The activity time estimate (in PERT/CPM) based on the assumption that the most unfavorable conditions will occur.

**slack:** The length of time an activity can be delayed without affecting the completion date of a project.

## ■ Review questions

1. What advantage does a PERT/CPM network have over a bar chart?

2. Define the following terms employed in a network:
   a. nodes
   b. activities
   c. events
   d. arcs
   e. branches

3. Explain the use of a dummy activity. Give an example to illustrate your explanation.

4. Explain the difference between *earliest start* and *earliest finish* times for each activity in a network. How are these related to the activity duration time?

5. Explain how the expected completion date for a project can be computed by making a *forward pass* through the network.

6. Explain how scheduled start and completion times for each specific activity in a network can be provided once a *forward pass* and a *backward pass* are made through the network.

7. Explain what is meant by the critical path.

8. Explain how it is possible, using PERT/CPM, to identify how long "noncritical" activities can be delayed before they cause a delay in the total project.

9. Identify the specific steps employed in the process of analyzing a project with PERT/CPM.

10. Explain the basic time/cost trade-off concept used in PERT/CPM.

11. List the four basic factors that must be known to compute the cost-slope factor used in crashing.

12. Identify the basic procedures for crashing a PERT/CPM network.

13. Identify the mathematical programming model for crashing a network.

14. Identify those factors, beyond developing an activity schedule and crashing, that must be employed in managing a project with PERT/CPM.

## ■ True/false questions

1. The first step in developing a PERT/CPM network is to lay out a bar chart.

2. Dummy activities are not required in every network, but they should be used to ensure that the proper activity relationships are depicted in the network.

3. A project network can have multiple (parallel) branches in the critical path.

4. The *earliest start* and *earliest finish* times for each activity are computed by using a backward pass through the network.

5. The critical path in a network can easily be identified once a forward pass has been made through the network.

6. The variability in the actual completion times for the activities in a network is modeled in PERT/CPM by employing a procedure that allows the user to input *optimistic, most likely,* and *pessimistic* estimates of the activity time.

7. In crashing a network, the activity that should be crashed first is the one with the lowest cost per time period.

8. Both the forward pass and the backward pass procedures are employed in crashing a network.

9. In crashing a network, one must recompute the critical path as well as slack time each time an activity time is crashed.

10. Computing the critical path and crashing activity times are the only two factors necessary in managing a project with PERT/CPM.

# ■ Problems

1. The Randell Company is a medium-sized construction and maintenance firm whose business is plumbing and piping systems. The principal area in which the firm operates is repair and maintenance of existing systems. Following are the activities involved in a steam pipe maintenance project.

   a. Move required material and equipment to site.
   b. Erect a scaffold and remove old pipe and valves.
   c. The new pipe can be fabricated while the activities noted in (b) are being done.
   d. After the old pipe and valves have been removed and the new pipe fabricated, the new pipe can be placed.
   e. The new valves, however, can be placed as soon as the old line is removed.
   f. Finally, when everything is in place, the pipe can be welded and insulated.

   Construct a PERT/CPM network for the project.

2. Assume that we have a project that consists of constructing a two-part table lamp base from two different types of wood. Part 1 is made of walnut and part 2 of white pine. The wood for each part must be ordered and delivered from two separate suppliers. After the wood for both parts is received, each part is turned to the correct diameter on a lathe. Lathe A is used to turn the walnut and lathe B the white pine. A hole is then drilled in the walnut piece, after which the walnut is glued to the white pine. This completes the base. The activity data are shown in Table P9-2.

**TABLE P9-2**

| Activity | | Estimated Duration |
|---|---|---|
| A | Ordering and shipping time for walnut | 3 |
| B | Ordering and shipping time for white pine | 4 |
| C | Lathe turning time for walnut | 3 |
| D | Lathe turning time for white pine | 2 |
| E | Drilling time for walnut | 2 |
| F | Time required to glue parts together | 1 |

Draw the associated PERT/CPM network diagram.

3. Construct the PERT/CPM network diagram comprising activities A, B, C, . . . , P for the following precedence relationships:

   a. A, B, C, the first activities of the project, can start simultaneously.
   b. Activities D, E, and F can start immediately after A is completed.
   c. Activities I and G can start after both B and D are finished.
   d. Activity H starts after both C and G are completed.
   e. Activities K and L succeed activity I.
   f. Activity J succeeds both E and H.
   g. Activities M and N succeed F, but cannot start until E and H are completed.
   h. Activity O succeeds M and I.
   i. Activity P succeeds J, L, and O.
   j. Activities K, N, and P are the terminal jobs of the project.

4. The B & B Motor Company assembles motors that are used in manufacturing by the automotive industry. The company purchases, from outside vendors, all the components used in fabricating the motors. Following are the activities. The associated times involved in the fabrication process are shown in Table P9-4.

   a. The first three activities can be performed simultaneously:
      (1) Purchase casting.
      (2) Purchase steel.
      (3) Purchase motor.
   b. After the casting has been received,
      (4) casting must be machined.
   c. After the steel is received,
      (5) fabricate frames, then
      (6) fabricate housings.
   d. After activities (4), (3), and (6) are complete,
      (7) assemble the three units into a single unit.
   e. After activity (7) is complete, unit can be
      (8) inspected,
      (9) packed, and
      (10) shipped.

**TABLE P9-4**

| Activity | Time (weeks) | Activity | Time (weeks) |
|----------|--------------|----------|--------------|
| 1 | 4 | 6 | 4 |
| 2 | 2 | 7 | 3 |
| 3 | 10 | 8 | 1 |
| 4 | 3 | 9 | 1 |
| 5 | 2 | 10 | 1 |

Sketch the PERT/CPM network for the fabrication project.

5. Following is a list of activities involved in constructing a brick patio. Develop the appropriate PERT/CPM network diagram.

   a. Three activities can begin simultaneously at the start of the project:
      (1) Rip redwood edge strips.
      (2) Lay out area.
      (3) Bring in bricks from street curb.

**b.** Two activities follow the area layout in the following order:
   (4) Place sand base.
   (5) Level and tamp sand base.

**c.** After activities (3) and (5) have been completed,
   (6) start laying bricks.

**d.** After activity (1) has been done,
   (7) precut edge strips to length.

**e.** Two activities can begin simultaneously after activity (6) is finished:
   (8) Begin lining up and leveling bricks.
   (9) Complete laying bricks.

**f.** After both (8) and (9) have been done, activity (10) can be carried out:
   (10) Complete lining up and leveling bricks.

**g.** Before activity (11) can begin, activities (7) and (8) must have been finished:
   (11) Start setting redwood edge strips.

**h.** Preceding activity (12), activity (8) must have been finished:
   (12) Begin sweeping sand into joints.

**i.** Activity (13) follows the completion of activities (10) and (12):
   (13) Complete sweeping sand into joints.

**j.** Following the completion of activities (10) and (11), activity (14) can begin:
   (14) Complete setting edge strips.

**k.** The final activity can begin after (13) and (14) have been finished:
   (15) Clean up.

**6.** Based on the PERT/CPM diagram developed in Problem 4 and the associated activity times given in the statement of the problem:

   **a.** Find the earliest start time and earliest finish time for each activity.

   **b.** Identify the critical path for the project.

   **c.** The project must be completed in 16 weeks. Are there any difficulties in meeting this deadline? Describe the situation in detail.

**7.** Given the project network of Figure P9-7:

**FIGURE P9-7**

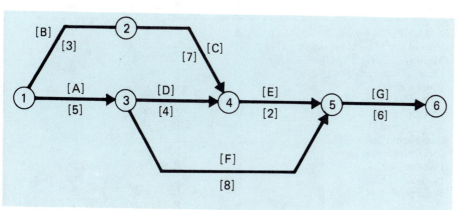

   **a.** Compute the early and late start times for all activities.

   **b.** Identify the critical path for the project.

   **c.** How much slack time, if any, exists for activity E?

8. A small maintenance project consists of the following ten jobs, whose precedence relationships are identified by their node numbers (see Table P9-8).

**TABLE P9-8**

| Job (Activity) | (Initial Node, Final Node) | Estimated Duration (days) |
|---|---|---|
| a | (1, 2) | 2 |
| b | (2, 3) | 3 |
| c | (2, 4) | 5 |
| d | (3, 5) | 4 |
| e | (3, 6) | 1 |
| f | (4, 6) | 6 |
| g | (4, 7) | 2 |
| h | (5, 8) | 8 |
| i | (6, 8) | 7 |
| j | (7, 8) | 4 |

a. Draw the PERT/CPM diagram representing the project.
b. Calculate the early and late start and the early and late finish times for each job.
c. How much slack does job d have? Job f? Job j?
d. Which jobs are critical?
e. If job b were to take 6 days instead of 3, how would the project finish date be affected?
f. Do any jobs have slack time? If so, which ones and how much?

**TABLE P9-9**

| Activity | Code | Immediate Predecessor | Activity Time (days) |
|---|---|---|---|
| Assemble crew for job | A | — | 10 |
| Use old line to build inventory | B | — | 28 |
| Measure and sketch old line | C | A | 2 |
| Develop materials list | D | C | 1 |
| Erect scaffold | E | D | 2 |
| Procure pipe | F | D | 30 |
| Procure valves | G | D | 45 |
| Deactivate old line | H | B, D | 1 |
| Remove old line | I | E, H | 6 |
| Prefabricate new pipe | J | F | 5 |
| Place valves | K | E, G, H | 1 |
| Place new pipe | L | I, J | 6 |
| Weld pipe | M | L | 2 |
| Connect valves | N | K, M | 1 |
| Insulate | O | K, M | 4 |
| Pressure test | P | N | 1 |
| Remove scaffold | Q | N, O | 1 |
| Clean up and turn over to operating crew | R | P, Q | 1 |

9. Table P9-9 shows activities, predecessor relationships, and activity times for an extended project for the Randell Company (see Problem 1).
   a. Develop a PERT/CPM project diagram.
   b. Determine the critical path.
   c. Determine the slack time for each activity not on the critical path.

10. Given the network diagram and the estimated activity times of Figure P9-10:

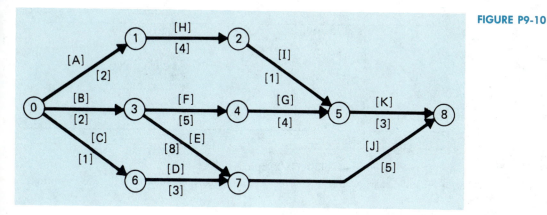

**FIGURE P9-10**

   a. Identify the critical path for the network.
   b. What is the impact on the critical path if activity E's time is reduced to 3?
   c. What is the slack time for activities G and H?

11. Given the network diagram of Figure P9-11:

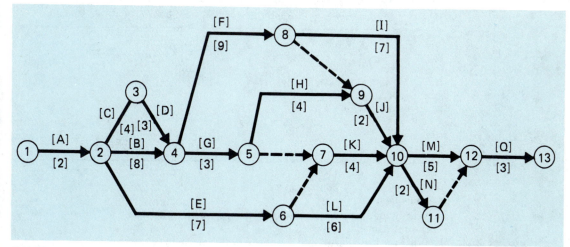

**FIGURE P9-11**

   a. Identify the earliest start and finish times for each activity.
   b. Identify the critical path for the network.
   c. How much slack time exists in activity J? In activity N?

12. A small project is composed of seven activities whose time estimates are listed in Table P9-12. Activity predecessor relationships are identified by beginning ($i$) and ending ($j$) node numbers.

**TABLE P9-12**

| | Node | | Estimated Duration (weeks) | | |
|---|---|---|---|---|---|
| Activity | $i$ | $j$ | Optimistic | Most Likely | Pessimistic |
| A | 1 | 2 | 1 | 1 | 7 |
| B | 1 | 3 | 1 | 4 | 7 |
| C | 1 | 4 | 2 | 2 | 8 |
| D | 2 | 5 | 1 | 1 | 1 |
| E | 3 | 5 | 2 | 5 | 14 |
| F | 4 | 6 | 2 | 5 | 8 |
| G | 5 | 6 | 3 | 6 | 15 |

a. Draw the appropriate PERT/CPM project network.
b. Calculate early and late occurrence times for each node. What is the expected project length?
c. Calculate slack for each activity.

13. Table P9-13 lists the jobs of a network along with their time estimates.

**TABLE P9-13**

| | Immediate | Estimated Duration (days) | | |
|---|---|---|---|---|
| Job | Predecessors | Optimistic | Most Likely | Pessimistic |
| A | — | 3 | 6 | 15 |
| B | — | 2 | 5 | 14 |
| C | A | 6 | 12 | 30 |
| D | A | 2 | 5 | 8 |
| E | C | 5 | 11 | 17 |
| F | D | 3 | 6 | 15 |
| G | B | 3 | 9 | 27 |
| H | E, F | 1 | 4 | 7 |
| I | G | 4 | 19 | 28 |

a. Draw the project network.
b. What is the approximate probability that jobs on the critical path will be completed by the due date of 41 days?
c. What is your estimate of the probability that the entire project will be completed by the due date? Explain.

14. Given the project network of Figure P9-14 and its associated data (Table P9-14, the times are expressed in days and the costs in dollars):

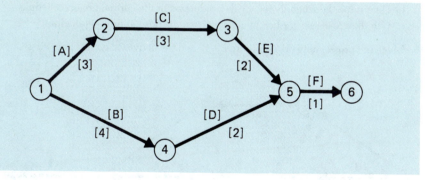

**FIGURE P9-14**

**TABLE P9-14**

|          | Duration |       | Cost   |       |
|----------|----------|-------|--------|-------|
| Activity | Normal   | Crash | Normal | Crash |
| A        | 3        | 2     | 20     | 50    |
| B        | 4        | 2     | 40     | 80    |
| C        | 3        | 1     | 35     | 65    |
| D        | 2        | 1     | 25     | 50    |
| E        | 2        | 1     | 20     | 30    |
| F        | 1        | 1     | 5      | 5     |

**a.** Compute the dollars/day value for each activity.

**b.** What is the impact of crashing activity E by 1 day?

**c.** Continue to compress the activity times until the project is fully "crashed."

15. A small maintenance project consists of six jobs. The normal time, a minimum (or crash) time (in days), and the cost in dollars per day of crashing each job are given in Table P9-15.

**TABLE P9-15**

|     | Node |     | Normal Time | Minimum (Crash) Time | Cost of Crashing |
|-----|------|-----|-------------|----------------------|------------------|
| Job | i    | j   | (days)      | (days)               | ($/days)         |
| A   | 1    | 2   | 9           | 6                    | 20               |
| B   | 1    | 3   | 8           | 5                    | 25               |
| C   | 1    | 4   | 15          | 10                   | 30               |
| D   | 2    | 4   | 5           | 3                    | 10               |
| E   | 3    | 4   | 10          | 6                    | 15               |
| F   | 4    | 5   | 2           | 1                    | 40               |

**a.** What is the normal project length? Minimum project length?

**b.** Determine the schedule for a 1-day reduction in the normal project schedule.

**c.** Can the project be crashed by 2 days (from the normal project schedule)?

16. Given the project network of Figure P9-16 and the activity data of Table P9-16:

**FIGURE P9-16**

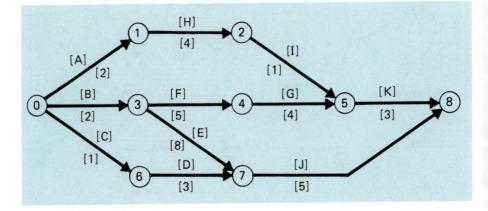

**TABLE P9-16**

| | Time | | Cost | |
|---|---|---|---|---|
| Activity | Normal | Crash | Normal | Crash |
| A | 2 | 2 | 20 | 20 |
| B | 2 | 1 | 30 | 70 |
| C | 1 | 1 | 10 | 10 |
| D | 3 | 2 | 50 | 100 |
| E | 8 | 6 | 200 | 400 |
| F | 5 | 3 | 150 | 490 |
| G | 4 | 4 | 100 | 100 |
| H | 4 | 2 | 300 | 600 |
| I | 1 | 1 | 50 | 50 |
| J | 5 | 4 | 80 | 80 |
| K | 3 | 2 | 50 | 90 |

Assume that the time units are in weeks and the costs are in $100's.

**a.** Determine the cost/week "crashing" values for each activity.

**b.** Determine the normal and minimum (crashed) completion times for the network.

**c.** Identify the two critical paths that result when activity J is compressed (crashed) by 1 day.

**d.** Compress the times for the network until it is fully "crashed."

**10**

# Transportation and Assignment Models

## ■ Introduction

In the preceding chapter on PERT/CPM, we discussed the concept of a **network** being made up of **arcs** and **nodes.** In the PERT/CPM case, the nodes, denoted by circles with numbers in them, represented events, whereas the arcs represented activities. Another important group of problems that can be denoted by networks are **transportation problems.** This type of problem is aimed at finding the least expensive group of routes over which to ship some commodity where there is a constant per unit cost. By this we mean that two units cost exactly twice as much as one unit, four units cost twice as much as two units, and so on. In the terminology of transportation problems, the nodes from which the commodity is sent are termed *source nodes* or *supply nodes*. The nodes to which the commodity is being sent are called *destination nodes* or *demand nodes*.

In this chapter we will consider how to formulate transportation problems as linear programming problems. We will also show how a special version of the simplex method called the *stepping stone method* can be used in a tabular format.

A special case of the transportation problem called the *assignment problem* will also be discussed in this chapter. A solution method termed the *Hungarian method* will be presented for the assignment problem.

As has been the practice in previous chapters, we will use a short case to motivate our discussion of the transportation problem. This example will be formulated as a linear programming problem and then solved by the stepping stone method.

*network*
*arcs*
*nodes*

*transportation problems*

## ■ Case

# Boor's Brewery Company

Boor's Brewery is a nationally known brewery that produces a beer in two locations, one in Silver, Washington, and one in Apple Chill, N.C. After being brewed and bottled, the beer is sent to four wholesalers, who handle any subsequent distribution. These wholesalers are located throughout the country, causing Boor's to incur significant costs for transporting the beer to the wholesalers. For this reason, Boor's is concerned about total costs of distributing the beer to the wholesalers.

Each month it is necessary for the distribution manager at Boor's, Walter Gunter, to try to find the least-cost distribution pattern that will meet each wholesaler's demand from the available supply at the two breweries. The necessary data to make this decision includes the distribution costs from each brewery to each wholesaler, the demand at each wholesaler, and the available supply at the two breweries. For this month, Walter has shown this information in Table 10-1. This includes the distribution costs per 100 cases to each wholesaler, the monthly supply from each brewery, and the monthly demand at each wholesaler.

In the past, Walter has used a trial-and-error method to solve this transportation problem. He has recently heard about a method to solve this problem that will always lead to the least-cost distribution pattern.

### Discussion of case

The Boor's Brewery Case is a classic example of the transportation problem where there are supplies and demands as well as routes over which the commodity is moved. If we represent the locations of the supplies and demands as circles (nodes) and the routes as arrows (arcs), we then have the network representation of the Boor's Brewery problem shown in Figure 10-1.

In the network representation of the transportation problem, we have numbered the supply nodes 1, 2, and so on. We have also numbered the demand nodes in the same fashion. The amount of the commodity shipped over the arcs between the nodes are denoted by $x_{ij}$, where $i$ refers to the supply node and $j$ refers to the demand node. Since the supply nodes ship only to demand nodes, there is no ambiguity in this numbering system. For example, while $x_{23}$ refers to the amount shipped between supply node 2 and the demand node 3, $x_{11}$ refers to the amount shipped between supply node 1 and demand node 1.

If we examine the transportation problem, it is easy to see that since it meets all of the assumptions of the linear programming problem, we can formulate it as one. The linear programming formulation of the Boor's Brewery problem is much like the B & Z Brewing Company discussed in Chapter 6. As noted above, we let

$$x_{ij} = \text{the amount shipped from supply node } i \text{ to demand node } j$$

In the linear programming formulation, we wish to minimize the total cost of transporting the total supply to meet total demand. This gives us an objective function of:

MINIMIZE $21x_{11} + 15x_{12} + 18x_{13} + 9x_{14} + 10x_{21}$
$$+ 14x_{22} + 16x_{23} + 23x_{24} \qquad (10.1)$$

In a transportation problem, one set of constraints ensures that the total amount shipped from each supply node equals the supply available at that node. A second set of constraints ensures that the total amount shipped to each demand node meets the requirements. These constraints are shown as follows:

| Brewery | Albany, N.Y. | Ames, Iowa | Luckenbach, Tx. | Needles, Calif. | Supply (100's of Cases) | | TABLE 10-1. Distribution Costs for Boor's Brewery Company |
|---|---|---|---|---|---|---|---|
| Silver, Wa. | $21 | $15 | $18 | $ 9 | 550 | | |
| Apple Chill, N.C. | $10 | $14 | $16 | $23 | 650 | | |
| Demand (100's of Cases) | 200 | 250 | 400 | 350 | | | |

SUBJECT TO:

$$x_{11} + x_{12} + x_{13} + x_{14} \qquad\qquad = 550 \tag{10-2}$$

$$x_{21} + x_{22} + x_{23} + x_{24} = 650 \tag{10-3}$$

$$x_{11} \qquad + x_{21} \qquad\qquad = 200 \tag{10-4}$$

$$x_{12} \qquad + x_{22} \qquad = 250 \tag{10-5}$$

$$x_{13} \qquad + x_{23} \qquad = 400 \tag{10-6}$$

$$x_{14} \qquad + x_{24} = 350 \tag{10-7}$$

$$x_{ij} \geq \text{ for all } i \text{ and } j$$

Several items should be noted about this formulation. First, the first two constraints required that the amount moved be equal to the amount available. Equal-to constraints are used here because the total supply equals the total demand, so all of the supply must be transported. This is referred to as a **balanced transportation problem.** Second,

the next four constraints require that the amount going to each demand node be equal to the demand at that node. Equal-to constraints are used here for the same reason as discussed above. It should be noted that for a balanced transportation problem, one of the constraints is not needed. If 1200 is the total supply transported and the first

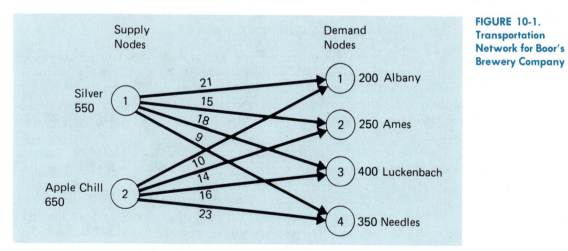

**FIGURE 10-1. Transportation Network for Boor's Brewery Company**

three demand nodes have absorbed 850 units, then the last demand node must absorb 350 units, so the last constraint is redundant and may be dropped. If this is done, then for this problem with 2 supply nodes and 4 demand nodes, there will be $2 + 4 - 1 = 5$ constraints. In general, a problem with *m supply nodes* and *n demand nodes* will have $m + n - 1$ *constraints*. This is an important result, since there will always be the same number of basic variables as there are constraints.

......................................................................................................

# ■ Stepping stone method for transportation problems

*stepping stone method*

A special form of the simplex method has been developed for transportation problems. This special simplex method is called the **stepping stone method.** The reason for this name will become clear later.

## The transportation tableau

*transportation tableau*

To formulate a transportation problem for solution by the stepping stone method, we use a special tableau known as the **transportation tableau.** To demonstrate this tableau, we will use the Boor's Brewery problem discussed previously. The information for this problem was given in Table 10-1. The transportation tableau for the problem is shown in Figure 10-2, where the large cells are equivalent to the arcs connecting the supply points and demand points, and the small cells in the upper left corner of the large cells contain the per-unit costs for each arc. We will use the empty space in the large cells for calculations.

In this problem, it should be noted that the total of the supplies equals the total of the demands. As noted earlier, when these totals are equal, the problem is said to be *balanced;* otherwise, the problem is *unbalanced.* For the time being, we will consider only balanced problems; we will discuss methods for unbalanced problems later.

## An initial solution

As with any linear programming problem (such as the transportation problem), we must find an initial basic feasible solution. If we used a standard linear programming tableau, we would use artificial variables, since the linear programming formulation of the transportation problem has equal-to constraints. However, we do not need to use artificial variables to find an initial basic feasible solution in the transportation tableau.

There are several approaches to finding an initial solution. In all of the methods, we try to find an allocation of the supplies to the demands in such a way that all of the supplies are used to satisfy all of the demands.

*minimum cost method*

An intuitive approach to making an initial allocation is termed the **minimum cost method.** In this approach, the cell (arc) having the least cost is given an allocation sufficient to exhaust the corresponding supply or demand, whichever is less. The supply and demand are then reduced by the amount allocated (obviously, one

FIGURE 10-2.
Transportation
Tableau for Boor's
Brewery Company

| | Albany | Ames | Luckenbach | Needles | Supply: |
|---|---|---|---|---|---|
| Silver | 21 | 15 | 18 | 9 | 550 |
| Apple Chill | 10 | 14 | 16 | 23 | 650 |
| Demand: | 200 | 250 | 400 | 350 | 1200 |

becomes equal to zero), then the next smallest cost cell is chosen and the process is repeated. If either the supply or demand, or both, are equal to zero, an allocation cannot be made to the cell being considered. This process continues until all supplies are exhausted and all demands are met.

As an example of this procedure, we have shown the allocation made to the least-cost cell in the tableau in Figure 10-3, and the completed initial allocation in Figure 10-4. In Figure 10-4, we have shown by a number in the upper right corner of each cell the order in which cells were allocated. If it was impossible to make an allocation to a cell, an $x$ is shown rather than a number. The impact of each allocation on each supply and demand is shown by crossing out the previous supply or demand and showing the new supply or demand. The cost for this initial allocation is $15,450. (Costs are in dollars and allocations are in hundreds of cases of beer.) This is not the optimal solution, but it does give us a relatively low-cost initial solution.

The minimum cost method for making an initial allocation for the transportation problem is one of several such allocation methods that attempt to use the cost structure to arrive at an initial solution. Other methods, similar to the minimum cost method, are the *row minimum cost method* and the *column minimum cost method*. The **row minimum cost method** allocates the maximum amount to the least-cost cell in a given row. If the total supply is used up for this row, then we move on to the next; otherwise, the next least-cost cell in that row is chosen for allocation and so on.

*row minimum cost method*

FIGURE 10-3.
Allocation to the
Least Cost Cell

| | Albany | Ames | Luckenbach | Needles | Supply: |
|---|---|---|---|---|---|
| Silver | 21 | 15 | 18 | 9 (350) | 550 200 |
| Apple Chill | 10 | 14 | 16 | 23 | 650 |
| Demand: | 200 | 250 | 400 | 350  0 | 1200 |

**FIGURE 10-4.**
**Completed Initial**
**Allocation**

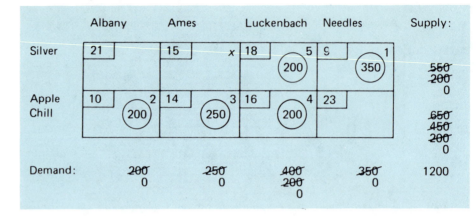

The **column minimum cost method** approaches the initial allocation similarily to the row minimum cost method *except* that columns are considered rather than rows. The result of using a row minimum cost initial allocation is shown in Figure 10-5, while the column minimum cost initial allocations are shown in Figure 10-6. In each case, the numbers in the upper right corner of each cell give the order in which the allocations were made. The effect of each allocation on the supplies and demands is also shown.

The total cost for the row minimum initial allocation is $15,250, which is less than the total cost for the column minimum initial allocation or the minimum cost initial allocation. Since these initial allocation methods are easy to apply, the user can try all three to determine the one with the least cost. The question as to whether any of these initial allocations are optimal will be considered next. If the least-cost initial solution is not optimal, one must apply a procedure for moving from the initial allocation to the optimal allocation. We will present this method next.

**FIGURE 10-5.**
**Row Minimum Initial Allocation**

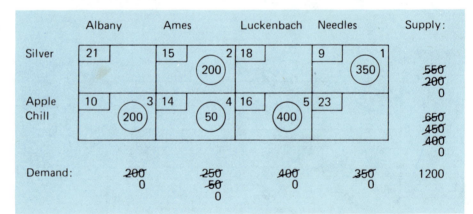

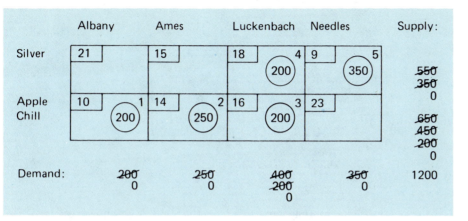

**FIGURE 10-6.**
**Column Minimum Initial Allocation**

## Calculation of improvement indices

To determine whether an initial solution is optimal or not, we need to compute a value for each empty cell to determine if a smaller total cost allocation exists. This value is known as the **improvement index** for each cell. Consider, for example, the minimum-cost initial allocation for the Boor's Beer problem as shown in Figure 10-7. (While this is not the least-cost initial allocation, we will use the allocation for purposes of explanation.)

*improvement index*

To determine if a better allocation exists, we need to compute the change in cost resulting from a reallocation of *one* unit to an empty cell, say the Silver to Albany cell. However, if one unit is reallocated to this cell, then it will be necessary to allocate one less unit to some other cell in order to keep the sum of the cells equal to the total supply for the first row. This in turn will necessitate an increase in the allocation for a second cell to balance the first decrease. This process will have to continue until all supplies and demands are balanced. We then will use these increases and decreases to determine the effect of this one-unit change on total cost.

To demonstrate how this procedure works, consider the effect of reallocating one unit to the Silver to Albany cell. This is shown in Figure 10-8. Here, the effect of reallocating one unit to the Silver–Albany cell ($x_{11}$ in the network formulation) must

**FIGURE 10-7.**
**Boor's Initial Allocation**

|  | Albany | Ames | Luckenbach | Needles | Supply: |
|---|---|---|---|---|---|
| Silver | 21 | 15 | 18 / 200 | 9 / 350 | 12  550 |
| | 12 | (16) | | | |
| Apple Chill | 10 / 200 | 14 / 250 | 16 / 200 | 23 / 13 | 10  650 |
| Demand: | 0  200 | 4  250 | 6  400 | 3  350 | 1200 |

FIGURE 10-8.
Reallocation of
One Unit to Cell
$x_{11}$

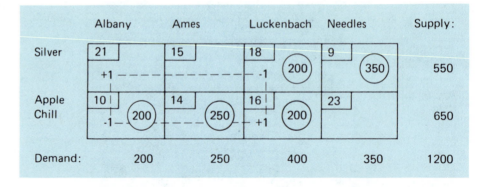

be balanced by the subtraction of one unit from the Silver–Luckenbach cell ($x_{13}$). The Silver–Needles cell ($x_{14}$) was *not* chosen because there would be no way to balance the decrease in $x_{14}$ by an addition to a currently allocated cell. This way, we do not have to consider the effect of increased allocations to more than one empty cell, and we will retain, in the end, a solution with $m + n - 1$ basic cells.

Given that we have subtracted one unit from $x_{13}$, we need to balance this by a one-unit increase in the Apple Chill–Luckenbach cell ($x_{23}$). We must then have a one-unit decrease in $x_{21}$ to balance both the increases in $x_{23}$ and $x_{11}$. Once again, $x_{22}$ is not considered because there does not exist another allocation in the second column. The cost effect of this path is found by adding and subtracting costs according to whether a unit is added or subtracted. In this case, the result is found to be

$$+21 - 18 + 16 - 10 = +9$$

In the case of reallocating one unit to the $x_{11}$ cell, the total cost would increase by $9 for each 100 cases of beer shipped from Silver to Albany. This value is termed the improvement index. If the improvement index is positive, then the reallocation to this cell would result in an increase in the total costs. Conversely, a negative value for the improvement index indicates a *decrease* in the total cost. Since we are interested in the *lowest* possible total cost allocation, we will be looking for cells with negative improvement indices. If there exist no cells with negative improvement indices, then the current allocation is optimal since any reallocations would cause an increase in the total cost. To perform this checking, improvement indices must be computed for *all* empty cells.

The process of computing improvement indices in the stepping stone method is analogous to the computation of the $(c_j - z_j)$ values in the simplex algorithm and serves the same purpose.

So far we have only considered the $x_{11}$ cell. Now consider the $x_{12}$ cell. If we reallocate one unit to the $x_{12}$ cell, we must then subtract one unit from the $x_{13}$ cell, add one unit to the $x_{23}$ cell, and subtract one unit from the $x_{22}$ cell to balance all supplies and demands. These additions and subtractions are shown in Figure 10-9.

The improvement index for cell $x_{12}$ can be computed by adding and subtracting the costs in the cells on the reallocation path in the same sequence as the $+1$'s and

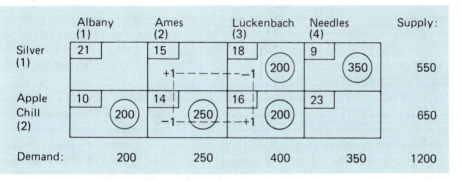

**FIGURE 10-9.**
**Reallocation of**
**One Unit to Cell**
$x_{12}$

$-1$'s. For $x_{12}$, the improvement index is found by

$$+15 - 18 + 16 - 14 = -1$$

Because the improvement index for $x_{12}$ is $-1$, we can reduce the total cost by \$1 for each 100 cases of beer that we reallocate to the Silver–Ames route.

Finally, we need to compute the improvement index for the last empty cell, $x_{24}$. To do this, we first find the reallocation path connecting $x_{24}$ to the allocated cells. In this case, the path is $x_{24} \rightarrow x_{23} \rightarrow x_{13} \rightarrow x_{14}$ and the resulting improvement index is found by

$$+23 - 16 + 18 - 9 = +16$$

Since $x_{12}$ has the only negative improvement index, we will reallocate to this cell. If there exists more than one cell with a negative improvement index, we reallocate to the cell with the most negative improvement index. Given that we wish to reallocate to $x_{12}$, we must now determine how much we can reallocate to the $x_{12}$ cell.

## Improving the current solution

Given that we have found the cell with the most negative improvement index, we would like to reallocate as much as possible to this cell. Recall that we assigned $+1$'s in cells where the reallocation process will bring about an increase over the current allocation and $-1$'s to the cells where there will be a decrease in the present allocation, in order to balance the increases. We would like to increase as much as possible the allocation in those cells with a $+1$, in order to maximize the resulting decrease in total cost. However, any increase in the $+1$ cells must be balanced by an identical decrease in those cells having a $-1$. We cannot have too large a decrease or some cell with a $-1$ assignment will become negative, which is not realistic. This limits the amount of the reallocation.

Referring to Figure 10-9, cells $x_{13}$ and $x_{22}$ both have $-1$'s in them so they will have a decrease in their allocation as a result of the reallocation process. The present allocation to $x_{13}$ is 200, while the present allocation to $x_{22}$ is 250. These are the maximum allowable decreases in allocation for each cell. Obviously, we must use the minimum of these two values as the amount to be reallocated. In the example, we may not reallocate more than 200 units to the $x_{12}$ cell. We then add 200 units to cells that have a $+1$ and subtract 200 units from cells having a $-1$, obtaining the result shown in Figure 10-10.

At this point, we once again must check each cell to determine if any cell has a negative improvement index. In each case, a path must be found that connects the cell being checked to a set of the allocated cells. The determination of these loops is fairly easy for problems such as Boor's Beer, but we need a systematic procedure for finding the loops. We will present just such a procedure next. This procedure was

*stone cells*
*water cells*

termed the stepping stone method because some of the early users of this method referred to the allocated cells as **stone cells** and the empty cells as **water cells.** Then, if starting at the cell to which an allocation is desired, we must find a reallocation loop by "stepping only on the stone cells" and not on any of the water cells (which would not support you!)—hence the name *stepping stone method.*

## A crossing-out method for finding loops

An easy procedure for finding the loop that will connect the cell being checked to the currently allocated cells involves *crossing out* those cells that will not be a part of the path. To find a cell that fits this criterion, look for one that is the *only* allocated cell in *either* its row or column. If one is found, *cross out* that row or column by drawing a line through it. In this procedure, consider the cell being checked as being allocated. When looking for cells that are the only allocated cells in their row or column, do not consider previously crossed-out cells. If no more cells can be found to be crossed out, the remaining group of allocated cells *plus* the cell being checked make up the path to use in computing an improvement index. All that is required is to place a $+1$ in the cell being checked, then a $-1$ in an allocated cell in the same *row*, then a $+1$ in an allocated cell in the same *column* as the first allocated cell. This process of alternating $+1$ and $-1$ with rows and columns continues until the cell being checked is again encountered. The final step is to compute the improvement index by adding the costs of cells having a $+1$ and subtracting the costs of the cells having a $-1$.

As an example of this procedure, consider again the Boor's problem *after* 200 units

**FIGURE 10-10.**
**Result of a Reallo-cation to Cell $x_{12}$**

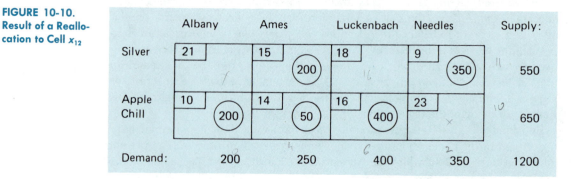

| | Albany | Ames | Luckenbach | Needles | Supply: |
|---|---|---|---|---|---|
| Silver | 21 | 15  200 | 18 | 9  350 | 550 |
| Apple Chill | 10  200 | 14  50 | 16  400 | 23 | 650 |
| Demand: | 200 | 250 | 400 | 350 | 1200 |

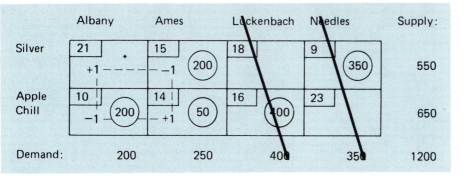

**FIGURE 10-11.**
**Crossing-out**
**Method**

are reallocated to the $x_{12}$ cell. The transportation tableau for this allocation is seen in Figure 10-10. To check cell $x_{11}$, we note that cells $x_{14}$ and $x_{23}$ do not have other allocated cells in their column. We, therefore, cross out the third and fourth columns. The result of this crossing out is seen in Figure 10-11.

After the third and fourth columns are crossed out, we see that each remaining allocated cell has other allocated cells in both its row and its column (including the cell being checked, $x_{11}$ which has an asterisk in it). Therefore, the remaining allocated cells complete the path to $x_{11}$. If we then put a $+1$ in the $x_{11}$ cell, a $-1$ in the $x_{12}$ cell, a $+1$ in the $x_{22}$ cell, and finally a $-1$ in the $x_{21}$ cell, we can use these values to compute the improvement index by

$$+21 - 15 + 14 - 10 = +10$$

To check the $x_{13}$ cell, we note that the $x_{14}$ and $x_{21}$ cells are the only allocated cells in their columns, so these columns may be crossed out. This leaves the path connecting $x_{13}$ to $x_{23}$ to $x_{22}$ to $x_{12}$. This is shown in Figure 10-12.

The improvement index is found to be

$$+18 - 15 + 14 - 16 = +1$$

Since it is positive, we go on to check the remaining empty cell, $x_{24}$.

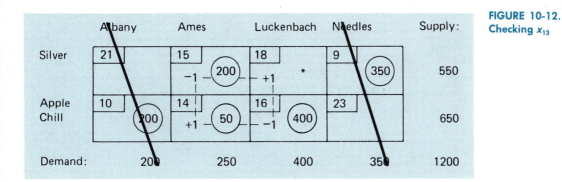

**FIGURE 10-12.**
**Checking $x_{13}$**

For $x_{24}$, we note that $x_{21}$ and $x_{23}$ are the only allocated cells in their columns, so we cross out these columns, leaving the remaining allocated cells to form a path with $x_{24}$. This result is shown in Figure 10-13.

The improvement index is found to be

$$+23 - 14 + 15 - 9 = +15$$

Since the improvement index for $x_{24}$ is positive, we would not want to allocate more to that cell.

We have now checked all nonallocated cells and found that all improvement indices are positive. This indicates that the present allocation is optimal.

## The stopping rule for optimality

From the previous discussion, it should be clear that the stepping stone method terminates with an optimal solution when the improvement indices for all nonallocated cells are nonnegative.

We will summarize the stepping stone method as a step-by-step procedure.

**Step 1.** Formulate the transportation problem in a transportation tableau.

**Step 2.** Using one of the least-cost procedures (total minimum, row minimum, column minimum), find an initial allocation for the problem.

**Step 3.** One by one, compute the improvement indices for each nonallocated cell. Select the nonallocated cell with the largest negative improvement index as the incoming allocated cell and go to step 4. If *no* nonallocated cell is found with a negative improvement index, stop. The present allocation is optimal.

**Step 4.** For the nonallocated cell with the most negative improvement index, determine the cell in the loop having a negative sign that has the smallest allocation. This is the amount that is to be used for the reallocation process. Add this amount to the cells in the loop having a positive sign and subtract this amount from those cells in the loop having a negative sign. Go to step 3.

**FIGURE 10-13.**
**Checking $x_{24}$**

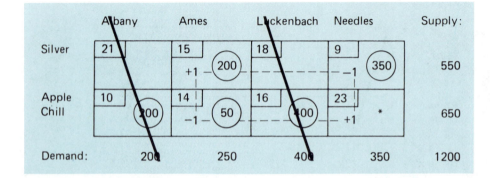

# ■ Extensions of the stepping stone method

So far we have considered only the simplest variety of transportation problems. In this section we will consider ways to handle complications that arise in some transportation problems.

## Unbalanced problems

So far we have only considered transportation problems where the sum of the supplies equals the sum of the demands. Obviously, total supply and demand are not exactly equal in all problems. Problems where this equality does not exist are referred to as **unbalanced problems.**

Since the stepping stone method as we have presented it works only for balanced problems, we will need to convert unbalanced problems into balanced problems. Fortunately, this is not difficult. As an example of an unbalanced problem, consider the distribution problem of the Myers Stone Company portrayed in a transportation tableau in Figure 10-14.

The Myers Stone Company moves crushed stone from quarries in Anthony, Reddick, and Otto to building sites in Erie and Greeneville at varying costs per ton. These costs are given in the transportation tableau in dollars per ton. Note from Figure 10-14 that the total supply at the quarries is 1100 tons while only 800 tons of crushed rock are required at the building sites. Consequently, the problem is unbalanced.

To rectify this problem, we add a *dummy* demand point with demand equal to the excess supply. This demand point represents the supply that *never* leaves the supply points. As such, the costs associated with this demand point are set to zero. With the new column (Figure 10-15) the problem now is balanced, and the stepping stone method may be used to solve the problem.

*unbalanced problems*

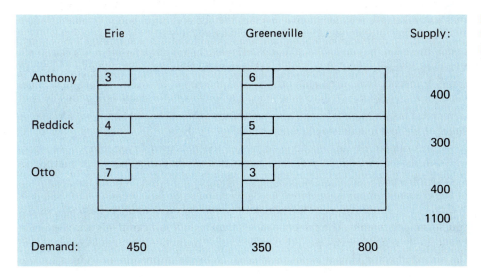

**FIGURE 10-14. Myers Stone Company Problem**

| | Erie | Greeneville | Supply: |
|---|---|---|---|
| Anthony | 3 | 6 | 400 |
| Reddick | 4 | 5 | 300 |
| Otto | 7 | 3 | 400 |
| | | | 1100 |
| Demand: | 450 | 350 | 800 |

**FIGURE 10-15.**
**Balanced Tableau**
**for Myers Stone**
**Company**

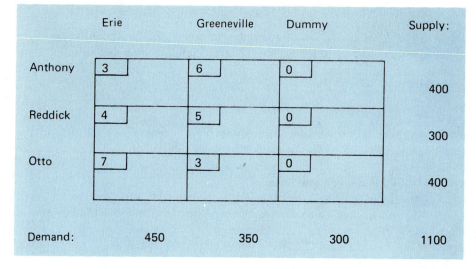

In the Myers Stone Company problem, the difference between the total supply and total demand is 300 tons. This is the demand at the dummy demand point as shown in the revised transportation tableau in Figure 10-15. If the total demand is greater than the total supply, a dummy supply point is added with supply equal to the excess demand. The costs in the new row are set equal to zero as for the dummy column. The interpretation of this row is that the amount allocated to the dummy supply point is the amount of demand that will be unsatisfied at each demand point.

## Degeneracy

Recall that in our linear programming formulation of the transportation problem (earlier in the chapter), we discovered that the last constraint was redundant. When this constraint was dropped, we were left with $(m + n - 1)$ total constraints. As a result, there will be $(m + n - 1)$ basic variables. In the transportation tableau, basic variables correspond to allocations, so that there will be $(m + n - 1)$ *allocations*. In some transportation problems, there will occur a situation where less than *degeneracy* $(m + n - 1)$ positive allocations will be necessary to absorb all of the supply and demand. This situation is known as **degeneracy** and will occur whenever a subset of supplies is equal to a subset of the demands.

As an example of this situation, consider the *modified* Myers Stone Company problem shown in Figure 10-16. We have used the row minimum cost method to find an initial allocation for the problem.

For this problem, we have 3 rows and 3 columns, so we have $m + n - 1 = 3 + 3 - 1 = 5$ necessary allocations. Our initial allocation has only 4 allocated cells, so the problem is degenerate. The presence of less than $m + n - 1$ positively allocated cells results in there not being a path that will join one or more of the unallocated cells to the allocated cells. Thus it is not possible to compute improvement indices for the

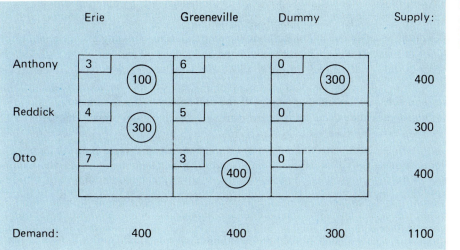

**FIGURE 10-16.
Modified Myers
Stone Company
Problem**

unallocated cells or to make reallocations from the allocated cells to the unallocated cells.

The resolution of degeneracy in the initial solution can be handled by the use of *place-holder* cells with zero allocations. This **degenerate cell** does not change the cost of the allocation but does allow us to apply the stepping stone method. The choice of the cell to be used for the zero allocation must be made in such a way as *not to form a loop with any previously allocated cells.* In Figure 10-17 we have shown one choice of a cell to have a zero allocation.

By making the zero allocation in cell $x_{12}$, we now have 5 allocations, and we did not form a closed loop with previously allocated cells. Had we made a zero allocation to the $x_{23}$ cell, however, we would have a closed path joining $x_{23}$ to $x_{13}$, $x_{11}$, and $x_{21}$. We

*degenerate cell*

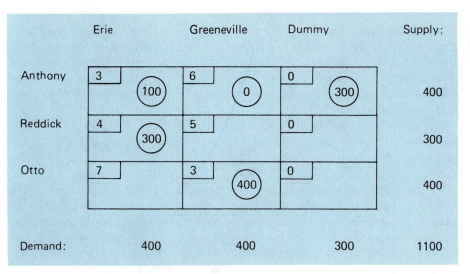

**FIGURE 10-17.
Initial Allocation
for Modified Myers
Stone Company**

would still have the same problems as before in terms of not being able to compute improvement indices or to make reallocations.

The only other consideration that we must give to choosing the degenerate or place-holder cell is that if it is the cell to be added and subtracted in the reallocation process, the result will be simply to move the location of the degenerate cell. This may seem pointless since it does not change the value of the allocation, but such reallocations must be made as a part of the movement to final optimality.

Degeneracy may occur at any time during the reallocation process. If there is a tie between two cells for the amount to be reallocated by addition and subtraction, then one of these cells will end up with no allocation (empty) and one will have a degenerate or zero allocation. We can resolve the problem of degeneracy by having one of the empty cells serve as an allocation cell. The choice of which cell is to be empty (unallocated) is completely arbitrary and does not affect the solution process.

## Maximization problems

So far in this discussion of transportation problems, we have considered only minimization problems. Obviously, there can exist problems where the objective is to maximize profits rather than to minimize costs. When such a problem is encountered, there are three possible ways to handle it. We can (1) change both the rule for choosing an empty cell for reallocation and the stopping rule, (2) multiply all profits by −1 and use the standard stopping rule, or (3) compute *opportunity costs* for each cell and use the standard rules to minimize opportunity costs. While all three methods will work, we suggest the use of the third method because it is simple to implement and does not require a change of the solution procedure.

*opportunity cost*

First we must define **opportunity cost.** This is the cost of not having made the best decision or choice possible. In the context of a maximization transportation problem, the opportunity cost for a cell is the difference between its profit and the profit for the highest-profit cell in the row. In other words, opportunity cost is the cost of not shipping everything over the highest-profit route.

To compute opportunity costs, we must simply subtract each cell's profit from the highest profit in the row. As an example, consider the Wacasassa Fish Company problem in Figure 10-18. In this problem, the values in each cell are profits per pound (expressed in cents) of fish shipped between the two fish houses and three wholesalers in Houston, Chicago, and New York. The objective of the problem is to maximize total profits.

In Figure 10-19, the Wacasassa Fish Company problem has been converted to a minimization problem by use of opportunity costs. For example, all profits in row one were converted by subtracting all profits from 6, the maximum profit in the row.

We are now ready to solve the problem using the stepping stone method. While this was a balanced problem, the opportunity cost approach is also valid for an unbalanced problem if the dummy row or column is added *before* the opportunity costs are computed. Otherwise, the dummy column will appear to have the lowest opportunity cost, and the optimal solution may not be the highest-profit allocation.

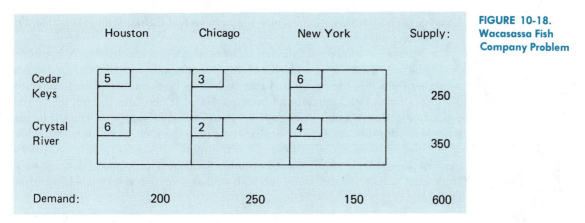

**FIGURE 10-18.**
**Wacasassa Fish**
**Company Problem**

## ■ An application of the transportation problem

In the field of production, a great deal of planning must take place in order to match the capacity of the production process and the demand for the end product. An example of a mismatch of capacity and demand is in the production of snow skis. The demand for skis usually occurs during the fall and early winter months, and demand will usually outstrip production capacity during this period.

We solve this dilemma by using inventory, which may be considered a means of "storing" production capacity. There are usually costs for holding inventory resulting from high capital investment, storage costs, deterioration costs, etc. These *holding costs* can be expressed either as a percentage of the production costs or as a per-unit cost for each period the inventory is held.

The question then becomes one of how to use the available capacity to meet present and future demands at a minimum cost, where both production and holding costs are to be considered.

This planning problem can be formulated as a transportation problem if we think of it as a problem of transporting production across time. Thus, the production

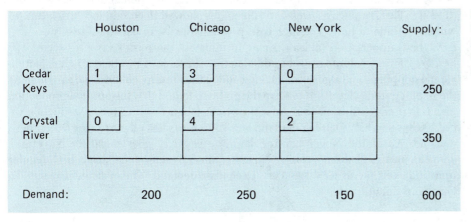

**FIGURE 10-19.**
**Opportunity Cost**
**Matrix for Wacas-**
**assa Fish Com-**
**pany Problem**

capacities in each time period become the supplies and the requirements per period become the demands.

For example, consider the situation faced by the Miller Electronics Company in the production of a TV game. The fourth-quarter demands (in 100's) and production capacities for Miller are shown in Table 10-2. Note that capacity exists to produce TV games by working regular and overtime hours. It may also be seen that while capacity remains constant through time, the demand increases for the Christmas sales. Note also that the December demand cannot be met solely from December production, so inventory must be used to "transport" previous production capacity forward through time to help meet December demand. The company does not have any initial inventory and does not wish to have any inventory on hand after December.

**TABLE 10-2.**
**Miller Electronics Monthly Demands and Capacities**

| Month | Demand | Regular Time Capacity | Overtime Capacity |
|---|---|---|---|
| October | 200 | 300 | 100 |
| November | 300 | 300 | 100 |
| December | 600 | 300 | 100 |

The costs for production of the TV games are $50 per 100 games if produced during regular production hours and $70 per 100 games if produced using overtime. It has been determined that inventory costs are $5 per 100 games per month.

These costs, demands, and capacities can now be combined to yield the transportation tableau shown in Figure 10-20. In this tableau, the costs are a combination of production costs and inventory costs. For example, to supply some of the December demand using November regular time production, the cost will be $50 + 5 = $55 per 100 games. Note that we have given very high arbitrary costs ($1000 per 100 games) to the cells that represent the satisfaction of a month's demand by using future capacity. This is known as *back ordering* and is allowed in certain industries, but we will not consider it here. The high costs preclude the use of back-order cells.

As the transportation tableau is now formulated, there is excess capacity of 100 lots, so a dummy column must be added before the tableau will be ready for solution via the stepping stone algorithm. Having added the dummy column, we can then use the stepping stone algorithm to solve the problem to find that the optimal production plan is to produce 300 lots in regular time in October. From October production we use 200 lots to satisfy October demand and 100 lots to satisfy a portion of December's demand. All of the November regular time capacity goes to satisfy November demand, and all of the remaining November and December capacity, both regular time and overtime, is used to satisfy December demand. The overtime capacity in October is not utilized.

| | Oct. Demand | Nov. Demand | Dec. Demand | | Supply: |
|---|---|---|---|---|---|
| Oct. Regular Time | 50 | 55 | 60 | | 300 |
| Oct. Overtime | 70 | 75 | 80 | | 100 |
| Nov. Regular Time | 1000 | 50 | 55 | | 300 |
| Nov. Overtime | 1000 | 70 | 75 | | 100 |
| Dec. Regular Time | 1000 | 1000 | 50 | | 300 |
| Dec. Overtime | 1000 | 1000 | 70 | | 100 |
| | | | | | 1200 |
| Demand: | 200 | 300 | 600 | 1100 | |

FIGURE 10-20. Production-Planning Transportation Tableau for Miller Electronics

# ■ The assignment problem

A special case of the *transportation problem* discussed earlier in this chapter is the **assignment problem,** which attempts to find the minimum cost assignment of workers to jobs. In this section we will discuss the assignment problem and a special method of solving this problem.

*assignment problem*

## *The Red Bank Swim Team*

As an example of an assignment problem, consider the Red Bank Swim Team, coached by Ray Mann. Coach Mann has a particularly strong group of girls on the team this year, and one problem facing him is selecting the best possible girls' 200-yard medley relay team. A medley relay is composed of backstroke, breaststroke, butterfly, and freestyle. Coach Mann has decided to use four girls on the relay team whose names are Lynn, Jodie, Missy, and Renee, but there is still a question about the assignment of swimmers to strokes. Each of the four girls can swim all four strokes very well, and Coach Mann wants to make assignments that will minimize the total time for the relay. The times for each girl in each stroke are shown in Table 10-3.

**TABLE 10-3. Red Bank Swim Team Times**

| *Swimmer* | *Stroke* | | | |
|---|---|---|---|---|
| | *Backstroke* | *Breaststroke* | *Butterfly* | *Freestyle* |
| Jodie | 35 sec | 37 sec | 33 sec | 28 sec |
| Missy | 37 sec | 37 sec | 33 sec | 30 sec |
| Renee | 36 sec | 39 sec | 32 sec | 30 sec |
| Lynn | 36 sec | 38 sec | 34 sec | 29 sec |

This problem may be viewed as a transportation problem having four supply nodes each having a supply of one unit, and four demand nodes, each having a demand on one unit. The supply nodes represent the available swimmers and the demand nodes represent the strokes. Since the supplies and demands are all equal to 1, the allocations in each cell will all be either 1 or 0. An allocation of 1 indicates that a swimmer is assigned to that stroke. The supplies and demands of 1 also force exactly one swimmer to be assigned to each stroke. The transportation tableau for this problem is shown in Figure 10-21.

While the assignment problem could be solved via the stepping stone method, the process would be very slow. This is caused by the large number of degenerate cells (cells with an allocation equal to zero). For an assignment problem with $n$ jobs and $n$ workers, there will always be $n - 1$ cells with an allocation of zero. When the stepping stone method is applied to an assignment problem, many iterations can be taken up just reallocating the zero allocations with no net improvement in the solution value. To address this slowness of solution using the stepping stone method, the **Hungarian method** was developed by an American mathematician, H. W.

*Hungarian method*

**FIGURE 10-21 Transportation Tableau for Red Bank Swim Team**

| | Backstroke | Breaststroke | Butterfly | Freestyle | |
|---|---|---|---|---|---|
| Jodie | 35 | 37 | 33 | 28 | 1 |
| Missy | 37 | 37 | 33 | 30 | 1 |
| Renee | 36 | 39 | 32 | 30 | 1 |
| Lynn | 36 | 38 | 34 | 29 | 1 |
| | 1 | 1 | 1 | 1 | |

FIGURE 10-22.
Assignment
Tableau for Red
Bank Swim Team

| Swimmer | Stroke | | | |
|---|---|---|---|---|
| | Backstroke | Breaststroke | Butterfly | Freestyle |
| Jodie | 35 | 37 | 33 | 28 |
| Missy | 37 | 38 | 34 | 30 |
| Renee | 36 | 39 | 32 | 30 |
| Lynn | 38 | 39 | 34 | 29 |

Kuhn. Since the method is based on the work of two Hungarians, Kuhn called it the "Hungarian method."

## The Hungarian method

To solve the assignment problem via the Hungarian method, it is first necessary to place the costs in an assignment tableau. This is done for the Red Bank Swim Team problem in Figure 10-22.

The first step in the Hungarian Method is to subtract the *smallest* value in each row from every value in that row. In our case this means that 28 is subtracted from every value in the first row, 30 from every value in the second row, and so on for all four rows. This results in Figure 10-23a.

FIGURE 10-23(a).
Assignment
Tableau after Row
Subtraction

| Swimmer | Stroke | | | |
|---|---|---|---|---|
| | Backstroke | Breaststroke | Butterfly | Freestyle |
| Jodie | 7 | 9 | 5 | 0 |
| Missy | 7 | 8 | 4 | 0 |
| Renee | 6 | 9 | 2 | 0 |
| Lynn | 8 | 10 | 5 | 0 |

**FIGURE 10-23(b). Assignment Tableau after Column Subtraction**

| Swimmer | Stroke: Backstroke | Breaststroke | Butterfly | Freestyle |
|---|---|---|---|---|
| Jodie | 1 | 1 | 3 | 0 |
| Missy | 1 | 0 | 2 | 0 |
| Renee | 0 | 1 | 0 | 0 |
| Lynn | 2 | 2 | 3 | 0 |

The next step in the Hungarian method is to subtract the smallest value in each column from all other elements in the column. If this is done, we arrive at the revised assignment tableau shown in Figure 10-23b.

Using the tableau resulting from the column subtraction, we move to the next step. This step involves finding the minimum number of vertical and horizontal lines necessary to *cover* all zeros in the tableau. In our case, this number is 3: a vertical line through the fourth column, a horizontal line through the second row, and a horizontal line through the third row. This covering pattern is shown in Figure 10-24.

If the minimum number of lines is *equal* to $n$, the number of workers and jobs, then the minimum cost assignment has been found. This assignment will be found by making the assignments corresponding to the zeros in the final tableau. Since only three lines are needed to cover the zeros in our tableau, we are not optimal and need to proceed to the next step.

**FIGURE 10-24. Covering Pattern with Three Lines**

| Swimmer | Stroke: Backstroke | Breaststroke | Butterfly | Freestyle |
|---|---|---|---|---|
| Jodie | 1 | 1 | 3 | 0 |
| Missy | 1 | 0 | 2 | 0 |
| Renee | 0 | 1 | 0 | 0 |
| Lynn | 2 | 2 | 3 | 0 |

A question that is often asked is: How do I know that I have used the *minimum* covering lines? For example, it would be possible to use four lines to cover the zeros in Figure 10-24 by using four horizontal lines. However, if too many covering lines are used, it will not be possible to find an assignment of exactly one worker to each task by using the zeros in the tableau. If we try this with Figure 10-24, we see that no assignment is possible with the zeros.

The next step in the assignment method involves determining the smallest *uncovered* element in the tableau. This smallest uncovered element is then *subtracted* from all *uncovered* elements in the tableau and *added* to all elements at the intersection of two covering lines. All *other* covered elements remain the same in the next tableau. In our example, the smallest uncovered element is 1. If this value is subtracted from all uncovered elements and added to elements at the intersection of the covering lines, we arrive at the tableau shown in Figure 10-25.

At this point, we return to the line-covering step to find the minimum number of lines necessary to cover all zeros. In this case, four lines are necessary, as shown in Figure 10-26.

Since four lines are necessary to cover all zeros in Figure 10-26, we have reached the optimal solution(s). There may be more than one optimal solution, but they will all have the same minimum value. The final step is to find the optimal assignment corresponding to the final tableau. This is done by looking for zeros that are the *only* zero in their row or column. When one is found, make this assignment and cross out the row and column. Continue this procedure until all workers are assigned to a job. In our example, we find that the Missy–Breaststroke element is the only zero in the second row. We make this assignment and cross out the second row and second column. The Lynn–Freestyle element is now the only zero in the fourth row, so we make this assignment and cross out the fourth row and fourth column. This leaves the Jodie–Backstroke as the only zero in the first row, so we make this assignment, leaving the Renee–Butterfly element as the only remaining zero. The complete

| | Stroke | | | |
|---|---|---|---|---|
| Swimmer | Backstroke | Breaststroke | Butterfly | Freestyle |
| Jodie | 0 | 0 | 2 | 0 |
| Missy | 1 | 0 | 2 | 1 |
| Renee | 0 | 1 | 0 | 1 |
| Lynn | 1 | 1 | 2 | 0 |

**FIGURE 10-25. Revised Tableau for Red Bank Swim Team**

**FIGURE 10-26.**
**Final Tableau for**
**Red Bank Swim**
**Team**

| Swimmer | Backstroke | Breaststroke | Butterfly | Freestyle |
|---------|------------|--------------|-----------|-----------|
| Jodie   | 0          | 0            | 2         | 0         |
| Missy   | 1          | 0            | 2         | 1         |
| Renee   | 0          | 1            | 0         | 1         |
| Lynn    | 1          | 1            | 2         | 0         |

(table column header group: **Stroke**)

assignment of swimmers to strokes is shown below:

> Jodie swims backstroke in 35 seconds
>
> Missy swims breaststroke in 38 seconds
>
> Renee swims butterfly in 32 seconds
> and Lynn swims freestyle in 29 seconds
> for a total time of 2 minutes 14 seconds.

To summarize the Hungarian method, we have listed it in a step-by-step fashion below for an assignment problem having $n$ rows and $n$ columns:

> **Step 1.** Determine the least-cost element in each row and subtract it from all other elements in that row.
>
> **Step 2.** Determine the least-cost element in each column and subtract it from all other elements in that column.
>
> **Step 3.** Use vertical and horizontal lines to cover all zeros in the tableau. If it is not possible to cover all zeros with less than $n$ lines, the optimal assignment has been found, so go to step 5. Otherwise, go to step 4.
>
> **Step 4.** Determine the smallest uncovered element and subtract it from all other uncovered elements. Also, add this element to all zeros at the intersection of two covering lines. Using the resulting tableau, return to step 3.
>
> **Step 5.** Determine an optimal assignment by finding any zero that is the only zero in its row or column. Make this assignment of worker to job and cross out the corresponding row and column. Continue this process until there are no rows and columns remaining.

## Complicating factors

In working with assignment problems, there are three complicating factors to be considered. These are multiple solutions, maximization, and unbalanced problems.

For the latter two factors—that is, maximization and unbalanced problems—the process to handle them is similar to that for transportation problems. For maximization problems it is necessary to convert the maximization problem to a minimization problem using the opportunity cost method. For unbalanced problems it is necessary to add a dummy row or column to ensure that the number of workers equals the number of jobs. The costs for the dummy row or column are equal to zero.

Multiple solutions can very easily occur in an assignment problem. These alternative solutions can be found by initiating step 5 of the solution process with a different element that is the only zero is a row or column. By so doing a different set of assignments will result.

## ■ An application of the assignment problem

An interesting application of the assignment problem is that of pilot scheduling, as, for example by an airline that has several flights between two cities each day. The airline is faced with deciding which flights should have their crews based in which cities so as to minimize the layover time in the other city. Consider the case of the Trans-Florida Airline, which operates a number of flights between Jacksonville and Miami each day. Each flight takes one hour. The scheduled departure and arrival times for flights coming into Miami are shown in Table 10-4; the scheduled departure and arrival times for flights arriving in Jacksonville are shown in Table 10-5. (All times are in hours after midnight.)

On the basis of these tables, we would like to determine which of the five crews should be stationed in Jacksonville, and which should be stationed in Miami so as to minimize crew layover time, that is, the time between the arrival of a crew and its departure on another flight.

| Flight Number | Departure Time | Arrival Time |
|---|---|---|
| 10 | 0500 | 0600 |
| 30 | 1000 | 1100 |
| 40 | 1200 | 1300 |
| 60 | 1800 | 1900 |
| 70 | 2100 | 2200 |

TABLE 10-4.
Miami Arrival
Times

| Flight Number | Departure Time | Arrival Time |
|---|---|---|
| 25 | 0800 | 0900 |
| 45 | 1300 | 1400 |
| 55 | 1500 | 1600 |
| 65 | 1700 | 1800 |
| 75 | 2200 | 2300 |

TABLE 10-5.
Jacksonville
Arrival Times

**TABLE 10-6.**
**Miami Layover**
**Times for**
**Jacksonville Crews**

*Jacksonville-to-Miami Flights*

| Arriving Flight No. | Departing Flight No. | | | | |
|---|---|---|---|---|---|
| | 25 | 45 | 55 | 65 | 75 |
| 10 | 2 | 8 | 9 | 11 | 16 |
| 30 | 21 | 2 | 4 | 6 | 11 |
| 40 | 19 | 0 | 2 | 4 | 9 |
| 60 | 13 | 18 | 20 | 22 | 3 |
| 70 | 10 | 15 | 17 | 19 | 0 |

To do this, we need to develop two more tables. First, Table 10-6 will show the layover time for crews stationed in Jacksonville who arrive in Miami and then pilot each possible return flight back to Jacksonville. Similarly, Table 10-7 shows the layover times in Jacksonville for crews stationed in Miami.

For example, a Jacksonville crew that pilots flight 30 into Miami would have a layover of 6 hours if it took flight 65 back to Jacksonville. Similarly, a Miami-based crew bringing flight 25 into Jacksonville would have a layover of 12 hours if it took flight 70 back to Miami.

Using these two tables, we now form a third table (Table 10-8), which has as its entries the minimum of the two corresponding entries from the two previous tables. We have circled the entries that come from the Jacksonville-based crews in order to keep up with where the minimum entry came from.

**TABLE 10-7.**
**Jacksonville**
**Layover Times for**
**Miami Crews**

*Miami-to-Jacksonville Flights*

| Departing Flight No. | Arriving Flight No. | | | | |
|---|---|---|---|---|---|
| | 25 | 45 | 55 | 65 | 75 |
| 10 | 20 | 15 | 13 | 11 | 6 |
| 30 | 1 | 20 | 18 | 16 | 11 |
| 40 | 3 | 22 | 20 | 18 | 13 |
| 60 | 9 | 4 | 2 | 0 | 19 |
| 70 | 12 | 7 | 5 | 3 | 22 |

**TABLE 10-8.**
**Minimum Layover**
**Times**

| Flight No. | Flight No. | | | | |
|---|---|---|---|---|---|
| | 25 | 45 | 55 | 65 | 75 |
| 10 | ② | ⑧ | ⑨ | ⑪ | ⑥ |
| 30 | 1 | ② | ④ | ⑥ | ⑪ |
| 40 | 3 | ⓪ | ② | ④ | ⑨ |
| 60 | 9 | 4 | 2 | 0 | ③ |
| 70 | ⑩ | 7 | 5 | 3 | ⓪ |

| Flight No. | to | Flight No. | Base |
|---|---|---|---|
| 10 |  | 25 | Jax |
| 30 |  | 45 | Jax |
| 40 |  | 55 | Jax |
| 60 |  | 65 | Miami |
| 70 |  | 75 | Jax |

**TABLE 10-9.**
**Optimal Crew**
**Assignment**

We can now solve the assignment problem to determine the minimum-layover assignment of arriving crews to departing flights using the Hungarian method or the stepping stone algorithm. The optimal solution can also tell where the various crews should be based. In this case, the optimal solution is to make the assignments shown in Table 10-9. The home bases for the crews are also shown in this table.

## ▪ Summary

In this chapter we have considered two special cases of networks, the transportation problem and the assignment problem. The transportation problem involves finding the least-cost set of routes to transport a commodity from a set of supply points to a set of demand points. For each route there exists a per-unit cost for transporting the commodity. The assignment problem is involved with assigning workers to jobs to find the minimum cost assignment and is a special case of the transportation problem with supplies and demands equal to 1.

For solving transportation problems, we discussed the use of the stepping stone method, which uses a special transportation tableau to arrive at a solution to the transportation problem. Based on this method, we showed extensions for variations of the standard transportation problem such as unbalanced problems, degenerate problems, and maximization problems. We also discussed an application of the transportation problem to production planning.

For solving assignment problems we discussed the use of the so-called Hungarian method. We also discussed ways of handling unbalanced problems and maximization problems. Finally, we presented an application of the assignment problem to airline crew assignments.

## ▪ Glossary of Terms

**arc:**   a path over which the flow will move in a network.

**assignment problem:**   the problem of finding the least-cost assignment of workers to jobs.

**balanced transportation problem:**   a transportation problem where the total supply equals total demand.

**degeneracy:**   the presence of one or more zero allocations in a transportation problem.

**degenerate cell:**   a place-holder cell in a transportation problem having a *zero* allocation, as opposed to an unallocated or empty cell.

**Hungarian method:**   a solution procedure for assignment problems.

**improvement index:**  the increase or decrease in total cost that would result from reallocating one unit to a currently empty cell.

**network:**  a combination of nodes and arcs.

**node:**  a supply or demand point in a transportation problem.

**opportunity cost:**  in a transportation problem, the difference between the highest-profit cell in a row and the profit of another cell in that row.

**row (column) minimum cost method:**  an initial solution to the transportation problem that is found by making allocations to the least-cost cell in each row (column) as long as supply (demand) exists to make each allocation in that row (column).

**stepping stone method:**  a special case of the simplex method that can be used to solve transportation problems.

**stone cell:**  an allocated cell.

**transportation problem:**  a problem where the objective is to transport a commodity from a set of supply points to a set of demand points for the minimum cost.

**transportation tableau:**  a tabular arrangement of supplies, demands, and costs used to represent a transportation problem.

**unbalanced problem:**  a transportation problem where the total supply does not equal the total demand.

**water cell:**  an unallocated cell.

## ■ Review questions

1. Why do we only need $m + n - 1$ constraints for a transportation problem having $m$ and $n$ demands?

2. Show how the transportation tableau relates to the LP formulation of the transportation problem.

3. In what cases could the use of, say, the row minimum allocation lead to a "bad" initial solution. (If the answer is not immediately obvious, make up some small problems that fit the situation.)

4. What does an improvement index of zero indicate about the reallocation of one unit to the empty cell?

5. Why must we choose to add and subtract the minimum allocation in cells (in the reallocation loop) having a negative one?

6. Why does the crossing out method always end up with the desired reallocation loop? (*Hint:* What kinds of cells are being crossed out?)

7. If there is greater demand than supply, we will add a dummy row to a transportation tableau. What is the physical meaning of this dummy row?

8. When adding a place-holding cell to a degenerate initial allocation, why must we avoid forming a loop with a previously allocated cell?

9. Why will there always be $n - 1$ degenerate cells in an assignment problem having $n$ rows and columns?

10. Why must the number of covering lines in the Hungarian method equal the number of workers or jobs?

11. Why must the number of jobs equal the number of workers?

# ■ True/false questions

1. The transportation problem is involved with determining the least-cost set of routes to use to transport a commodity between a set of supply points and a set of demand points.

2. A balanced transportation problem has the same number of supply points as demand points.

3. The stepping stone algorithm is used because the transportation problem cannot be solved via the simplex algorithm.

4. A row or column minimum initial solution to the transportation problem can lead to a high-cost initial solution.

5. Using opportunity costs is one way of handling an unbalanced transportation problem.

6. In the production-planning problem, the objective is to transport production over time using inventory at the least possible cost.

7. The assignment problem has as its objective the minimum-cost assignment of workers to jobs.

8. In the assignment problem, it is not necessary to have the same number of workers as jobs.

9. The Hungarian method is used to solve the assignment problem because assignment problems are too large for the stepping stone algorithm.

10. Opportunity costs can be used to solve maximization assignment problems.

# ■ Problems

1. Consider the transportation tableau formulation of a transportation problem provided in Figure P10-1.

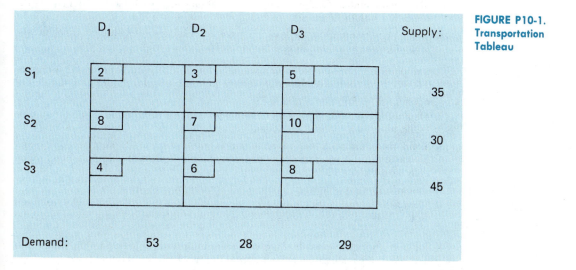

**FIGURE P10-1.
Transportation
Tableau**

a. Find an initial solution using the method of minimum cost initial allocation and compute the total cost of this allocation.

b. Repeat part (a) using the row-minimum initial allocation.

c. Repeat part (a) using the column-minimum initial association.

d. Compare the total cost resulting from parts (a), (b), and (c). Which method yields the least cost initial solution?

e. Check to determine if the least cost initial solution found in part (d) is optimal. If not, proceed with the stepping stone algorithm to find the optimal solution.

2. Consider the transportation problem shown in Figure P10-2.

**FIGURE P10-2.**
**Transportation**
**Tableau**

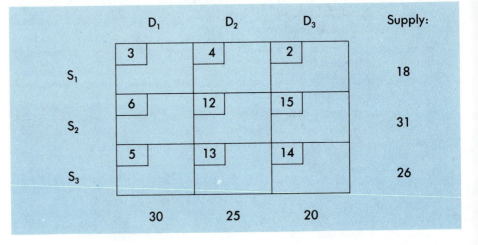

a. Find initial solutions using the row minimum, column minimum, and minimum cost allocation methods. Compare the total allocation cost of each method and choose the allocation with the least cost.

b. Using the allocation with the least initial cost, check to see if it is optimal. If not, use the stepping stone algorithm to move to the optimal solution.

3. A transportation problem for which we have found a solution is presented in Figure P10-3. We have computed the improvement indices for each cell and have decided to reallocate some unknown amount to cell (1, 4).

a. Determine the reallocation loop to be used to make a reallocation to cell (1, 4). This reallocation loop includes which cells?

b. Using the reallocation loop found in part (a) place a +1 in the empty cell (1, 4) and alternate −1, +1, etc. around the reallocation cells. Which cells have a −1 and which cells have a +1?

c. Based on part (b), which cell having a −1 has the smallest allocation?

d. Complete the reallocation process by adding the amount found in part (c) to each cell in the reallocation loop having a +1 and subtract this amount from the cells having a −1.

e. Is this new solution optimal? If not, determine improvement indices for the empty cells and repeat the reallocation process until the optimal solution is found.

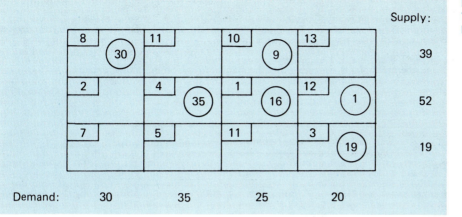

**4.** Consider the transportation problem shown in Figure P10-4. An initial allocation is shown for this problem, which we have determined is not optimal. We have computed improvement indices and have decided to reallocate to cell (2, 2).

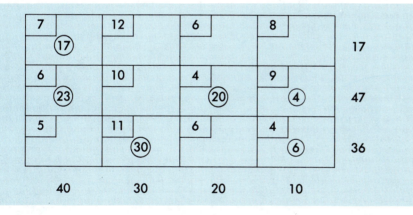

**a.** Determine the reallocation loop to be used to make the reallocation to cell (2, 2) and assign +1 and −1 to cells around the loop.

**b.** Determine which cell with a −1 assigned to it has the minimum allocation.

**c.** Complete the reallocation process by adding this minimum to the cells with a +1 and subtracting it from the cells with a −1 in them.

**d.** Is this new allocation optimal? If not, determine improvement indices for the empty cells and repeat the reallocation process until the optimal solution is found.

**5.** The Marion Fruit Company has orange groves at three different sites throughout central Florida. It also has three plants for turning fruit into orange juice concentrate. The fruit must be picked and transported from the groves to the concentrate plant. The transportation costs depend directly upon the distances from the grove to the plant. The supply of oranges (in tons) at each grove and the capacity of each plant (also in tons) are shown along with the distances from each grove to each plant in Table P10-5. Solve this as a transportation problem to find the minimum distance allocation of orange supply to concentrate plants, assuming that the plants are to be used to their capacity.

**TABLE P10-5.**
**Marion Fruit**
**Company**

|  | *Distance (miles) to Plant at* | | | |
|--------|--------|---------|----------|--------|
| *Grove* | *Ocala* | *Orlando* | *Leesburg* | *Supply* |
| Lynne | 21 | 70 | 40 | 250 |
| Eustis | 35 | 30 | 15 | 400 |
| Clermont | 80 | 10 | 25 | 300 |
| Capacity | 200 | 525 | 225 | |

6. Solve the transportation problem given in Figure P10-6. At each stage of the solution, show the calculations used to determine the incoming cell and the "tour" used to perform each transformation.

**FIGURE P10-6.**
**Transportation**
**Problem**

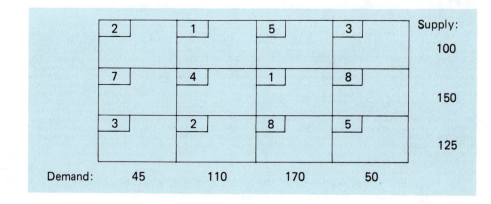

7. Solve the transportation problem given in Figure P10-7.

8. For the grove-to-plant distances shown in Problem 5, the transportation costs have been determined to be 10¢/ton/mile. Due to differences in plant efficiency, the plants have been found to have different gross profit values (not including transportation costs). The

gross profit values for each plant are

>Ocala: $9.50/ton
>
>Orlando: $8.50/ton
>
>Leesburg: $5.00/ton

Using these values, compute an optimal distribution of fruit so as to maximize profit.

| | | | Supply: |
|---|---|---|---|
| 50 | 100 | 100 | 110 |
| 200 | 300 | 200 | 160 |
| 100 | 200 | 300 | 150 |
| Demand: 140 | 200 | 80 | |

**FIGURE P10-7.**
**Transportation Problem**

9. The transportation problem in Figure P10-9 is unbalanced. Revise the problem to make it balanced, and solve it by the stepping stone method.

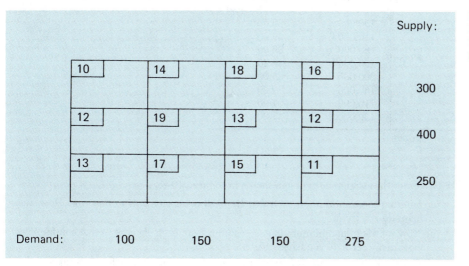

| | | | | Supply: |
|---|---|---|---|---|
| 10 | 14 | 18 | 16 | 300 |
| 12 | 19 | 13 | 12 | 400 |
| 13 | 17 | 15 | 11 | 250 |
| Demand: 100 | 150 | 150 | 275 | |

**FIGURE P10-9.**
**Unbalanced Transportation Problem**

10. The transportation in Figure P10-10 is unbalanced. Revise this problem to make it balanced and then solve it via the stepping stone algorithm.

**FIGURE P10-10.**
**Unbalanced**
**Transportation**
**Problem**

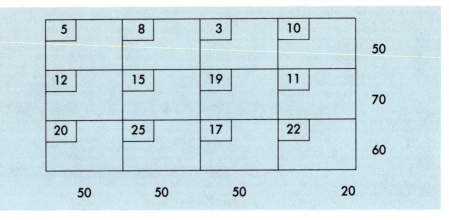

11. The E.L. Griffith Company has the opportunity to produce boots in advance of sales with a $1.00 per month per pair of boots storage cost. The company cannot produce more than 170,000 pairs of boots per month. Using the monthly demands and production costs in Table P10-11, formulate this problem as a transportation problem to minimize total costs.

**TABLE P10-11. E. L. Griffith Company**

| Month° | Forcasted Demand | Projected Cost (per pair) |
|--------|------------------|---------------------------|
| 1 | 150,000 | $36.00 |
| 2 | 110,000 | 42.00 |
| 3 | 180,000 | 38.00 |
| 4 | 100,000 | 40.00 |
| 5 | 200,000 | 35.00 |
| 6 | 180,000 | 39.00 |
| 7 | 110,000 | 37.00 |
| 8 | 120,000 | 41.00 |

12. Consider the assignment problem shown in Figure P10-12.

   a. Subtract the minimum in each row from all other elements in that row. How many zeros do you have?
   b. Now subtract the minimum in each column from each element in that column. Now, how many zeros do you have?
   c. Cover all zeros with the minimum number of lines. How many lines does it require?
   d. Your answer to the second part of (c) above should have been two lines. Now subtract the minimum uncovered element from all other uncovered elements and add it to the element at the intersection of the two lines. How many lines are needed now to cover

the zeros? If it is three lines, compute an assignment using the zero elements. Otherwise, repeat this step until an assignment can be determined.

|   | I | II | III |
|---|---|----|-----|
| x | 3 | 2  | 4   |
| y | 4 | 10 | 12  |
| z | 2 | 11 | 9   |

FIGURE P10-12.
Assignment
Problem

13. Consider the assignment problem shown in Figure P10-13.
  a. Subtract the minimum in each row from all other elements in that row. How many zeros do you have?
  b. Now subtract the minimum in each column from each element in that column. Now, how many zeros do you have?
  c. Cover all zeros with the minimum number of lines. How many lines does it require?
  d. Your answer to the second part of (c) above should have been two lines. Now subtract the minimum uncovered element from all other uncovered elements and add it to the element at the intersection of the two lines. How many lines are needed now to cover the zeros? If it is three lines, compute an assignment using the zero elements. Otherwise, repeat this step until an assignment can be determined.

|   | 1   | 2   | 3  |
|---|-----|-----|----|
| A | 50  | 40  | 20 |
| B | 110 | 130 | 60 |
| C | 140 | 120 | 30 |

FIGURE P10-13.
Assignment
Problem

14. Solve the assignment problem of Figure P10-14 to minimize costs.

15. Solve the assignment problem of Figure P10-15 to minimize costs.

**FIGURE P10-14.**

|   | 1 | 2 | 3 | 4 |
|---|---|---|---|---|
| A | 8 | 7 | 2 | 5 |
| B | 6 | 3 | 8 | 10 |
| C | 4 | 7 | 9 | 9 |
| D | 8 | 10 | 8 | 1 |

**FIGURE P10-15.**

|   | 2 | 3 | 4 | 5 |
|---|---|---|---|---|
| W | 20 | 40 | 80 | 50 |
| X | 30 | 10 | 20 | 30 |
| Y | 90 | 100 | 110 | 120 |
| Z | 60 | 80 | 70 | 100 |

16. Add a column to the unbalanced assignment problem in Figure P10-16 and then solve the resulting problem.

**FIGURE P10-16.**

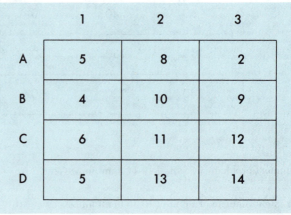

|   | 1 | 2 | 3 |
|---|---|---|---|
| A | 5 | 8 | 2 |
| B | 4 | 10 | 9 |
| C | 6 | 11 | 12 |
| D | 5 | 13 | 14 |

17. Convert the maximization assignment problem shown in Figure P10-17 to a minimization problem using opportunity costs and then solve the resulting problem for the highest-profit assignment.

|     | 1   | 2   | 3   | 4   |
|-----|-----|-----|-----|-----|
| I   | 100 | 120 | 140 | 110 |
| II  | 50  | 60  | 40  | 100 |
| III | 30  | 40  | 20  | 130 |
| IV  | 20  | 50  | 40  | 150 |

18. Coach Flakey Waters of the Oconee High School football team has three players he can use interchangeably in his backfield. All three players can play the quarterback, fullback, or tailback position. For the upcoming state championship game, Coach Waters wishes to maximize the combined yardage gained from the three players by placing them in their best position. He has looked at their past performance at each position and computed the average yards gained per game. The results of this investigation are shown in Table P10-18.

**TABLE P10-18. Average Yards Gained per Game**

| Player  | Position       |          |          |
|---------|----------------|----------|----------|
|         | Quarterback    | Fullback | Tailback |
| Allman  | 102            | 95       | 65       |
| Griffen | 55             | 70       | 60       |
| Gurley  | 90             | 80       | 75       |

Solve this as an assignment problem to maximize total yardage.

**11**

# Other Network Models

## ■ Introduction

The topic of network models is one of the most interesting of those being studied today by management scientists. We have already discussed three special types of networks, the PERT/CPM network, the transportation problem, and the assignment problem. In this chapter we will look at networks in general and show how they can be formulated as linear programming. We will then show four applications of LP networks.

As in previous chapters, we will begin our discussion with a case study of classical example of a network. We will formulate this case as a linear programming problem and discuss the characteristics of this formulation. We will present definitions and terminology that are used in the study of networks.

The chapter will be formulation oriented in that we will be interested in showing that several different network problems all have similar formulations that can be solved by linear programming. While there is a special linear programming algorithm similar to the stepping stone method that can be used to solve very large network problems quickly, we will not go into that in this chapter.

■ **Case**

## Toyoson Motors, Inc.

The scheduling manager of Toyoson Motors, Inc., in the eastern United States, Sam Jenkins, is interested in developing a weekly plan for shipping cars from their port of entry to various regional distributors. To develop a shipping plan, he has gathered data on cross-country shipping costs per car, monthly needs for cars of each distributor, and monthly arrivals of cars to each port of entry. Cars can be shipped directly to each distributor or a load of cars may be shipped to a

distributor, some unloaded, and the remainder shipped to another distributor. The distributor demands and port-of-entry supplies are shown on the map in Figure 11-1. In each case, the needs of local distributors at the port of entry have been subtracted from port-of-entry supplies.

The shipping costs between port-of-entry cities, transfer cities, and final destination cities are shown in Table 11-1 in dollars per car. In those cases where no direct link exists between a pair of cities, no cost is given.

Sam needs to determine how many cars should be shipped from Jacksonville and New Orleans to

**FIGURE 11-1.  Toyoson Distribution Network**

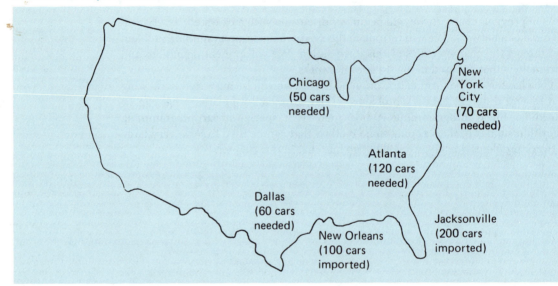

**TABLE 11-1.  Toyoson Motors, Inc.: Shipping Costs per Car**

| From: City | To: City Atlanta | Dallas | New York | Chicago |
|---|---|---|---|---|
| Jacksonville | $75 | — | $150 | — |
| New Orleans | $125 | $100 | — | — |
| Atlanta | — | — | $125 | $150 |
| Dallas | — | — | — | $100 |

**FIGURE 11-2. Revised Toyoson Distribution Network**

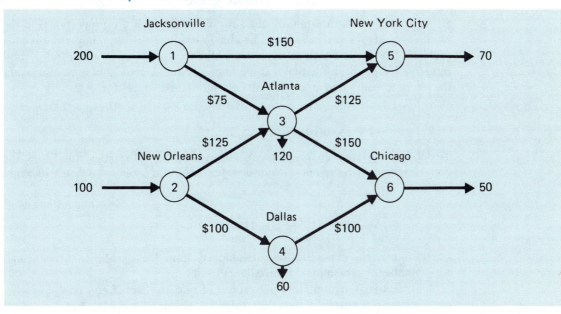

each of the other cities to be either sold there or transferred to another city. He realizes that it is not difficult to find a shipping plan that will meet all cities' needs, *but* will it be the cheapest such plan? Since Sam has a BBA degree, he is aware of mathematical models such as linear programming that can be used to determine a least cost allocation of some resources subject to some set of constraints. But he is not sure how a model like linear programming would fit a problem such as this. A couple of things worried him about using LP. First, there is the divisibility assumption. Would an LP solution send a fraction of a car to one city? Such a solution obviously would not be usable. Second, while the East Coast problem appeared to be fairly small, if the entire United States were to be considered, the size of the distribution problem could be very large. Would linear programming be able to handle *all* of the various city-to-city combinations that could exist?

## Discussion of Toyoson Motors, Inc.

Sam Jenkins' problem is to determine how to ship the cars in such a way as to minimize costs while meeting all distributor needs. To assist in understanding this problem, it has been redrawn in a different form (Figure 11-2), with circles representing each port of entry and distributor, and arrows representing the linkages between them. The supplies and demands are shown at each city by arrows also. An arrow into a city denotes cars coming into that city for distribution, and an arrow out of a city denotes the demand for that city. For example, Dallas has a demand of 60 cars, which it must get from New Orleans, but it may also act as a transfer point for cars going to Chicago. We may notice that the total demand at the distributors is equal to the total supply at the ports of entry. While this is not a necessity for formulating the problem, it simplifies matters.

# ■ Formulation of the case

Since Jenkins wants to minimize the sum of costs, which are proportional to the number of cars shipped, we should be able to use linear programming to solve the problem. The question then arises as to what the constraints are. The constraints must represent the physical situation relating to supply and demand and must also satisfy the physical reality that at any city all cars must be accounted for.

## LP formulation

To define the variables in this problem, we have numbered the cities from 1 to 6. The variables then will represent *the number of cars shipped between each pair of cities,* that is,

$$x_{ij} = \text{number of cars shipped from city } i \text{ to city } j$$

For example, $x_{13}$ = number of cars shipped from Jacksonville to Atlanta, and $x_{36}$ = number of cars shipped from Atlanta to Chicago.

Our objective is to minimize the total cost of shipping cars. If $c_{ij}$ = cost of moving one car from city $i$ to city $j$, then the total cost over this route is $c_{ij}x_{ij}$. For example, if we are looking at the Jacksonville-to-Atlanta route, we have a cost of $75x_{13}$. Then our objective function is

MINIMIZE:     $75x_{13} + 150x_{15} + 125x_{23} + 100x_{24} + 125x_{35} + 150x_{36} + 100x_{46}$

At Jacksonville (city 1), we must write a constraint to account for all cars that arrive. At this port of entry, the 200 cars that arrive each month must be shipped to either Atlanta or New York City. Mathematically, this constraint would be

$$x_{13} + x_{15} = 200$$

$$\frac{\text{number of cars}}{\text{departing Jacksonville}} = \frac{\text{number of cars}}{\text{arriving Jacksonville}}$$

Similarly for New Orleans, we must ship all of the incoming cars to either Atlanta or Dallas. Mathematically, this is represented as

$$x_{23} + x_{24} = 100$$

$$\frac{\text{number of cars}}{\text{departing New Orleans}} = \frac{\text{number of cars}}{\text{arriving New Orleans}}$$

At Atlanta, we have incoming cars, outgoing cars, and cars that stay in Atlanta. The key thing to remember here is that the difference between the number of cars that arrive and the number that leave must be equal to the number that stays in

Atlanta. Mathematically, this is written as

$$x_{13} + x_{23} - x_{35} - x_{36} = 120$$

$$\underbrace{\text{number of cars}}_{\text{arriving in Atlanta}} - \underbrace{\text{number of cars}}_{\text{departing Atlanta}} = \underbrace{\text{demand in}}_{\text{Atlanta}}$$

This same sort of relationship also holds for Dallas, where the constraint would look as follows:

$$x_{24} - x_{46} = 60$$

$$\underbrace{\text{number of cars}}_{\text{arriving in Dallas}} - \underbrace{\text{number of cars}}_{\text{departing Dallas}} = \underbrace{\text{demand in}}_{\text{Dallas}}$$

In New York City and Chicago, we have only cars arriving to meet the demand of these cities. In this case, the sum of cars that arrive must be equal to the demand. Mathematically, for New York City, the constraint is

$$x_{15} + x_{35} = 70$$

$$\begin{array}{c}\text{number of cars arriving} \\ \text{New York City}\end{array} = \begin{array}{c}\text{demand in} \\ \text{New York City}\end{array}$$

Finally, the constraint for Chicago would be as follows:

$$x_{36} + x_{46} = 50$$

$$\begin{array}{c}\text{number of cars} \\ \text{arriving Chicago}\end{array} = \begin{array}{c}\text{demand in} \\ \text{Chicago}\end{array}$$

As a whole, our linear programming formulation of the Toyoson Motors, Inc., case is

MINIMIZE: $\quad 75x_{13} + 150x_{15} + 125x_{23} + 100x_{24} + 125x_{35} + 150x_{36} + 100x_{46}$ (11.1)

SUBJECT TO:

$$x_{13} + x_{15} = 200 \tag{11.2}$$
$$x_{23} + x_{24} = 100 \tag{11.3}$$
$$x_{13} + x_{23} - x_{35} - x_{36} = 120 \tag{11.4}$$
$$x_{24} - x_{46} = 60 \tag{11.5}$$
$$x_{15} + x_{35} = 70 \tag{11.6}$$
$$x_{36} + x_{46} = 50 \tag{11.7}$$

$$x_{13}, x_{15}, x_{23}, x_{24}, x_{35}, x_{36}, x_{46} \geq 0$$

This problem could now be solved as a linear programming problem using standard simplex procedures. If this were done, we would find the optimal solution to be

$$x_{15} = 70, \qquad x_{13} = 130, \qquad x_{24} = 100, \qquad x_{46} = 40, \qquad x_{36} = 10$$

for a total cost of $35,750.

## Characteristics of LP formulation

Looking at the linear programming formulation of the Toyoson Motors problem [equations (11.1) through (11.7)], we note two important characteristics. First, each column has at most two nonzero variable coefficients. Second, all nonzero coefficients are $+1$ or $-1$. These characteristics are common to all linear programming formulations of network problems. Conversely, if a linear programming problem has these two characteristics, then there exists a network representation of the linear programming problem. It is also evident that in this linear programming formulation there exists *one constraint for each node* and *one variable for each arc*. This will be true in general for network problems.

Finally, it can be shown that *all network problems that have discrete supplies and demands will have a linear programming solution that is also discrete*. These results insure that in the linear programming solution to problems such as that of Toyoson Motors there will not be a fractional car sent between any cities.

These results have allowed for the development of extremely efficient, special-purpose linear programming methods for solving network problems. These methods, when computerized, have made it possible to solve network problems with a number of variables in excess of one million. These methods have also been shown to be at least one *hundred* times faster than comparable commercial linear programming computer packages.[1] For this reason, the study of network applications today is one of the most exciting areas of study in management science/operations research.

## Basic types of network problems

We shall consider four important types of network problems. These are (1) the *transshipment problem*, (2) the *shortest path problem*, (3) the *maximum flow problem*, and (4) the PERT/CPM problem. The Toyoson Motors case is a typical example of *transshipment problems* since we have supplies and/or demands at each city, *and* some cities can both receive and send cars to other cities. The other types of problems are illustrated later in the chapter. We will emphasize the commonalities among these problems and show that all four problems can be formulated similarly *minimum cost* as what are called **minimum cost flow problems.**
*flow problems*

---

[1]Fred Glover and Darwin Klingman, "Network Application in Industry and Government," *AIIE Transactions*, December 1977, pp. 363–375.

Before we can do that, we need to discuss some of the terminology of network problems.

## ■ Network terminology

Any network can be considered to be made up of three components: (1) the nodes, (2) the arcs, and (3) the flow over the arcs. Consider Figure 11-3, which illustrates this. As in Chapter 6, the circles are the **nodes** and they are joined by **arcs.** In this figure there are two types of arcs, *directed* and *undirected*. A directed arc is one over which flow can move in only one direction, while flow may move either direction over an undirected arc. The arc that joins nodes 1 and 2 is a directed arc; the arc joining nodes 1 and 3 is an undirected arc.

*nodes*
*arcs*

Nodes are usually numbered, as we have shown in Figure 11-3, while arcs are denoted by the nodes they join. For example, the arc joining nodes 1 and 2 would be referred to as arc 12. The flow between the nodes over the arcs is the unknown factor in a network and is denoted as $x_{ij}$ for the flow between nodes $i$ and $j$.

The flow in a network may consist of many different goods or products. A few examples are: natural gas in a pipeline; distribution of goods from wholesalers to retailers, or between factories and warehouses; and allocation of production over time periods. The per-unit cost of the flow over each arc is denoted as $c_{ij}$ for nodes $i$ and $j$. In the Toyoson Motors case, the *cities* are the *nodes* and the *shipping routes* between cities are the *arcs*. The cost per car over each route is the *flow cost*. In some problems, there may exist *capacities* over each arc that limit the amount of flow on the arcs.

We may define a *network* as a series of nodes, arcs, and flows over the arcs between the nodes. Within a network, there will exist certain combinations of nodes and arcs having special properties. A **chain** is a series of nodes and arcs that connect a node $L$ to a node $K$. In Figure 11-3, the series of nodes 1, 2, 3, 4 and the corresponding arcs form a chain as shown in Figure 11-4. A chain that connects a node to itself is a **loop.** For example, in Figure 11-3, the chain that connects node 1 to itself through nodes 2 and 3 is a loop. This is presented in Figure 11-5.

*chain*

*loop*

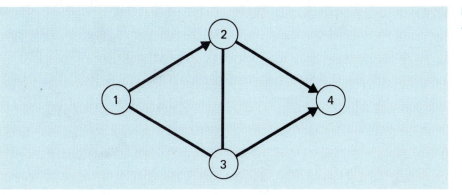

**FIGURE 11-3.
A Network**

**FIGURE 11-4.**
**A Chain**

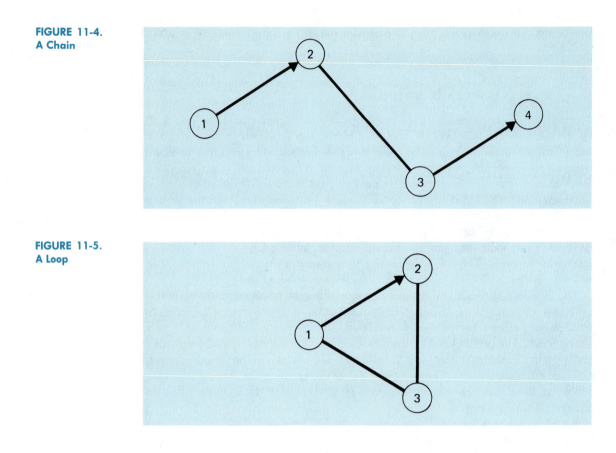

**FIGURE 11-5.**
**A Loop**

*spanning tree*

A subset of the arcs from the original network that serves to connect every node, but does not contain any loop, is referred to as a **spanning tree.** An example of a spanning tree for Figure 11-3 is shown in Figure 11-6. Notice that the chain in Figure 11-4 is also a spanning tree.

**FIGURE 11-6.**
**A Spanning Tree**

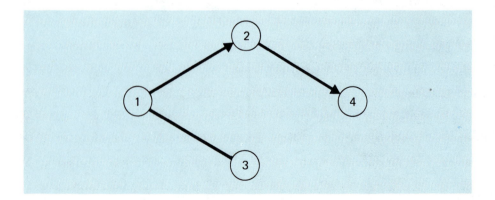

# ■ Formulation of network models

## *Transshipment problem*

If a network problem is concerned with minimizing the cost of the flow of some product between nodes, where each node may be a supply point, a demand point, or both, then the network problem is considered a *transshipment problem*. The Toyoson Motors problem is a very good example of a transshipment problem. There exist three types of nodes in a transshipment problem. If a node acts only as a sender of flow, it is referred to as a *source*.

If a node acts only as a receiver of flow, then the node is referred to as a *sink*. If a node acts as both a sender and receiver of flow, the node is termed a **transshipment node.** The transshipment problem is the most general of all network problems, since each node can have both supply and demand and there are no restrictions on flows or types of nodes.

As an example of a transshipment problem, consider the following: The Ahab Oil Company has a single oil field from which all crude oil is piped to one of two shipping centers, where it is then placed on tankers to be sent to oil refineries in the United States. The daily supply at the oil field is 2000 barrels. We must consider pipeline costs, shipping costs, and capacities on the amount of oil that can be shipped via the pipelines. The pipeline costs and daily pipeline capacities are shown in Table 11-2. The shipping costs to each refinery from each shipping depot and the daily refinery demands are shown in Table 11-3. This problem is formulated as a network in Figure 11-7.

In the network formulation, node 0 is the oil field, nodes 1 and 2 are the shipping nodes, and nodes 3 and 4 represent the refineries in New Jersey and Houston, respectively. The pipeline capacities are shown on the arcs within the semicircle, and the costs are shown above the arcs.

We may formulate this as a linear programming problem by letting

$$x_{ij} = \text{barrels shipped from node } i \text{ to node } j$$

*transshipment node*

| Shipping Depot | Per-Barrel Cost | Pipeline Capacity (barrels) |
|---|---|---|
| 1 | $0.20 | 1000 |
| 2 | $0.15 | 500 |

**TABLE 11-2.**
**Ahab Oil Company: Pipeline Costs and Capacities**

| Refinery | | Shipping Cost/Barrel | | |
|---|---|---|---|---|
| Number | Location | From Depot 1 | From Depot 2 | Daily Demand |
| 1 | New Jersey | $0.10 | $0.15 | 600 |
| 2 | Houston | $0.20 | $0.25 | 800 |

**TABLE 11-3.**
**Ahab Oil Company: Shipping Costs and Demand**

**FIGURE 11-7.**
**Ahab Oil Com-**
**pany Network**

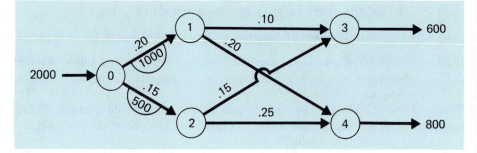

Then the problem is

MINIMIZE:     $.2x_{01} + .15x_{02} + .10x_{13} + .2x_{14} + .15x_{23} + .25x_{24}$     (11.8)

SUBJECT TO:   $x_{01} + \quad x_{02} \qquad\qquad\qquad\qquad\qquad \le 2000$     (11.9)

$x_{01} \qquad\qquad - \quad x_{13} - \quad x_{14} \qquad\qquad\qquad = 0$     (11.10)

$x_{02} \qquad\qquad\qquad - \quad x_{23} - \quad x_{24} = 0$     (11.11)

$x_{13} \qquad + \quad x_{23} \qquad\qquad = 600$     (11.12)

$x_{14} \qquad\qquad + \quad x_{24} = 800$     (11.13)

$x_{01} \qquad\qquad\qquad\qquad\qquad\qquad \le 1000$     (11.14)

$x_{02} \qquad\qquad\qquad\qquad\qquad \le 500$     (11.15)

all $x_{ij}$'s $\ge 0$

This problem is a little different from the Toyoson Motors problem in that capacities exist on some of the arcs. These appear as upper-bound constraints. The supply constraint appears as a less-than-or-equal-to constraint rather than an equality constraint, since the total demand is less than the available supply.

If we were to solve the Ahab Oil Company problem via linear programming, we would arrive at the following optimal solution:

| Variable: | $x_{01}$ | $x_{02}$ | $x_{13}$ | $x_{14}$ | $x_{23}$ | $s_1$ | $s_7$ |
|---|---|---|---|---|---|---|---|
| Flow: | 1000 | 400 | 200 | 800 | 400 | 600 | 100 |

This solution has a total cost of $500.

## Shortest path problem

If a network is defined so that the coefficients on each arc are nonnegative (such as distance measures), then we may be interested in finding the shortest path between two nodes in the network. This problem is then referred to as the *shortest path problem*.

As an example of a shortest path problem, consider the problem of driving from New Orleans to Atlanta in the shortest legal time. The roads connecting New Orleans and Atlanta form the network shown in Figure 11-8, where "distances" are the driving times in minutes.

Note that, in order to formulate this problem as a minimum cost flow problem, at any node, we may choose to follow only one arc. This implies that we want to have the following arc flows:

$$x_{ij} = \begin{cases} 1 \text{ if the road between city } i \text{ and city } j \text{ is traversed} \\ 0 \text{ otherwise.} \end{cases}$$

If we traverse the $(i, j)$ route, this means that no other route starting with city $i$ may be traversed. For example, if we traverse the New Orleans to Mobile road, then the flow between these cities will be equal to 1 while $x_{13}$ will be zero.

These conditions may be met by using an imaginary flow of one unit in the network. This flow will begin at the starting or *origin* node and end at the ending or *terminal* node. In other words, there is a *supply* of one unit at the origin and a *demand* of one unit at the terminal node. In our example, there would be a supply of one unit at New Orleans and a demand of one unit at Atlanta.

The only question that remains is: What costs should be used on this minimum flow problem? To answer this question, note that if $x_{ij} = 1$, then it will be necessary to travel the distance between nodes $i$ and $j$. If these distances are denoted by $d_{ij}$, and if the route between $i$ and $j$ is traversed, then the *cost* over this route becomes $d_{ij}x_{ij}$. Since $x_{ij}$ is 0 or 1, the cost over any route will be $d_{ij}$ or 0. Thus we can use the distances, $d_{ij}$, as the costs for the minimum cost flow problem. We may then write this problem as:

MINIMIZE: $\qquad 210x_{12} + 210x_{13} + 192x_{24} + 315x_{25} + 210x_{34} + 180x_{35} + 192x_{46} + 180x_{56}$ $\qquad$ (11.16)

SUBJECT TO:

New Orleans: $\quad x_{12} + \quad x_{13} \qquad\qquad\qquad\qquad\qquad\qquad = 1$ $\qquad$ (11.17)

Mobile: $\qquad x_{12} \qquad - \quad x_{24} - \quad x_{25} \qquad\qquad\qquad = 0$ $\qquad$ (11.18)

Meridian: $\qquad\qquad x_{13} \qquad\qquad - \quad x_{34} - \quad x_{35} \qquad\qquad = 0$ $\qquad$ (11.19)

Montgomery: $\qquad\qquad x_{24} \qquad + \quad x_{34} \qquad - \quad x_{46} \qquad = 0$ $\qquad$ (11.20)

Birmingham: $\qquad\qquad\qquad x_{25} \qquad + \quad x_{35} \qquad - \quad x_{56} = 0$ $\qquad$ (11.21)

Atlanta: $\qquad\qquad\qquad\qquad\qquad\qquad\qquad x_{46} + \quad x_{56} = 1$ $\qquad$ (11.22)

$$x_{ij} \geq 0 \text{ all } i \text{ and } j$$

For discussion purposes, we have noted the city to which each constraint is related. The New Orleans constraint states that either the road to Mobile or the road to Meridian is traversed, but not both. We know that linear programming solutions to

**FIGURE 11-8.
Driving Routes
from New Orleans
to Atlanta**

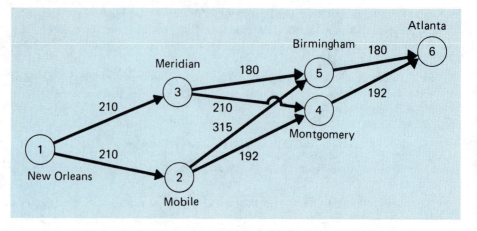

network problems are integers, so we are assured that $x_{12} = 1$ or 0, and that $x_{13} = 1$ or 0, while the constraint requires that either $x_{12} = 1$ or $x_{13} = 1$, but not both.

The constraints at Mobile, Meridian, Montgomery, and Birmingham all require that the flow into each of these nodes (cities) must equal the flow out of these nodes since there is no demand at any of these nodes. The constraint for Atlanta requires that Atlanta must be reached from either Birmingham or Montgomery by forcing the sum of the flows to be equal to 1.

In a shortest path problem, there can be directed and undirected arcs. In our example, we have only directed arcs. For an undirected case we would have a variable from $i$ to $j$ and from $j$ to $i$. It would not be difficult to modify the formulation to handle variables in both directions.

If we solve this problem by either standard linear program or a special network version of the simplex method, we arrive at the solution

$$x_{13} = 1$$

$$x_{35} = 1$$

$$x_{56} = 1$$

or New Orleans to Meridian to Birmingham to Atlanta for a total distance of 570 miles.

There also exist special-purpose algorithms that have been developed for this problem. One such algorithm will be discussed in the chapter on dynamic programming (Chapter 22).

The reader should be aware that there are several variations of the shortest path problem and only one is presented here. Two of these variations are (1) find the shortest path between some node to every other node in the network; (2) find the shortest path between any pair of nodes in the network. As with the version presented here, the various other shortest path problems can be formulated as minimum cost flow problems. There are also special-purpose algorithms for other versions of the problem.

## PERT/CPM problem

In the PERT/CPM models discussed in Chapter 9 it was assumed that there exists a project that is being planned, and that the project consists of tasks to be performed. In general, we assume that some tasks precede others. The object in these models is to find the sequence of activities or tasks that requires the *longest* time to complete. This sequence of tasks is referred to as the *critical path* since the entire project under consideration cannot be completed until this critical path is completed. As an example of an activity network analysis, consider the following situation:

The Motown University School of Business is planning a conference for business executives. The activities that must be accomplished before the conference can take place are listed in Table 11-4 along with the estimated time to complete each activity. Any preceding activities that must be completed before each activity may be begun are also shown. This planning problem is also shown in a network format (Figure 11-9), where the activity labels and estimated time required to complete the activity are shown directly on the arcs; the nodes are also numbered.

Since we are attempting to discover the longest path through this network, we have the opposite of the shortest path problem. Nevertheless, this problem may be formulated in a similar manner. In this case, the estimated times on each arc are used as "distances," which we maximize rather than minimize. Once again, we introduce an imaginary supply of one unit of flow at the first node and an imaginary demand of one unit at the last node. The linear programming formulation of this problem then becomes

MAXIMIZE: 
$$3x_{12} + 5x_{13} + 4x_{24} + 9x_{26} + 2x_{35} + 3x_{46} + 4x_{56} + 1x_{67} \qquad (11.23)$$

SUBJECT TO:

$$x_{12} + x_{13} = 1 \qquad (11.24)$$

$$x_{12} - x_{24} - x_{26} = 0 \qquad (11.25)$$

$$x_{13} - x_{35} = 0 \qquad (11.26)$$

$$x_{24} - x_{46} = 0 \qquad (11.27)$$

$$x_{35} - x_{56} = 0 \qquad (11.28)$$

$$x_{26} + x_{46} + x_{56} - x_{67} = 0 \qquad (11.29)$$

$$x_{67} = 1 \qquad (11.30)$$

$$x_{ij} \geq 0 \text{ for all } i \text{ and } j$$

If we solve this problem, we arrive at the following solution:

$$x_{12} = 1$$

$$x_{26} = 1$$

$$x_{67} = 1$$

or a critical path made up of activities A, C, and H with a total time of 13 weeks.

**TABLE 11-4.**
**Motown University, School of Business: Conference Activities**

| Activity | Description | Estimated Time (weeks) | Preceding Activities |
|----------|-------------|------------------------|----------------------|
| A | Develop program | 3 | — |
| B | Gather mailing list of attendees | 5 | — |
| C | Contact speakers for attendance | 9 | A |
| D | Put together brochure on program | 2 | B |
| E | Make physical arrangements | 4 | A |
| F | Send out brochures | 4 | D |
| G | Prepare conference program | 3 | E |
| H | Last minute details | 1 | C,G,F |

## Max flow problem

In the previous problems, we were interested in the value generated by some flow through a network. This value may be in terms of money, distance, time, or some other measure. There exist problems where the value of the flow is not as important as the *amount of flow* through the network. Gas pipelines and electric transmission lines are examples of this situation. Problems where we are concerned with determining the maximum flow through a network are termed *max flow problems*.

To study max flow problems, it is necessary to assume that there exist *capacity restrictions* on the arcs. Otherwise, the maximum flow through the network would be infinite. As an example of a max flow problem, consider the problem of moving natural gas from a gas field in Louisiana to Chicago through a network of pipelines. This network is shown in Figure 11-10. The values in the semicircles on each arc are the capacity restrictions in millions of cubic feet of gas per hour.

**FIGURE 11-9. Conference Planning Network**

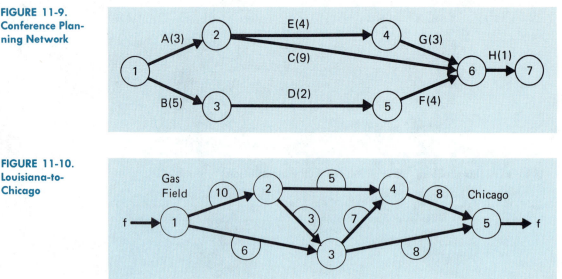

**FIGURE 11-10. Louisiana-to-Chicago**

In Figure 11-10, we have also shown some unknown amount of flow, $f$, entering the pipeline at node 1 (the gas field) and leaving the pipeline at node 5 (Chicago terminal). Using this flow, $f$, we could then formulate this problem as follows:

$$\text{MAXIMIZE:} \quad f \tag{11.31}$$

$$\text{SUBJECT TO:} \quad x_{12} + x_{13} \qquad\qquad\qquad = f \tag{11.32}$$

$$x_{12} \quad - x_{23} - x_{24} \qquad\qquad = 0 \tag{11.33}$$

$$x_{13} + x_{23} \qquad - x_{34} - x_{35} \qquad = 0 \tag{11.34}$$

$$x_{24} + x_{34} \qquad - x_{45} = 0 \tag{11.35}$$

$$x_{35} + x_{45} = f \tag{11.36}$$

$$x_{12} \le 10, \quad x_{13} \le 6, \quad x_{23} \le 3, \quad x_{24} \le 5 \tag{11.37}$$

$$\vdots$$

$$x_{34} \le 7, \quad x_{35} \le 8, \quad x_{45} \le 8 \tag{11.43}$$

$$x_{ij} \ge 0 \text{ for all } i \text{ and } j$$

This formulation does not fit our standard minimum cost flow linear programming formulation since the unknown flow, $f$, appears both as an objective function variable *and* as a right-hand-side value for the constraints. Formulated in this manner, it is not possible to use a minimum cost flow approach to solve the problem.

To circumvent this difficulty, we first drop the flow $f$ and introduce a dummy arc connecting node 5 to node 1. The objective then becomes to maximize the flow over this dummy arc. Maximizing the return flow from node 5 to node 1 over a dummy arc with no capacity will yield the amount of flow going from node 1 to node 5 over the capacitated network. Figure 11-11 shows the pipeline network redrawn with the return arc. Then, using the revised pipeline, as shown in Figure 11-11, we have a

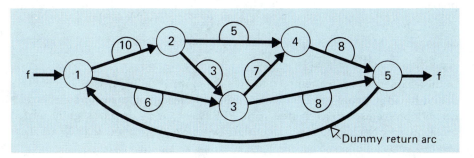

**FIGURE 11-11.**
**Revised Natural Gas Pipeline Network**

revised formulation, where the objective is to maximize $x_{51}$:

| MAXIMIZE: | $x_{51}$ | | (11.44) |

SUBJECT TO:

$$x_{51} - x_{12} - x_{13} \qquad\qquad\qquad\qquad = 0 \qquad (11.45)$$

$$x_{12} \qquad - x_{23} - x_{24} \qquad\qquad\qquad = 0 \qquad (11.46)$$

$$x_{13} + x_{23} \qquad - x_{34} - x_{35} \qquad\qquad = 0 \qquad (11.47)$$

$$x_{24} + x_{34} \qquad - x_{45} = 0 \qquad (11.48)$$

$$-x_{51} \qquad\qquad\qquad + x_{35} + x_{45} = 0 \qquad (11.49)$$

$$x_{12} \le 10,\ x_{13} \le 6,\ x_{23} \le 3,\ x_{24} \le 5,\ x_{34} \le 7,\ x_{35} \le 8,\ x_{45} \le 8 \qquad (11.50)$$

$$x_{ij} \ge 0 \text{ for all } i \text{ and } j$$

Now the max flow problem is formulated as a standard network linear programming problem except that there are no supplies and demands. Problems such as this are referred to as *circular networks*.

If we solve this problem, we find that the maximum flow is represented by

| arc ONE–TWO ($x_{12}$): | 8 million cubic feet |
| arc ONE–THREE ($x_{13}$): | 6 million cubic feet |
| arc TWO–THREE ($x_{23}$): | 3 million cubic feet |
| arc TWO–FOUR ($x_{24}$): | 5 million cubic feet |
| arc THREE–FOUR ($x_{34}$): | 1 million cubic feet |
| arc THREE–FIVE ($x_{35}$): | 8 million cubic feet |
| arc FOUR–FIVE ($x_{45}$): | 6 million cubic feet |
| arc FIVE–ONE ($x_{51}$): | 14 million cubic feet |

The flow on the return arc (FIVE–ONE) is the maximum flow over the network, while the other flows give the amount flowing over each leg of the pipeline.

As with the other network problems, there are special algorithms for the max flow problem.

## ■ Summary

In this chapter we have attempted to give a somewhat different view of networks than is found in many texts similar to this one. Instead of approaching the various network problems such as shortest path, PERT, etc., as a group of slightly related problems each having its own algorithm, we have shown you that all of these problems can be modeled in such a way as to use linear programming to solve them. We are not suggesting that this is the only way (or even the best way in all cases) to solve many of these problems, but we feel that it is important for you to realize that all of these network problems can be modeled similarly.

The general case we used to model all other problems is the minimum cost flow problem. This problem seeks to minimize the cost of achieving a desired level of flow into and out of a set of nodes. We then showed that the shortest path problem, the PERT/CPM, the maximum flow problem, and the transshipment problem can all be formulated as minimum cost flow problems.

## ■ Glossary of terms

**arc:**   A path over which the flow will move in a network.

**chain:**   A series of arcs and nodes that connect two specified nodes.

**loop:**   A chain that connects a node to itself.

**max flow problem:**   A problem that seeks to maximize the flow between two nodes. It may be formulated as a minimum cost flow problem using a dummy arc joining the first and last node. The objective is to maximize the flow over this dummy arc. There are no costs on any of the arcs, but there are capacities on one or more of the arcs.

**minimum cost flow problem:**   A network problem with the objective of minimizing the cost of satisfying all demands using available supplies.

**network:**   A series of nodes connected by arcs.

**node:**   A supply, demand, or connecting point within a network.

**PERT/CPM problem:**   A minimum cost flow problem where the objective is to maximize the cost of moving one unit of flow between two specified nodes. Each cost is the negative of the time to accomplish the task that is represented by the arc. This serves to find the longest time to complete the desired set of tasks.

**shortest path problem:**   A problem with the objective of determining the shortest path between two specified nodes. It may be formulated as a minimum cost flow problem by minimizing the cost of moving one unit of flow between two specified nodes. The costs are the distances between each pair of nodes.

**spanning tree:**   A subset of arcs from the original network that will connect all nodes but does not contain any loops. It corresponds to a basic solution to the LP formulation of the network problem.

**transshipment problem:**   A minimum cost flow problem where each node may be a supply point, a demand point, both a supply and a demand point simultaneously, or only a connecting point.

## ■ Review questions

1. Can a network have only one node and one arc? What is the relationship between numbers of nodes and numbers of arcs?

2. Write down a simple minimum cost flow network problem and formulate it as an LP problem.

3. How would you handle a transshipment problem that has greater supply than demand? (*Hint:* Recall how we handled this for transportation problems.)

4. If we were to write the dual of the LP formulation for a minimum cost flow problem, what would be the relationship between nodes, arcs, variables, and constraints?

5. What is the relationship between transshipment problems and transportation problems?

6. Why do we ship only one unit of flow through a shortest path network? (How does the optimal solution yield the shortest path?)

7. Compare the algorithm used in Chapter 9 for the PERT/CPM problem to the minimum cost flow formulation discussed here.

8. Why did we have to add a dummy arc to a max flow problem to convert it to a minimum cost flow problem?

## ▪ True/false questions

1. In an LP formulation of a network problem, there exists one constraint for each node and one variable for each arc.

2. All network problems may be formulated as maximum profit flow problems.

3. Flow can move in either direction on a directed arc.

4. All spanning trees correspond to a basic feasible solution.

5. A sink is a node that acts only as a receiver of flow.

6. In a shortest path problem, there is a supply of one unit at the origin and a demand of one unit at the terminal node.

7. A transportation problem is so called because it contains transshipment nodes.

## ▪ Problems

1. Given the network representation of a minimum cost flow problem in Figure P11-1, write its linear programming formulation where costs are shown for each arc.

2. Write the linear programming formulation for the network problem of Figure P11-2.

3. Write the linear program formulation for the network problem of Figure P11-3.

4. The Jones Shipping Company has a contract to pick up shipments of automobile parts in Raleigh and Columbia for shipment to Asheville, Charlotte, and Greensboro. The route structure is such that shipments from Columbia to Asheville go through Charlotte and shipments from Raleigh to Asheville or Charlotte go through Greensboro. It is possible to ship directly from Columbia to Greensboro. Due to union agreements and distances involved, the per-unit shipping charges vary between pairs of cities. The pertinent per-unit cost information is given in Table P11-4.

   Raleigh has a net supply of 250 boxes, and Columbia has a net supply of 150 boxes. It is possible for boxes to be shipped from Raleigh to Columbia but not vice versa. Greensboro has a demand for 125 boxes, Asheville's demand is 100 boxes, and Charlotte's demand is for 175 boxes.

   a. Draw the network representation of this problem.

   b. Formulate this problem as a linear programming problem.

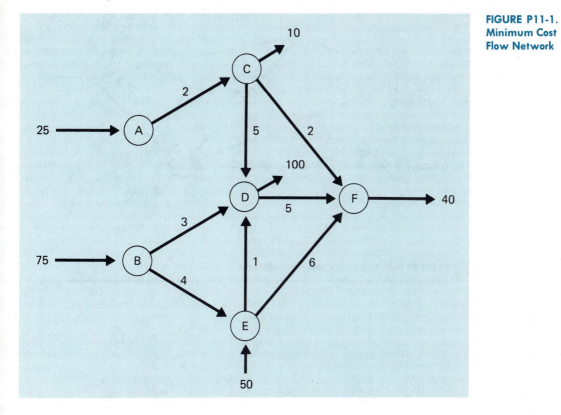

**FIGURE P11-1.**
**Minimum Cost**
**Flow Network**

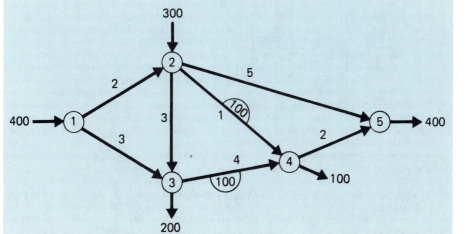

**FIGURE P11-2.**

**FIGURE P11-3.**

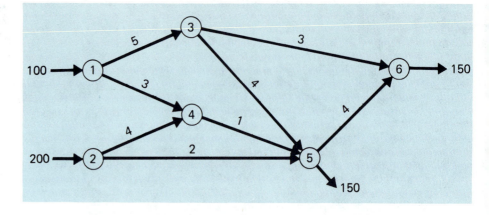

**TABLE P11-4.  Shipping Costs for Problem 4**

| From | To | | | |
| --- | --- | --- | --- | --- |
| | Greensboro | Columbia | Charlotte | Asheville |
| Raleigh | $7/box | $10/box | — | — |
| Columbia | $11/box | — | $8/box | — |
| Charlotte | — | — | — | $6/box |
| Greensboro | — | — | $5/box | $6/box |

5. The Duvall Fruit Company ships apples over a three state area from the groves in Cedartown. The cities in their shipping area are shown in Table P11-5a along with the supply and demand at each city in bushels.

**TABLE P11-5a.  Supplies and Demands**

| City | Supply | Demand |
| --- | --- | --- |
| Cedartown | 2000 | 0 |
| Johnson City | 0 | 500 |
| Gainesville | 0 | 200 |
| High Point | 0 | 500 |
| Franklin | 0 | 800 |

The intercity distances are shown in Table P11-5b. The cost of shipping one bushel one mile is $0.003.

a. Using this information, draw the network.
b. Write the linear programming formulation for this problem.

**TABLE P11-5b. Intercity Distances**

|  | Johnson City | Gainesville | High Point | Franklin |
|---|---|---|---|---|
| Cedartown | 220 | 100 | 200 | — |
| Gainesville | 100 | — | 120 | 80 |

6. What is the network representation of the following LP formulation where $x_{ij}$ = the flow between nodes $i$ and $j$?

MINIMIZE:

$$5x_{12} + 6x_{13} + 4x_{14} + 8x_{25} + 2x_{32} + 2x_{34} + 7x_{45}$$

SUBJECT TO:

$$x_{12} + x_{13} + x_{14} \qquad\qquad = 75$$
$$x_{12} \qquad\quad - x_{25} + x_{32} \qquad = 20$$
$$x_{13} \qquad\quad - x_{32} - x_{34} \qquad = 0$$
$$x_{14} \qquad\qquad + x_{34} - x_{45} = 20$$
$$x_{25} \qquad\qquad + x_{45} = 35$$
$$x_{ij} \geq 0$$

7. For the following LP formulation, draw the associated network.

MINIMIZE:    $3x_{12} + 5x_{14} + 2x_{23} + 4x_{24} + 2x_{34}$

SUBJECT TO:

$$x_{12} + x_{14} \qquad\qquad = 100$$
$$x_{12} \quad - x_{23} - x_{24} \qquad = 50$$
$$x_{23} \qquad - x_{34} = 0$$
$$x_{14} \quad + x_{24} + x_{34} = 50$$
$$x_{ij} \geq 0$$

8. A recent graduate of the North Avenue Trade School (Athens, Ga.) is planning a vacation to Las Vegas. Being short of money, he wishes to determine the cheapest air route to follow. The recent increase in certain airfares has complicated the task of finding the cheapest route. The graduate has looked into various options and has listed the information he has gathered.

| Leg of Journey | Cost |
|---|---|
| Athens to Las Vegas | $350 |
| Athens to Atlanta | $16 |
| Athens to Los Angeles | $250 |
| Athens to Phoenix | $275 |
| Atlanta to Las Vegas | $345 |
| Los Angeles to Las Vegas | $25 |
| Phoenix to Las Vegas | $25 |
| Atlanta to Los Angeles | $245 |

On the basis of this information, formulate a network representation of this problem as a shortest path problem.

9. For the network shown in Figure P11-9, set up the linear programming formulation to find the shortest path from point A to point H.

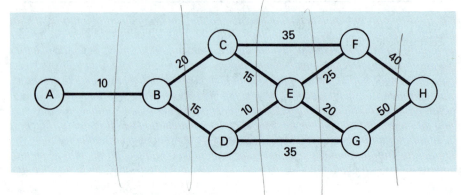

10. Curtis Beville, an underpaid college professor, is planning the construction of a garage. He is going to do much of the work himself, so he wishes to plan out the process well in advance. He has determined the major tasks to be completed, their estimated time, and any immediate procedures. This information is shown in Table P11-10.

a. Draw a network formulation of this activity sequence.

b. Formulate as a minimum cost flow linear programming problem.

**TABLE P11-10. Garage Construction Time**

| Activity | Description | Time (days) | Preceding Activities |
|---|---|---|---|
| A | Pour slab | 2 | — |
| B | Contact brick mason | 1 | — |
| C | Order lumber | 3 | — |
| D | Frame in walls | 4 | A, C |
| E | Put up roof | 3 | D |
| F | Put on brick siding | 2 | B, D |
| G | Put on shingles | 3 | E |
| H | Electrical work | 3 | F |
| I | Finish interior | 5 | G, H |

| 11. Event | Predecessor Activity | Time Required |
|---|---|---|
| 1. Design | None | 5 |
| 2. Make A, B, and C | Design | A—4, B—5, C—3 |
| 3. Test A | Make A | 2 |
| 4. Assembly of A and B | Test A, make B | 2 |
| 5. Attach C | Assemble A and B, make C | 1 |
| 6. Test final product | Attach C | 1 |

**a.** Draw a network for this problem.

**b.** Formulate this problem as an LP problem.

12. For the pipeline network in Figure P11-12:

    **a.** Redraw as a transshipment problem to find the max flow.

    **b.** Write the linear programming formulation of the revised network.

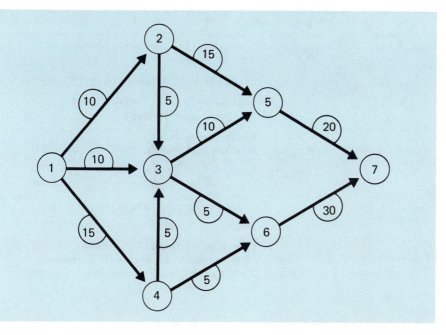

**FIGURE P11-12.**
**Pipeline Network**

13. For the network shown in Figure P11-13 with capacities as shown on each arc, set up the linear programming formulation to find the maximum flow between point 1 and point 7.

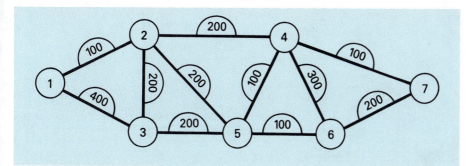

**FIGURE P11-13.**
**Arc Capacities**

**12**

# Goal Programming

## ■ Introduction

Goal programming (GP) is primarily a variation of linear programming. It was first identified and studied by Charnes and Cooper in the early 1960s. The technique was refined and extended by Ijiri in the mid-60s, and detailed descriptions and numerous applications were developed by Ignizio and Lee in the 1970s.[1] A key factor that differentiates goal programming from linear programming is the structure and use of the objective function. In linear programming, only one goal is incorporated into the objective function, while in goal programming all goals, whether one or many, are incorporated. This is accomplished by expressing the goal in the form of a constraint, including a deviational variable in the constraint to reflect the extent to which the goal is or is not achieved, and incorporating the deviational variable in the objective function. In linear programming, the objective is either maximized or minimized, while in goal programming the objective is to minimize the deviations from the specified goals (that is, *all goal programming problems are minimization problems*).

Since the deviations from the set of goals are minimized, a GP model can handle multiple goals with different dimensions or units of measure. Conflicting goals, likewise, can be considered. If multiple goals exist, an ordinal ranking or priority can be specified, and the GP solution process will operate in such a manner that the goal with the highest priority is satisfied as closely as possible before considering goals of lower priority. Whereas linear programming seeks to identify the *optimal* solution from a set of feasible solutions, goal programming identifies the point that *best satisfies* a problem's set of goals (that is, *GP minimizes the deviations from the goals, taking into consideration the hierarchy of priorities*).

One of the key advantages of goal programming is that it can provide information beyond that provided by linear programming, and thus is more useful as an aid to management in its decision-making process. For example, assume that the management of a firm has employed linear programming to maximize profits in the production of its products. Assume further that the company is committed to an order of 100 units for a specific product and that the company's goal is to meet that commitment. In an LP formulation, the goal would be specified as a constraint; and,

---

[1] A. Charnes and W. W. Cooper, *Management Models and Industrial Applications of Linear Programming* (New York: Wiley), 1961; Y. Ijiri, *Management Goals and Accounting for Control* (Chicago: Rand-McNally), 1965; James P. Ignizio, *Goal Programming and Extensions* (Lexington, Mass.: D. C. Heath), 1976; and Sang Lee, *Goal Programming for Decision Analysis* (Philadelphia: Auerbach), 1972.

if sufficient production capacity existed, the linear programming model would provide a solution. If insufficient capacity exists, however, an infeasible solution will result. The goal programming treatment of the problem would provide a solution regardless. If sufficient capacity exists, the GP solution will be the same as the LP solution; but where insufficient capacity exists, the GP and LP solutions will clearly differ. The exact GP solution would depend upon the order of priorities, the cost of overtime, and profits, but a solution would be provided. From the GP solution, management would be able to determine the required overtime and profits foregone to meet the goal of customer satisfaction.

Throughout this chapter we will examine these as well as other goal programming concepts. We will present the GP solution process and discuss interpretation of the output from a goal programming computer code. As in other chapters, however, our main emphasis will be on formulation and use of results.

We will first present a case in order to illustrate the need for such multicriteria mathematical programming techniques as goal programming. The case is formulated as a GP problem and solved later in the chapter.

# ■ Case

## The Rewlings Company

The Rewlings Company manufactures three lines of men's topcoats: Sports-Wear (A), Young-Executive (B), and Top-Executive (C). The company is a family-owned-and-operated business, but the majority of employees of the firm are not members of the family. Because of the competitive nature of the business and the high demand for labor in the industry, it is extremely important that employee satisfaction be maintained. Management at Rewlings feels that a key step toward meeting the needs of its employees is offering full employment, even if this requires excess production and write-off. Fortunately, management expects the demand for its products to remain relatively high. As a matter of fact, to meet some demand it may be necessary to employ overtime operations.

All three lines of topcoats at Rewlings are fabricated in two departmental operations. Table 12-1 is a schedule of the weekly labor and material requirements used in the fabrication process. The unit prices of the three lines are $100, $150, and $250, respectively. Management has determined that at the normal production level the variable costs are $70, $80, and $100 per coat, respectively. Overtime costs are $2 per hour above the normal rate for department 1 and $3 per hour above the normal rate for department 2.

Extra material can be acquired at a cost of $2 per yard above the normal cost.

Management at Rewlings has forecast that the market demand for the sportswear topcoat is 1000 units per week, while the demand for the other two lines is 500 and 200 units, respectively. The breakeven level of production is 100 units of product 1 (sportswear), and 50 units each of the two remaining products.

To aid in analyzing the problem, management at Rewlings has identified, in priority order, the following goals:

1. Utilize all available production capacity, i.e., no idle time should exist in either department.

2. Meet the breakeven production levels in each of the product lines.

3. Since labor shortages will likely exist in department 2, and since personnel can be shifted, on overtime, to department 2, overtime in this department can be greater than that in department 1. However, overtime in department 2 should be limited to 600 hours. Overtime in department 1 should not exceed 200 hours.

4. Achieve a weekly profit goal of $20,000.

5. Meet all market demands. Within this goal, differential weights should be used to reflect the normal unit contribution to profits.

**TABLE 12-1. Time and Material Requirements and Resources for Rewlings**

|  | Product Requirements (per Unit) | | | Resources (Labor and Material) |
|---|---|---|---|---|
|  | Sports-Wear | Young-Executive | Top-Executive |  |
| Dept. 1 | 4 hours | 12 hours | 10 hours | 8000 hours |
| Dept. 2 | 6 hours | 6 hours | 16 hours | 4000 hours |
| Material | 8 sq yd | 6 sq yd | 12 sq yd | 8000 sq yd |

# ■ Foundations: Goal programming terminology/concepts

We cannot solve Rewlings's problem with linear programming, since more than one objective (goal) is sought. We can, however, solve Rewlings's problem with goal programming. But before we can formulate the problem in a GP framework, we must develop a general understanding of the framework and how it relates to linear programming. To aid in this objective, we will take a simple problem, formulate it as an LP problem and then reformulate it as a GP problem. We will then modify the GP problem to include multiple goals, and multiple goals with priorities. After developing these GP concepts, we will examine the Rewlings case.

## *Single-goal models*

To obtain a clear understanding of the GP–LP relationship, we begin with a single-goal problem. Consider the case where a firm produces two products. Each product requires time in two production departments: product 1 requires 20 hours in department 1 and 10 hours in department 2; product 2 requires 10 hours in department 1 and 10 hours in department 2. Production time is limited in department 1 to 60 hours and in department 2 to 40 hours. Contribution to profits for the two products is \$40 and \$80, respectively. Management's objective (goal) is to maximize profits. The LP formulation of the problem is

MAXIMIZE: $\qquad Z = 40x_1 + 80x_2$ $\hfill$ (12.1)

SUBJECT TO: $\qquad 20x_1 + 10x_2 \leq 60$ $\hfill$ (12.2)

$\qquad\qquad\quad\ 10x_1 + 10x_2 \leq 40$ $\hfill$ (12.3)

$$x_1, x_2 \geq 0$$

where $\qquad x_1$ = number of units of product 1 to produce

$\qquad\qquad x_2$ = number of units of product 2 to produce

The optimal solution to the problem, which can be solved by the simplex method, is $x_1 = 0$, $x_2 = 4$, and $Z = \$320$. Twenty hours of slack time remain in department 1 ($s_1 = 20$), and no time remains in department 2 ($s_2 = 0$).

The goal programming formulation of the problem is

MINIMIZE: $\qquad Z = d^-$ $\hfill$ (12.4)

SUBJECT TO: $\qquad 20x_1 + 10x_2 \qquad\qquad\ \leq 60$ $\hfill$ (12.5)

$\qquad\qquad\quad\ 10x_1 + 10x_2 \qquad\qquad\ \leq 40$ $\hfill$ (12.6)

$\qquad\qquad\quad\ 40x_1 + 80x_2 + d^- - d^+ = 1000$ $\hfill$ (12.7)

$$x_1, x_2, d^-, d^+ \geq 0$$

where the $x$'s represent decision variables and the $d$'s represent deviational variables.

The key difference between the LP model [(12.1) through (12.3)] and the GP model [(12.4) through (12.7)] is the objective function, where deviational variables have been used and equation (12.7) has been added. Equation (12.7) appears very much like a constraint, but is actually the goal equation for the model—in this case, the profit goal. Since we are seeking to maximize profits, we set an arbitrarily high goal, $1000 in this example. The two nonnegative variables, $d^-$ and $d^+$, are the *deviational variables* for the goal. They represent, respectively, the amount by which we underachieve ($d^-$) or overachieve ($d^+$) the profit goal of $1000.

While, in the majority of applications, both $d^+$ and $d^-$ deviationals will appear in a goal equation, at most only one of the two variables will take on a positive value in any solution. For example, it is impossible to underachieve the profit goal of $1000 at the same time as it is overachieved. If the goal is achieved *exactly*, both deviational variables will be zero; if the goal cannot be achieved, then one or the other of the variables will be zero.

Since our objective is to maximize profit, the objective function of the GP model, equation (12.4), contains only a deviational variable; the profit function that appeared in the LP model is written as a goal constraint. Only the deviational variables associated with the goal (objective) appear in the objective function. For this problem only the $d^-$ deviational variable is included. This results from the fact that our objective, in GP form, is to minimize the underachievement of the profit goal; and since underachievement is undesirable, we would like to drive $d^-$ as close to zero as possible. If overachievement of the profit goal were considered undesirable (which is unlikely here since we are considering profits, but likely if we were considering overtime), then only $d^+$ would be included in the objective function. If the decision maker were interested in achieving the profit goal *exactly*, then both deviational variables would be included in the objective function.

Since the deviational variables can be treated like any other variable, we can solve the GP formulation of the problem with the traditional LP solution algorithm (the simplex method), and thereby obtain the final tableau shown in Table 12-2. We see

| $c_B$ | $c_j \rightarrow$ Variables in the Basis | Right-hand Side (Solution) | 0 $x_1$ | 0 $x_2$ | −1 $d^-$ | 0 $d^+$ | 0 $s_1$ | 0 $s_2$ |
|---|---|---|---|---|---|---|---|---|
| 0 | $s_1$ | 20 | 10 | 0 | 0 | 0 | 1 | −1 |
| 0 | $x_2$ | 4 | 1 | 1 | 0 | 0 | 0 | .10 |
| −1 | $d^-$ | 680 | −40 | 0 | 1 | −1 | 0 | −8 |
| | $z_j$ | −680 | 40 | 0 | −1 | 1 | 0 | 8 |
| | $c_j − z_j$ | | −40 | 0 | 0 | −1 | 0 | −8 |

**TABLE 12-2.**
**Solution to the Single-Goal Model**

that the optimal solution is $x_1 = 0$, $x_2 = 4$, $s_1 = 20$, $s_2 = 0$, and $d^- = 680$. This solution is identical to the solution for the LP formulation, except for the difference in the Z value; for the LP formulation, Z = \$320; in the GP formulation Z = \$680. (The Z value is actually −\$680 in Table 12-2, but recall that we are solving a minimization problem using the maximization logic of the simplex method.) The Z value for the GP solution reflects the extent by which we underachieved our profit goal of \$1000, so the actual maximum profit for the problem is \$320 (that is, \$1000 − \$680), identical to the LP solution.

We might conclude from this example that little is gained from going to a GP solution framework, but the advantages of GP become obvious in more complex problems. Consider an example where there exists a single goal that *cannot* be solved via linear programming. The Beta Corporation is considering the allocation of a \$150,000 advertising budget to two magazines (A *and* B). Rated exposures per hundred dollars of advertising expenditures are 1000 and 750, respectively, for the two magazines; and it has been forecast that on the average \$10 in sales results from each advertisement exposure. Management has decided that no more than 75% of the advertising budget can be expended in magazine A. The company has indicated that it would like to achieve exactly 1.5 million exposures from its advertising program. Management's objective is to allocate its monies to advertising in such a manner that sales (\$) are maximized.

The LP formulation for the problem is

$$\text{MAXIMIZE:} \qquad Z = 10{,}000x_1 + 7{,}500x_2 \quad \textit{sales} \tag{12.8}$$

$$\text{SUBJECT TO:} \qquad x_1 + \quad x_2 \le 1{,}500 \tag{12.9}$$

$$x_1 \qquad \le 1{,}125 \tag{12.10}$$

$$1{,}000x_1 + \quad 750x_2 = 1{,}500{,}000 \quad \textit{exposures} \tag{12.11}$$

$$x_1, x_2 \ge 0$$

where        $x_1$ = hundreds of dollars spent on advertising in magazine A

$x_2$ = hundreds of dollars spent on advertising in magazine B

If we were to attempt to solve this with the simplex method, the results would be an infeasible solution. With an LP structure, no feasible solution results because it is impossible to achieve 1,500,000 exposures without violating constraint (12.10).

If we examine the problem closely, we can see that in maximizing sales the company is in essence maximizing exposures, since each magazine exposure results in \$10 in sales. Since Beta has set a target goal of 1,500,000 exposures, achieving this goal also means Beta is maximizing sales. Therefore, expressed in a GP framework, the problem is

$$\text{MINIMIZE:} \qquad Z = \qquad\qquad d^- + d^+ \tag{12.12}$$

$$\text{SUBJECT TO:} \qquad x_1 + \quad x_2 \qquad \le 1{,}500 \tag{12.13}$$

$$x_1 \qquad \le 1{,}125 \tag{12.14}$$

$$1,000x_1 + 750x_2 + d^- - d^+ = 1,500,000 \qquad (12.15)$$

$$x_1, x_2, d^-, d^+ \geq 0$$

As the problem was originally stated, Beta is interested in achieving the exposure goal exactly. Both deviational variables, therefore, are included in the objective function.

Using the simplex method to solve the GP formulation of Beta's single-goal advertising problem results in the following: $x_1 = 1{,}125$, $x_2 = 375$, $d^+ = 0$, and $d^- = 93{,}750$. This indicates that Beta underachieved its exposure goal of 1.5 million by 93,750. The GP model does not result in achieving the impossible—management is still unable to achieve 1.5 million exposures—but the model does provide a *feasible mathematical solution*. In the next section, we will find that by including deviational variables in the budget constraint, equation (12.13), and establishing a second goal of attempting to stay within the budget, the additional budget dollars required to meet the exposure goal can be identified.

## Multiple-goal models

In this section we will examine multiple goal models. Three types of models exist: *multigoal with equal (no) priorities, multigoal with priorities*, and *multigoal with priorities and weights*. In the real world the third formulation is most useful; however, we can gain a better understanding of the concept of priorities and weights by examining each type of model.

**Multiple goals with equal (no) priorities.** The multigoal equal-priority model is easy to deal with mathematically but is the least practical of the three formulations. Some actual cases may exist where all goals have equal priorities, but the output from an equal-priority model should be examined carefully for compatibility. Consider the following problem. Assume we modify the single-goal production problem in the previous section so that in addition to the profit goal, at least two units of each type of product are desired. Management considers this second goal to be as important as the profit goal, which is maximizing profit. Under these conditions, management is saying that a deviation of $1 from the profit goal is considered to be equal to a one-unit deviation from the production goal. The GP formulation for this problem is

| | | | | | |
|---|---|---|---|---|---|
| MINIMIZE: | $Z =$ | $d_1^-$ | $+ d_2^-$ | $+ d_3^-$ | (12.16) |
| SUBJECT TO: | $20x_1 + 10x_2$ | | | $\leq 60$ | (12.17) |
| | $10x_1 + 10x_2$ | | | $\leq 40$ | (12.18) |
| | $40x_1 + 80x_2 + d_1^- - d_1^+$ | | | $= 1000$ | (12.19) |
| | $x_1$ | $+ d_2^- - d_2^+$ | | $= 2$ | (12.20) |
| | $x_2$ | | $+ d_3^- - d_3^+ = 2$ | | (12.21) |

$$x_1, x_2, d_1^-, d_1^+, d_2^-, d_2^+, d_3^-, d_3^+ \geq 0$$

**TABLE 12-3. Solution to the Production Problem with Multiple Goals and No Priorities**

| $c_B$ | Variables in the Basis | Right-hand Side (Solution) | $x_1$ | $x_2$ | $d_1^-$ | $d_1^+$ | $d_2^-$ | $d_2^+$ | $d_3^-$ | $d_3^+$ | $s_1$ | $s_2$ |
|---|---|---|---|---|---|---|---|---|---|---|---|---|
| $c_j \rightarrow$ | | | 0 | 0 | -1 | 0 | -1 | 0 | -1 | 0 | 0 | 0 |
| 0 | $s_1$ | 20 | 10 | 0 | 0 | 0 | 0 | 0 | 0 | 0 | 1 | -1 |
| 0 | $d_3^+$ | 2 | 1 | 0 | 0 | 0 | 0 | 0 | -1 | 1 | 0 | .1 |
| -1 | $d_1^-$ | 680 | -40 | 0 | 1 | -1 | 0 | 0 | 0 | 0 | 0 | -8 |
| -1 | $d_2^-$ | 2 | 1 | 0 | 0 | 0 | 1 | -1 | 0 | 0 | 0 | 0 |
| 0 | $x_2$ | 4 | 1 | 1 | 0 | 0 | 0 | 0 | 0 | 0 | 0 | .1 |
| | $z_j$ | -682 | 39 | 0 | -1 | 1 | -1 | 1 | 0 | 0 | 0 | 8 |
| | $c_j - z_j$ | | -39 | 0 | 0 | -1 | 0 | -1 | -1 | 0 | 0 | -8 |

Since the deviational variables in the objective function have no priorities, we can continue to use the standard simplex algorithm to solve the problem. Table 12-3 is the final tableau that results from applying the simplex method. The solution is $x_1 = 0$, $x_2 = 4$, $s_1 = 20$, $s_2 = 0$, $d_1^- = 680$, $d_1^+ = 0$, $d_2^- = 2$, $d_2^+ = 0$, $d_3^- = 0$, $d_3^+ = 2$, and $Z = 682$. In terms of production ($x_1 = 0$, $x_2 = 4$) and profits ($1000 - $680$), this solution is identical to the single-goal model. The 682 value for Z indicates that we missed the profit goal by 680 and one of the production goals by 2. (The Z value of 682 reflects the sum of the extent by which we missed *all* goals.) The model did not achieve the production goals of at least two units of $x_1$ and two units of $x_2$ because no priorities were specified for the goals; the model simply ought to minimize the *sum* of the deviations for *all* goals.

**Multiple goals with priorities.**　When management has multiple goals, it most likely will have some priority scale for the goals. Goal programming provides for the preferential ordering of goals through the use of priority coefficients ($P$'s). All goals (deviational variables) that have a top or first priority are assigned an objective function value of $P_1$, the goals considered to be second in priority are assigned a $P_2$ value, and this process is continued until all goals have been ranked. The coefficients, $P_1$, $P_2$, etc., are not parameters or variables. They do not, in general, assume a numerical value; they simply represent levels for the priorities. Since the priority coefficients appear in the objective function, the standard simplex algorithm cannot be used to solve such problems. However, the simplex method can be modified to handle the priority coefficients and assure that the deviations for the first-priority goals are minimized before lower priorities are examined, and so on.

The use of priority goals can be demonstrated by considering the production problem we just examined. Assume management has established the following goal priorities:

$P_1$ (priority 1): Meet production goals of 2 units for each product.

$P_2$ (priority 2): Maximize profits.

The model for this problem would be identical to the previous no-priority model [equations (12.16)–(12.21)] with the exception of the addition of priority coefficients in the objective function. The revised model is

MINIMIZE: $\quad Z = P_1 d_2^- + P_1 d_3^- + P_2 d_1^-$ $\hfill$ (12.22)

SUBJECT TO: $\quad 20x_1 + 10x_2 \qquad\qquad\qquad\qquad\qquad \leq 60$ $\hfill$ (12.23)

$\qquad\qquad\quad 10x_1 + 10x_2 \qquad\qquad\qquad\qquad\qquad \leq 40$ $\hfill$ (12.24)

$\qquad\qquad\quad 40x_1 + 80x_2 + d_1^- - d_1^+ \qquad\qquad = 1000$ $\hfill$ (12.25)

$\qquad\qquad\qquad x_1 \qquad\qquad +d_2^- - d_2^+ \qquad\quad = 2$ $\hfill$ (12.26)

$\qquad\qquad\qquad\qquad x_2 \qquad\qquad + d_3^- - d_3^+ = 2$ $\hfill$ (12.27)

$$x_1, x_2, d_1^-, d_1^+, d_2^-, d_2^+, d_3^-, d_3^+ \geq 0$$

The standard simplex algorithm cannot be used to solve this problem since priority indexes are in the objective function. We can, however, use a *modified GP simplex algorithm*. (The structure, use, and output from the GP simplex algorithm are described later in the Solution Methodology section.)

The solution to the problem of multiple priority goals is $x_1 = 2$, $x_2 = 2$, $s_1 = 0$, $s_2 = 0$, $d_1^- = 760$, $d_1^+ = 0$, $d_2^- = 0$, $d_2^+ = 0$, $d_3^- = 0$, $d_3^+ = 0$, and $Z = 760P_2$. With respect to achievement of the goals the following occurred:

> Goal 1 ($P_1$) is achieved: Two units of $x_1$ and 2 units of $x_2$ are produced.
>
> Goal 2 ($P_2$) is not achieved: The total contribution to profits is \$240 (that is, \$1000 − 760); the goal is underachieved by \$760 (that is, $d_1^- = 760$).

Comparing this result with the results of the previous goal (no-priority) model, it can be seen that management must sacrifice profits (\$240 versus \$320) in order to meet the goal of producing at least 2 units of each product.

A second example demonstrating the use of priority ranking of goals can be given by modifying the media-mix problem [model (12.12)–(12.15)]. Recall that Beta had a single goal of achieving 1.5 million exposures but because of budget constraints was unable to achieve the goal. If we modify the problem so that the budget constraint is set as a goal, we can determine the budget requirements necessary to meet the exposure goal. Specifically the goals are:

> $P_1$ (priority 1): Achieve an exposure goal of exactly 1.5 million exposures.
>
> $P_2$ (priority 2): Minimize the budget requirements.

The model for the problem would require replacing constraint (12.13) with the following goal:

$$x_1 + x_2 + d_2^- - d_2^+ = 1,500 \tag{12.28}$$

where $d_2^-$ is the amount by which the $150,000 is underspent and $d_2^+$ is the amount of overexpenditure. The complete model is

MINIMIZE:　　Z = $\qquad\qquad\qquad\qquad P_1 d_1^- + P_1 d_1^+ \qquad + P_2 d_2^+$　　　　(12.29)

SUBJECT TO:　　　$x_1 + \quad x_2 \qquad\qquad\qquad + d_2^- - \quad d_2^+ = 1{,}500$　　　　(12.30)

$\qquad\qquad\qquad x_1 \qquad\qquad\qquad\qquad\qquad \le 1{,}125$　　　　(12.31)

$\qquad 1{,}000 x_1 + 750 x_2 + \quad d_1^- - \quad d_1^+ \qquad\qquad = 1{,}500{,}000$　　　　(12.32)

$$x_1, x_2, d_1^-, d_1^+, d_2^-, d_2^+ \ge 0$$

The solution to the problem is $x_1 = 1125$, $x_2 = 500$, $d_1^- = 0$, $d_1^+ = 0$, $s_1 = 0$, $d_2^- = 0$, $d_2^+ = 125$, and $Z = 125 P_2$, where $s_1$ is a slack variable associated with constraint (8.31). With respect to achievement of the goals, the following results were achieved:

> Goal 1 $(P_1)$ is achieved: 1.5 million exposures have resulted: 1,125,000 exposures result from spending $112,500 for advertisements in magazine A, and 375,000 exposures result from spending $50,000 for advertisements in magazine B.

> Goal 2 $(P_2)$ is exceeded: The second goal is exceeded by 125; in terms of the actual expenditure this means the advertising budget is exceeded by $12,500. This is the additional expenditure necessary to achieve 375,000 exposures in order to meet the 1.5 million exposures that result in goal 1.

*differential weight*

**Multiple goals with priorities and weights.**　Both problems in the preceding section can be said to have multiple goals with the same priority index [refer to the $P_1$ goals in equations (12.22) and (12.29)]. Sometimes we may wish to give some of the equally ranked goals more importance than others. If this is the case, a **differential weight** is used to reflect the difference of importance within the same priority level. Suppose, for example, that profits and overtime for a given problem both have the same priority rank. If no weights are assigned, the decision maker is implicitly stating that a $1 deviation from the profit goal is equal in importance to one hour of overtime. If this is not true, then weights can be assigned that reflect the proper relationship. If the decision maker decides that 6 hours of overtime is equivalent to $1 of profits, then a 6 to 1 ratio of weights will be employed.

To demonstrate, let us again consider the production example in model (12.22)–(12.27). Assume we modify the goals of the problem slightly. Instead of having a goal of producing 2 units of each type of product, we will set a goal of producing a minimum of 4 units of product 1 and 6 units of product 2. Since product 2 contributes twice as much to profits as product 1, we should produce product 2 before producing product 1. Overtime will be required in producing either quantity of the specified products. [Recall that in model (12.22)–(12.27) we used all the production capacity in producing 2 units of each product.] We will assume that 50 hours of overtime is available. Suppose we set the following priorities for goal attainment:

$P_1$ (priority 1): Limit total overtime in the two production operations to 50 hours.

$P_2$ (priority 2): Meet minimum production goals of 4 units of product 1 and 6 units of product 2. Use differential weights of 1 and 2, respectively, since these reflect the "weighted contribution to profits" of $40 and $80.

$P_3$ (priority 3): Maximize profits.

Since overtime is required in this modified problem, it will be necessary to add deviational variables to constraints (12.23) and (12.24). We must also add a goal constraint to reflect the goal of limiting overtime to 50 hours. To allow comparisons with the previous model we will use the previous deviational variable numbers. The modified model would appear as follows:

MINIMIZE:  $Z = P_1 d_6^+ + 1P_2 d_2^- + 2P_2 d_3^- + P_3 d_1^-$  (12.33)

SUBJECT TO:

$$20x_1 + 10x_2 \qquad\qquad + d_4^- - d_4^+ \qquad\qquad = 60 \qquad (12.34)$$

$$10x_1 + 10x_2 \qquad\qquad + d_5^- - d_5^+ \qquad = 40 \qquad (12.35)$$

$$40x_1 + 80x_2 + d_1^- - d_1^+ \qquad\qquad = 1000 \qquad (12.36)$$

$$x_1 \qquad + d_2^- - d_2^+ \qquad\qquad = 4 \qquad (12.37)$$

$$x_2 + d_3^- - d_3^+ \qquad\qquad = 6 \qquad (12.38)$$

$$d_4^+ + d_5^+ + d_6^- - d_6^+ = 50 \qquad (12.39)$$

$$x_1, x_2, d_1^-, d_1^+, d_2^-, d_2^+, d_3^-, d_3^+, d_4^-, d_4^+, d_5^-, d_5^+, d_6^-, d_6^+ \geq 0$$

The $d_4^+$ and $d_5^+$ represent, respectively, the overtime required in operations 1 and 2. The $d_6^-$ deviational variable reflects the extent to which the 50 hours of total overtime is underutilized. A $d_6^+$ variable is included in goal constraint (12.39) to reflect the possibility of exceeding the 50 hours.

The solution to the modified problem is $x_1 = 1$, $x_2 = 6$, $d_4^- = 0$, $d_4^+ = 20$, $d_5^- = 0$, $d_5^+ = 30$, $d_1^- = 480$, $d_1^+ = 0$, $d_2^- = 3$, $d_2^+ = 0$, $d_3^- = 0$, $d_3^+ = 0$, $d_6^+ = 0$, $d_6^- = 0$, and $Z = 3P_2 + 480P_3$. Note that:

Goal 1 ($P_1$) is achieved: Overtime is exactly 50 hours; 20 overtime hours ($d_4^+$) were used in operation 1; and 30 ($d_5^+$) hours were used in operation 2.

A portion of goal 2 ($P_2$) was met: Six units of product 2 were produced since this portion of the goal had the largest differential weight, but only one unit of product 1 was produced before the overtime limit on goal 1 occurred.

Goal 3 ($P_3$) was not achieved: The total contribution to profits is $520 (that is, $1000 − $480). The goal is underachieved by $480 (that is, $d_1^- = $480).

The results from this revised model indicate that additional profits can be achieved by going to overtime, but the production goals cannot be met since overtime is limited to 50 hours. Because of the differential weights used on the production goals, all 6 units of product 2 were produced before producing any units of product 1. Had the weights been reversed, the 50 hours of overtime plus regular time would have been used to produce 4 units of product 1 and 1.5 units of product 2.

The importance of the ordering (ranking) of priorities can easily be demonstrated if we reverse the first two goals for the revised model. Assume that goal 1 $(P_1)$ is to produce 4 units of product 1 and 6 units of product 2 and goal 2 $(P_2)$ is to limit total overtime to 50 hours. We can accomplish this by modifying equation (8.33). The new objective function would be

MINIMIZE:        $Z = 1P_1d_2^- + 2P_1d_3^- + P_2d_6^+ + P_3d_1^-$        (12.40)

The solution to this problem is $x_1 = 4$, $x_2 = 6$, $d_4^- = 0$, $d_4^+ = 80$, $d_5^- = 0$, $d_5^+ = 60$, $d_1^- = 360$, $d_1^+ = 0$, $d_2^- = 0$, $d_2^+ = 0$, $d_3^- = 0$, $d_3^+ = 0$, $d_6^- = 0$, $d_6^+ = 90$, and $Z = 90P_2 + 360P_3$. Comparing these results with those from the previous model, (12.33)–(12.39), it can be seen that because the production goals have top priority, both production levels are met $(x_1 = 4, d_2^- = 0, \text{ and } x_2 = 6, d_3^- = 0)$. But this occurs at a cost of an additional 90 hours of overtime $(d_6^+ = 90)$. This means that 140 overtime hours are required in order to meet the production goals.

Yet another solution would result if the profit goal were set at the priority 1 level while the production and overtime goals had lower priorities. Oftentimes, exploring the output for different goal priorities will give a *sensitivity of goal attainment*.

## ■ Formulation: application of goal programming

The previous section highlights the concepts of priority coefficients (the $P$'s) and differential weights (the $w$'s) and identifies the role each plays in a goal programming model. In this section we will concentrate on formulating a GP model.

Before examining this example, three summary comments should be made regarding the formulation of GP models. First, two types of variables will be a part of any formulation: (1) *decision variables* (the $x$'s), and (2) *deviational variables* (the $d^+$s and $d^-$s). Second, two classes of constraints can exist in a given GP model: (1) *structural constraints*, which are generally considered environmental constraints not directly related to goals; and (2) *goal constraints*, which are directly related to goals. [In model (12.29)–(12.32), constraints (12.30) and (12.32) are goal constraints while (12.31) is a structural constraint.] Finally, while in most cases a goal constraint will contain both an underachievement $(d^-)$ and an overachievement $(d^+)$ deviational variable, even when both do not appear in the objective function, it is not mandatory that both be included. Omission of either type of deviational variable in the goal

*bounds*

constraint, however, **bounds** the goal in the direction of the omission. That is, omission of $d^+$ places an upper bound on the goal, while omission of $d^-$ forces a lower bound on the goal. Thus omission of deviational variables on goals of lower priority can limit achievement of high-priority goals. An example is given in the Solution Methodology section that highlights this point.

Assuming that there are $m$ goals, $p$ structural constraints, $n$ decision variables, and $K$ priority levels, the general model can be expressed as follows:

MINIMIZE:

$$Z = \sum_{k=1}^{K} P_k \sum_{i=1}^{m} (w_{i,k}^+ d_i^+ + w_{i,k}^- d_i^-) \qquad (12.41)$$

SUBJECT TO:

$$\sum_{j=1}^{n} a_{ij} x_j + d_i^- - d_i^+ = b_i, \qquad i = 1, \ldots, m \qquad (12.42)$$

$$\sum_{j=1}^{n} a_{ij} x_j \qquad (\leq = \geq) b_i, \qquad i = m + 1, \ldots, m + p \qquad (12.43)$$

$$x_j, d_i^+, d_i^- \geq 0, \qquad j = 1, \ldots, n; i = 1, \ldots, m \qquad (12.44)$$

where

$P_k$ = the priority coefficient for the $k$th priority

$w_{i,k}^+$ = the relative weight of the $d_i^+$ variable in the $k$th priority level

$w_{i,k}^-$ = the relative weight of the $d_i^-$ variable in the $k$th priority level

........................................................................

### ■ Example

## *The Rewlings Company case*

In the early part of the chapter we presented the case of the Rewlings Company, a manufacturer of men's topcoats. Recall that the company produces three lines of coats: Sports-Wear, Young-Executive, and Top-Executive. Each product passes through two production departments in the production process and requires a certain amount of raw materials. The company identified breakeven production levels for each product line and forecasted the market demand for each product. Following are the goals that Rewlings identified:

$P_1$ (priority 1): Utilize all available production capacity, i.e., no idle time should exist in either department.

$P_2$ (priority 2): Meet the breakeven production levels in each of the product lines.

$P_3$ (priority 3): Limit overtime in department 2 to 600 hours. Limit overtime in department 1 to 200 hours.

$P_4$ (priority 4): Achieve a weekly profit of $20,000.

$P_5$ (priority 5): Meet all market demand. Employ differential weights to reflect the normal unit contribution to profit.

### ■ Solution

## *Objective (verbal)*

Management at Rewlings would like to determine the quantity of each type of topcoat to produce. The company's primary goal is to maintain full employment. In addition, the company has four other goals, as noted above. The solution output will reflect the quantity to produce on each product line in order to achieve or satisfy these goals as closely as possible.

## *Variables/constraints (math structure)*

Three decision variables are required.

$x_1$ = number of Sports-Wear topcoats that should be produced during the week

$x_2$ = number of Young-Executive topcoats that should be produced during the week

$x_3$ = number of Top-Executive topcoats that should be produced during the week

Twelve goal constraints are required.

**Goal Constraints 1–2: Utilize all production capacity.**

Since two production departments exist, two goal constraints are necessary. For department 1 the constraint is

$$4x_1 + 12x_2 + 10x_3 + d_1^- - d_1^+ = 8000$$

where $d_1^- =$ number of hours by which production time in department 1 falls short of production capacity (8000 hours)

$d_1^+ =$ number of hours of overtime [i.e., amount (hours)] by which production time in department 1 exceeds 8000 hours

The 4, 12, and 10 coefficients reflect the hours of production time required in production of one unit of the respective product. For department 2 the constraint is

$$6x_1 + 6x_2 + 16x_3 + d_2^- - d_2^+ = 4000$$

where $d_2^- =$ number of hours by which production time in department 2 falls short of production capacity (4000 hours)

$d_2^+ =$ number of hours of overtime [i.e., amount (hours)] by which production time in department 2 exceeds 4000 hours

**Goal Constraints 3–5: Meet breakeven production levels.**

Three goal constraints are required—one for each product. For product A (Sports-wear), the constraint is

$$x_1 + d_3^- - d_3^+ = 100$$

where $d_3^- =$ amount (units) by which the production of Sports-Wear topcoats falls short of the breakeven level of 100 units

$d_3^+ =$ amount (units) by which the production of Sports-Wear topcoats exceeds the breakeven level of 100 units

For product B (Young-Executive), the constraint is

$$x_2 + d_4^- - d_4^+ = 50$$

where $d_4^- =$ amount (units) by which the production of Young-Executive topcoats falls short of 50

$d_4^+ =$ amount (units) by which the production of Young-Executive topcoats exceeds 50

For product C (Top-Executive), the constraint is

$$x_3 + d_5^- - d_5^+ = 50$$

where $d_5^-$ = amount (units) by which the production of Top-Executive topcoats falls short of 50

$d_5^+$ = amount (units) by which the production of Top-Executive topcoats exceeds 50

Both deviational variables are required in these constraints even though only the underachievement variables ($d^-$'s) will appear in the objective function. If the $d^+$ variables were omitted from the constraints, production would be bounded to 100, 50, and 50 units, respectively, for the three products. This could unnecessarily limit the achievement of lower priority goals.

> **Goal Constraints 6–7: Limit overtime in the two departments to 200 and 600 hours, respectively.**

Two goal constraints are required—one for each department. For department 1 the constraint is

$$d_1^+ + d_6^- - d_6^+ = 200$$

where $d_6^-$ = amount (hours) by which overtime in department 1 falls short of 200 hours

$d_6^+$ = amount (hours) by which overtime in department 1 exceeds 200 hours

For department 2 the constraint is

$$d_2^+ + d_7^- - d_7^+ = 600$$

where $d_7^-$ = amount (hours) by which overtime in department 2 falls short of 600 hours

$d_7^+$ = amount (hours) by which overtime in department 2 exceeds 600 hours

Both deviational variables are also required in these constraints. If the underachievement variables ($d^-$'s) were omitted from these constraints, we would force the departments to utilize 200 and 600 hours of overtime. Only the $d^+$ variables would appear in the objective function.

> **Goal Constraints 8–9: Achieve a weekly profit of $20,000.**

We need two goal constraints to address the goal of achieving a $20,000 profit since profits result from the production of goods on both regular time and overtime. Profits that result from regular time production are $30 ($100 price − $70 cost), $70 ($150 price − $80 cost), and $150 ($250 price − $100 cost), respectively, for the three products. If overtime or extra material is required, then these costs ($2 per hour for department 1, $3 per hour for department 2, and $2 per unit of material) must be charged against profits. The deviational variables that reflect overtime in the respective departments ($d_1^+$ and $d_2^+$) were introduced in goal constraints 1 and 2, but the deviational variable reflecting material usage above 8000 square yards has not been identified. This can be expressed in the following goal constraint:

$$8x_1 + 6x_2 + 12x_3 + d_8^- - d_8^+ = 8000$$

where      $d_8^-$ = amount (expressed in square yards) by which material usage falls below 8000 square yards

           $d_8^+$ = amount (expressed in square yards) by which material usage exceeds 8000 square yards

Neither of the deviational variables for the constraint will appear in the objective function, since no priority goal level was established for minimizing or maximizing the use of material.

The goal constraint for profit can now be expressed as follows:

$$30x_1 + 70x_2 + 150x_3 - 2d_1^+ - 3d_2^+ - 2d_8^+ + d_9^- - d_9^+ = 20{,}000$$

where      $d_9^-$ = amount ($) by which profits fall short of $20,000

           $d_9^+$ = amount ($) by which profits exceed $20,000

> ### Goal Constraints 10–12: Meet all market demand.

Three goal constraints are required, one for each of the products. The goal constraint for the first product is

$$x_1 + d_{10}^- = 1000$$

where      $d_{10}^-$ = amount (units) by which production of Sports-Wear topcoats falls short of 1000 units

The goal constraint for the second product is

$$x_2 + d_{11}^- = 500$$

where      $d_{11}^-$ = amount (units) by which production of Young-Executive topcoats falls short of 500 units

For the third product, the goal constraint is

$$x_3 + d_{12}^- = 200$$

where $\qquad d_{12}^- =$ amount (units) by which production of Top-Executive topcoats falls short of 200 units

The overachievement deviational variables ($d^+$'s) are not included in these constraints, since it is assumed that the maximum the market will take is 1000, 500, and 200 units, respectively, of the three products. By omitting the $d^+$ variables we assure that the solution, if a solution exists, will not result in the production of more than these quantities.

## Objective function (math structure)

The objective function for the problem is

MINIMIZE: $\qquad Z = P_1(d_1^- + d_2^-) + P_2(d_3^- + d_4^- + d_5^-) + P_3(d_6^+ + d_7^+)$

$$+ P_4(d_9^-) + P_5(30d_{10}^- + 70d_{11}^- + 150d_{12}^-)$$

The highest priority coefficient ($P_1$) is associated with ($d_1^- + d_2^-$). This indicates that Rewlings' primary goal is to utilize all production capacity in both departments. If $d_3^-$, $d_4^-$, and $d_5^-$ are driven to zero at a $P_2$ priority level, then the breakeven production level goals will be achieved. Management is indifferent as to which breakeven level is achieved first. Inclusion of $d_6^+$ and $d_7^+$ at a $P_3$ priority level reflects management's third goal of limiting overtime in the two departments. If $d_6^+$ and $d_7^+$ are zero, then overtime will be no greater than 200 and 600 in the respective departments.

The fourth goal is to achieve \$20,000 in profits. If $d_9^-$ is driven to zero at a $P_4$ priority level, then profits will be at least \$20,000. The $d_{10}^-$, $d_{11}^-$, and $d_{12}^-$ deviational variables included in the objective function at a $P_5$ priority level reflect management's goal of meeting market demand for the three products. If the deviational variables are zero, the demands are met exactly. Different weights are used to indicate the order of achievement of the multiple goals at the $P_5$ priority level.

## Math formulation

The complete GP model is

MINIMIZE: $\qquad Z = P_1(d_1^- + d_2^-) + P_2(d_3^- + d_4^- + d_5^-) + P_3(d_6^+ + d_7^+)$

$$+ P_4d_9^- + P_5(30d_{10}^- + 70d_{11}^- + 150d_{12}^-) \qquad (12.45)$$

SUBJECT TO:

$$4x_1 + 12x_2 + 10x_3 + d_1^- - d_1^+ = 8{,}000 \qquad (12.46)$$

$$6x_1 + 6x_2 + 16x_3 + d_2^- - d_2^+ = 4{,}000 \qquad (12.47)$$

$$x_1 + d_3^- - d_3^+ = 100 \qquad (12.48)$$

$$x_2 + d_4^- - d_4^+ = 50 \qquad (12.49)$$

$$x_3 + d_5^- - d_5^+ = 50 \qquad (12.50)$$

$$d_1^+ + d_6^- - d_6^+ = 200 \qquad (12.51)$$

$$d_2^+ + d_7^- - d_7^+ = 600 \qquad (12.52)$$

$$8x_1 + 6x_2 + 12x_3 + d_8^- - d_8^+ = 8{,}000 \qquad (12.53)$$

$$30x_1 + 70x_2 + 150x_3 - 2d_1^+ - 3d_2^+ - 2d_8^+ + d_9^- - d_9^+ = 20{,}000 \qquad (12.54)$$

$$x_1 + d_{10}^- = 1{,}000 \qquad (12.55)$$

$$x_2 + d_{11}^- = 500 \qquad (12.56)$$

$$x_3 + d_{12}^- = 200 \qquad (12.57)$$

$$x_1, x_2, x_3, d_1^-, d_1^+, d_2^-, d_2^+, d_3^-, d_3^+, d_4^-, d_4^+, d_5^-, d_5^+,$$

$$d_6^-, d_6^+, d_7^-, d_7^+, d_8^-, d_8^+, d_9^-, d_9^+, d_{10}^-, d_{11}^-, d_{12}^- \geq 0$$

# ■ Solution methodology

Up to this point in the chapter we have developed the general structure of goal programming models and have identified the process for formulating these models. In this section we will discuss the methodology for solving GP problems. Two solution procedures are identified: (1) a graphical method and (2) a GP algorithm. The purpose in presenting the graphical method is to give the reader a better understanding of how goal programming works. The purpose in presenting the GP algorithm is to provide a tableau procedure that will handle problems with more than two decision variables. The tableau can be used to determine when specific goals are achieved and what trade-offs occurred in achieving the goals. It will be shown that the GP algorithm is a modification of the standard simplex method.

The output from the computerized version of the GP algorithm is presented in the latter part of the chapter.

## Graphical solution of GP problems

As is the case for solving LP problems, a graphical approach can be used to solve GP problems with two decision variables. Five procedural steps are employed in the process, assuming the problem has been formulated.

1. Graph or plot all *structural constraints* and identify the feasible region. If no structural constraints exist, the feasible region is that area where both $x_1$ and $x_2$ are $\geq 0$ (the nonnegative quadrant).

2. Graph the lines corresponding to the *goal constraints*. This is accomplished by setting the deviational variables in the goal constraint to zero and plotting the resulting equation.

3. Identify the top-priority solution (5). This is accomplished by determining the point or points within the feasible region that satisfy the highest priority goal.

4. Move to the goal having the next highest priority and determine the "best" solution(s), such that this "best" solution does not degrade the solution(s) already achieved for goals of higher priority.

5. Repeat step 4 until all priority levels have been investigated.

To demonstrate the graphical procedure, consider the following problem: The Davidson Camera Company manufactures two types of 35-mm cameras. The production process for manufacturing the cameras is such that two departmental operations are required. To produce their standard camera requires 2 hours of production time in department 1 and 3 hours in department 2. To produce their deluxe model requires 4 hours of production time in department 1 and 3 hours in department 2. Currently, 80 hours of labor are available each week in each of the departments. This labor time is a somewhat restrictive factor since the company has a general policy of avoiding overtime, if possible. The manufacturer's profit on each standard camera is $30, while the profit on the deluxe model is $40. Management at Davidson has set the following goals:

$P_1$ (priority 1): Avoid overtime operations in each department.

$P_2$ (priority 2): Prior sales records indicate that, on the average, a minimum of 10 standard and 10 deluxe cameras can be sold weekly. Management would like to meet these sales goals. Since production time may limit producing this number of each camera, and since the deluxe camera has a higher profit margin, the sales goals should be weighted by the profit contribution for the respective cameras, that is, $30 for the standard camera, $40 for the deluxe camera. (We could also use weights of 3 and 4 since they have the same ratios as the profit contributions.)

$P_3$ (priority 3): Maximize profits.

The GP model for the problem is

MINIMIZE: $\quad Z = P_1 d_1^+ + P_1 d_2^+ + 30 P_2 d_3^- + 40 P_2 d_4^- + P_3 d_5^-$  (12.58)

SUBJECT TO:
$$2x_1 + 4x_2 + d_1^- - d_1^+ \qquad\qquad\qquad = 80 \quad (12.59)$$
$$3x_1 + 3x_2 \qquad + d_2^- - d_2^+ \qquad\qquad = 80 \quad (12.60)$$
$$x_1 \qquad\qquad\qquad\qquad + d_3^- - d_3^+ = 10 \quad (12.61)$$

$$x_2 \qquad\qquad\qquad\qquad\qquad + d_4^- - d_4^+ \qquad\qquad\qquad = 10 \qquad (12.62)$$

$$30x_1 + 40x_2 \qquad\qquad\qquad\qquad\qquad + d_5^- - d_5^+ = 1200 \qquad (12.63)$$

$$x_1, x_2, d_1^-, d_1^+, d_2^-, d_2^+, d_3^-, d_3^+, d_4^-, d_4^+, d_5^-, d_5^+ \geq 0$$

The 1200 value for the right-hand side of equation (12.63) is an arbitrarily high profit goal.

Given that the model has been formulated, we can proceed with graphing.

> **Step 1:** *Graph all structural constraints.* Since no structural constraints exist, the feasible region is the nonnegative quadrant. That is, the feasible region is the area where $x_1 \geq 0$ and $x_2 \geq 0$.
>
> **Step 2:** *Graph all goal constraints.* By setting the deviational variables to zero in each constraint, we can plot the resulting goal equations. These are identified in Figure 12-1 as $GC_1$, $GC_2$, ..., $GC_5$.

The effect of a deviational variable on a goal equation is to shift the equation so that the new equation is parallel to the original equation. The value of the deviational variable reflects the degree of shift. The directed arrows in Figure 12-1

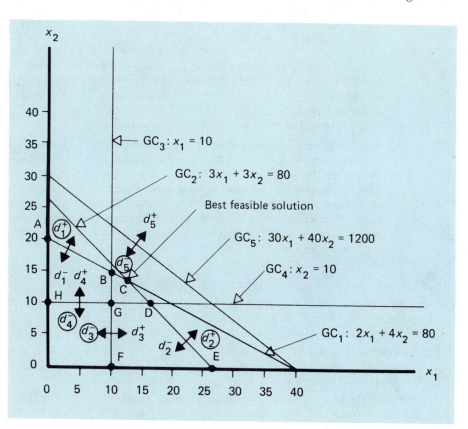

**FIGURE 12-1. Graphical Representation of Davidson Camera Company Problem**

emanating from each goal equation reflect the impact of the deviational variables on the equation. The particular deviational variables to be minimized in the objective function have been circled.

> **Step 3:** *Identify the top-priority solution.* The $d_1^+$ and $d_2^+$ deviational variables have a priority coefficient of $P_1$ in the objective function; therefore, goal constraints 1 and 2 must be considered first. The objective is to minimize $d_1^+$ and $d_2^+$. If we set $d_1^+$ to zero, the area of feasibility (in Figure 12-1) is that area *below* the $GC_1$ equation. If we set $d_2^+$ to zero, the area of feasibility is that area below the $GC_2$ equation. The feasible area common to both is that below line segments AC and CE. Any point in this area will satisfy the condition $d_1^+ = 0$ and $d_2^+ = 0$.

Note that it is incorrect to now conclude that point C is the *optimal* solution to the top-priority goal, since the entire feasible area satisfies the condition $d_1^+ = 0$ and $d_2^+ = 0$.

> **Step 4:** *Move to next highest priority and determine "best" solution, without violating prior goals.* The $d_3^-$ and $d_4^-$ deviational variables have a priority coefficient of $P_2$ in the objective function; therefore, we examine these goal constraints next. Since the $P_2 d_4^-$ factor has a differential weight of 40 while the $P_2 d_3^-$ factor has a weight of 30, we should seek to drive $d_4^-$ to zero before considering $d_3^-$. In this example, we can drive both $d_4^-$ and $d_3^-$ to zero and still remain within the feasible region identified in step 3. Driving these variables to zero, however, will reduce the feasible region. The new feasible region is identified by line segments BC, CD, DG, and GB. Any point in this feasible area will satisfy the condition $d_1^+ = 0, d_2^+ = 0, d_3^- = 0, d_4^- = 0$.

> **Step 5:** *Repeat step 4 until all priorities are investigated.* The last priority level is $P_3$; the deviational variable associated with this priority is $d_5^-$. We have been able to drive the first four deviational variables to zero, which means we have met the goal with which these variables are associated. If we can drive $d_5^-$ to zero, we will have achieved all the goals. However, if we examine Figure 12-1, we note that goals equation $GC_5$ lies outside the current feasible region. Since $GC_5$ is not feasible, the $P_3$ level goal can only be achieved at the expense of goals with higher priorities.

To have an acceptable solution that does not destroy the achievement of goals with a higher priority, $d_5^-$ must be $> 0$. Obviously we would like $d_5^-$ to be as small as possible. If we draw lines parallel to $GC_5$ until we contact the feasible region (BCDGB), we can identify the solution that best satisfies our objective of minimizing $d_5^-$. This is point C on the feasible region. Since goal equations 1 and 2 (i.e., $GC_1$ and $GC_2$) intersect at point C, we can solve these simultaneously to find the final solution values for the decision variables: $x_1 = 13.33$ and $x_2 = 13.33$.

To determine the solution values for the deviational variables, we must employ both the solution graph and the original goal constraints, equations (12.58)–(12.63).

In Figure 12-1 the values for the deviational variables are as follows:

$$d_1^- = 0, \quad d_1^+ = 0$$
$$d_2^- = 0, \quad d_2^+ = 0$$
$$d_3^- = 0,$$
$$d_4^- = 0,$$
$$d_5^+ = 0$$

Substituting this information, along with the values for $x_1$ and $x_2$, into the respective goal constraints, we can determine that

$$d_3^+ = 3.33, \quad d_5^- = 266.67$$
$$d_4^+ = 3.33$$

Using the graphical procedure, the solution to Davidson's problem is as follows:

> By producing 13.33 units/week of each camera, the company can achieve its first two objectives and can maximize profits. Exactly 80 hours will be used in each departmental operation and profits will be \$933.33. The company will underachieve its objective of \$1200 profit by \$266.67.

Note that this solution calls for the production of a fractional number of units. In implementing this solution, fractional units would be carried forward into the next time period (week). To find an integer solution for the problem, we would have to restrict the solution process in much the same manner as in solving an LP problem for integer variables. Some research has been devoted to developing integer-goal programming algorithms; however, that material is beyond the scope of this text.

## Simplex method applied to GP problems

The standard simplex method can be used to solve goal programming problems. Table 12-2 showed the solution of a *single-goal model* solved via the simplex method. Table 12-3 showed the solution of a *multigoal model without priorities*. The simplex method can also be used to solve other GP models. As a matter of fact, any goal programming problem can be solved with the standard algorithm. As indicated in the discussion of the modified production example, equations (12.22)–(12.27), this is accomplished by assigning values to the priority coefficients in the objective function. These values should be assigned so that the values reflect the same order of relationship as the priorities. For example, for a three-priority model, $P_1$ could be assigned a value of 100, $P_2$ a value of 10, and $P_3$ a value of 1.

For the revised production problem, the objective function would appear as follows:

MINIMIZE: $\qquad Z = 100d_2^- + 10d_3^- + 1d_1^-$ $\hfill$ (12.64)

For the extended model, (12.33)–(12.39), the objective function would be

MINIMIZE: $\qquad Z = 100d_6^+ + (1)(10)d_2^- + 2(10)d_3^- + 1d_1^-$  (12.65)

For the previous graphical problem, equations (12.58)–(12.63), the objective function would be

MINIMIZE: $\qquad Z = 1000d_1^+ + 1000d_2^+ + (30)(10)d_3^- + 40(10)d_4^- + d_5^-$  (12.66)

In this latter case, $P_1$ was assigned a value of 1000 and $P_2$ a value of 10. Had we assigned $P_1$ a value of 100, the second set of goals ($30P_2d_3^-$ and $40P_2d_4^-$) would have taken precedence over the first priority goal since the weights of 30 and 40 are employed in the second-level goals.

The advantage of expressing the objective function in this manner is that any GP problem can then be solved without having a GP algorithm. However, if a GP algorithm is available, it should be employed, since the tableau-to-tableau output from the algorithm provides some useful information. Use of a GP algorithm can also be justified by the fact that additional effort is required to interpret the output of a GP model solved via the standard simplex method.

## The GP algorithm: Extended simplex method

In Chapter 7 we described in detail the steps and procedures of the simplex method. In this section we will demonstrate how the algorithm can be modified to solve a goal programming model. As is the case for most algorithms, the GP algorithm is intended for use on the computer; however, if the student is to gain any appreciation or feeling for the method, several problems must be calculated by hand. As was the case for the simplex method, output from a computerized version of the algorithm is given in the chapter.

Six procedural steps are employed in the GP algorithm. These are:

1. Establish the initial, modified simplex tableau. This tableau will include a $(z_j - c_j)$ row for each priority level. Set $k = 1$, where $k$ is a pointer that represents the $(z_j - c_j)$ row associated with the $P_k$ priority. Go to step 2.

2. Check for optimality by examining the Right-hand Side (solution) value in the $(z_j - c_j)$ row for the $P_k$ priority. If a zero exists, then the $P_k$ priority goal has been met; therefore, go to step 6. If a zero value does not exist, proceed to step 3.

3. Determine the new entering variable by examining the $(z_j - c_j)$ row for the $P_k$ priority. Examine each *positive* coefficient in the $P_k$ row. Identify the largest positive coefficient for which there are no negative coefficients at a higher priority in the same column. The variable in the column associated with the largest positive coefficient is the incoming variable. If a tie exists in the values of the coefficients that determine the entering variable, it can be broken arbitrarily. If no positive coefficient exists in the

$P_k$ row that meets the above conditions, then go to step 6; otherwise, go to step 4.

4. Determine the departing variable by using the standard procedure from the simplex method.

5. Develop the new tableau. The standard procedure of the simplex method is used to update the coefficients in the body of the tableau. The new $(z_j - c_j)$ rows are computed in the same manner used in developing the initial tableau. Go to step 2.

6. Evaluate the next-lowest priority level by setting $k = k + 1$. If $k$ exceeds $K$, where $K$ is the total number of priority levels, then stop; the solution is optimal. If $k \le K$, then the $(z_j - c_j)$ row for the $P_k$ priority level must be examined; therefore, go to step 2.

To demonstrate the algorithm, consider again the problem of the Davidson Camera Company, which we solved graphically. The GP model for the problem was formulated as follows [refer to equations (12.58)–(12.63)]:

MINIMIZE: $\quad Z = P_1 d_1^+ + P_1 d_2^+ + 30 P_2 d_3^- + 40 P_2 d_4^- + P_3 d_5^-$

SUBJECT TO:

$$2x_1 + 4x_2 + d_1^- - d_1^+ \qquad\qquad = 80$$

$$3x_1 + 3x_2 \qquad + d_2^- - d_2^+ \qquad\qquad = 80$$

$$x_1 \qquad\qquad + d_3^- - d_3^+ \qquad\qquad = 10$$

$$x_2 \qquad\qquad + d_4^- - d_4^+ \qquad = 10$$

$$30x_1 + 40x_2 \qquad\qquad\qquad + d_5^- - d_5^+ = 1200$$

$$x_1, x_2, d_1^-, d_1^+, d_2^-, d_2^+, d_3^-, d_3^+, d_4^-, d_4^+, d_5^-, d_5^+ \ge 0$$

**Step 1:** *Establish the initial tableau.* The procedures for creating the initial tableau are identical to those of the simplex method, with the exception of the last row(s) of the tableau. We begin by determining if an initial feasible solution exists within the coefficients of the constraints. If a $d^-$ variable is associated with each goal constraint, it will be the basic variable for that constraint. If structural constraints exist, the slack variables will be in the initial basis; if slack variables do not exist, artificial variables are added. For the current problem, $d_1^-$ through $d_5^-$ form the basis for the first tableau.

The initial tableau for the problem is presented in Table 12-4. The coefficients in the $c_j$ row, the $c_B$ column, and the body of the tableau are transferred into the tableau in the same manner used in the simplex method. The difference between this tableau and any initial simplex tableau is the $(z_j - c_j)$ row. Three changes have been made:

1. The $z_j$ row has been omitted.

2. $(z_j - c_j)$ is computed rather than $(c_j - z_j)$.

3. Multiple $(z_j - c_j)$ rows exist.

**TABLE 12-4. Initial Tableau for Davidson Camera**

| $c_j$ | | | 0 | 0 | 0 | $P_1$ | 0 | $P_1$ | $30P_2$ | 0 | $40P_2$ | 0 | $P_3$ | 0 |
|---|---|---|---|---|---|---|---|---|---|---|---|---|---|---|
| $c_B$ | Variable in the Basis | Right-hand Side (Solution) | $x_1$ | $x_2$ | $d_1^-$ | $d_1^+$ | $d_2^-$ | $d_2^+$ | $d_3^-$ | $d_3^+$ | $d_4^-$ | $d_4^+$ | $d_5^-$ | $d_5^+$ |
| 0 | $d_1^-$ | 80 | 2 | 4 | 1 | -1 | 0 | 0 | 0 | 0 | 0 | 0 | 0 | 0 |
| 0 | $d_2^-$ | 80 | 3 | 3 | 0 | 0 | 1 | -1 | 0 | 0 | 0 | 0 | 0 | 0 |
| $30P_2$ | $d_3^-$ | 10 | 1 | 0 | 0 | 0 | 0 | 0 | 1 | -1 | 0 | 0 | 0 | 0 |
| $40P_2$ | $d_4^-$ | 10 | 0 | ① | 0 | 0 | 0 | 0 | 0 | 0 | 1 | -1 | 0 | 0 |
| $P_3$ | $d_5^-$ | 1200 | 30 | 40 | 0 | 0 | 0 | 0 | 0 | 0 | 0 | 0 | 1 | -1 |
| | $P_3$ | 1200 | 30 | 40 | 0 | 0 | 0 | 0 | 0 | 0 | 0 | 0 | 0 | -1 |
| $z_j - c_j$ | $P_2$ | 700 | 30 | 40 | 0 | 0 | 0 | 0 | 0 | -30 | 0 | -40 | 0 | 0 |
| | $P_1$ | 0 | 0 | 0 | 0 | -1 | 0 | -1 | 0 | 0 | 0 | 0 | 0 | 0 |

The $z_j$ row has been omitted simply to avoid complicating the tableau. The tableau can be determined easily without this row.

Recall that we solved minimization LP problems with the simplex method by multiplying each coefficient in the objective function by $-1$. Since every GP problem is a minimization problem, logic would tell us that we must multiply the objective function by $-1$ before employing the simplex method. We can avoid this by changing our procedure slightly—instead of computing $c_j - z_j$ in each tableau, we can simply compute $z_j - c_j$. By doing this, we avoid having to multiply the objective function by $-1$.

The multiple $(z_j - c_j)$ rows are computed in the same manner as would be used in the simplex method. The difference is the tabular representation of the results. Recall that $z_j$ is computed by multiplying the value in the $j$th column by the values in the $c_B$ column and summing the component parts. For example, for the $x_1$ column

$$z_1 = (2)(0) + (3)(0) + (1)(30P_2) + (0)(40P_2) + (30)(P_3)$$

The value of $c_1$ (from the $c_j$ row) associated with $x_1$ is zero. Therefore,

$$z_1 - c_1 = 0 + 0 + 30P_2 + 0 + 30P_3 - 0$$

Rather than transfer this into a single cell in a single $(z_1 - c_1)$ row, we can break it into parts where the parts are associated with the priority levels. In this case we have

$$\begin{array}{ll} 30 & P_3 \\ 30 & P_2 \\ 0 & P_1 \end{array}$$

By performing this procedure for each column, we develop the multiple $(z_j - c_j)$ rows. By expressing the $(z_j - c_j)$ rows in this manner, we can in later steps in the algorithm seek to satisfy each goal in priority order.

We begin examining the initial tableau by checking the $(z_j - c_j)$ row associated with the $P_1$ priority level (that is, the index pointer, $k$, is set to 1).

> **Step 2:** *Check for optimality.* Recall that, in the simplex method, optimality exists when the value of every coefficient in the $(c_j - z_j)$ row is zero or negative. For the GP algorithm, two checks can be used to test for optimality: (1) Is there a zero in the Right-hand Side (Solution) column (the RHS column) in the $P_k$ row or (2) are all values in the $P_k$ row zero or negative? A zero in the RHS column of a given row indicates that the associated goal has been achieved. For our problem, the RHS value in the $P_1$ row is zero; therefore, the $P_1$ goal has been met. A quick check of all values in the $P_1$ row verifies this.

In the RHS column, the 700 associated with the $P_2$ row and the 1200 associated with the $P_3$ row indicate the extent to which the goals at these priority levels have not been satisfied. By examining the solution values in the tableau, we can explain these achievement levels as well as that of $P_1$.

The solution at this step is $d_1^- = 80$, $d_2^- = 80$, $d_3^- = 10$, $d_4^- = 10$, and $d_5^- = 1200$; all other variables are zero since they are nonbasic variables. The top-priority goal $(P_1)$ is to avoid overtime in either department; since $d_1^+$ and $d_2^+$ are zero, we have achieved this goal. The second priority goal $(P_2)$ is to meet production goals of 10 units of $x_1$ and 10 units of $x_2$. We missed both of these goals by 10, since $d_3^-$ and $d_4^-$ are each 10. The weighted value of $d_3^-$ is 30 and the weighted value of $d_4^-$ is 40 (at the $P_2$ level). Therefore, 700 is the *weighted* value of our underachievement of the total production goal. The third priority goal is to achieve a profit of $1200, if possible. Since no units are produced, we underachieved this goal by $1200 ($d_5^- = 1200$).

Since the top-priority goal is met, the GP algorithm indicates that we should set the $k$ index pointer to 2 and examine the $(z_j - c_j)$ row associated with $P_2$.

From the above analysis, we already know that $P_2$ is not achieved. A check of the values of the coefficients in the $(z_j - c_j)$ row verifies this since a $+30$ exists in the $x_1$ column and a $+40$ exists in the $x_2$ column. Since no negative values exist in column $x_1$ or $x_2$ at the $P_1$ level, we can proceed to step 3.

**Step 3:** *Determine the new entering variable.* The largest positive coefficient in the $(z_j - c_j)$ row associated with $P_2$ is 40; therefore, the *incoming variable* is $x_2$.

**Step 4:** *Determine the departing variable.* To determine the departing variable, we use the standard simplex procedure of dividing the positive coefficients in the $x_2$ column into the values in the RHS column and selecting the smallest ratio. In this case we have $80/4 = 20$; $80/3 = 26.66$; $10/0 = \infty$; $10/1 = 10$, and $1200/40 = 30$. The smallest ratio is associated with $d_4^-$; therefore, $d_4^-$ is the *outgoing variable*.

**Step 5:** *Develop the new tableau.* The new tableau is developed by employing the updating procedure used in the simplex method: the incoming row is computed by dividing the outgoing row by the pivot element; all remaining rows are updated by use of the new incoming row and the old row in the tableau. The new $(z_j - c_j)$ rows are computed using the procedure employed in the initial tableau. Table 12-5 is the second tableau (Tableau II) for the problem.

Examination of Tableau II indicates that the second priority goal $(P_2)$ has not been attained, since the RHS value in the $(z_j - c_j)$ row for $P_2$ is 300 and a positive value exists in the $x_1$ column. However, the solution at this point is a better solution since the weighted deviations from the $P_2$ goal have been reduced from 700 to 300. This reduction occurs because $d_4^-$ has been driven to zero and $d_4^-$ is weighted by 40 in the objective function.

The solution values for Tableau II are $d_1^- = 40$, $d_2^- = 50$, $d_3^- = 10$, $x_2 = 10$, and $d_5^- = 800$. These indicate that 40 hours of unused capacity remain in department 1; 50 hours of unused capacity remains in department 2; the production goal of $x_1$ is still underachieved by 10 units; 10 units of $x_2$ are produced; and the profit goal is still underachieved by $800. From this information and from the solution in the initial tableau, we can conclude that the production of 10 units of $x_2$ required 40 hours in

**TABLE 12-5. Tableau II for Davidson Camera**

| $c_j \rightarrow$ | | | 0 | 0 | 0 | $P_1$ | 0 | $P_1$ | $30P_2$ | 0 | $40P_2$ | 0 | $P_3$ | 0 |
|---|---|---|---|---|---|---|---|---|---|---|---|---|---|---|
| $c_B$ | Variables in the Basis | Right-hand Side (Solution) | $x_1$ | $x_2$ | $d_1^-$ | $d_1^+$ | $d_2^-$ | $d_2^+$ | $d_3^-$ | $d_3^+$ | $d_4^-$ | $d_4^+$ | $d_5^-$ | $d_5^+$ |
| 0 | $d_1^-$ | 40 | 2 | 0 | 1 | -1 | 0 | 0 | 0 | 0 | -4 | 4 | 0 | 0 |
| 0 | $d_2^-$ | 50 | 3 | 0 | 0 | 0 | 1 | -1 | 0 | 0 | -3 | 3 | 0 | 0 |
| $30P_2$ | $d_3^-$ | 10 | ①  | 0 | 0 | 0 | 0 | 0 | 1 | -1 | 0 | 0 | 0 | 0 |
| 0 | $x_2$ | 10 | 0 | 1 | 0 | 0 | 0 | 0 | 0 | 0 | 1 | -1 | 0 | 0 |
| $P_3$ | $d_5^-$ | 800 | 30 | 0 | 0 | 0 | 0 | 0 | 0 | 0 | -40 | 40 | 1 | -1 |
| $z_j - c_j$ | $P_3$ | 800 | 30 | 0 | 0 | 0 | 0 | 0 | 0 | 0 | -40 | 40 | 0 | -1 |
| | $P_2$ | 300 | 30 | 0 | 0 | 0 | 0 | 0 | 0 | -30 | -40 | 0 | 0 | 0 |
| | $P_1$ | 0 | 0 | 0 | 0 | -1 | 0 | -1 | 0 | 0 | 0 | 0 | 0 | 0 |

$\leftarrow$

department 1 and 30 hours in department 2, and resulted in $400 of profit (which moves us $400 closer to achieving the profit goal of $1200).

Since we were not able fully to achieve the second priority goal ($P_2$), we must check to determine if we can continue the tableau process. (This action sends us back to step 2 in the GP algorithm.) The positive 30 that exists under the $x_1$ column in the $(z_j - c_j)$ row for $P_2$ indicates that $x_1$ is a candidate for entering the basis. Since a negative number does not exist under the $x_1$ column in the $(z_j - c_j)$ row of $P_1$, we can bring $x_1$ into the basis without violating the existing goal achievement at the $P_1$ level.

A quick check of the ratio of the values in the $x_1$ column and the RHS values (40/2, 50/3, 10/1, 10/0, 800/30) indicates that $d_3^-$ should be removed from the basis.

If we compute the new tableau that results from removing $d_3^-$ and bringing $x_1$ into the basis, it will be discovered that the first two priority goals are fully achieved. However, this will not be the best solution, that is, the optimality criteria will not be met. We thus should continue the pivoting procedure.

**Step 6:** *Evaluate the next lowest priority goal(s).* To evaluate the next priority goal (third in this case), we add one to the pointer index, $k$ (recall that $k$ was equal to 2, which pointed us to the $P_2$ priority level) and evaluate the new $P_k$ row of the current tableau. This would indicate what we already know, that $P_3$ should be examined for optimality. If we perform this step, a new tableau (fourth, in this case) will result. As was the case for the third tableau, this fourth tableau will not provide the best solution. However, the fifth tableau, which would result from one additional pivot, will provide the best solution. This tableau is shown in Table 12-6.

Interpreting this tableau, we note that we are now $266.66 short of the profit goal of $1200—but we are still underachieving the goal. We have used all the available production capacity ($d_1^- = 0$, $d_2^- = 0$). We cannot, therefore, logically improve our profit goal without going to overtime (which would violate the $P_1$ goal). A check of the $(z_j - c_j)$ row for $P_3$ confirms that this is true—a positive value (6.6) exists in the $d_2^+$ column in the $(z_j - c_j)$ row of $P_3$ but a negative value ($-1$) exists in the same column in the $(z_j - c_j)$ row of $P_1$; likewise, a positive value (5) exists in the $d_1^+$ column in the $(z_j - c_j)$ row of $P_3$ but a negative value ($-1$) exists in the same column in the $(z_j - c_j)$ row of $P_1$. We must conclude, therefore, that this is the best solution for the defined problem. This solution is identical to the graphical solution:

$$x_1 = 13.33 \qquad d_1^- = 0 \qquad d_1^+ = 0$$

$$x_2 = 13.33 \qquad d_2^- = 0 \qquad d_2^+ = 0$$

$$d_3^- = 0 \qquad d_3^+ = 3.33$$

$$Z = 266.66 P_3 \quad d_4^- = 0 \qquad d_4^+ = 3.33$$

$$d_5^- = 266.66 \quad d_5^+ = 0$$

**TABLE 12-6. Optimal Tableau for Davidson Camera**

| | $c_j \rightarrow$ | | 0 | 0 | 0 | $P_1$ | 0 | $P_1$ | $30P_2$ | 0 | $40P_2$ | 0 | $P_3$ | 0 |
|---|---|---|---|---|---|---|---|---|---|---|---|---|---|---|
| $c_B$ | Variables in the Basis | Right-hand Side (Solution) | $x_1$ | $x_2$ | $d_1^-$ | $d_1^+$ | $d_2^-$ | $d_2^+$ | $d_3^-$ | $d_3^+$ | $d_4^-$ | $d_4^+$ | $d_5^-$ | $d_5^+$ |
| 0 | $d_4^+$ | 3.33 | 0 | 0 | .5 | -.5 | -.33 | .33 | 0 | 0 | -1 | 1 | 0 | 0 |
| 0 | $d_3^+$ | 3.33 | 0 | 0 | -.5 | .5 | .66 | -.66 | -1 | 1 | 0 | 0 | 0 | 0 |
| 0 | $x_1$ | 13.33 | 1 | 0 | -.5 | .5 | .66 | -.66 | 0 | 0 | 0 | 0 | 0 | 0 |
| 0 | $x_2$ | 13.33 | 0 | 1 | .5 | .5 | -.33 | .33 | 0 | 0 | 0 | 0 | 0 | 0 |
| $P_3$ | $d_5^-$ | 266.66 | 0 | 0 | -5 | 5 | -6.6 | 6.6 | 0 | 0 | 0 | 0 | 1 | -1 |
| $z_j - c_j$ | $P_3$ | 266.66 | 0 | 0 | -5 | 5 | -6.6 | 6.6 | 0 | 0 | 0 | 0 | 0 | -1 |
| | $P_2$ | 0 | 0 | 0 | 0 | 0 | 0 | 0 | -30 | 0 | -40 | 0 | 0 | 0 |
| | $P_1$ | 0 | 0 | 0 | 0 | -1 | 0 | -1 | 0 | 0 | 0 | 0 | 0 | 0 |

## *Special problems in GP*

A number of special problems can occur in the GP–simplex solution process, such as ties for the departing variable, infeasible solutions, alternate optimal solutions, and negative right-hand side values. Since some of these can have an impact on the solution, a few words of caution are in order.

**Tie for departing variable.**   In constructing a GP–simplex tableau, the departing variable is determined by the smallest nonnegative ratio that results when the coefficients in the incoming column are divided into the Right-hand Side. If two or more rows have the same ratio, the tie may be broken by selecting the row with the highest associated priority level (located in the $c_B$ column). In some cases, the variable being considered for removal will not have an associated priority level. In such cases, ties may be broken arbitrarily. Although theory would indicate that this could cause cycling because of degeneracy, this has not occurred in practice.

**Infeasible solution.**   As indicated earlier in the chapter, infeasible solutions occur in linear programming, but not in goal programming. Occasionally, however, an *unexpected* solution may occur. One should not expect that, when a given priority goal is not achieved, every lower-priority goal will likewise not be achieved. It is possible to have a solution in which the top-priority goal is not achieved but lower-priority goals are met. This generally occurs when absolute objectives (goals) exist and limits (bounds) are placed on resources.

**Alternate optimal solutions.**   Alternate optima can occur in goal programming just as in linear programming. The existence of alternate optimal solutions is indicated by an entire column of zeros in the $(z_j - c_j)$ rows for a nonbasic variable and the existence of at least one positive $a_{ij}$ element in the corresponding column. The alternate solution is determined by computing the new tableau, using the standard update procedure.

**Negative right-hand-side values.**   The GP–simplex tableau procedure generally cannot accept negative right-hand-side values, although some computer codes have special procedures to accept such conditions. One can avoid negative right-hand-side values simply by multiplying the entire goal constraint by $-1$. The modification should be made after the deviational variables have been added. For example, for the goal constraint

$$3x_1 - 4x_2 - 5x_3 + d_1^- - d_1^+ = -50$$

would be modified to

$$-3x_1 + 4x_2 + 5x_3 - d_1^- + d_1^+ = 50$$

The appropriate variable to appear in the objective function is determined from analysis of the original constraint, not the new constraint. That is, if the goal were to achieve or exceed $-50$, then $d_1^-$ would be placed in the objective function; if the goal were to underachieve $-50$, then the $d_1^+$ would appear in the objective function. (In some computer codes the deviational variables are added automatically—which means they would be added to the modified constraint—therefore, it may be necessary to reverse the variables when they are analyzed in the output.)

## ■ Summary

Decision makers in an organization often are faced with problems that have multiple (and often conflicting) goals. In this chapter we have demonstrated that if such problems can be described by linear goal equations (constraints), and if the goals can be prioritized (ranked) in terms of importance, then goal programming is a viable multicriteria math programming technique for generating solutions to the problems.

Obviously, goal programming does not provide answers to all multicriteria problems. The technique will provide solutions for problems where goals are to be met in a preferential order. Research is needed, however, in the areas of sensitivity analysis and solutions that will allow a small deviation from a higher-priority goal in order to achieve a substantial reduction in a lower-priority goal or goals. Research into understanding duality theory's relationship to goal programming should also broaden the use of the technique. If the technique is to be fully functional, it should also provide integer solution values for problems where this is a strict requirement.

## ■ Glossary of terms

**bounds:**   Omission of either the $d^-$ or $d^+$ deviational variable in a goal constraint *bounds* the goal in the direction of the omission.

**deviational variables:**   The $d^-$ and $d^+$ variables incorporated into a goal equation—they reflect the extent to which the goal is underachieved ($d^-$) or exceeded ($d^+$).

**differential weight:**   A numeric value (weight) assigned to goals (deviational variables) at the same priority level to reflect goal preference within the level.

**goal equation:**   Used synonymously with the term *goal constraint*. A goal equation is a goal expressed in mathematical equation form by inclusion of deviational variables.

**goal programming:**   A multicriteria mathematical programming technique identified and studied by A. Charnes and W. W. Cooper in the early 1960s.

**GP–simplex method:**   The modified simplex method (algorithm) used in solving a goal programming problem.

**multicriteria mathematical programming techniques:**   Mathematical programming techniques that have the flexibility to incorporate more than one objective into the objective function. Goal programming is a multicriteria mathematical programming method; other methods exist.

**multiple goals with equal priorities:**   A model in which deviational variables from more than one goal are incorporated into the objective function; all variables take on the same priority level.

**multiple goals with priorities:**   A model in which deviational variables from more than one goal are incorporated into the objective function; all variables are assigned a priority coefficient ($P$) that reflects the preferential ordering of the goals.

**multiple goals with priorities and weights:** A multiple-goal priority model in which differential weights are employed in one or more priority levels to differentiate goal preference within the level.

**priorities (P's):** Coefficients assigned to goals (deviational variables) at the same priority level to reflect goal preference within the level.

**single-goal model:** A model in which the deviational variables associated with a single goal are incorporated into the objective function.

**structural constraints:** Environmental constraints that do not directly relate to the goals of the problem. Deviational variables are not incorporated into these constraints; therefore, the constraints are not incorporated into the objective function. These constraints place operational bounds (constraints) on a problem.

## ▪ Review questions

1. Explain how goal programming differs from linear programming.

2. How are deviational variables employed in goal programming? What do they indicate in regard to the goal constraint in which they are incorporated?

3. What advantage does goal programming have over linear programming in regard to generating a solution?

4. What is the purpose of priority coefficients in goal programming? of differential weights?

5. Does every goal programming problem employ priority coefficients? differential weights?

6. Differentiate between a goal constraint (equation) and a structural constraint.

7. Will every goal constraint contain both a $d^-$ and a $d^+$ deviational variable? What does the omission of a deviational variable in the goal constraint imply in relation to the solution to the problem?

8. Can the standard simplex algorithm be applied to any GP problem? If yes, explain how this is accomplished; i.e., what modification in the GP model is necessary?

9. Explain how the GP–simplex tableau differs from the standard simplex tableau.

10. Explain the optimality test associated with the GP–simplex algorithm.

## ▪ True/false questions

1. The simplex method used in linear programming can be used to solve any GOAL programming problem, if properly employed.

2. Artificial variables are never required in solving a GP problem.

3. One of the advantages of goal programming is that a solution to the problem is always possible—an infeasible solution will not result.

4. Every GP problem will employ both *priorities* and *weights* in the formulation process.

5. Every goal constraint will contain both a $d^-$ and $d^+$ deviation variable.

Questions 6 and 7 relate to the following goal programming problem:

MINIMIZE:    $Z = P_1 d_4^+ + P_2 d_5^- + P_3 d_1^- + P_4(d_2^+ + d_3^+)$

| $c_B$ | $c_j$ Variable in the Basis | Right-hand Side (Solution) | 0 $x_1$ | 0 $x_2$ | $P_3$ $d_1^-$ | 0 $d_1^+$ | 0 $d_2^-$ | $P_4$ $d_2^+$ | 0 $d_3^-$ | $P_4$ $d_3^+$ | 0 $d_4^-$ | $P_1$ $d_4^+$ | $P_2$ $d_5^-$ |
|---|---|---|---|---|---|---|---|---|---|---|---|---|---|
| $P_3$ | $d_1^-$ | 66 | 0 | 0 | 1 | -1 | 0 | 0 | -6 | 6 | 0 | 0 | 2 |
| 0 | $d_2^-$ | 1 | 0 | 0 | 0 | 0 | 1 | -1 | -2 | 2 | 0 | 0 | 1 |
| 0 | $x_1$ | 1 | 1 | 0 | 0 | 0 | 0 | 0 | 1 | -1 | 0 | 0 | -1 |
| 0 | $d_4^-$ | 16 | 0 | 0 | 0 | 0 | 0 | 0 | 0 | 1 | 1 | -1 | 0 |
| 0 | $x_2$ | 7 | 0 | 1 | 0 | 0 | 0 | 0 | 0 | 0 | 0 | 0 | 1 |
| | $P_4$ | 0 | 0 | 0 | 0 | 0 | 0 | -1 | 0 | -1 | 0 | 0 | 0 |
| $z_j - c_j$ | $P_3$ | 66 | 0 | 0 | 0 | -1 | 0 | 0 | -6 | 6 | 0 | 0 | 2 |
| | $P_2$ | 0 | 0 | 0 | 0 | 0 | 0 | 0 | 0 | 0 | 0 | 0 | -1 |
| | $P_1$ | 0 | 0 | 0 | 0 | 0 | 0 | 0 | 0 | 0 | -1 | 0 | 0 |

TABLE Q12-6/7.
Tableau for
Questions 6 and 7

SUBJECT TO:

$$6x_1 + 4x_2 + d_1^- - d_1^+ = 100$$

$$2x_1 + x_2 + d_2^- - d_2^+ = 10$$

$$x_1 + x_2 + d_3^- - d_3^+ = 8$$

$$3x_1 + 2x_2 + d_4^- - d_4^+ = 34$$

$$x_2 + d_5^- = 7$$

$$x_1, x_2, d_1^-, d_1^+, d_2^-, d_2^+, d_3^-, d_3^+, d_4^-, d_4^+, d_5^- \geq 0$$

and the tableau in Table Q12-6/7.

6. In this solution process, if either $d_3^+$ or $d_5^-$ were brought into the basis, we would move closer to the $P_3$ goal.

7. Currently the first, second, and fourth goal constraints are met exactly.

8. A GOAL programming problem can constrain both goal constraints as well as environmental constraints.

# ■ Problems

1. Keystone Electronics produces and markets novelty video devices. The company is organized on a profit-center basis, that is, the performance of each operating center (unit) in the company is determined by the weekly profit it generates. The circuit-board profit center produces two types of circuit boards, which are used in a variety of end products produced by the company. Circuit board #1 requires 15 minutes to fabricate; circuit board #2 requires 24 minutes of fabrication time. The normal hours of operation of the center are 240 hours per week. The unit profits for the circuit boards are $4 for board #1

and $5 for board #2. The profit-center manager has listed, in priority order, the following goals:

**Goal 1.**  Achieve a profit goal of at least $4000 per week.

**Goal 2.**  Limit the overtime operation of the center to 24 hours.

**Goal 3.**  Meet committed orders for 100 units of board #1 and 150 units of board #2.

**Goal 4.**  Meet forecasted demand for each circuit board: board #1 = 500 units; board #2 = 400 units.

**Goal 5.**  Utilize all existing man-hours available as regular operating hours.

    **a.** Formulate the goal programming model for the problem.

    **b.** How would the model be changed (i.e., reformulated), if management stated that "committed orders must be met regardless of cost or man-power requirements"?

2. The T & L Machine Company produces three different types of rollers used in textile manufacturing equipment. All rollers are produced in a milling operation. The manufacturing time required to produce a *basic* roller is 5 hours, while the *high-precision* roller requires 12 hours of production time. The *general-purpose* roller requires 8 hours of production time. The company has 340 hours per week of production capacity. The per-unit profits resulting from the sale of the rollers are: $1000, *basic* roller; $1450, *general-purpose* roller; $2500, *high-precision* roller. The marketing department at T & L has indicated that demand for the rollers is such that the company can sell all the rollers produced. Management at T & L has listed the following goals (in order of importance).

**Goal 1.**  Utilize all existing production capacity.

**Goal 2.**  Meet weekly sales goals for each type of roller: 20 basic; 24 general-purpose; and 15 high-precision. Assign differential weights according to the relative profit for each roller.

**Goal 3.**  Limit overtime to 40 hours per week.

**Goal 4.**  Maximize profits.

Formulate the goal programming model for the problem.

3. Delta Manufacturing Inc. produces two types of products (A and B). Manufacturing of both products requires two operations. The first operation is performed in department #1. The production of product A requires 3 hours in the first operation while product B requires 4 hours in the first operation. The second operation can be performed in either department 2 or department 3. The required production time in department 2 for each unit of A is 3 hours; for each unit of B, 6 hours. If department 3 is employed, the production time for each unit of A is 8 hours, while each unit of B requires 10 hours. There are 3000, 3600, and 5000 hours of production time available in the respective departments. Labor costs associated with the three departments are as follows:

Department #1: $6.50 per hour

Department #2: $8.00 per hour

Department #3: $5.00 per hour

Delta has demand for 400 units of product A and 620 units of product B. The company has established the following goals (listed in priority order).

**Goal 1.** Satisfy customer demand.

**Goal 2.** Limit overtime in department 2 to 1000 hours.

**Goal 3.** Minimize total costs.

**Goal 4.** Minimize overtime in departments 1 and 3.

Formulate the goal programming model for the problem.

4. Lonestar Distilleries blends and distributes fine whiskey. The company produces three distinct whiskeys: Prairie High, Lone Wolf, and Wild West. The blends are produced by mixing different grades of raw whiskey. Blending requirements as well as availability and price (cost) per fifth for the raw stock are as follows (availability in fifths/day):

| Stock | Cost per Fifth | Availability |
|---|---|---|
| Grade I | $6.50 | 1800 |
| Grade II | $5.00 | 2000 |
| Grade III | $3.50 | 1200 |

| Blend | Requirements | Selling Price |
|---|---|---|
| Prairie High | No more than 12% of Grade III At least 50% of Grade I | $6.00 |

| Blend | Requirements | Selling Price |
|---|---|---|
| Lone Wolf | No more than 40% of Grade III At least 25% of Grade I | $5.25 |

| Blend | Requirements | Selling Price |
|---|---|---|
| Wild West | No more than 50% of Grade III At least 10% of Grade II | $4.75 |

Lonestar has established the following goals:

**Goal 1.** Produce at least 2000 fifths of Prairie High and 1000 fifths of Lone Wolf per day.

**Goal 2.** Maximize profits.

**Goal 3.** Utilize all available daily supplies of raw stocks.

Formulate the goal programming model for the problem that will indicate the number of fifths of each grade to blend in each mix in order to meet the above goals.

5. Sigma Paper Company Inc. is in the process of building a new plant. Labor requirements for the new facility are: 2000 nonprofessionals and 850 professionals. Recruiting costs average $570 for each nonprofessional position and $1290 for each professional position.

Because of labor market shortages in both categories, costs for recruiting women and minorities are greater than the above figures. Specifically, the cost for recruiting women is: nonprofessional, $685; professional, $1450. For recruiting minorities (men or women) the cost is: nonprofessional, $740; professional, $1560. The company has budgeted $2.4 million for recruiting purposes. Management at Sigma has established the following objectives (goals).

**Goal 1.**  The company would like to have at least 45% of the new labor force consist of women.

**Goal 2.**  Minorities should constitute at least 40% of the labor force. A minority woman is counted both as a minority and as a woman employee.

**Goal 3.**  Minimize the amount of dollars required for recruiting.

**Goal 4.**  Limit the recruiting cost overrun to $300,000.

Formulate the goal programming model for the problem that will indicate the number of recruiting dollars that should be expended in each labor category.

6. Assume that a given individual is limited to a diet of milk, beef, and eggs. The individual is not restricted in the quantity of any item chosen, but it is important that certain minimum daily vitamin requirements be met and that cholesterol intake be minimized. Table P12-6 reflects the quantity (mg) of vitamin A, B, and C contained in each of the food products as well as the level (units) of cholesterol. The table also includes the minimum daily vitamin requirements and the cost of each food product. Assume the following goals have been established (listed in order of importance).

**Goal 1.**  Satisfy the minimum daily vitamin requirements. It is twice as important that the vitamin A requirement be met, compared to both vitamin B and vitamin C requirements.

**Goal 2.**  Minimize the cholesterol intake.

**Goal 3.**  Minimize the cost associated with the diet.

**TABLE P12-6. Diet Information for Problem 6**

| Food Components | Food Product | | | Minimum Daily Requirement (mg) |
|---|---|---|---|---|
| | Milk (mg/gal) | Beef (mg/lb) | Eggs (mg/doz) | |
| Vitamin A | 2 | 2 | 20 | 2 |
| Vitamin C | 200 | 20 | 20 | 60 |
| Vitamin D | 20 | 200 | 20 | 10 |
| Cholesterol | 140 units/gal | 100 units/lb | 240 units/doz | |
| Cost | $2.00/gal | $2.75/lb | $1.20/doz | |

Formulate a goal programming model for the problem.

7. Sneed Manufacturing produces auxiliary gas tanks for subcompact automobiles. The company produces one type of tank that fits a variety of automobiles. Currently the company is faced with a large demand and a fixed production capacity. In an attempt to meet demand the company is considering (1) running a multishift overtime operation, (2) subcontracting some orders to outside companies, and/or (3) hiring temporary employees.

   Management is somewhat concerned about going to outside subcontractors or hiring temporary employees because this might reduce the quality of work. In some cases the costs will even be higher. The data in Table P12-7 describe the labor requirements, costs, and average quality levels associated with the different alternatives. With the existing labor force, the company can support 200 total hours of operations (180 regular hours plus 20 overtime hours) per week. After such discussion and analysis the company came up with the following set of goals:

   **Goal 1.** Current demand for the gas tank is 100 units per week. The company would like to meet this demand; however, because of limited storage, the company would like to avoid overproduction. Management has decided it is twice as important to meet demand than to avoid overproduction.

   **Goal 2.** Achieve an average quality level of 98%.

   **Goal 3.** Minimize the total costs associated with all operations.

   Formulate the goal programming model for the problem that will indicate the number of units of the product to produce by each employment alternative.

**TABLE P12-7. Sneed Manufacturing**

|  | In-house Operations: | | Subcontracting | Temporary Employment |
|---|---|---|---|---|
|  | Regular | Overtime | | |
| Hours required | 4.0 | 4.0 | 5.0 | 6.0 |
| Cost per hour | $12.00 | $18.00 | 10.00 | 10.00 |
| Average quality level | 99% | 98% | 94% | 90% |

8. The Dixon Company is a wholesale merchandiser (i.e., the company buys from the manufacturer and sells to retail outlets). The company handles a single product and has limited capital on which to operate. Because the selling price of the product is somewhat seasonal, and thus can vary from month to month, it is to the advantage of the company to buy in some months for sale in later months. The firm has definite information concerning the cost at which it can buy and the price at which it can sell in the next four months. These data are as follows:

| Month | | | |
|---|---|---|---|
| 1 | 2 | 3 | 4 |
| Cost | 8 | 8 | 10 | 12 |
| Price | 12 | 10 | 7 | 9 |

Sales are made at the beginning of the month, followed by purchases. The quantity of the purchases is based entirely upon the revenue generated from sales. Purchases are restricted by the storage capacity of the firm; currently the firm can store 3000 units of the products (an additional 1000 units can be stored, but this is considered undesirable). Currently (beginning with month 1) there are 2000 units in the warehouse at $6 per unit. Management at Dixon's has identified the following goals (listed in order of importance).

**Goal 1.**  Only the normal capacity of the warehouse should be used in month 1.

**Goal 2.**  The company would like to hold at least $2000 in reserve, each month, for operational contingencies.

**Goal 3.**  At least $4000 should be available at the beginning of month 4, after purchases. This money will be used to meet an outside financial commitment.

**Goal 4.**  The company would like to maximize total profits over the entire four-month period.

Formulate a GP model for the problem that will indicate the quantity of the product that should be purchased each month in order to meet the above goals.

9. A major West Coast university has a large endowment fund; a funds manager has been assigned the responsibility of determining the "best" investment portfolio. The manager has decided that the funds can be fully invested in stocks, provided certain "risk policies" are employed. The manager has identified six acceptable stock alternatives. Data describing these alternatives are given in Table P12-9. Return on each of the investment alternatives is determined as follows:

$$\text{Return} = \frac{[\text{current price per share} \times \text{growth rate}] + [\text{dividends}]}{\text{current price per share}}$$

**TABLE P12-9. Stock Alternatives for Problem 9**

|  | Stock Number | | | | | |
|---|---|---|---|---|---|---|
|  | 1 | 2 | 3 | 4 | 5 | 6 |
| Current price per share | $90.00 | $25.00 | $70.00 | $125.00 | $35.00 | $140.00 |
| Av. annual growth rate | .09 | .08 | .06 | .04 | .03 | .01 |
| Av. annual dividend per share | $1.15 | $0.20 | $1.90 | $2.15 | $0.80 | $3.40 |
| Risk factor | .07 | .09 | .10 | .04 | .03 | .04 |

Currently, $1.5 million exist in the endowment. After careful evaluation of a number of different investment objectives the manager identified the following goals (listed in order of importance).

**Goal 1.**  Achieve a return on investment of at least 8%.

**Goal 2.**  Achieve a dividend goal of at least $18,000 per year.

**Goal 3.**  Invest at least 35% of the total dollars in the three stocks that have the lowest risk factors.

**Goal 4.**   Limit the weighted risk factor of the portfolio to 6% or less.

**Goal 5.**   Maximize the dollars invested in alternatives 1, 2, and 3.

**Goal 6.**   Limit the total dollars invested in the three low-risk alternatives to $700,000.

Formulate a goal programming model for the problem.

10. The Brooks Hall Investment Company problem was formulated as an LP model in Chapter 6. Formulate this problem as a goal programming model, given that management has specified the following set of goals.

**Goal 1.**   At least $50,000 should be invested in investment type 1 in years 1, 3, and 4.

**Goal 2.**   Meet a $50,000 financial obligation at the end of years 2 and 4. These monies will be withdrawn from the fund.

**Goal 3.**   Limit idle funds in any one year to $5,000.

**Goal 4.**   At least $100,000 should be invested in investment type 5.

**Goal 5.**   The company would like to maximize its total investment return at the end of year 6.

11. The TRC Publishing Company has four sales territories to which its salespersons are assigned. The company has found that sales are a function of salesperson-days per month. Data show that daily sales per salesperson-day are $2,000, $1600, $900, and $800, respectively, for the four territories.

**TABLE P12-11. Preference Index for TRC Publishing Company Sales Personnel**

| Salesperson | Territory | | | |
|---|---|---|---|---|
| | 1 | 2 | 3 | 4 |
| 1 | 5 | 4 | 2 | 2 |
| 2 | 4 | 3 | 5 | 1 |
| 3 | 3 | 5 | 0 | 2 |
| 4 | 5 | 4 | 1 | 3 |

The company has a four-person sales force; all salespersons work a 20-day month. Since all of the sales territories are in very close proximity, salespersons are not restricted to a single sales territory, rather the company requires that each salesperson work at least 2 territories. As an incentive for sales the company tries to honor each salesperson's preference for working given territories. The preference index in Table P12-11 (where 5 reflects top preference) reflects each salesperson's territory work preference. Management at TRC has established the following goals (listed in order of importance).

**Goal 1.**   Maximize sales.

**Goal 2.**   Maximize the weighted preference index for each salesperson, where the weighted index is the salesperson's index for a territory multiplied by the percentage of his/her time spent in the territory, summed over all territories visited.

**Goal 3.** At least 10 salesperson-days must be spent in each territory.

Formulate the GP model for the problem.

12. A certain Midwestern city is composed of three public school districts, each of which has a different proportion of resident black and white students. The city would like to develop a busing plan that will, to the greatest extent possible, balance the proportions of blacks and whites within the three school districts. Existing records indicate that the following numbers of black and white school-age children live within the respective districts:

| District | White | Black |
| --- | --- | --- |
| 1 | 22,049 | 3,165 |
| 2 | 22,590 | 8,700 |
| 3 | 6,980 | 13,215 |

In order to achieve balanced racial proportions within the districts, the Board of Education for the city has agreed to "overoccupy" any of the districts, if necessary. The Board has agreed that no district should be required to accommodate more than 110% of its "student capacity." Currently, the capacity levels for the respective districts are: 91.3%, 99.7%, and 109.6%. The cost associated with transporting a student between district 1 and district 2 is $42.10 per student per month. Between district 1 and district 3 the cost is $69.75 per student per month. A cost of $38.90 per student per month is incurred when any student is transported between district 2 and district 3. The Board has identified the following goals (listed in priority order):

**Goal 1.** Achieve a racial balance within the three districts. An acceptable balance would be one in which the proportions in each district are within ±.10 of the proportions for the combined school system.

**Goal 2.** Achieve, as close as possible, a balanced occupancy level within each district.

**Goal 3.** Achieve, as close as possible, an equal number of transfers from among the districts; that is, one district should not have a large percentage of transfers while another has a very small transfer ratio.

**Goal 4.** Minimize the transportation costs associated with the busing plan.

13. Given the following programming problem:

MINIMIZE:     $Z = P_1 d_1^- + P_2 d_4^+ + 5 P_3 d_2^- + 3 P_3 d_3^- + P_4 d_1^+$

SUBJECT TO:

$$x_1 + x_2 + d_1^- - d_1^+ \qquad\qquad\qquad = 40$$

$$x_1 \qquad\qquad + d_2^- \qquad\qquad = 30$$

$$x_2 \qquad\qquad + d_3^- \qquad\qquad = 30$$

$$x_1 + x_2 \qquad\qquad + d_4^- - d_4^+ = 50$$

$$x_1, x_2, d_1^-, d_1^+, d_2^-, d_3^-, d_4^-, d_4^+ \geq 0$$

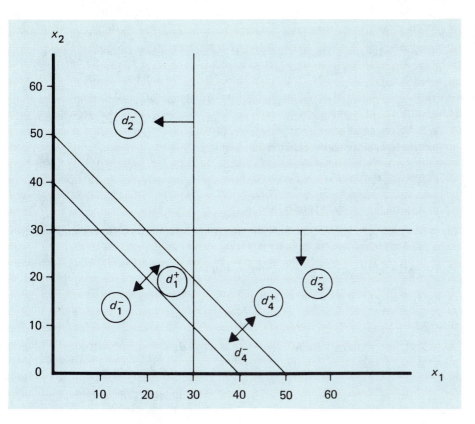

and the graph in Figure P12-13, identify the most satisfactory solution for the problem (that is, identify the values for the decision variables and the deviational variables). Explain your results.

14. Given the following goal programming problem: The E-Z Paint Company specializes in manufacturing two types of outdoor paints, a water-base and an enamel paint. The production of each 100 gallons of the water-base paint requires 10 hours of labor while each 100 gallons of enamel requires 15 hours of labor. Forty hours of labor are available weekly. Additional help is not available and overtime will not be employed. Both paints provide a profit of $1.00 per gallon. The owner of E-Z Paint has established the following goals:

> **Goal 1.**  Avoid overtime operations.
>
> **Goal 2.**  Achieve a weekly profit of $1000.
>
> **Goal 3.**  Produce at least 700 gallons of enamel paint per week.

And, given the following formulation of the problem,

MINIMIZE:        $Z = P_1 d_1^+ + P_2 d_2^- + P_3 d_3^-$

SUBJECT TO:
$$10x_1 + 15x_2 + d_1^- - d_1^+ = 40$$
$$100x_1 + 100x_2 + d_2^- - d_2^+ = 1000$$
$$x_2 + d_3^- - d_3^+ = 7$$
$$x_1, x_2, d_1^-, d_1^+, d_2^-, d_2^+, d_3^-, d_3^+, \geq 0$$

**a.** Solve graphically.

**b.** Solve graphically if the objective function is

$$P_1 d_2^- + P_2 d_1^+ + P_3 d_3^-$$

**c.** Explain the results in parts (a) and (b).

**15.** Solve Problem 1a graphically. Interpret the results. Solve the problem assuming priorities 1 and 3 are interchanged; explain the results.

**16.** Given the following goal programming problem:

MINIMIZE:
$$Z = P_1 d_1^+ + P_2 d_2^- + P_3 d_3^-$$

SUBJECT TO:
$$10x_1 + 15x_2 + d_1^- - d_1^+ = 40$$
$$100x_1 + 100x_2 + d_2^- - d_2^+ = 1000$$
$$x_2 + d_3^- - d_3^+ = 7$$
$$x_1, x_2, d_1^-, d_1^+, d_2^-, d_2^+, d_3^-, d_3^+ \geq 0$$

**a.** Solve graphically.

**b.** Solve using the GP-simplex algorithm.

**17.** Given the following goal programming problem:

MINIMIZE:
$$Z = P_1 d_4^+ + P_2 d_5^- + P_3 d_1^- + P_4(d_2^+ + d_3^+)$$

SUBJECT TO:
$$6x_1 + 4x_2 + d_1^- - d_1^+ = 100$$
$$2x_1 + x_2 + d_2^- - d_2^+ = 10$$
$$x_1 + x_2 + d_3^- - d_3^+ = 8$$
$$3x_1 + 2x_2 + d_4^- - d_4^+ = 34$$
$$x_2 + d_5^- = 7$$
$$x_1, x_2, d_1^-, d_1^+, d_2^-, d_2^+, d_3^-, d_3^+, d_4^-, d_4^+, d_5^- \geq 0$$

and the tableau in Table P12-17.

**a.** Interpret the results of this tableau. That is, what is the solution at this step; which goals have been met; what are the values of the decision variables?

**b.** If the solution in part (a) is not optimal, identify the incoming variable and the outgoing variable.

**c.** Interpret the goal trade-off that will occur if an additional tableau is computed.

**TABLE P12-17. Tableau for Problem 17**

| $c_B$ | Variable in the Basis | Right-hand Side (Solution) | $x_1$ | $x_2$ | $d_1^-$ | $d_1^+$ | $d_2^-$ | $d_2^+$ | $d_3^-$ | $d_3^+$ | $d_4^-$ | $d_4^+$ | $d_5^-$ |
|---|---|---|---|---|---|---|---|---|---|---|---|---|---|
| $c_j \rightarrow$ | | | 0 | 0 | $P_3$ | 0 | 0 | $P_4$ | 0 | $P_4$ | 0 | $P_1$ | $P_2$ |
| $P_3$ | $d_1^-$ | 66 | 0 | 0 | 1 | −1 | 0 | 0 | −6 | 6 | 0 | 0 | 2 |
| 0 | $d_2^-$ | 1 | 0 | 0 | 0 | 0 | 1 | −1 | −2 | 2 | 0 | 0 | 1 |
| 0 | $x_1$ | 1 | 1 | 0 | 0 | 0 | 0 | 0 | 1 | −1 | 0 | 0 | −1 |
| 0 | $d_4^-$ | 16 | 0 | 0 | 0 | 0 | 0 | 0 | 0 | 0 | 1 | 1 | −1 |
| 0 | $x_2$ | 7 | 0 | 1 | 0 | 0 | 0 | 0 | 0 | 0 | 0 | 0 | 1 |
| $z_j - c_j$ : $P_4$ | | 0 | 0 | 0 | 0 | 0 | 0 | −1 | 0 | −1 | 0 | 0 | 0 |
| $P_3$ | | 66 | 0 | 0 | 0 | −1 | 0 | 0 | −6 | 6 | 0 | 0 | 2 |
| $P_2$ | | 0 | 0 | 0 | 0 | 0 | 0 | 0 | 0 | 0 | 0 | 0 | −1 |
| $P_1$ | | 0 | 0 | 0 | 0 | 0 | 0 | 0 | 0 | 0 | 0 | −1 | 0 |

18. Mr. B. M. Higgins has $100,000 he wishes to invest so that his return on investment *each* year is maximized. Mr. Higgins has identified the investment alternatives and the dollar (ranges) he is willing to invest in each (see Table P12-18). Mr. Higgins contacted a financial analyst and asked for specific recommendations regarding his investments. After analyzing the problem, the analyst informed Mr. Higgins that it was impossible to meet the investment conditions, but that a close-as-possible solution could be identified if the investment conditions were to have priorities. After examining the investment alternatives, Mr. Higgins identified the following priority goals:

**Goal 1.** Satisfy as best possible the bond and savings account goals, taking into consideration that the savings account goal is twice as important as the bonds goal.

**Goal 2.** Meet the business venture goal if possible, i.e., provide at least $60,000.

**Goal 3.** Meet the mutual funds investment objective, if possible.

**Goal 4.** Achieve at least $8000 return on investments, if possible.

**TABLE P12-18. Investment Alternatives in Problem 18**

| Type of Investment | Return on Investment | Dollars to Be Invested |
|---|---|---|
| Bonds | 6% | At least $40,000 |
| Savings account (bank) | 5% | $10,000–$30,000 |
| Mutual funds | 8% | No more than $20,000 |
| Business venture | 7% | At least $60,000 |

**a.** Formulate an LP model of the problem to demonstrate why the analyst concluded that Mr. Higgins could not meet his initial investment objectives. Explain what would occur if one were to attempt to solve the LP problem.

**b.** Formulate the GP model for the problem. Solve the problem using a GP algorithm. Explain the results.

19. Solve Problem 4 using the GP–simplex algorithm. Interpret the results. What impact will occur if priorities 1 and 2 are switched?

# Integer Programming

## ■ Introduction

In Chapters 5 through 12 we discussed linear models. These models have satisfied a number of assumptions discussed in Chapter 5. Briefly these assumptions are additivity, proportionality, divisibility, and nonnegativity. The third assumption, divisibility, implies that fractional solutions to linear problems are permissible. Obviously, there will exist situations where all of the above assumptions except divisibility will hold. In these cases, integer solutions rather than fractional solutions are required by the circumstances surrounding the problem. Up to now we have largely ignored the fact that in some of the linear programming problems we have formulated integer solutions would be required.

An example of a linear programming problem that could be required to have integer rather than fractional solutions is the Hickory Desk Company production problem in Chapter 6. In this problem we formulated the production of two types of desks as an LP problem. Obviously, desks cannot be produced in fractional parts. The problem is an integer programming problem, because the solution must be in discrete values.

Since many problems fit all of the assumptions of linear programming with the exception of the requirement of integer solutions, a large body of knowledge has developed that addresses this type of problem. This field of study is called integer programming. Unfortunately, except for rare problems and the broad class of problems known as networks, linear programming will not be guaranteed to yield integer solutions. And since no one algorithm, such as the simplex method, has been developed to solve an integer programming problem, a large portion of the work in integer programming (IP) has been directed toward developing better ways of solving IP problems. Much of this work is beyond the scope of this text, so we will concentrate our discussion on formulating integer programming problems. We will give examples of the three generic types of IP problems and then discuss several well-known problems that have been investigated in some depth. Finally, we will discuss solution procedures for IP problems. As usual we begin our discussion with a case.

## ■ Case
# JCL, Inc.

JCL, Inc., is involved in the development and production of minicomputers for use by businesses. Fred Wilson, the Vice-President for Planning and Research for JCL, is considering five possible research projects. Each of these projects has potential as a big profit maker for JCL, but each is also fairly expensive. Table 13-1 shows the forecasted profit potential and development cost for each of the five projects.

While JCL would like to maximize the profit potential, the company is constrained by having only $9 million available for research and development. The projects under consideration are such that partial development of a project is not allowed. That is, if a project is chosen for development, then the total development funds for the project must be allocated.

Fred Wilson must determine which projects to develop. Clearly, not all of the projects can be developed since the sum of the costs is $18 million, which is greater than the $9 million available for research and development. He realizes that the problem has some aspects of linear programming, but the requirement that projects be completely funded or not funded at all seems to preclude the use of linear programming.

Since Fred did not immediately see a way to formulate and solve this problem to find a maximum profit allocation of funds, he called Patti Winkler of the Management Science Department to see if she had any ideas. Patti has an MBA with a specialization in Management Science and had done a good bit of development in mathematical programming software packages for JCL.

Patti agreed to look at the problem. That same afternoon, Fred went down to Patti's office and explained his problem. She immediately got a big smile on her face and said, "I think I can handle this one. It belongs to a well-known class of problems known as knapsack problems and involves the use of integer-valued variables."

"Is it like linear programming?" asked Fred, trying to sound knowledgeable.

"Quite a bit," said Patti, "The formulation process is very much the same, and LP is often used as part of the solution process. However, we don't have a single algorithm that solves all such problems as the simplex method does for LP."

"How do we solve such a problem?" asked Fred.

"First, let's formulate your problem. Then we'll use some integer programming software I've been working on to find a solution. We'll use a special type of integer variables, namely, the values zero and one, in our formulation."

"Why zero and one?" interrupted Fred.

"We'll let a variable be one if that project is chosen and zero if not. No fractional values will be allowed since its all or nothing for each project. If we use zero–one variables, then the formulation is fairly easy to see."

Patti then went to her blackboard and wrote the following formulation of Fred's problem:

MAXIMIZE:

$$Z = 12x_1 + 15x_2 + 8x_3 + 5x_4 + 11x_5$$

SUBJECT TO:

$$2x_1 + 5x_2 + 4x_3 + 1x_4 + 6x_5 \leq 9$$
$$x_1, x_2, x_3, x_4, x_5 = 0 \text{ or } 1$$

"Why, except for the last line, that looks just like the LP problem we discussed in my last executive development class!"

"That's right," grinned Patti, "it is like LP except

**TABLE 13-1. Profit and Cost Data for JCL, Inc.**

| Project | Profit Potential | Development Cost |
|---------|------------------|------------------|
| A | $12 million | $2 million |
| B | 15 million | 5 million |
| C | 8 million | 4 million |
| D | 5 million | 1 million |
| E | 11 million | 6 million |

for the zero–one variables. They make a big difference, though! I'll run this on the computer and get back to you with a solution tomorrow."

"Great!" exclaimed Fred, "I appreciate your help on this. Maybe you could look at a few other projects I've been working on recently."

"Anytime," said Patti, as visions of managerial opportunities came to her mind.

........................................................................................................................................

# ■ Overview of integer programming

The JCL case is a good example of a problem where integer solutions are required. In many such problems, the structure is much like linear programming except that some or all of the decision variables are constrained to take on only integer solutions. Before discussing the JCL case, we will look at various types of IP problems. To understand what the integer requirement does to the geometry of the problem, consider the following example:

MAXIMIZE: $\quad Z = 3x_1 + 5x_2$ $\hfill (13.1)$

SUBJECT TO: $\quad 5x_1 + 8x_2 \leq 20$ $\hfill (13.2)$

$\qquad x_1, x_2 \leq 0$ and integer $\hfill (13.3)$

Except for the requirement that the variables be integers, this is a linear programming problem. The effect of the integer requirement can be seen in Figure 13-1. In this figure, we have marked the integer points with a + and/or have given their coordinates. These points are often referred to as **lattice points.** Note that the lattice point $(0, 3)$ is not feasible since it does not fall within the LP feasible region (the shaded area in Figure 13-1). Similarly, all points that are linear programming feasible but are not lattice points are also not IP feasible. So for a point to be IP feasible, it must satisfy the linear programming constraints *and* be a lattice point. In this case, this criterion is met by points A through I as shown in Table 13-2 (the objective value is also shown for each feasible point). The optimal LP solution is found at the point $(0, 2.5)$ that has a Z value of 12.5. However, if we refer to the list of feasible lattice points above, we find that the optimal integer programming solution does not occur anywhere near the optimal LP solution. In fact, the optimal IP solution occurs at the lattice point $(4, 0)$, which has a Z value of 12.

*lattice points*

## *Comparison of integer and linear programming*

The previous example serves to point up several important differences between linear and integer programming. To understand some of these differences better, it is first necessary to discuss the difference between a **global optimum** and a **local optimum.** A global optimum is the best solution (highest or lowest, as the case may be) of all feasible solutions. A local optimum, on the other hand, is the best solution when compared only with feasible solutions within close proximity. In linear programming, the simplex algorithm always finds the global optimum because the proportionality assumption guarantees that there are no local optima. However, in

*global optimum*
*local optimum*

**FIGURE 13-1.**
**Geometry of an IP**
**Problem**

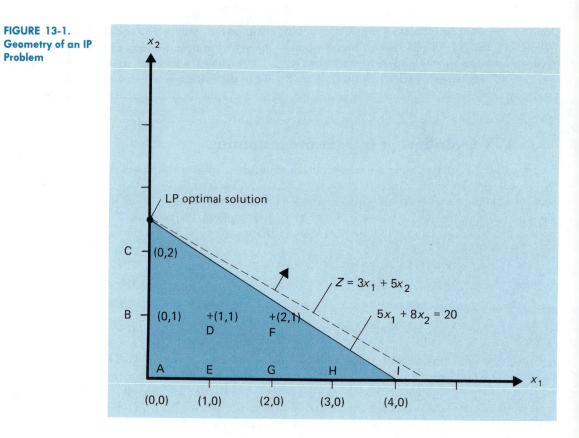

integer programming, there are often numerous local optima that must be considered in the search for a global optimum.

In our example, consider point F. If we were to compare this point only with other feasible points close to it (that is, points D, E, G, and H), we would find that F has the

**TABLE 13-2.**
**Feasible Lattice**
**Points**

| Point | Variable $x_1$ | $x_2$ | Objective Value |
|-------|------|------|-----------------|
| A | 0 | 0 | 0 |
| B | 0 | 1 | 5 |
| C | 0 | 2 | 10 |
| D | 1 | 1 | 8 |
| E | 1 | 0 | 3 |
| F | 2 | 1 | 11 |
| G | 2 | 0 | 6 |
| H | 3 | 0 | 9 |
| I | 4 | 0 | 12 |

highest objective value. Therefore, point F is a *local optimum*. But if F is compared with all feasible points, we find that *point I*, rather than point F, is the *global optimum*. Searching for a global optimum is one factor that makes integer programming problems much *more* difficult to solve than corresponding linear programming problems. While there exist computer codes that will solve linear programming problems with several thousand variables, the largest integer programming problems (with the exception of a few specially structured problems) that can currently be solved have *only* a few hundred variables.

The ease of solution for linear programming problems arises because the simplex method allows one to pivot until the global optimal solution is reached. Once this optimal point has been reached, any additional pivoting will *always* lead to a solution with a less desirable objective value. On the other hand, there exists no procedure comparable to the simplex method for solving integer programming problems. For an IP problem, usually it is necessary to *search* among the local optimal solutions to find a global optimal solution, and the searching process can take a large amount of time and effort. The best known and most efficient search procedure is called **branch and bound.** Solution procedures will be discussed further in a later section of this chapter. First, however, we will discuss types of IP problems and their formulations.

*branch and bound*

# ■ Types of integer programming problems

Integer programming problems may be divided into three main categories according to the type of variables or combination of variables used to formulate the problem. These are (1) *general integer programming problems;* (2) *binary or 0–1 integer programming problems;* and (3) *mixed integer programming problems.* We will discuss each type briefly.

### *General integer programming problems*

The variables in general integer programming problems must all take on integer values. The integer variables may have upper and lower bounds, but they are not restricted to a specific subset of values, and usually there is no special structure to the problem. Some of the linear programming problems discussed in Chapters 5–8 are really general integer programming problems since the variables should take on integer values. In general, any linear programming problem that requires the variables to take on discrete values is a general integer programming problem.

### *Binary integer programming problems*

Binary or 0–1 integer programming problems have variables that are restricted to only the values 0 or 1. By having 0–1 variables, we are in essence modeling all-or-nothing or go–no-go situations. This type of problem is very important because all-or-nothing situations are very common in such areas as capital budgeting, site selection, and scheduling. The JCL, Inc., case in this chapter is an example of a binary integer programming problem.

### Mixed integer programming problems

Problems in which some but not all variables are required to be integer are referred to as mixed integer programming problems. These problems allow the mixing of integer and continuous variables. The integer variables may be either *general integer* or *binary integer* variables depending on the situation being modeled.

## ■ Examples of integer programming problems

Now we will present examples to illustrate each type integer programming problem. In each case, we will discuss which type of problem the scenario represents and show how the variables are used to model the situation given in the scenario.

■ **Example**

## *Cross Country Airlines*

Due to a ticket price war, demand for tickets on Cross Country Airlines has grown greatly over the last few months. Demand has grown so much that the airline now intends to purchase several new planes. There are three types of aircraft from which to choose, the DC-33, the Boeing 797, and the Lockheed Bi-Star. The cost, capacity, and required maintenance time per month for each type are shown in Table 13-3. Cross Country wishes to buy the new planes at the minimum possible cost, subject to capacity and maintenance time requirements. The new planes must carry a combined total of at least 3400 passengers and have a combined total maintenance time of no more than 250 hours per month. The decision as to which planes to purchase is further complicated by the availability of only five Bi-Stars for purchase by Cross Country.

■ **Formulation**

This problem is much like a linear programming problem except that the variables must take on integer values. There is no way to purchase a part of an airplane or to carry over the purchase to another time period to circumvent the integer requirement. In this case, a *whole* number of aircraft must be bought at one time. Thus we have an integer programming problem.

To formulate the problem, let

$x_1$ = number of DC-33's purchased

$x_2$ = number of B-797's purchased

$x_3$ = number of Bi-Stars purchased

Since our objective is to minimize total purchase cost, the objective function becomes

MINIMIZE:    $Z = 10x_1 + 15x_2 + 12x_3$                    (13.4)

| Aircraft | Cost ($000,000) | Capacity | Maintenance Time (hrs./mos.) |
|----------|-----------------|----------|------------------------------|
| DC-33 | 10 | 350 | 25 |
| Boeing 797 | 15 | 450 | 15 |
| Lockheed Bi-Star | 12 | 400 | 15 |

**TABLE 13-3.**
**Aircraft Data**

The requirements on capacity and maintenance time per month can be formulated as:

CAPACITY REQUIREMENT:        $350x_1 + 450x_2 + 400x_3 \geq 3400$                     (13.5)

MAINTENANCE TIME:        $25x_1 + 15x_2 + 15x_3 \leq 250$                     (13.6)

In addition, we must include the Bi-Star availability in the model:

$$x_3 \leq 5 \tag{13.7}$$

Finally, we have the nonnegativity conditions *and* the integrality requirements:

$$x_1, x_2, x_3 \geq 0 \text{ and integer} \tag{13.8}$$

As a whole, the problem can be stated as

MINIMIZE:        $Z = 10x_1 + 15x_2 + 12x_3$                     (13.4)

SUBJECT TO:        $350x_1 + 450x_2 + 400x_3 \geq 3400$                     (13.5)

$25x_1 + 15x_2 + 15x_3 \leq 250$                     (13.6)

$x_3 \leq 5$                     (13.7)

$x_1, x_2, x_3 \geq 0 \text{ and integer}$                     (13.8)

This is an example of a general integer programming problem since there are only integer variables *and* the integer variables are *not* restricted to be 0 or 1.

■ **Example**

## *The Ferguson Company*

The Ferguson Company wishes to choose the most profitable combination of projects from among several alternative projects, subject to a limited source of capital. There are four possible projects that need to be funded over four years. The pertinent data are shown in Table 13-4.

Because a project can be either undertaken or not, with nothing in between, the problem is a *0–1 or binary integer programming problem*. This approach to the problem yields the following formulation:

MAXIMIZE:        $Z = 180,000x_1 + 20,000x_2 + 72,000x_3 + 80,000x_4$                     (13.9)

SUBJECT TO:        $30,000x_1 + 12,000x_2 + 30,000x_3 + 20,000x_{4_4} \leq 65,000$                     (13.10)

$40,000x_1 + 8,000x_2 + 20,000x_3 + 40,000x_4 \leq 80,000$                     (13.11)

$40,000x_1 \qquad\qquad + 20,000x_3 + 40,000x_4 \leq 80,000$                     (13.12)

$$30,000x_1 + 4,000x_2 + 20,000x_3 + 10,000x_4 \leq 50,000 \qquad (13.13)$$

where $\qquad x_j = \begin{cases} 1 \text{ if project } j \text{ is selected} \\ 0 \text{ otherwise} \end{cases} \quad j = 1, 2, 3, 4 \qquad (13.14)$

In this formulation the objective function is the sum of the estimated net present values for each project, while each constraint relates to the availability of capital funds for each year.

The use of **binary variables** (0–1) in this formulation ensures either complete funding or rejection of a project.

*binary variables*

| Project | Estimated Net Present Value | Capital Requirements | | | |
|---|---|---|---|---|---|
| | | Year 1 | Year 2 | Year 3 | Year 4 |
| Plant expansion | $180,000 | $30,000 | $40,000 | $40,000 | $30,000 |
| New machinery | 20,000 | 12,000 | 8,000 | 0 | 4,000 |
| New product research | 72,000 | 30,000 | 20,000 | 20,000 | 20,000 |
| Warehouse expansion | 80,000 | 20,000 | 40,000 | 40,000 | 10,000 |
| Available capital funds | | $65,000 | $80,000 | $80,000 | $50,000 |

**TABLE 13-4.
Ferguson
Company Values**

## ■ Example
### *Agro-Tech Inc. Revisited*

Recall from Chapters 5 and 8 that we discussed a situation where Agro Tech Inc. was seeking to determine a product mix that maximized contribution to profit. In the final formulation in Chapter 8, the production manager, Tom Anderson, was attempting to determine production levels of 5-5-10, 5-10-5, and 5-5-5 fertilizers subject to limited availabilities of the raw materials (nitrate, phosphate, and potash). This problem was formulated as a linear programming problem as follows:

MAXIMIZE: $\qquad Z = 18.5x_1 + 20x_2 + 14.5x_3 \qquad (13.15)$

SUBJECT TO: $\qquad .05x_1 + .05x_2 + .05x_3 \leq 1100 \qquad (13.16)$

$\qquad .05x_1 + .10x_2 + .05x_3 \leq 1800 \qquad (13.17)$

$\qquad .10x_1 + .05x_2 + .05x_3 \leq 2000 \qquad (13.18)$

$$x_1, x_2, x_3 \geq 0$$

where $\qquad x_1 = \text{tons of 5-5-10 produced}$
$\qquad x_2 = \text{tons of 5-10-5 produced}$
$\qquad x_3 = \text{tons of 5-5-5 produced}$

In this problem, the optimal LP solution yielded a product mix of 8000 tons of 5-5-10 ($x_1$), 14,000 tons of 5-10-5 ($x_2$), and none of the 5-5-5 ($x_3$). However, let us now add a restriction that complicates Mr. Anderson's planning process. He has been reminded that the company had recently produced fertilizers only in batches of 10,000 tons or more. The current solution is no longer allowable since it proposed to produce only 8,000 tons of 5-5-10. How then could the problem be reformulated to account for the batch-size restriction?

We can resolve this issue by using integer variables. If we let $M_j$ be an upper bound on the production of product $x_j$ and $L_j$ be the corresponding batch size (lower bound), then the addition of the following two constraints per variable will force the production of amounts greater than or equal to the batch size *or no* production at all:

$$x_j - M_j y_j \leq 0 \tag{13.19}$$

$$x_j - L_j y_j \geq 0 \tag{13.20}$$

where        $y_j = 0$ or 1.

If $y_j = 0$, then $x_j = 0$ for both constraints. If $y_j = 1$, the first constraint is no longer binding and the second constraint becomes

$$x_j \geq L_j \tag{13.21}$$

which forces at least a batch-size production.

In our problem, $L_j = 10,000$ for all variables. We can calculate the $M_j$ values for each variable by letting all other variables be zero and computing the maximum value for the variable under study. (This approach will not work if there are any negative $a_{ij}$ coefficients.) For example, $M_1$ may be found by computing the minimum ratio for $x_1$ under all constraints, that is,

$$M_1 = \min \{1,100/.05, 1,800/.05, 2,000/.10\}$$

$$= \min \{22,000, 36,000, 20,000\}$$

$$= 20,000$$

Also, we can use similar reasoning to find

$$M_2 = \min \{1,100/.05, 1,800/.10, 2,000/.05\}$$

$$= \min \{22,000, 18,000, 40,000\}$$

$$= 18,000$$

and

$$M_3 = \min \{1,100/.05, \ 1,800/.05, \ 2,000/.05\}$$

$$= \min \{22,000, \ 36,000, \ 40,000\}$$

$$= 22,000$$

We now add two new constraints for each variable to arrive at a new formulation that includes the batch-size requirements:

| | | |
|---|---|---|
| MAXIMIZE: | $Z = 18.5x_1 + 20x_2 + 14.5x_3$ | (13.22) |
| SUBJECT TO: | $.05x_1 + .05x_2 + .05x_3 \qquad\qquad\qquad \leq 1,100$ | (13.23) |
| | $.05x_1 + .10x_2 + .05x_3 \qquad\qquad\qquad \leq 1,800$ | (13.24) |
| | $.10x_1 + .05x_2 + .05x_3 \qquad\qquad\qquad \leq 2,000$ | (13.25) |
| | $x_1 \qquad\qquad - 20,000y_1 \qquad\qquad\quad \leq 0$ | (13.26) |
| | $x_1 \qquad\qquad - 10,000y_1 \qquad\qquad\quad \geq 0$ | (13.27) |
| | $x_2 \qquad\qquad - 18,000y_2 \qquad\quad \leq 0$ | (13.28) |
| | $x_2 \qquad\qquad - 10,000y_2 \qquad\quad \geq 0$ | (13.29) |
| | $x_3 \qquad\qquad - 22,000y_3 \leq 0$ | (13.30) |
| | $x_3 \qquad\qquad - 10,000y_3 \geq 0$ | (13.31) |
| | $x_1, x_2, x_3 \geq 0$ | (13.32) |
| | $y_1, y_2, y_3 = 0 \text{ or } 1$ | (13.33) |

## ▪ Specific problems

In integer programming, many of the problems that arise in actual applications have certain basic similarities in their structure. While these problems can be classified according to the generic categories mentioned earlier, they occur so often that they are treated as special cases. Also, since they seem to occur in many different situations, special algorithms, that are much more efficient than a general-purpose integer programming algorithm have been developed to solve these special cases. For this reason, it is very important that one be able to recognize the special structures of these cases rather than group all integer programming problems together. The ability to *recognize* a special problem and use the right solution procedure can mean the difference between solving or not solving a given problem.

In general, a discussion of these specialized algorithms is beyond the scope of this text.

## El Cheapo Grocery Store

Leonard Myers is the manager of the El Cheapo Grocery Store. At present, he is considering using 50 square feet of shelf space for various tobacco displays. The displays take up different amounts of shelf space and Myers would be paid differing amounts for each display by the tobacco companies. Leonard wishes to maximize his income from the tobacco companies while not using more than the allotted 50 square feet of display space.

The potential payments from each tobacco company and the required shelf space are given in Table 13-5. In formulating this problem, we should note several characteristics. First, it is an all-or-nothing problem, since partial displays are not possible. Second, it is impossible to provide space for all of the displays; therefore, Myers must choose the most beneficial displays. Finally, we have a single objective function and a single constraint.

The formulation must begin with a definition of the variables. If we let

$$x_j = \begin{cases} 1 \text{ if product } j \text{ is displayed} \\ 0 \text{ if product } j \text{ is not displayed} \end{cases}$$

then our objective function becomes

MAXIMIZE:        $Z = 100x_1 + 75x_2 + 115x_3 + 50x_4 + 135x_5$        (13.34)

and the constraint is

$$17x_1 + 15x_2 + 20x_3 + 15x_4 + 20x_5 \le 50 \tag{13.35}$$

The complete problem is then

MAXIMIZE:        $Z = 100x_1 + 75x_2 + 115x_3 + 50x_4 + 135x_5$        (13.34)

SUBJECT TO:        $17x_1 + 15x_2 + 20x_3 + 15x_4 + 20x_5 \le 50$        (13.35)

each $x_j = 0$ or $1$        (13.36)

**TABLE 13-5.
Values for El
Cheapo Grocery**

| Product No. | Tobacco Co. | Payments ($) | Space Required (square feet) |
|---|---|---|---|
| 1 | Puffo | 100 | 17 |
| 2 | Hack & Hack | 75 | 15 |
| 3 | L. Porrilland | 115 | 20 |
| 4 | Krogo | 50 | 15 |
| 5 | Browntooth | 135 | 20 |

Problems of this type, that is, with binary variables and a single constraint, are known as **binary knapsack problems.** The name comes from the concept of a hiker who wishes to fill a knapsack (pack) of limited size with as many items as possible, where each item has a different weight (or volume) and value to the hiker.

*binary knapsack problems*

Knapsack problems are important for several reasons. First, several other integer programming problems have been expressed as knapsack problems, enabling the solution procedure derived for knapsack problems to be applied to other integer programming problems. Also, knapsack problems have been embedded in procedures to help solve various other problems. This has been done since solution procedures for knapsack problems are quite efficient—for example, problems with 1000 variables have been solved on a modern computer in less than 2 seconds.

## Capital budgeting problems

If a problem has all the characteristics of a knapsack problem *except* that it has more than one constraint, it is often referred to as a **capital budgeting problem.** The name comes from the fact that problems of this type often occur in the allocation of capital (or any funds for development) to various projects. Capital budgeting may involve building projects, research projects, or any situation where funds must be allocated to a project in a lump sum. Under capital budgeting, projects may not be funded partially.

*capital budgeting problem*

The various types of capital can refer to either funding available at different time periods or the availability of some resource that must be used in lump amounts, say, manpower.

An example of a capital budgeting problem is the Ferguson Company problem formulated earlier in this chapter as equations (13-9)–(13-14).

## Revised diet problem

Consider again the diet problem from Chapter 6. Recall that in this problem our objective was to determine a minimum-cost food mixture that would meet certain dietary standards. In that problem we assumed that the only costs were ingredient costs. However, ordering costs may also be a factor. In general, ordering costs may vary from ingredient to ingredient depending upon the ordering procedure. Let us assume that in this problem, the ordering costs for the food sources are $5.00 and $7.50, respectively. The costs do not depend on how much food is ordered, but rather on the fact that an order is placed.

For this problem, the pertinent information is given in Table 13-6. Our objective is to determine the number of ounces of each food source that should be ordered so that the required units of each nutrient are met at a minimum total cost. If we let

$x_1$ = number of ounces of food source #1 used

$x_2$ = number of ounces of food source #2 used

$y_1$ = 1 if food source #1 is used, 0 otherwise

$y_2$ = 1 if food source #2 is used, 0 otherwise

TABLE 13-6.
Diet Information
for Senora
Hospital

|  | Units of Nutrients in Food Source #1 | Units of Nutrients in Food Source #2 | Required Units of Nutrients |
|---|---|---|---|
| Nutrient A | 100 | 200 | 1000 |
| B | 400 | 250 | 2000 |
| C | 200 | 200 | 1500 |
| Cost per ounce for food source | $0.375 | $0.50 | |
| Ordering costs for food source | $5.00 | $7.50 | |

then the formulation is

MINIMIZE:

$$.375x_1 + .50x_2 + 5y_1 + 7.50y_2 \qquad (13.37)$$

SUBJECT TO:

$$100x_1 + 200x_2 \geq 1000 \qquad (13.38)$$

$$400x_1 + 250x_2 \geq 2000 \qquad (13.39)$$

$$200x_1 + 200x_2 \geq 1500 \qquad (13.40)$$

$$x_1 \leq M_1 y_1 \qquad (13.41)$$

$$x_2 \leq M_2 y_2 \qquad (13.42)$$

$$x_1, x_2 \qquad \geq 0 \quad \text{and} \quad y_1, y_2 = 0 \text{ or } 1 \qquad (13.43)$$

In this formulation, $M_1$ and $M_2$ are upper bounds on the use of food sources #1 and #2, respectively (these may be a part of the statement of the problem or an arbitrarily large value may be used).

Note that the first three constraints are linear programming constraints while the last two constraints serve to tie the continuous and 0–1 variables together. If an $x_j$ is positive, then the corresponding $y_j$ is forced to take on a positive value to satisfy these constraints. This type of problem is referred to as the **fixed charge** problem.

*fixed charge*

In a fixed charge problem, there is a conditional relationship between a set of continuous (LP) variables and a set of binary (0–1) variables. This problem can occur in situations like our example, or in production problems where both a *per-unit* cost and a *setup* cost is incurred. Setup costs occur due to the cost of making a machine ready for production or ordering a batch of given ingredients, and are incurred only if a product is produced. The cost structure for a fixed charge problem is shown graphically in Figure 13-2.

Note that this cost structure differs from a standard LP problem in that there is a discontinuity in the objective function caused by the setup cost.

A special case of the fixed charge problem is the *fixed charge transportation problem*, which is simply a transportation problem with lump-sum charges on one or more routes in addition to the continuous costs on the routes. If any positive amount

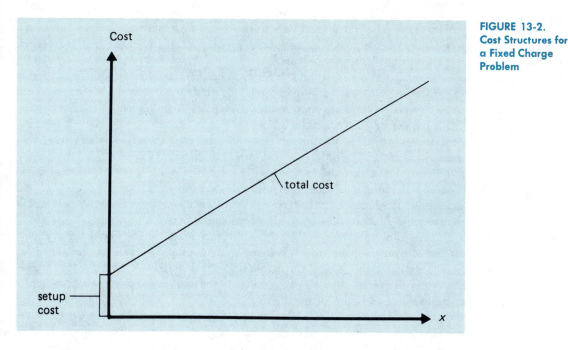

**FIGURE 13-2.**
**Cost Structures for a Fixed Charge Problem**

is shipped over a route having a fixed charge, then the entire fixed charge must be paid. This problem has a network structure, so we could employ the network formulation process of Chapter 11 to address the problem.

## Jones Cigar Company

Dave Renfro, a salesman for the Jones Cigar Company, is based in Tampa and must travel to four other cities in Florida each week before returning home. The cities and their distances from Tampa and from each other are given in Table 13-7.

Not wishing to travel any further than necessary, Dave wants to find the shortest route to travel so that each city is visited before he returns home. Dave considers it inefficient to visit any city more than once each week, so the route chosen must take this restraint into account.

Dave Renfro's problem belongs to a broad class of integer programming problems known as *scheduling-problems*. This class of problems, as the name implies, involves determining the best sequence or schedule of activities. The term *best* can refer to cost, time, distance, or some other criterion that one wishes to minimize. The

**TABLE 13-7.**
**Inter-city Distances**

|              | Tampa | Jacksonville | Ft. Myers | Miami | Orlando |
|--------------|-------|--------------|-----------|-------|---------|
| Tampa        | —     | 194          | 125       | 268   | 83      |
| Jacksonville | —     | —            | 319       | 349   | 145     |
| Ft. Myers    | —     | —            | —         | 143   | 208     |
| Miami        | —     | —            | —         | —     | 236     |

*traveling
salesman
problems*

activities can be tasks that must be performed on one or more machines, or the cities to be visited by salesmen. This last situation is the one discussed here and is referred to as **traveling salesman problems.**

In general, the objective of a traveling salesman problem is to determine the least-distance route that a salesman can take so that he/she leaves a home city, visits each of several other cities *once and only once*, and then returns to the home city. Such a sequence of visits to cities is referred to as a *tour*. If the salesman visits a city more than once or returns to the home city before visiting all other cities, this involves a *subtour*. The difference is shown in Figure 13-3.

In Figure 13-3a, the salesman traces a tour from "Home" to A–B–C–D–E–Home. Figure 13-3b shows a salesman who returns home after visiting cities A, B, and C and *then* visits cities E and D in that order. The second case involves two subtours and is not a feasible solution to the traveling salesman problem.

The traveling salesman problem may be formulated mathematically as a 0–1 integer network problem, but it is much more common to see it formulated in a manner similar to the personnel assignment problem as discussed in Chapter 11. The city-to-city distances are placed in a table with the tour requirement being implicitly understood as part of the formulation.

Using this approach, Dave's problem (visiting each city once and only once while traveling the minimum possible distance) is formulated in Table 13-8. In this formulation, the cities on the left are considered cities to be traveled from (origins) while the cities across the top are destinations. Note that we have used a distance of infinity for a city to itself. This insures that the traveler does not return to the city just visited by making that choice too expensive. Note also that this is a symmetric traveling salesman problem since distances between cities remain constant whether coming from or going to a city. Later we will look at an asymmetric problem.

**FIGURE 13-3.
Traveling Sales-
man Travel Routes**

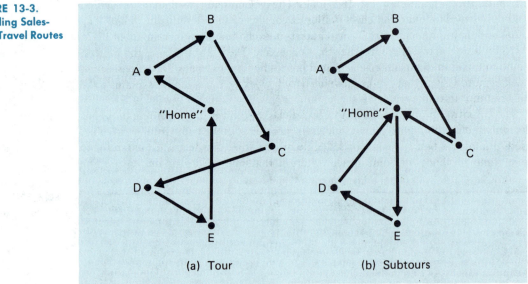

(a)  Tour                    (b)  Subtours

| Origin City | Destination City | | | | |
|---|---|---|---|---|---|
| | *Tampa* | *Jacksonville* | *Ft. Myers* | *Miami* | *Orlando* |
| Tampa | ∞ | 194 | 125 | 268 | 83 |
| Jacksonville | 194 | ∞ | 319 | 349 | 145 |
| Ft. Myers | 125 | 319 | ∞ | 143 | 208 |
| Miami | 268 | 349 | 143 | ∞ | 236 |
| Orlando | 83 | 145 | 208 | 236 | ∞ |

**TABLE 13-8.**
**Traveling Salesman Formulation**

The traveling salesman problem is also an example of a *combinational problem,* so named because a large number of combinations could possibly be optimal. Recall that there were $n!$ solutions for the personnel assignment problem; for the traveling salesman problem, there will exist $(n - 1)!$ solutions for an $n$-city problem. The difference occurs because the solution must start at some origin city. For Dave Renfro's problem, there will be $(5 - 1)! = 24$ possible solutions. The factorial (!) function increases very rapidly as $n$ increases. For example, if $n = 11$ cities, then $(n - 1)! = 3,628,800$ possible solutions!

## Christopher Paint Company

While the original application of the traveling salesman problem was to problems such as the one discussed above, recent work has shown that many other problems can be formulated as traveling salesman problems. For example, consider a company that uses a mixing machine to mix different types of paints and stains. The machine must be cleaned thoroughly between paint jobs to avoid contamination of succeeding paint jobs, and the cleaning time depends to a large degree upon the order in which the paints are used. For example, if a latex-based paint is used prior to an oil-based paint, the cleanup time may be shorter than vice versa. If a series of paint jobs with different types of paint must be completed using the same painting machine, the sequence of paint jobs will have an effect on the total time to complete all jobs. In this way, the problem becomes a traveling salesman problem.

As an example, consider the Christopher Paint Company, which has a contract for a series of paint jobs using a high-speed paint machine. The jobs are labeled A–D in Table 13-9. The table gives the cleanup times (expressed in minutes) for all possible orders of jobs. In this case, the objective is to minimize the sum of the cleanup times

| Job | Job | | | |
|---|---|---|---|---|
| | *A* | *B* | *C* | *D* |
| A | — | 30 | 15 | 40 |
| B | 25 | — | 45 | 20 |
| C | 35 | 15 | — | 30 |
| D | 20 | 50 | 25 | — |

**TABLE 13-9.**
**Job Cleanup Times**

by selecting the best sequence of paint jobs. Note that this is an example of an *asymmetric traveling salesman problem* since the "distances" depend on the direction traveled.

## ■ Solution procedures

There are five primary procedures for solving integer programming problems. We will discuss all five briefly. Whenever possible, we will use our original example to demonstrate the procedure.

The five solution procedures are:

1.   graphical methods
2.   rounding-off the LP optimal solution
3.   complete enumeration
4.   cutting planes
5.   branch and bound

### *Graphical methods*

Graphical methods may be of some use in solving problems with two integer variables. As with LP, solving an IP problem graphically involves a four-step process, the first three steps are identical to those for LP, but the fourth step differs. These steps are:

1.   State the problem mathematically.
2.   Graph or "plot" the constraints.
3.   Graph the objective function.
4.   Solve for the values of the lattice point variables having the highest profit.

The fourth step requires that the objective function be moved outward until the lattice point for the highest profit that is also LP feasible is found. No longer do we look solely at the vertices of the LP feasible region; we must also consider the lattice points inside the LP feasible region.

To illustrate this process, we will solve our initial example by a graphical approach. Recall that this problem had the following mathematical formulation:

MAXIMIZE:     $Z = 3x_1 + 5x_2$                                           (13.1)

SUBJECT TO:     $5x_1 + 8x_2 \leq 20$                                      (13.2)

$x_1, x_2 \geq 0$ and integer                                             (13.3)

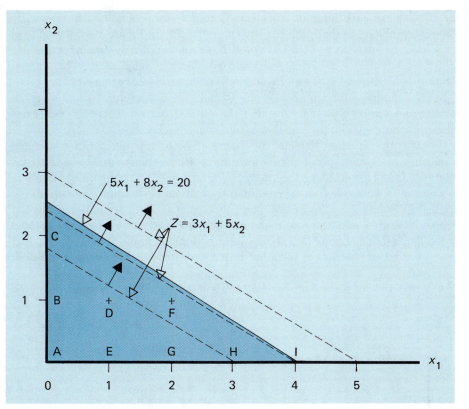

FIGURE 13-4.
Graphical Solution

In Figure 13-4 we have plotted the constraint for this problem and have placed a series of iso-profit lines on the graph with values of 9, 12, and 15, respectively. We have also shown the lattice points for this problem. From this we may see that the LP optimal solution occurs at the vertex having coordinates of $x_1 = 0$ and $x_2 = 2.5$ for a value of $Z = 12.5$. We can also see that an iso-profit line having value $Z = 12$ passes through the lattice point $x_1 = 4$, $x_2 = 0$ (point I). Since this is the highest iso-profit line that passes through a lattice point, the optimal IP solution must be $x_1 = 4$, $x_2 = 0$ for $Z = 12$.

## Rounding off the LP optimal solution

The term *rounding off*, when applied to integer programming problems, refers to using the integer part of a linear programming solution as the solution to the integer programming problem. The usual approach is to attempt to remain feasible by rounding down if the problem is a maximization problem and rounding up for minimization problems. While rounding is a very common procedure for solving practical integer programming problems, in certain cases it can lead to difficulties.

First, there will be some cases where the rounded LP solution will not be optimal for the integer programming problem. Consider, for example, the previously discussed problem. In that problem, shown graphically in Figure 13-4, the optimal LP solution occurred at $x_2 = 2.5$ and $x_1 = 0$. If we round down to remain feasible, we find the solution $x_2 = 2$ and $x_1 = 0$, with an objective value of 10. The optimal solution, however, was $x_1 = 4$ and $x_2 = 0$, which has an objective value of 12.

In that example, although we were able to find a feasible solution by rounding, the solution had a lower objective value than the optimal solution. There also exist cases where the rounded solution is neither optimal nor even feasible.

Consider the situation depicted in Figure 13-5. In this integer programming problem, we are attempting to maximize the objective function. The optimal LP solution is found at point A on the graph. However, point A is not an integer solution, so we must look elsewhere for the optimal IP solution. If we round down from the optimal LP solution, we find either point B or point C. Both are lattice points but neither is feasible; so in this case rounding leads to infeasible solutions. The optimal IP solution is found at point D. This may be an extreme example of the problems that may occur when rounding is used, but it demonstrates that care must be taken in rounding.

As an example of the use of rounding as a solution procedure, consider again the

**FIGURE 13-5.**
**Infeasible Solution**
**by Rounding**

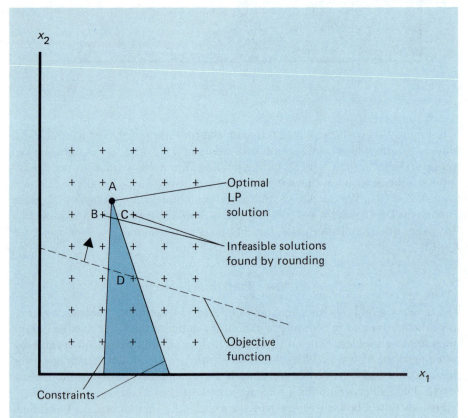

Cross Country Airline problem. The IP formulation for this problem is

MINIMIZE: $\quad Z = 10x_1 + 15x_2 + 12x_3$ (13.4)

SUBJECT TO: $\quad\quad 350x_1 + 450x_2 + 400x_3 \geq 3400$ (13.5)

$$25x_1 + 15x_2 + 15x_3 \leq 250 \qquad (13.6)$$

$$x_3 \leq 5 \qquad (13.7)$$

$$x_1, x_2, x_3 \geq 0 \text{ and integer} \qquad (13.8)$$

If this problem is solved via linear programming by dropping the integrality requirement, we obtain the following solution:

$$x_1 = 9\tfrac{5}{7}, \quad x_2 = 0, \quad x_3 = 0$$

for a total cost of $\$97\tfrac{1}{7}$.

If this solution is rounded up, we obtain a solution of

$$x_1 = 10, \quad x_2 = 0, \quad x_3 = 0$$

for an integer feasible cost of \$100. Note that rounding down leads to an infeasible solution.

## Complete enumeration

The use of complete or total enumeration of all lattice points, as in the initial example (Figure 13-4), is impractical for many problems. The number of values that must be enumerated can grow quite large rather quickly. For example, if an integer programming problem has 100 variables, each of which is restricted to the values 0 or 1 (usually referred to as a binary or 0–1 problem), then there are $2^{100}$ possible lattice points that must be enumerated. This is far too many to make the use of complete enumeration a practical solution procedure.

## Cutting plane methods

One of the first theoretical approaches to finding the global optimal solution, proposed by Gomory in 1958, is called the *cutting plane method*. In the cutting plane method, the procedure searches for the optimal IP solution by successively *cutting* off part of the continuous (LP) feasible region. The process is continued until the optimal LP solution to the reduced problem is integer. This then is the optimal IP solution.

To demonstrate graphically how this would work, consider again the initial example problem:

MAXIMIZE:       $Z = 3x_1 + 5x_2$                                    (13.1)

SUBJECT TO:       $5x_1 + 8x_2 \leq 20$                              (13.2)

$x_1, x_2 \geq 0$ and integer                     (13.3)

and the graphical LP solution in Figure 13-6.

Since the optimal LP solution is not integer, we will add a new constraint that will "cut off" the optimal LP solution. It is not necessary to go into how this new constraint is generated except to say that it does exclude the old LP solution while *not* excluding any lattice points. If enough of the region between $x_2 = 2$ and $x_2 = 2.5$ is cut off, then the new LP solution will become point I at (4, 0). Graphically, we could have the result shown in Figure 13-7, where the cutting plane constraint cuts off enough of the old feasible region to cause the new optimal LP solution to occur at a lattice point (I); and point I is the optimal IP solution.

In this example, the cutting plane method appears to work well. Unfortunately,

**FIGURE 13-6.
Graphical LP Solution**

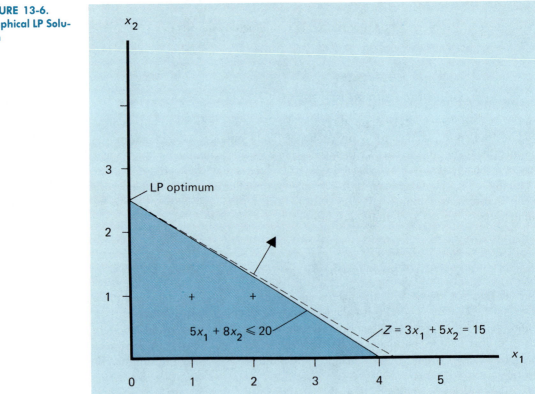

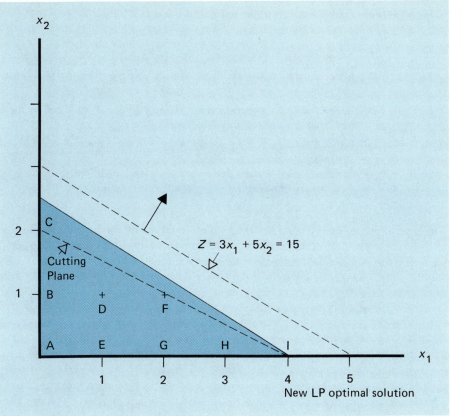

**FIGURE 13-7.
Cutting Plane
Method**

experience with cutting planes has shown that quite often many additional constraints (that is, many additional "cuts") are required in order to end up with an all-integer solution to the reduced LP problems.

## Branch and bound methods

Cutting plane methods use additional constraints to exclude noninteger LP solutions. In contrast, branch and bound methods attempt to do the same thing by a strategy of "divide and conquer." This involves splitting the feasible region into segments such that the previous noninteger LP solution is not included in the new feasible region. Splitting the feasible region into segments results in additional problems that must be solved; but since the feasible regions of these new "subproblems" are smaller than the feasible region of the main problem, the solution process at the subproblem level should be easier. The process of splitting and resplitting continues until it can be shown that none of the subproblems has an integer solution that is better than a previously computed integer solution.

There are four possible outcomes for each subproblem.

1. If a problem is infeasible, we do not investigate it further.

2. If the LP solution to the problem is integer, we record this as possibly the best solution and do not investigate this problem further.

3. If the LP solution is worse than some integer solution already known, then we do not investigate this problem any further.

4. If the LP solution is fractional but better than any integer solution known so far, we divide up the feasible region for that subproblem so that a fractional part of the solution has been excluded. This procedure is continued until no further subproblems exist to be investigated.

In general, branch and bound has been found to be the most efficient method for solving integer programming problems. Numerous computerized versions of branch and bound are now available on most computer systems.

## *Heuristic programming*

While branch and bound is a very important approach to finding optimal solutions, many times the effort necessary to find the *optimal* solution is not considered worth the computer time required. Many times it is necessary to resort to *heuristic programming,* that is, the use of a rule of thumb or another common-sense approach to find a good approximate solution to an integer programming problem. The practice of rounding the LP solution, for example, is a heuristic programming method that has application in practical integer programming problems.

For each of the specific problems discussed earlier, there exists a heuristic programming method that was designed to find "good" approximate solutions. For example, the *greedy solution* approach is used on the knapsack problem. This approach involves first finding the benefit-to-cost ratio for each variable, then accordingly ranking the variables from largest to smallest. Finally, assignments are made in the order of this ranking. For the El Cheapo Grocery Store problem, the benefits (payments), costs (amount of space required), and benefit-to-cost ratios are given in Table 13-10.

If we now rank the variables according to the payment–space ratio, we find the following ranking:

$$x_5, x_1, x_3, x_2, x_4$$

We now set $x_5$ to 1 since by so doing we get the greatest payment for the space required. This leaves $50 - 20 = 30$ feet of space. Next, we assign $x_1 = 1$, leaving 13 feet of space. Since setting any other variables to one would require more than 13

| Variable | Payment | Space Required | Payment/Space |
|----------|---------|----------------|---------------|
| $x_1$ | 100 | 17 | 5.88 |
| $x_2$ | 75 | 15 | 5.00 |
| $x_3$ | 115 | 20 | 5.75 |
| $x_4$ | 50 | 15 | 3.33 |
| $x_5$ | 135 | 20 | 6.75 |

**TABLE 13-10.
Benefit-to-Cost
Ratios for El
Cheapo Grocery
Store**

feet of space, we cannot make any more assignments, and the "greedy" approach terminates with $x_5 = x_1 = 1$ for a total payment of \$235.

If we compare this heuristic solution with the optimal solution of $x_2 = x_4 = x_5 = 1$ for a total payment of \$260, we see that the greedy approach is not as good. This is not surprising, since heuristic procedures cannot be expected to do as well as procedures that guarantee optimal solutions.

As another example of a heuristic programming method, consider the "closest unvisited city" method for the traveling salesman problem. As the name implies, the rule used for choosing a city to visit is fairly simple: Go to the nearest (closest) city that has not been visited. In the Jones Cigar Company problem, if Dave Renfro used this rule, he would leave Tampa and go to Orlando. From Orlando, the closest city other than Tampa is Jacksonville. From Jacksonville the closest unvisited city is Ft. Myers, and from Ft. Myers the closest unvisited city is Miami. From Miami the only choice is to return to Tampa. The total distance is then $83 + 145 + 319 + 143 + 268 = 958$ miles. The reader should be aware that this method can lead to situations where the only choice left for a visit may entail a long-distance trip. You are encouraged to try your hand at finding a better solution to this problem than the heuristic one provided.

Many times, heuristic methods are combined with branch and bound algorithms to achieve improved results. In these procedures, the heuristic method provides a good initial solution to the problem to be used in the branch and bound portion of the procedure.

## ■ Summary

In this chapter, we have looked at optimization problems where the divisibility assumption of linear programming does not hold due to the requirement that some solution value be integers. These are called integer programming problems. The difficulty in solving such problems, due to the presence of local optimal points, was discussed and various general solution procedures for the problems were presented. The procedures discussed were a graphical method, rounding off the LP solution, total enumeration, cutting planes, and branch and bound.

The emphasis of the chapter was on formulating important types of integer programming problems and showing how integer variables can be used to yield desired formulations of other problems. The specific integer programming problems formulated in this chapter were the knapsack problem, the capital budgeting problem, the fixed charge problem, and the traveling salesman problem.

## ■ Glossary of terms

**binary variables:**    Variables that are restricted to be either 0 or 1.

**branch-and-bound method:**    A solution method for integer programming that uses a "divide and conquer" strategy to exclude noninteger solutions to the original problem.

**capital budgeting problems:**    Binary IP problems having multiple constraints.

**complete enumeration:**    A solution method for integer programming that enumerates all possible integer solutions in order to find the optimal solution.

**cutting plane method:**    A solution method for integer programming that searches for the optimal solution by adding constraints to exclude noninteger LP solutions. The procedure terminates when an all-integer LP solution is encountered.

**fixed charges:**    Costs that are incurred in order for a continuous variable or a set of continuous variables to be positive.

**global optimal solution:**    A feasible solution that is the best solution relative to all other feasible solutions.

**integer programming:**    Problems that have all of the characteristics of linear programming except that only integer values are accepted as solutions.

**knapsack problems:**    Binary IP problems that have only a single constraint.

**lattice point:**    A feasible solution in which all variables are integer valued.

**local optimal solution:**    A solution that is feasible and is the best solution relative to other solution values near it.

**traveling salesman problems:**    Scheduling problems originally associated with finding a shortest path through a series of cities.

## ■ Review questions

1. Which of the following coordinate pairs are lattice points? (a) $(1, 2)$; (b) $(1/2, 2)$; (c) $(3/2, 3/2)$; (d) $(0, 10)$; (e) $(10, 11\frac{1}{2})$.

2. Is it possible for an integer programming problem to be infeasible because no lattice points are in the feasible region? If so, draw such a situation in two dimensions.

3. Discuss why rounding off the LP problem associated with an integer programming problem could lead to (a) a very poor solution that is feasible; (b) an infeasible solution in the integer programming problem.

4. Discuss why the name "cutting plane" was applied to the solution procedure bearing that name.

5. Discuss why the branch and bound method is called a "divide-and-conquer" strategy.

6. Can you describe a quick way of solving a continuous version of the knapsack problem by linear programming? (*Hint:* Use the ratio of the objective function to the constraint coefficients to rearrange the variables in decreasing order of ratios.)

7. In a fixed charge problem, what is the effect of the constraints $x_j \le M_j y_j$?

**8.** If the LP solution to an integer programming problem turns out to be integer, is it the optimal solution? Why?

## ■ True/false questions

**1.** A good way to solve an integer programming problem is to use linear programming and round off the LP answers.

**2.** Lattice points and vertices are different names for the same thing in integer programming.

**3.** In integer programming, the presence of many local optima causes finding the global to be a difficult task.

**4.** Branch and bound is a method for solving integer programming problems that involves cutting off parts of the feasible region to arrive at an optimal solution.

**5.** The fixed charge problem is an example of a pure 0–1 integer programming problem.

**6.** The traveling salesman problem requires that the solution be a route that visits each city once and only once.

**7.** When heuristic methods are used to find a solution to an integer programming problem, the solution will always be close to the optimal solution.

## ■ Problems

**1.** Solve the following problem graphically by enumerating all lattice points.

MAXIMIZE: $\qquad 6x_1 + 8x_2$

SUBJECT TO: $\qquad 3x_1 + 4x_2 \leq 12$

$\qquad\qquad\quad 5x_1 + 2x_2 \leq 10$

$\qquad\qquad\qquad x_1, x_2 \geq 0$ and integer

**2. a.** Solve the following as an LP problem. Determine an integer solution by rounding off the LP solution.

MAXIMIZE: $\qquad 2x_1 + 3x_2$

SUBJECT TO: $\qquad 2x_1 + 6x_2 \leq 12$

$\qquad\qquad\quad x_1 + \;\; x_2 \leq 3$

$\qquad\qquad\quad x_1 \qquad\;\; \leq 2$

$\qquad\qquad\qquad x_1, x_2 \geq 0$ and integer

**b.** Solve the problem graphically to determine the true optimal integer programming solution. How does it compare with the solution you found in (a)?

**3.** Joe Jock plays football at North Avenue Trade School. As a requirement to stay eligible, he must carry at least 13 hours per semester. Joe has narrowed his course selection down to six possible courses. These courses and the minimum study hours required per week (as per a knowledgeable upper classman) are

| Course | Credit Hours | Study Hours |
|--------|--------------|-------------|
| Math 100 | 5 | 10 |
| P.E. 101 | 2 | 2 |
| Chem. 110 | 4 | 7 |
| Soc. Stud. 113 | 3 | 6 |
| Drawing 112 | 3 | 1 |
| Eng. 102 | 4 | 5 |

Joe wishes to meet his eligibility requirement while having to study as few hours per week as possible. Formulate this as an integer programming problem.

4. An investor is attempting to maximize her income from $25,000 by investing in a series of bond issues. The bonds, their return after one year, and the denominations in which they are available are shown in Table P13-4. Formulate this as an integer programming problem to find the maximum return after one year.

**TABLE P13-4. Bond Choices**

| Bond | Return | Denomination |
|------|--------|--------------|
| AABCO | $  800 | $10,000 |
| Bixby | 1,080 | 12,000 |
| Caribe | 350 | 5,000 |
| Southco | 640 | 8,000 |
| Pacific | 1,040 | 13,000 |
| Elby | 400 | 4,000 |

5. The Albany, N.Y., metropolitan area (Albany, Schenectady, and Troy) has received a federal grant to build a set of new facilities to treat alcoholics. The Albany planners have divided the metro area into seven regions and are considering five possible sites for the alcoholism treatment centers. They also have determined which sites are within a half-hour's driving distance of each region since their grant requires that there be a

**TABLE P13-5. New York Treatment Centers**

| Region | Possible Centers | | | | |
|--------|--------|------|--------|--------|--------|
|        | Albany | Troy | Schen. | Cohoes | Delmar |
| I      |        |      |        | 1      |        |
| II     | 1      | 1    |        |        | 1      |
| III    | 1      |      | 1      | 1      |        |
| IV     |        | 1    |        |        |        |
| V      | 1      |      | 1      |        |        |
| VI     |        | 1    |        | 1      | 1      |
| VII    | 1      | 1    |        |        |        |
| Cost ($000) | 400 | 250 | 350 | 200 | 500 |

treatment center within this distance from each member of the population. Table P13-5 shows the metro regions, the possible treatment centers, and the estimated cost of building each treatment center. A one is shown for a treatment center and a region if they meet the half-hour driving time criterion.

Formulate an integer programming problem to choose the centers to be built so that all regions are served and building costs are minimized. (*Hint:* Let $x_j = 1$ if center $j$ is built, 0 otherwise, and note that at least *one* center must serve each region.)

6. Assuming a salesman lives in Atlanta, use the closest unvisited city approximation to find a tour for the following traveling salesman problem (where "distances" are travel times in hours).

| City | Athens | Birmingham | Chattanooga | Columbia |
|------|--------|------------|-------------|----------|
| Altanta | 1 | 3 | 2 | 3 |
| Athens | — | 4 | 3 | 2 |
| Birmingham | — | — | 3 | 5 |
| Chattanooga | — | — | — | 4 |

7. The Johnson Company has two plants and three warehouses. The cost of shipping products from each plant to the warehouses consists of a variable portion and a fixed portion. The variable portion of the cost is determined by multiplying the miles from the plant to the warehouse by $0.020, while the fixed portion is a function of truck rental costs and driver salaries. Table P13-7 shows the two plants and the three warehouses with the mileage and the fixed costs for each plant–warehouse pair, the supply at each plant, and the demand at each warehouse. Formulate this problem to find the minimum cost to meet the warehouse demands.

**TABLE P13-7.**

| Plant | Warehouse | | | Supply |
|-------|-----------|-----------|-----------|--------|
| | A | B | C | |
| 1 | 300/$10 | 200/$20 | 150/$20 | 2000 |
| 2 | 100/$25 | 400/$50 | 250/$30 | 1000 |
| Demand | 1500 | 1000 | 500 | |

8. The New Dominion College of Management is in the process of selecting a new dean. The chairman of the faculty wants to appoint a committee of four to work during the summer on the selection. Each member of the committee will be paid a summer salary of 10% of his/her yearly salary.

The various departments have each nominated one professor to serve on the committee. These professors and their department and yearly salary are given in Table P13-8. Also given is their rank, years in service, and time available for working on the dean search. The faculty chairman wishes to select a committee that will minimize cost subject to the following restrictions:

(1) four members

(2) an average of at least 5 years in service

(3) a total committee work time of 100 hours

**(4)**    a minimum of one committee member from each rank

**(5)**    the professors from Management and from Management Science do not agree on anything, so both should not be on the committee

**TABLE P13-8. Nominations for Dean-Search Committee**

| Name | Salary | Department | Rank | Years | Hours Available |
|------|--------|-----------|------|-------|-----------------|
| J. Kools | 25,000 | Management | Prof. | 10 | 30 |
| B. Long | 20,000 | Accounting | Asst. Prof. | 2 | 35 |
| B. Boatright | 30,000 | Marketing | Prof. | 15 | 40 |
| J. Cooper | 15,000 | Insurance | Asso. Prof. | 10 | 30 |
| D. Nesmith | 20,000 | Real Estate | Asst. Prof. | 4 | 15 |
| J. Rainey | 15,000 | Finance | Asst. Prof. | 3 | 10 |
| D. Rubin | 20,000 | Man. Sci. | Asso. Prof. | 6 | 20 |
| P. Earey | 25,000 | Economics | Prof. | 20 | 40 |

9. Game Shows, Inc., produces four game shows, which are sold to local TV stations to be broadcast during nonprime time hours. These shows are the Franklin Squares, Low Rollers, Name That Show, and Trivia Times. The company must rent studio space from one of the national networks and the rental is on a per-hour basis. The time to actually tape the game show is the same for all shows, *but* the time to break down one show and set up the next depends upon the sequence of the taping.

   If the Franklin Squares (FS) precedes Low Rollers (LR), the setup time is 2 hours; if FS precedes Name That Show (NTS), the setup time is 3 hours; and if FS precedes Trivia Times (TT), the setup time is 1 hour.

   For LR preceding the other three shows, the shows and setup times are

   LR before FS: 4 hours

   LR before NTS: 2 hours

   LR before TT: 2 hours

   For NTS preceding the other three shows, the shows and setup times are

   NTS before FS: 1 hour

   NTS before LR: 3 hours

   NTS before TT: 1 hour

   For TT preceding the other three shows, the shows and setup times are

   TT before FS: 5 hours

   TT before LR: 2 hours

   TT before NTS: 3 hours

   a. Formulate this problem as an integer programming problem. Assume that FS is always first and that the studio must be set for FS after the last show. Is it a special type of problem?

**b.** Use heuristic programming methods to find an approximate solution to this problem.

**c.** Compare your solution with the optimal solution of 6 hours.

10. Coach Sam "Gator" Jones is attempting to decide which basketball players to take on a cross-country road trip. He has 11 players to choose from, but he only wants to take nine. "Gator" wishes to maximize the average points for the traveling team subject to several restrictions. Formulate an IP to maximize points.

    **(1)**  There must be at least three guards.

    **(2)**  There must be at least three forwards.

    **(3)**  There must be at least two centers.

    **(4)**  If Stafford goes, then Jacobson must stay home, and vice versa.

    **(5)**  If Burton goes, then Coach Jones also wants to take Greve along, but not necessarily vice versa.

The names, positions, and points per game average for the 11 players are given below:

| Name | Position | Points per Game |
|------|----------|-----------------|
| Hanson | C | 12.0 |
| Stafford | C | 9.0 |
| Jacobson | C | 8.0 |
| Greve | F | 15.0 |
| Burton | F | 10.0 |
| Ellwanger | F | 5.0 |
| Ford | G | 20.0 |
| Davis | F | 18.0 |
| O'Koren | G | 12.0 |
| Sims | G | 7.0 |
| Scholle | G | 2.0 |

11. Formulate Problem 4 in Chapter 6 again, but this time assume that the Lord Manufacturing company will not produce diskettes, cassettes, or cleaning kits in lot sizes of less than 10 units.

12. Two heuristic policies that can be used to find solutions to knapsack problems are the following:

    **(1)**  Simply go by the profit values and put items in the knapsack in decreasing order of profit, that is, highest profit item assigned first, second highest profit item assigned second, and so on.

    **(2)**  Compute the ratio of profit to constraint values, that is, the benefit-to-cost ratio discussed in the chapter, and make the assignments in decreasing order of this ratio.

For the JCL case formulated at the beginning of the chapter, compare the solutions found using these two methods.

14

# Inventory Models

## ■ Introduction

Throughout the text we have emphasized linear deterministic models—that is, linear programming, integer programming, network models, transportation models, goal programming, and the like. However, one of the first areas in which quantitative models was employed was inventory analysis. In 1915, F. W. Harris developed what has become known as the economic order quantity model (the EOQ model), a model for determining the optimal quantity of materials or items to purchase or manufacture. Harris' model was expanded by F. E. Raymond in the early 1930s. Building upon the initial works of these researchers, the field has grown tremendously; today the literature of management science includes models that address the problem of economic order quantity, optimal order points, back ordering, inventory balancing, and quantity discounts, among others.

It should not be surprising that inventory analysis is a key topic in management science, since inventories are an integral part of most organizations. Inventory is often the largest item appearing in the asset side of a company's balance sheet, in many corporations representing as much as 35 to 40% of total assets. When one considers this fact, it becomes apparent that a reduction in inventories, even by a small percentage, can represent very large dollar savings.

Viewed as a claim on the organization's capital, inventories should be reduced, but before reducing them, it is desirable to consider the effect this will have on other aspects of the organization. Manufacturers as well as retailers hold inventories to satisfy customer demand, regardless of whether the customer is a wholesaler or retailer. If inventories are raised to high levels, then customer service can be maximized. From the customer's point of view, then, high inventories are desirable.

Obviously a firm cannot simultaneously reduce inventories to reduce asset investment and hold large inventories to satisfy customer demand. But a balance can be achieved between customer satisfaction and asset investments through good inventory management supported by basic inventory models. The objective of this chapter is to introduce some basic inventory management concepts and identify specific models that can be employed in inventory analysis. This chapter will deal with deterministic models, such as the classic economic order quantity model, EOQ models with noninstantaneous replenishment, and quantity discount models. The latter sections of the chapter deal with other inventory concepts.

Before we consider some of the basic concepts of inventory analysis, let us examine a typical inventory problem.

# ■ Case
## Video Inc.

Video Inc. is a retailer of cathode-ray video systems used in conjunction with minicomputers. Video orders directly from the manufacturer and sells to retail customers. John Jefferson, the purchasing agent for Video, has generally ordered only one or two video systems at a time since the manufacturer has always provided immediate delivery on all orders. Because of increased demand, however, Jefferson decided to order 20 systems last month. His decision to order a larger quantity of systems was based on the fact that the cost of processing an order was $20. He reasoned that a smaller number of orders should result in a significant saving in ordering costs. Adequate space exists for holding 20 systems in inventory.

Bob Benson, president of Video, reviewed the monthly operating report for the company and pointed out to Jefferson that the inventory cost for the company had increased drastically. Benson elaborated: "We have projected that the annual holding cost for each video system is approxi-

mately 20% of the purchase price of $500. This means the company will incur $100 on each system that we hold in inventory for the year. It appears to me that purchasing 20 systems is not a wise decision, even if we can save on ordering costs. I would like you to justify your decision further." Benson indicated that the forecasted demand for the year was approximately 365 systems.

Jefferson returned to his office and began to analyze the problem, particularly the inventory cost factor. Using the data supplied by Benson, he reasoned that if the company incurred a $100 cost for each unit held in inventory for a year, then the daily inventory costs would be

$$\frac{\$100/\text{year}}{365 \text{ days/year}} \qquad \text{or} \qquad \$0.274 \text{ per day per unit}$$

He then reasoned that the number of units (systems) in inventory per day was a function of daily demand and the size of the order placed with the manufacturer. If demand were 365 units per year, this would mean daily demand would, on the average, be 1 unit.

**FIGURE 14-1.**
**Inventory Picture**

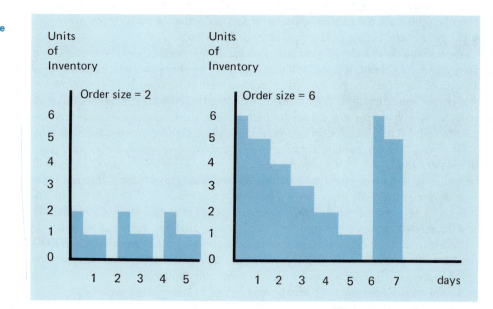

Jefferson then needed to determine inventory based on different order sizes, assuming demand was 1 unit per day. To determine this he sketched what he reasoned would be an "inventory picture" (Figure 14-1). For an order size of 2, the inventory would be 2 units for the first half-day (assuming the order for the day is shipped during the day), 1 unit until midday the following day, and zero units through the remainder of the second day. A new shipment would be received at the end of the day. From one shipment to another the company thus would incur 2 unit-days of inventory, that is,

$$(\frac{1}{2})(2) + (1)(1) + (\frac{1}{2})(0) = 2$$

For an order of 6, the inventory would be 18 unit-days, i.e.,

$$(\frac{1}{2})(6) + (1)(5) + (1)(4) + (1)(3) + (1)(2)$$
$$+ (1)(1) + (\frac{1}{2})(0) = 18$$

Using these data, Jefferson computed the inventory holding cost between each order, i.e., per inventory cycle, as follows:

$$(.274)(2) = \$0.548 \text{ per inventory cycle}$$

This result convinced Jefferson that his decision to order more than 2 units was sound; the ordering

cost for 2 units was $20.00 whereas the holding cost between orders was approximately $0.55. Jefferson recalled that in a short, in-plant course on inventory control the instructor had indicated that in the least-cost inventory arrangement holding cost is near or equal to ordering cost.

He then examined his order size of 20. For this order size, he determined that the inventory would be 200 unit-days. This meant that the inventory costs incurred between orders would be

$$(.274)(200) = \$54.8$$

compared with the ordering cost of $20. This cost was very high. Ordering 20 units thus was not a good decision.

Jefferson then decided to develop a table that would reflect the inventory cost for different order sizes. Table 14-1 is the result of his efforts. Based on these data, Jefferson concluded that the best decision would be to purchase 12 units per order, since the ordering cost of $20.00 would be almost balanced with the holding costs that would be incurred between each order.

He returned to Benson's office to discuss his findings. Benson was pleased with the analysis, but raised several questions:

Will your results hold throughout the year? What would be the impact on your results if the manufac-

**TABLE 14-1. Inventory Holding Cost for Varying Ordering Sizes—Video Inc.**

| Order Size (units) | Inventory (unit-days) | Holding Cost per Unit-day ($) | Total Holding Cost Between Orders ($) |
|---|---|---|---|
| 2 | 2 | .274 | .548 |
| 4 | 8 | .274 | 2.192 |
| 6 | 18 | .274 | 4.932 |
| 8 | 32 | .274 | 8.768 |
| 10 | 50 | .274 | 13.700 |
| 12 | 72 | .274 | 19.728 |
| 14 | 98 | .274 | 26.852 |
| 16 | 128 | .274 | 35.072 |
| 18 | 162 | .274 | 44.388 |
| 20 | 200 | .274 | 54.800 |

turer could not deliver immediately? Or more realistically, what if the manufacturer has a varying delivery time? Also, if we are going to purchase a number of systems, can we obtain price discounts—how does this affect your results?

Jefferson's enthusiasm was somewhat deflated after his review with Benson; some of the questions that Benson had raised did not appear to have solutions.

# ■ Concepts and terminology

A simple order quantity model will help answer some of the questions raised by Benson and resolve Mr. Jefferson's dilemma. Before we develop a model, however, we need a better understanding of the terminology of inventory analysis and some of the cost trade-offs that must be considered. In the following section we examine some of these concepts and relationships.

## Functions performed by inventories

Broadly defined, inventories are usable resources that are idle at a given point in time. In a manufacturing environment this would include raw materials, semifinished goods (work in process), and finished goods. In retail firms, inventory is generally viewed as the stock of goods for sale. Inventories, however, may also include nonphysical assets such as cash, accounts receivable, and personnel.

From the traditional point of view, inventory is associated with manufacturing and retail firms; however, equipment, supplies, and personnel are integral inventories for organizations such as hospitals, universities, and other public service organizations. Inventory models are thus applicable for these areas as well as for manufacturing and retailing.

The basic function of inventories is that of *decoupling*. Within a manufacturing firm, inventories decouple the production, distribution, and marketing activities. *Raw material inventories* permit short-run production decisions to be made independent of the raw materials market (supply) activity. For example, raw materials are often accumulated because of price breaks (for large quantity purchases), as a hedge against price inflation, or as a hedge against union strikes against suppliers. *Work-in-process inventories* permit decoupling of the stages of the production process, i.e., these inventories allow the various production departments to operate without direct reliance on the schedule of output of prior departments. *Finished goods inventories* decouple the production function and customer demand. For example, when demand for an item is known to be variable or seasonal, it may be more economical to carry inventories rather than allow the level of production to oscillate. This can occur when the costs of acquiring and training new workers, unemployment compensation, overtime required to meet peak demand, additional setups, backordering, and the like are higher than the costs of carrying additional inventory.

The decoupling function of inventories is not limited to manufacturing: it is equally applicable to retailing. A shopper expects the retailer to carry the item wanted. If an item is not available at the time the customer demands, then the retailer loses a customer on that item and possibly on future items. To absorb fluctuations in demand and thus provide better customer service, retailer inventories are required. From the opposite point of view, the retailer must maintain inventories in order to decouple the variability of replenishment (delivery) times from suppliers.

In the home, food supplies (inventories) permit dietary planning and food preparation activities to be decoupled from the food purchasing. In hospitals, medical supplies decouple daily health care and operating room activities from medical supplies. In the environmental area, dams and reservoirs decouple the variability of rainfall and water needs of communities. In this latter case the cost trade-off is the cost of building the dam or reservoir versus the cost of communities being depleted of water during variable periods of time.

## Terminology

Inventory analysis is similar to queuing analysis in that a single model is not applicable for every inventory problem. Rather, a number of models exist, depending on the characteristics of the problem. Following are some of the typical characteristics of different models.

**Retail models versus production models.**  Retail models are those in which replenishment inventories are purchased from supplies outside the firm. Production models are those in which the replenishment inventories are produced internally by the company. The key item that differentiates these models is the manner in which the inventories are replenished. Retail models assume the inventories are replenished instantaneously upon receipt of a shipment, while production models most often assume that replenishment occurs over time.

**Demand.**  If demand is known with certainty and is assumed to be constant over time, then the model is referred to as a deterministic demand model. However, just because a model is classified as deterministic does not imply that demand is constant; demand can be "lumpy" and the model still be deterministic. In the cases we will examine it will be assumed that demand is constant.

**Lead time (delivery delay).**  Lead time is the time between the initiation of the replenishment activity (ordering or production) and receipt or delivery of replenishment inventories. As is the case for demand, lead time can be constant and known with certainty or it can be probabilistic in nature. We will examine only models where lead time is constant and known with certainty. In Chapter 21 (Simulation) we will consider the case where lead time is variable.

**Ordering policy.**  Two basic decisions that must be resolved in any inventory system are what quantity should be ordered (or produced) and when to order. The

*order point*
*periodic review*

*reorder point*

latter decision depends a great deal on the order system the model employs. Two types of order systems exist: **order-point** and **periodic review** systems. Order-point systems, often referred to as "perpetual inventory systems," are those in which a perpetual inventory record is maintained. The records are reviewed on a continual basis. When the inventory reaches a predetermined level, referred to as the **reorder point,** a replenishment order (activity) for a fixed quantity of items is initiated. Order-point systems are often used when the number of items demanded per transaction is relatively large and inventory costs are significant.

In a periodic review system, inventories are not reviewed continuously; rather, checks are made at predetermined fixed intervals of time. The replenishment inventories ordered (produced) vary. The inventory on hand is compared with the desired inventory level; the difference between the two levels is the quantity ordered (produced).

Variations and combinations of order-point and periodic review systems exist. For example, one could periodically review the inventory level, estimate the probability of a stockout (a completely depleted inventory) during the fixed time interval, and then order a variable replenishment quantity based on the probability estimate.

In this chapter we will only consider order-point systems.

**Shortage (stockouts).**    Inventory shortages occur when demand exceeds the quantity of inventory on hand. Shortages may either be accidental or planned. Regardless of the cause of the shortage, a policy must be developed that addresses the problem of shortage. A model that takes into consideration shortages by fulfilling the shortages at a later date employs what is known as **backordering.**

*backordering*

**System structure.**    Inventory systems are either single-stage systems or multistage systems. A single-stage system is one in which the inventories are used directly to satisfy demand. Examples would be the inventories that a retailer holds in order to meet consumer demand; the finished goods inventories that a manufacturer holds in order to meet retailer demand; medical supplies that a hospital would maintain in order to meet daily medical needs. Multistage systems are those in which multiple inventory banks or stock points exist. If we were to view the manufacturer-to-retailer and retailer-to-consumer cycle as a system, we would have a multistage system. Likewise, a manufacturing firm could be appropriately labeled as a three-stage system since raw material inventories, work-in-process inventories, and finished-goods inventories could exist, each serving a different demand. In essence, multistage systems are single-stage systems treated jointly rather than independently. Because of the complexity of multistage models, we will examine only single-stage systems.

**Time horizon of the model.**    Inventory models have either a finite or an infinite time horizon. In the earlier chapters where linear, integer, goal programming, and transportation algorithms were applied to production-inventory problems, the time horizon was finite. In most of these cases, single time periods were considered, but in several cases we examined multiple time periods. In the models we examine in this chapter, the time horizon will be considered to be infinite.

## Cost criteria

A number of factors could be considered in any inventory analysis, such as return on investment, asset turnover, and product life cycle. Many of these factors are considered and reviewed in monthly financial statements of the firm. Unfortunately, including these factors in continuous time-interval inventory models requires complex analytical techniques. Most basic inventory models, therefore, rely on cost trade-offs as the criteria for analysis. In general, four cost factors are considered: (1) ordering (setup) costs; (2) carrying (holding) costs; (3) shortage (stockout) costs; and (4) purchase (production) costs.

**Ordering (setup) costs.**   Ordering (setup) cost is incurred whenever an inventory replenishment activity occurs. For retail models, the term **ordering costs** is used. This cost consists primarily of clerical and administrative costs associated with all the steps and activities from the time a requisition for purchase is issued until the order is received, placed in inventory, and paid for. Typical elements of ordering costs include processing and expediting purchase orders, transportation, receiving, inspection, placement in inventory, accounting and auditing, and payment to supplier. Ordering costs are generally considered to be independent of the order size; typically a fixed charge per order is employed.

*ordering costs*

In production models, the term **setup costs,** is used in lieu of ordering costs. Setup costs usually include many clerical and administrative costs associated with production support (such as requisitioning, receiving, inspection, inventory placement, and accounting); however, the key cost items most often are the labor and material cost associated with setting up machinery for production.

*setup costs*

For the models we will examine, we will assume that the ordering (setup) cost is constant; that is, the cost is independent of the number of units ordered or the number of units in a production run.

**Carrying (holding) costs.**   Carrying (holding) costs are the costs associated with holding a given level of inventory over a specific time period. In essence this cost consists of the explicit and implicit costs associated with maintaining and owning inventory. The cost includes opportunity cost of money invested in inventory, the cost of physical storage (rent, heating, lighting, refrigeration, record keeping, security, etc.), depreciation, taxes, insurance, and product obsolescence and deterioration. Carrying cost is expressed as a cost per unit of time. To simplify the analysis it is assumed to be proportional to the average number of units in inventory.

**Shortage (stockout) costs.**   Shortage (stockout) cost is the cost that occurs when an item cannot be supplied upon demand. The magnitude of the cost depends upon whether backordering is permitted. If backordering is not allowed, then an inventory shortage will result in the permanent loss of sales for those items demanded but not available. An additional "goodwill cost" may be incurred if the customer takes future business elsewhere.

When backordering is permitted, the relevant shortage costs are the clerical and administrative costs associated with backordering—these include the cost of special clerical and administrative efforts, overtime, expediting and special transportation, and follow-up. Backordering shortages may result in the loss of some customers; therefore, "goodwill costs" may also be incurred. Safety stock is generally carried as a hedge against shortages.

Shortage cost is computed differently, depending upon the situation. The most general case assumes a fixed cost per shortage, regardless of the size of the shortage or the period of time over which the shortage occurs. A more direct approach is to assume a per-unit shortage cost. In some situations it may be more applicable to consider both the number of units short and the period of the shortage. Obviously, if a contractual agreement has been established that prescribes a certain penalty cost for shortage, the cost computation must include this factor.

**Purchase (production) costs.**   For retailer models, the direct cost associated with the actual purchase of an item is referred to as the purchase cost. For production models, this cost is referred to as the production cost. In either case the cost per unit is generally assumed to be constant, regardless of the quantity purchased or produced. This assumption, however, must be relaxed if quantity and/or price breaks are allowed for specific order sizes or if unit costs can be reduced for large production runs. The latter case can occur as a result of economies of scale. We will examine the case where quantity discounts are considered; however, the major focus of the chapter will be directed at those models where the per-unit cost is constant.

## ■ Deterministic models

In this section we develop a series of basic inventory models and concepts. Specifically we will examine

1.   the classic economic order quantity (EOQ) model
2.   reorder point and lead time and how they relate to order quantity
3.   sensitivity analysis as related to the classic EOQ model
4.   EOQ models with price breaks
5.   the production lot-size model

We discuss the basic model first, followed by increasingly complex models. As we move from one model to the next, one or more assumptions in the basic model will be relaxed. In all of the models we assume that the objective is to minimize total cost. Within this objective we will identify the optimal order quantity ($Q°$), the optimal order point ($R°$), and some additional factors, such as time between orders and total costs.

### *Classic economic order quantity (EOQ) model*

The simplest inventory model is the classic model, often referred to as the EOQ model. In discussing this model, as well as other models in this section (with the exception of the production lot size model), we will assume the model relates to a *retail* function.

**Model assumptions.**    The following assumptions characterize the classic model:

1.  Demand is known with certainty and is constant over time.

2.  Lead time is zero; that is, an order is received at the instant it is placed.

3.  An order-point system is employed, thus inventories are reviewed continuously.

4.  Inventory is replenished when inventory is exactly zero. No safety stock is employed and no shortages (stockouts) are allowed.

5.  Inventory replenishment is instantaneous; that is, the entire order is received in a single batch.

6.  The order quantity is constant for each replenishment order.

7.  The problem involves a single-stage system.

8.  An infinite continuous time horizon is assumed.

9.  All costs are assumed to be constant over the infinite time horizon.

Figure 14-2 is a pictorial representation of the inventory behavior of the classic model based on the above assumptions. The downward-sloping line indicates that the inventory is being reduced at a constant rate over time, that is, demand is constant. Since lead time is zero and replenishment is instantaneous, the reorder point, $R$, is determined automatically when inventory reaches zero. The quantity ordered at each replenishment point is $Q$.

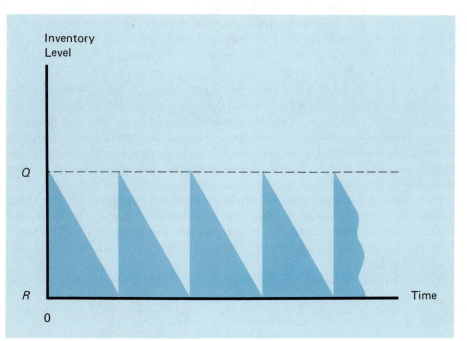

**FIGURE 14-2.**
**Inventory Behavior: Classic Model**

FIGURE 14-3.
Inventory Costs:
Classic Model

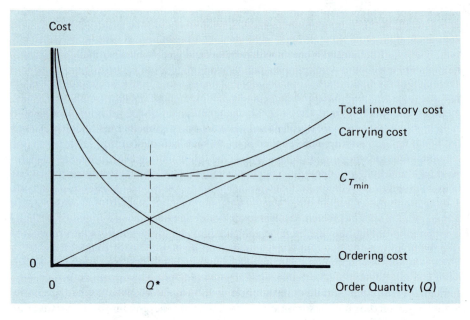

**Formulation of the model.** The objective of this model, as noted earlier, is to determine the optimal order quantity $(Q°)$ and order point $(R°)$ such that total inventory costs are minimized. Since by logical deduction we have determined that the optimal reorder point, $R°$, is zero, the objective is simply to determine the economic order quantity, $Q°$. (The label "EOQ model" thus is appropriate.)

Since we have assumed that no shortages occur, shortage cost is zero; therefore, we will minimize the sum of the inventory ordering costs and carrying costs. To develop the model we need to examine the relationship between ordering costs and carrying costs. Figure 14-3 illustrates the behavior of these costs as the order quantity, $Q$, varies. As the order quantity (number of units per order), increases, fewer orders are necessary; therefore, the ordering costs will decrease. On the other hand, as the order size increases, more units are held in inventory; therefore, carrying cost increases. Since ordering costs and carrying costs respond in opposing manners with increasing ordering size, the optimal order quantity, $Q°$, is the point where ordering costs are equal to carrying costs.[1] (This is shown in Figure 14-3 where the two curves intersect.)

Our objective is to minimize total inventory costs. Note in Figure 14-3 that total inventory cost first decreases as the order size increases, due to the decreasing ordering costs, and then increases as the carrying costs become the predominant cost. Note also that the minimum point on the total cost curve $(C_{T_{min}})$ is where carrying cost is equal to ordering cost.

To develop the general mathematical model that represents the inventory cost

[1]It should be noted that ordering cost is equal to carrying cost at $Q°$ for an inventory problem that meets the basic assumption of the classic model. This is not true for all inventory models.

structure, as shown in Figure 14-3, we must define the variables and parameters for the model. Symbols used in the model are as follows:

$C_O$ = ordering cost per order placed $C_3$

$C_C$ = carrying cost per unit per time period holding $C_1$

$C_T$ = total inventory cost per time period

$Q$ = quantity ordered (order size) per order

$D$ = units demanded per time period

The decision variable for the model, that is, the variable for which a solution value is sought, is the quantity ordered, $Q$. The criterion to be minimized is the total inventory cost, $C_T$. $C_O$ and $C_C$ are parameters for the model since, as we shall see shortly, they are constants used to determine ordering cost and carrying cost for varying order sizes.

A general statement of the model is

MINIMIZE:          total inventory cost = ordering cost + carrying cost          (14.1)

Ordering cost is simply the ordering cost per order, $C_O$, times the number of orders per time period. Since the demand per time period, $D$, is known, the number of orders per time period is the quantity demanded divided by the order size $(D/Q)$. Ordering cost thus is

$$\text{ordering cost} = C_O \times D/Q \qquad (14.2)$$

Carrying cost is equal to the carrying cost per unit per time period, $C_C$, times the average number of units held in inventory. To determine carrying costs we thus must first compute the average inventory.

Average inventory is slightly different from the unit-days of inventory that Jefferson computed for the Video Inc. problem. In the Video case, we computed the total number of units that were held between orders and multiplied this by the daily unit holding cost. We could have computed average inventory per day and multiplied this by the cost for the time period. For example, for an order size of 6 we computed the total units of inventory to be 18. If we average this over 6 days the average inventory is 3 units. The holding cost would then be

$$\text{holding cost} = \binom{\text{average inventory}}{\text{per day}} \times \binom{\text{cost per unit}}{\text{for 6-day time period}}$$

$$= (3) \times (.274)(6)$$

$$= 4.932$$

This cost is identical to the cost figure shown in Table 14-1 for an order size of 6.

FIGURE 14-4.
**Average Inventory
Level for Classic
Model**

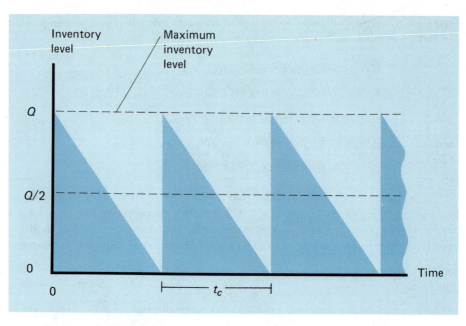

From Figure 14-2 it should be obvious that average inventory is $Q/2$. To demonstrate this, consider the inventory picture as shown in Figure 14-4. Theoretically, average inventory is the area under the inventory curve divided by the length of the time period. The length of each sawtooth portion of the inventory is defined as the inventory cycle $t_c$. Average inventory thus is computed as follows:

$$\text{Average inventory} = \frac{\text{area under an inventory curve}}{\text{length of time period}}$$

$$= \frac{\frac{1}{2} \times \text{height} \times \text{base}}{t_c}$$

$$= \frac{\frac{1}{2} \times Q \times t_c}{t_c}$$

or

$$\text{average inventory} = \frac{Q}{2} \qquad\qquad (14.3)$$

If we compute the inventory over several inventory cycles, we should still arrive at an average inventory of $Q/2$. For example, if we examine four inventory cycles,

$$\text{average inventory} = \frac{4 \times \frac{1}{2}(Q)(t_c)}{4t_c} = \frac{Q}{2}$$

Carrying cost thus is expressed as follows:

$$\text{carrying cost} = C_C \times Q/2 \qquad (14.4)$$

The problem can now be expressed as

MINIMIZE:     $C_T = C_O \times D/Q + C_C \times Q/2$ $\qquad$ (14.5)

**Solution to the model.**     In Figure 14-3, we indicated graphically that the optimal order quantity, $Q°$, was at the point where ordering cost is equal to carrying cost. We can demonstrate, using differential calculus, that this is the case if we optimize (minimize) equation (14.5). To optimize $C_T$ we first take the derivative; that is,

$$\frac{dC_T}{dQ} = \frac{-C_O D}{Q^2} + \frac{C_2}{2}$$

Setting the resulting equation to zero (since the slope of the $C_T$ curve is zero at the minimum point on the curve) and solving for $Q$, we have

$$\frac{-C_O D}{Q^2} + \frac{C_C}{2} = 0$$

$$\frac{Q^2}{C_O D} = \frac{2}{C_C}$$

$$Q^2 = \frac{2C_O D}{C_C}$$

Therefore,

$$Q° = \sqrt{2C_O D/C_C} \qquad (14.6)$$

If $Q°$ is the optimal order quantity, ordering cost should be equal to carrying cost at that order quantity value. We can check this by squaring both sides of equation (14.6), cross-multiplying by $C_C$, and dividing both sides of the equation by $2Q°$.

$$\frac{Q° C_C}{2} = \frac{C_O D}{Q°}$$

Therefore, the costs are equal and equation (14.6) is the optimal order quantity model.

$Q°$ and $R°$ provide the optimal order quantity and order point for the model; however, quite often a manager is interested in knowing the number of orders per time period that will be issued under the optimal policy and the time between orders. More than likely it is also desirable to know the total cost that will result if the optimal order policy is employed. We can compute these once we know $Q°$; however, we can also develop general formulas for these factors.

The optimal number of orders per time period, based upon the optimal order quantity, $Q°$, is simply the demand per time period divided by $Q°$ that is, $N° = D/Q°$. Substituting $Q° = \sqrt{2C_0D/C_C}$ into the equation we have,

$$N° = \frac{D}{\sqrt{2C_0D/C_C}}$$

$$= \frac{\sqrt{D^2C_C}}{\sqrt{2C_0D}}$$

Therefore,

$$N° = \sqrt{DC_C/2C_0} \tag{14.7}$$

The time between orders, or the inventory cycle $t_c$, is the inverse of the optimal number of orders, $N°$, so $t_c = 1/N°$. Substituting $N° = \sqrt{DC_C/2C_0}$ into the equation, we have

$$t_c = \frac{1}{\sqrt{DC_C/2C_0}}$$

Therefore,

$$t_c = \sqrt{2C_0/DC_C} \tag{14.8}$$

We should note that time units of measure of $t_c$ will be the same as those associated with demand, $D$. If $D$ is expressed as demand per year, then $t_c$ will be expressed in *years*.

To determine the cost that will be associated with the optimum order policy, we simply substitute $Q°$ into the total cost formula [equation (14.5)], that is,

$$C_T° = C_0 \times \frac{D}{Q°} + C_C \times \frac{Q°}{2}$$

Substituting $Q° = \sqrt{2C_0D/C_C}$ into the equation, we have

$$C_T° = \frac{C_0 \times D}{\sqrt{2C_0D/C_C}} + \frac{C_C \times \sqrt{2C_0D/C_C}}{2}$$

$$= \frac{2C_0D + C_C \times \sqrt{2C_0D/C_C} \times \sqrt{2C_0D/C_C}}{2\sqrt{2C_0D/C_C}}$$

$$= \frac{2C_0D + 2C_0D}{2\sqrt{2C_0D/C_C}}$$

$$= \frac{\sqrt{(2C_0D)^2}}{\sqrt{2C_0D}} \times \sqrt{C_C} = \sqrt{\frac{4C_0^2D^2C_C}{2C_0D}}$$

Therefore,

$$C_T^\circ = \sqrt{2C_oC_cD} \tag{14.9}$$

By employing equations (14.6) through (14.9), we can fully describe the inventory policy for the classic EOQ model.

**Classic model applied to Video Inc.**   To test the model, we can examine the Video Inc. case. The model parameters for the model are

$$C_O = \$20 \text{ per order}$$

$$C_C = \$100 \text{ per unit per year}$$

$$D = 365 \text{ units per year}$$

Applying equation (14.6), the optimal economic order quantity is

$$Q^\circ = \sqrt{\frac{2C_oD}{C_c}}$$

$$= \sqrt{\frac{(2)(20)(365)}{100}}$$

$$= \sqrt{146}$$

$$= 12.08$$

This compares very closely to the value that Jefferson computed using a single-cycle analysis.

The optimal number of orders per year, using equation (14.7), is

$$N^\circ = \sqrt{\frac{DC_c}{2C_o}}$$

$$= \sqrt{\frac{(365)(100)}{(2)(20)}}$$

$$= \sqrt{912.5}$$

$$= 30.2$$

The time between orders, or the inventory cycle in this case, using equation (14.8),

is

$$t_c = \sqrt{\frac{2C_o}{DC_c}}$$

$$= \sqrt{\frac{(2)(20)}{(365)(100)}}$$

$$= .0331 \text{ years}$$

If we wish to express $t_c$ in days, then we must multiply this result by 365. Therefore

$$t_c = (365)(0.331)$$

$$= 12.08 \text{ days}$$

The total cost associated with the optimal policy of $Q^\circ \approx 12$ units, using equation (14.9), is

$$C_T^\circ = \sqrt{2C_oC_cD}$$

$$= \sqrt{(2)(20)(100)(365)}$$

$$= \sqrt{1,460,000}$$

$$= \$1208.30$$

**Units of measure associated with model parameters.** In applying the classic model to the Video Inc. case, the time period for analysis was one year ($T = 1$ year). Note also that demand, $D$, was expressed on an annual basis, and the carrying cost, $C_C$, was expressed as $ per unit per year. In applying the model it is important that these parameters, $D$ and $C_C$, be expressed on the same time period base. It is not necessary to express the parameters on an annual basis, but they must be consistent with the defined length of the analysis. For example, assume we express the time period for Video Inc. as 6 months. Demand, $D$, would then be 182.5 units per 6 months and carrying cost, $C_C$, would be $50 per unit per 6 months. Using the data, the economic order quantity would remain 12.08. That is,

$$Q^\circ = \sqrt{\frac{2C_oD}{C_c}}$$

$$= \sqrt{\frac{2(20)(182.5)}{50}}$$

$$= \sqrt{146}$$

$$= 12.08$$

The remaining factors ($N^\circ$, $t_c$, and $C_T^\circ$) likewise can be computed using the 6-month time frame.

## *Reorder point and lead time*

One of the assumptions of the classic EOQ model is that lead time is zero. In practice, it is unlikely that this assumption will hold true. In this section, we will examine a situation where lead time is known and greater than zero and demand is constant.

Eight basic assumptions were made when we defined the basic EOQ model. To define a situation where lead time is greater than zero, we can relax assumptions 2 and 4. Relaxing these assumptions will not affect the optimal order quantity, $Q°$; therefore, equation (14.6)—as well as equations (14.7)–(14.9)—is still relevant when an order for replenishment is released. The order size thus is $Q°$; the question that must be addressed is when the order should be released.

Two lead-time situations exist that relate to reorder point. The first is where lead time $t_L$ is less than the inventory cycle $t_c$. This is illustrated in Figure 14-5.

Demand during any lead time period is $t_L D$. For the situation where $t_L < t_c$, demand during lead time is less than $Q°$ since $Q° = t_c D$ and $t_L < t_c$. Therefore, if we reorder when the inventory level reaches $R°$, where $R° = t_L D$, the replenishment inventory will arrive at the end of the inventory cycle. The replenishment order will drive the inventory level to $Q°$.

One of the basic requirements for this, as well as a number of other inventory models, is the arrival of the replenishment inventory at the end of the inventory cycle; reordering at the $R°$ level assures this will occur.

A second situation that can occur is where lead time is greater than the cycle time ($t_L > t_c$). This is illustrated in Figure 14-6.

Demand during lead time is $t_L D$ for the $t_L > t_c$ situation, just as it was when $t_L < t_c$. However, lead time demand now is greater than the order quantity $Q°$. This means that we must order in a prior period(s) rather than the current period in order to satisfy demand during lead time. In essence, the inventory we have on hand at the time of reorder (which would be $R°$) plus replenishment inventories that arrive during the lead-time period, are used to satisfy demand during lead time. Thus,

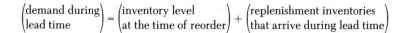

$$\begin{pmatrix} \text{demand during} \\ \text{lead time} \end{pmatrix} = \begin{pmatrix} \text{inventory level} \\ \text{at the time of reorder} \end{pmatrix} + \begin{pmatrix} \text{replenishment inventories} \\ \text{that arrive during lead time} \end{pmatrix}$$

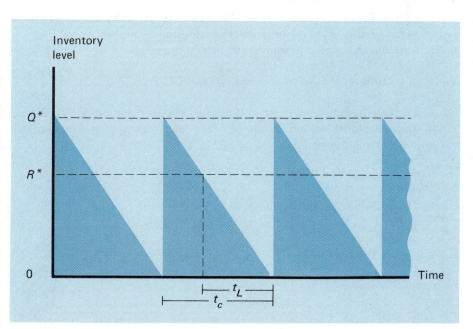

**FIGURE 14-5.
Reorder Points
When Lead Time Is
Less Than Cycle
Time**

FIGURE 14-6.
Reorder Points
When Lead Time Is
Greater Than Cy-
cle Time

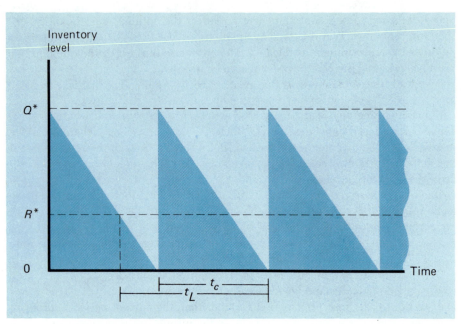

Expressed mathematically,

$$t_L D = R° + \begin{pmatrix} \text{replenishment inventories} \\ \text{that arrive during lead time} \end{pmatrix}$$

If we recognize that the number of replenishment orders that arrive during lead time is equal to the number of complete inventory cycles, and recall that $Q°$ is the size of each replenishment, then the replenishment inventories will be

$$(\text{number of complete inventory cycles}) \times Q°$$

Recognizing that the number of complete inventory cycles is determined by dividing $t_L$ by $t_c$ and taking the whole number (integer) portion of this division operation, the replenishment inventories will be

$$[t_L / t_c] \times Q°$$

where $[t_L/t_c]$ is the whole number (integer) portion that results when $t_L$ is divided by $t_c$. The complete mathematical model thus becomes

$$t_L D = R° + [t_L/t_c]Q°$$

Solving for $R$, we have

$$R° = t_L D - [t_L/t_c]Q° \tag{14.10}$$

This reorder-point model can be used when $t_L > t_c$, but is equally applicable when $t_L < t_c$ (situation #1). To demonstrate this point, assume that for Video Inc. lead time is 7 days ($t_L = 7$). From the previous analysis we know that $Q° \approx 12$ units, $D = 1$ unit per day (365 units per year), and $t_c \approx 12$ days. Substituting into equation (11.10), we have

$$R° = (7 \text{ days}) \times (1 \text{ unit/day}) - [7 \text{ days}/12 \text{ days}] \times (12 \text{ units}) = 7 \text{ units}$$

where $[7/12] = 0$. This checks with the results we described in the situation where $t_L < t_c$, where $R° = t_L D$.

Consider the case where lead time is 30 days. Substituting into equation (14.10), we have

$$R° = (30 \text{ days}) \times (1 \text{ unit/day}) - [30 \text{ days}/12 \text{ days}] \times (12 \text{ units})$$

$$= 30 \text{ units} - [2.5] \times (12 \text{ units})$$

$$= 30 \text{ units} - 24 \text{ units}$$

$$= 6 \text{ units}$$

These results indicate that if we reorder 12 units ($Q° \approx 12$) each time the inventory level drops to 6 units, sufficient replenishment inventories will be incoming to satisfy demand during lead time. In this case, the 30 units required to meet lead-time demand would be 6 units in inventory at the time of reorder, 12 units that would arrive 6 days after reordering, and 12 that would arrive 18 days after the reorder. At the end of the 30th day, the replenishment inventory arrives.

For the case where $t_L < t_c$, replenishment inventories arrive at the end of the current inventory cycle. For the case where $t_L > t_c$, replenishment inventories arrive at the end of an inventory cycle in the future.

### *Sensitivity analysis*

In the discussion of the classic EOQ model [equation (14.6)], we implicitly assumed that the ordering cost, $C_O$; carrying cost per unit per time period, $C_C$; and demand per time period, $D$, are known with certainty. In reality, each of these factors is usually estimated. Because of potential estimation erring, it would be desirable to have some means for evaluating the impact on $Q°$ of errors in the estimates. In addition, we may not be able to order exactly $Q°$ units; for example, if suppliers impose order quantity restrictions, we may be required to order some quantity of units other than $Q°$. Thus, we need a technique to examine the impact of variations in model parameters or ordering in amounts other than $Q°$. Sensitivity analysis can be employed to examine these issues.

We should point out that sensitivity analysis used in inventory models differs from that employed earlier in conjunction with linear models. In linear programming, we only considered the effects of changing one variable at a time; in inventory analysis, we will simultaneously evaluate the effect of changing several variables.

**Model formulation.** In developing the sensitivity analysis model it is desirable to express the effect of errors or changes in the variables and/or parameters as a ratio of the actual economic order quantity to the estimated optimal economic order quantity. Therefore, let

$D'$ = *actual* value of demand    $D$ = *estimated* value of demand

$C'_O$ = *actual* value of ordering cost    $C_O$ = *estimated* value of ordering cost

$C'_C$ = *actual* value of carrying cost    $C_C$ = *estimated* value of carrying cost

The estimated economic order quantity is then represented (as noted earlier) by equation (14.6), while the actual economic order quantity is

$$Q' = \sqrt{\frac{2C'_O D'}{C'_C}}$$

If we then define $k$ as the ratio of the actual EOQ (that is, $Q'$) to the estimated *EOQ* (that is, $Q°$), then

$$k = \frac{Q'}{Q°} = \frac{\sqrt{2C'_O D'/C'_C}}{\sqrt{2C_O D/C_C}} \tag{14.11}$$

Expressed more succinctly,

$$k = \sqrt{\left(\frac{D'}{D}\right)\left(\frac{(C'_O/C'_C)}{C_O/C_C}\right)} \tag{14.12}$$

We can use this expression to evaluate the effect of errors or variations in the parameters and/or variables. For example, assume that for a given problem the actual cost factors are exactly equal to the estimated cost factors, but actual demand, $D'$, is 1450 units, while the estimated demand, $D$, was 2265. Substituting into the equation, we find

$$k = \sqrt{(1450/2265)\,(1)}$$

$$= \sqrt{.64}$$

$$= .80$$

Since $k = Q'/Q°$, and 2265/1450 is 156.2%, this tells us that a 56.2% error in estimating demand results in a 20% error in the size of the order quantity. That is, the actual order quantity, $Q'$, is only 80% as large as the estimated economic order quantity, $Q°$. (A similar analysis could be performed for errors or changes in the cost factors, if these exist.)

**Impact on cost of not employing $Q^\circ$.**    Using equation (14.12), we can evaluate the effects of errors or changes on the order quantity. Now we wish to evaluate how such changes affect the total cost.

Assume that the actual order quantity is $Q'$, rather than the estimated order quantity, $Q^\circ$. Using equation (14.5), we know that estimated total cost is

$$C_T = (C_O)(D/Q) + (C_C)(Q/2)$$

Therefore, the actual total cost would be

$$C'_T = (C_O)/(D/Q') + (C_C)(Q'/2)$$

Since $k = Q'/Q^\circ$, we know that $Q' = kQ^\circ$; therefore, $C'_T$ can be expressed as

$$C'_T = (C_O)(D/kQ^\circ) + (C_C)(kQ^\circ/2)$$

Substituting the value of $Q^\circ$ from equation (14.6), we then have

$$C'_T = (C_O)\left[ D \div \left( k\sqrt{\frac{2C_O D}{C_C}} \right) \right] + (C_C)\left( k\sqrt{\frac{2C_O D}{C_C}} \div 2 \right)$$

Collecting terms gives

$$C'_T = \left(\frac{1}{k}\right)\sqrt{\frac{C_O C_C D}{2}} + k\sqrt{\frac{C_O C_C D}{2}}$$

$$= \left( k + \frac{1}{k} \right)\sqrt{\frac{C_O C_C D}{2}} = \frac{k + 1/k}{2}\sqrt{2C_O C_C D}$$

From equation (14.9), $C^\circ_T = \sqrt{2C_O C_C D}$; therefore,

$$C'_T = \left( \frac{k + 1/k}{2} \right) C^\circ_T$$

Dividing both sides of the equation by $C^\circ_T$, we have

$$\frac{C'_T}{C^\circ_T} = \frac{k + 1/k}{2}$$

Recognizing that $C'_T/C^\circ_T$ is the ratio of total cost with an order quantity of $Q'$ to the total cost when the order quantity is $Q^\circ$, and defining this ratio as $l$, that is,

$$l = \frac{C'_T}{C^\circ_T}$$

we can write

$$l = \frac{k + 1/k}{2} \qquad (14.13)$$

The $k$ ratio thus provides a relative measure of the effect of changes on $Q°$, while the $l$ ratio provides a relative measure of the effect of changes on $C_T°$. In addition, we can relate the impact of changes in $Q$ on $C_T°$, since $l$ is a function of $k$. To get a better understanding of the $k$ and $l$ ratios and how they relate to order quantity, let us examine the total cost curve we developed earlier. Figure 14-7 is the total cost curve taken from Figure 14-3. The $k$ ratio is simply the quantity $Q_1'$ or $Q_2'$ divided by $Q°$. If $Q'$ is less than $Q°$, which is the case for $Q_1'$, then the ratio is less than 1; if $Q'$ is greater than $Q°$, which is the case for $Q_2'$, then $k$ is greater than 1. (When $Q' = Q°$, $k = 1$.) The $l$ ratio is $C_T'$ divided by $C_T°$. Note, however, that $l$ will never be less than 1 since the cost increases regardless of whether $Q'$ is less than or greater than $Q°$. In addition, note that the $l$ ratio ($C_T'/C_T°$) is the same for both $Q_1'/Q°$ and $Q_2'/Q°$.

We can check this latter point by using the $k$ and $l$ equations. Assume that $Q_1'$ is 20% less than $Q°$, and $Q_2'$ is 25% greater than $Q°$. For example, if $Q° = 300$, then $Q_1' = 240$ and $Q_2' = 375$. Therefore,

$$k_1 = Q_1'/Q° = 240/300$$

$$= 0.80$$

Using equation (14.13),

$$l_1 = \frac{k_1 + 1/k_1}{2} = \frac{.8 + 1/.8}{2}$$

$$= 2.050/2$$

$$= 1.025$$

For $Q_2'$ we have

$$k_2 = 375/300$$

$$= 1.25$$

From equation (14.13)

$$l_2 = \frac{1.25 + 1/1.25}{2}$$

$$= 2.050/2$$

$$= 1.025$$

Thus if $Q'$ is 25% too high or 20% too low, the total cost will increase by 2.5%. This tells us two things; first, in general, the costs of the EOQ model are insensitive to order quantities error (e.g., a +25% or −20% error in the order quantity results in only a 2.5% increase in $C_T^\circ$). Second, the EOQ model is more sensitive to $Q'$ values less than $Q^\circ$ than to those greater than $Q^\circ$. This latter point is what we would expect from analyzing the cost curve; note from Figure 14-7 that the curve has a steeper slope on the left side of $Q^\circ$ than on the right.

To illustrate the use of the $k$ and $l$ ratios, assume that we have estimated the values of $C_O$, $C_C$, and $D$, and computed $Q^\circ = 250$ units using the EOQ model, but we can only order units in lots of 100. Our choice thus would be to order 200 or 300 units. For $Q' = 200$ units, $k = .80$ and $l = 1.025$; for $Q' = 300$ units, $k = 1.2$ and $l = 1.0167$. We thus should order 300 units since the cost penalty for ordering 200 is 2.5% compared with a 1.67% increase for ordering 300.

**Sensitivity of time between orders, $t_c$.**   Using equation (14.8), we can compute the optimal time between orders, $t_c$ (based on the estimated $C_C$, $C_O$, and $D$); however, quite often one is faced with the decision of ordering at times other than the computed optimal. Just as it is important to know the impact of employing an order quantity that differs from the estimated optimal order size, it is important to know what impact differing order times will have on total cost.

Since $t_c = 1/N^\circ$ and $N^\circ = D/Q^\circ$, $t_c = Q^\circ/D$. To be consistent with the notations we have used throughout sensitivity analysis, we will let $t^\circ = t_c$; therefore,

$$t^\circ = Q^\circ/D$$

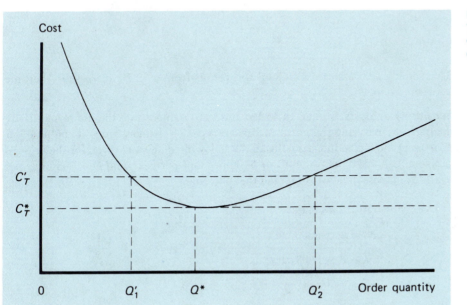

**FIGURE 14-7.**
**Total Cost Curve:**
**Cost Versus Order**
**Quantity**

If we then let $t'$ represent a time between orders other than $t°$, then

$$t' = Q'/D$$

Expressing these two relationships as a ratio, we then have

$$\frac{t'}{t°} = \frac{Q'/D}{Q°/D} = \frac{Q'}{Q°} = k \tag{14.14}$$

Since $k = Q'/Q°$, $t'/t°$ thus is equal to $k$. We can thus employ the $l$ ratio, equation (14.13), to determine the effect on cost for a change in time between orders.

To illustrate, assume that for a given problem we have estimated the values of $C_O$, $C_C$, and $D$, and have computed [using equation (14.8)] the optimal time between orders $t°$ to be 22.6 days. Assume also that management has a policy of placing orders only once each month (each 30 days). To determine the impact of this decision on cost we first compute $k$:

$$k = \frac{t'}{t°} = \frac{30}{22.6} = 1.327$$

Applying equation (14.13), then

$$l = \frac{k + 1/k}{2}$$

$$= \frac{1.327 + 1/1.327}{2}$$

$$= 1.0403$$

Thus, only a 4.03% increase in total cost results from a 32.7% increase in the time between orders.

**Sensitivity analysis applied to Video Inc.**   To demonstrate the use of sensitivity analysis for analyzing the effect of various types of changes, we will continue our analysis of the Video Inc. case. Recall the following data were given for the original problem: $C_O = \$20$ per order, $C_C = \$100$ per unit per year, and $D = 365$ units per year. From these data we computed the following:

$$Q° = 12.08 \text{ units}$$

$$N° = 30.2 \text{ orders per year}$$

$$t_c = t° = 12.08 \text{ days}$$

$$C_T° = \$1208.30$$

Now assume that Jefferson recognizes that it is difficult to order fractional units and that the actual order size would be 12 units rather than 12.08 units. He thus would like to determine the impact of rounding the order size down to 12. Since $k = Q'/Q°$, the ratio thus is

$$k = \frac{12.00}{12.08} = .99338$$

Therefore,

$$l = \frac{k + 1/k}{2} = \frac{.99338 + 1.00667}{2} = 1.000022$$

Then, since $l = C'_T/C°_T$, $C'_T = lC°_T$,

$$C'_T = (1.000022)(1208.30)$$

$$= \$1208.33$$

The new time between orders, $t'$, would be computed as follows:

$$\frac{t'}{t°} = k$$

Therefore,

$$t' = kt°$$

$$= (.99338)(12.08)$$

$$= 12 \text{ days}$$

By rounding the order quantity down to 12, Jefferson can order every 12 days. The effect of this decision would be negligible since the cost only increases $0.03 (from $1208.30 to $1208.33).

Now let us assume that after Jefferson completed his analysis he wanted to test the sensitivity of the original results (i.e., when $Q° = 12.08$) to changes in the cost factors. He reasoned that this would help in his review with Benson. Jefferson posed the following problem: "Suppose the carrying cost were $70 rather than the current value of $100. What would be the order size, and what would be the associated cost?"

Since the $k$ ratio is expressed as follows,

$$k = \sqrt{\left(\frac{D'}{D}\right)\left(\frac{C'_o/C'_c}{C_o/C_c}\right)}$$

and since neither demand nor the ordering is affected, the ratio of $C'_o/C'_c$ to $C_o/C_c$

will be in the proportion of 1/70 to 1/100. Therefore,

$$k = \sqrt{(1)\left(\frac{1/70}{1/100}\right)}$$

$$= \sqrt{1.4286}$$

$$= 1.19524$$

Since $k = Q'/Q°$, we know that $Q' = kQ°$. Therefore, the resulting order size is:

$$Q' = (1.19524)(12.08) = 14.44 \text{ units}$$

To compute the total cost associated with this order size, we must use equation (14.9). Equation (11.13) is not applicable at this point; it holds only for the case where $Q$ changes but $C_O$, $C_C$, and $D$ are constant. The associated cost thus is

$$C_T' = \sqrt{2C_O' C_C' D}$$

$$= \sqrt{2 \times 20 \times 70 \times 365}$$

$$= \$1010.94$$

With a 30% reduction in holding cost (from \$100 to \$70), total cost changes by 16.33% (from \$1208.30 to \$1010.94).

## EOQ Model with price breaks (quantity discounts)

In all the models presented thus far we assumed that the unit purchasing price was constant, thus purchasing cost was not included as a factor in the models. In practice it is not uncommon for suppliers to allow purchase price discounts if the replenishment orders are sufficiently large. Several different discount situations (policies) are possible; however, we will only consider the case where a single discount is allowed.

**Model structure.** One approach for evaluating the impact of a single discount is to compare the total cost for the optimal inventory policy without discounts with the total cost if the discount is accepted. Recall from our discussion of the classic EOQ model that total cost was defined as follows:

$$C_T = (C_O)(D/Q) + (C_C)/(Q/2) \tag{14.5}$$

The total-cost equations for evaluating discounts must include purchasing cost per time period; therefore, the total-cost equations would be:

$$C_{T_1} = (C_O)(D/Q°) + (C_C)(Q°/2) + (D)(P_{\text{no discount}}) \tag{14.15}$$

for the no-discount case,

where'    $P_{\text{no discount}}$ = per unit no discount price

and    $C_{T_2} = (C_O)(D/Q_{\text{discount}}) + (C_C)(Q_{\text{discount}}/2) + (D)(P_{\text{discount}})$    (14.16)

for the discount case,

where    $Q_{\text{discount}}$ = quantity purchased at the discount price

$P_{\text{discount}}$ = per-unit quantity discount price

$C_{T_1}$ is actually the minimum point on the total cost curve, while $C_{T_2}$ is the point on the quantity discount cost curve where $Q$ is the minimum quantity required for receiving the discount.

Note that in both the discount case [equation (14.16)] and the no-discount case [equation (14.15)] the carrying cost, $C_C$, is constant, even though $C_C$ was defined originally to be a function of the purchase price. A constant, $C_C$, is not a mandatory condition for developing the equations; however, it simplifies the analysis. Throughout the analysis we will assume that $C_C$ is constant and is a function of the original no-discount price.

The cost trade-off relationship that occurs when quantity discounts are considered is shown pictorially in Figure 14-8. The cost curve when no discount is considered will be higher than for the discount case since the product price is higher without a

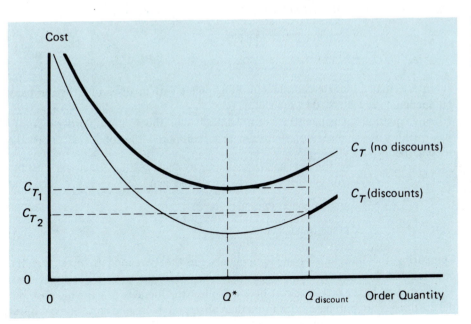

**FIGURE 14-8.**
**Inventory Struc-**
**ture for Quantity**
**Discount**

discount. The minimum order quantity required to receive a price discount is labeled $Q_{discount}$.

The actual cost curve that is applicable for the discount analysis is the darkened portion of the two curves. If the order quantity is less than $Q_{discount}$, the price discount is not allowed; therefore, the upper curve is relevant. If the order quantity is equal to or greater than $Q_{discount}$, we use the lower curve.

The objective in the discount analysis is to determine whether the lower point on the cost curve with no discount, $C_{T_1}$, is less than or greater than the lower limit on the discount cost curve, $C_{T_2}$. If $C_{T_1} > C_{T_2}$ (which is the case in Figure 14-8), then the discount should be "considered." We use the word "considered" because factors such as lack of storage space, tying up of capital (cash), inability of the receiving area to accommodate the additional volume of goods, spoilage, and other factors may well override the fact that $C_{T_1} > C_{T_2}$.

**Quantity discounts applied to Video Inc.**  To demonstrate the application of quantity discount analysis, let us assume that just as Jefferson was completing the evaluation of his ordering policy the manufacturer called and offered to provide a discount of 2% off the normal cost of $500 per unit for Video purchases in quantities of 20 or more. Jefferson was very excited, since this was exactly the quantity he had purchased last month.

Using the values $P = \$500$ per unit, $D = 365$ units per year, $Q° = 12.08$ units (rounded to a practical lot size, $Q° = 12$), $C_O = \$20$ per order, and $C_C = \$100$ per unit per year, Jefferson computed the total cost at the optimal order point [equation (14.15)].

$$C_{T_1} = (20)(365)/(12.08) + (100)(12.08/2) + (365)(500)$$

$$= 604.33 + 600 + 182,500$$

$$= \$183,704.33$$

This means that if Jefferson employs an EOQ policy with no discounts, the company will incur a cost of $183,704.33 per year.

Using equation (14.16), with $P = \$490$ and $Q = 20$ (the minimum order quantity that qualifies for a discount), Jefferson then computed the total cost under the discount policy.

$$C_{T_2} = (20)(365/20) + (100)(20/2) + (365)(490)$$

$$= 365 + 1000 + 178,850$$

$$= \$180,215.00$$

Comparing the individual cost components for the two models, note that the ordering cost decreases for the larger order size, while the carrying cost increases. The reduction in the ordering cost does not offset the increase in carrying cost, but the 2% discount in purchase price more than offsets the increased cost. The net result is a savings of $3489.33. Jefferson was elated.

## *Production lot-size model*

In all of the models considered thus far, we have assumed that the entire replenishment order was received instantaneously. For most retail establishments, this is a valid assumption; but in a production situation, the replenishment results from a production run, and the production run may take a significant time to complete. Figure 14-9 is a pictorial representation of inventory behavior in a production operation where the production-line output goes into the finished stock inventory and goods demanded are shipped from inventory.

Figure 14-9 illustrates the case of a production inventory replenishment operation with zero lead time and where stockouts are not allowed. We can relax these assumptions just as we did previously, but in this section we will concentrate only on the basic model. The term "production lot-size model" is the label used to describe this basic model. The decision variable for the model is $Q°$, the optimal production lot-size.

**Formulation of the model.**   With the exception of the fifth assumption, all of the assumptions associated with the classic EOQ model are applicable for the lot-size model. Based on these assumptions, one might conclude that the optimal lot size would equal $Q°$ for the classic model. However, from Figure 14-9 it can be seen that the maximum inventory level for the lot-size model is less than $Q$. The average inventory thus will be less than $Q/2$, which was the average inventory for the EOQ model. Since the average inventory is less, the carrying cost will be less than that for the classic model.

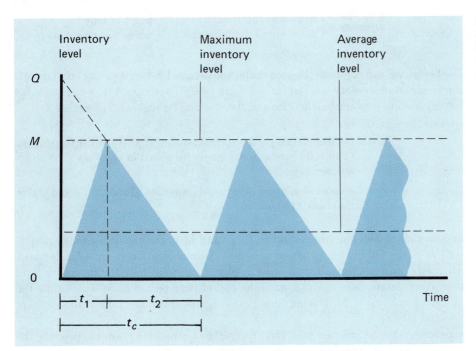

**FIGURE 14-9.
Inventory Behavior: Noninstantaneous Replenishment**

With this basic overview of the model, let us begin by giving the general statement of the lot-size model:

MINIMIZE:        total inventory cost = setup cost + holding cost                    (14.17)

Note that we use different terminology for costs. Instead of ordering cost, we now have setup cost, consisting of the labor and material costs associated with setting up machinery for a production run. Instead of carrying cost we use the term holding cost.

If we let $C_O$ = setup cost per production lot-size run, then the setup cost component is identical to the ordering cost component for the classic model. Therefore,

$$\text{setup cost} = (C_O)(D/Q)$$

If we let $C_C$ = holding cost per unit per time period, then the holding cost component of the lot-size model can be defined similarly to the carrying cost component for the EOQ model, i.e., holding cost is equal to $C_C$ times the average number of units held in inventory. As we have just indicated, however, average inventory for the lot-size model differs from the classic model. Before we can develop the holding cost equation, we must compute average inventory.

Average inventory per inventory cycle is defined as follows:

$$\begin{matrix} \text{average} \\ \text{inventory} \\ \text{per cycle} \end{matrix} = \left( \begin{matrix} \text{area under the demand} \\ \text{curve when inventory exists} \end{matrix} \right) \div \left( \begin{matrix} \text{length of time} \\ \text{when inventory exists} \end{matrix} \right)$$

But before we can compute the area under the demand curve, we must compute $M$, the maximum inventory level (refer to Figure 14-9). To compute $M$, we must define the production (replenishment) rate and the demand (usage) rate. Therefore, let

$r_1 =$    number of units per time period resulting from the production process. (This is the rate at which goods are placed in inventory. The rate is assumed to be constant.)

$r_2 =$    number of units per time period demanded. (This is equivalent to $D$ in the classic EOQ model.)

In a feasible model, the production rate, $r_1$, must be greater than the usage rate, $r_2$ (i.e., $r_1 > r_2$). Otherwise, production wouldn't be able to keep up with demand. Therefore, immediately after an order is placed in production, the inventory level rises at a constant rate $(r_1 - r_2)$, until the end of time period $t_1$, at which time the inventory is equal to $M$. During time period $t_2$, the inventory falls at the constant demand rate, $r_2$.

Since $r_1$ is the production rate, $Q/r_1$ is equal to $t_1$, the time period to produce the entire order. The number of units demanded during time period $t_1$ is $r_2 \times t_1$.

Substituting $t_1 = Q/r_1$,

$$\text{demand during} \atop \text{time period } t_1 = (Q/r_1)r_2$$

Therefore,

$$M = Q - (Q/r_1)r_2 = Q - Q\left(\frac{r_2}{r_1}\right) \qquad (14.18)$$

Having defined $M$, we can now compute the average inventory per cycle,

$$\text{average inventory} \atop \text{per cycle} = \frac{(1/2)Mt_1 + (1/2)Mt_2}{t_1 + t_2}$$

$$= \frac{(1/2)[Q - Q(r_2/r_1)]t_1 + (1/2)[Q - Q(r_2/r_1)]t_2}{t_1 + t_2}$$

$$= \frac{(1/2)[Q - Q(r_2/r_1)](t_1 + t_2)}{t_1 + t_2}$$

$$= \left(\frac{Q}{2}\right)\left(1 - \frac{r_2}{r_1}\right)$$

Since the inventory behavior is repetitive, the average inventory taken over a large number of inventory cycles would also be $(Q/2)(1 - r_2/r_1)$. Therefore, the holding cost is expressed as

$$\text{holding cost} = \left(\frac{Q}{2}\right)\left(1 - \frac{r_2}{r_1}\right)C_C \qquad (14.19)$$

Combining the setup and holding cost factors, the production lot-size model thus is

MINIMIZE: $\qquad C_T = (C_O)(D/Q) + (C_C)(Q/2)[1 - (r_2/r_1)] \qquad (14.20)$

**Solution to the model.** Since only two cost factors are involved in the $C_T$ cost function, we can find the lot size, $Q^\circ$, that minimizes $C_T$ by employing differential calculus. We will leave this exercise as well as that of finding $C_T^\circ$, $t_c^\circ$, and $N^\circ$ to the reader. The final equations are expressed as follows:

$$Q^\circ = \sqrt{\frac{2C_O D}{C_C[1 - (r_2/r_1)]}} \qquad (14.21)$$

$$C_T^\circ = \sqrt{2C_O C_C D[1 - (r_2/r_1)]} \qquad (14.22)$$

$$N^\circ = \sqrt{\frac{C_C D[1 - (r_2/r_1)]}{2C_O}} \qquad (14.23)$$

$$t_c^\circ = \sqrt{\frac{2C_O}{C_C D[1 - (r_2/r_1)]}}$$

(14.24)

**Application of the lot-size mode.** To demonstrate usage of the lot-size model, consider the following problem: The Hammel Company has decided to begin manufacturing a part that it has previously been purchasing from an outside vendor. The demand is 1000 units per month; the setup cost per run is $20, and holding cost is $5 per unit per year. Once a machine is running, it can produce parts at a rate of 2500 units per month. The company normally operates approximately 300 working days per year. Management at Hammel would like to know the production lot size to run, how often production runs should be made, and the total cost associated with the recommended run size.

From the information given, we note the following:

$$C_O = \text{setup cost} = \$20$$

$$C_C = \text{holding cost per unit per year} = \$5$$

$$r_1 = \text{production rate in units per month} = 2500$$

$$r_2 = D = \text{demand, in units per month} = 1000$$

The optimal lot size $Q^\circ$, thus is

$$Q^\circ = \sqrt{\frac{(2)(20)(1000)(12)}{(5)[1 - (1000/2500)]}}$$

$$= 400 \text{ units per lot}$$

Note that we multiplied $D$ (i.e., 1000) by 12 in order to express demand on an annual basis.

Using equation (14.24), we can compute the time between production runs.

$$t_c^\circ = 300 \sqrt{\frac{(2)(20)}{(5)(1000)(12)[1 - (1000/2500)]}}$$

$$= (300)(.0333)$$

$$= 10 \text{ days}$$

Using equation (14.22), the total inventory system cost associated with using a lot size of 400 is

$$C_T^\circ = \sqrt{(2)(20)(5)(1000)(12)[1 - (1000/2500)]}$$

$$= \sqrt{1,440,000}$$

$$= \$1200$$

Although it was not requested, we could compute the maximum inventory level, $M$, as follows: The production rate, $r_1$, is 2500 units per month or 100 units per day (assuming a 25-day month, i.e., $300/12 = 25$). For a lot size of 400, four days would be required to make the production run. Demand, $r_2$, is 1000 units per month or 40 units per day (i.e., $1000/25 = 40$). The inventory level for the first four days thus increases at 60 units per day (100 produced $-$ 40 used $=$ 60 inventoried). The maximum production level thus is 4 times 60 or 240 units. Using equation (14.18),

$$M = Q - Q(r_2/r_1)$$

$$= 400 - 400(1000/2500)$$

$$= 400 - 400(.4)$$

$$= 240 \text{ units}$$

## ▪ Other inventory concepts

Throughout the chapter we have focused our attention on order-point models. Lest one conclude that these are the most frequently used inventory control systems, we will briefly review some general inventory control concepts and some other inventory models (systems).

### The A-B-C classification system

The models we have examined throughout the chapter have dealt with single items. For a number of firms and businesses it is impractical to exercise control over every single item by use of EOQ analysis; rather, different inventory systems should be employed, depending on the value-volume analysis of the inventoried item.

One method of differentiating inventory items is the A-B-C classification system. The classification method segregates all inventory items into three groups, A, B, and C, based on some control criterion, such as cost, annual dollar inventory value, frequency of use, or some other factor. For discussion purposes we will use dollar inventory value as the classification criterion.

Figure 14-10 is a pictorial representation of the A-B-C inventory classification scheme, where the $x$-axis represents the percent volume of inventory and the $y$-axis represents the percent inventory value of the items. Category A usually includes that 10% of a firm's items that generally constitute approximately 70% of the total annual dollar value (cost) of the inventory. Detailed procedures, such as EOQ analysis and models, should be used for items in this category. Category B items account for another 10% of the items in inventory but are typically worth only approximately 20% of the total inventory value. Items in this group warrant less control than those items in category A. EOQ analysis is applicable for items in the group but the frequency with which the inventory is adapted and reviewed is less than category A. Category A and B items together constitute approximately 20% of the total items in the inventory and may account for approximately 90% of the dollar value of the inventory. Category C thus accounts for about 80% of the total items but only 10% of

**FIGURE 14-10.**
**Inventory Classifi-**
**cation**

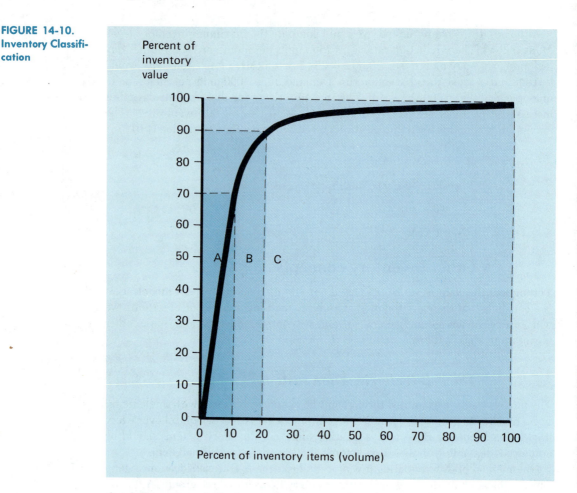

the dollar value of the inventory. EOQ analysis is not required for items in this category. Category C items are typically of such low value that the effort required to determine the economic order quantity or to review frequently is not economically justified.

## Periodic review systems

Many of the items that fall into the category B classification can be handled via a periodic review system. Recall from the introduction that in a periodic review system, inventories are not reviewed continuously; rather, checks are made at predetermined *fixed* intervals of time. Figure 14-11 is a pictorial representation of such a system.

If the inventory level is below the predesignated reorder level $R$, when inventory is reviewed (at fixed intervals of time), an order is placed of size $Q_i$ where $Q_i$ is the difference between the maximum inventory level ($S$) and the existing inventory level at the beginning of the $i$th review (or at the end of the $(i-1)$ review).

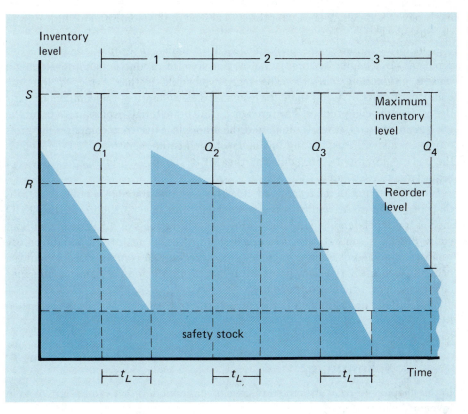

The major disadvantages of a periodic review system are that a relatively large safety stock is required, and nonuniform order sizes may lead to extra expense and inconvenience.

## Material requirements planning (MRP)

Order-point and periodic review systems both require a forecast of the demand for each inventory item. However, the demand for all inventory items is not necessarily *independent*, so employing an order-point system for *all* inventory items is not necessarily a good policy. Consider, for example, a manufacturing operation that produces lamps. Once a forecast has been made for the number of lamps required and a production plan for the assembly of the lamps has been established, the demand for the component parts that go into the assembly can be calculated. Demand for the component parts is completely determined by assembly needs; therefore, the term *dependent* demand more appropriately describes this situation. Assume for our example that 400 lamps are demanded monthly (every 4 weeks). Weekly demand for lamp shades would then be 0, 0, 0, 400. If we used an average demand of 100 units per week as the forecasted independent demand and used one of the order-point models to establish the order point and order quantity, we would likely have too much inventory for three weeks out of the month and too little during the final week.

A material requirements planning (MRP) system can be used to resolve this problem. MRP begins by forecasting the end item of production and developing a *master production schedule*. The master schedule is then *exploded* into the component parts by using the *bill of materials* that describes the component parts that go into the end product. The result of the bill of materials explosion is a list of the *gross requirements*, listed by item and the amounts. MRP then compares the gross requirements with the existing inventory of each component item and determines the *net requirements*. In addition, the MRP system identifies *when* the net requirements are needed.

From experience in the recent past, it has been demonstrated by a number of firms that an MRP system results in fewer stockouts and lower inventories than EOQ models for dependent demand items. However, the benefits of MRP are not without costs. Forecasts, master production schedules, bills of materials, and inventory replenishment activities need to be described precisely. A computerized system is a necessity because large data bases are required; and extensive data maintenance changes occur frequently (often daily).

A detailed description of the structure and use of MRP is described by J. Orlicky.[2]

## ▪ Summary

In this chapter we have attempted to develop basic models that can be employed in inventory planning and control.

As is the case for queuing theory, the inventory model required for a given inventory problem is a function of both the problem and its associated environment. For example, the classic economic order quantity model (the EOQ model) is relevant for a retail establishment where demand is constant, lead time is zero, no safety stock is required, and replenishment is instantaneous. The production lot-size problem is identical to the retail problem, except that replenishment occurs over time rather than instantaneously.

We developed a number of models in the chapter including those where lead time was not equal to zero, and those where price breaks were allowed. In each case, closed-form solutions were developed that allowed direct computation of $Q^\circ$, $R^\circ$, $N^\circ$, $t_c^\circ$, and $C_T^\circ$. In addition, sensitivity analysis was developed for the basic EOQ model with constant lead time.

Obviously these models provide only approximate solutions if the assumptions of the model do not reflect the environment of the problem being modeled. However, quite often the approximated values are far removed from the optimal.

It should be obvious from this chapter that inventory modeling is more complex than modeling linear systems and that a number of basic assumptions are made in

[2]J. Orlicky, *Material Requirements Planning* (New York: McGraw-Hill), 1974.

most models. This does not reduce the credibility of the models; rather, it reinforces the fact that modeling should be used as an aid to decision making, not a replacement for the process.

The inventory models covered in this chapter highlight the different classes of models, but this coverage, is only at an introductory level. Extensive research has been conducted in many of the model areas. This level of presentation, however, is beyond the scope of this text.

## ■ Glossary of terms

**A-B-C classification system:** A classification method for segregating inventory items into three groups, A, B, and C, based on some control criterion such as cost, annual dollar inventory value, frequency of use, or some other factor.

**backordering:** Demand that is delayed because of inventory shortage. The demand is accumulated and fulfilled when replenishment inventories are received (produced).

**carrying (holding) costs:** Those costs associated with holding a given level of inventory over a specified time period.

**classic EOQ model:** Refers to the basic inventory model where demand is constant, lead time is zero, inventory replenishment is instantaneous, and no shortages are allowed. The decision variable for the model is the order quantity that balances carrying costs, $C_C$, with ordering costs, $C_O$.

**lead time:** The time between the initiation of the replenishment activity (ordering production) and receipt of replenishment inventories.

**material requirement planning (MRP):** An inventory control system that operates by forecasting end-item demand, developing a master production schedule, exploding the schedule using a bill of materials, and finally determining net requirements by comparing gross requirements with existing inventory levels.

**order costs:** Cost associated with the inventory replenishment activity. This cost consists primarily of clerical and administrative costs associated with the steps and activities from the time a requisition for purchase is issued until the order is received, placed in inventory, and paid for.

**order-point system:** An inventory system in which a perpetual inventory record is maintained. Replenishment orders are issued when the inventory drops to a predetermined level referred to as the reorder point.

**periodic review system:** An inventory system in which inventories are reviewed at fixed intervals of time. The order quantity under this system is the difference between actual and desired inventory.

**production costs:** The cost associated with manufacturing replenishment inventories.

**production lot-size model:** Basic EOQ model where inventory replenishment occurs over time rather than instantaneously.

**production models:** Those models in which replenishment inventories are produced internally by the firm.

**purchase costs:** The cost associated with the actual purchase of an item for replenishing inventories.

**reorder point:** The level at which replenishment orders are released in an order-point inventory system.

**retail models:** Those models in which replenishment inventories are purchased from suppliers outside the firm.

**setup costs:** Primarily the labor and material costs associated with setting up machinery for production.

**shortage costs:** The cost associated with a stockout.

**shortage (stockout):** A condition when demand exceeds the quantity of inventory on hand.

## ▪ Review questions

1. Differentiate between deterministic and stochastic inventory models.

2. Identify the basic functions performed by inventories.

3. Differentiate between a retail model and a production model.

4. Define each of the following terms.
   a.   lead time
   b.   shortage
   c.   backordering
   d.   system structure
   e.   time horizon of the model

5. What cost factors are considered in most inventory models? Explain the cost trade-off of these factors.

6. What are the basic assumptions upon which the classic EOQ model is built?

7. Sketch the inventory/cost trade-off relationship for the classic EOQ model.

8. How is $R°$, the optimal reorder point, determined for the classic EOQ model?

9. Explain the relationship between reorder point, lead time, and constant demand.

10. Sketch the "inventory picture" for the basic inventory model where lead time is greater than zero, $t_L > 0$, and inventory cycle time, $t_c$, is less than lead time, i.e., $t_L > t_c$. Explain the model for this situation.

11. How does one handle the case for variable demand for the case presented in Question 10?

12. Explain the key difference in sensitivity analysis used for inventory analysis and that used for linear models. What are the benefits of sensitivity analysis from a practical point of view?

13. How does the production lot-size model differ from the classic EOQ model? Use pictorial diagrams in your explanation.

14. Explain the A-B-C classification system. Use a pictorial diagram in your explanation.

15. Define the term *material requirement planning*. Differentiate how *independent* and *dependent* demand are handled by an MRP system.

## ▪ True/false questions

1. Inventory analysis is similar to queuing analysis in that a single model is not applicable for every inventory problem.

2. A deterministic demand inventory model means that demand is known with certainty and constant.

3. The classic economic order quantity (EOQ) model assumes that no safety stock is required and no shortages (stockouts) are allowed.

4. The optimal number of orders per time period (for the classic EOQ model) is equal to the optimal order quantity, $Q°$, divided by the demand per time period.

5. The following reorder-point model

$$R° = t_L D - [t_L/t_c]Q°$$

is applicable when $t_L > t_c$ but not when $t_L < t_c$.

6. Inventory models are available that will allow one to evaluate the effect of errors or variations in the parameters and/or variables, such as $D$, $C_O$, and $C_S$, of a basic model. In using such models, it would not be unusual to have a 50% error in estimating demand, $D$, result in a 50% error in the size of the order quantity, $Q$.

7. For the production lot-size model, all assumptions associated with the classic EOQ model—with the exception of instantaneous replenishment of inventory—are applicable, and the maximum inventory levels for the two models are equal.

## ■ Problems

1. Heath Manufacturing Company purchases part no. 644, used in the production of stereophonic equipment, from an outside vendor. During the year, Heath expects to produce approximately 100,000 systems that utilize part no. 644. The demand for the part throughout the year is relatively constant. The cost associated with ordering is $25. The inventory cost policy that Heath has traditionally employed is to charge 20% of the purchase cost as the annual inventory holding cost for any item in inventory. The purchase price that Heath pays for each part no. 644 is $6.25.

   a. Determine the optimal order quantity that Heath should employ in order to minimize cost.
   b. What is the total cost associated with the optimal order quantity?
   c. How many orders would Heath place during the year?
   d. What assumptions have you made in solving parts (a), (b), and (c)?

2. The Delta Shoe Company purchases large quantities of leather for production of its shoes. Currently the company purchases all of its leather from the Reggins Company since Reggins has always been able to provide immediate delivery on standard leather stock. Because Delta has been able to get immediate delivery on its orders, the company has not employed any particular ordering policy. The new plant manager at Delta is of the opinion that savings can result by employing an appropriate ordering policy. It has been determined that the cost associated with ordering is approximately $20 per order. The cost of carrying one unit of leather (approximately 20 square feet) in inventory for one year is $40. Delta has forecast that approximately 6400 units of leather will be needed during the year. Demand for the leather is fairly constant throughout the year. The plant manager at Delta would like to determine the following.

   a. The optimum order quantity per order.
   b. The average (expected) inventory level.
   c. The total cost associated with the policy computed in step (a).
   d. The number of *days* between orders for the ordering policy in step (a). Assume the company operates 360 days per year.
   e. The optimal number of orders per year.

3. Graph the inventory level for Problem 2.

4. Usage for a certain product is constant at 100 items per month; ordering cost is $5 per unit; and inventory carrying cost is $0.40 per month per unit. Determine the economic order quantity and the associated minimum cost. How many weeks elapse between orders? (Assume 1 month = 4 weeks.)

5. Compute the optimal order quantity for Problem 4 if usage is 8000 units per month, ordering cost is $15 per unit, and carrying cost is $0.30 per week.

6. Assume that the Heath Company (Problem 1) operates 50 weeks out of the year and 6 days per week.

   a. Compute the reorder point associated with the optimal ordering policy if lead time for an order is 4 days.

   b. Compute the reorder point if the lead time is 8 days; 10 days.

7. Compute the reorder point for Delta Shoe Company (Problem 2) if the lead time is 9.0 days.

8. The Heath Company (Problems 1 and 6) has decided to order every 2 weeks with an order quantity of 4000 units. Compute the cost penalty the company will incur by employing this policy.

9. Because of an internal reorganization, the Delta Shoe Company (Problem 2) would like to consider placing all orders every 10 days. Determine the impact of this proposed policy.

10. Home Mart Inc., a large furniture distributor, purchases items in large quantities. The company is currently examining the purchasing policy for each item it handles. The cost of ordering and handling a particular item is $40 per order. The item costs the distributor $240. The annual cost that Home Mart incurs on inventoried items is 25% of the purchase cost. Historical records show that annual demand is essentially constant at 240 units.

    a. Compute the optimal order quantity that Home Mart should employ.

    b. Compute the optimal order quantity if the company is only allowed to purchase the item in multiples of 10 units.

11. The D & H Manufacturing Company is a specialty company that produces motors for garage door and overhead opening systems. The company has forecast, from past data, that 20,000 motors will be demanded during the coming year. The past data show that this demand is reasonably constant throughout the year. The company operates 250 days annually and can produce 160 motors per day. The production setup cost associated with each production run is $150. The annual carrying/holding cost for any motor produced but stored in inventory is $16.

    a. Compute the optimal production lot size that D & H should employ.

    b. What is the cost associated with the production plan in part (a)? Identify the component parts.

    c. What is the time (in days) between production runs?

12. The Acoustic Sound Company produces and sells stereophonic sound components and systems. The company is a multinational organization with offices and sales outlets throughout the world. The company has projected that 60,000 A1-X amplifiers will be required each month during the coming year. The company has decided, because of construction constraints and other resource limitations, to purchase half of the amplifiers from an outside vendor. (The vendor has an amplifier system that is equivalent to the A1-X.) The vendor can deliver the amplifiers the same day in which they are ordered. The

A1-X costs Acoustic $30.00 to produce; the vendor price is $34.80. The ordering cost associated with purchasing the units externally is $35.00 per order. Annual carrying/holding cost is 15% of the purchase price/production cost. The setup cost associated with producing the A1-X is $50.00. Acoustic has the production capacity to produce 150,000 A1-X amplifiers per month.

**a.** Compute the optimal order quantity to be purchased from the outside vendor.

**b.** Determine the optimal in-house production lot size.

**c.** What is the total inventory cost for the A1-X?

**d.** Compute the optimal number of purchase orders per month.

**e.** Compute the optimal number of production runs per month.

13. The Ethel Company manufactures a gear system used in earth-moving equipment. The gear system is produced on a continuous assembly line that operates at a rate of 120 units per day. A subassembly part used in the gear system is manufactured on a special lathe. The lathe operation can run at a rate of 400 subparts per day. Because the lathe operation can run at a higher rate than the assembly line, it handles a number of jobs, including the production of the gear system parts. When parts are being run on the lathe, deliveries are made directly to the assembly area; otherwise, the assembly line draws parts from inventory. Given the following information:

> Inventory holding cost per piece = $2 per year
>
> Setup cost = $110
>
> Lead time = 10 working days
>
> Work days per year = 250

**a.** Determine the economic production (ordering) quantity for the lathe operation that would be requested by the assembly line.

**b.** Determine the reorder point.

**c.** Assume the production rate of the assembly line increases (decreases). Would this alter the answers in part (a)? How?

14. A limousine service company uses gasoline at the rate of 11,900 gallons/month. The gasoline costs $1.12/gallon, with a setup (delivery) cost of $500. The inventory holding cost is $0.02/gallon/month.

**a.** Assuming shortages are not allowed, determine the quantity and timing (how often) of orders.

**b.** Assuming that shortages cost $0.45/gallon/month, determine the quantity and timing of orders.

**c.** Assuming that the cost for the gasoline drops to $1.02/gallon if at least 65,000 gallons are purchased, determine the quantity and timing of orders. (Assume that no shortages are allowed.)

15. the XYZ Import Company imports olives, as well as other items used by specialty restaurants. The company has determined that the ordering costs on an order of Extra Fancy olives is $90 and the carrying charges are 40% of the average value of the inventory. XYZ buys approximately $1,350,000 of the olives annually. Currently the company is importing the olives on an optimal EOQ basis, but has been given the option of purchasing the olives for 50% discount if purchases are made exactly six times a year. Should the company accept this arrangement? Explain.

16. The Beta Corporation employs storage/shipping crates to package its specialty products. The corporation purchases the crates from an outside vendor. The quantity discount schedule the vendor will provide is,

| Order Quantity | Price per Crate |
| --- | --- |
| 1–599 | $12.00 |
| 600–1199 | 11.50 |
| 1200–1799 | 11.10 |
| 1800–over | 11.00 |

It has been determined that ordering cost is $16 per order. The inventory policy for the corporation is to charge an inventory carrying cost of 20% of the purchase price for the average inventory held during the year. Beta has forecast that 2200 crates will be needed during the year. What order quantity should Beta employ in order to minimize total cost? (Holding cost remains constant regardless of discounts taken.)

**15**

# Probability Review

## ■ Introduction

Many of the decision-making topics presented in this book are based on the assumption of deterministic information. We often simplify our decision task by assuming, at least as an initial step, that the values of all problem parameters are known with certainty, and that the future holds no surprises for us. In the chapter on breakeven analysis, we assumed that we knew the market demand for our product for each different pricing policy that we might wish to examine. In our discussion of inventory, we assumed that such parameters as demand and order lead time were known with certainty. In the chapters on networks and mathematical programming, we assume certainty of our information to facilitate the solution of complex problems, and then test the effects of different degrees of inaccuracies in that information on the solutions we have derived.

For certain other types of decision problems, however, we cannot assume certainty of information and then test the criticality of that assumption, because the uncertainty is the crux of the problem and must be dealt with directly if any meaningful decisions are to be made. It is these decisions under uncertainty, or decisions influenced by the likelihood of future events, that are the concern of the next six chapters. Decision analysis, game theory, Markov chains, queuing analysis, and simulation are techniques designed to deal with uncertainty.

In order to understand these topics as they are presented, it is necessary to have an understanding of basic statistics, especially probability and probability distributions. This chapter provides a basic introduction to probability and probability distributions, along with examples of the application of these concepts.

## ■ Probability

We have all heard statements such as "He has only a one-in-five chance of winning the election," "There is a 60% chance of snow in New York today," "His horse has a better-than-ever chance of finishing the race," or "Making it through the winter without a cold is a long shot." Each of these and the other similar statements that we hear daily are attempts by people to describe their perceptions as to the likelihood that some future event will happen. If these statements can be quantified, the resulting measure of one's belief in an outcome is called a **probability.**

*probability*

There are three major concepts as to the derivation of probabilities. They are the theoretical concept, the subjective evaluation concept, and the frequency concept of

*theoretical*
*concept*

probability. The **theoretical concept** relies on some theory or known phenomenon to suggest the relevant probabilities. While available data may suggest parameters that define the realm within which events can occur, it is some theory that provides the actual form of the probabilities. Examples include gambling theories that suggest likelihoods, or theories in chemistry or the other physical sciences that suggest the form of probability outcomes.

*subjective*
*probabilities*

As the name implies, **subjective probabilities** are those probabilities resulting from the subjective assessment of some individual, normally an expert in the area within which the probability fits. Such subjective assessments are necessary in cases where historical data is not available and experimentation is not possible, leaving expert opinion as the only choice. Economists are often called on to render subjective probability assessments as to future behavior of interest rates, consumer spending, and so on.

*frequency*
*concept*

The **frequency concept** relies on experimentation as a basis for probability assessment. If we select a sample of our product and 20% of the units in the sample are faulty, we might infer from this frequency that there is a 20% chance that any unit selected from our product output will be faulty. In similar fashion, past history may be viewed as an experiment or a sample of what is to come. If in the past it has rained one day out of every three, in the absence of any meteorological data we might infer that there is a $\frac{1}{3}$ chance of rain tomorrow. Of course, when we make such assessments we had better be sure that we have lots of past data on which to estimate the frequency, and that we are exhausting all information that might bear on the likelihood of the future event.

*statistics*
*parameters*

The frequency concept parallels the general purpose of statistics, that of making inferences about a large body of data, called the population, based on information contained in some subset of the population, called a sample. We calculate numerical descriptors from the sample called **statistics,** and use them to estimate population values called **parameters.** The true probability of some future event is a parameter, and our estimate of that probability from a sample is a statistic. In the following sections we will look at some different types of probabilities and some rules for calculating them.

## *Sample space*

*events*

Every experiment results in one or more outcomes out of a set of possible outcomes. We will call these possible outcomes of an experiment **events.** As an example, suppose that we draw a playing card from a normal deck with 52 cards. Immediately, we can identify 52 different outcomes or events that could result. The card could be a two of clubs, or an ace of diamonds, or any of the other unique 50 cards in the deck. However, there are other events that could occur, depending on how we define our events and exactly what we are interested in. A possible event is that the card drawn could be a four. Another possible event is that it could be from the suit of spades. Yet another is that the value of the card may be less than five. You will notice a difference between the first set of 52 possible events and the last several that were named. The difference is that the latter events are combinations of the first 52 events. There are four different cards that could be drawn that would result in the card simply being a four. One-fourth of all the cards are spades and would result in that event. Sixteen different cards have values less than five.

The first type of event that cannot be decomposed is generally called a **simple event.** Any experiment will always result in one and only one simple event. The other events that were made up of simple events and could be decomposed into those simple events are referred to as **compound events.** The only limit to the possible number of compound events is the number of pertinent ways that the simple events can be combined. We will use the notation $E$ to represent simple events, and any other capital letter to represent compound events. Thus, our example had 52 simple events, $E_1$, $E_2$, ..., $E_{52}$, and we also defined three compound events, call them $A$, $B$, and $C$.

*simple event*

*compound events*

As another example, suppose that we toss two coins into the air and record the outcomes. There are four possible simple events:

$E_1$     (head, head)

$E_2$     (head, tail)

$E_3$     (tail, head)

$E_4$     (tail, tail)

Can you think of some compound event definitions? One possibility is the compound event that we observe at least one head. This compound event, call it $A$, will occur if any of the simple events $E_1$, $E_2$, or $E_3$ occurs. Another possibility is the event that we observe the same outcome on both coins (call this compound event $B$). This would happen if either $E_1$ or $E_4$ occurs. Again, the number of compound events depends on how many we are interested in and choose to define.

The set of all simple events for an experiment is generally referred to as its **sample space,** since all possible outcomes or samples, simple or compound, may be found within this set. Venn diagrams are often used to illustrate the concept of sample space. Figure 15-1 is the Venn diagram illustrating the sample space for our coin-toss example. Note that we have indicated our compound events by encircling all simple events contained within the compound event.

*sample space*

Such a framework makes it easier to define probabilities, especially probabilities of compound events. If we assign a probability to each simple event in the sample space, call them $P(E_i)$ for each simple event $i$, which conform to the requirements of probability

$$0 \le P(E_i) \le 1 \qquad \text{for each simple event } i$$

$$\sum_i P(E_i) = 1$$

then the probability of any compound event is equal to the sum of the probabilities of all simple events making up the compound event. Let us return to our coin-toss example. If both coins are "fair" coins and produce either a head or a tail with equal likelihood, then each of the four simple events we defined earlier should have an equal chance of occurrence. That is, $P(E_1) = P(E_2) = P(E_3) = P(E_4) = \frac{1}{4}$. For the compound event $A$ (at least one head), the probability of this event is $P(A) = P(E_1) +$

FIGURE 15-1.
Venn Diagram of
the Coin-Toss
Example

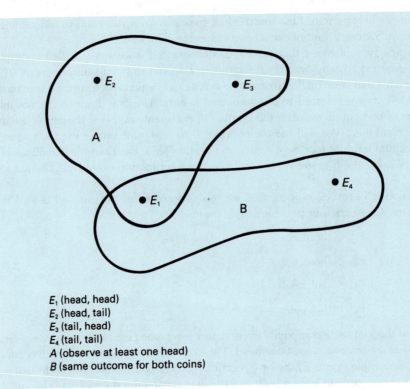

$E_1$ (head, head)
$E_2$ (head, tail)
$E_3$ (tail, head)
$E_4$ (tail, tail)
A (observe at least one head)
B (same outcome for both coins)

$P(E_2) + P(E_3) = \frac{1}{4} + \frac{1}{4} + \frac{1}{4} = \frac{3}{4}$. For the event $B$ (both coins result in the same outcome), the probability is $P(B) = P(E_1) + P(E_4) = \frac{1}{4} + \frac{1}{4} = \frac{1}{2}$.

As another example of summing simple event probabilities, suppose that we have five units of a particular product in our inventory, call them units 1, 2, 3, 4, and 5. Let us further suppose that, unknown to us, units 1 and 2 are defective. A customer calls in an order for three units of the product, and, not knowing that any units are bad, we choose three of the units at random and ship them to the customer. What are the possible contents of the shipment? In other words, what are the different simple events that make up the sample space? Enumerating all possible combinations of the five units taken three at a time, we get:

|        | Items in Shipment |
| --- | --- |
| $E_1$ | (1, 2, 3) |
| $E_2$ | (1, 2, 4) |
| $E_3$ | (1, 2, 5) |
| $E_4$ | (1, 3, 4) |
| $E_5$ | (1, 3, 5) |
| $E_6$ | (1, 4, 5) |
| $E_7$ | (2, 3, 4) |
| $E_8$ | (2, 3, 5) |
| $E_9$ | (2, 4, 5) |
| $E_{10}$ | (3, 4, 5) |

Because we did not know which units were defective and selected the units to be included in the shipment entirely at random, each of the 10 simple events in our list should have an equal probability of $\frac{1}{10}$ of being the actual shipment. Using this information about the probabilities of the simple events, we can examine the probabilities of some more interesting compound events:

1.  *What is the probability that the entire shipment is good?* This compound event occurs only if items 3, 4, and 5 comprise the shipment. Therefore, $P(\text{entire shipment is good}) = P(E_{10}) = \frac{1}{10}$.

2.  *What is the probability that there is no more than one bad item in the shipment?* This happens only if items 1 and 2 are *not* both in the shipment. Thus, $P(\text{no more than one bad item in the shipment}) = P(E_4) + P(E_5) + \cdots + P(E_{10}) = \frac{7}{10}$.

3.  *What is the probability of* exactly *one bad item in the shipment?* This is the same as the previous event, except that it excludes event $E_{10}$, where there are no bad items. Therefore, $P(\text{exactly one bad item in ship-ment}) = \frac{6}{10}$.

The main difficulty with this method of computing event probabilities is the effort involved in enumerating the entire sample space. If we modified our previous example slightly, 15 units in inventory with three to be shipped would result in 455 possible shipments in our sample space! In the next few sections we will present some further rules for computing and combining probabilities that often make it unnecessary to enumerate the entire sample space.

## Probability laws and relations

There are several laws governing the computation of the probability of an event from the probabilities of other events, and some event relations that are useful in applying these laws. We will discuss some of the most important ones.

**1.** If $A$ is an event, the **complement** of $A$ is the set containing all points in the sample space that are not in $A$. $A'$ is the notation used to represent the complement of *complement* $A$. Figure 15-2 is a Venn diagram that illustrates the concept of a complement. Because the sum of the probabilities of all points in the sample space is 1, it is clear that $P(A) + P(A') = 1$, since everything is in either $A$ or $A'$. This relation can also be written as $P(A) = 1 - P(A')$. Sometimes it is easier to find the probability of the complement of an event and work backward in this manner rather than attempt to find the event probability directly.

**2.** The **union** of two events $A$ and $B$ is the set of all simple events contained within *union* $A$ or $B$ or both. For this reason the union is also called the "or" operation, and instead of saying "union," people sometimes say "$A$ or $B$." If a game can result in either a win, a loss, or a tie for a particular team, then the compound event {win or tie} is the union of the two simple events {win} and {tie}. The union is written $A \cup B$. Figure 15-3 illustrates the union of $A$ and $B$. The union can be applied to as many events as

FIGURE 15-2.
Venn Diagram of
an Event and Its
Complement

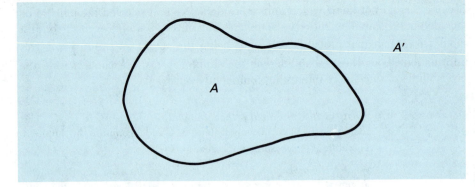

*(caption, left margin)*
**FIGURE 15-2.**
**Venn Diagram of**
**an Event and Its**
**Complement**

we wish. The union of the four events $A$, $B$, $C$, and $D$ would be written $[(A \cup B) \cup C] \cup D$, and is the collection of all points within $A$ or $B$ or $C$ or $D$.

*intersection*

**3.** The **intersection** of two events $A$ and $B$ is the set of points that are contained within both $A$ and $B$. For this reason, it is called the "and" operation, and instead of intersection, people sometimes say "$A$ and $B$." If $A = \{E_1, E_2, E_3\}$ and $B = \{E_3, E_4\}$, then the intersection of $A$ and $B$, written $A \cap B$, would be $\{E_3\}$. Figure 15-4 is a Venn diagram of an intersection. The intersection operation may be extended to as many events as we wish, and would be written $[(A \cap B) \cap C]$ . . . for multiple events. If the intersection of two or more events is empty (i.e., the events have no points in

*mutually*
*exclusive*

common), the events are said to be **mutually exclusive.**

**4.** It is sometimes the case that the probability of occurrence of one event depends on whether or not some other event has occurred. Suppose that we have a bin with 10 golf balls in it and two of the balls are painted red. The probability of drawing out a red ball on a random draw is $\frac{2}{10}$. If we draw out a ball and keep it out, the result of a second draw is definitely dependent on the result of the first draw. If the first ball was red, there would be one red ball left among the nine remaining balls, for a $\frac{1}{9}$ chance of drawing a red ball on the second try. If the first ball was not red, there would be two red balls left among the nine remaining balls, for a $\frac{2}{9}$ chance of drawing a red ball on the second try. Thus, $P$(draw two is red given that draw one was red) $= \frac{1}{9}$ and $P$(draw two is red given that draw one was not red) $= \frac{2}{9}$. This type of

FIGURE 15-3.
Venn Diagram of
a Union of Two
Events (Shaded
Area Is the Union)

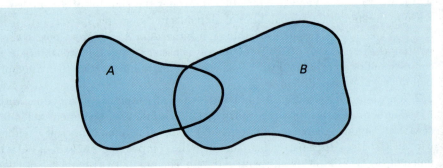

*(caption, left margin)*
**FIGURE 15-3.**
**Venn Diagram of**
**a Union of Two**
**Events (Shaded**
**Area Is the Union)**

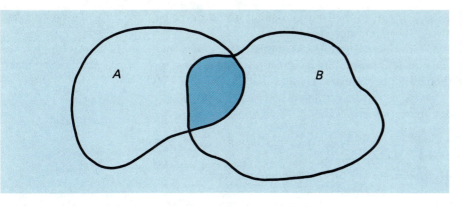

FIGURE 15-4.
Venn Diagram of
an Intersection of
Two Events
(Shaded Area Is
the Intersection)

probability where one event's likelihood is conditional on another event is called a
**conditional probability.** Obviously, we are more interested in business problems
such as the probability that a product will be successful given that its test marketing
was successful than we are in drawing golf balls from a bin, but the principle is the
same.

    If we are interested in the probability of an event $A$ given that another event $B$ has
occurred, we use the notation $P(A|B)$, and can calculate the conditional probability
with the formula

*conditional
probability*

$$P(A|B) = \frac{P(A \cap B)}{P(B)}$$

Likewise, for the reverse situation the formula is

$$P(B|A) = \frac{P(A \cap B)}{P(A)}$$

Two events $A$ and $B$ are said to be **independent** if $P(A|B) = P(A)$ or $P(B|A) = P(B)$.
If this is not true, the events are dependent. Put simply, if the probability of one
event is not conditional on the probability of another event, they are independent of
one another.

*independent*

    To illustrate the formulas and the concept of dependence, suppose that $A$ =
(successful new product introduction) and $B$ = (successful test marketing). Suppose
further that $P(A) = .30$, $P(B) = .50$, and $P(A \cap B) = .20$. Using the first formula,
$P$(successful new product introduction given successful test marketing) is

$$P(A|B) = \frac{.20}{.50} = .40$$

Because $P(A|B)$ is not equal to $P(A)$, the outcome of the product introduction *is*
dependent on the outcome of the test marketing. Notice that $P(B|A)$ does not make

sense here, given that test marketing would never be done after the product has already been introduced.

**5.** Given our definitions of intersection, union, and conditional probability, we can state four probability laws that relate these three types of probabilities and make them easier to calculate. These probability laws are as follows:

*Multiplication law:*

$$P(A \cap B) = P(A) \times P(B|A)$$

*Multiplication law for independent events:*

$$P(A \cap B) = P(A) \times P(B)$$

*Addition law:*

$$P(A \cup B) = P(A) + P(B) - P(A \cap B)$$

*Addition law for mutually exclusive events:*

$$P(A \cup B) = P(A) + P(B)$$

These laws are simply stating what is already obvious if you have examined the earlier Venn diagrams closely. The probability of an intersection is the percentage of one event that overlaps another event. The probability of a union is the probability of one event plus the probability of the other event, minus the overlap or intersection probability so that we do not count it twice. The modifications for independent events and mutually exclusive events follow from our earlier observations that if two events are independent, then $P(B|A) = P(B)$; and if two events are mutually exclusive, then $P(A \cap B) = 0$.

*marginal*
*probabilities*
*joint*
*probabilities*

In the preceding paragraphs, we have looked at rules involving single event probabilities, often called **marginal probabilities,** intersectional probabilities, often called **joint probabilities,** and conditional probabilities. The implementation of these rules will make more sense as we look at some examples using them. It is also useful to examine two different ways that we may structure what we are given to make understanding of the required steps a little easier. The following two examples illustrate these two alternatives.

# ■ Example

## *Personnel screening*

The personnel department of a large company has past data on employee applications. These data indicate that 20% of all applicants for assembly-line jobs in the past have had prior experience in the area. They also know that of those people with experience, 70% pass the mandatory written personnel test the company gives, and of those without experience, 50% pass. Furthermore, experienced applicants who pass the exam have about a 60% chance of being hired, while inexperienced applicants who pass have about a 30% chance of being hired. Applicants who fail the exam are automatically rejected. The company is beginning to wonder if they should even test those individuals without prior experience.

How do we organize our thoughts to tackle this problem? First, we should define some "events" that pertain to the problem. Having experience, passing the exam, and being hired are three obvious events that may occur. The complements of these events are also possible outcomes. The total list of possible outcomes is

$A$ = have prior assembly experience

$A'$ = do not have prior assembly experience

$B$ = pass the personnel exam

$B'$ = do not pass the personnel exam

$C$ = hired by the company

$C'$ = not hired by the company

The data that we were given about event $A$ is marginal information. That is, it is a simple probability that any given applicant will have experience. Knowing the probability of $A$ automatically gives us the probability of $A'$. The other probabilities of passing and being hired were stated conditionally, and also give us knowledge of their complements. Therefore we know several event probabilities, but we need some way to organize it.

A probability tree like the one shown in Figure 15-5 is one way of arranging our problem. Once again, the branches marked $A$ and $A'$ are marginal probabilities, and the $B$, $B'$, $C$, and $C'$ branches are conditional probabilities. In order to know whether it is worthwhile to test inexperienced applicants, we need to know the percentage of inexperienced applicants who are hired [the conditional probability of being hired given that you are inexperienced, $P(C|A')$] in relation to the percentage of experienced applicants who are hired [the conditional probability of being hired given that you are experienced, $P(C|A)$]. Before we can get these, we need certain joint probabilities.

Looking at the top set of branches in Figure 15-5, how do we calculate $P[(A \cap B) \cap C]$? Remembering that $P(A \cap B) = P(A) \times P(B|A)$, we can get

FIGURE 15-5.
Probability Tree for
the Assembly-Line
Hiring Example
(Values in Paren-
theses Are Branch
Probabilities—
Marginals for *A*
and Conditionals
for *B* and *C*)

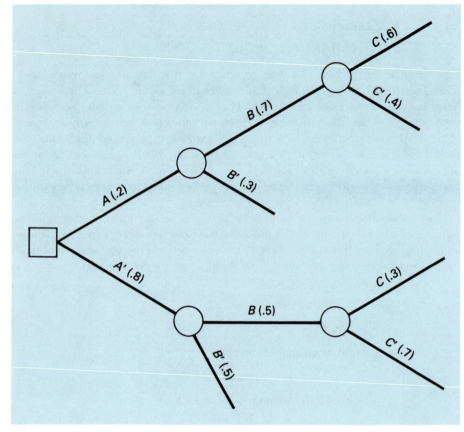

$P(A \cap B)$ by multiplying .2 times .7. Now, $P[(A \cap B) \cap C] = P(A \cap B) \times P(C|A \cap B)$, or .2(.7) times .6, for a joint probability of .084. Because the $B$ and $C$ probabilities are already conditionals, we can get the joint probability for any possible path through the tree by multiplying the probabilities along the path. Figure 15-6 is the same probability tree with all of the joint probabilities computed. Now we can calculate the conditional probabilities that we wanted. Remembering our multiplication law,

$$P(A \cap C) = P(A) \times P(C|A)$$

we can cross-multiply and get:

$$P(C|A) = \frac{P(A \cap C)}{P(A)}$$

Recognizing that $P(A \cap C)$ is the same as $P[(A \cap B) \cap C]$, since you cannot be

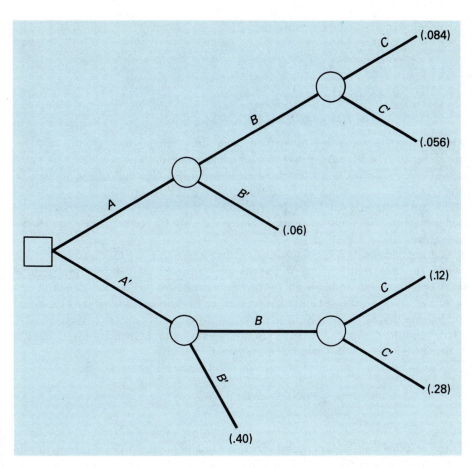

FIGURE 15-6.
Probability Tree for
the Assembly-Line
Hiring Example
with Path (Joint)
Probabilities

hired without passing the exam,

$$P(C|A) = \frac{.084}{.2} = .42$$

42% of the experienced applicants are eventually hired. In like fashion:

$$P(C|A') = \frac{P(A' \cap C)}{P(A')} = \frac{.12}{.80} = .15$$

Only 15% of all inexperienced applicants are eventually hired.

Though the 15% figure is much lower than the 42% figure, the company may wish to continue testing inexperienced applicants, because 15% is a reasonable success rate. The important aspect of this problem is not so much the recommendation that we decide to make to the company, but rather the development of a methodology for structuring what we know to make analysis a little easier.

- ■ **Example**
  ## *Machine replacement*

Our company has two machines used to produce our product. One is an older machine, and the other is a newer machine. The older machine produces about 40% of our output, and the newer machine accounts for the other 60% of our product. In the past, 3% of our output has been defective. Approximately 70% of the defective items can be traced back to the older machine. If we are to consider replacing the older machine, we must know its defect rate in relation to the defect rate on the newer machine.

A 2 × 2 table could be used to illustrate this problem. Figure 15-7 is an event table where the probabilities shown in the margins represent the marginal probabilities that a product came from the old or the new machine, or that it was a defective or a good item. The cells, as yet empty, represent the joint probabilities of the events that intersect at that cell. The only given information that we have not shown on the table is the conditional probability that an item came from the old machine given that it is a defective item, that is, $P$(old machine/defective) = .70.

We can use this conditional probability to fill in the rest of the table:

$$P(D \cap O) = P(O|D) \times P(D)$$

$$= .7 \times .03 = .021$$

Once we know that the joint probability that a unit of product will come from the old machine and be defective is .021, the rest of the joint probabilities follow from subtraction, because the sum of the row or column cell probabilities must sum to the

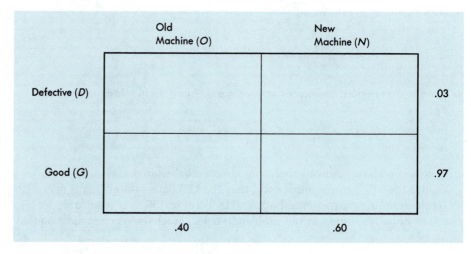

**FIGURE 15-7.**
**Event Probability Table for the Machine Defect Problem with Marginal Probabilities Illustrated**

| | Old Machine (O) | New Machine (N) | |
|---|---|---|---|
| Defective (D) | | | .03 |
| Good (G) | | | .97 |
| | .40 | .60 | |

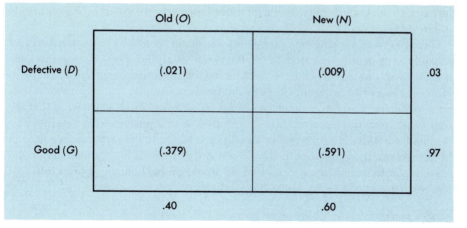

FIGURE 15-8.
Event Probability
Table for the Machine Defect Problem

marginal probability for that row or column. Figure 15-8 is the same table with the joint probabilities computed and filled in. Now we can calculate the defect rates, which are nothing more than the conditional probabilities that an item will be defective given that it comes from a particular machine:

$$P(D|O) = \frac{P(D \cap O)}{P(O)} = \frac{.021}{.4} = .0525$$

$$P(D|N) = \frac{P(D \cap N)}{P(N)} = \frac{.009}{.6} = .015$$

Thus, we see that the older machine has a defect rate more than three times that of the newer machine.

Again, the interesting aspect is the use of a graphic aid for solving the problem. Both probability trees and tables can be very useful for structuring our thoughts.

## ■ Bayes' theorem

We used the last example to illustrate the structure of a probability table for arranging our thoughts. There is another interesting aspect to the last example that is worth elaborating. In that example we were able to start with a conditional probability going in one direction and calculate the conditional probability going in the opposite direction. Specifically, we knew that $P$(item came from old machine/item is defective) = .7. What we really wanted to know was the reverse probability, $P$(item is defective/item came from old machine). Through our calculations, we found that $P(D|O) = .0525$. The main reason for wanting this probability is the additional information that it offers beyond what we already knew. Initially, we knew only that typically 3% of our output is defective. After the calculations, we were able to revise our perception based on knowledge of which machine produced the parts. Given that the old machine produced the parts, we expect 5.25% of them to be defective.

This process of revising our probability estimates as new information becomes available is generally referred to as **Bayesian analysis.** The original marginal probability estimate that we have, such as the 3% defective in the last example, is referred to as a **prior probability.** The conditional probability that updates or revises our perception given the occurrence of some other event, such as knowing that the parts came from the older machine, is referred to as a **posterior probability.** The formula for computing posterior probabilities is basically the same one we used in the last section. If we enhance the formula slightly by expanding the numerator and denominator to include those items that we would probably know as prior information, we arrive at what is known as **Bayes' theorem.**

*Bayes' theorem:* If $A$ and $B$ are events such that $P(B)$ is not zero, then

$$P(A|B) = \frac{P(A \cap B)}{P(B)}$$

$$= \frac{P(B|A) \times P(A)}{P(B|A) \times P(A) + P(B|A') \times P(A')}$$

This version of Bayes' theorem assumes that there are only two events, with one conditional on the other. If we have more than two events, we can state Bayes' theorem in a more general form:

If $A_1, A_2, \ldots, A_n$ are a set of collectively exhaustive (the set contains all possibilities) and mutually exclusive events conditional on $B$, where $P(B)$ is not equal to zero, then:

$$P(A_i|B) = \frac{P(B|A_i) \times P(A_i)}{\Sigma_j P(B|A_j) \times P(A_j)} \qquad \text{for } j = 1, 2, \ldots, n$$

Let us return to our previous example of defective parts and apply the version of Bayes' theorem for two events to find $P(D|O)$. The only other piece of information we need is $P(O|G)$, which is $P(O \cap G)/P(G) = .379/.97 = .39072$. Now:

$$P(D|O) = \frac{P(O|D) \times P(D)}{P(O|D) \times P(D) + P(O|D') \times P(D')}$$

$$= \frac{P(O|D) \times P(D)}{P(O|D) \times P(D) + P(O|G) \times P(G)}$$

$$= \frac{.7(.03)}{.7(.03) + .39072(.97)}$$

$$= \frac{.021}{.021 + .37899}$$

$$= \frac{.021}{.39999}$$

$$= .0525$$

*Marginal notes:* Bayesian analysis · prior probability · posterior probability · Bayes' theorem

Thus, we arrive at the same answer using the single formula known as Bayes' theorem that we arrived at after many individual steps in the previous section.

Now that we have seen an example of Bayes' theorem applied to two events in our defective products example, let us look at one with more than two events. Suppose that there are only three serums available for preventing a particular strain of flu, each made by a different company. We will define our multiple events to be

$$S_i = \text{take flu serum } i$$

$$F = \text{catch the flu}$$

We know from past history that the probability of catching the flu given that you have taken serum $i$ and the percentage of people taking each serum is

$$P(F|S_1) = .05 \quad P(S_1) = .30$$

$$P(F|S_2) = .04 \quad P(S_2) = .50$$

$$P(F|S_3) = .07 \quad P(S_3) = .20$$

We can use this information to compute the posterior probabilities:

| Serum | $P(F \cap S_i) =$ $P(F|S_i) \times P(S_i)$ | $P(S_i|F) =$ $P(F|S_i) \times P(S_i)/\Sigma_j P(F|S_j) \times P(S_j)$ |
|-------|---------------------------------------------|----------------------------------------------------------------------|
| 1 | $.05 \times .3 = .015$ | $.015/.049 = .3061$ |
| 2 | $.04 \times .5 = .02$ | $.02/.049 = .4082$ |
| 3 | $.07 \times .2 = \underline{.014}$ | $.014/.049 = .2857$ |
|   | $P(F) = .049$ | |

From this example, we see the principle of revising our perception given additional information. Based on the prior probabilities, if we picked out a person at random from among those who had taken one of the three serums, the probability would be .50 that they had taken serum 2. However, if that person had the flu, the posterior probability that they had taken serum 2 given that they had the flu would be .4082. This example may sound trivial, and you may say that we could just ask the person which serum they took or look at their medical records. If we look beyond this simple example at situations where a patient is unconscious or has no medical records, we begin to see the logic of posterior probabilities.

## ■ Discrete probability distributions

Thus far we have been dealing with situations where the number of different outcomes of an experiment has been relatively small. In cases where the possible outcomes are numerous, or perhaps there are an infinite number of outcomes, the solution space enumeration method becomes useless. However, there is a format for displaying the probabilities of outcomes no matter how many outcomes there may be. This format is called a probability distribution. More specifically, a **probability distribution** is a listing of, or function for determining, the probabilities of every

*probability distribution*

possible outcome of an experiment. We typically use some letter, such as $x$, to represent the variable outcomes of the experiment. Because these outcomes generally occur in some chance or random order, we refer to the variable as a *random variable*.

If the number of different outcomes that a random variable can assume is finite, or if the number of outcomes is infinite but the values themselves have spaces between consecutive values, as with integers, we call it a **discrete random variable.** As an example of a discrete random variable and its probability distribution, suppose that demand for a certain product always occurs in lots of 1, 2, 3, or 4 cases. Letting $p(d)$ represent the probability of each of the discrete demands, the discrete probability distribution might look like the following:

*discrete random variable*

| Demand | P(demand) |
|--------|-----------|
| 1 | .2 |
| 2 | .25 |
| 3 | .3 |
| 4 | .25 |

Figure 15-9 is a picture called a probability histogram that illustrates our simple demand distribution. Such pictures are used to convey the tendency of a random variable quickly.

While the example above has few possible outcomes for the random variable, many real examples involve distributions with many possible outcomes. In order to

**FIGURE 15-9. Probability Histogram for the Simple Discrete Demand Distribution**

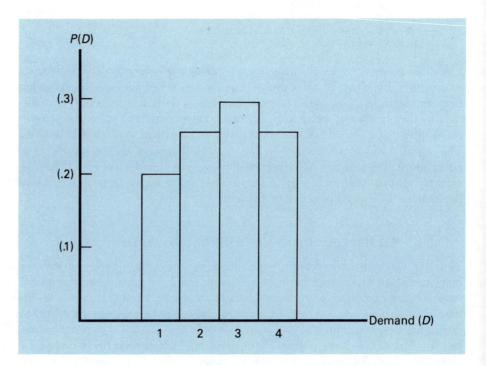

summarize what we know about a probability distribution and make it easier to see the tendencies of a discrete random variable, we often compute its *expected value* and *variance*.

The **expected value,** or mean, of a random variable is a measure of the variable's central tendency. Letting $E(x)$, or $\mu$, represent the expected value of $x$, the formula for expectation is

*expected value*

$$E(x) = \mu = \sum xp(x)$$

For our demand example, the expected value is

$$E(x) = 1(.2) + 2(.25) + 3(.3) + 4(.25)$$

$$= 2.6$$

While this expected value is not even a possible outcome, it is nonetheless the expected average over a large number of realizations of the random variable.

**Variance** is a measure of the dispersion of a random variable (how widely the outcomes vary around the expected value). It is the average squared amount by which the outcomes differ from the expected value. The variance of a discrete random variable is

*Variance*

$$\sigma^2 = E(x - \mu)^2 = \sum(x - \mu)^2 p(x)$$

Looking at the formula, it is clear why we square the differences. If we did not, the summation of differences when weighted by the probabilities would always be zero because, by definition, the expected value has exactly the same amount of deviation above it as it does below. For our numerical example, the variance is

$$\sigma^2 = (1 - 2.6)^2(.2) + (2 - 2.6)^2(.25) \ldots$$

$$= 1.14$$

Another measure of dispersion that is commonly used is the standard deviation. It is equal to the positive square root of the variance. The main advantage of the standard deviation is that the measure is in the same units as the random variable (pounds, feet, etc.) rather than being in units squared as is the variance. The standard deviation for our numerical example is the positive square root of 1.14.

We mentioned earlier that a probability distribution is either a list of probabilities for each outcome or a function for computing the probability of each outcome. The previous example was a list of probabilities. There are several discrete random variables for which there are formulas to calculate their probabilities. We will briefly review two of the most common ones.

## The binomial distribution

Many experiments are such that only two outcomes are possible: 0 and 1. These two outcomes may also be success or failure, good or bad, approve or disapprove, and so forth. We call such an experiment a *binomial experiment* (literally meaning two numbers), provided that it satisfies the following conditions:

1. The experiment consists of $n$ identical trials.

2. Each trial has only two possible outcomes.

3. The probabilities are stationary over the experiment (i.e., the probability of a "success" is the same for each trial of the experiment).

4. The trials are independent.

If we are interested in the probability distribution of $x$, where $x$ is the number of successes out of $n$ trials, it is called the binomial distribution. Letting $p$ be the probability of a success on any given trial and $q = (1 - p)$ be the probability of a failure, the binomial formula is

$$p(x) = \frac{n!}{x!(n - x)!} p^x q^{n-x} \qquad \text{for } x = 0, 1, 2, \ldots, n$$

where $n! = n(n - 1)(n - 2) \cdots (3)(2)(1)$. The mean of a binomial random variable is $E(x) = np$, and the variance is $\sigma^2 = npq$.

The tossing of a coin is an example of a binomial experiment, and you will find that if you apply the sample point approach we developed earlier for such problems, you will get precisely the same terms and the same answer by using the formula, probably with much less work. As a numerical example, suppose that we have a production process where the long-run fraction defective is known to be .05. If we select five items from our inventory, what is the probability that one or less of the items is defective?

The characteristic of interest is a defective part, so we will define success to be the observance of a defective part. The probability of this is $p = .05$, the probability of a good part is $q = .95$, and the number of identical "trials" is $n = 5$. We need the probability of 1 or less successes (bad parts), so we need to find $p(x = 0)$ and $p(x = 1)$:

$$p(0) = \frac{5!}{0!5!} (.05)^0 (.95)^5$$

$$= [1](1)(.7738)$$

$$= .7738$$

$$p(1) = \frac{5!}{1!4!} (.05)^1 (.95)^4$$

$$= [5](.05)(.8145)$$

$$= .2036$$

Therefore, the probability that one or less of the five parts will be defective is .7738 + .2036 = .9774.

For relatively small sample sizes, direct application of the binomial formula is simple. (For larger sample sizes, a binomial table is available in the Appendix.)

### The Poisson distribution

The Poisson distribution is most commonly used as a model for the number of events observed within a unit of space or time. For instance, the Poisson distribution would apply to the number of telephone calls coming into a switchboard per hour, or the number of people arriving at a toll booth per hour, or the number of demands for a product within a week, and so on. The Poisson random variable $x$ represents the number of such events over a period of time or space. It has an infinite, though discrete, range. Assuming that $\mu$ is the expected number of such events over the interval, the Poisson distribution can be written as

$$p(x) = \frac{\mu^x e^{-\mu}}{x!}$$

where $e$ is the base of the natural logarithm (Table A-3 in Appendix A provides values of $e^x$ and $e^{-x}$).

As an illustration of the Poisson calculation procedure, suppose that a bank normally receives loan applications at a rate of four per hour. What is the probability of only two applications coming in within any given hour? We are interested in $x = 2$, where $\mu = 4$. The probability is

$$p(2) = \frac{4^2 e^{-4}}{2!}$$

$$= \frac{16 e^{-4}}{2}$$

$$= \frac{16(.018)}{2}$$

$$= .144$$

Thus, the probability of exactly two applications coming in within a given hour is .144.

## ■ Continuous probability distributions

When a variable can assume the infinitely many values across its range with no gaps or restricted values, it is referred to as a **continuous random variable.** Given that we could measure accurately enough, height of human beings is a continuous random variable as there are an infinite number of heights over some range that people may

*continuous random variable*

take on. Such random variables are called continuous because a graph of their values would be a continuous, unbroken line.

Obviously, if there are an infinite number of different values that can occur for a continuous random variable, we cannot build a probability distribution for it using a list of outcomes with assigned probabilities as we did in the discrete case. We will have to develop formula-based distributions for such variables. In fact, since there are an infinite number of outcomes, the individual probability of any exact value for the random variable will be approximately zero, and our formula-based distributions can only be used to find the probability that the outcome of the random variable will be within some range.

The area under a continuous probability distribution between any two points is equal to the probability that the random variable will take on a value in that range. Sometimes we can use geometry to find such an area, but more often than not we must use integral calculus to find these areas. Suppose that we have a probability distribution $f(x) = 2x$ for $x$ over the range 0 to 1, as shown in Figure 15-10. We can find the probability (area) between any two points by taking the integral of the probability density function $f(x)$ and evaluating the integral between those points.

**FIGURE 15-10.**
**Continuous Distri-**
**bution Curve for**
**the Distribution**
$f(x) = 2x, 0 \le$
$x \le 1$

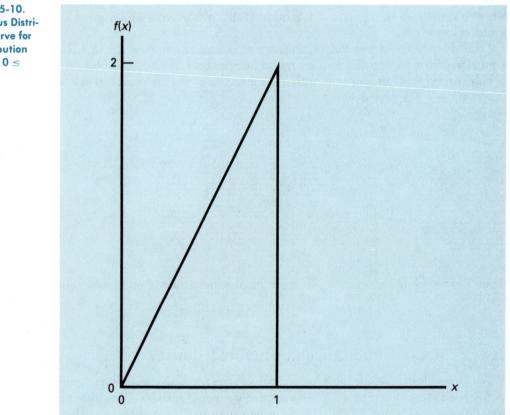

For example, the area between 0 and 1 is

$$\int_0^1 f(x)\, dx = \int_0^1 2x\, dx = x^2 \Big|_0^1 = (1)^2 - (0)^2 = 1$$

This is to be expected, because the probability of any distribution over its entire range must be 1. If we wanted to know the probability of the random variable $x$ taking on a value between .2 and .7, we would repeat the above procedure for those limits:

$$\int_{.2}^{.7} 2x\, dx = x^2 \Big|_{.2}^{.7} = (.7)^2 - (.2)^2$$
$$= .49 - .04$$
$$= .45$$

Thus, there is a 45% chance that $x$ will be between .2 and .7 for this distribution for any realization of $x$.

We also find the expected value and variance of continuous random variables using calculus. The expected value is found by taking

$$\mu = E(x) = \int_a^b x f(x)\, dx$$

where $a$ and $b$ are the limits of the distribution. For our example, the expected value is

$$E(x) = \int_0^1 x(2x)\, dx = \int_0^1 2x^2\, dx = \frac{2x^3}{3} \Big|_0^1 = \frac{2(1^3)}{3} - \frac{2(0^3)}{3}$$
$$= \frac{2}{3} - 0$$
$$= \frac{2}{3}$$

The variance of a continuous random variable is

$$\sigma^2 = \int_a^b [x - \mu]^2 f(x)\, dx$$
$$= \int_a^b x^2 f(x)\, dx - [\mu]^2$$

For the above example, this is

$$\sigma^2 = \int_0^1 x^2(2x)\,dx - \left[\frac{2}{3}\right]^2$$

$$= \int_0^1 2x^3\,dx - \frac{4}{9}$$

$$= \frac{2x^4}{4}\bigg|_0^1 - \frac{4}{9}$$

$$= \frac{1}{2} - 0 - \frac{4}{9}$$

$$= \frac{1}{18}$$

As was true with discrete distributions, there are a number of continuous distributions that seem to fit many situations and are worth a quick look. We will finish our review of probability by looking at three of these continuous distributions.

## The uniform distribution

When every outcome of a random variable has exactly the same probability of occurring, we say that the random variable is uniformly distributed. Such random variables might occur in a computer simulation where equally likely random numbers are required, or in a case where little other information is available to suggest some alternative distributional shape. If the random variable were discrete, it would simply mean that each of the $n$ possible discrete outcome in our list has a probability of $1/n$ of occurring. In a continuous sense, it means that the probability function or density function is constant or flat over the range of values of the random variable.

Assuming that the random variable $x$ is uniformly distributed over the range $a$ to $b$, the uniform probability density function is

$$f(x) = \frac{1}{b - a} \qquad a \le x \le b$$

The expected value of a uniformly distributed variable is $E(x) = (b + a)/2$, and the variance is $\sigma^2 = (b - a)^2/12$. Figure 15-11 is an illustration of a uniform distribution with limits $a \le x \le b$. The rectangular geometry of the uniform distribution also makes it easy to verify that the total density of the probability distribution is a probability of 1. If we take the length of a rectangle, which is $b - a$ in this case, and multiply by the height, $1/(b - a)$, we get the area, which in this case is exactly 1.

As we saw in our previous discussion of continuous random variables, it is always some area that we are concerned with, since the probability of any single outcome

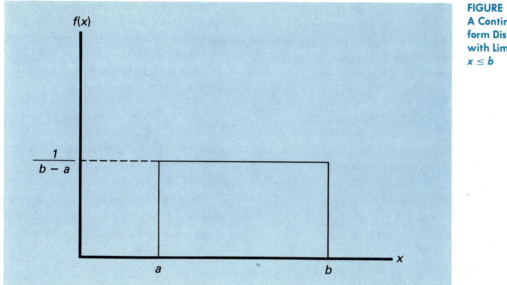

for a continuous random variable is always zero. If we are interested in the area or probability over some range $c$ to $d$ of a uniform distribution where $a \le c$ and $d \le b$, we would take the integral as follows:

$$\int_c^d \frac{1}{(b-a)}\,dx = \frac{x}{(b-a)}\bigg|_c^d = \frac{d}{(b-a)} - \frac{c}{(b-a)}$$
$$= \frac{d-c}{(b-a)}$$

In other words, the area of the range of interest is equal to the ratio of the length of that range to the length of the range of the uniform random variable. For $x$ distributed uniformly between 0 and 10, for example, there is a probability of .10 that $x$ will be between 0 and 1. Likewise, there is a .10 probability that $x$ will be between 3 and 4, or between 7 and 8. For the same distribution, there is a .40 chance that $x$ will be between 2 and 6, and so on.

## The exponential distribution

The exponential is to the time domain what the Poisson distribution was to the rate domain. If customers arrive to a toll booth at a rate of five per hour distributed Poisson, their average time between arrivals is one-fifth of an hour, and the times between arrivals are distributed exponentially. Though the exponential distribution has many applications, the modeling of these arrival times, service times, repair times, and so on, are the most common applications within the realm of quantitative analysis as defined in this text.

Figure 15-12 illustrates three of the many possible exponential curves that exist. The shape of the exponential curve is always the same, but its flatness or steepness depends on its single parameter $\lambda$. In the above examples, $\lambda$ is the average rate of occurrence, and $1/\lambda$ is the average time between arrivals, average time of service, average repair time, and so on. The probability distribution for an exponential random variable $x$ depends on this parameter $\lambda$, and is of the form

$$f(x) = \lambda e^{-\lambda x}$$

where $x$ and $\lambda$ must both be $\geq 0$. Also, the mean of an exponential is $E(x) = 1/\lambda$ and the variance is $\sigma^2 = (1/\lambda)^2$.

We find exponential probabilities just as we did for the simple continuous distribution $f(x) = 2x$. Suppose that we can repair knitting machines at an average rate of $\lambda = \frac{1}{3}$ machine per hour (i.e., the mean repair time for a knitting machine is $1/\lambda = 3$ hours). What is the probability of the machine being repaired within 2 hours?:

$$\int_0^2 \left[\tfrac{1}{3}\right] e^{-x/3} \, dx = -e^{-x/3} \Big|_0^2 = -e^{-2/3} - (-e^{-0/3})$$

$$= -.514 + 1$$

$$= .486$$

As with all continuous distributions, only probabilities within a range may be calculated.

## The normal distribution

The normal distribution is the most important distribution in statistics. It has been found to be applicable to many natural processes. Also, any variable that is an average of values or sum of values is likely to be normally distributed. It is this phenomenon that makes it so useful in statistics for determining the distribution of sample statistics.

The normal distribution is a bell-shaped symmetric distribution. Figure 15-13 illustrates several different normal distributions with the same means but with different variances. The density function for the normal distribution is

$$f(x) = \frac{1}{\sigma \sqrt{2\pi}} e^{-(1/2)[(x-\mu)/\sigma]^2}$$

where $\mu$ and $\sigma$ are the mean and standard deviation of the particular normal distribution, and $\pi$ and $e$ are constants equal to 3.14159 and 2.71828, respectively.

The difficulty in working directly with the normal density as we did with the exponential arises when we try to take the integral of the density. As you might expect from looking at the function, this integral is not easily evaluated. To avoid

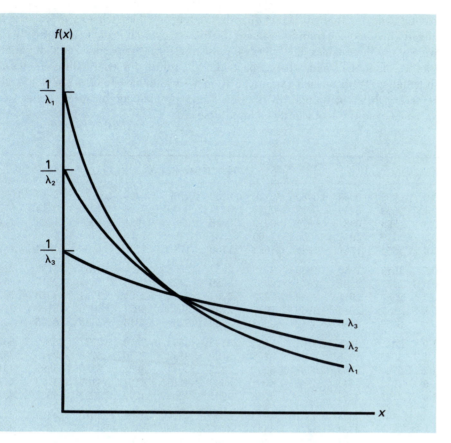

FIGURE 15-12.
Exponential Distribution for Three Different Values of $\lambda$ ($\lambda_1 > \lambda_2 > \lambda_3$)

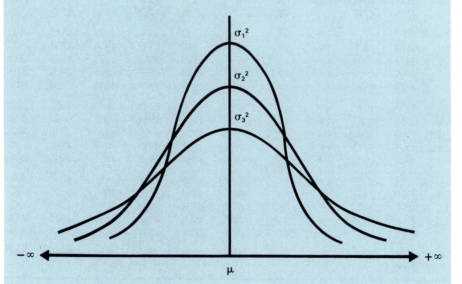

FIGURE 15-13.
Normal Distributions with the Same Mean but Different Variances
($\sigma_1^2 < \sigma_2^2 < \sigma_3^2$)

having to deal with the function directly, we rely on tables, where someone else has already invested the time to evaluate the density over all possible intervals. Before we can use these tables, however, we must transform the normal random variable into a common format where one table will suffice for every different normal distribution. Without such a transformation, we would have to have a separate table for every different normal distribution (every possible combination of mean and variance), and this is obviously an impossible task.

**TABLE 15-1.**
**Probability Table for the Standard Normal Distribution**

| Z | 0.00 | .01 | .02 | .03 | .04 | .05 | .06 | .07 | .08 | .09 |
|---|---|---|---|---|---|---|---|---|---|---|
| 0.0 | 0.0000 | 0.0040 | 0.0080 | 0.0120 | 0.0160 | 0.0199 | 0.0239 | 0.0279 | 0.0319 | 0.0359 |
| 0.1 | .0398 | .0438 | .0478 | .0517 | .0557 | .0596 | .0636 | .0675 | .0714 | .0753 |
| 0.2 | .0793 | .0832 | .0871 | .0910 | .0948 | .0987 | .1026 | .1064 | .1103 | .1141 |
| 0.3 | .1179 | .1217 | .1255 | .1293 | .1331 | .1368 | .1406 | .1443 | .1480 | .1517 |
| 0.4 | .1554 | .1591 | .1628 | .1664 | .1700 | .1736 | .1772 | .1808 | .1844 | .1879 |
| 0.5 | .1915 | .1950 | .1985 | .2019 | .2054 | .2088 | .2123 | .2157 | .2190 | .2224 |
| 0.6 | .2257 | .2291 | .2324 | .2357 | .2389 | .2422 | .2454 | .2486 | .2517 | .2549 |
| 0.7 | .2580 | .2611 | .2642 | .2673 | .2704 | .2734 | .2764 | .2794 | .2823 | .2852 |
| 0.8 | .2881 | .2910 | .2939 | .2967 | .2995 | .3023 | .3051 | .3078 | .3106 | .3133 |
| 0.9 | .3159 | .3186 | .3212 | .3238 | .3264 | .3289 | .3315 | .3340 | .3365 | .3389 |
| 1.0 | .3413 | .3438 | .3461 | .3485 | .3508 | .3531 | .3554 | .3577 | .3599 | .3621 |
| 1.1 | .3643 | .3665 | .3686 | .3708 | .3729 | .3749 | .3770 | .3790 | .3810 | .3830 |
| 1.2 | .3849 | .3869 | .3888 | .3907 | .3925 | .3944 | .3962 | .3980 | .3997 | .4015 |
| 1.3 | .4032 | .4049 | .4066 | .4082 | .4099 | .4115 | .4131 | .4147 | .4162 | .4177 |
| 1.4 | .4192 | .4207 | .4222 | .4236 | .4251 | .4265 | .4279 | .4292 | .4306 | .4319 |
| 1.5 | .4332 | .4345 | .4357 | .4370 | .4382 | .4394 | .4406 | .4418 | .4429 | .4441 |
| 1.6 | .4452 | .4463 | .4474 | .4484 | .4495 | .4505 | .4515 | .4525 | .4535 | .4545 |
| 1.7 | .4554 | .4564 | .4573 | .4582 | .4591 | .4599 | .4608 | .4616 | .4625 | .4633 |
| 1.8 | .4641 | .4649 | .4656 | .4664 | .4671 | .4678 | .4686 | .4693 | .4699 | .4706 |
| 1.9 | .4713 | .4719 | .4726 | .4732 | .4738 | .4744 | .4750 | .4756 | .4761 | .4767 |
| 2.0 | .4772 | .4778 | .4783 | .4788 | .4793 | .4798 | .4803 | .4808 | .4812 | .4817 |
| 2.1 | .4821 | .4826 | .4830 | .4834 | .4838 | .4842 | .4846 | .4850 | .4854 | .4857 |
| 2.2 | .4861 | .4864 | .4868 | .4871 | .4875 | .4878 | .4881 | .4884 | .4887 | .4890 |
| 2.3 | .4893 | .4896 | .4898 | .4901 | .4904 | .4906 | .4909 | .4911 | .4913 | .4916 |
| 2.4 | .4918 | .4920 | .4922 | .4925 | .4927 | .4929 | .4931 | .4932 | .4934 | .4936 |
| 2.5 | .4938 | .4940 | .4941 | .4943 | .4945 | .4946 | .4948 | .4949 | .4951 | .4952 |
| 2.6 | .4953 | .4955 | .4956 | .4957 | .4959 | .4960 | .4961 | .4962 | .4963 | .4964 |
| 2.7 | .4965 | .4966 | .4967 | .4968 | .4969 | .4970 | .4971 | .4972 | .4973 | .4974 |
| 2.8 | .4974 | .4975 | .4976 | .4977 | .4977 | .4978 | .4979 | .4979 | .4980 | .4981 |
| 2.9 | .4981 | .4982 | .4982 | .4983 | .4984 | .4984 | .4985 | .4985 | .4986 | .4986 |
| 3.0 | .4987 | .4987 | .4987 | .4988 | .4988 | .4989 | .4989 | .4989 | .4990 | .4990 |
| 3.1 | .4990 | .4991 | .4991 | .4991 | .4992 | .4992 | .4992 | .4992 | .4993 | .4993 |
| 3.2 | .4993 | .4993 | .4994 | .4994 | .4994 | .4994 | .4994 | .4995 | .4995 | .4995 |
| 3.3 | .4995 | .4995 | .4995 | .4996 | .4996 | .4996 | .4996 | .4996 | .4996 | .4997 |
| 3.4 | .4997 | .4997 | .4997 | .4997 | .4997 | .4997 | .4997 | .4997 | .4997 | .4998 |
| 3.6 | .4998 | .4998 | .4999 | .4999 | .4999 | .4999 | .4999 | .4999 | .4999 | .4999 |
| 3.9 | .5000 | | | | | | | | | |

The transformation we are referring to is called standardization of the normal random variable. If we let

$$z = \frac{(x - \mu)}{\sigma}$$

$z$ is called a standard normal random variable. The mean of $z$ is 0, and the variance of $z$ is 1. The actual meaning of $z$ is the number of standard deviations that the value $x$ is away from its mean.

For example, suppose that we are interested in the value $x = 11$, where $x$ is normally distributed with a mean of 3 and a standard deviation of 4. The standardized normal variable is $z = (11 - 3)/4 = 2$. In other words, the value 11 is 2 standard deviations away from its mean. Likewise, suppose that a normal variable $y$ has mean 20 and standard deviation 12, and we are interested in the value $y = 44$. The standard normal value is $z = (44 - 20)/12 = 2$. Again, this value of $y$ is 2 standard deviations away from its mean. Though we are working with two totally different normal distributions, through this $z$ transformation we are able to express values from both of them in common terms. Note that $z$ will take on negative values for random variable values below the mean. The negative sign implies only that the original value was below the mean; it does not affect its interpretation.

Table 15-1 is a list of areas under the standard normal curve. The one-decimal-place row headings and the two-decimal-place column headings allow you to locate $z$ values from 0 up to about 3 in increments of .01. Negative $z$ values are not shown, as the normal is a symmetric distribution. The area entries in the table represent the area under the normal curve from the mean outward to the specific $z$ value (positive or negative). As an example of how to use the table, suppose that we want to know the area under the standard normal curve between $z = -1.2$ and $z = +1.83$. Figure 15-14 is a drawing of the area we are interested in. From the

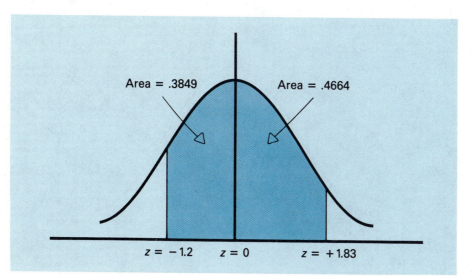

**FIGURE 15-14.**
**Area Under the Standard Normal Curve Between $z = -1.2$ and $z = +1.83$**

Area = .3849

Area = .4664

$z = -1.2$    $z = 0$    $z = +1.83$

**FIGURE 15-15.**
**Area Under the**
**Normal Curve be-**
**tween 4.9 and 5.2**
**for $\mu = 5$ and**
**$\sigma = 1$.**

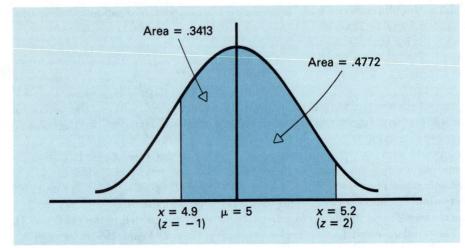

normal table, the area from the center of the distribution out to $z = -1.2$ is .3849, and the area from the center out to $z = +1.83$ is .4664. Therefore, the total area we were looking for is $.3849 + .4664 = .8513$.

To further illustrate usage of the normal table, suppose that the diameter of a part that we produce is a random variable due to fluctuating machine performance, and is known to be normally distributed with $\mu = 5$ inches and $\sigma = .1$ inches. What is the probability that the diameter of a single unit of this part will be between 4.9 and 5.2? What we are asking for is the area under the normal curve between 4.9 and 5.2. Since the mean is 5, if we find the area between 4.9 and 5 and add it to the area between 5 and 5.2, we will have the answer. For $x = 4.9$, $z = (4.9 - 5)/.1 = -1$. By sym-

**FIGURE 15-16.**
**Area Under the**
**Normal Curve Be-**
**low $x = 4.9$ for**
**$\mu = 5$ and $\sigma = .1$**

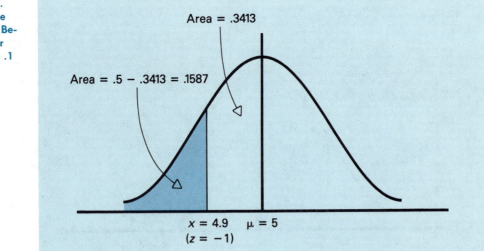

metry, the area from the mean out to $z = -1$ is the same as the area from the mean to $z = +1$, which, from the table, is .3413. For $x = 5.2$, $z = (5.2 - 5)/.1 = 2$. The area from the mean out to $z = 2$ is .4772. Therefore, $P(4.9 \leq x \leq 5.2) = .3413 + .4772 = .8185$ (Figure 15-15 illustrates the area for this example).

Suppose that we wanted to know the probability that the same part would have a diameter less than 4.9. The total area (probability) under any density is 1.0, and because the normal is symmetric, the area in each half of the distribution is .5. That is, the area from the mean downward is .5, as is the area from the mean upward. If the area between the mean and $x = 4.9$ is .3413 as we calculated a moment ago, the area below 4.9 has to be $.5 - .3413 = .1587$ (see Figure 15-16). It especially helps in cases like these where the area we are looking for is a composite of several areas to draw a picture of the normal curve and shade in the area. By using our knowledge of the symmetry of the distribution and the standard normal table, we can calculate any conceivable normal probability.

## ■ Summary

In this chapter we have reviewed a number of concepts related to probability. Beginning with the most basic level of experimental outcomes, we have developed an understanding of how to compute probabilities using certain relations and laws, and how to summarize variable outcome probabilities using probability distributions.

Though we have covered a lot of things in this chapter, we have focused the discussion on concepts of probability. We have not even scratched the surface as to the varied uses of probability information, such as statistical inference. Whole texts are devoted to such topics, so it is not practical to review them here. We have covered those items necessary for an understanding of the quantitative analysis topics to be presented in the following chapters. The reader interested in knowing more about probability and inference is encouraged to seek out additional information in texts devoted to the subject.

## ■ Glossary of terms

**Bayesian analysis:**  The process of revising probability estimates as new information becomes available.

**complement:**  An event set that contains all points within the sample space that are not contained within an original event set.

**compound event:**  An event that is composed of two or more simple events.

**conditional probability:**  When the probability of occurrence of one event is dependent on or affected by the outcome of some other event.

**continuous random variable:**  A variable that may randomly assume the infinitely many values across its range with no gaps or restricted values.

**discrete random variable:**  A random variable that either has a finite number of outcomes or, if the number of outcomes is infinite, there are spaces between the consecutive values of the random variable.

**events:**   The possible outcomes of an experiment.

**expected value:**   A measure of the central tendency of a random variable; it is the mean value that would result if infinitely many values of the random variable were to occur.

**frequency concept:**   The use of experimentation and/or past history as a basis for probability assessment.

**independence:**   The situation where the probability of one event is not dependent on the outcome of some other event.

**intersection:**   A set containing only those events that are contained in both of two other sets; that is, the overlap of two sets.

**joint probability:**   The probability associated with an intersectional set.

**marginal probability:**   The probability of a single event.

**mutually exclusive:**   When the intersection of two events is empty; that is, when it is not possible for two events to occur at the same time.

**parameter:**   Numerical descriptors of a population.

**posterior probability:**   A conditional probability that revises our perception of the probability of one event given new information or the occurrence of some other event.

**prior probability:**   An original marginal probability estimate that is subject to revision as more information becomes available.

**probability:**   A measure of one's belief in the likelihood of an outcome.

**probability distribution:**   A format for describing the probability of all possible outcomes of a random variable.

**sample space:**   The set of all possible simple events for an experiment.

**simple event:**   An event that cannot be further decomposed.

**statistic:**   Numerical descriptor of a sample.

**subjective evaluation concept:**   The use of expert opinion for assessing probabilities.

**theoretical concept:**   Reliance on some theory or known phenomena to suggest the form of probabilities.

**union:**   The set of all events contained within either of two other sets.

**variance:**   A measure of the dispersion of a random variable; it is the average squared amount by which outcomes differ from the expected value.

## ■ Review questions

1. Discuss the three concepts related to the derivation of probabilities.

2. Define the following terms:
   a. simple event
   b. compound event
   c. sample space

3. Name and describe at least three event relations.

4. Describe the four probability laws that relate intersectional probabilities, union probabilities, and conditional probabilities.

5. Explain the decision process known as Bayesian analysis. Name at least three decision situations where Bayesian analysis might be useful.

6. Explain the difference between discrete random variables and continuous random variables. Why is it necessary to use the probability distribution format in order to represent random variables?

7. List the four conditions necessary for an experiment to qualify as a binomial experiment.

8. Explain the relationship between the Poisson distribution and the exponential distribution.

9. Describe the procedure for calculating the expected value and variance of a continuous random variable.

10. Why are we only interested in finding the probability that the random variable will take on a value within some range rather than a specific value when working with continuous random variables?

11. Explain the concept of standardization of normal random variables. Why is it necessary to make this transformation?

## ■ True/false questions

1. The frequency concept for probability assessment relies on the number of experts in the area that agree with our perception.

2. Any compound event can always be decomposed into exactly two simple events.

3. All possible outcomes of an experiment, simple or compound, may be found within the experiment's sample space.

4. An event and its complement are always mutually exclusive.

5. Joint probability is just another term for the probability of the intersection of two events.

6. The purpose of Bayesian analysis is to allow us to calculate marginal prior probabilities based on conditional posterior probabilities.

7. A discrete random variable always has a finite number of possible outcomes or values.

8. The binomial distribution is an example of a discrete probability distribution.

9. The area under a continuous probability distribution between any two points is equal to the probability that the random variable will take on a value within that range.

10. The exponential distribution is to the rate domain what the Poisson distribution is to the time domain.

11. A standard normal random variable is one whose variance is exactly one more than its mean.

12. A negative standard normal value indicates that the original number before standardization was negative.

## ■ Problems

1. Suppose that we toss a pair of fair dice and record the numerical outcome on each of the die. List the simple events that make up each of the following, and calculate the probability of each:

   a. the sample space
   b. event $A$: the sum of the two dice is 6
   c. event $B$: the first die has a value of 2

    **d.** event $C$: the product of the two dice is 18

    **e.** event $D$: the sum of the two dice is less than 4

2. Larson Accounting Services is finishing up an audit of a client, and there are five accounts left to certify. Suppose that Larson only has time to look at two randomly chosen accounts from the five. Answer the following:

    **a.** If there is one incorrect account among the five, what is the probability that the audit will catch this account?

    **b.** If there are two incorrect accounts among the five, what is the chance that the audit will catch both of them? What is the probability that it will catch at least one of the two incorrect accounts?

3. Referring to Problem 1, use the simple event approach to find the probability of each of the following:

    **a.** $A'$

    **b.** $A \cup B$

    **c.** $A \cup D$

    **d.** $B \cap D$

    **e.** $C \cap D$

4. A parts bin contains four units of a certain part. Two of the units are bad. Suppose that we randomly draw one unit from the bin and inspect it, then without replacing that unit we draw a second unit for inspection. Given the event definitions:

    $A$:   obtain a bad unit on the first draw

    $B$:   obtain a bad unit on the second draw

    $C$:   obtain a good unit on the second draw

find the following probabilities:

    **a.** $P(A)$

    **b.** $P(B)$

    **c.** $P(C)$

    **d.** $P(A \cap B)$

    **e.** $P(A \cap C)$

    **f.** $P(B|A)$

    **g.** $P(C|A)$

5. Rolph Construction is currently bidding for the contract to build a shopping center. Because of all the restrictions and because of intangibles such as builder reputations, the lowest bidder does not automatically receive the contract. Letting $A$ = (receive the contract) and $B$ = (submit the low bid), we know that $P(A) = .2$, $P(B) = .3$, and $P(A \cap B) = .15$. Assuming that we submit the lowest bid, what is our likelihood of receiving the contract? Is the probability of receiving the contract dependent on submitting the lowest bid?

6. Given $P(A) = .5$, $P(B) = .3$, and $P(A \cup B) = .6$, use the probability laws from the chapter to calculate $P(A \cap B)$ and $P(A|B)$.

7. First Investors Bank routinely makes small business loans. Past data indicates that 18% of all loan applicants already have an established credit rating. Of those applicants who already have a credit rating, 60% have sufficient collateral to back up the loan. Only 40%

of those without a credit rating have collateral. Applicants with both a credit rating and collateral have about a 90% chance of receiving a loan, while applicants without an established credit rating who have sufficient collateral have a 55% chance of receiving the loan. Applicants without sufficient collateral are never given a loan. The bank is beginning to wonder whether it should even accept applications from businesses without an established credit rating, since this is the first step in the screening process. Draw a probability tree to help organize your thoughts and then calculate the percentage of applicants with a credit rating who eventually get a loan and the percentage of applicants without a credit rating who eventually get a loan. What do you think the bank should do?

8. Art and Bill are the only two salesmen working a particular sales district. In the past, Art has accounted for about 57% of all calls made on customers. Across both salesmen, about 5% of all sales calls have actually resulted in a sale. Approximately 65% of the sales were made by Art. Find the probability that a sales call will result in a sale, given that Art makes the call.

9. Workers in a particular textile industry belong to one of three different unions. We are interested in those hourly paid workers who make more than $14,000 annually. Defining events as:

$$L_i = \text{belonging to labor union } i$$
$$W = \text{having annual wages in excess of } \$14,000$$

we know from historical data that the proportion of workers in each union that make over $14,000 and the percentage belonging to each union are

$$P(W|L_1) = .04 \qquad P(L_1) = .25$$

$$P(W|L_2) = .035 \qquad P(L_2) = .35$$

$$P(W|L_3) = .046 \qquad P(L_3) = .40$$

Using the Bayesian analysis formulas, find the posterior probabilities $P(L_i|W)$ (that is, the probability that someone who makes over $14,000 belongs to union $i$ for $i = 1, 2, 3$). How might a company use such information?

10. Given the discrete probability distribution

| $x$ | $P(x)$ |
| --- | --- |
| 2.5 | .21 |
| 4.0 | .30 |
| 5.5 | .25 |
| 7.8 | .24 |

Calculate the mean and variance for this distribution. What is the probability that $x$ will take on a value less than or equal to 4.0? A value less than 6?

11. Suppose that the percentage of customers entering our store who finally make a purchase is .14. If six customers enter our store, what is the probability that exactly one will make a purchase? Exactly two will make a purchase? Five or less will make a purchase? What is the expected number of purchases?

12. Only 4% of the population has blood type AB negative. If eight blood donors show up for a blood drive, what is the probability of getting no type AB negative for the blood bank? What is the probability of getting 1 pint of AB negative.?

13. The blood donors in Problem 12 arrive to the donation center at a rate of three per hour. What is the probability of exactly five donors coming in within a given hour? What is the probability of no donors arriving within a given hour? What is the probability of two or more donors arriving within a given hour?

14. For the probability density

$$f(x) = 3x^2 \qquad 0 \le x \le 1$$

Find the mean and standard deviation. What is the probability that $x$ will assume a value between .3 and .5?

15. Suppose that $y$ is a continuous random variable uniformly distributed over the range 30 to 60. Find the expected value and variance of $y$. What is the probability that $y$ will assume a value between 36 and 45?

16. Cars arrive to a garage for service at a rate of four per hour. What is the probability that a car will arrive within the first 6 minutes after the garage opens in the morning?

17. Given a standard normal distribution, find the following probabilities:

   a. $P(-.6 \le z \le 1.75)$
   b. $P(.71 \le z \le 1.92)$
   c. $P(z \ge -1.33)$
   d. $P(z \ge .66)$

18. Suppose that the life of a certain brand of computer chip is known to be normally distributed with a mean life of 5000 hours and a standard deviation of 300 hours. What is the probability that one of the randomly selected chips will last longer than 5500 hours? Between 4500 and 5500 hours? Less than 4800 hours?

**16**

# Decision Models I

## ■ Introduction

Every day we, as human beings, make many decisions. Most of these decisions are relatively inconsequential and are made from habit. Occasionally we make an important decision that can have immediate and/or long-term effects on our lives. Such decisions as where to attend school, whether to continue in school or accept a job, which job offer to accept, whether to rent or to buy, or whether your company should accept a merger proposal are important decisions for which we would prefer to make the correct choice. Often these decisions are made on the basis of emotion or intuition, but is this proper?

In the next two chapters we will discuss the process of making decisions and present decision models that can be used possibly to improve the process of decision making. Regardless of whether you actually use any of these models to make a decision, they provide a standard against which the decision you make can be compared.

It is important to understand what these decision models *can* and *cannot* do. First, these models provide a *structure* for examining the decision-making process. In some situations, there is no need to justify how a decision has been made. However, in a world where most managers are not the owners of the businesses they manage, it becomes necessary to use a justifiable process in making a decision.

Second, these models can be used to avoid arbitrary, inconsistent decisions that are not based on all the available data. Unfortunately many times we make decisions that fall into this category without realizing that we are doing so. These models do not tell us what decisions to make; rather, they tell us how to go about making them, or how to analyze past decisions.

Finally, even if we used these models in all decisions, we would not be guaranteed that the outcome would always be favorable. In other words, *good decisions do not guarantee good outcomes*. For example, consider two college roommates who are both faced with the same decision at a county fair. A game of chance is played that pays $100 for a $10 bet and the odds are 10 to 1 against winning. The first student pays his $10 and wins the $100 prize. The second student pays his $10 and loses. They both made the same decision, which most people would consider to be a good one, yet they had different outcomes. So making a good decision does not always result in a favorable outcome.

While good decision-making procedures can, and do, result in bad outcomes, one would expect that the use of better-than-average decisions will be reflected in better-than-average outcomes. The successful manager will be the one who consistently makes good decisions.

## Types of decision models

Throughout this text, we have discussed the use of decision-making models in management. We have seen that such models as linear, goal, and integer programming can be used to determine a course of action that will lead to a maximum profit or a minimum cost subject to some sort of constraints. In all of these situations, it has been assumed that the parameters or coefficients were known with certainty. That is, the models we have used were deterministic, and the outcome of any course of action would not be subject to any uncertainty.

Not all decision-making models are deterministic, however. In many cases, the parameters of the model vary due to uncertainty. In Chapter 1 we referred to models of this type as stochastic models. In this and the next chapter we will discuss some stochastic decision-making models. Such decision-making models can be broadly divided into two categories depending on whether or not the decision will be made using prior data related to the occurrence of events. This chapter will discuss decision models that do not use prior data; the next chapter will take up decision models that use prior data to help in the decision-making process. Various decision models will be discussed for both types of decisions. We will take care to discuss the circumstances where a given decision model is appropriate, since choosing the correct model is an important part of any decision.

Before we begin our discussion of decision-making models, it is worthwhile to discuss the decision-making process itself, so we can better understand when it is appropriate to use the models discussed in these chapters. This discussion will apply to the decision models that do not use prior data discussed in this chapter as well as the models using prior data discussed in the next chapter.

## The Decision-making process

A *decision* may be defined as the process of choosing a solution to a problem, given that at least two alternative solutions exist. It is obvious that before a decision can be made, several steps must be carried out. These steps may be summarized as follows (where DM = decision maker):

**Step 1.** DM becomes aware of existence of problem.

**Step 2.** DM gathers data on the problem.

**Step 3.** DM develops a model that describes the problem.

**Step 4.** DM uses model to generate alternative solutions to the problem.

**Step 5.** DM chooses from alternative solutions.

We will not discuss step 1 in detail because it has to do with how a person might recognize and perceive a problem, and that is beyond the scope of this text. Suffice it to say that once the decision maker has become aware of a problem, the next step is to gather more information about the problem. This additional information can be both quantitative and qualitative in nature and serves to help the DM move to step 3, wherein a model that describes the problem is developed. As discussed in Chapter 1, a model is a *simplified version of reality* that retains the important characteristics of the problem. Modeling helps the DM to understand the key parts of complex problems that otherwise would be beyond human comprehension. Using the model, which also may be quantitative or qualitative, the DM moves on to step 4 and generates alternative solutions to the problem. This may be done by "brainstorming," by mathematical techniques, or by other methods. From a behavioral viewpoint, having too many solution alternatives can be worse than having too few since the DM can be overwhelmed by the sheer magnitude of the selection process that comes in step 5. It is at step 5 that quantitative models can differ most from qualitative models. Quantitative models may explore all possible alternative solutions in an attempt to find *the one best*, or *optimal* solution; qualitative models may seek to find *any satisfactory* solution to the problem. This latter approach, known as *satisficing*, takes into account the behavioral aspects of decision making and is often used where resources may be unavailable or the costs of finding the optimal solution are prohibitive.

This five-step decision-making process can be related to the first three steps of the MS/OR problem-solving process discussed in Chapter 1. Those first three steps were:

1. problem recognition, observation, and formulation
2. model construction
3. solution generation

Steps 1 and 2 of the decision-making process relate to step 1 of the problem-solving process; step 3 of the decision-making process relates to step 2 of the problem-solving process. Finally, steps 4 and 5 of the decision-making process correspond to step 3 of the problem-solving process.

In these chapters, we use both quantitative and qualitative approaches. We will use the satisficing concept to restrict the number of alternatives, and then use quantitative techniques to choose one of these alternatives.

## ■ Case

## Ashley's Pizzeria

Ashley Washington has become very successful with her novel approach to making and selling pizzas to students at State College. By mixing up the main ingredients for the pizzas and baking them in advance, she has been able to keep the waiting time for customers very short compared with that at competing restaurants. Because of the possibility of a shift of students away from the older dormitories near Ashley's present location, Ashley is considering moving her pizzeria to a new location. She has decided that there are only three alternatives from which she will choose. These are: stay where she is, move onto Baxter Street near the new dormitories, or move out on Epps Bridge Road where it is rumored that a new student-oriented apartment complex will be built. Her decision will be influenced by external actions over which she has no control. These external actions are the decisions that other persons will make. Besides the rumored new apartment complex, there is also a question as to whether the university administration will close the pre-1900 dorms and move those students to the new dorms on Baxter Street. With the help of a financial consultant, Ashley has forecast the present value of each decision considering the two external actions (which are felt to be mutually exclusive) plus the

possibility that neither external action will occur. These values are shown in Table 16-1.

Since this decision of location is to be made only once, there are no previous data to use in making such a decision. However, Ashley must somehow make a decision.

### Preliminary discussion of Ashley's Pizzeria Case

The decision that Ashley faces as to whether or not to move and, if the decision is to move, where to move, is an example of a decision that must be made without any prior data. Decisions of this type are usually made only once; if they were made repetitively, there would be prior data to use in the later decisions. These decisions must be based on the possible outcomes that can occur and how they will affect the user. To make such decisions, the decision maker can use decision-making criteria that do not use any probabilities. Recall that probability is a way of assessing the likelihood of an event occurring. If $p$ is the probability of an event occurring, then $0 \leq p \leq 1$. The closer $p$ is to 1, the more likely the event is to occur. While decision making without prior data can be made without resorting to probabilities, the decision maker can use *subjective probabilities* to determine a decision. Subjective probabilities are generated by each individual decision maker without the use of prior data.

**TABLE 16-1.**
**Present Values of Location Decision**

| Decision | External Action | | |
| --- | --- | --- | --- |
| | *None* | *Close Old Dorms* | *New Apts. Built* |
| Don't move | +$100,000 | +$50,000 | +$20,000 |
| Baxter St. | +$40,000 | +$150,000 | +$25,000 |
| Epps Bridge Rd. | −$20,000 | +$20,000 | +$200,000 |

# ■ Types of decisions

There are essentially three major types of decisions.

1. decisions under certainty
2. decisions where prior data can be used to compute probabilities to use in making decisions
3. decisions where no prior data exist for computing probabilities

We will discuss each type of decision and give the conditions under which each type occurs.

## Decision making under certainty

Whenever there exists only one outcome for a decision, we are making decisions under certainty. Examples of this are linear and integer programming. In both cases, if a group of variables is chosen to be positive—that is, if a decision is made—there is no question as to what the profit associated with this decision will be. We will not be interested in this type of decision since a great deal of attention was given to it in earlier chapters. Instead, we will direct our attention to situations in which the outcome associated with any decision is not known for certain—that is, more than one outcome can result from any single decision.

## Decision making using prior data

Whenever a decision must be made on a repeated basis with multiple outcomes being possible, and the circumstances surrounding the decision are always the same, we have what may be called decisions using prior data. Since it is possible to use past experience to develop probabilities that each outcome will occur, this type of decision making uses probability-based decision-making models.

There are three conditions necessary for this type of decision making:

1. decisions are made under the same conditions
2. there exists more than one outcome for each decision
3. there exists previous experience that can be used to derive probabilities for each outcome

If any one of these conditions does not hold, then it is not considered to be a decision based on prior data. In the next chapter we will consider decision models for this situation.

### Decision making without prior data

In cases where a decision is not made repeatedly or there is no past experience to use in computing probabilities or the circumstances surrounding the decision change from instance to instance, we consider the decision to be made without prior data. It is so termed because the same decision will only be made once, and as such, no past experience is available to help in the decision-making process.

For this type of decision problem, we can take one of two approaches. We can use only the outcomes for each decision to determine the decision that best fits our view of the external factors surrounding the problem. On the other hand, we may choose to use subjective estimates (not based on prior data) known as **subjective probabilities** to determine a decision.

*subjective*
*probabilities*

## ■ Terminology of decision-making models

As with any type of model, decision-making models have a terminology of their own. This terminology describes the three essential parts of a decision:

*alternative*
*decisions*

1. the **alternative decisions** from which the DM may choose

*states-of-nature*

2. the **states-of-nature,** or external actions facing the decision maker

*outcome*

3. the **outcome** resulting from the use of a given alternative when a certain state-of-nature occurs

*decision tree*

We will discuss these three parts separately, before we go into the various decision-making models. We will also discuss the use of the **decision tree** as a means of structuring these three essential parts of a decision.

### Alternative decisions

When a DM is faced with a problem requiring a decision, one of the first actions he/she must take before actually arriving at a decision is to determine the alternatives upon which the final decision must be based. In the case of Ashley's Pizzeria, Ashley has three alternatives related to location (no move, Baxter Street, or Epps Bridge). This case illustrates the fact that doing nothing is also an alternative that the DM must consider. Notice that only truly viable alternatives are considered. The consideration of only truly viable alternatives is a form of **satisficing** as discussed previously.

*satisficing*

### The states-of-nature

A decision maker faced with a decision situation where multiple outcomes result for a given strategy is facing multiple *states-of-nature*, or external actions. States-of-nature are the circumstances that affect the outcome of the decision but are beyond the control of the DM. They are also referred to as external actions because they are situations that are external to the DM.

Regarding her decision on location, Ashley again faces three states-of-nature over which she has no control. These states-of-nature are influenced by someone else's decisions on the old dorms and the new apartments. The decisions will have a decided effect on the present value of profits regardless of which decision Ashley makes regarding location.

The primary concept to remember about states-of-nature is that they are external conditions that have an effect on the outcomes resulting from the various alternative decisions. Once again, as in the selection of alternatives, it is important to consider only environmental conditions that will have a significant effect on the outcomes.

## Outcomes

For each combination of a strategy and a state-of-nature there will exist an *outcome*. This outcome may be expressed in terms of profits (as it was for the problem of selecting the number of pizzas to prebake), it may be expressed in terms of present values (as was the case in the location decision), or it may be expressed in terms of some *nonmonetary* measure.

To determine the outcomes, it is necessary to look at all possible combinations of alternative decisions and states-of-nature to determine the outcome that would result *if* a given alternative were employed and a particular state-of-nature occurred. For example, in the pizzeria location problem, if Ashley decided not to move and the old dorms were closed, the outcome was computed to be $50,000. In that situation, since there were three alternatives and three states-of-nature, there are $3 \times 3 = 9$ outcomes to compute. In general, if there are $k$ alternatives and $n$ states-of-nature, there will be $(k \times n)$ outcomes to calculate. Quite often, outcomes are also referred to as *payoffs*, and a table of outcomes is referred to as a **payoff table.**

*payoff table*

## Decision trees

A clear, easy way to structure the decision-making process is through a *decision tree*. The decision tree is made up of *action nodes*, *chance nodes*, and *branches*. In our decision trees, action nodes will be denoted by a square (□) and will represent places in the decision-making process where a decision is made. Chance nodes will be denoted by a circle (○) and will represent places in the decision-making process where some state-of-nature will occur. The branches are used to denote the decisions or the states-of-nature. Probabilities can also be placed on the branches to denote the probability of a given state-of-nature occurring. Finally, payoffs are placed on the end of the final state-of-nature branches to show the result of making a particular decision and then having that particular state-of-nature occur. As an example of a decision tree, consider the example of the college professor who is trying to decide whether or not to carry an umbrella to work today. The decision on carrying the umbrella is shown as an action node in Figure 16-1.

FIGURE 16-1.
Action and
Chance Nodes

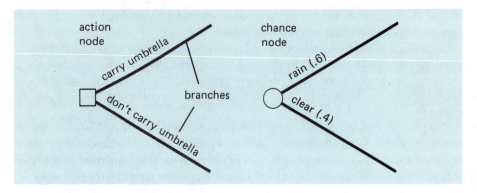

At the end of each branch that begins at an action node, there will be a chance node or another action node. The possible states-of-nature will begin at the chance nodes. The possible states-of-nature for the professor's decision are also shown in Figure 16-1. In this case, we have also placed on the chance branch the probabilities of rain and clear as given by the local weather bureau.

Now if we combine the action nodes and chance nodes with the payoffs for each such combination, we have a decision tree. The professor has determined the various payoffs associated with the four possible combinations of decisions and states-of-nature. These payoffs are placed at the end of the final chance branches. The professor has decided on the following payoffs:

| | |
|---|---|
| carry umbrella and no rain | $-1$ |
| carry umbrella and rain | $+20$ |
| don't carry umbrella and no rain | $+5$ |
| don't carry umbrella and rain | $-40$ |

Using these payoffs, a final decision tree can be constructed. This tree is shown in Figure 16-2.

Using the terminology of alternatives, states-of-nature, outcomes, and decision trees, we will now discuss decision models for both decision making using prior data and decision making without prior data.

## ■ Decision making without prior data

In this section, we will look at a group of decision models that can be used for decision making without prior data. It is not possible to say that one of these models is any more correct than any other. The appropriateness of each model depends upon the outlook of the DM and whether or not the DM wishes to use subjective probabilities. As we discuss each model, we will describe under what circumstances it would be appropriate to use that decision model, and we will use the Ashley's Pizzeria location problem as an application of that model. The first three models do not use subjective probabilities to make a decision, while the latter two models do.

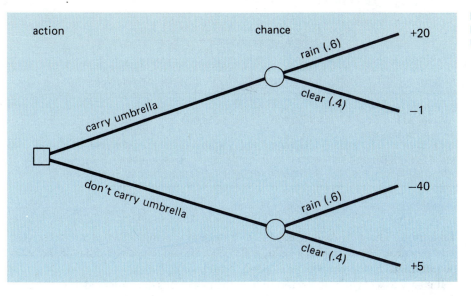

**FIGURE 16-2.**
**Decision Tree for Umbrella Decision**

action — carry umbrella — chance — rain (.6) → +20 — clear (.4) → −1

don't carry umbrella — rain (.6) → −40 — clear (.4) → +5

## Pessimist's decision model

The decision maker who is pessimistic about the states-of-nature or who feels, because of economic insecurity, that high losses must be avoided at the risk of losing possibly high profits, will lean toward using the decision model known as the *pessimist's decision model*. The major concept behind this model is the avoidance of high or unacceptable losses.

To implement this concept of loss avoidance, we determine the lowest outcome for each strategy and then select the strategy having the highest of these lowest outcomes. Since we are maximizing the minimum outcomes, this decision model is also known as the *maximin criterion*. The procedure may be described as follows:

> **Step 1.** For each alternative, determine the lowest-valued outcome and record this in a list.
>
> **Step 2.** From the list of outcomes, choose the maximum value. The alternative associated with this maximum outcome is the strategy to employ.

As an example of the use of the pessimist's decision model, consider the outcome for the Ashley's Pizzeria location decision (Table 16-2). If we now apply step 1 of the pessimist's decision model to this problem, we can list the minimum outcomes (payoffs) and the state-of-nature associated with each minimum outcome (Table 16-3).

If we then apply step 2 of the pessimist's decision model, we maximize the values in Table 16-3 and find that the alternative selected is A2 (move to Baxter Street) with a minimum payoff of $25,000. (This is the alternative marked with an asterisk in

**TABLE 16-2.**
**Payoff Table for**
**Location Problem**
**(from Table 16-1)**

|  | State-of-Nature | | |
|---|---|---|---|
| *Alternative* | *No Change (N1)* | *Old Dorms Closed (N2)* | *Apartments Built (N3)* |
| Remain at present lo-cation (A1) | +$100,000 | +$50,000 | +$20,000 |
| Move to Baxter Street (A2) | +$40,000 | +$150,000 | +$25,000 |
| Move to Epps Bridge Road (A3) | −$20,000 | +$20,000 | +$200,000 |

Table 16-3.) That is, if Ashley selects the strategy of moving to Baxter Street, then the least payoff she could expect would be $25,000. Should she select either of the other two alternatives, the payoff *could* be less than this.

It is easy to see why this is referred to as the pessimist's decision model. We assume the worst will happen and then seek to do the best we can under this assumption. In other words, we view the environment as being hostile and work on this basis.

Another reason why we might choose to use this decision model is the set of circumstances surrounding the decision. In some cases, we cannot afford some of the payoffs that could occur. So we make our choice in such a way as to avoid what could be ruinous payoffs. For example, while the Baxter Street strategy has a minimum payoff of $25,000, the Epps Bridge Road minimum payoff has a loss of $20,000. If Ashley's Pizzeria cannot afford a loss such as this, it is necessary to avoid the possibility of having this occur by not choosing the Epps Bridge strategy.

In Figure 16-3, Ashley's moving problem has been placed in a decision tree. In this case, there are three decision branches, which correspond to don't move, move to Baxter Street, and move to Epps Bridge Road. For each decision branch there are three state-of-nature branches associated with a chance node. These correspond to no change, close the dorms, and build new apartments. Finally, for each action/chance combination there is a payoff, which we have put at the right end of each ending branch.

To set up the minimum payoff table for the pessimist's decision model, all we need to do is to select the minimum payoff associated with each decision branch.

**TABLE 16-3.**
**Minimum Payoffs**
**for Location**
**Problem**

| *Alternative* | *Minimum Payoff* |
|---|---|
| A1 | $20,000 (N3) |
| A2° | $25,000 (N3) |
| A3 | −$20,000 (N1) |

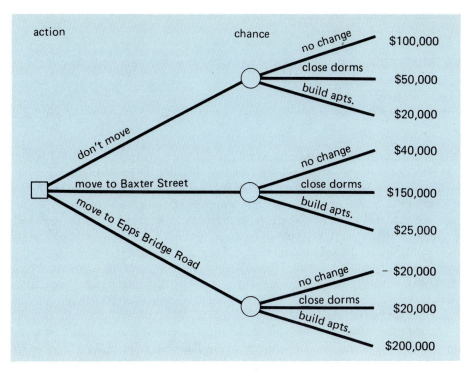

**FIGURE 16-3.
Decision Tree for
Ashley's Moving
Decision**

## Optimist's decision model

The DM who chooses to view the environment as being friendly will be optimistic about the outcome rather than pessimistic. Under such an assumption, the DM determines the highest payoff for each alternative and then chooses the maximum of these.

The procedure for implementing the optimist's decision model is the same as that for the pessimist's decision model with one important exception. Step 1 should be revised as follows:

> **Step 1:** For each alternative, determine the highest-valued outcome and record it in a list.

> **Step 2:** From the list of outcomes, choose the maximum value. The alternative associated with this maximum outcome is the strategy to employ.

As an example of the use of the optimist's decision model, consider again Ashley's problem of deciding whether to move or not. If we apply this decision model to Ashley's problem, step 1 yields the list shown in Table 16-4.

If we then apply step 2 of the optimist's decision model, we will maximize the values in Table 16-4 and find that the alternative selected is A3 (move to Epps Bridge Road) with a payoff of $200,000. That is, if Ashley selects the alternative of moving

**TABLE 16-4.**
**Maximum Payoffs**

| Alternative | Maximum Payoff |
|---|---|
| A1 | +$100,000 (N1) |
| A2 | +$150,000 (N2) |
| A3° | +$200,000 (N3) |

to Epps Bridge Road, then the maximum payoff she could expect is $200,000. Should she select any other alternative, the payoff will definitely be less than this value.

This decision model is known as the optimist's decision model because the DM has an optimistic outlook about the environment. The DM might also decide to use this decision model in a situation where the amount of money to be lost (negative payoff) is small compared with the profit to be made. In such a case, it is assumed that the DM can *afford* the losses that might occur if the optimist's decision model is used. In our example, alternative A3 might have been chosen because of the size of the return, $200,000, which was large compared with the *loss* that might have occurred by choosing this alternative, $20,000. The DM did not consider $20,000 a large potential loss when the payoff was considered.

As with the pessimist's decision model, it is easy to use a decision tree in the optimist's decision model. The only change is that instead of making a list of the minimum payoffs for each decision branch, we make a list of the maximum payoffs.

### Minimization-of-regret decision model

Another decision model that represents a fairly pessimistic view of the environment is that of minimization-of-regret, also known as *minimizing opportunity losses*.

*opportunity loss*          To understand this decision model, we need to define an **opportunity loss.** For a given state-of-nature, there always exist one or more alternatives that yield the highest payoff. If we choose a strategy that results in a payoff lower than the maximum for this given state-of-nature, then we incur an opportunity loss equal to the difference between the highest payoff and the payoff for the chosen strategy—and feel regret. In other words, for a particular state-of-nature,

$$\text{opportunity loss} = \text{maximum payoff} - \text{payoff for chosen alternative} \quad (16.1)$$

**TABLE 16-5.**
**First**
**State-of-Nature**
**Payoffs**

| Alternative | No Change (N1) |
|---|---|
| A1 | +$100,000 |
| A2 | +$40,000 |
| A3 | −$20,000 |

TABLE 16-6.
Opportunity Loss
Calculation for N1

| Alternative | Maximum Payoff | − | Alternative Payoff | = | Opportunity Loss |
|---|---|---|---|---|---|
| A1 | $100,000 | | $100,000 | | 0 |
| A2 | $100,000 | | $40,000 | | $60,000 |
| A3 | $100,000 | | −$20,000 | | $120,000 |

Opportunity losses are the amount we lose when the alternative chosen was not the best. If our decision leads to the highest payoff for a particular state of nature, there is no opportunity loss—and we feel no regret.

As an example of the opportunity loss, or regret decision model, consider the first state-of-nature (no change) for Ashley's location problem. This column of the payoff table is shown in Table 16-5.

Using the values in Table 16-5, we determine that the maximum payoff is $100,000 and occurs for A1 (don't move). Using this value and equation (16.1), we can compute opportunity loss for each alternative (see Table 16-6).

Using the same procedure, we can compute the opportunity loss for the second and third states-of-nature. When the opportunity values for all states-of-nature are placed in a combined table, we have a *regret table*. Such a table for Ashley's moving problem is shown in Table 16-7.

We seek to avoid high regret values since these are associated with high opportunity loss. This kind of decision making is similar to the pessimist's decision model with the exception that here we seek to minimize maximum opportunity losses. A step-by-step procedure for the minimization-of-regret decision model may be stated as follows:

**Step 1.** For each state-of-nature:

**a.** Determine the highest payoff.
**b.** Compute opportunity losses for each alternative using equation (16.1).
**c.** Place these opportunity loss values in a regret table.

**Step 2.** For each alternative in the regret table, determine the maximum opportunity loss and place this value in a list.

TABLE 16-7.
Regret Table

| | State-of-Nature | | |
|---|---|---|---|
| Alternative | No Change (N1) | Close Old Dorms (N2) | Build New Apartments (N3) |
| Don't move (A1) | 0 | $100,000 | $180,000 |
| Move to Baxter Street (A2) | $60,000 | 0 | $175,000 |
| Move to Epps Bridge Road (A3) | $120,000 | $130,000 | 0 |

**Step 3.** Using the list from step 2, determine the *minimum* of the maximum opportunity losses. The corresponding alternative is the alternative to be selected.

If we use this step-by-step procedure to generate the regret table in Table 16-7, we arrive, in step 2, at the list of maximum opportunity loss values shown in Table 16-8. Using step 3, we then choose alternative A3 (move to Epps Bridge Road), since it is the smallest value in the list of maximum opportunity losses, with a value of $130,000. This alternative is marked with an asterisk in Table 16-8.

In this decision model, the DM is seeking to avoid high opportunity losses via a *minimax* approach to the regret table. In so doing, the DM minimizes the maximum difference that can occur between the best outcome for a given state-of-nature and each outcome. In choosing an alternative, the DM has been assured that the maximum regret or opportunity loss has been minimized.

## *Maximization-of-average-payoff decision model*

*average payoff*

Whenever a decision maker is faced with multiple alternatives with each alternative in turn having multiple outcomes, a common practice is to find the **average payoff** for each strategy, and then choose the alternative with the highest average payoff. In this decision model, if there exist $n$ outcomes for each alternative with

$O_{ij}$ = payoff for $i$th alternative given $j$th state-of-nature, and

$V_i$ = average payoff for the $i$th alternative

then

$$V_i = \frac{1}{n} \sum_{j=1}^{n} O_{ij}$$   (16.2)

For example, in the Ashley Pizzeria moving problem, the average payoff for the first alternative is given by

$$V_1 = (100,000 + 50,000 + 20,000)/3 = \$56,667 \quad (A1)$$

while

$$V_2 = (40,000 + 150,000 + 25,000)/3 = \$71,667 \quad (A2)$$

**TABLE 16-8.**
**Maximum Regret Values**

| Alternative | Maximum Opportunity Loss |
|---|---|
| A1 | $180,000 (N3) |
| A2 | $175,000 (N3) |
| A3° | $130,000 (N2) |

and

$$V_3 = (-20,000 + 20,000 + 200,000)/3 = \$66,667 \qquad (A3)$$

Using these values, the DM will make up a list of average values similar to that in the three previous decision models. In this case, the list is shown in Table 16-9. When we then maximize over these average payoffs, we choose strategy A2 (move to Baxter Street). This alternative is marked with an asterisk in Table 16-9.

The step-by-step description of the maximum-average-payoff decision model is given below:

> **Step 1.** For each alternative, compute the average payoff over all states-of-nature and put these values in a list.
>
> **Step 2.** Determine the largest value from the list of average payoffs. The alternative corresponding to this payoff is the one to be selected.

Intuitively, the maximum-average-payoff decision model would not appear to depend upon probabilities. However, by taking the average of the outcomes for each decision, we are implicitly saying that the outcomes are *equally likely*. In terms of probabilities, the probability of each outcome occurring is equal to $1/n$ where there are $n$ outcomes. In other words, if $p_i$ = probability of the $i$th outcome, then $p_1 = p_2 = \cdots = p_n = 1/n$.

These probabilities can then be used to compute the **expected monetary value** (EMV) of each decision. The **EMV decision model** is based upon the concept of *expected value* from probability theory. If there are, say, $n$ outcomes for an experiment, with each outcome having return $r_j$ and probability of occurrence $p_j$, then the expected value of such an experiment is given by

*EMV decision model*

$$\text{expected value} = \sum_{j=1}^{n} p_j r_j \qquad (16.3)$$

where

$$\sum_{j=1}^{n} p_j = 1 \qquad (16.4)$$

For example, if we were to roll a single die having six equally likely sides and the return were equal to the number showing, then the expected value for such an

| Alternative | Average Payoff |
|---|---|
| A1 | $56,667 |
| A2° | $71,667 |
| A3 | $66,667 |

experiment would be

$$\text{expected value} = (\tfrac{1}{6})(1) + (\tfrac{1}{6})(2) + (\tfrac{1}{6})(3) + (\tfrac{1}{6})(4) + (\tfrac{1}{6})(5) + (\tfrac{1}{6})(6)$$

$$= 3\tfrac{1}{2}$$

If the return is in terms of money, then the expected value becomes expected monetary value.

In the case of equally likely probabilities,

$$\text{EMV} = \sum_{j=1}^{n} p_j r_j = \sum_{j=1}^{n} \frac{1}{n} r_j \tag{16.5}$$

This is the same as the formula given in equation (16.2), which demonstrates that the maximum-average-payoff decision model is the same as using a maximum EMV approach with equal probabilities.

## Subjective probabilities model

While it is not always possible to use prior data to compute probabilities for the occurrence of various outcomes, it is possible to use subjective probabilities. Such probabilities are based on a multitude of prior experiences that the DM can use to assign probabilities to outcomes. Subjective probabilities are the basic concept upon which betting is based. Each bettor assigns a different probability to the various outcomes of a race or other game of chance and then evaluates the outcomes to decide how to bet. Many things go into each bettor's assignment of probabilities, including the number of options, the bettor's assessed strength of each option, and prior experience in the event.

In business, the DM must often assign probabilities to the occurrence of various outcomes based on personal judgment of market conditions, a competitor's future actions, the strength of the product being considered, and on and on. Sometimes intuition, or "gut feeling," will lead a DM to make assignments of probabilities for reasons that he/she cannot define.

Once the subjective probabilities have been assigned, the DM must then decide whether the dollar values for the payoffs (both positive and negative) are adequate to be used in expected value computations. In other words, is there a linear relationship

*utility*

between the money involved and the DM's **utility** for each outcome? In this case, utility refers to the *nonmonetary* consequences of an outcome occurring. To understand this concept better, consider the situation facing Gene Van Etten, an industrious college student who has worked all summer to earn the $3,000 he needs to pay expenses for the next school year. Gene has also earned an extra $1,000, which he plans to apply toward the purchase of a car. Gene figures he needs an additional $1,000 to buy the MG he wants; so he has decided to bet in a local football pool. He has investigated the betting pool and determined that for a $1,000 bet on this week's semipro game between the Winemucca Road Runners and the Waynesville Critters he could win $1,000 if he picked the winning team. He also found out that on a $4,000 bet, he could win $6,000. In the first bet he would end up with either $3,000 or $5,000, while in the second bet, he could have either nothing or $10,000. The decision facing Gene is which bet to invest in.

If Gene uses straight expected-value calculation and believes that he has a 50–50 chance of winning in either bet, for Bet 1 the EMV is $(.5)(5,000) + (.5)(3,000) = \$4,000$. Similarly, for Bet 2, the EMV is $(.5)(10,000) + (.5)(0) = \$5,000$. So if Gene used the expected monetary value as a decision criterion, he would obviously choose Bet 2 since the EMV is higher. But what about the *nonmonetary* consequences? If Gene takes Bet 1, he will either win enough money to buy a car or he will lose the $1,000. If he takes Bet 2, he will be much wealthier than before if he wins, but if he loses, he will not be able to attend school this year. If Gene were asked to assign some sort of utility values to each of these outcomes on, say, a scale of 1 to 10 (any scale will do), he might give the following values:

| Outcome | Utility Value |
|---|---|
| Have $5,000 (Bet 1) | 8 |
| Have $3,000 (Bet 1) | 4 |
| Have $10,000 (Bet 2) | 9 |
| Not attend school (Bet 2) | 1 |

If Gene computed the expected nonmonetary values of Bet 1 and Bet 2, he would find that the **expected utility value** (EUV) of Bet 1 is $(.5)(8) + (.5)(4) = 6$ and the EUV of Bet 2 is $(.5)(9) + (.5)(1) = 5$. Using EUV, Gene would choose Bet 1. This type of reasoning fits the concept of the rational person who constantly seeks to maximize expected utility.

*expected utility value*

If we apply expected utility analysis to Ashley's Pizzeria and her decision concerning moving, we will need to solicit two types of information from Ashley. First, we must know if the dollars in the payoff table (Table 16-2) truly represent all consequences of each decision, monetary as well as nonmonetary. If not, then Ashley will need to develop a table of utility values. This can be done as in the previous example or through various structured methods. Second, we must solicit Ashley's estimation of the probability of each outcome occurring. (We will not discuss the calculations of utilities and subjective probabilities here but the interested reader can find a further discussion in the references listed at the end of the chapter.) Then we may use expected value to choose an alternative. Let us assume that Ashley is satisfied with the dollar values in the payoff table as a representation of the consequences of each decision. She estimates that there is a .4 probability of no external action (outcome 1), a .3 probability of the old dorms being closed (outcome 2), and a .3 probability of the new apartments being built (outcome 3). Now we can compute expected utility values for each decision:

A1: $\quad EUV_1 = (.4)(100,000) + (.3)(50,000) + (.3)(20,000) = \$61,000$

A2: $\quad EUV_2 = (.4)(40,000) + (.3)(150,000) + (.3)(25,000) = \$68,500$

A3: $\quad EUV_3 = (.4)(-20,000) + (.3)(20,000) + (.3)(200,000) = \$58,000$

Using the subjective probability approach, Ashley would choose A2 (move to Baxter Street).

If we used a decision tree to present this decision, the tree would look like the one shown in Figure 16-3 except that we now include probabilities on each outcome branch (Figure 16-4). These probabilities are simply multiplied by the outcome at the end of their branch and summed over outcomes for each strategy branch to compute the expected value (either EMV or EUV) for each alternative.

As an example of the expected value calculations using a decision tree, consider the A1 (don't move) branch. On this branch, if we multiply the outcomes at the end of each state-of-nature branch by the probabilities on the branch, and then sum, we get

$$(.4)(100{,}000) + (.3)(50{,}000) + (.3)(20{,}000) = \$61{,}000$$

which is the same as the EUV calculated earlier for A1, only now we have used the decision tree in the calculation.

Note that EUV would be exactly the same for the maximum-average-payoff approach if we replace the subjective probabilities by the equally likely probabilities. In this case, the probabilities on every branch would become .3333 since there are three outcomes for each decision branch.

**FIGURE 16-4.**
**Decision Tree for**
**Moving Decision**

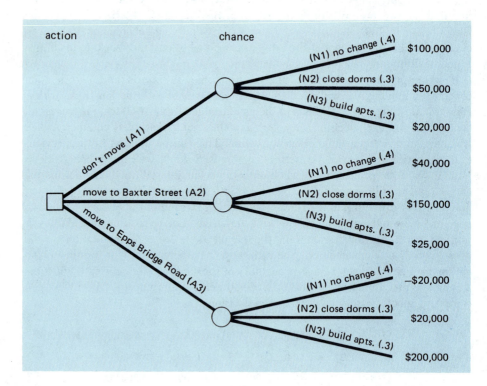

**TABLE 16-10.**
**Pitfalls of the**
**Pessimist's Model**

|              | State-of-Nature |         |
|--------------|-----------------|---------|
| Alternative  | N1              | N2      |
| A1           | −10             | 400,000 |
| A2           | 0               | 0       |

## A warning about decision models

In this section, we have discussed both probability- and nonprobability-based decision models for situations where no prior experience exists. It should be noted that one must be careful in the use of these models because it is very easy to create problems where unrealistic results can occur. In the case of the nonprobability-based models (the pessimist's decision model, optimist's decision model, and minimization-of-regret model), it is possible in each case to develop a problem where the use of that model can lead to very bad decisions. For example, consider the decision problem shown in Table 16-10.

If, in Table 16-10, we take the worst that can happen for each alternative, A1 and A2, and make a list, we have Table 16-11. Using the pessimist's decision model, we would then choose alternative A2 since 0 is greater than −10. We have completely neglected the fact that the $400,000 positive payoff exists.

This example may appear to be extreme, but it serves to point out the type of results that can occur when one fails to consider all existing information while making a decision. There exist other nonprobability-based models that attempt to incorporate the degree of optimism the DM feels; but the fact that these models do not account for the probabilistic nature of the environment leaves them open to criticism.

On the other hand, one must also be aware of the problems that can occur in using an EMV approach to decision making *without* considering the nonmonetary consequences. As we saw in our example of the college student who was considering two gambling opportunities, always choosing the alternative with the highest EMV can lead to disastrous consequences. And as we noted in our maximum-average payoff example, the average or expected value calculated may not actually occur. In the college student example, the highest EMV was $5,000, yet the two outcomes were $10,000 and $0. Only when the nonmonetary and monetary consequences are combined into a *utility* scale can we have confidence in using expected value as a

**TABLE 16-11.**
**Minimum Payoffs**
**for the Pessimist's**
**Model**

| Alternative | Minimum Payoff |
|-------------|----------------|
| A1          | −10            |
| A2°         | 0              |

decision criterion where prior data do not exist and subjective probabilities are used.

## ■ Summary

In this chapter on decision models, we have introduced the concept of decision making when the outcome is uncertain. To do this, we first discussed a step-by-step procedure for making decisions and compared it with the problem-solving method of Chapter 1.

Next we consider three types of decisions: decisions under certainty, decisions without prior data, and decisions using prior data. Our discussion centered around decisions without prior data, since decisions under certainty were discussed in detail earlier and decisions with prior data are discussed in the next chapter.

In discussing decisions without prior data, we considered several models that ignored the probabilistic nature of the decisions. We then included the concepts of utility and subjective probability as aids in reaching a decision. We used subjective probabilities, since these decisions assume there are no prior data to be used in computing probabilities. In this discussion, we encountered the terms *alternative*, *stage-of-nature*, and *payoff*, which describe the decision-making problem.

## ■ Glossary of terms

**average payoff decision model:**    A decision model that chooses the alternative that has the average maximum payoff.

**decision making:**    Choosing between alternatives.

**decision tree:**    A diagrammatic portrayal of the various states-of-nature and decision alternatives.

**EMV decision model:**    A decision model that chooses the alternative with maximum EMV.

**environment:**    Equivalent to states-of-nature.

**expected monetary value:**    For each alternative, the sum of each payoff times the probability for the corresponding state-of-nature.

**expected utility value:**    For each alternative, the sum of each utility times the subjective probability for the corresponding state-of-nature.

**minimization-of-regret decision model:**    A decision model that chooses the alternative that minimizes the maximum opportunity loss (regret).

**opportunity loss:**    The decrease in payoff for a particular state-of-nature that results from using an alternative other than the highest-payoff alternative.

**optimist's decision model:**    A decision model that chooses an alternative that maximizes the maximum payoff for each alternative.

**outcome:**    The result of using a particular alternative when a particular state-of-nature occurs. There exists one outcome for each combination of alternative and state-of-nature.

**payoff table:**    A table of the payoffs (outcomes) for all possible alternatives and states-of-nature.

**pessimist's decision model:**   A decision model that chooses an alternative that maximizes the minimum payoff for each alternative.

**probability:**   A measure of the likelihood of an event occurring.

**states-of-nature:**   The circumstances surrounding a decision over which the decision maker has no control.

**strategies:**   The alternative decisions from which the decision maker must choose.

**subjective probability:**   A set of probabilities based upon the decision maker's prior experience.

**utility:**   The nonmonetary consequences of any decision.

## ■ Review questions

1. Distinguish between deterministic decision making and stochastic decision making.

2. Discuss briefly the difference between *optimizing* and *satisficing*.

3. Why should "doing nothing" be considered an alternative in all decisions?

4. Using the Ashley's Pizzeria case, show how the decision-making algorithm can be applied.

5. Classify each of the following decisions as being either decision making using prior data or decision making without prior data and explain your choice:
   a. building a new basketball coliseum
   b. choosing a college to attend
   c. deciding on a route to use to go to work each day
   d. choosing a sample size to use to test for defects on an assembly line
   e. choosing a number of newspapers to order for sale each day

6. Discuss briefly the conditions under which a decision maker would use each of the decision-making-without-prior-data decision models.

7. Suggest a situation in which the average payoff decision model could lead a decision maker possibly to make a catastrophic decision.

8. Another name for the average payoff criterion is the *equally likely* criterion since it is implicitly assumed that each state-of-nature is equally likely to occur. Does this mean we are actually using an EMV approach when we apply the average payoff criterion? Why?

9. Can you suggest another nonprobability decision model or derive a combination of the four discussed here?

## ■ True/false questions

1. A decision maker should always try to make the optimal decision by searching out and analyzing all alternatives.

2. Integer programming is an example of decision making under certainty.

3. The use of computers has made the concept of satisficing obsolete.

4. Gambling on a football game is an example of the use of subjective probabilities.

5. In decision making without prior data, the decision model used depends a great deal on the amount the DM can afford to risk.

6. The EMV decision model is always appropriate if probabilities are available.

7. Everyone's utility functions are very similar.

## ■ Problems

1. Consider the following matrix of payoffs for a decision problem where past data are not available. Use each of the decision models discussed in the chapter to select an alternative to follow (where Q, R, S, and T are states-of-nature).

| Alternative | Q | R | S | T |
|---|---|---|---|---|
| 1 | 1000 | 250 | 600 | 100 |
| 2 | 2000 | 125 | 1280 | 100 |

2. Using each of the decision models discussed in the chapter, select an alternative to follow for the table profits shown in Table P16-2. Compare the alternatives selected in each case.

**TABLE P16-2. Matrix of Profits for Problem 2**

| Alternative | State-of-Nature | | |
|---|---|---|---|
| | X | Y | Z |
| 1 | 300 | 400 | 700 |
| 2 | 400 | 500 | 500 |
| 3 | 200 | 600 | 200 |

3. Consider the following matrix of *losses* for a decision problem where past data are not available. Use each of the decision models discussed in the text to select an alternative to follow (A, B, C, and D are states-of-nature).

| Alternative | A | B | C | D |
|---|---|---|---|---|
| I | 10 | 100 | 0 | 50 |
| II | 75 | 50 | 60 | 40 |
| III | 30 | 40 | 25 | 25 |

a. Why would the pessimist's decision model become a minimax approach rather than the maximin approach used for the payoff tables in the chapter?

b. Why is the optimist's decision model a minimin approach rather than maximax?

c. How does the calculation of *opportunity costs* for a loss table differ from a payoff table?

d. Does the average approach for losses differ from other decision-making approaches?

4. If the matrix of losses shown in Table P16-4 is used in making a decision, show the alternative that would be chosen under each of the decision models discussed in the chapter.

**TABLE P16-4. Matrix of Losses for Problem 4**

| Alternative | State-of-Nature | | | |
|---|---|---|---|---|
| | A | B | C | D |
| I | -10 | -20 | -30 | -40 |
| II | -30 | 0 | -50 | -20 |
| III | 40 | -25 | -30 | -25 |

5. **a.** Given a decision tree as shown in Figure P16-5, write the problem in a payoff matrix form.

   **b.** Determine a decision to maximize total expected return using the given probabilities.

**FIGURE P16-5.**

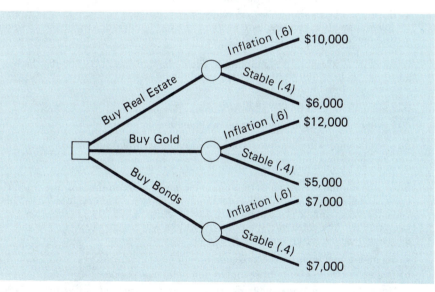

6. Given a decision tree as shown in Figure P16-5, write the problem as a loss matrix. Use the pessimist's model to choose an alternative and relate this back to the decision tree.

7. Coach Jim Dooley has recently become interested in using decision models to help him choose plays for this football team to run. In this case, the states-of-nature are the defenses the other team uses, and his plays are the alternatives. Table P16-7 shows the gain/loss matrix that Coach Dooley has estimated for each play under each of the defenses. Using this information and the decision models discussed in the chapter, select alternatives for each model. If you were Coach Dooley, which model would you use?

**TABLE P16-7. Gain/Loss Matrix for Problem 7**

| Play | Defensive Arrangement | | |
| --- | --- | --- | --- |
| | Goal Line | 5–3–3 | 4–3–2–2 |
| Pass | +15 | +5 | 0 |
| Sprint draw | −3 | +5 | +6 |
| End sweep | −4 | +3 | +10 |

8. Chip Conley is a young contractor who has the opportunity to choose between building a speculative house and doing two additions during the next two months. If he builds the spec house and is able to sell it, he will clear $10,000. However, if the housing market declines due to increases in the mortgage interest rate, Chip will not be able to sell the house and stands to loose $5,000. On the other hand, he can make $7,000 on the two house additions regardless of the housing market.

   a. Set up a payoff table for this problem.

   b. Draw a decision tree for this problem.

   c. Choose an alternative to follow using each of the nonprobability decision models appropriate for this type of problem.

   d. If Chip has decided that the probability of the mortgage rate increasing is .6, and the dollar amounts are an adequate measure of Chip's utility, determine the appropriate strategy for Chip to follow.

9. Professor E. Z. Gradum is attempting to decide how to spend $10,000 that he has just inherited. He has three possible ways to spend the money.

   (1)  buy canal front property in Florida

   (2)  invest in a colleague's new gas-saving invention

   (3)  put the money in a five-year bank investment that will return (after compounding) 10% per year

   Professor Gradum's major concern is a possible gas shortage in the next five years. If this occurs and gas rationing results, the canal front property will increase in value to $14,000, while the gas-saving device will produce a total return of $25,000. On the other hand, if gas rationing does not occur, the property will be worth $23,000, while the gas-saving device will yield a total return of only $5,000.

   a. Set up a payoff table for this problem.

   b. Draw a decision tree for Professor Gradum's decision problem.

   c. Use each of the nonprobability decision models discussed in this chapter to choose an investment plan.

   d. If Professor Gradum feels the probability of a gas shortage is .65 and the monetary returns are an adequate measure of his utility, determine an appropriate strategy for Professor Gradum to follow.

10. Tom Jacobson is faced with the decision as to whether to repair his present car or to buy a new car. If he repairs his present car and it still "dies" within the year, the present value of his total cost will be the repairs plus buying a new car anyway or $6000. On the other hand, he figures that if the present car lasts more than one year but less than three, the present value of the costs will be $3500. Finally, if the present car makes it to five more

years, the present value of his cost will be only $2000. If he sells the unrepaired present car and buys a new car right away, his cost is $5000 regardless of what would have happened to the present car.

**a.** Set up a *cost* table for his problem.
**b.** Draw a decision tree for Tom's decision problem.
**c.** Use the pessimist's decision model to select a decision to implement.
**d.** Use the optimist's decision model to select an alternative.
**e.** Use the average value approach to select an alternative.

11. In Problem 10, Tom Jacobson has computed probabilities of his car's future use to be .3 for less than one year's use, .5 for one to three year's use, and .2 for more than three year's use. He has also assigned utilities of 1, 5, and 10 to each outcome. Compare the decisions resulting from the use of EMV and of EUV.

12. Evelyn Brown is the dispatcher for the Shope Trucking Company out of Silver City, N. Dak. In this job, she must choose which routes the trucks will take to make their deliveries. One particular route from Silver City to Franklin has been known to cause problems in the past. These troubles are caused by rock slides and flooding whenever it rains. The map in Figure P16-12 shows the various possible roads from Franklin to Silver City and the troublesome areas. The driving times over possible legs of this trip from Silver City to Franklin are as follows.

| Leg of Trip | Driving Time |
| --- | --- |
| A–B | 30 |
| A–C | 15 |
| A–C–D | 20 |
| A–B–E | 45 |
| A–C–D–E | 50 |
| D–B | 15 |
| D–E | 30 |

If a truck is dispatched from Silver City via Route 64 and the bridge is out, it will have to return to Silver City and then go to Cowee Road. Similarly, if a truck goes via Cowee Road and there are rock slides, then the truck will have to go back along Rt. 64 to Country Road 1101. It has just rained, and Evelyn is seeking to determine the best way to send a convoy of trucks in such a way as to avoid delay as much as possible. (*Note:* There may be flooding and rock slides at the same time.)

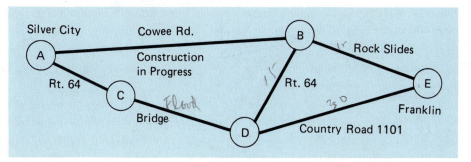

**FIGURE P16-12.
Truck Routes for
Problem 12**

**a.** Set up a cost matrix showing all possible alternatives, states-of-nature, and corresponding driving times.

**b.** Choose a decision model to use in making a decision as to which alternative should be used and apply it to this problem.

**c.** Do the same using a second-decision model.

13. Joe Patrick of the Patrick Manufacturing Company has the opportunity to bid on one of three big government research projects. These projects are code named Zeus, Thor, and Atlas. Joe can bid on each of the three projects but there are different preparation costs and levels of funding for each. The states-of-nature are the three projects that can be funded. The cost of bidding on each project and the gross amount of the grant for each of the three states-of-nature are as follows:

| Project | Cost | Grant |
|---------|------|-------|
| Thor | $40,000 | $80,000 |
| Zeus | $50,000 | $150,000 |
| Atlas | $100,000 | $125,000 |

**a.** Set up a payoff matrix based on *net* funding to the Patrick Company.

**b.** Apply each of the appropriate decision models to this problem to pick a strategy for the Patrick Company to use.

**c.** Joe has assigned subjective probabilities of .4, .3, and .3 to the funding of Thor, Zeus, and Atlas. If the net funding values reflect Joe's utility scale, use the EUV model to choose an alternative.

**17**

# Decision Models II

## ■ Introduction

In the last chapter we discussed the use of decision models as an aid to decision making with particular emphasis on decision without prior data. In this chapter we consider decision making using prior data. Decisions using prior data are those that occur repetitively under similar circumstances, where past experience exists that may be used in making these decisions. The expected value model discussed in the last chapter is the most appropriate model for this situation. We will also discuss the difference between classical statistical decision making and Bayesian decision making, but our emphasis will be on Bayesian methods.

■ **Case**
## Ashley's Pizzeria (Continued)

In the last chapter we met Ashley Washington, who had made a name for herself by prebaking pizzas. In so doing she was able to reduce the time that students for State College had to wait for a pizza. While the students like this approach very much, and a large number of pizzas have been sold, there have been occasions when Ashley has been forced to discard a large number of pre-baked pizzas. This occurred when demand was less than anticipated. For this reason Ashley is seeking a policy to use in deciding how many pizzas to bake in order to maximize profit.

Ashley has narrowed her alternatives down to four possibilities: baking 150, 160, 170, or 180 pizzas. She has studied previous demand patterns to determine the number of pizzas demanded each day over the last 100 days. Her findings are as follows (we have rounded the number of pizzas to the nearest multiple of 10):

| Number of pizzas demanded | 150 | 160 | 170 | 180 |
|---|---|---|---|---|
| Number of days | 20 | 40 | 25 | 15 |

Ashley has determined that she has seldom had demand less than 150 pizzas or more than 180; so we may restrict our alternatives to 150, 160, 170, and 180 pizzas per day. This is an example of using *satisficing* to reduce the number of alternatives.

Ashley has determined that she makes $2 on each pizza sold and loses $1 on each pizza left unsold. With this information, it is possible to construct a profit table that gives the profit for each baking policy and each sales level (see Table 17-1). In this table, if demand for pizzas is higher than the number that has been baked, it is assumed that the customer will not wait and the profit from that customer will be lost.

To illustrate the computations involved in Table 17-1, consider the case where 160 pizzas were prebaked, but only 150 were demanded. In this situation, the gross profit would be $2 × 150 = $300, with $10 being lost due to the extra pizzas not being sold, hence a net profit of $290 is realized. Table 17-1 can be used to determine the number of pizzas to be prebaked in order to maximize profit for Ashley's Pizzeria.

**TABLE 17-1.**
**Profit Table for**
**Ashley's Pizzeria**

| No. of Pizzas Prebaked | No. of Pizzas Demanded | | | |
|---|---|---|---|---|
| | 150 | 160 | 170 | 180 |
| 150 | 300 | 300 | 300 | 300 |
| 160 | 290 | 320 | 320 | 320 |
| 170 | 280 | 310 | 340 | 340 |
| 180 | 270 | 300 | 330 | 360 |

## ■ Decision making using prior data

Whenever a decision must be repeated a number of times under similar conditions and past experience exists that may be used in making these decisions—this is termed decision making using prior data. In the case of Ashley's Pizzeria, the problem of determining how many pizzas to prebake is an example of decision making using prior data. In that situation, we have assumed that demand is for 150, 160, 170 or 180 pizzas each night, but it is not possible to know in advance exactly what this demand will be on a given night. We do have past experience to help us in making this decision, and we assume that the conditions surrounding the decision will be the same each night. On those occasions when conditions may differ, say, after a football game or during a snowstorm, it would not be appropriate to use the earlier approach based solely on previous experience with daily demand.

Using the data from Table 17-1, we wish to make decisions about the number of pizzas to prebake each night. There are two methods of analyzing the data to use in making decisions—classical and Bayesian. We will consider both types of analysis, but will emphasize Bayesian analysis for decision making.

### Bayesian versus classical analysis for decision making

When prior data are available to help us make a decision, there are two types of analysis that can be used. These are broadly defined as *Bayesian analysis* and *classical analysis*. In **Bayesian analysis,** the prior data (or subjective probabilities) are combined with sample or test data using the formula developed by the English minister Thomas Bayes.

*Bayesian analysis*

In **classical analysis,** the prior data are used to develop a decision rule and then a test is run or a sample taken. Based on the outcome of the test or sample, a decision is made. This is the type of analysis that is usually taught in introductory statistics courses under the name *tests of hypothesis*. For example, in the Ashley Pizzeria case, the expected demand can be found by the following calculation:

*classical analysis*

$$\text{Expected demand} = (.2)(150) + (.4)(160) + (.25)(170) + (.15)(180)$$

$$= 163.5$$

Based on this expected demand, Ashley could expect that demand would, on the average, exceed 160 pizzas per night. To test this expectation, classical analysis could be used.

To use classical analysis, we would first set up the following null hypothesis using the expected value computed from the prior data:

$$H_0 = \mu \geq 160$$

This null hypothesis says that the prior data indicate that the long-run average demand, or mean, $\mu$, will be greater than or equal to 160 pizzas. Using the prior data, we set up an alternative hypothesis that demand is less than 160 pizzas:

$$H_1: \mu < 160$$

or mean demand is less than 160 pizzas.

To make a decision, we would take a sample of demand values for some number of nights. On the basis of this sample, we may accept the null hypothesis and assure

Ashley that mean demand is indeed 160 or more pizzas per night. On the other hand, the sample may lead us to reject the null hypothesis and to tell Ashley that the mean demand does not appear to be 160 or more pizzas after all.

*prior analysis*
*preposterior*
*analysis*

In Bayesian analysis, a decision martrix is developed that contains the monetary consequences of various decisions. With this decision matrix, Bayesian analysis first makes a **prior analysis** using the prior data. This is followed by a second or **preposterior analysis,** which determines whether or not additional testing or sampling would be useful. If the preposterior analysis shows that the testing or sampling will be economically useful, then the testing or sampling will be performed. If a test is run or a sample taken, the results are used to modify the prior probabilities to produce after-the-testing or **posterior probabilities.** These posterior probabilities combine both the prior data and the test or sample results.

*posterior*
*probabilities*

In comparing classical and Bayesian analysis, we see that the classical analysis *always* performs a test or gathers a sample but that Bayesian analysis will do this only after a preposterior analysis of the data has shown that additional testing or sampling would be economically worthwhile. It is this decision whether or not to test or sample combined with the modification of probabilities based on testing that gives Bayesian analysis its advantages over classical analysis for economic decision making.

In the remainder of this chapter, we will present an introduction to Bayesian analysis and apply this analysis to the Ashley's Pizzeria case.

## Bayesian analysis

To begin a Bayesian analysis of the Ashley's Pizzeria case, we first need a decision matrix showing the economic consequences of various decisions. To do this, we will expand Profit Table 17-1 into Profit Table 17-2. This expanded table includes the payoff values for each state-of-nature and each alternative, and the fraction of time that each state-of-nature occurred. This fraction is found by dividing the number of days for each state-of-nature by the total number of days for all states-of-nature. There were $20 + 40 + 25 + 15 = 100$ days; so for the first state-of-nature the fraction is $\frac{20}{100} = .20$. These fractions are equivalent to probabilities since their sum is equal to one and they reflect the proportion of time that each state-of-nature did occur. We believe that the same proportion will be observed in the future.

**TABLE 17-2.**
**Profit Table**

| No. of Pizzas Prebaked | No. of Pizzas Demanded | | | |
|---|---|---|---|---|
| | 150 | 160 | 170 | 180 |
| 150 | 300 | 300 | 300 | 300 |
| 160 | 290 | 320 | 320 | 320 |
| 170 | 280 | 310 | 340 | 340 |
| 180 | 270 | 300 | 330 | 360 |
| Fraction of time | .20 | .40 | .25 | .15 |

Using this information, if there are $n$ states-of-nature, we can compute the EMV for each alternative by the following formula:

$$EMV_i = \sum_{j=1}^{n} O_{ij}p_j \qquad (17.1)$$

where

$O_{ij}$ = payoff using $i$th alternative if $j$th state-of-nature occurs

$p_j$ = probability that $j$th state-of-nature will occur

$EMV_i$ = expected monetary value for $i$th alternative

If we apply this decision model to the Ashley's Pizzeria problem of deciding how many pizzas to bake, we have the following computations:

$$EMV_1 = (.20)(300) + (.40)(300) + (.25)(300) + (.15)(300) = \$300.00$$

$$EMV_2 = (.20)(290) + (.40)(320) + (.25)(320) + (.15)(320) = \$314.00$$

$$EMV_3 = (.20)(280) + (.40)(310) + (.25)(340) + (.15)(340) = \$316.00$$

$$EMV_4 = (.20)(270) + (.40)(300) + (.25)(330) + (.15)(360) = \$310.50$$

These expected monetary values are then placed in a list from which the maximum such value is determined (see Table 17-3). We find that the maximum EMV is $316 and occurs for a decision to prebake 170 pizzas. The interpretation of this value is that if Ashley prebaked 170 pizzas every night, then the *long-run average* profit would be $316 per night. Note that at no time would this value actually occur; it is an average value over many applications of the alternative under similar conditions. This alternative is marked with an asterisk in Table 17-3.

A step-by-step procedure for the EMV decision model follows:

**Step 1:** Compute probabilities, $p_j$, for the occurrence of each state-of-nature.

**Step 2:** Compute EMV's for all alternatives using equation (17.1) and place these values in a list.

**Step 3:** Using the list of EMV's computed in step 2, determine the maximum value. The alternative that corresponds to the maximum EMV is the decision to be selected.

This is the *prior analysis* portion of a Bayesian analysis.

| Alternative | EMV |
| --- | --- |
| 150 (A1) | $300.00 |
| 160 (A2) | 314.00 |
| 170 (A3) | 316.00° |
| 180 (A4) | 310.50 |

**TABLE 17-3.**
**Expected**
**Monetary Values**

## Using decision trees for problems with prior data

As with decision problems where no prior data are available, it is possible (and many times advisable) to use decision trees in the determination of a decision. In the case of problems where prior data exist, we construct a decision tree in exactly the same way as for other types of problems. The only difference is that we include the calculated probabilities on the chance branches and use these in making the EMV calculation. In the case of the Ashley's Pizzeria decision as to how many pizzas to prebake, there will be four decision branches corresponding to prebaking either 150, 160, 170, or 180 pizzas. At the end of each decision branch, there will be a chance node having four states-of-nature corresponding to 150, 160, 170, or 180 pizzas being demanded. On each state-of-nature branch, there will also be a probability of that state-of-nature occurring. Finally there will be an outcome or profit for each decision and state-of-nature at the end of the state-of-nature branch. The decision tree for Ashley's Pizzeria is shown in Figure 17-1.

Using the profit values and probabilities for each state-of-nature branch, we compute the EMV for each chance node using equation (17.1). This is easily done by multiplying each probability by the corresponding profit and summing over all such products for each chance node. The EMV's are written below each chance node, and the maximum of the EMV's is written below the decision point. The decision to which the EMV corresponds is the maximum long-run number of pizzas to prebake, in this case 170 pizzas for a daily profit of $316.

This problem is commonly referred to as the *newsboy problem*. The name comes from the situation of a newsboy deciding how many papers to buy each day for resale. The concept is exactly the same as deciding on the number of pizzas to prebake.

## The value of perfect information

The question often arises: What would the decision maker be willing to pay for additional information on what the environment will be? Before we can answer this question, we need to know the value of the information itself. If the information is perfect, that is, if the information tells us exactly what will occur, we can answer this question fairly easily. We will reserve consideration of imperfect information to a later section.

If we know exactly which state-of-nature will occur, it is easy to determine the alternative to choose. We would choose the alternative that yields the highest payoff for each state-of-nature. In the Ashley's Pizzeria case, for a given number of pizzas demanded, we would choose to prebake the number of pizzas that would maximize the net profit. For example, for the situation where we know that 160 pizzas would be demanded, the maximum profit will occur if we prebake 160 pizzas, and this profit will be $320. If we computed this for each state-of-nature, the list in Table 17-4 would be generated.

Since each state-of-nature only occurs a fraction of the time, we may compute the expected monetary value for the perfect-information case using the maximum

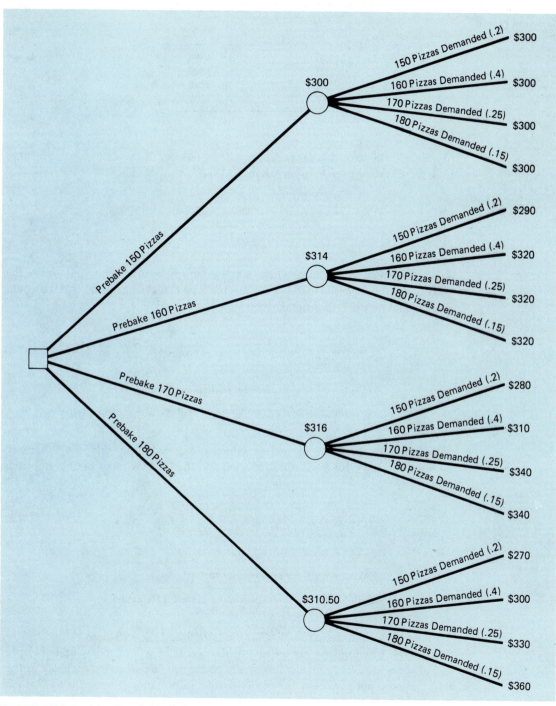

**FIGURE 17-1. Decision Tree for Prebaking Pizzas**

TABLE 17-4.
Maximum Payoffs

| Pizzas Demanded (state-of-nature) | Maximum Payoff Decision | Payoff |
|---|---|---|
| 150 | 150 | $300 |
| 160 | 160 | $320 |
| 170 | 170 | $340 |
| 180 | 180 | $360 |

payoffs and the probabilities for each state-of-nature. In the case shown in Table 17-4, the EMV for perfect information ($EMV_{PI}$) is computed as

$$EMV_{PI} = (.2)(300) + (.4)(320) + (.25)(340) + (.15)(360)$$

$$= \$327$$

So if we knew in advance which state-of-nature would occur and chose the maximum profit decision to use each time, the long-run average profit that we would make would be $327. In general, this is stated as

$$EMV_{PI} = \sum_{j=1}^{n} O_{ij}^{\circ} p_j \qquad (17.2)$$

where        $O_{ij}^{\circ}$ = the maximum profit for each state-of-nature

$p_j$ = the probability of each state-of-nature

To compute the value of perfect information, we simply take the difference between the EMV for perfect information and the EMV without perfect information:

$$VPI = EMV_{PI} - EMV^{\circ} \qquad (17.3)$$

where        VPI = value of perfect information

$EMV_{PI}$ = EMV for perfect information

$EMV^{\circ}$ = maximum EMV without perfect information

In the Ashley's Pizzeria case, $EMV_{PI}$ = $327 and $EMV^{\circ}$ = $316, so VPI = $327 − $316 = $11. From this we can see that Ashley would be willing to pay up to $11 per day to know in advance exactly how many pizzas will be demanded each day. If the information is not perfect or the cost of perfect information is more than $11, then she would be better off without the advance information.

## The value of test information

In the previous section, we presented the calculation of the value of perfect information. In practical terms, however, information generally results from some sort of imperfect testing procedure. By this we mean that the test information does not always correctly predict the state-of-nature that will occur. For example, a meteorologist may, on the basis of some test, predict rain, yet this state of nature (rain) may actually occur only 70% of the time that this prediction is made.

Due to this imperfection in the predictive power of testing, the calculation of the value of test information is somewhat more complex than that for perfect information. To understand the procedure used to make this calculation, let

$$P(N \mid R) = \text{probability that event } N \text{ will actually occur}$$
$$\text{given that the test result was } R$$

Since the test is imperfect, $P(N \mid R) < 1$. For example, if a weather forecaster is correct 70% of the time, then $P(N \mid R) = .7$ where $N$ = rain occurs and $R$ = rain predicted.

However, we usually do not know values of $P(N \mid R)$—which is read "the probability of $N$, given $R$"—since these are known only *after* the test has been used long enough to gather data to calculate probabilities. What *is* usually known is the reverse, that is, the probability that the test result will occur given the corresponding outcome. This probability is $P(R \mid N)$, and may be calculated by using historical data to determine how the test would have worked had it been used.

Unfortunately, the probability $P(R \mid N)$ is not the test probability $P(N \mid R)$ that we need since it was computed *after* the outcome was known. To compute $P(N \mid R)$ we use a well-known result from probability called *Bayes's law*. This result says that

$$P(N \mid R) = \frac{P(R \mid N)P(N)}{P(R)} \tag{17.4}$$

Two of the values in this formula are usually available from the test data, and a third may be calculated from the other two. The probability that the test is accurate, given that the actual outcome is known, $P(R \mid N)$, and the probability that the given outcome occurs regardless of any testing, $P(N)$ are easily calculated from prior data. $P(N)$ may also be a subjective probability based on the DM's experience with such situations. This latter probability, $P(N)$, is referred to as the prior probability since it is calculated before any testing, while the former are conditional probabilities.

The third probability in Bayes's law, $P(R)$, is the probability that the test result $R$ will occur. This probability may be computed by way of the following result from probability theory:

$$P(R) = P(R \mid N)P(N) + P(R \mid \overline{N})P(\overline{N}) \tag{17.5}$$

where $\overline{N}$ means "not $N$." Since $\overline{N}$ includes all events other than $N$, $P(\overline{N})$ and $P(R \mid \overline{N})$ may be sums of several values. The values $P(R \mid \overline{N})$ and $P(\overline{N})$ may be calculated at the same time as $P(R \mid N)$ and $P(N)$ are found.

Combining (17.4) and (17.5), we arrive at a revised version of Bayes's law:

$$P(N \mid R) = \frac{P(R \mid N)P(N)}{P(R \mid N)P(N) + P(R \mid \overline{N})P(\overline{N})} \tag{17.6}$$

The final result, $P(N \mid R)$, the probability that event $N$ occurs given that the test result is $R$, is known as the *posterior* probability since it is found after the testing procedure. Once the posterior probability values are known, they can be used to perform the preposterior analysis to determine whether or not the testing or sampling should be done.

## Application to Ashley's Pizzeria

Let us now consider the use of a prediction procedure for Ashley's Pizzeria. We will be following the steps outlined in our discussion using a tabular approach to compute the various probabilities and expected values. Recall that Ashley prebakes all of her pizzas and needs to know the highest-profit baking decision.

Since Ashley's is in a university town, a marketing research professor at the Business School, Carolyn Myers, has offered to use an experimental test to predict the number of pizzas that will be purchased each day. For this service, she will charge Ashley $5 per day. The question is: Should Ashley subscribe to this prediction service?

If the professor's predictions were 100% accurate, then we determined earlier that their value would be $11. However, her predictions have been found not to be 100% accurate, so their value will be something less than this. Using the previous day-by-day sales data, the professor has compiled the table of test probabilities shown in Table 17-5. The states-of-nature shown across the top of the table are the number of pizzas *actually* demanded; the values down the side are the number of pizzas the professor's test would have predicted. The probabilities in the body of the

**TABLE 17-5.**
**Test Probabilities**

| Number of Pizzas Predicted | Number of Pizzas Demanded | | | |
|---|---|---|---|---|
| | 150 | 160 | 170 | 180 |
| 150 | $\frac{1}{2}$ | $\frac{1}{4}$ | 0 | 0 |
| 160 | $\frac{1}{3}$ | $\frac{1}{2}$ | $\frac{1}{6}$ | $\frac{1}{6}$ |
| 170 | $\frac{1}{6}$ | $\frac{1}{4}$ | $\frac{2}{3}$ | $\frac{1}{3}$ |
| 180 | 0 | 0 | $\frac{1}{6}$ | $\frac{1}{2}$ |

table are the probabilities that the test would have predicted each number of pizzas, *given* the number actually demanded. For example, on those days that 160 pizzas were actually demanded, the predictive test would have predicted 160 pizzas one-half of the time, 150 pizzas one-fourth of the time, 170 pizzas one-fourth of the time, and 180 pizzas none of the time. These are the conditional probabilities that we have discussed earlier, that is, $P(R \mid N)$.

Notice from this table that the sum of the probabilities in each column is equal to 1, while the sum in each row is not equal to 1. The reason for this is that for a given number sold, some number *has* to be predicted, while there exists no relationship between number predicted and number sold.

In order to convert the $P(R \mid N)$ probabilities in Table 17-5 to $P(N \mid R)$ probabilities, we need to calculate the $P(R)$ for each number of pizzas predicted using Equation (17.7):

$$P(R) = P(R \mid N)P(N) + P(R \mid \overline{N})P(\overline{N}) \tag{17.7}$$

In Table 17-5, for $R = 150$, we find that $N = 150$ and $\overline{N} = 160$, 170, and 180. To calculate probabilities of $P(N)$ and $P(\overline{N})$, we now use the prior-experience values for the number of pizzas demanded; that is, we use the fraction of time each number of pizzas was demanded from Table 17-2:

$$P(150 \text{ demanded}) = .2 = \tfrac{1}{5}$$

$$P(160 \text{ demanded}) = .4 = \tfrac{2}{5}$$

$$P(170 \text{ demanded}) = .25 = \tfrac{1}{4}$$

$$P(180 \text{ demanded}) = .15 = \tfrac{3}{20}$$

From this and the values from Table 17-5, we get

$$
\begin{aligned}
P(150 \text{ predicted}) = \ & P(150 \text{ predicted} \mid 150 \text{ demanded})P(150 \text{ demanded}) \\
& + P(150 \text{ predicted} \mid 160 \text{ demanded})P(160 \text{ demanded}) \\
& + P(150 \text{ predicted} \mid 170 \text{ demanded})P(170 \text{ demanded}) \\
& + P(150 \text{ predicted} \mid 180 \text{ demanded})P(180 \text{ demanded}) \\
= \ & (\tfrac{1}{2})(\tfrac{1}{5}) + (\tfrac{1}{4})(\tfrac{2}{5}) + (0)(\tfrac{1}{4}) + (0)(\tfrac{3}{20}) \\
= \ & \tfrac{2}{10}
\end{aligned}
$$

Similarly,

$$P(160 \text{ predicted}) = (\tfrac{1}{3})(\tfrac{1}{5}) + (\tfrac{1}{2})(\tfrac{2}{5}) + (\tfrac{1}{6})(\tfrac{1}{4}) + (\tfrac{1}{6})(\tfrac{3}{20})$$

$$= \tfrac{1}{3}$$

$$P(170 \text{ predicted}) = (\tfrac{1}{6})(\tfrac{1}{5}) + (\tfrac{1}{4})(\tfrac{2}{5}) + (\tfrac{2}{3})(\tfrac{1}{4}) + (\tfrac{1}{3})(\tfrac{3}{20})$$

$$= \tfrac{7}{20}$$

$$P(180 \text{ predicted}) = (0)(\tfrac{1}{5}) + (0)(\tfrac{2}{5}) + (\tfrac{1}{6})(\tfrac{1}{4}) + (\tfrac{1}{2})(\tfrac{3}{20})$$

$$= \tfrac{7}{60}$$

Notice that these calculations can be made by working with the values in each row. Each $P(R)$ value is simply the sum of the products of the state-of-nature probabilities and the corresponding probabilities in each row. It may also be noted that if we sum these probabilities of each number of pizzas being predicted, we get:

$$\tfrac{2}{10} + \tfrac{1}{3} + \tfrac{7}{20} + \tfrac{7}{60} = 1$$

This is to be expected since some number of pizzas, 150, 160, 170, or 180, must be predicted.

Using each element of each sum that gave us the $P(R)$ values as an entry in a new table, we have Table 17-6, where each entry is either $P(R \mid N)P(N)$ or $P(R \mid \overline{N})P(\overline{N})$. For example, the entry in the third row, first column, is equal to

$$P(170 \text{ predicted} \mid 150 \text{ demanded})P(150 \text{ demanded})$$

From equation (17.8), we know that the posterior probabilities are found by

$$P(N \mid R) = \frac{P(R \mid N)P(N)}{P(R \mid N)P(N) + P(R \mid \overline{N})P(\overline{N})} \tag{17.8}$$

By using the values in Table 17-6, the values in this equation are easy to find. The numerator comes from the values in this table, and the denominator is the sum for

**TABLE 17-6.**
**Revised Table of**
**Joint Probabilities**

| Number of Pizzas Predicted | Number of Pizzas Demanded | | | | Sum |
|---|---|---|---|---|---|
| | 150 | 160 | 170 | 180 | |
| 150 | $\frac{1}{10}$ | $\frac{1}{10}$ | 0 | 0 | $\frac{2}{10}$ |
| 160 | $\frac{1}{15}$ | $\frac{1}{5}$ | $\frac{1}{24}$ | $\frac{1}{40}$ | $\frac{1}{3}$ |
| 170 | $\frac{1}{30}$ | $\frac{1}{10}$ | $\frac{1}{6}$ | $\frac{1}{20}$ | $\frac{7}{20}$ |
| 180 | 0 | 0 | $\frac{1}{24}$ | $\frac{3}{40}$ | $\frac{7}{60}$ |

each row. As two examples, consider $P(150$ demanded $\mid 150$ predicted$)$ and $P(150$ demanded $\mid 160$ predicted$)$. For the first probability, we go to the first row, first column, of Table 17-6 to get the numerator, $P(150$ predicted $\mid 150$ demanded$)P(150$ demanded$)$ and use the sum of the 150 predicted row for the denominator. The result is:

$$P(150 \text{ demanded} \mid 150 \text{ predicted}) = \frac{1/10}{2/10} = 1/2$$

This means that one-half of the time that 150 pizzas are predicted to be demanded, 150 are actually demanded. Similarly,

$$P(150 \text{ demanded} \mid 160 \text{ predicted}) = \frac{P(160 \text{ predicted} \mid 150 \text{ demanded})P(150 \text{ demanded})}{\text{sum of row}}$$

$$= \frac{1/15}{1/3} = 1/5$$

This value means that if the test predicts that 160 pizzas will be demanded, one-fifth of the time 150 pizzas will actually be demanded.

If we make this calculation for each value in Table 17-6, we arrive at a table of values where each value is $P(N$ pizzas will be demanded $\mid R$ pizzas were predicted$)$. These values are given in Table 17-7.

The values in Table 17-7 are the desired probabilities, $P(N \mid R)$, that will tell us how useful Professor Myers's test will be. Each row of this table is now a complete posterior probability distribution and can be used to predict demanded levels *via preposterior analysis*.

Now we can proceed to compute the expected monetary value of the professor's test via preposterior analysis. We do this by first choosing the best alternative for each possible test result using the EMV criteria. This is done on a result-by-result basis.

If the professor's test predicts that 150 pizzas will be demanded, we use the probabilities from the first row of Table 17-7 to calculate EMV's from the payoff table. This gives us Table 17-8, from which we see that if 150 pizzas are predicted, the highest EMV alternative is to prebake 160 pizzas. Tables 17-9, 17-10, and 17-11 show these calculations for prediction values of 160, 170, and 180 pizzas.

| Number of Pizzas Predicted | Number of Pizzas Demanded | | | |
|---|---|---|---|---|
| | 150 | 160 | 170 | 180 |
| 150 | $\frac{1}{2}$ | $\frac{1}{2}$ | 0 | 0 |
| 160 | $\frac{1}{5}$ | $\frac{3}{5}$ | $\frac{1}{8}$ | $\frac{3}{40}$ |
| 170 | $\frac{2}{21}$ | $\frac{2}{7}$ | $\frac{10}{21}$ | $\frac{1}{7}$ |
| 180 | 0 | 0 | $\frac{5}{14}$ | $\frac{9}{14}$ |

**TABLE 17-7.**
**Posterior**
**Probabilities**

**TABLE 17-8.**
**EMV Calculation Given 150 Pizzas Predicted**

| Pizzas Prebaked | Number of Pizzas Demanded | | | | EMV | |
|---|---|---|---|---|---|---|
| | 150 | 160 | 170 | 180 | | |
| 150 | 300 | 300 | 300 | 300 | $300.00 | |
| 160 | 290 | 320 | 320 | 320 | 305.00 | ← Preferred Alternative |
| 170 | 280 | 310 | 340 | 340 | 295.00 | |
| 180 | 270 | 300 | 330 | 360 | 285.00 | |
| Probability | $\frac{1}{2}$ | $\frac{1}{2}$ | 0 | 0 | | |

By using our preferred alternative for each possible test result and the probability of each test result occurring (from Table 17-7), we can calculate the EMV using the professor's test:

$$\text{EMV(test)} = (\text{max EMV given 150 predicted})P(150 \text{ predicted})$$

$$+ (\text{max EMV given 160 predicted})P(160 \text{ predicted})$$

$$+ (\text{max EMV given 170 predicted})P(170 \text{ predicted})$$

$$+ (\text{max EMV given 180 predicted})P(180 \text{ predicted})$$

Substituting in the proper values, we get

$$\text{EMV(test)} = (305.00)(\tfrac{2}{10}) + (314.00)(\tfrac{1}{3}) + (325.70)(\tfrac{7}{20}) + (349.30)(\tfrac{7}{60})$$

$$= \$320.41$$

So the EMV resulting from using the professor's test is $320.41. Recall that the EMV without the test was $316.00. Therefore, the *net* value of the professor's test is $320.41 − $316.00 = $4.41 per day. Since this value is less than the $5.00 per day charge for using the test, Ashley would be better off not using Professor Myers's prediction service.

**TABLE 17-9.**
**EMV Calculation Given 160 Pizzas Predicted**

| Pizzas Prebaked | Number of Pizzas Demanded | | | | EMV | |
|---|---|---|---|---|---|---|
| | 150 | 160 | 170 | 180 | | |
| 150 | 300 | 300 | 300 | 300 | $300.00 | |
| 160 | 290 | 320 | 320 | 320 | 314.00 | ← Preferred Alternative |
| 170 | 280 | 310 | 340 | 340 | 310.00 | |
| 180 | 270 | 300 | 330 | 360 | 302.25 | |
| Probability | $\frac{1}{5}$ | $\frac{3}{5}$ | $\frac{1}{8}$ | $\frac{3}{40}$ | | |

TABLE 17-10.
EMV Calculation
Given 170 Pizzas
Predicted

| Pizzas Prebaked | Number of Pizzas Demanded | | | | EMV |
| | 150 | 160 | 170 | 180 | |
|---|---|---|---|---|---|
| 150 | 300 | 300 | 300 | 300 | $300.00 |
| 160 | 290 | 320 | 320 | 320 | 317.10 |
| 170 | 280 | 310 | 340 | 340 | 325.70  ← Preferred Alternative |
| 180 | 270 | 300 | 330 | 360 | 320.00 |
| Probability | $\frac{2}{21}$ | $\frac{2}{7}$ | $\frac{10}{21}$ | $\frac{1}{7}$ | |

The use of this analysis is summarized below:

**Step 1.** Develop a table of test probabilities, i.e., $P$(test result will be $R$ | actual outcome was $N$), and a set of prior probabilities, $P(N)$, for each state-of-nature, $N$.

**Step 2.** For each row of the table of test probabilities, multiply each element by the corresponding prior state-of-nature probability, $P(N)$. Each product is an element in a revised table of probabilities, $P(R \mid N)P(N)$. The sum of these probabilities for each row is now $P(R)$.

**Step 3.** Divide each element of the revised probability matrix by the sum for its row, i.e., $P(R \mid N)P(N)/P(R)$, to obtain elements of the prediction table, $P(N \mid R)$.

**Step 4.** Using the payoff matrix, calculate separately for each test result the maximum EMV using the probabilities in the row of the prediction matrix corresponding to the test result.

**Step 5.** Using the maximum EMVs for each test result, calculate the EMV (test) by multiplying the maximum EMV for each test result times the probability of that test result occurring, $P(R)$, and summing over all test results.

**Step 6.** Calculate the net value of the test by computing the difference between the EMV of the test calculated in step 5 and the maximum EMV possible without the test.

TABLE 17-11.
EMV Calculation
Given 180 Pizzas
Predicted

| Pizzas Prebaked | Number of Pizzas Demanded | | | | EMV |
| | 150 | 160 | 170 | 180 | |
|---|---|---|---|---|---|
| 150 | 300 | 300 | 300 | 300 | $300.00 |
| 160 | 290 | 320 | 320 | 320 | 320.00 |
| 170 | 280 | 310 | 340 | 340 | 340.00 |
| 180 | 270 | 300 | 330 | 360 | 349.30  ← Preferred Alternative |
| Probability | 0 | 0 | $\frac{5}{14}$ | $\frac{9}{14}$ | |

Note that in the Ashley's Pizzeria case, we decided from our preposterior analysis that testing would not be economically advantageous. If we had used a classical analysis, we would not have considered the economics of the testing.

## ■ Summary

When prior data are available for decision making, we considered two methods of analyzing these data—classical analysis and Bayesian analysis—but emphasized the latter. In Bayesian analysis, there are two stages, prior and preposterior. In the prior analysis, the prior data are used to compute probabilities, which are, in turn, used to calculate the expected monetary value (EMV) of each decision. The EMV of each decision is the long-run average return on that decision. In the preposterior analysis, we used posterior probabilities calculated using Bayes's theorem to determine whether testing or sampling should be performed. In this discussion, we learned about the value of perfect information and the value of test information.

## ■ Glossary of terms

**Bayesian analysis:**   A form of decision making that combines prior data or subjective probabilities with test or sample data using Bayes' theorem.

**classical analysis:**   A form of decision making that uses prior data to make hypotheses and then gathers samples to make decisions.

**posterior probabilities:**   Probabilities calculated by combining prior data or subjective probabilities with test or sample data.

**preposterior analysis:**   A set of calculations made using posterior probabilities to determine whether testing or sampling is economically worthwhile.

**prior analysis:**   A set of calculations that are used to make a decision. These calculations are made using only prior data or subjective probabilities.

**value of perfect information:**   The net value to the decision maker of knowing in advance exactly which state-of-nature is going to occur.

**value of test information:**   The net value to the decision maker of information derived from a predictive test.

## ■ Review questions

1. Why do we refer to expected value as the "long-run average"?

2. What definition of probability are we using when we calculate probabilities from past experience?

3. Discuss ways for a decision maker to determine subjective probabilities.

4. Can the value of perfect information ever be less than the value of test information? Why or why not?

## ■ True/false questions

1. In Bayesian analysis, either prior data or subjective probabilities must be used in the prior analysis.

2. If, in a maximization problem, the value of test information plus the cost of the test is less than the prior EMV value, we will go ahead with the test.

3. Bayesian analysis differs from classical analysis in that sampling or testing is used in classical but not in Bayesian.

## ■ Problems

1. For a certain decision problem, the payoff matrix in Table P17-1 has been computed. Using the EMV decision model, compute the highest expected payoff decision.

**TABLE P17-1. Payoff Matrix**

| Alternative | State-of-Nature | | |
|---|---|---|---|
| | N1 | N2 | N3 |
| A1 | 30 | 35 | 25 |
| A2 | 15 | 40 | 25 |
| A3 | 30 | 30 | 30 |
| A4 | 20 | 30 | 45 |
| Probability | .4 | .3 | .3 |

2. For the matrix of losses given in Table P17-2 and the probabilities for each state-of-nature, use the EMV decision model to compute the minimum expected cost decision.

**TABLE P17-2. Matrix of Costs for Problem P17-2**

| Alternative | State-of-Nature | | |
|---|---|---|---|
| | X | Y | Z |
| 1 | 300 | 400 | 700 |
| 2 | 400 | 500 | 500 |
| 3 | 200 | 600 | 200 |
| 4 | 400 | 300 | 500 |
| Probability | .4 | .3 | .3 |

3. The Kinsey Bake Shop specializes in peach pie. These pies are sold to the public for a price of $3.50 and cost $2.00 to produce. Any pies not sold on the day after they are produced may be sold to an institutional supplier for only $1.25. The owner of the Kinsey Bake

Shop, Laura Kinsey, has collected some statistics on previous demand:

| Daily demand | 0 | 10 | 20 | 30 | 40 | 50 | 60 or more |
|---|---|---|---|---|---|---|---|
| Number of days | 5 | 5 | 15 | 10 | 10 | 5 | 0 |

    **a.** For each production alternative, compute the net profit.

    **b.** Using the EMV decision model, determine the best production alternative.

    **c.** What is the value of perfect information for this decision?

**4.** Every three days, the Bishop Produce Company must decide how many boxes of strawberries to order for the next three days. Ben Jones, manager of Bishop Produce Company, has determined that if the weather is generally good during this three-day period, he can sell 100 boxes, while if the weather is unsettled, he can only sell 75 boxes. If the weather is bad, sales are very poor, and he can sell only 50 boxes during the three days. Since the shelf life of strawberries is only three days, any strawberries not sold must be thrown away with no salvage value. Ben can buy strawberries for $0.50 a box and sell them at $1.00 a box.

    Past records of the weather have shown that for any three-day period, the weather is good 50% of the time, unsettled 20% of the time, and bad 30% of the time. On the basis of the given data:

    **a.** Define Ben's alternatives and the states-of-nature (three alternatives are assumed).

    **b.** Set up a payoff matrix.

    **c.** Determine the highest-profit alternative that Ben should use in ordering strawberries.

    **d.** What is the value of perfect information for this problem?

**5.** At each of the Yeehaw State University home football games, local high school students sell programs. These programs can be purchased by the students at a cost of $1.00 and the selling price is $1.50. Any sold programs are worthless after the game, so the students suffer a loss.

    The number of programs an individual student can sell depends upon the size of crowd for that game. Since many fans purchase tickets at the gate, there is no way to know in advance how large the crowd will be for any given game. In studying past attendance records, Gay Bugbee, a local program salesperson, has determined that there is a sellout 50% of the time, a 90% of capacity crowd 30% of the time, and a 80% of capacity crowd 20% of the time. Her sales records show that when there is a capacity crowd, she can sell 200 programs; when there is a 90% of capacity crowd, she can sell 150 programs; and when there is an 80% of capacity crowd, she can sell only 100 programs. If you were a friend of Gay's, how many programs would you suggest she buy for each home game?

**6.** What is the value of perfect information for Problem 1? Similarly, what is the value of perfect information for Problem 2?

**7.** Using the table of test probabilities for Problem 1 shown in Table P17-7:

    **a.** Determine a revised table of joint probabilities.

    **b.** Determine a table of posterior probabilities.

    **c.** Compute the value of test information.

TABLE P17-7. Table of Test Probabilities for Problem 1

| | State-of-Nature Actually Occurring | | |
|---|---|---|---|
| State-of-Nature Predicted | N1 | N2 | N3 |
| N1 | .40 | .25 | .15 |
| N2 | .30 | .50 | .25 |
| N2 | .30 | .25 | .60 |

8. Using the table of test probabilities for Problem 2 shown in Table P17-8:

   **a.** Determine a revised table of joint probabilities.

   **b.** Determine a table of posterior probabilities.

   **c.** Determine the value of the test information.

TABLE P17-8. Table of Test Probabilities for the Kinsey Bake Shop

| | Actual Daily Demand | | |
|---|---|---|---|
| Daily Demand Predicted | X | Y | Z |
| X | .60 | .20 | .10 |
| Y | .25 | .70 | .35 |
| Z | .15 | .10 | .55 |

9. Mike Dirr, vice-president for marketing for Super-Cola, is considering which of two advertising plans to use for a new caffeine-free cola. Plan I will cost $500,000 while a more conservative approach, Plan II, will cost only $100,000. Table P17-9 shows the projected gross (before advertising) profits on the new cola for each advertising plan under two possible states-of-nature—complete acceptance of the new cola and limited acceptance.

TABLE P17-9. Gross Profits

| | State-of-Nature | |
|---|---|---|
| Advertising Plan | Limited Acceptance | Complete Acceptance |
| Plan I | $400,000 | $1,000,000 |
| Plan II | $300,000 | $500,000 |

Mike estimates that there are equal chances of complete and limited acceptance of the new cola.

   **a.** Set up a net profit payoff matrix.

   **b.** Use Mike's subjective probability estimates to choose an advertising plan.

c. What is the value of perfect information in this situation?

d. A survey costing $50,000 can be run to test-market the product. In past uses, this survey has been shown to predict complete acceptance in 60% of the cases where there was complete acceptance and predicted limited acceptance 70% of the time when there was limited acceptance. Use this information to determine whether this survey should be used to help decide on an advertising plan.

e. Use a decision tree to show your analysis.

10. Lynn Miller has recently come into enough money to consider seriously the various types of investments that are available to her. After studying the various forms of investments, Lynn has decided that only three types suit her needs. These are money funds, stocks, and bonds. The choice of an investment depends on the prime rate since the return on the investment will be a function of this interest rate.

Currently the prime rate is 12%, but is considered quite volatile and can go up or down significantly over the coming year. On the basis of the current return on investments, Lynn has developed the following table showing the value of a $100,000 investment after one year depending on the prime rate at the end of the year.

**TABLE P17-10a.  Return on $100,000 Investment**

|  | Prime Rate at End of Year | | |
| --- | --- | --- | --- |
| Option | 8% | 12% | 15% |
| Stocks | $125,000 | $110,000 | $ 60,000 |
| Bonds | 140,000 | 112,000 | 75,000 |
| Money market | 108,000 | 112,000 | 115,000 |

a. Lynn has polled various economics professors and has determined that 40% believe the prime rate will drop, 30% believe it will remain the same, and 30% believe it will go up. Use these values as subjective probabilities to make a prior analysis of the decision.

b. What is the value of perfect information?

c. Lynn has been told that the Niemi Forecasting Service claims to be able to forecast future interest rates. This service is available for a $5000 fee. Table P17-10b shows the past performance of the forecasting service.

**TABLE P17-10b.  Performance of Forecasting Service**

| Predicted Change in Prime Rate | Actual Change in Prime Rate | | |
| --- | --- | --- | --- |
|  | Rise | Same | Fall |
| Rise | 60% | 10% | 20% |
| Same | 20% | 60% | 20% |
| Fall | 20% | 30% | 60% |

Use the results from this table together with the prior probabilities to determine whether Lynn should use the forecasting service.

11. Ben Jones of the Bishop Produce Company (see Problem 4) has started subscribing to a special weather service that costs him $10 per three-day period. The company that markets this service has provided Ben with information on how well their service would have performed had it been available over the past five years. This information is in the form of the percentage of instances that the company would have predicted correctly each type of weather that occurred. Using Table P17-11, advise Ben as to whether or not he should subscribe to the weather prediction service.

**TABLE P17-11. Weather Prediction Probabilities**

| Weather That Would Have Been Predicted | Weather That Actually Occurred | | |
|---|---|---|---|
| | Bad | Unsettled | Good |
| Bad | 50% | 30% | 20% |
| Unsettled | 30% | 40% | 40% |
| Good | 20% | 30% | 40% |

12. A local expert on crowd size in Yeehaw claims that he can predict the size of the crowds that will attend the home games at Yeehaw State (Problem 5). He has worked out a table of conditional probabilities from past data. Use the information in Table P17-12 to determine the value of the test information.

**TABLE P17-12. Predicting Crowd Size**

| Crowd Size That Would Have Been Predicted | Actual Crowd Size | | |
|---|---|---|---|
| | 80% Capacity | 90% Capacity | 100% Capacity |
| 80% capacity | 60% | 20% | 10% |
| 90% capacity | 30% | 70% | 10% |
| 100% capacity | 10% | 10% | 80% |

**18**

# Markov Processes

## ■ Introduction

In previous chapters we have been concerned with *static models,* that is, models whose parameters remain the same throughout the planning period. In this chapter we will consider a family of dynamic models that are stochastic as well as time dependent. This family of models is known as *Markov processes.*

Besides being stochastic, Markov processes are different in another way. Markov processes are used to describe various situations. In particular, Markov processes are descriptive in that they seek to determine, in a sequential fashion, the probabilities that certain events will or will not occur. Markov processes are named for the Russian mathematician A. A. Markov, who first formalized the theory concerning events whose current condition depends solely on their condition one period before. Such events are described as being *Markovian* and are thought of as being *memoryless* because anything that occurred more than one period prior to the current period has no effect on the current condition.

In this chapter we will first discuss the general topic of Markov processes as it applies to the case. We will then apply the model to other areas. Finally, we will extend the basic model to consider another situation that has the same basic assumptions.

## ■ Case
## Move-U Truck Rental Company

The Move-U Truck Rental Company specializes in renting trucks to individuals who wish to do their own moving. The distribution manager for the company, G. I. Miller, is considering instituting a "drop-charge" to cover the cost of relocating trucks from areas where there is a surplus to areas where there is a need for the trucks. Before G. I. decides whether to add the drop-charge to the rental cost of trucks that are going to the surplus areas, he wants to determine the proportion of the total number of trucks that will, over the long run, end up in each of the rental areas. If the proportions are approximately the same, a drop-charge will be unnecessary. Otherwise, the drop-charge will depend on the proportion of the total ending up in each region.

G. I. has divided the portion of the United States served by the company into three regions—north, central, and south. From previous records, it has been determined that of the trucks rented each month in the north, 20% go to a city in the north, 30% end up in the central region, and 50% of the trucks are returned to the company in the south region.

Similarly, the company has determined that on a monthly basis, 40% of the trucks rented in the central region are returned in the same region, 30% are returned in the north, and 30% are returned in the south.

Finally, of the trucks rented each month in the south region, 20% are returned in the north, 40% are returned in the south, and 40% are returned to the central region.

At the present time, 40% of the trucks are in the north, 30% are in the central, and 30% are in the south region.

Given the pattern of truck movement, the Move-U Company is interested in knowing the answers to the following:

1. What proportion of the trucks will be in each region after one month? Two months?

2. What proportion of the trucks will be in each region after a "long" period of time?

### Discussion of case

To summarize the information on the proportion of trucks leaving an origin region and arriving at a destination region, a table such as that shown in Table 18-1 may be used. In this table, the region where the truck is rented is listed along the side and the region where the truck is returned is listed across the top of the table. For example, on looking in the first row of the table and the first column, we find that 20% of the trucks rented in the north region are returned in the north region. Another way to state this relationship is that there is a .2 probability that a truck rented in the north will be returned in the same region.

Note that for any row, the sum of the probabilities is one. This means that a rental truck must go somewhere. Note also that the region to which a truck is returned depends *only* on the region in which it was rented. In other words, the ending status of the truck depends only on the most recent status of the truck. That a truck was once rented from the central region does not affect in any way

**TABLE 18-1.**
**Fraction of Trucks Returned to Each Region**

| Rental Region | Return Region | | |
|---|---|---|---|
| | North | Central | South |
| North | .2 | .3 | .5 |
| Central | .3 | .4 | .3 |
| South | .2 | .4 | .4 |

where that truck will be returned if it is rented now in the north.

The fact that a probability is associated with where any truck will be returned and that the region to which a truck is returned depends only on the region from which it was rented means that this situation satisfies the primary assumptions of Markov processes. An additional assumption for problems of this type is that there will be repeated occurrences of the event under study.

To summarize, the primary assumptions of Mar-kov processes as applied to our example are:

1. there is uncertainty as to which region a truck will be returned and this uncertainty can be measured by probabilities;

2. the region to which a truck will be returned depends only on the region from which it was rented;

3. there will be repeated occurrences, or trials, of trucks being rented under the same conditions.

## ■ Markov processes: Assumptions and terminology

### States, trials, and transition probabilities

Markov processes, like most models we have studied, have a terminology of their own. For example, the initial and ending conditions of a Markov process are referred to as **states.** The repeated occurrences of the event under study are termed **trials,** and the probability of going from a current state to the next state is referred to as a **transition probability.**

*states*

*trials*

*transition probability*

In our example, the regions that a truck is rented from and returned to are the states. The probabilities in Table 18-1 are the transition probabilities. Finally, each month will be considered as a trial.

To simplify our discussion somewhat, we will make three additional assumptions:

1. finite number of states exist
2. constant transition probabilities exist
3. equal time periods occur

These assumptions taken together with the three primary assumptions discussed earlier define special types of Markov processes called **Markov chains.** For a text such as this, where we have attempted to emphasize formulation and interpretations, a study of Markov chains will be sufficient to present the possible uses of Markov processes in general.

*Markov chains*

### A tree presentation of Markov chains

An illustrative method of answering the first of the questions about the truck fleet is to use a "tree" approach. In Figure 18-1, we have shown the tree diagram for a truck that is rented in the north region in month 0. The nodes of the tree are the locations in

**FIGURE 18-1.**
**Tree Diagram for**
**Move-U Company**

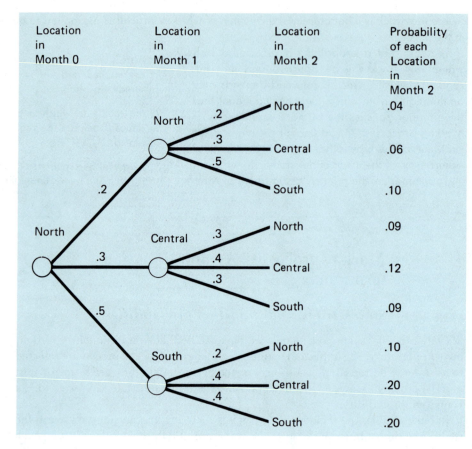

months 0, 1, and 2, and the probabilities of each transition are shown on the branches of the tree.

The probabilities of being in each state in month 2 are computed by multiplying together the individual transition probabilities. For example the probability of being in the north in all three months is given by $(.2)(.2) = .04$.

To find the probability of a truck being in the north after two months, we add up all three of the probabilities of being in the north:

$P$(being in north in month 2 given in north in month 0) $= .04 + .09 + .10 = .23$

Similarly,

$P$(being in central in month 2 given in north in month 0) $= .06 + .12 + .20 = .38$

and

$P$(being in south in month 2 given in north in month 0) $= .10 + .09 + .20 = .39$

If we use matrix notation, these calculations for month 1 would look as follows (see Chapter 2 for discussion of matrix operations):

$$
\begin{array}{c} \text{N} \quad \text{C} \quad \text{S} \\ [1 \quad 0 \quad 0] \end{array}
\begin{array}{c} \text{N} \quad \text{C} \quad \text{S} \\ \begin{bmatrix} .2 & .3 & .5 \\ .3 & .4 & .3 \\ .2 & .4 & .4 \end{bmatrix} \end{array}
=
\begin{array}{c} \text{N} \quad \text{C} \quad \text{S} \\ [.2 \quad .3 \quad .5] \end{array}
$$

Probability vec- One-month transi- Probability vector
tor for starting  tion matrix  after one month
in north

For the second month, we repeat the calculation:

$$
\begin{array}{c} \text{N} \quad \text{C} \quad \text{S} \\ [.2 \quad .3 \quad .5] \end{array}
\begin{array}{c} \text{N} \quad \text{C} \quad \text{S} \\ \begin{bmatrix} .2 & .3 & .5 \\ .3 & .4 & .3 \\ .2 & .4 & .4 \end{bmatrix} \end{array}
=
\begin{array}{c} \text{N} \quad \text{C} \quad \text{S} \\ [.23 \quad .38 \quad .39] \end{array}
$$

Probability vector One-month transi- Probability vector
after one month  tion matrix  after two months

Note that this series of calculations can be combined into one calculation as follows:

$$
\begin{array}{c} \text{N} \quad \text{C} \quad \text{S} \\ [1 \quad 0 \quad 0] \end{array}
\begin{array}{c} \text{N} \quad \text{C} \quad \text{S} \\ \begin{bmatrix} .2 & .3 & .5 \\ .3 & .4 & .3 \\ .2 & .4 & .4 \end{bmatrix} \end{array}
\begin{array}{c} \text{N} \quad \text{C} \quad \text{S} \\ \begin{bmatrix} .2 & .3 & .5 \\ .3 & .4 & .3 \\ .2 & .4 & .4 \end{bmatrix} \end{array}
=
\begin{array}{c} \text{N} \quad \text{C} \quad \text{S} \\ [.23 \quad .38 \quad .39] \end{array}
$$

Probability vector One-month transi- One-month transi- Probability vector
for starting in  tion matrix  tion matrix  after two months
north

The calculation of the probability vector after two months depends upon the probability vector in month 0 and the one-month **transition matrix.** In the above calculation, we used an initial probability vector that represented a truck that started in the north. To calculate the proportion of trucks that will be in each region after two months, we simply substitute the original proportion of trucks in each region as the initial probability vector, that is, [.4  .3  .3]. So the calculation becomes:

*transition matrix*

$$
\begin{array}{c} \text{N} \quad \text{C} \quad \text{S} \\ [.4 \quad .3 \quad .3] \end{array}
\begin{array}{c} \text{N} \quad \text{C} \quad \text{S} \\ \begin{bmatrix} .2 & .3 & .5 \\ .3 & .4 & .3 \\ .2 & .4 & .4 \end{bmatrix} \end{array}
\begin{array}{c} \text{N} \quad \text{C} \quad \text{S} \\ \begin{bmatrix} .2 & .3 & .5 \\ .3 & .4 & .3 \\ .2 & .4 & .4 \end{bmatrix} \end{array}
=
\begin{array}{c} \text{N} \quad \text{C} \quad \text{S} \\ [.236 \quad .377 \quad .387] \end{array}
$$

Truck proportion One-month transi- One-month transi- Truck proportion in
in month 0  tion matrix  tion matrix  month 2

From this calculation, we see that 23.6% of all trucks will be in the north, 37.7% will be in the central region, and 38.7% will be in the south after two months.

**TABLE 18-2.**
**Solution of**
**Move-U Problem**

| Month | North | Central | South |
|-------|-------|---------|-------|
| 1 | .23 | .36 | .41 |
| 2 | .236 | .377 | .387 |
| 3 | .2377 | .3764 | .3859 |
| 4 | .2376 | .3763 | .3862 |
| 5 | .2376 | .3763 | .3862 |
| 6 | .2376 | .3763 | .3862 |
| 7 | .2376 | .3763 | .3862 |
| 8 | .2376 | .3763 | .3862 |

The second question we are interested in answering is what proportion of trucks will be in each region after a "long period" of time? To answer this question, we have programmed a computer to repeat the calculation of the probability vector for 8 months. This series of calculations is shown in Table 18-2.

In Table 18-2 we note that the probability vector changes from its initial value of [.4   .3   .3] to [.238   .376   .386] over 8 months. Note also that the *change* between subsequent vectors decreases as the number of months increases. This pattern of

*steady state*

practically unchanging probability vectors indicates that a **steady-state** condition has been reached where the proportion of trucks in each region will remain the same. This steady-state proportion of trucks is 23.8% in the north, 37.6% in the central, and 38.6% in the south.

## Mathematical development

The previous discussion can be summarized if we use the following notation:

$p_{ij}$ = probability of going from state $i$ to state $j$ in one step

$P$ = a matrix made up of the $p_{ij}$ values (the transition matrix)

$s_i(t)$ = probability of being in state $i$ in period $t$

$S(t)$ = vector of state probabilities in period $t$

For example,

$$p_{11} = .2, \qquad p_{23} = .3, \qquad s_1(0) = .4, \qquad S(0) = [.4 \quad .3 \quad .3]$$

Using this notation, several key results may be stated. First, we have that the sum of state probabilities must be equal to 1:

$$s_1(t) + s_2(t) + s_3(t) + \cdots + s_n(t) = 1 \tag{18.1}$$

for a case with $n$ states.

Similarly, for each row of the transition matrix, $P$, we have the sum:

$$p_{i1} + p_{i2} + p_{i3} + \cdots + p_{in} = 1 \tag{18.2}$$

for $i = 1, 3, \ldots, n$. Recall that this implies that a transition must be made to some state in each step.

The transition from one period to the next is embodied in the following equation:

$$S(t + 1) = S(t)P \tag{18.3}$$

For the first time period, this becomes

$$S(1) = S(0)P \tag{18.4}$$

And for the second period, we have

$$S(2) = S(1)P = S(0)P^2 \tag{18.5}$$

In general, this result becomes

$$S(t) = S(0)P^t \tag{18.6}$$

Now, for a steady-state condition we have

$$S = S(t + 1) = S(t) \tag{18.7}$$

where $S = $ steady-state probability vector, which is the same regardless of time period. This implies that

$$S = SP \tag{18.8}$$

That is, the steady-state vector remains the same after a one-step transition. For our example, this results in

$$S = [s_1 \quad s_2 \quad s_3] = [s_1 \quad s_2 \quad s_3] \begin{bmatrix} .2 & .3 & .5 \\ .3 & .4 & .3 \\ .2 & .4 & .4 \end{bmatrix}$$

Completing the calculation, we arrive at a system of equations:

$$s_1 = .2s_1 + .3s_2 + .2s_3 \tag{18.9}$$

$$s_2 = .3s_1 + .4s_2 + .4s_3 \tag{18.10}$$

$$s_3 = .5s_1 + .3s_2 + .4s_3 \tag{18.11}$$

We also know that the sum of the state probabilities is equal to one, so we have

$$1 = s_1 + s_2 + s_3 \tag{18.12}$$

If we solve for $s_1$, $s_2$, and $s_3$ using equations (18.9)–(18.12), we arrive at the steady-state probabilities:[1]

$$s_1 = .238, \qquad s_2 = .376, \qquad s_3 = .386$$

These values are the same steady-state proportions as were found using the computer printout. However, we were able to find these values by solving a system of linear equations rather than iterating until the difference between the values for two months becomes small.

An important point to recognize about this steady-state condition is that it *does not* depend on the beginning state. If we start off with a proportion vector of [.5   .25   .25] or one of [.33   .33   .34], in the long run we will always end up with the same steady-state proportion vector, [.238   .376   .386].

To summarize our development of Markov chains, if there exists a one-step transition matrix $P = [p_{ij}]$ and a state vector for time period $t$, $S(t)$, then we have that

$$S(t + 1) = S(t)P$$

But since

$$S(t + 1) = S(t)P = S(t - 1)P^2 = \cdots = S(1)P^{t-1} = S(0)P^t$$

we may say that

$$S(t) = S(0)P^t$$

Also, a steady-state or equilibrium probability vector, $S$, may be found by solving the system of equations defined by

$$S = SP \qquad \text{and} \qquad \sum_{i=1}^{n} s_i = 1$$

to find the appropriate values of $s_i$ that make up $S$, the equilibrium vector.

## ■ Markov chains with absorbing states

To illustrate the concept of *Markov chains with absorbing states,* consider the following problem. Helderberg Junior College is a state-supported, two-year school that offers associate degrees. The administration of HJC is interested in knowing how

---

[1]Since we have four equations in three unknowns, we will use any two of the first two equations plus the last to solve for the three unknowns.

many students will graduate each year, continue in school, or drop out of school. This information is helpful in planning for future faculty–staff needs and for obtaining funding from the state.

Since HJC is a two-year school, students completing their first year may either continue in school or transfer to another school (a student who drops out is considered a transfer). If the students continue in school, they may either take second-year courses or repeat first-year courses. Students completing their second year of school will either graduate with an associate's degree, continue in school to complete requirements for the degree, or transfer to another school without finishing the necessary courses for an associate's degree. In any case, a student's status in the next school year (HJC does not have summer school classes and does not accept transfers) depends entirely upon their status this year.

Based upon previous data, the registrar at HJC has determined the proportion of students who fall into each category based upon their prior year's status. This information is shown in the following transition matrix:

|          | 1st year | 2nd year | Grad. | Trans. |
|----------|----------|----------|-------|--------|
| 1st year | .1       | .7       | 0     | .2     |
| 2nd year | 0        | .2       | .6    | .2     |
| Grad.    | 0        | 0        | 1     | 0      |
| Trans.   | 0        | 0        | 0     | 1      |

This transition matrix is different than the ones we have seen earlier for two reasons. First, it is not possible to go to all other states from a starting state. For example, a student in the first year cannot graduate. Second, a student who reaches the graduate state or the transfer state cannot go to any other state. For this reason, these two states, graduate and transfer, are known as **absorbing states** since once they are reached, they cannot be left.

*absorbing states*

In a *Markov chain with absorbing states*, the question is no longer what proportion of the total will reach a given state, since all of the total will eventually be in one of the two absorbing states. In other words, the steady-state condition will have everything in an absorbing state. Given this result, the question then becomes: What proportion of the nonabsorbing original states will end up in each absorbing state? In the Helderberg Junior College example, the question becomes: What proportion of students in the first or second year will graduate, and what proportion will transfer to another school or drop out?

To compute these proportions, we need first to define a special matrix called the **fundamental matrix** $Q$. The matrix is found by the following procedure:

*fundamental matrix*

1. Delete the rows corresponding to the absorbing original states.

2. Divide the matrix that remains into absorbing states and nonabsorbing states. Call the part of the matrix under absorbing states, $G$, and the part under nonabsorbing states, $H$.

3. Compute $Q = (I - H)^{-1}$, where $I$ = the identity matrix (ones on the diagonal, zeros elsewhere) and the $-1$ superscript refers to the inverse of a matrix.

If we apply this procedure to the Helderberg Junior College case, we have the following:

**Step 1.** Delete absorbing rows.

|  | 1st year | 2nd year | Grad. | Trans. |
|---|---|---|---|---|
| 1st year | .1 | .7 | .0 | .2 |
| 2nd year | 0 | .2 | .6 | .2 |

**Step 2.** Divide remaining rows into absorbing and nonabsorbing states.

$$G = \begin{bmatrix} 0 & .2 \\ .6 & .2 \end{bmatrix}$$

$$H = \begin{bmatrix} .1 & .7 \\ 0 & .2 \end{bmatrix}$$

**Step 3.** Compute $Q = (I - H)^{-1}$.

$$Q = \begin{bmatrix} (1 - .1) & (0 - .7) \\ (0 - 0) & (1 - .2) \end{bmatrix}^{-1} = \begin{bmatrix} .9 & -.7 \\ 0 & .8 \end{bmatrix}^{-1}$$

$$= \begin{bmatrix} 1.111 & .972 \\ 0 & 1.250 \end{bmatrix}$$

Using $Q$, we can compute the proportions of students that will reach each absorbing state. Let this matrix of proportions be called $R$, where $r_{ij}$ = proportion of students in an initial state $i$ that eventually go into absorbing state $j$. Then we have

$$R = QG$$

In our example,

$$Q = \begin{bmatrix} 1.111 & .972 \\ 0 & 1.250 \end{bmatrix} \quad \text{and} \quad G = \begin{bmatrix} 0 & .2 \\ .6 & .2 \end{bmatrix}$$

so

$$R = \begin{bmatrix} 1.111 & .972 \\ 0 & 1.250 \end{bmatrix} \begin{bmatrix} 0 & .2 \\ .6 & .2 \end{bmatrix} = \begin{bmatrix} .583 & .417 \\ .750 & .250 \end{bmatrix}$$

In the context of the Helderberg Junior College case, the values in the $R$ matrix may be interpreted as follows:

$r_{11} = .583 = $ proportion of students in their first year who will eventually graduate

$r_{12} = .417 = $ proportion of students in their first year who will transfer rather than graduate

$r_{21} = .750 = $ proportion of students in their second year who will graduate

$r_{22} = .250 = $ proportion of students in their second year who will transfer

If there are now 1000 first-year students at Helderberg Junior College and 800 second-year students, we may expect that

$(.583)(1000) = 583$ first-year students will eventually graduate

$(.417)(1000) = 417$ first-year students will transfer

$(.750)(800) \ = 600$ second-year students will graduate

$(.250)(800) \ = 200$ second-year students will transfer

If the Helderberg Junior College wishes to graduate, on the average, 700 students, then it will need to increase its first-year class to $(700 \div .583) = 1201$ students (assuming that the new students admitted will be from the same population as the previously admitted students).

We can further interpret the fundamental matrix $Q$ by using the following result: *The entries of the fundamental matrix $Q$ give the average number of periods the system will be in each nonabsorbing state until absorption occurs.* In the Helderberg Junior College case, this means that the average first-year student will spend 1.111 years in the first year before either dropping out of school or going on to the second year. By the same token, the average first-year student will spend .972 year in the second year. Similarly, the average second-year student will spend no time in the first year (as would be expected!), but will spend 1.250 years in the second year.

Another result that can be found by looking at $Q$ is that the sum of the rows yields the average number of periods to absorption in one of the absorbing states. In the Helderberg case, this means that if a student is in the first year, it will take, on the average, 2.083 years either to graduate or drop out of school. If a student is in the second year, the average time to graduation or dropping out of school is 1.250 years.

# ▪ Summary

Markov processes are a set of quantitative models that act in a sequential manner with wide and varying applications for managerial decision making. Markov processes are stochastic models that are descriptive and give us a means of determining probabilities that a given event will occur as a result of a recurring transition from one situation to another.

In terms of assumptions, Markov processes assume that there exist a set of states or conditions and a matrix of probabilities, $P_{ij}$, that give the probability of moving from state $i$ to state $j$ in one step. It is also assumed that the condition of the previous step is the only one that affects the condition of the current state. In this chapter, we considered a special case of Markov processes known as Markov chains.

We showed how Markov chains can be used to determine long-term effects of movements of rental trucks. We also looked at Markov chains where there were absorbing states and used this concept to determine the result of a college's student retention and admission policies.

# ▪ Glossary of terms

**absorbing state:**   A state such that once entered cannot be left.

**fundamental matrix:**   A matrix derived from the transition matrix for a Markov chain with absorbing states; used to calculate end probabilities.

**Markov chains:**   A special case of Markov processes that assumes a finite number of states, constant transition probabilities, and equal-length periods.

**Markovian assumption:**   The assumption that the condition of any process depends only on its condition at the immediately previous period.

**state:**   The condition of the process under study at any period.

**steady state:**   The condition where the probability of being in a given state does not change from period to period.

**transition matrix:**   A matrix of all transition probabilities for all possible one-step transitions.

**transition probability:**   The probability that the process will move from state $i$ to state $j$ in one step.

**trials:**   The repeat occurrences of the event of process under study.

# ▪ Review questions

1. Can there be a situation where the number of initial states is not equal to the number of final states? Why or why not?

2. Why do the probabilities in each column of the transition matrix not have to sum to one?

3. Discuss under what assumptions the following processes could be considered Markovian:
   a. prices on the stock market
   b. the weather on a day-to-day basis
   c. a patient's condition in the hospital
   d. the progress of a hurricane on an hour-to-hour basis
   e. the status of machines in a factory with regard to being functioning or in need of repair

4. Why can we obtain steady state probabilities by solving systems of equations?

5. Why is it true that $S = SP$ in a Markov Chain?

6. What happens when one attempts to apply the standard approach for determining steady-state proportions to problems having absorbing states?

7. Can a Markov chain have only absorbing states? What does this imply?

## ■ True/false questions

1. In a Markov process the probability of being in any state depends on the two most previous states.

2. Markov processes can be defined as descriptive, stochastic, and dynamic models.

3. A Markov chain is a Markov process with transition probabilities that change from trial to trial.

4. In a transition matrix the probabilities in each column must sum to one.

5. In a Markov chain a steady-state condition has been reached when the probability of being in a given state is the same from trial to trial.

6. The steady-state probabilities are dependent on the initial state.

7. In a Markov chain with absorbing states, the steady-state probabilities for the nonabsorbing states are always zero.

8. The entries in the fundamental matrix give the average number of periods the system will be in in each absorbing state.

## ■ Problems

1. For the following transitions matrix, compute the probability of being in state A or B after three periods for an initial state of [.5    .5].

|   | A | B |
|---|---|---|
| A | .3 | .7 |
| B | .5 | .5 |

2. For the transition matrix in Problem 1, compute the steady-state probabilities for states A and B.

**3. a.** For the following transition matrix, compute the probabilities of being states X, Y, or Z after two periods, if the initial state was (.3   .4   .3):

|   | X | Y | Z |
|---|---|---|---|
| X | .2 | .2 | .6 |
| Y | .8 | .1 | .1 |
| Z | .7 | 0 | .3 |

**b.** What are the steady-state probabilities for X, Y, and Z?

**4.** For the following transition matrix, compute the steady-state probabilities of being in states I, II, and III.

|     | I | II | III |
|-----|----|-----|------|
| I   | .5 | .25 | .25 |
| II  | .3 | .5  | .2  |
| III | .2 | .2  | .6  |

**5.** Yogi Bear, manager of the Gotham City Yankees, is attempting to determine the steady-state probabilities of opposing pitchers so that his hitters can have a better idea of what to expect. Using the following transition matrix, determine the steady-state matrix for the Metropolitan Giants' best pitcher, "Big" Jim Palmer.

| Pitch | Current-Pitch | | |
|-------|--------|-------|----------|
|       | Slider | Curve | Fastball |
| Slider   | .40 | .40 | .20 |
| Curve    | .30 | .50 | .20 |
| Fastball | .20 | .20 | .60 |

**6.** Avertz Company rents its fleet of 500 cars. Once a week each car is inspected. During this time it may have been rented or had maintenance performed or both. In the first week in June, it was determined that 400 of the cars were in good working condition, 80 of the cars needed minor repairs, and 20 of the cars needed major repairs. In the second week of June, 350 of the cars that were in good working condition were in the same condition, 40 needed minor repairs, and 10 needed major repairs. Of the 80 cars needing minor repairs, 50 were in good working order, 25 still needed minor repairs, and 5 now needed major repairs. Finally, of the 20 cars needing major repairs, 15 were in good condition, 3 needed minor repairs, and 2 were still in need of major repairs. Set up a transition matrix for this problem.

**7.** In a faraway galaxy, a long time ago, there existed a planet where the weather on any day depended only upon the previous day's weather. For example, the probability that it rains today depends only on what happened yesterday. Only three types of weather exist on this planet, fair, rain, and snow. The daily transition matrix for these types of weather is shown below.

|      | Fair | Rain | Snow |
|------|------|------|------|
| Fair | .5 | .3 | .2 |
| Rain | .4 | .4 | .2 |
| Snow | .3 | .3 | .4 |

**a.** Compute the state probabilities for the day after tomorrow if it rained today.

**b.** What are the steady-state probabilities for each type of weather?

8. In the "light" beer industry, three brands share about 75% of all such sales—Sudco, Mills, and Schotz. These three are in intense competition for the "light" beer customer. Recently, Sudco had an outside agency perform a study on how customers were reacting to the ads. The results of the study showed that after three months, 50% of Sudco's customers still preferred Suds Lite, 30% preferred Mills Light Beer, and 20% preferred Schotz Easy Beer. Of Mills' customers, 60% still preferred Mills Light, 30% preferred Suds Lite, and 10% preferred Schotz Easy. Of Schotz's customers, 40% still preferred Schotz, 30% preferred Sudco and 30% preferred Mills.

**a.** Set up the transition matrix for this brand-switching problem.

**b.** Find the steady-state percentage of customers that prefer each type of beer.

9. Tarheel Computers is a new firm specializing in producing minicomputers. However, the company's cash flow position does not allow it to produce more than two machines per month. The demand each month will be either one or two machines. There is a .3 probability of a demand for one machine and a .7 probability of a demand for two machines. Tarheel Computers feels it must meet the demand level, whatever it is. This requires that it develop a production policy to meet demand. One possible policy is shown.

| Initial Inventory | Production |
|-------------------|------------|
| 0                 | 2          |
| 1                 | 2          |
| 2                 | 1          |

**a.** Develop a transition matrix for this situation where the initial state is the initial inventory for each period.

**b.** Find the steady-state probabilities of each inventory value.

10. Bulldog Construction Company has won a contract to build a road into the Mount St. Helens area of Washington. This road will help in studying the effects of the 1980 volcanic explosion. Bulldog has determined that the volcanic dust will clog up engine filters very quickly and cause trucks to stop running. Filters are checked each day and classified as being either newly cleaned, partially clogged, or totally clogged. Prior experience has shown that a newly cleaned filter has a .1 probability of remaining clean, a .8 probability of being partially clogged, and a .1 probability of being totally clogged. A partially clogged filter has a .5 probability of remaining in that state and a .5 probability of being totally clogged. A totally clogged filter must be cleaned before the truck can be used.

**a.** Set up a transition matrix for this problem.

**b.** If a truck goes out of operation, it costs the company $100 for lost work time and $20 to clean the filter. How much will it cost the company to follow a policy of not cleaning filters until the truck stops?

11. If, in the situation described in Problem 10, the Bulldog Construction Company decides to keep a spare filter in the truck and to replace partially clogged filters, what will be the cost of this policy if the additional filter will cost $20?

12. A large regional department store, Silverland's, has a store charge account plan. Each month, these accounts are classified four ways: paid, up, balance due, balance overdue, and bad debt. Paid-up accounts are those that have no balance due this month;

balance-due accounts are those that have no balance due from the previous month but that have been billed for purchases made this month; overdue accounts are those that have an outstanding balance for more than one month but less than three months. Finally, bad-debt accounts are those that have a balance that is more than three months old and are not expected to be collected.

From store records, it has been found that 60% of the amount in the balance-due accounts is paid up the next month, 30% remain as balance due, and 10% become overdue. It has also been determined that 40% of the overdue accounts become balance due, 30% become paid up, 20% remain overdue, and 10% are written off as bad debts. Once an account reaches the bad-debt category, it is closed. Similarly, once an account moves to the paid category, that money is no longer part of the accounts receivable.

**a.** Write the transition matrix for this problem.

**b.** If the accounts receivable currently has $100,000 in the paid-up category, $50,000 in the balance-due category, $20,000 in the overdue category, and $5000 in the bad-debt category, what amount will be in each category next month? the month after?

**c.** In the steady-state condition, what percentage of the accounts receivable dollars will be in either the paid category or the bad-debt category?

**13.** The transition matrix for a certain Markov chain is shown in Table P18-13. For this transition matrix, compute the probability of being in each absorbing state once the steady-state condition is reached.

**TABLE P18-13. Transition Matrix**

| Initial State | Final State | | | |
|---|---|---|---|---|
| | *I* | *II* | *III* | *IV* |
| I | .2 | .4 | .3 | .1 |
| II | 0 | 1 | 0 | 0 |
| III | 0 | 0 | 1 | 0 |
| IV | .5 | .2 | .1 | .2 |

**14.** Using the transition matrix shown in Table P18-14, compute the probability of being in each absorbing state once the steady-state condition is reached.

**TABLE P18-14. Transition Matrix**

| Initial State | Final State | | | |
|---|---|---|---|---|
| | *A* | *B* | *C* | *D* |
| A | 1 | 0 | 0 | 0 |
| B | .2 | .3 | .3 | .2 |
| C | .1 | .2 | .4 | .3 |
| D | 0 | 0 | 0 | 1 |

**15.** The Summer Sun Tanning Salon has a single tanning room and waiting room for two customers. The tanning process takes exactly 20 minutes. Slim Goodbody, the manager, is interested in knowing the probability that a newly arrived customer will not be able to find a seat in the waiting room. Slim has determined that the probability distribution of arriving customers during the 20 minute service interval is as shown below:

| Number of arrivals | 0 | 1 | 2 | 3 or more |
|---|---|---|---|---|
| Probability | .3 | .6 | .1 | 0.0 |

Assume that new customers do not arrive at exactly the same time as the previously served customers depart.

a. Set up the transition matrix for this problem. (*Hint:* If there are no waiting customers, a tanning session will begin only upon arrival. Otherwise, a tanning session will begin immediately. Let the number of waiting customers during the previous session be the initial state and the number of customers during the current session be the final state.)

b. Find the steady-state probability vector. How do you answer Slim Goodbody's question regarding customers leaving because there exists no waiting room?

# 19

# Game Theory

## ▪ Introduction

In Chapters 16 and 17 we discussed the topic of decision theory. In each of the problems discussed in those chapters, the decision maker was attempting to arrive at an optimal decision based on his or her perception of the likelihood of different outcomes or states of nature. In each of these situations, the decision maker was acting alone and did not have to take into account possible actions of opponents or competitors whose actions might have an effect on the outcomes of his or her decisions. In reality, many business situations do involve competitors such that the outcome of the situation depends not only on one's own strategy but also on the strategies of competitors. These types of situations fall under the category of game theory. Examples of these adversarial situations include labor-management negotiations where one party is seeking to secure contract gains while the other party is seeking to minimize concessions, competition for market share of a product where the share captured by one party is market share lost by a competitor, or military strategy decisions where territory gained by one player represents territory lost by another player.

Since the development of game theory in 1944, the research literature has abounded with theoretical developments and applications. However, it has typically been the case that real adversarial situations involving many players with many possible strategies available to them have not been solvable. Perhaps the most important aspect of game theory is the understanding that it provides for general decision problems. In this chapter we will study the very basic structure of game theory and some simple solution methods that may be applied.

## ■ Case
## Sunbelt Airlines

Sunbelt Airlines is a small commuter airlines that operates primarily in the Southeast region of the country. The airlines has several multiengine aircraft, each requiring both a pilot and co-pilot as crew. Therefore Sunbelt employs a large number of pilots. The company's pilots are represented by the Airline Pilots Union (APU), and next month the current contract with the APU will be expiring. Consequently, both Sunbelt and the APU are preparing to sit down at the bargaining table to work out the details of a new contract for the pilots. In preparation for the negotiations, each side has developed certain proposals for the contents of the new contract. The union's ideas may be categorized into three different contract proposals, call them proposals 1, 2, and 3. The airlines' counterproposals may also be categorized into three groups, call them contracts A, B, and C. Both parties are aware of the financial aspects of each proposal-contract combination. The following table indicates the value of each combination in hundreds of thousands of dollars.

These values are the contract gains that the APU would secure, and also the cost the company would have to bear.

|     |   | Sunbelt | | |
|-----|---|-----|-----|-----|
|     |   | A | B | C |
| APU | 1 | 8.5 | 7 | 7.5 |
|     | 2 | 12 | 9.5 | 9 |
|     | 3 | 9 | 11 | 8 |

What is going to happen when the two parties come together for negotiations? Will there be a clear-cut contract combination agreeable to both parties, or will the parties find it necessary to submit to arbitration in order to arrive at some sort of compromise?

## ■ Two-person, zero-sum games

Competitive games are typically categorized according to two criteria: the number of players in the game and the structure of the game's outcomes. In terms of the number of players, when a game has exactly two players it is referred to as a two-person game. For more than two players, it is known as an $n$-person game. While much has been written about the two-person game, relatively little progress has been made toward solving $n$-person games where $n$ is reasonably large.

In terms of the outcome structure, in many situations the sum of one player's gain and the other player's loss will equal zero. In the case of Sunbelt Airlines, the gain that the union secures represents an equal cost to the company. In situations like this, *zero-sum game* we refer to the payoffs as being **zero-sum**. When the sum of one player's gain and the other player's loss do not equal zero, it is called a non-zero-sum situation. An example of this would be where both players gain something, but the degree of their respective gains is affected by their opponent's choice. Once again, while much is known about zero-sum games, relatively less has been developed in the way of efficient solution procedures for non-zero-sum games. In this chapter we will concentrate on the two-person, zero-sum game in order to acquire a basic understanding of the principles of game theory.

Our Sunbelt case is an example of a two-person, zero-sum game. There are exactly two players, the union and the airlines, and the potential gain to one party will be exactly equal to the potential cost to the other. The matrix used to present the "payoffs" for each proposal-contract combination happens to be the typical method for organizing information for a two-person, zero-sum game. Typically, the player who stands to gain is listed in the left margin of the matrix, and the player who is attempting to prevent that gain is listed along the top of the matrix. Each cell in the matrix represents the payoff for the particular row and column combination of strategies selected by the two players. The assumption in two-person, zero-sum games is that the players will make their strategy choices simultaneously with full knowledge of the options available to their opponent and the possible payoffs. Naturally, each player will attempt to choose that strategy which best accomplishes some objective set forth before the decision is made.

If the union were to adopt proposal 3 while Sunbelt offered contract C, the outcome would be 8, the value in row 3, column C, representing $800,000 in gain by the union and $800,000 in cost to the company. This amount is known as the *value* of the game. In the next section we will look at some possible methods for determining the optimal strategy for each of the two players and for determining the value of the game.

## ■ Games with pure strategies

### *The maximin (minimax) criterion*

The criterion most often used to solve games is the minimax decision criterion. Under this criterion, each player tries to select a strategy in order to minimize his or her maximum losses. The player in the left-hand margin will attempt to select the strategy that maximizes the minimum payoff, i.e., the maximin strategy. The player across the top of the matrix will select that strategy which minimizes the maximum loss, i.e., the minimax strategy. If each player's strategy choice results in the same payoff, such that in subsequent plays of the game the players would again choose the same strategies over and over, we say that the game has a **pure strategy.** Because in pure strategy situations the maximum of the minimum payoffs is equal to the minimum of the maximum loss, we say that the optimal strategies represent an **equilibrium point** or **saddle point.**

*pure strategy*

*saddle point*

To illustrate the application of the minimax decision criterion, let us return to the payoff matrix for the Sunbelt Airlines case, as shown in Figure 19-1.

First we will determine the union's optimal strategy. In Figure 19-1 the minimum payoff for each possible union strategy (i.e., the minimum payoff in each row) has been circled. We see that the value 9 in the second row is the maximum of these minimum payoffs. Consequently, under the maximin criterion, the union would select strategy 2 as its optimal strategy. The logic behind this has to do with our assumption that both decision makers are rational. The union knows that if it selects

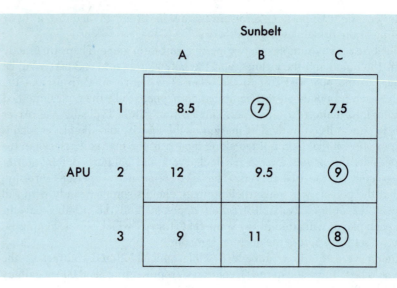

strategy 1, Sunbelt, in order to minimize its outlay, will choose strategy B, resulting in a $700,000 gain to the union. If the union chooses strategy 3, Sunbelt can be expected to select contract C, resulting in a gain to the union of $800,000. Thus, under the assumption that Sunbelt is a rational bargainer, the union will choose strategy 2 in order to maximum the minimum gain that the company's choice will allow.

The Sunbelt negotiators will be applying the same type of logic in order to minimize their maximum payout to the union. Figure 19-2 is our original payoff matrix with the maximum payoff in each column circled. The company will select strategy C, as this represents the minimum of the maximum costs they would incur. The logic is the same as before. If Sunbelt chooses strategy A, they realize that a

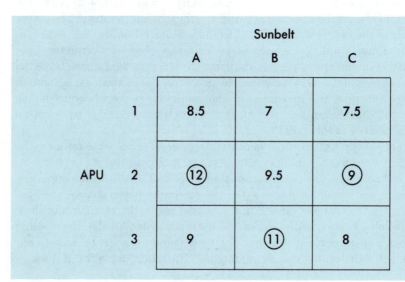

rational union would opt for strategy 2 in order to maximize its gains at 12. If it chooses strategy B, the union will select strategy 3 in order to achieve a payoff of 11. Therefore, Sunbelt will choose strategy C, because the maximum loss the company can incur in this case is 9.

We see that both of the players in this game will select a strategy that has the same value. Both arrive at a single strategy that they would not opt to change, and the game has a pure strategy. The minimum value in row 2 is also the maximum value in column C, so our solution is an equilibrium point or saddle point as discussed earlier.

### *Dominance*

In some cases it is possible to reduce the size of the payoff matrix before any analysis is performed, thereby reducing the task of identifying optimal strategies. Looking at our Sunbelt matrix once again, we notice that union strategy 1 has a lower payoff than strategy 2 regardless of what strategy is chosen by Sunbelt. Since the union is seeking to maximize its gain, there is no conceivable circumstance under which they would choose strategy 1 as opposed to strategy 2. Therefore, we say that strategy 2 **dominates** strategy 1. As such, strategy 1 can be removed from the payoff matrix. For strategies 2 and 3, neither dominates the other. Depending on the strategy selected by Sunbelt, either strategy 2 or 3 could result in the higher payoff.

*dominance*

From a column standpoint, we can do the same type of reduction. Since Sunbelt is seeking to choose the lowest payouts possible, we see that strategy A always has a higher loss to the company than strategy C regardless of the union's action. Consequently, Sunbelt would never choose strategy A, and it may be removed from the matrix. Strategies B and C must be retained, as neither dominates the other. Figure 19-3 illustrates the payoff table with dominated rows and columns crossed out.

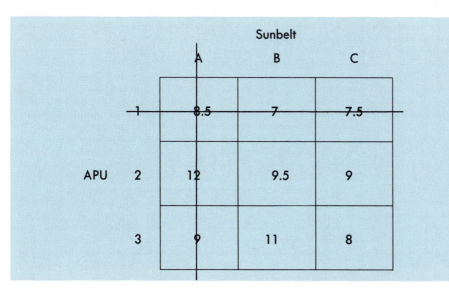

**FIGURE 19-3.
Payoff Matrix for
Sunbelt Airlines
with Dominated
Strategies Crossed
Out**

Note that the remaining matrix still must be analyzed by the minimax principle, but we have less values to consider than in the original matrix. For a 3 × 3 matrix such as our example, application of the dominance criterion does not substantially reduce the amount of effort necessary to select the optimal strategies. In a larger problem, or one where pure strategies do not exist, application of the dominance criterion may be very useful in reducing the computational aspects of the problem.

## ■ Games with mixed strategies

*mixed strategies*

When a game is such that neither party can settle on a single strategy (i.e., no equilibrium strategy exists), we say that the game has **mixed strategies.** As an example, suppose that we modify our Sunbelt payoffs to come up with the game matrix shown in Figure 19-4.

Checking for dominance, we see that row 2 and column B are both dominated strategies. Removing these from the payoff matrix, we get Figure 19-5.

If we apply the minimax criterion to Figure 19-5, we get a different result from that of the original situation. The minimum payoff in row 1 is 7, and the minimum payoff in row 3 is 6. Therefore, the union would choose strategy 1, since it is the maximum of these minimum gains. The maximum payoff in column A is 9.5, and the maximum payoff in column C is 10. Therefore, the company would choose strategy A in order to minimize its maximum cost.

We notice immediately that the value of the union's strategy is 7 but the value of the company's strategy is 9.5. Since these two are not the same, there is no single value for the game. What does this mean? Let's look at the play of the game sequentially. The union will begin by selecting strategy 1 and the company will begin by selecting strategy A. Immediately, the company will notice the union's

**FIGURE 19-4. Game Matrix for Sunbelt Airlines with Modified Payoffs**

|  |  | Sunbelt A | B | C |
|---|---|---|---|---|
|  | 1 | 9.5 | 12 | 7 |
| APU | 2 | 7 | 8.5 | 6.5 |
|  | 3 | 6 | 9 | 10 |

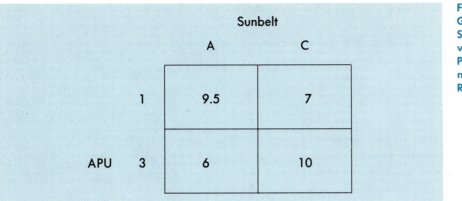

FIGURE 19-5.
Game Matrix for
Sunbelt Airlines
with Modified
Payoffs and Domi-
nated Strategies
Removed

choice and begin to question its own strategy. By switching to strategy C while the union is at strategy 1, the company will reduce its cost from 9.5 to 7. As soon as the company switches to strategy C, the union will realize that it can increase its gain from 7 to 10 by switching to strategy 3. But as soon as the union moves to strategy 3, the company will go back to strategy A in order to lower its costs, and so on. Because there is no equilibrium, the players will continue to switch their strategies, always attempting to benefit from the last move by their opponent.

In order to resolve this conflict arising from mixed strategies, we apply the concept of expected gain and loss. The idea here is to derive long-run probabilities that each player will select each strategy such that, if the game were played many times, the expected gain to the one player and the expected loss to the other player would be the same and would not depend on the strategy chosen by the opponent. Suppose that we let the probability that on any given play of the game the union selects strategy 1 be $p$, and let $1 - p$ be the probability that the union will select strategy 3. Under these circumstances, if the company selects strategy A, the expected gain to the union will be

$$\text{expected gain} = p(9.5) + (1 - p)(6)$$

$$= 3.5p + 6 \tag{19.1}$$

If the company selects strategy C, the expected gain is

$$\text{expected gain} = p(7) + (1 - p)(10)$$

$$= 10 - 3p \tag{19.2}$$

Since we want to select probabilities such that our expected gain will be the same regardless of our opponent's strategy selection, we can equate the two expected gains in order to arrive at those probabilities:

$$3.5p + 6 = 10 - 3p$$

$$6.5p = 4$$

$$p = \frac{4}{6.5} = .6154 \qquad\qquad (19.3)$$

Thus, 61.54% of the time we would select strategy 1 and $(1 - .6145) = .3846$ or 38.46% of the time we would select strategy 3. Using this approach, regardless of the strategy chosen by our opponent, our expected gain over many plays of the game is $3.5p + 6 = 10 - 3p = 8.1538$.

If we do the same analysis for the company, assuming that $p$ is the probability of selecting strategy A and $1 - p$ is the probability of selecting strategy C, the expected loss if the union chooses strategy 1 is

$$\text{expected loss} = p(9.5) + (1 - p)(7)$$

$$= 2.5p + 7 \qquad\qquad (19.4)$$

and if the union chooses strategy 3,

$$\text{expected loss} = p(6) + (1 - p)(10)$$

$$= 10 - 4p \qquad\qquad (19.5)$$

Equating the two expected losses so that we will be indifferent as to our opponent's selection, we get

$$2.5p + 7 = 10 - 4p$$

$$6.5p = 3$$

$$p = \frac{3}{6.5} = .4615 \qquad\qquad (19.6)$$

Therefore, the company will select strategy A 46.15% of the time and strategy C $(1 - .4615) = .5385$ or 53.85% of the time. Once again, the expected loss will be $2.5p + 7 = 10 - 4p = 8.1538$. Given the probabilities derived for each player, the expected gain and the expected loss over multiple plays of the game are equal, and we once again have an equilibrium situation. It is also interesting to note that the mixed strategy value of the game is better for both players than their original strategies under the straight minimax criterion. The union has increased its expected gain from 7 to 8.1538, while the company has reduced its expected cost from 9.5 to 8.1538. This is to be expected for a mixed strategy.

# ■ Graphical solution procedure

As long as a particular player of a game faces only two alternative strategies to choose from, it is possible to draw a graph of the player's decision situation. Figure 19-6 is a graph of the options facing the union in our mixed strategies example. Each of the vertical axes represents one of the two strategies available to the union, and the horizontal axis represents the probability scale for choosing strategy 1. The probabilities range from 1 at the left vertical axis, which represents strategy 1, to 0 at the right vertical axis, representing strategy 3.

The lines drawn on the graph represent gains to the union given the possible strategy choices by the company. Assuming that the company chooses strategy A, the union's gains vary from 9.5 if the union selects strategy 1 to 6 if the union selects strategy 3. For any probability level of choosing strategy 1 (which also determines the probability of choosing strategy 2, since there are only two alternatives), the line represents the expected gain to the union given that the company has selected strategy A. Assuming that the company chooses strategy C, the gains vary from 7 if the union selects strategy 1 to 10 if its selects strategy 3. Again, the line connecting these two points represents the expected gain to the union if the company selects strategy C.

The shaded area underneath the gain lines represents the area from which our gain would have to be taken, since the company would be expected to force us onto

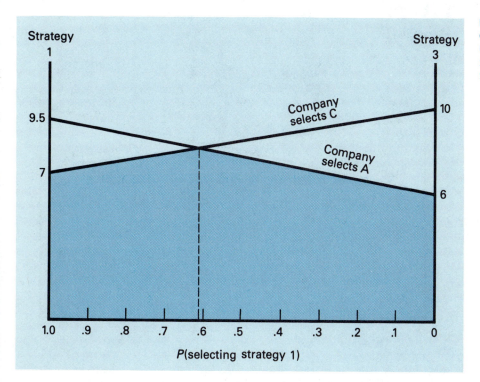

**FIGURE 19-6.**
**Graph of the Union's Mixed Strategies for the Sunbelt Case**

the lower of the two gain lines through its strategy choices. The point of intersection of the two gain lines is obviously the point that maximizes our expected gain, as it is the highest point in the shaded area. Dropping a line down from the point to the probability scale, we see that, as before, the optimal probability for the union of selecting strategy 1 is .6154.

Figure 19-7 is the graph for determining the strategy probabilities for the company. Once again, the two alternatives available to the company are represented on the vertical axes, and the probability of choosing strategy A is shown on the horizontal axis. The lines represent the expected loss to the company for each possible union strategy, and the shaded area is the region of company loss. The intersection point of the two lines is the lowest expected loss that the company can hope to attain. This point corresponds to a probability level of .4615 that the company will select strategy A.

It is also possible to graph situations where one opponent faces more than two alternatives, provided that the other player faces only two alternatives. Figure 19-8 is an example of what such a graph would look like. We would only be able to determine the strategy for the player with two alternatives, because we could not graph the other player's alternatives.

In cases where one or both of the players face more than two alternatives, we have seen the shortcomings of the solution methods presented thus far. There are two

**FIGURE 19-7.**
**Graph of the Company's Mixed Strategies for the Sunbelt Case**

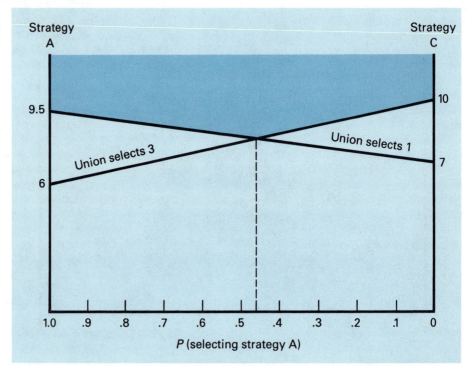

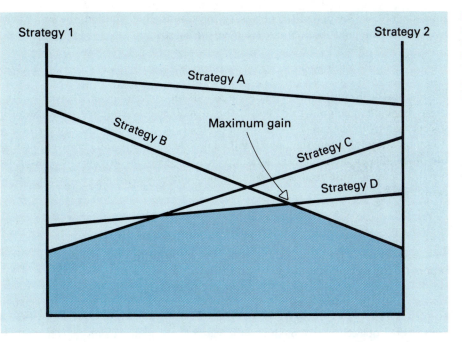

FIGURE 19-8.
Graph for Mixed
Strategies Where
One Player Has
Two Strategies
and the Other Has
Four Strategies

other methodologies that offer assistance in solving these more complex problems: linear programming and the method of subgames. We will conclude this chapter by looking at the procedures necessary to apply these two methodologies.

## ■ Linear programming formulation

Although the true value of the linear programming approach to solving games is that it allows us to solve efficiently games with numerous strategies for each player, it will probably facilitate understanding of the approach if we return to the simple mixed strategy example we are already familiar with. Returning to Figure 19-5, let us look at the linear programming formulation that could be used to solve this game.

Just as in the earlier solution approaches, it is possible to view the game from two vantage points, that of the Airline Pilots Union and that of Sunbelt Airlines. Since APU is the "offensive" player in this game, we will formulate the linear programming model from their point of view first. APU has two decisions to make. They must decide with what probability they will choose strategy 1 and with what probability they will choose strategy 3. Let us define the two decision variables:

$p_1$ = the probability of selecting strategy 1

$p_2$ = the probability of selecting strategy 3

Immediately, we see one of the necessary constraints. By definition, the sum of the two probabilities must be 1, and so we have the constraint:

$$p_1 + p_2 = 1 \tag{19.7}$$

We will also need constraints to relate the payoffs for each strategy to the value of the game. Looking at column 1 of Figure 19-5, if APU selects strategy 1 while Sunbelt selects strategy A, the payoff to APU will be 9.5. Likewise, if the strategy 3, strategy A combination is chosen, the payoff will be 6. When these payoffs are weighted by the probability of choosing each strategy (i.e., the decision variables), the resulting weighted payoff must be at least equal to the value of the game. This results in the constraint

$$9.5p_1 + 6p_2 \geq v \tag{19.8}$$

where $v$ represents the value of the game. Using the same logic, the constraint that represents the second column of the game matrix is

$$7p_1 + 10p_2 \geq v \tag{19.9}$$

Since APU's objective is to maximize the value of the game which represents their gain, we can write the linear programming model as

MAXIMIZE:        $Z = v$                                                         (19.10)

SUBJECT TO:      $9.5p_1 + \phantom{1}6p_2 \geq v$                                (19.11)

$\phantom{SUBJECT TO:}7p_1 + 10p_2 \geq v$                                       (19.12)

$\phantom{SUBJECT TO:}p_1 + \phantom{1}p_2 = 1$                                  (19.13)

$\phantom{SUBJECT TO:}p_1, p_2 \geq 0$                                            (19.14)

The model is not in exactly the form we want, since we have nonconstant values on the right-hand side of the first two constraints. If we divide both sides of each constraint by $v$, we get:

MAXIMIZE:        $Z = v$                                                         (19.10a)

SUBJECT TO:      $\dfrac{9.5p_1}{v} + \dfrac{6p_2}{v} \geq 1$                     (19.11a)

$\dfrac{7p_1}{v} + \dfrac{10p_2}{v} \geq 1$                                       (19.12a)

$\dfrac{p_1}{v} + \dfrac{p_2}{v} = \dfrac{1}{v}$                                  (19.13a)

$p_1, p_2 \geq 0$                                                                 (19.14a)

To further simplify matters at this point, let us define

$$x_1 = \frac{p_1}{v} \qquad (19.15)$$

$$x_2 = \frac{p_2}{v} \qquad (19.16)$$

so that our model becomes

MAXIMIZE:     $Z = v$                                         (19.17)

SUBJECT TO:   $9.5x_1 + 6x_2 \geq 1$                          (19.18)

$\phantom{SUBJECT TO:}\ \ 7x_1 + 10x_2 \geq 1$               (19.19)

$$x_1 + x_2 = \frac{1}{v} \qquad (19.20)$$

$\phantom{SUBJECT TO:}\quad x_1, x_2 \geq 0$                 (19.21)

One final change will put the model into a very familiar form. APU's objective is the maximization of $v$. This is equivalent to minimizing $1/v$, since larger values of $v$ result in smaller values of $1/v$. Since, from the third constraint, $1/v$ is equal to the sum of $x_1$ and $x_2$, we may rewrite the model as

MINIMIZE:     $Z = x_1 + x_2$                                (19.22)

SUBJECT TO:   $9.5x_1 + 6x_2 \geq 1$                          (19.23)

$\phantom{SUBJECT TO:}\ \ 7x_1 + 10x_2 \geq 1$               (19.24)

$\phantom{SUBJECT TO:}\quad x_1, x_2 \geq 0$                 (19.25)

This model could now be easily solved by the simplex method. Of course, the Z value in the solution will be equal to $1/v$, and each variable $x_i$ will be equal to $p_i/v$. It will be necessary to compute the value of the game from the value of Z, and then compute the strategy probabilities $p_i$ from our knowledge of $v$ and the values of $x_1$ and $x_2$.

To illustrate the conversion, the solution to the above linear programming model is

$$x_1 = .0754716$$

$$x_2 = .0471698$$

$$Z = .1226414$$

This means that the value of the game is $v = 1/Z = 8.1538$. Likewise, since $x_1 = p_1/v$, then $p_1 = x_1 \times v = .0754716(8.1538) = .6154$. Also, $p_2 = .0471698(8.1538) = .3846$.

These are exactly the same values that we arrived at earlier using the methods appropriate only for $2 \times 2$ games.

We could also formulate the model for the game from Sunbelt's viewpoint. Given that Sunbelt will try to minimize the value of the game representing their payout, the model would be

MAXIMIZE:    $Z = y_1 + y_2$ (19.26)

SUBJECT TO:    $9.5y_1 + 7y_2 \leq 1$ (19.27)

$6y_1 + 10y_2 \leq 1$ (19.28)

$y_1, y_2 \geq 0$ (19.29)

(Go through the formulation steps and verify for yourself that this formulation is correct.) The value of the game resulting from the solution to this model will be the same value of the game we just computed, and the strategy probabilities will be the same as the ones we found earlier for Sunbelt. It is interesting to note that the model for Sunbelt is the dual of the APU model. Thus, it is not necessary to formulate both, as the solution to either will provide all necesssary information.

While this example of solving games by linear programming relied on a $2 \times 2$ situation, the real power of linear programming becomes evident when we face larger $M \times M$ games. In the next section we will see another method that can be applied to games larger than $2 \times 2$.

## ■ Subgames

*subgames*

It is sometimes possible to break down a game matrix into smaller matrices called **subgames** for the purpose of analysis. Consider the following example:

|  |  | Player 2 A | Player 2 B |
|---|---|---|---|
| Player 1 | 1 | 7 | 2 |
|  | 2 | 6 | 8 |
|  | 3 | 5 | 9 |

This is an example of a $3 \times 2$ game. None of the strategies is dominant, so the game matrix cannot be reduced. However, the matrix can be decomposed into the three $2 \times 2$ subgames that follow:

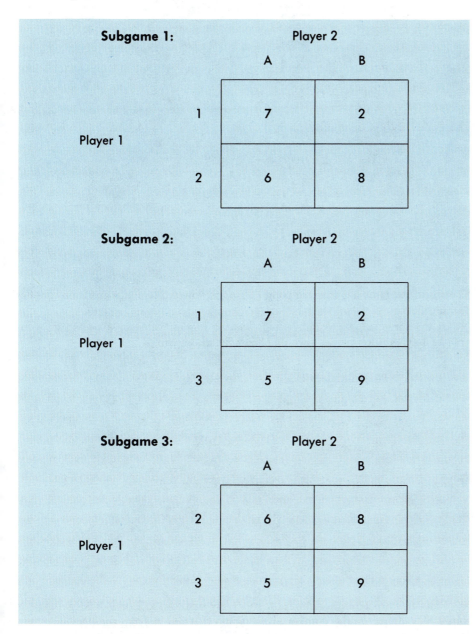

**Subgame 1:**

| | Player 2 | |
| --- | --- | --- |
| | A | B |
| Player 1  1 | 7 | 2 |
| Player 1  2 | 6 | 8 |

**Subgame 2:**

| | Player 2 | |
| --- | --- | --- |
| | A | B |
| Player 1  1 | 7 | 2 |
| Player 1  3 | 5 | 9 |

**Subgame 3:**

| | Player 2 | |
| --- | --- | --- |
| | A | B |
| Player 1  2 | 6 | 8 |
| Player 1  3 | 5 | 9 |

Using expected gain as a criterion and assuming that player 1 has control of the game since he or she has more alternatives to choose from, we can analyze each subgame.

The first subgame has a value to player 1 of

$$p(7) + (1 - p)(6) = p(2) + (1 - p)(8)$$

$$p + 6 = 8 - 6p$$

$$7p = 2$$

$$p = \tfrac{2}{7}, \quad (1 - p) = \tfrac{5}{7}$$

$$\text{value} = p + 6 = \tfrac{2}{7} + 6 = 6\tfrac{2}{7} \tag{19.30}$$

The value of the second subgame is

$$p(7) + (1 - p)(5) = p(2) + (1 - p)(9)$$

$$2p + 5 = 9 - 7p$$

$$9p = 4$$

$$p = \tfrac{4}{9}, \quad (1 - p) = \tfrac{5}{9}$$

$$\text{value} = 2p + 5 = 2\tfrac{4}{9} + 5 = 5\tfrac{8}{9} \tag{19.31}$$

The third subgame has a saddle point in the first row, first column and therefore has a value of 6.

Of the three subgames, subgame 1 has the highest value or expected gain for player 1. Therefore, player 1 would choose his strategy to be

$$P(\text{select strategy 1}) = \tfrac{2}{7}$$

$$P(\text{select strategy 2}) = \tfrac{5}{7}$$

$$P(\text{select strategy 3}) = 0$$

$$\text{expected gain} = 6\tfrac{2}{7}$$

Likewise, calculating player 2's strategy for subgame 1 yields

$$P(\text{select strategy A}) = \tfrac{6}{7}$$

$$P(\text{select strategy B}) = \tfrac{1}{7}$$

$$\text{expected loss} = 6\tfrac{2}{7}$$

While this procedure is simple for relatively small $M \times 2$ or $2 \times M$ games, for large $M \times M$ games the number of subgames that results from the decomposition may be extremely large. For large $M \times M$ games, the recommended approach is to formulate the game situation as a linear program as we did in the last section.

# ■ Summary

In this chapter we have looked at the fundamentals of game theory restricted to two-person, zero-sum games. We have discussed the minimax (maximin) principle for strategy selection, the dominance principle for reducing problem size, and a method for resolving the conflict that occurs when no equilibrium strategy exists. We also presented a graphical procedure for analyzing $2 \times 2$ games with mixed strategies, and went on to discuss linear programming and the subgame procedure for decomposing $M \times M$ games into $2 \times 2$ games to facilitate solution.

We have purposefully avoided discussing games with more than two players or games with non-zero-sum payoffs. The mathematics needed to attack these problems is generally beyond the scope of this text, and successful applications of these structures have not been documented. Still, there is substantial theoretical value in these developments which aids understanding of other decision problems, so the reader interested in knowing more about these more complicated game structures is encouraged to seek out the literature.

# ■ Glossary of terms

**dominance:**   When one strategy is always preferrable to another strategy regardless of the opponent's actions.

**equilibrium point:**   See "saddle point."

**mixed strategy:**   A strategy made up of probabilities of choosing each available strategy on repeated plays of the game; used where no pure strategy exists.

**pure strategy:**   The situation where each player's strategy choice results in the same payoff, such that in subsequent plays of the game the players would again choose the same strategies over and over.

**saddle point:**   The optimal point in a pure strategy situation.

**subgame:**   A game matrix arrived at by decomposing a larger matrix.

**two-person game:**   A game with only two players.

**value of the game:**   The value representing the optimal gain to one player and the optimal loss to the other player.

**zero-sum game:**   When the sum of one player's gain and the other player's loss is zero.

# ■ Review questions

1. Discuss the criteria used to categorize games. For which categories has the majority of work been done?

2. Explain the maximin (minimax) criterion for solving games.

3. Explain the concept of equilibrium as it relates to a game with a pure strategy.

4. Describe the principle of dominance in games.

5. If a game with a mixed strategy is played only once, what does this do to the concept of game value?

6. Explain the restrictions on the size game that may be solved graphically.

7. Describe the steps involved in formulating a linear program for a game. Could LP be used in a situation where a pure strategy exists?

8. How many $2 \times 2$ subgames are contained within a $4 \times 4$ game?

## ▪ True/false questions

1. The most important aspect of game theory is the understanding it provides for other decision problems.

2. In a game, one player's gain always represents another player's loss.

3. The major assumption in two-person, zero-sum games is that each player must make his or her strategy decision without any significant knowledge as to the options facing the opponent.

4. In a zero-sum game, the value of the game is always the same to both players.

5. All zero-sum games have a saddle point.

6. It is possible that the identification of dominance could be sufficient to solve a game.

7. The main concept underlying mixed strategies is that of expected gain and loss.

8. In a mixed strategy situation, one player will always benefit at the expense of the other in comparison to a maximin (minimax) solution.

9. We can not solve any games graphically where either player faces more than two strategy alternatives.

10. The main advantage to formulating a game as a linear program is that we can solve games with more than two players.

11. The linear programming formulations for the two players in a two-person game will always bear a primal-dual relationship to each other.

12. Subgames are a type of adversarial training exercise that the Navy uses to teach strategy to ship captains.

## ▪ Problems

1. Given the game matrix:

|  |  | Player 2 Strategies | |
|---|---|---|---|
|  |  | A | B |
| Player 1 Strategies | 1 | 25 | 46 |
|  | 2 | 23 | 17 |

**a.** Apply the maximin (minimax) criterion and identify the optimal strategy for each player.

**b.** Does this game have a pure strategy? Why?

**c.** Are any of the strategies in the matrix dominant? Explain.

2. Given the game matrix:

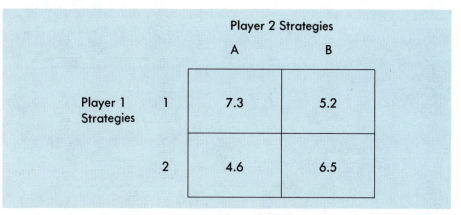

|  |  | Player 2 Strategies | |
|---|---|---|---|
|  |  | A | B |
| Player 1 Strategies | 1 | 7.3 | 5.2 |
|  | 2 | 4.6 | 6.5 |

**a.** Apply the maximin (minimax) criterion and identify the optimal strategy for each player.

**b.** Does this game have a pure strategy? Why?

**c.** Are any of the strategies in the matrix dominant? Explain.

3. American Marketing competes directly with one other firm, Consolidated Marketing, for market share of a particular product. Consolidated has historically controlled the market, but American is aggressively trying to take away some of Consolidated's share. The following payoff table represents the monthly sales in thousands that American stands to gain (and Consolidated stands to lose) given different combinations of marketing strategy that each firm may adopt:

|  |  | Consolidated's Strategies | | |
|---|---|---|---|---|
|  |  | A | B | C |
|  | 1 | 15 | 17 | 16 |
| American's Strategies | 2 | 19 | 24 | 18 |
|  | 3 | 22 | 18 | 16 |

a. Determine the optimal strategy for each player.
b. Does this game have a pure strategy or mixed strategies? Why?
c. Are any of the strategies in the matrix dominant? Explain.

4. Suppose that the payoffs for Problem 3 were modified as follows:

**Consolidated's Strategies**

|                          |   | A  | B  | C  |
|--------------------------|---|----|----|----|
|                          | 1 | 24 | 14 | 19 |
| American's Strategies    | 2 | 15 | 20 | 21 |
|                          | 3 | 22 | 23 | 18 |

This game now has no saddle point.

a. Determine the initial strategy each player would adopt.
b. For subsequent plays of the game, each player would switch his or her strategy, always attempting to benefit from the last move by his or her opponent. For several subsequent steps, explain the strategy switching that would occur.

5. Consider the following mixed strategy game:

**Player 2 Strategies**

|                     |   | A   | B   |
|---------------------|---|-----|-----|
|                     | 1 | 120 | 145 |
| Player 1 Strategies | 2 | 130 | 115 |
|                     | 3 | 118 | 160 |

a. Determine the initial strategy each player would adopt.

b. For several subsequent steps, explain the strategy switching that would result as each player attempts to benefit from the last move of his or her opponent.

6. Pat Filibuster and Mike Porkbarrel are both running for the office of mayor of Smallville. Mike currently holds the lead in the polls, and can probably hope only to hang on to that lead at best. Pat hopes to gain on Mike in the polls and is preparing to go on the offensive with a change in campaign strategy. The following matrix gives the percentage gains to Pat (losses to Mike) in the polls for two strategies facing each of the candidates:

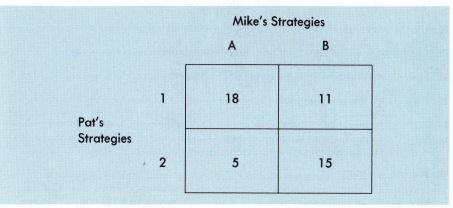

|  | | Mike's Strategies | |
|  | | A | B |
|---|---|---|---|
| Pat's Strategies | 1 | 18 | 11 |
|  | 2 | 5 | 15 |

a. Determine the initial strategy each candidate would adopt.

b. Does this game have a pure strategy?

c. Use the expected gain/loss method to determine the optimal mixed strategy for each of the candidates.

7. The Unified Miner's Union (UMU) is getting ready to negotiate a new contract with Deep Shaft Mining and Drilling. The union has three different contract proposals that they are willing to submit (different combinations of pay raises, benefits, etc.), and Deep Shaft has two proposals they are willing to discuss. The following matrix represents the gains by the union in millions of dollars (cost to the company) for each of the proposal combinations:

|  | | Deep Shaft's Strategies | |
|  | | A | B |
|---|---|---|---|
| UMU's Strategies | 1 | 35 | 50 |
|  | 2 | 30 | 42 |
|  | 3 | 40 | 25 |

a. Determine the initial strategy each player would adopt.

b. Use the expected gain/loss method to determine the optimal mixed strategy for the union and for the company.

8. Use the graphical solution procedure to solve for the optimal mixed strategies for the game in Problem 2.

9. Use the graphical solution procedure to solve for the optimal mixed strategies for the game in Problem 5. What are the limitations of using graphical analysis on a problem like this one?

10. Use the graphical solution method to find the optimal strategies for Problem 6.

11. Use the graphical solution method to find the optimal strategies for Problem 7.

12. Formulate a linear programming model for finding the optimal strategies in Problem 4.

13. Formulate a linear programming model for finding the optimal strategies in Problem 5.

14. Formulate a linear programming model for finding the optimal strategies in Problem 6. Solve the LP model using the simplex method and transform the solution so that it can be compared to the solution by the expected gain/loss method in Problem 6.

15. Formulate a linear programming model for finding the optimal strategies in Problem 7. Solve the LP model using the simplex method and transform the solution so that it can be compared to the solution by the expected gain/loss method in Problem 7.

16. Hi-Tech Industries is in the process of bidding against General Technology, its major competitor, for several government contracts. The following matrix indicates the gain to Hi-Tech and loss to General Technology in millions of dollars of contract awards for each of the bidding strategy combinations facing the companies:

|  |  | General Technology's Strategies | |
|---|---|---|---|
|  |  | A | B |
|  | 1 | 30 | 28 |
| Hi-Tech's Strategies | 2 | 36 | 22 |
|  | 3 | 25 | 29 |

Use the method of subgames to find the optimal strategies for the two players.

17. Use the method of subgames to solve for the optimal strategies in Problem 5.

# Queuing Analysis: Waiting-Line Problems

## ■ Introduction

At one time or another in their lives, most individuals in our modern society have waited in line for service of some sort. Waiting could include (but definitely is not limited to) such situations as

> waiting in a line to be checked out of a grocery store
>
> waiting in line at a gas station to purchase gasoline
>
> waiting to be answered when one telephones the utility company to discuss the power bill
>
> waiting for a teller in a bank to transact some financial business
>
> standing in line to buy tickets to a big sporting or entertainment event.

Such a list could be extended indefinitely and still not exhaust all possible situations where people wait in a line, or **queue,** to be serviced. But waiting lines involve more than just people. Although we probably have not considered such lines, when a machine breaks down and requires maintenance, it too must wait in a queue for the service person to reach it. So we can say that a waiting line, or queue, forms when some unit (person, machine, etc.) requires service and the service is not instantly forthcoming.

*queue*

Since waiting lines are so prevalent in our modern society, it is not surprising that a field of knowledge developed from the study of queues. This field of knowledge, commonly referred to as *queuing theory*, traces its beginnings to a Danish telephone engineer, A. K. Erlang, who in 1910 did the early work on queuing problems. Erlang was interested in the problems callers encountered at a telephone switchboard.

In this chapter, we will often speak of a **queuing system.** By this we refer to all components that make up the queuing arrangement—units demanding service, the actual waiting line, the service facilities, and the units leaving after service.

*queuing system*

Unlike a single model such as linear programming, queuing theory encompasses a very large group of models with each relating to a different type of queuing situation. However, all of these models have some things in common. First, these models do not attempt to "solve" queuing problems; rather, they describe the queue by computing the *operating characteristics* of the waiting line. Operating characteristics include such things as the average number of units waiting to be served and the average time a unit waits to be served. To compute the operating characteristics, the user must specify certain *parameters* of the queuing system, such as how the units arrive to be serviced and how the actual service is handled. Description rather than optimization is the objective of queuing models, and any optimization that takes place must be done by the user varying the system parameters to obtain different sets of operating characteristics. The set of operating characteristics that most closely matches the user's needs defines the "best" system structure. For this reason, queuing models are usually *descriptive* rather than *normative*.

Since many of the parameters of queuing models are not known with certainty, queuing models are *stochastic* rather than *deterministic*. Such parameters as arrival rates or service rates are described by probability distributions; so average or expected values are employed in the queuing model. At the same time, queuing models are *static* and *nonlinear* rather than *dynamic* and *linear* because we assume that the parameters do not vary with time and, as we shall see, changes in the operating characteristics are not proportional to changes in the model parameters.

# ■ Case
## Guarantee Bank and Trust Company, Inc.

Mr. James T. Smith of the Guarantee Bank and Trust Company is the new Assistant Vice-President for Customer Service at the bank. His first assignment is to investigate a new arrangement to shorten the waiting time for customers to be processed by the drive-in tellers. Usually, in selecting a drive-in teller the customer selects the shortest line. But this procedure does not always work well since, due to differences in transaction times, some lines tend to move faster than others. Quite often, then, a customer who picks a short line must wait an inordinate period of time if the customers in front of him have long transactions.

Mr. Smith has investigated ways in which other banks handle the problem. One method he found popular involves having all drive-in customers wait in a single line. Each customer then moves to the first drive-in teller who becomes available when his/her car reaches the front of the line. In comparing the present with the proposed procedure, the criterion for deciding whether to implement the single-line operation will be the average time a customer spends waiting in line. If the new single-line method is found to yield a shorter average waiting time, then it will be adopted without further investigation into other procedures. Both procedures are illustrated in Figure 20-1.

In Figure 20-1a, we see drive-in customers in four individual lines waiting for service, while in Figure 20-1b, the drive-in customers wait in a single line for one of four drive-in tellers to become free for service.

Mr. Smith's prior study of the problem has shown that the customers arrive at an average rate of 16 per hour and each drive-in teller handles transactions at an average rate of 8 per hour.

To analyze the case, we need to determine the operating characteristics of each queuing system. Since a great deal of research has been done on queuing models, a sensible starting point for the analysis would be to determine if either arrangement fits one of the available models. If it does, then we may simply apply the known model to the situation at hand to compute the desired operating characteristics of the queuing system.

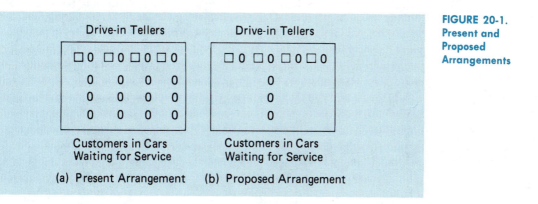

**FIGURE 20-1.**
**Present and Proposed Arrangements**

## ■ Classification of queuing systems

In order to check whether or not a given queuing situation fits a known model, we need a method of classifying waiting lines. Such a classification must answer questions such as the following:

1. Does the queuing system have only one point of service or are there multiple service points in sequence?

2. Is there only one service facility or are there multiple service facilities from which a unit can receive service?

3. Do the units that require service arrive in any pattern or do they arrive randomly?

4. Does the time required for service occur in any pattern or does the service take random lengths of time?

### *Number of stages and number of service channels*

To answer questions 1 and 2, we must first decide whether a unit must pass through one service point or through a series of service points. If we have the former case, then there is only *input* to the service point and *output* from the service point. This is called a *single-stage* system. If the output from the first service point becomes the input to the second service point and so on, we have a *multiple-stage* queuing system, which is much more complex and difficult to analyze than the single-stage system. For this reason we will consider single-stage systems only.

Both queuing structures are shown diagramatically in Figure 20-2. Note that in the multiple-stage system, the output of the first stage is the input to the second stage, and so on down through the stages.

If we restrict ourselves to single-stage systems, then we need to be concerned only with the number and arrangement of waiting lines at a single stage. Three important cases of single-stage systems are shown in Figure 20-3. The first case (a) is a single-service facility, or **channel** as it is often termed, with a single waiting line. The second case (b) has multiple service facilities or channels and multiple waiting lines. These are essentially single lines in parallel and may be analyzed as such. This is the present system at the bank. The third case (c) is a single waiting line serviced by

*channel*

**FIGURE 20-2.**
**Single- and**
**Multiple-Stage**
**Systems**

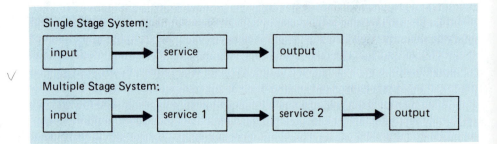

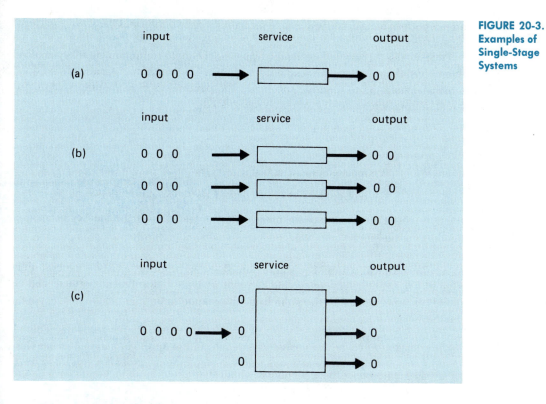

FIGURE 20-3.
Examples of
Single-Stage
Systems

multiple service facilities. This is the proposed arrangement for the bank. In both cases (b and c), it is usually assumed that all service facilities are of equal efficiency.

## Kendall notation

Arrival and service rates are generally not known with certainty but are stochastic, or probabilistic, in nature. That is, the arrivals and service times must be described by probability distributions, and the probability distributions chosen must describe the manner in which the arrivals or service times occur.

Three fairly common probability distributions are employed in queuing:

1. Markovian
2. deterministic
3. general

A *Markovian* distribution (from A. A. Markov, a mathematician who recognized memoryless events) is used to describe random occurrences, that is, occurrences that can be said to have no memory of past events. A *deterministic* distribution is one in which the events occur in a constant, unchanging manner. Finally, a *general* distribution would be any other probability distribution. It is quite possible for the arrival pattern to be described by one probability distribution and the service pattern by another.

To allow researchers and students in queuing theory to communicate easily among themselves about various queuing systems, Kendall, a British mathematician, set up a shorthand notation to describe succinctly the parameters of a queuing system. In **Kendall notation** a queuing system is designated

*Kendall notation*

A/B/C

where      A is replaced by a letter that denotes the arrival distribution

B is replaced by a letter that denotes the service distribution

C is replaced by a positive integer that denotes the number of service channels.

Kendall notation also uses M = Markovian, D = deterministic, and G = general. For example, a queuing system having random arrivals, deterministic service, and 3 service channels would be shown in Kendall notation as

M/D/3

In all cases, we assume there is only one input line.

## Other considerations

There are obviously attributes other than those discussed above that must be taken into consideration when one is discussing a queuing system. These include

size of the population from which those that will enter the queuing system are selected (the "calling population")

the manner in which units arrive to enter the queuing system, e.g., singly or in groups

the queue discipline, or order in which units are served (are units served in the order in which they arrive—first-come–first-served—or is there another priority system for service?)

whether or not units *balk* at the length of the line and do not enter the system

whether they *renege* and leave the system after they have gotten into line

whether or not there is enough room for all arrivals to join the waiting line

The various answers to questions such as these, along with the different probability distributions and number of service channels, serve to generate a host of different types of queuing systems to be analyzed. In this introductory discussion of queuing, we will restrict ourselves to the simplest cases; in particular we will assume:

> an infinite calling population
>
> arrivals come individually
>
> arrivals are serviced in a first-come–first-served manner
>
> arrivals neither balk nor renege at the length of the waiting line
>
> there is always enough room for the waiting line to form

## ■ Analysis of Guarantee Bank and Trust Company case

Returning to Guarantee Bank's problem, we need to classify both present and proposed queuing systems to see if they can be described by any known models. If a model exists, then the operating characteristics of each queuing system can be calculated and compared according to Mr. Smith's criterion, average customer waiting time, to determine the best system.

### Comparison of present and proposed systems

The two systems are similar in several ways. First, they are definitely one-stage systems. Second, they share the same calling population and the arrival pattern is the same for both systems. Finally, the service pattern will also be the same once a customer reaches a drive-in teller.

We also need to consider the other questions, i.e., size of population, arrival of individuals, service pattern, and balking or reneging. For the Guarantee Bank and Trust Company drive-in teller situation, we can assume the population of customers is so large that for all practical purposes it can be considered infinite. Since customers arrive in cars, they will usually come individually. Also, since the customers are in cars, they will be served on a first-come–first-served basis and they cannot renege once they are in the teller line. While they could balk, this is not the usual case since most people need to transact their business and will usually wait to have this done.

The major difference between the two systems lies with the arrangement of service facilities. Referring to Figure 20-3, the present system is made up of four lines in parallel (Figure 20-3b) while the proposed system is made up of a single line with four service centers (Figure 20-3c). We can classify the present system as four distinct but identical single-channel queuing systems and the proposed system as a single system with multiple service centers. The current system will work as four parallel queues since once a car has entered a line, it cannot easily change lines.

### Patterns of arrival and service

Let us now examine arrival and service patterns. It seems logical to assume that arrival of customers will be random since the majority of customers arriving to transact business with a drive-in teller will usually have no connection with other customers wishing to do the same. It might also be assumed that service times are random, since most transactions will have no connection with other transactions. Some transactions will take only a short time while others may be quite lengthy, but overall the distribution of service times will be random. Currently, there are four separate input lines, each having equal inputs. That is, the incoming customers will, on the average, distribute themselves equally among the four lines. On the service side, there are four single servers, each having an equal service rate. In this case, there are four queues that would be classified in Kendall notation as M/M/1 queues—that is, random input, random service time, and one service channel.

For the proposed system, we can still assume random arrivals and random service times, but with four service channels. So, in Kendall notation, this situation would be described as an M/M/4 queue.

We will consider in this chapter primarily M/M/1 and M/M/S queuing systems (where S is an integer greater than one indicating the number of service channels). We emphasize these types of queues for two major reasons. First, occurrence of random input rate and service time is extremely common in day-to-day situations. Second, operating characteristics of M/M/1 and M/M/S queues are easy to compute. We also briefly examine other queuing systems.

# ■ M/M/1 queuing characteristics

### Random arrivals

Examples of random arrivals are commonly found in everyday situations, since arrivals will be random any time one arrival does not affect other arrivals. A classic example of random arrivals is calls coming to a telephone switchboard or an emergency service.

*Poisson distribution*

Random occurrences of a special type have been found to be described by a well-known discrete probability distribution, the **Poisson distribution.** This special type of random arrivals assumes two characteristics about the input stream. First, arrivals are assumed to be completely independent of each other or the state of the system. Second, the probability of a given arrival during a specific time period does not depend on when the time period occurs but rather only on the length of the interval. Such occurrences are said to be *memoryless*. If we know the average number of occurrences per time period, we may calculate probabilities about the number of events that will occur in a given time period by using known properties of the Poisson distribution. In particular, if there is an average of $\lambda$ arrivals in a time period $T$, the probability of $n$ arrivals in the same time period is given by

$$P[n \text{ arrivals in the time } T] = \frac{e^{-\lambda T}(\lambda T)^n}{n!} \tag{20.1}$$

where         $e = 2.71828$

$$n! = (n)(n-1)(n-2)\ldots(2)(1)$$

For example, if there is an average of 6 random arrivals per hour, the probability that there will be only 3 arrivals during an hour is given by

$$P[3 \text{ arrivals in one hour}] = \frac{e^{-6}(6)^3}{3!} = .0892$$

### Random service times

As with random arrivals, the occurrence of random service times that are memory-less is a fairly common event in everyday waiting-line situations. And as with random arrivals, memoryless random service times are described by a probability distribution. The difference between random arrivals and random service times is that random service times are described by a continuous distribution while the arrivals are described by the discrete Poisson distribution. If service times are random in length, the **negative exponential distribution** describes the service times. If $\mu$ is the average service rate, that is, the inverse of the average service time, then this distribution is given by

*negative exponential distribution*

$$f(t) = \mu e^{-\mu t} \tag{20.2}$$

We can use this formula to compute the probability that the service will take longer than some specified length of time $T$. That is,

$$P(\text{service takes longer than } T) = P(t > T)$$

where $t$ = service time. Using the negative exponential, we find

$$P(t \leq T) = 1 - e^{-\mu T} \tag{20.3}$$

which shows that

$$P(t > T) = e^{-\mu T}$$

since

$$P(t > T) = 1 - P(t \leq T) \tag{20.4}$$

### Comments on probability distributions

The previously discussed Poisson and negative exponential distributions can be thought of as being *dual distributions*. That is, if arrivals occur according to the Poisson distribution, then the *time between arrivals* (the interarrival time) will be distributed according to the negative exponential distribution. This says that if

$$P(0 \text{ arrivals in time } T) = \frac{e^{-\lambda T}(\lambda T)^0}{0!} = e^{-\lambda T} \tag{20.5}$$

where        $0! = 1$

then this is equivalent to

$$P(\text{first arrival is after time } T) = e^{-\lambda T} \tag{20.6}$$

So when the *service time* distribution follows a negative exponential distribution, the *number of services* follows a Poisson distribution. Thus, random occurrences and random times between occurrences are equivalent. We see examples of both the Poisson and the negative exponential distribution in Figure 20-4.

An important property of randomness is that occurrences tend to clump together. Contrary to intuition, occurrences do not occur evenly, but rather in groups. Anyone who has worked in a situation where customers arrive randomly will testify to this. The fact that we are working with average rates does not guarantee that each event will occur at this rate during any given period of time; but, on the average, this rate occurs in the long run.

## Steady-state conditions

*steady-state conditions*

In many queuing situations, there is a start-up period at the beginning of the period under study. This start-up period has many transient characteristics that are not similar to the long-run average values found when the queuing system has settled down. An example of a transient period is the initial rush of customers into a bank when the doors first open. We are not interested in this period. We want to investigate the long-run average characteristics that occur when the system has reached the *steady state*. These are the so-called **steady-state conditions** we will compute for M/M/1 and M/M/S queues. We look at these steady-state values because they do not depend on the length of time the system has been operating. While it is true that some systems do not ever reach the steady state, many will come close enough that the steady-state characteristics are useful in describing the system.

## Data collection and probability distributions

In order to use a given queuing model we must first validate the model; that is, we must show that the actual queuing situation "fits" that model. In our case, in order to use the M/M/1, we are interested in showing that the arrivals come randomly and that the service times are random in length. To do this, we need to show that the actual arrival rate fits the Poisson distribution and that the actual service time fits the negative exponential distribution. First, we must collect the data on arrivals and

FIGURE 20-4.
Distribution
Patterns

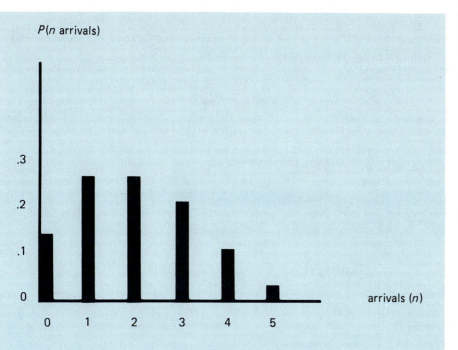

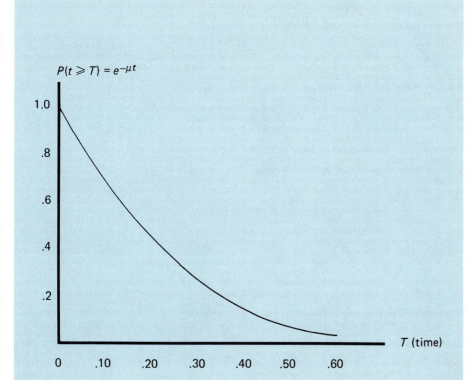

service times. Then we can use a well-known statistical technique called the Chi-Squared ($\chi^2$) Goodness-of-Fit Test to determine if the data do indeed match the Poisson and negative exponential distributions.

To fit a particular model, say M/M/1, we need to gather data on the average arrival rate, $\lambda$, and the average service time, $1/\mu$. To find the average arrival rate, we keep a tally of the number of arrivals per unit of time, hour, day, or whatever. Then it is a fairly simple matter to compute the average over all periods for which data have been collected. Of course, care must be taken to ensure that the arrival rate is not fluctuating so greatly as to make the use of a single value of $\lambda$ unrealistic.

Measuring service times is harder, since we cannot simply count the number of instances of service that occur during a period. Obviously, in the long run, this number will always be equal to the arrival rate, so it would not be a valid measure of the average service time. We must time the service instances individually. Then these times can be used to compute an average service time, $1/\mu$.

## Assumptions for M/M/1 queues

In order to use an M/M/1 queuing model, we must assume Poisson arrivals and negative exponential service distribution. To derive characteristics for this type of waiting line, we must also make several other assumptions. First there must be only one service channel, which arrivals enter one at a time. Second, it is assumed that there is an infinite population from which arrivals originate. It is also assumed that there is infinite room to hold arrivals waiting for service. Finally, we assume that arrivals are served on a first-come–first-served basis (also known as first-in–first-out, or FIFO). The following list includes all of the assumptions for the M/M/1 queue:

> random single arrivals (Poisson distribution)
>
> random service times (negative exponential distribution)
>
> steady-state situation exists
>
> single-service channel
>
> infinite calling population
>
> infinite waiting room
>
> first-come–first-served service discipline
>
> no balking
>
> no reneging

We have already discussed the first three assumptions in detail. The fourth assumption, the single-service channel, is self-explanatory. The next two assumptions, infinite calling population and infinite waiting room, simply mean that customers will always be arriving and that adequate room exists for these arrivals to wait. These assumptions insure that the waiting line situation does not become complicated by dependence between arrivals or arrivals leaving the system for lack of room in which to wait in line. The first-come–first-served assumption insures that later arrivals are not served sooner than earlier arrivals.

## *Operating characteristics for M/M/1 queues*

To compute the operating characteristics of an M/M/1 queue, we first should note that if $\lambda$ = average arrival rate and $\mu$ = average service rate, then $\lambda$ must be less than $\mu$. Otherwise, the average arrivals will outnumber the average number being served, and the number of units waiting will become infinitely large. If we let $\rho = \lambda/\mu$, we can term $\rho$ the **utilization factor.** This value, $\rho = \lambda/\mu$, is the *average fraction of time that the system is busy* (busy is defined as one or more units waiting and/or being served). Note that $\rho$ can also be looked upon as the *average number of units being served at any point in time*. In terms of probability,

*utilization factor*

$$P_W = \text{probability of the system being busy}$$

$$= \frac{\lambda}{\mu} = \rho \qquad (20.7)$$

Then the probability that the system is idle, $P_0$, can be found by

$$P_0 = 1 - P_W = 1 - \lambda/\mu = 1 - \rho \qquad (20.8)$$

From this, we can find the *probability of n units in the system, $P_n$,* by

$$P_n = (P_0)(\lambda/\mu)^n = P_0\rho^n \qquad (20.9)$$

where $n$ is any nonnegative integer. This crucial result allows us to compute operating characteristics of the waiting lines.

The first operating characteristic we will compute is the *average number of units in the system*, either waiting or being served. We will call this average number of units $L$. The average or expected value for a discrete probability distribution is given by

$$E(X) = \sum_{X=0}^{\infty} XP(X)$$

Thus the expected number of units in the system is given by

$$L = \text{expected number of units in the system}$$

$$= \sum_{n=0}^{\infty} nP_n = \sum_{n=0}^{\infty} nP_0\rho^n$$

so

$$L = \frac{\rho}{1-\rho} = \frac{\lambda}{\mu - \lambda} \qquad (20.10)$$

We can now use $L$, the expected number of units in the system, to compute all other desired characteristics. First, we would like to know the *average number of units that are waiting to be served* or $L_q$. Since $L$ is the average number of units either waiting or being served, and $\rho$ is the average number of units being served at any one time, then $L = L_q + \rho$. From this it is easy to see that

$$L_q = L - \rho$$

or

$$L_q = \frac{\rho^2}{1 - \rho} = \frac{\lambda^2}{\mu(\mu - \lambda)} \qquad (20.11)$$

Let us now examine waiting time. We will let $W$ be the *average or expected time that a unit is in the system*. To find $W$, we note that if $L$ is the expected number of units in the system and $\lambda$ is the average number of units that arrive to be served per time period, then the average time that any arriving unit has to be in the system is given by

$$W = \text{expected time a unit is in the system}$$

$$= \frac{L}{\lambda} = \frac{1}{\mu - \lambda} \qquad (20.12)$$

Similarly, the *expected or average time a unit has to wait before being served*, $W_q$, is given by

$$W_q = \frac{L_q}{\lambda} = \frac{\lambda}{\mu(\mu - \lambda)} \qquad (20.13)$$

Note that $W = W_q + 1/\mu$. This says that total time spent in the system, $W$, equals waiting time ($W_q$) plus service time ($1/\mu$).

## Illustrative example

Before turning our attention to the Guarantee Bank and Trust case, let us look at a simple example of an M/M/1 queue. Let $\lambda = 20$ units per hour and $\mu = 30$ units per hour so that $\rho = 2/3 < 1$. We can now compute the characteristics of this queuing system using equations (20.7)–(20.13). First

$$P_W = \text{probability of the system being busy}$$

$$= \rho = 2/3$$

Then

$$P_0 = \text{probability the system is idle}$$

$$= 1 - \rho = 1/3$$

And

$P_n$ = probability of $n$ units in the system

$= P_0(\rho)^n$

$= (1/3)(2/3)^n$

In Figure 20-5, we have graphed the probability distribution for values of $n = 0, 1, 2, \ldots$ that is, $P_n = (1/3)(2/3)^n$. Note that the probability of 0 units in the system, $P_0$, is always greater than $P_n$ for any $n > 0$. We have also marked the average number of units in system $L$. This value is found by

$L$ = expected number of units in the system

$= \dfrac{\rho}{1 - \rho}$

$= \dfrac{2/3}{1 - 2/3} = 2$ units

So there will be an average of 2 units in the system.

Using equation (20.11) we can compute $L_q$:

$L_q$ = expected number of units waiting to be served

$= L - \rho = \dfrac{\rho^2}{1 - \rho}$

$= 2 - 2/3 = 4/3$

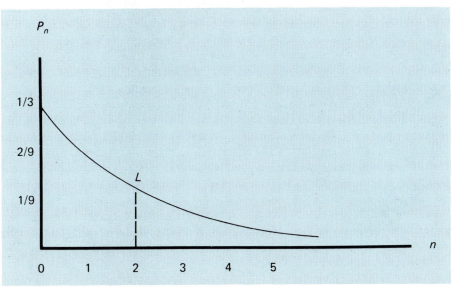

**FIGURE 20-5.**
**Distribution of $P_n$**

On the average, then, there will be 4/3 units waiting to be served and 2/3 of a unit being served.

We can compute the average time in the system using equation (20.12):

$$W = \text{expected time a unit spends in the system}$$

$$= \frac{L}{\lambda} = \frac{2 \text{ units}}{20 \text{ units per hour}} = \frac{1}{10} \text{ hour}$$

$$= 6 \text{ minutes}$$

Similarly, the average time a unit spends waiting to be served is given by equation (20.13):

$$W_q = \text{expected time a unit spends waiting to be served}$$

$$= \frac{L_q}{\lambda} = \frac{4/3 \text{ units}}{20 \text{ units per hour}} = \frac{1}{15} \text{ hour}$$

$$= 4 \text{ minutes}$$

Note that since the service rate $\mu = 30$ units/hour, then the service time is $1/\mu$ or $1/30$ hour ($= 2$ minutes). Using this, we can see that

$$W = W_q + 1/\mu$$

$$= 4 \text{ minutes} + 2 \text{ minutes}$$

$$= 6 \text{ minutes}$$

At this point, it is useful to look at the effect of changing the service rate. Above, we found that for $\lambda = 20$/hour and $\mu = 30$/hour, $P_0 = 1 - 2/3 = 1/3$. This says that $1/3$ of the time the system is idle. We might conclude that there is some slack in the system that could be taken up by reducing the service rate by, say, reducing the number of workers in the service facility. To investigate this effect, we have constructed Table 20-1 for various values of $\mu$, the service rate.

From this table, we see that when the idle time decreases from $1/3$ to $1/11$, the average line length increases by a factor of 5 from 2 units to 10 units. We also see that the time a unit spends in the system also increases by a factor of 5, from 6 minutes to 30 minutes. This demonstrates a key characteristic of queuing systems, namely, *idle time is necessary for any queuing system to operate efficiently*. Idle time would not be necessary if the arrivals and service rates were constant, but in the M/M/1 system, arrivals occur randomly so it is necessary to have slack in the system to handle the periods of time when the arrival rate is greater than the average. Otherwise the system would quickly become overloaded by a greater-than-average influx of units requiring service. A nonlinear change in operating characteristics due to a change in parameters is common to queuing models.

**TABLE 20-1.**
**Queuing**
**Characteristics**
**with $\lambda = 20$**

| $\mu$ (units/hour) | $P_0$ | $L$ (units) | $L_q$ (units) | $W$ (minutes) | $W_q$ (minutes) |
|---|---|---|---|---|---|
| 30 | 1/3 | 2 | $1\frac{1}{3}$ | 6 | 4 |
| 28 | 2/7 | $2\frac{1}{2}$ | $1\frac{11}{14}$ | $7\frac{1}{2}$ | $5\frac{5}{14}$ |
| 25 | 1/5 | 4 | $3\frac{1}{5}$ | 12 | $9\frac{3}{5}$ |
| 22 | 1/11 | 10 | $9\frac{1}{11}$ | 30 | $27\frac{3}{11}$ |

## Comments on the Guarantee Bank and Trust case

In the Guarantee Bank and Trust case, drive-in customers arrive randomly at the rate of 16 per hour. Each drive-in teller can handle transactions at the rate of 8 per hour. Service is first-come–first-served, and there is enough room in the parking lot of the bank to hold as many cars as necessary. Since there currently exist four lines in parallel that work independently of one another, we can divide up the input rate equally among the lines. If this is done, we have four lines each with $\lambda = 4$ and $\mu = 8$.

We can now analyze the four drive-in tellers individually and combine the results. In this case, $\rho = 4/8 = 1/2$ and $P_0 = 1 - 1/2 = 1/2$. Therefore,

$$L = \frac{1/2}{1 - 1/2} = \text{an average of 1 car in the system}$$

$$L_q = 1 - 1/2 = \text{an average of } 1/2 \text{ car in line}$$

$$W = 1/4 \text{ hour} = \text{an average of 15 minutes in the system}$$

$$W_q = \frac{1/2}{4} = 1/8 \text{ hour} = \text{an average of } 7\frac{1}{2} \text{ minutes}$$
$$\text{in line for each drive-in teller.}$$

Mr. Smith's criterion for making his decision is the average length of time a customer spends waiting in line. In the present setup, the average time a customer waits for service is $7\frac{1}{2}$ minutes. In a later section we will compare this value with the value resulting from the new system of using one line to feed all four drive-in tellers.

## ■ M/M/S queuing characteristics

The model that assumes random arrivals and random service times for multiple service channels has all of the same assumptions as the single service channel (M/M/1) model except that now there is a single input line feeding multiple service channels with equal service rates. The calculation of waiting-line characteristics for the M/M/S model are quite a bit more complicated than the calculations for the single-channel case, and since we are primarily interested in the implications of these characteristics rather than the formulas necessary to calculate them, we will resort to the use of tables developed from these formulas to make these calculations.

## Operating characteristics

In the M/M/S model, if $\mu$ is the average service rate for each of the $S$ service channels, then we no longer require that $\mu > \lambda$, but $S\mu$ must be greater than $\lambda$ to avoid infinite buildup of waiting lines. In the M/M/S case, the key characteristic that will be used to make all other calculations is the probability that the system is busy. In other words, this is the probability that there are $S$ or more units in the system. In that case, all service channels will be in use, so the system is said to be busy. We write this as

$$P(\text{system busy}) = P(n \geq S) \tag{20.14}$$

and it may be calculated using the formula

$$P(\text{system busy}) = \frac{\rho^S(\mu S)}{S!\,(\mu S - \lambda)} \times P_0 \tag{20.15}$$

where

$$P_0 = 1 \div \left[ \sum_{n=0}^{n=S-1} \frac{1}{n!}\left(\frac{\lambda}{\mu}\right)^n + \frac{1}{S!}\left(\frac{\lambda}{\mu}\right)^S\left(\frac{S\mu}{S\mu - \lambda}\right) \right] \tag{20.16}$$

Finding $P(\text{system busy})$ using equation (20.15) is not difficult given the value for $P_0$ but the calculation of $P_0$ using equation (20.16) is tedious. Rather than having to perform the time-consuming task of calculating $P_0$ each time it is needed, one could develop a table that would provide a $P_0$ value for various values of $\rho$ (i.e., $\lambda/\mu$) and $S$. Such a table is provided for your use in Table A-1 in Appendix A at the end of the text.

We may now use this system characteristic to calculate all other system characteristics. In the M/M/S model, as in the M/M/1 model, we have $L = L_q + \rho$, but here we use the value of $P(\text{system busy})$ to calculate $L_q$:

$$L_q = P(\text{system busy}) \times \frac{\rho}{S - \rho} \tag{20.17}$$

We then calculate $L$:

$$L = P(\text{system busy}) \times \frac{\rho}{S - \rho} + \rho \tag{20.18}$$

In the M/M/S case, as in the M/M/1 case, $W = L/\lambda$ and $W_q = L_q/\lambda$, so we have

$$W = \frac{1}{\lambda}\left[ P(\text{system busy}) \times \frac{\rho}{S - \rho} + \rho \right] \tag{20.19}$$

$$W_q = \frac{1}{\lambda}\left[ P\text{(system busy)} \times \frac{\rho}{S - \rho} \right] \qquad (20.20)$$

All we need to do is to use the parameters that define the particular situation, $\rho$ and $S$, to find a value for $P_0$ in Table A-1. Then this value is used to calculate $P$(system busy) and all other operating characteristics.

## Illustrative example

As an example of the M/M/S model assume there are five service channels with average service rates of $\mu = 6$ and an input rate $\lambda$ of 24 units per hour. This implies that $S = 5$ and

$$\rho = \frac{\lambda}{\mu} = \frac{24}{6} = 4$$

From Table A-1 we find that for an $S = 5$ and $\rho = 4$, $P_0 = .0130$. Then, using equation (20.15), $P$(system busy) $= .5547$. Employing this value, we have

$$L_q = P\text{(system busy)} \times \frac{\rho}{S - \rho}$$

$$= (.5547)\left(\frac{4}{5 - 4}\right) = 2.2188 \text{ units}$$

$$L = 2.2188 + 4 = 6.2188 \text{ units}$$

Using equations (20.19) and (20.20),

$$W = \frac{L}{\lambda} = \frac{6.2188 \text{ units}}{24 \text{ units per hour}} = .2591 \text{ hour}$$

$$W_q = \frac{L_q}{\lambda} = \frac{2.2188}{24} = .0925 \text{ hour}$$

## Comments on the Guarantee Bank and Trust case (continued)

To continue our comparison of multiple single servers (the present situation) with the proposed multiple-service channel setup at Guarantee Bank and Trust, we need first to calculate line characteristics for the latter case using the results for the M/M/S model presented in the previous section.

The proposed system consists of four service channels, all having equal service rates of 8 per hour. The input rate is 16 customers per hour. So the parameters are $\rho = 16/8 = 2$ and $S = 4$. For these values we find $P_0 = .1304$ in Table A-1 and compute $P$(system busy) $= .1739$ using equation (20.15). Using this value of $P$(system busy), we may calculate line characteristics as follows:

$$L_q = P(\text{system busy}) \times \frac{\rho}{S - \rho}$$

$$= (.1739)\left(\frac{2}{4 - 2}\right) = \text{an average of .1739 car in line}$$

$$L = L_q + \rho = \text{an average of 2.1739 cars in the system}$$

$$W = \frac{L}{\lambda} = \frac{2.1739}{16} = \text{an average time in the system}$$
$$\text{of .1359 hour or 8.154 minutes}$$

$$W_q = \frac{L_q}{\lambda} = \frac{.1739}{16} = \text{an average time in line of .0109 hour or .654 minute}$$

If we compare $W_q$ of $7\frac{1}{2}$ minutes for 4 individual lines (the present system at Guarantee) with a $W_q$ of .654 minutes for a single line, we have a drastic improvement in service.

## ■ An economic example

In the Guarantee Bank and Trust Company case, we were concerned with the time that customers waited before being served rather than with the total time a customer is in the system, since the average customer probably does not consider the time being served as time spent waiting. On the other hand, there are very definite examples where the time in the system is the key determinant of service. As an example, consider the Wheat-n-Corn Shipping Company.

The Wheat-n-Corn Shipping Company loads cargo vessels with wheat, corn, oats, and other grains for shipment overseas. The company does *not* own the ships that it loads but simply sells the grain to the shipowner whenever a ship arrives to be loaded. There is no fixed schedule of ship arrivals because arrivals depend on weather, the price of the grain, international conditions, etc., so the ships can be assumed to arrive randomly. Ships arrive at an average rate of one per day. Due to varying vessel capacities and cargo configurations, the company cannot be sure exactly how long it will take to load a ship. At the present time, there is only room for one cargo vessel to be loaded at a time. Also, due to various union agreements, all ship loadings must be done by employees of the Wheat-n-Corn Company and not by the crew of the cargo vessel. This restriction means that while the vessel is waiting to be loaded and while it is being loaded, the crew of the ship is idle. Since the shipowner's profit depends upon a quick turn-around time (the time from arrival to be loaded until the time the vessel is loaded), and since the Wheat-n-Corn Company faces a buyer's market due to the surplus of U.S. grain products, the Wheat-n-Corn Company has agreed to pay each shipowner $1000 per day for each complete day the ship is being loaded *or* waiting to be loaded. This payment is to compensate the shipowner for profit lost while the ship is being loaded at the Wheat-n-Corn dock.

According to company records, a loading team of three men can load ships at the rate of 1/4 of a ship per day on the average. Teams can work together without interference between teams, so the resulting loading rate is given by

$$\text{ships loaded/day} = (\text{number of teams})(\tfrac{1}{4}\text{ ship/day/team})$$

For example, 3 teams could load 3/4 of a ship per day of work. At the present time, the teams work an 8-hour day, 7 days a week, and workers on each team cost the company \$10/hour.

We need to determine how many teams to have available for loading the cargo vessels. We would like to minimize the total costs, that is, the sum of the per-day fee paid to the ships that are in the loading system and the cost of the loading teams.

The problem facing Wheat-n-Corn is one of a trade-off. If a single team is employed, a small labor cost (loading cost) will likely result, but a large dock fee (waiting cost) will be incurred. If a large number of teams is employed, a smaller dock fee will result, but so will high labor costs. The trade-off of loading costs and waiting costs is shown in Figure 20-6.

Since waiting-line models are *descriptive* rather than *normative* models, we cannot solve for the optimal number of teams by using an algorithm. We will have to compute waiting-line characteristics and costs for varying numbers of teams, and then pick the situation yielding the least cost. To aid in this analysis, we can use a tabular approach that lists the numbers of teams, their waiting-line characteristics, and associated costs.

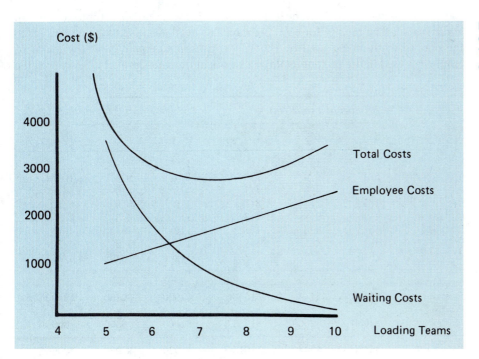

**FIGURE 20-6.**
**Comparison of Total, Employee, and Waiting Costs**

## Solution of example for M/M/1 case

First note that ship arrival rates and loading times are random, and that only one service facility exists; hence, an M/M/1 queuing situation exists. In this case $\lambda = 1$ per day and $\mu = (m)(1/4)$ where $m =$ number of teams. Obviously $m$ must be greater than 4 in order that $\mu > \lambda$. Note also that each team will cost $240 per day ($10 per hour × 8 hours × 3 men). Recall also that the company is paying $1000 per day per ship in the system. So the total daily cost, $TC$, is given by

$$\text{employee costs + ship fees}$$

that is,

$$TC = 240m + 1000L \tag{20.21}$$

Using this relationship, we will now solve for values of $TC$ for various numbers of teams. To do this we need to compute waiting-line characteristics. Results are shown in Table 20-2.

We see that the Wheat-n-Corn Company would minimize costs by employing 8 teams to load the incoming ships. The minimum cost is $2920 per day. The average ship will be in the system for one day and will spend 1/2 of that day waiting to be served.

## Solution of example for M/M/S case

Let us now assume that the Wheat-n-Corn Company has an opportunity to rent an additional loading facility for $500 per day. The available facility is very similar to the one presently being used by the Wheat-n-Corn Company, and the teams of employees used in the present facility can work at the same level of efficiency in the

**TABLE 20-2.**
**Costs for One**
**Loading Facility**

| | Number of Teams (m) | | | | | |
|---|---|---|---|---|---|---|
| | 5 | 6 | 7 | 8 | 9 | 10 |
| $\lambda$ | 1 | 1 | 1 | 1 | 1 | 1 |
| $\mu$ | 5/4 | 6/4 | 7/4 | 8/4 | 9/4 | 10/4 |
| $\rho$ | 4/5 | 4/6 | 4/7 | 4/8 | 4/9 | 4/10 |
| $P_0$ | 1/5 | 1/3 | 3/7 | 1/2 | 5/9 | 6/10 |
| $L$ | 4 | 2 | 4/3 | 1 | 4/5 | 2/3 |
| $L_q$ | 16/5 | 4/3 | 16/21 | 1/2 | 16/45 | 4/15 |
| $W$ | 4 | 2 | 4/3 | 1 | 4/5 | 2/3 |
| $W_q$ | 16/5 | 4/3 | 16/21 | 1/2 | 16/45 | 4/15 |
| Employee costs | $1200 | $1440 | $1680 | $1920 | $2160 | $2400 |
| Waiting costs | $4000 | $2000 | $1333.3 | $1000 | $800 | $666.7 |
| Total costs | $5200 | $3440 | $3013.3 | $2920 | $2960 | $3066.7 |

rented facility. The company wishes to determine whether it would be cheaper to rent the second facility or to stay with the present arrangement.

The two-facility case is an example of an M/M/S queuing situation with $S = 2$. To examine the case, we will assume that equal numbers of teams will be placed in each facility. For this case $\lambda = 1$ and $\mu = (m)(1/4)$ where $m$ = number of teams in each facility. In this situation, we must have

$$\lambda < \mu S \quad \text{or} \quad 1 < (m)(1/4)\,(2)$$

since $\lambda = 1$, then $m > 2$ in each facility.

First, we need to compute

$$P(\text{system busy}) = \frac{\rho^S \mu S}{S!(\mu S - \lambda)} \times P_0$$

for various values of $m > 2$. Then we need to find the waiting-line characteristics and costs for these values of $m$. If the minimum cost for the two-facility arrangement is less than that for the one facility, we recommend that the Wheat-n-Corn Company rent the additional facility.

For the two-facility case, the total daily cost is given by

$$\text{employee cost} + \text{ship fees} + \text{rental costs}$$

or

$$TC = (2)(m)(240) + (L)(1000) + 500 \tag{20.22}$$

Note that the employee cost has been doubled because $m$ teams are used in each facility. Calculations necessary to compute the minimum cost arrangement are presented in Table 20-3.

| | Number of Teams per Facility (m) | | | |
|---|---|---|---|---|
| | 3 | 4 | 5 | 6 |
| $\lambda$ | 1 | 1 | 1 | 1 |
| $\mu$ | 3/4 | 1 | 5/4 | 6/4 |
| $\rho$ | 4/3 | 1 | 4/5 | 2/3 |
| $P_0$ | .1993 | .3333 | .4286 | .5050 |
| $P(\text{system busy})$ | .5315 | .3333 | .2286 | .1683 |
| $L_q$ | 1.0630 | .3333 | .1524 | .0842 |
| $L$ | 2.3963 | 1.3333 | .9524 | .7509 |
| $W_q$ | 1.0630 | .3333 | .1524 | .0842 |
| $W$ | 2.3963 | 1.3333 | .9524 | .7509 |
| Employee costs | $1440 | $1920 | $2400 | $2880 |
| Ship fees | 2396 | 1333 | 952 | 751 |
| Rental fee | 500 | 500 | 500 | 500 |
| Total costs | $4336 | $3753 | $3852 | $4131 |

TABLE 20-3.
Costs for Two
Facilities

From this table, we see that the least cost configuration for the two-facility case has a cost of $3753 and uses four teams per facility ($m = 4$). This cost is higher than the cheapest configuration using only one loading facility, so it would *not* be advisable for the Wheat-n-Corn Company to rent and staff the additional facility.

## ■ Other queuing models

As we discussed at the beginning of the chapter, there are many types of queuing models other than the M/M/1 and M/M/S models that we have discussed so far. Unfortunately most of the formulas needed to calculate operating characteristics for these other queuing models are too complicated to be presented in a text such as this. We will consider three other cases in this section. These are the M/G/1, M/D/1, and Erlang's Lost Call Formula models.

### The M/G/1 case

The first case we will consider is the situation in which the arrivals are distributed according to the Poisson distribution as in the previous cases but the service times are not necessarily distributed according to the negative exponential distribution. If we consider the case where there is only one channel, we are considering the M/G/1 case, i.e., Markovian arrivals, general service time, and one service channel. Note that this case encompasses the M/D/1 case also.

The reason we can consider the M/G/1 case is that the formulas to use in calculating the operating characteristics are fairly simple. As with the M/M/S case, we cannot calculate $L$, the expected number of units in the system, directly. Instead we must calculate $L_q$, the number of units waiting to be served, and use the result that $L = L_q + \rho$ to find the value of $L$. To calculate $L_q$ we must know the value of the standard deviation of the distribution that does describe the service times, $\sigma$. If the service time distribution is unknown, we cannot determine the operating characteristics. However, if we do know the standard deviation and mean of the service time distribution, the formula for the value of $L_q$ can be found from equation (20.23).

$$L_q = \frac{\lambda^2 \sigma^2 + (\lambda/\mu)^2}{2(1 - \lambda/\mu)} \tag{20.23}$$

Using $L_q$, we can now determine the value of $L$ via (10.24):

$$L = L_q + \rho \tag{20.24}$$

As with the operating characteristics for the M/M/1 and M/M/S cases, we can determine $W$, the expected time in the queuing system, and $W_q$, the expected time before being served, by dividing $L$ and $L_q$ by the value of $\lambda$, that is,

$$W = L/\lambda \tag{20.25}$$

and

$$W_q = L_q/\lambda \tag{20.26}$$

For example, assume that for the Guarantee Bank and Trust case the service times for the drive-in tellers have been found to be distributed according to the normal distribution with a mean, $1/\mu$, of $1/8$ hour and a standard deviation of $1/12$ hour. Using these values together with an arrival rate, $\lambda$, of 4 per hour in equations (20.23)–(20.26), we get:

$$L_q = \frac{4^2(1/12)^2 + (4/8)^2}{2(1 - 4/8)} = \text{an average of .36 person in line}$$

$$L = .36 + .5 = \text{an average of .86 person in the system}$$

$$W_q = .36/4 = .090 \text{ hour or 5.4 minutes in line}$$

$$W = .86/4 = .2150 \text{ hour or 12.9 minutes in line}$$

If we compare these values with those for the M/M/1 case, we find that the M/M/1 values are greater. This is so because the standard deviation of the negative exponential distribution is equal to the mean, i.e., $1/8$, which is greater than the standard deviation of the distribution in our revised example, $1/12$. This higher value of the standard deviation results in a value of $L_q$, .5 person in line, which is greater in the case of the negative exponential distribution than for the normal distribution case.

## *The M/D/1 case*

The case where the service times are deterministic is the M/D/1 case, which is a special case of the M/G/1 case discussed above where the standard deviation is equal to zero. In this case, the value for $L_q$ is found by the following formula:

$$L_q = \frac{(\lambda/\mu)^2}{2(1 - \lambda/\mu)} \tag{20.27}$$

and all other operating characteristics can be found from this value.

For example, assume that Guarantee Bank and Trust has decided to install an automated drive-in teller for those persons who wish only to make either a withdrawal or a deposit. The bank has discussed this automated unit with the manufacturer and has been told that in such cases the service time is *constant* at $7\frac{1}{2}$ minutes (8 per hour). To determine the operating characteristics of this new system, we need to use equation (20.27) to find the value of $L_q$ with the standard deviation set to zero, since there is no variance in the service times:

$$L_q = \frac{(4/8)^2}{2(1 - 4/8)} = .25 \text{ person in line}$$

From this we get

$$L = .25 + .5 = .75 \text{ person in the system}$$

$$W = .25/4 = .0625 \text{ hour or } 3.75 \text{ minutes}$$

$$W_q = .75/4 = .1875 \text{ hour or } 11.25 \text{ minutes}$$

Note that these times are even less than those for the general case. Once again this is the result of the smaller (in this case, zero) standard deviation.

### Erlang's Lost Call Formula

A useful result that does not depend on the probability distributions that describe the arrivals or the service times is known as Erlang's Lost Call Formula after the originator of the study of queuing. This formula allows us to determine the probability that a call coming into a switchboard will be "lost" because the caller receives a busy signal. This formula assumes that the number of lines coming into the switchboard is equal to the number of operators ready to answer calls and is very useful in determining the number of telephone lines needed at an emergency center.

The formula is

$$P(\text{call lost}) = \frac{\dfrac{\rho}{n!}}{\displaystyle\sum_{k=0}^{n} \dfrac{\rho^k}{k!}} \tag{20.28}$$

where $n$ is the number of lines and $\rho = \lambda/\mu$.

As an example of the use of this formula, assume that we have three lines and three operators with an arrival rate of 10 calls per hour and an average length of call of 3 minutes. This gives us an arrival rate, $\lambda$, of 10 and a service rate, $\mu$, of 20, which results in a value of $\rho = .5$. In plugging these values into the Lost Call Formula, we find that the probability of a call not being answered is .050 for three lines and operators.

### ■ Summary

In this chapter, we have looked at the broad field of study known as *queuing theory* and its application to problems in such areas as consumer service and economics. These are but two of the many applications of queuing theory.

We noted that queuing models are *descriptive* and *stochastic*. We also saw that various queuing models are differentiated by the underlying assumptions of each model, and that each model is distinguished by such *parameters* as arrival rate and number of service channels. Using these parameters, *operating characteristics* may be calculated for each model. Since the models are descriptive, optimization can only be carried out by changing the model parameters and recalculating the operating characteristics until the set of parameters is found that best fits the needs of the user.

This process was applied to two well-known queuing models. In Kendall notation, these were the M/M/1 and M/M/S models. In both cases, the arrivals and services are assumed to occur randomly. In the former case, there is only a single service channel while in the latter case there are S service channels. Operating characteristics were given for both cases as functions of the arrival rate, $\lambda$, and service rate, $\mu$. These models were then applied to a consumer service problem and an economic problem to determine the best arrangement of facilities and/or workers.

In addition to the M/M/1 and M/M/S models, we also discussed the M/G/1 and M/D/1 models. The operating characteristics for queuing systems that have Markovian arrivals and general or deterministic service times can be computed using the formulas presented for these models. In the case of the M/G/1 model, it is necessary to know the standard deviation of the service time distribution. We also discussed Erlang's Lost Call Formula, which does not depend on particular arrival or service time distributions and can be used to determine the probability that an incoming call to a switchboard is not answered.

Readers should not think that M/M/1, M/M/S, M/G/1, and M/D/1 are the only queuing models they may ever encounter. On the contrary, in almost every issue of either *Operations Research* or *Management Science*, new work appears on more complex queuing models. Recent examples include work on server queuing systems and on queuing systems under transient rather than steady-state conditions.

This chapter was meant to introduce the fundamental concepts and uses of queuing theory. A list of references is included at the end of the chapter for those who wish to go further into this interesting topic.

## ■ Glossary of terms

**arrival rate ($\lambda$):**   The average number of arrivals per unit of time.

**channel:**   A service facility.

**Kendall notation:**   A shorthand method for describing a queuing system.

**M/D/1:**   A queuing system with random arrivals, constant service time, one service line, and one waiting line.

**M/G/1:**   A queuing system with random arrivals, general service time distribution (for which the standard deviation is assumed known), one service channel, and one waiting line.

**M/M/S queuing system:**   A queuing system with random arrivals, random service, S service channels, and one waiting line.

**multichannel queuing system:**   A queuing system with service facilities arranged in parallel.

**multistage queuing system:**   A queuing system with service facilities arranged in series.

**negative exponential distribution:**   The probability distribution that describes the time between random occurrences.

**operating characteristics:**    Average values that describe how the queuing system performs, e.g., average waiting time.

**Poisson distribution:**    The probability distribution that describes the number of random occurrences in a given time period.

**queue:**    One or more units (people, machines, etc.) waiting to be served.

**queuing system:**    All units either in line to be served or actually being served.

**random arrivals (service):**    Arrivals (service) that occur in such a way that the occurrence of an arrival (service) is in no way affected by other arrivals (service). Often referred to as Markovian arrivals (service).

**service rate ($\mu$):**    The average number of units that could be serviced per unit of time.

**steady-state condition:**    The condition of a queuing system where startup conditions do not affect the calculation of operating characteristics.

**utilization factor:**    The ratio of the average arrival rate ($\lambda$) to the average service rate ($\mu$). This is the fraction of time the system is busy.

# ■ Review questions

1. Discuss why we always assume that $\lambda < \mu$. Can you conceive of a situation where it would be acceptable for $\lambda$ to equal $\mu$?

2. Which of the assumptions of the M/M/1 queuing model do you find the least realistic? Why?

3. Pick an everyday waiting line that you are familiar with and answer the questions on page 614 in order to classify the appropriate queuing model. Write the Kendall notation for the situation you have chosen.

4. In reference to Question 3, what operating characteristic of the model you have chosen is the most important? Why?

5. Name at least one waiting line situation you are familiar with that fits the assumptions of the M/M/1 (or M/M/S) model.

6. With reference to Question 5, discuss data collection and model validation procedures for the situation you selected to discuss.

7. Think of other waiting-line situations that you have encountered that *might* fit each of the following models:

   **a.** M/D/1    **b.** D/M/1    **c.** D/D/1    **d.** M/G/1

# ■ True/false questions

1. Queuing models are both descriptive and deterministic at the same time.

2. The operating characteristics for queuing models are long-run average values rather than values that may actually occur.

3. In a multistage queuing system where the first stage is M/M/1, the arrival pattern to the second stage will be deterministic.

4. A queuing system with parallel lines where customers can switch lines (called "jockeying") can still be modeled as a multiple M/M/1 system.

5. A characteristic of the Poisson distribution is the "clumping" of events.

6. To compute the average service time, it is only necessary to count the number of occurrences per hour and take the reciprocal of this number.

7. The average number of units in the system must always be greater than the average number of units in line.

8. It is possible to remove "slack" from the queuing system by increasing the service rate without adversely affecting the waiting time for customers.

9. In an M/M/S model, the system is not considered "busy" unless all service channels are full.

10. Erlang's Lost Call Formula only works when the arrivals are Poisson and the service times are negative exponential.

# ▪ Problems

1. Using Kendall notation, describe each of the following queuing situations.

   a. Students randomly arriving to use a copy machine where each student makes only one copy.

   b. Bottles coming off an assembly line at a constant rate to be inspected. The inspection time is random in length and there are 4 inspectors.

   c. Students randomly arriving to preregister for fall quarter. The registration time is random in length and there is one advisor available for registering.

2. Customers arrive randomly at a rate of 5 per hour to use an automatic teller machine at a bank. Answer the following questions using Table A-2 in the appendix.

   a. What is the probability that more than 3 customers will arrive for service during a one-hour period?

   b. What is the probability that no customers will require service during a one-hour period?

   c. What is the probability of exactly two customers in an hour? Three customers?

3. Assuming the teller machine handles requests for service randomly at an average rate of 10 customers per hour, answer the following questions using Table A-3 in the appendix.

   a. What is the average length of time to service a customer?

   b. What is the probability that a customer will take longer than 10 minutes to be serviced?

   c. What percent of the customers will be serviced in less than 3 minutes?

4. Assume that for the teller machine in the two previous problems, customers arrive randomly and the time necessary to service a customer is also random. Assume further that the arrival rate is 5 per hour and the service rate is 10 customers per hour. Answer the following questions.

   a. What is the probability that a customer will be serviced immediately upon arrival at the teller machine?

   b. What is the average length of time a customer will spend at the teller machine (both waiting to be served and being served by the teller machine)?

   c. Draw the graph of $P_n$ versus $n$, where $n$ = number of customers in the system. Mark the expected value of $n$ on your graph.

   d. How many customers are, on the average, waiting in line to be served by the teller machine?

5. Discuss each of the following queuing situations as to whether they fit the assumptions of either the M/M/1 or M/M/S model.

   a. A fast-food restaurant with multiple service positions. These positions are opened as the need arises.

   b. A fast-food restaurant with a single service line through which all customers must pass to place and pick up their orders (of varying volume and complexity).

   c. The drive-in window at a bank.

   d. A car wash with a single line leading into multiple wash stalls.

   e. A large grocery store in a college town with multiple check-out counters.

6. The "express" line at the K-Roger Supermarket handles only customers with 12 items or less and, as a result, is much faster for these customers than the regular line. The manager, Wayne Edwards, has studied this line and found that the customers arrive at a random rate of 30 per hour and that, on the average, the time to service one customer is one minute. Assuming the service rate is also random, answer the following questions:

   a. What are $\mu$ and $\lambda$ for the express line?

   b. On the average, how many customers are waiting or being served?

   c. On the average, how long must a customer wait before being checked out?

7. Students arrive randomly at the book counter at the main library at the University of Hard Knocks (school colors are black and blue). At the check-out counter they must open any bags, briefcases, etc., for the attendant to look for stolen books, magazines, or documents. The time required to make this check is random in length due to the differing number of books and bags carried by the students. The average arrival rate has been found to be 20 students per hour and the average time to complete the bag check has been found to be one minute.

   a. What are $\lambda$ and $\mu$ for this problem?

   b. What is the utilization factor?

   c. How long will it take the average student to pass through the bag check?

   d. How many students, on the average, will be waiting in line at any one time?

   e. During what fraction of the time will the bag-check attendant be free to study?

8. The Oconee Drive-In Theatre has three ticket booths, each of which serves a line of customers. The cars arrive at the theatre at a total rate of 90 cars per hour and each booth can service 40 cars per hour. Both arrivals and service are completely random. Based on this information, answer the following questions.

   a. What type of queuing situation is this (be precise)?

   b. What is the probability that if we consider only one of the ticket windows, it will be idle? Will it have three cars being serviced or waiting in line?

   c. What is the average number of cars in each ticket booth's queuing system (waiting and being serviced)?

   d. What is the average length of time a car waits *before* reaching the ticket window?

   e. If the theatre goes to a single line for all ticket sales at the three booths, which operating characteristic do you expect to change the most? Why?

9. The TV Shak computer repair center in McLeod, Montana, handles repair of microcomputers sold by TV Shak. A common repair problem is the alignment of disk drives. As micros arrive at the repair center, they are assigned on a rotating basis to one of three technicians for alignment. For quality control reasons, once a micro is assigned to a tecnician, it will not be reassigned to another. Assuming the arrival and service rates are

random at 30 per month and 2 per day for each technician (20 work days per month), answer the following questions:

a. What will be the average length of time a micro will remain at the service center?

b. On the average, how many micros will each technician have waiting for service at any one time?

c. How would you answer the above questions if an incoming micro went to the first technician available for service rather than being assigned on a rotating basis?

10. The U-Drive-'em Car Rental Company operates its own car wash and cleanup facility to prepare its cars for rental. Cars arrive at the cleanup facility randomly at a rate of 5 cars per day. The rental company has determined that the cars can be cleaned at a rate of $2n$ cars per day where $n$ is the number of persons working on a car. For example, if 4 people are at the shop, the cleanup rate is 8 cars per day. This cleanup procedure has been found to fit the negative exponential distribution. The company pays its workers $30 per day and has determined that the cost of a car not available for rental is $25 per day.

a. Compute the least cost number of employees to hire for the cleanup facility.

b. Compute the operating characteristics $L$, $L_q$, $W$, and $W_q$ for the number of employees chosen.

11. The Ozella Fish Company uses its own shrimp boats to net shrimp, which it then packs for shipment elsewhere. When these boats arrive during the season, they must be unloaded as quickly as possible so that they can return to sea. The production manager of the Ozella Fish Company estimates the cost of a shrimp boat being idle at $50 per hour (this includes wages as well as lost shrimping time). The workers who unload the shrimp boats earn $8 per hour whether working or idle. If the arrival pattern for the shrimp boats is random and the time to unload is also random, what is the least-total-cost number of workmen that Ozella should use to unload the shrimp boats? The shrimp boats arrive at an average rate of one per hour and each workman can unload an average of $\frac{1}{2}$ boat per hour.

12. In a study of a local hamburger emporium known as Sally Jo's, students from the North Avenue Trade School made the following observations: Customers appear to arrive randomly; customers all stand in a single line to place and receive their orders; due to differences in the volume and complexity of the orders, the time to serve each customer is random in length.

   The students then collected data on arrivals and service times. Arrivals were observed for a 1-hour period and the number of arrivals were noted during each 10-minute period during the hour. The results of this check are as follows:

| Internal | Arrivals |
| --- | --- |
| 0–10 min | 14 |
| 10–20 min | 5 |
| 20–30 min | 10 |
| 30–40 min | 8 |
| 40–50 min | 12 |
| 50–60 min | 7 |

For a random sampling of the above arrivals, the service times (in seconds) were as follows:

| | | |
| --- | --- | --- |
| 25 | 20 | 45 |
| 25 | 13 | 52 |
| 35 | 25 | 25 |

| 45 | 25 | 38 |
| 42 | 55 | 45 |
| 15 | 70 | 20 |
| 28 | 30 | 55 |
| 32 | 58 | 65 |
| 10 | 85 | 50 |
| 13 | 10 | 30 |
| 45 | 15 | 30 |

Using the assumption that these arrivals and service times do indeed fit the Poisson and negative exponential probability distributions:

a. calculate the average arrival rate and service rate.

b. determine the following operating characteristics: $P_0$, $L$, $L_q$, $W$, and $W_q$.

13. Father Mulcahy presently uses two confessionals with separate lines to handle the needs of his parishioners. The arrivals have been noted to be random, at an average rate of 30 persons per hour, and the service time tends to be random, since the amount of sin per individual can differ greatly. The average time in the confessional has been found to be 3 minutes. The arrivals have been found to be equally distributed between the two lines. Father Mulcahy is considering going to a system that will use a single line that will feed into both confessionals. The Father wishes to know which system (the present or the proposed), will lead to the shortest average time in the system for his parishioners.

14. The U-Drive-'em Car Rental Company (Problem 10) is considering adding an additional cleanup shop due to an increase in their business. The new arrival rate is 8 cars per day while the cleanup rate for each shop will remain at $2n$ where $n$ = the number of employees in each shop. The company has determined that the additional cost of the new shop is $50 per day.

   a. Under these new conditions, determine whether the U-Drive-'em Company should add the additional facility or not.

   b. Calculate the operating characteristics for the plan you determine to have the least cost.

15. For the Ozella Fish Company (Problem 11), a new opportunity has just arisen. It may rent a neighboring dock for $20 per hour to use in unloading the shrimp boats during the heavy shrimping season. Determine whether it would be profitable for Ozella Fish Company to rent the additional dock space. You may assume that all other values remain the same as in the original problem.

16. The admissions officer at a well-known business school handles M.B.A. applications on a first-come–first-served basis. These applications arrive randomly at a rate of 5 per day. The probability distribution of the service times is such that the standard deviation is $1/10$ day and the mean is $1/9$ day. What is the average time that an application waits to be processed? On the average, how many applications are waiting to be processed at any one time?

17. First National Bank is planning to install a special variety of automatic teller machines in the bookstore at the local junior college. This teller machine will be special in that it will allow only withdrawals (a common need at a college). Since the teller only allows withdrawals, it will have a deterministic service time of 60 seconds. If arrivals are random at 30 per hour, what will be the average time a student will spend in line and in making a withdrawal? On the average, how many students will be waiting to make withdrawals?

**18.** A local hospital is planning a service to the general population. This service will involve providing medical information on various topics to those persons calling the hospital's public information number. The hospital forecasts that there will be approximately 10 calls per hour and these will be random in length. The caller will reach an operator who will attempt to answer the caller's question. Past experience has shown that the average call will last 5 minutes. The hospital wishes to reduce the probability of a caller receiving a busy signal to less than .05 by adding enough telephone lines. There will be only one telephone line per operator. Use Erlang's Lost Call Formula to calculate the number of telephone lines needed to achieve the desired probability level for the hospital.

**21**

# Simulation

## ■ Introduction

If one were to examine the MS/OR literature, it would quickly be noted that **simulation** is one of the most widely used tools in the management-science field. Simulation has been applied to production, inventory control, transportation systems, market strategy analysis, industrial and urban growth patterns, environmental control, and numerous other areas. Simulation, however, differs significantly from other models and techniques. The problems we examined in previous chapters were modeled and solved analytically (mathematically), but we made a number of basic assumptions about the problem environment in order to model the problems. Many of the assumptions required to model problems so they can be solved analytically are not required in simulation; thus, larger and more complex systems can be studied. In many situations, simulation is the only viable means for analysis. For example, the operating characteristics of complex queuing systems can be approximated using simulation but are not amenable to solution by way of analytical methods.

*simulation*

In this chapter, we will focus on the structure and use of simulation models. Specifically, we will

1. give a broad definition of simulation,

2. identify a simulation/modeling framework,

3. identify and define the terminology common to simulation,

4. identify and describe an application of simulation,

5. give a brief overview of some of the more common simulation languages, and

6. identify some of the operational problems that can occur in developing and implementing a **simulation model.**

*simulation model*

Obviously, in a text of this nature, it is impossible to address each of these areas in detail. The material in the chapter should be viewed as an introduction to the area, not a complete coverage.

Before we define what we mean by simulation and describe the framework used in simulation modeling, we will introduce a sample case.

## ■ Case

## B & D Manufacturing, Inc.

Management at B & D Manufacturing, Inc., has noted that the down time on machinery in the production area is causing significant production losses, increasing backlogs, and leading to lost business. Management is of the opinion that the problem can be reduced significantly by employing an adequate number of maintenance personnel. The hourly wage (including fringe benefits) for maintenance personnel is $8. Management feels

that $30 per hour is lost when a machine is not in operation; this cost includes lost profit as well as idle operator cost. B & D needs to determine the optimal number of maintenance personnel. That is, the company needs to know at what point the cost of maintenance personnel balances the expected lost profits and idle operator cost.

The production manager at B & D has collected data on the time between breakdowns. These data are given in Table 21-1. No data were collected on the length of time that maintenance personnel spend repairing a machine; however, the manager provided a rough estimate of service times and associated probabilities shown in Table 21-2.

We will proceed with the solution of B & D's problem after we discuss some simulation concepts and methodology.

**TABLE 21-1.**
**Time Between Machine Breakdowns**

| Time Between Breakdowns (minutes) | Frequency of Occurrence |
|---|---|
| 15 | 7 |
| 16 | 14 |
| 17 | 15 |
| 18 | 28 |
| 19 | 36 |
| 20 | 27 |
| 21 | 15 |
| 22 | 8 |
| Total | 150 |

**TABLE 21-2.**
**Service Time Estimates for Repair of Machinery**

| Service Time (minutes) | Probability |
|---|---|
| 5–15 | .05 |
| 15–25 | .25 |
| 25–35 | .40 |
| 35–45 | .25 |
| 45–55 | .05 |

## ■ Concepts and terminology

### Definition of simulation

A number of different definitions and types of simulation exist. For practical purposes we will define simulation as *the process of developing a model of a problem and estimating measures of the problem's performance by performing sampling experiments on the model.*

For a better understanding of this definition we can examine the relationship between simulation and the models we employed in previous chapters. Simulation differs significantly from the modeling-solution framework emphasized previously. In previous chapters we stressed the formulation and development of mathematical models and the analytical or mathematical solution to the models. In most cases the analytical solutions were in the form of algorithms that yielded "optimal" solutions. Simulation emphasizes neither of these factors—it is a descriptive modeling process as opposed to a normative process. The modeling process associated with simulation generally involves collecting data that describe input and operational factors and defining the interrelationship of the factors (variables), inputs, and other components of the problem being studied. The output from a simulation model is in the form of performance *descriptors*. By exercising the model, the characteristics of the problem can be explored.

It should be noted, as was pointed out in Chapter 1, that simulation can also be employed to generate solutions to models that are impractical to solve analytically. We should also point out that although simulation output is always descriptive in nature, a "search routine" can be included in the simulation model to provide an optimal or *near-optimal* solution. We use the term *near optimal* because the solution may be optimal in terms of the defined model, but this does not guarantee the solution is a global optimal. Optimality in simulation thus may be an approximation of optimality that occurs in mathematical programming.

## Simulation-modeling process

Figure 21-1 is a detailed representation of the simulation-modeling process.

The *first step, problem identification,* involves the collection of data that describe different input variables, identification of system boundaries, definition of problem components and their interrelationships, and so on.

The *second step* of the simulation process, *model formulation,* is concerned with constructing the simulation model and defining the statistical procedures (experimental design) that will be used in exercising the model. Since simulation involves conducting sampling experiments on a model of the real-world system, the results obtained are sample observations or sample statistics. The objective of the statistical analysis is to insure that the problem is adequately addressed statistically, that is, that the number of model conditions and cases examined is sufficient for drawing valid statistical inferences from the results.

Validation, the *third step,* is concerned with assuring that the simulation inputs are adequately modeled and that the model responds to these inputs in a manner similar to the actual (real-world) problem. A number of statistical tests and procedures are used in validation. (Some of these will be examined in detail in later sections of the chapter.) If a given model does not adequately simulate the response of the actual system, then the first two stages (problem identification and model formulation) must be reexamined in order to identify overlooked factors or relationships.

Once the model has been validated, the actual simulation process (analysis) can begin. This involves (1) generating system inputs, (2) exercising the model, and (3) collecting the simulated data. Two items must be addressed in the simulation process. First, for a given set of model conditions, one must be assured that an adequate number of sampling experiments (iterations of the simulation) are performed. Each iteration of the simulation is analogous to a single observation; running $n$ iterations, therefore, is analogous to drawing a sample of size $n$. In statistical terminology, the mean of the $n$ sample items would be $\bar{X}$, the sample mean. If one is to make some

**FIGURE 21-1.
Simulation-model-
ing Process**

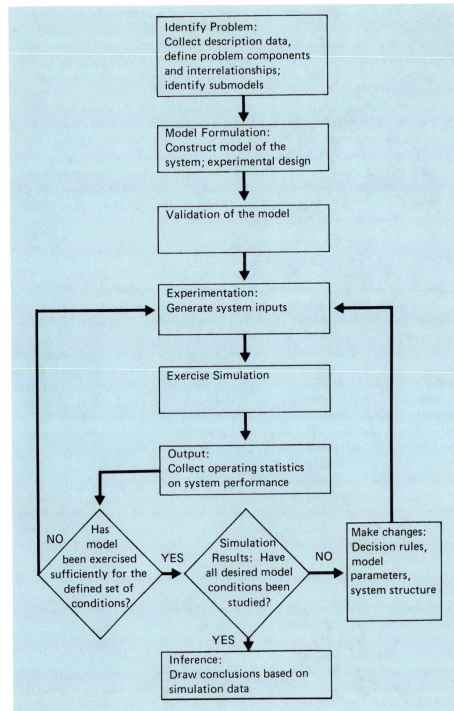

inference about the population mean ($\mu$) for the real-world problem, then an adequate sample size must be employed. Whether or not the sample mean approximates the population mean depends upon the starting condition of the simulation and the number of iterations employed. Comments will be made in the latter part of the chapter regarding how to determine the adequate sample size, i.e., number of iterations of the simulation. The left side of Figure 21-1, containing the feedback loop, highlights the sampling process.

The second item that must be addressed in the simulation process is that if inferences are to be made regarding the functioning of the real-world problem, different conditions and model parameters must be analyzed. The conditions, decision rules, and system structures that are to be examined are identified as part of the experimental design (second step). The right-hand feedback loop in Figure 21-1 depicts the simulation process associated with different design configurations.

## Moving a simulation through time

One must be aware of the different sampling problems involved with simulation, but one must also be aware of the necessity for keeping track of the timing of all events (arrivals, departures, failures, customer orders, shipments, etc.) that occur with the passage of time. In the B & D case, for example, we must keep track of when a breakdown occurs, when a repair person begins the repair activity, and when the repair is complete and the machine is once again available for service. There are two basic approaches for tracking events in a simulation: **fixed-time-increment** (often referred to as time-slicing) and **variable-time-increment** (often referred to as event sequencing).

*fixed-time-increment variable-time-increment*

In fixed-time-increment simulation the system clock is advanced a fixed time increment ($\Delta t$). At each successive point in simulated time, the model is scanned to determine whether any events have occurred in the time increment. When an event is found to have occurred, the model is updated; if no events occur in the time increment, the system clock is incremented again. The major advantage of the fixed-increment method is that the actual sequence of events need not be recorded since the possible occurrence of each event is checked at each time increment. The disadvantage of the method is that the time increments must be short in comparison with the average event time; thus unnecessary scanning can occur since, during some time increments, nothing is happening.

In the variable-time-increment simulation, the system clock is advanced to the time of the next event, regardless of whether it is one day or months away in simulated time. In using the variable-increment method a *time calendar* must be kept for each event, but this is computationally more efficient.

Most simulations employ the variable-time-increment method, and the majority of simulation languages are built upon this concept. We will employ only variable-time-increment simulation in this chapter, but in the section on simulation languages, later in the chapter, we will identify languages that employ both methods.

For a general overview of the simulation process, we will return to the B & D Manufacturing case. But before we examine the case we will identify what we mean by Monte Carlo sampling.

# ■ Monte Carlo sampling

*Monte Carlo sampling*

The origin of modern simulation methods is rooted in what is known as **Monte Carlo sampling,** a technique first employed by J. von Neumann and a number of other researchers in conjunction with military and war efforts during World War II. Since the mid-1940s, the procedure has been successfully applied to a variety of problem areas such as probabilistic financial planning, valuation of insurance, and inventory modeling, to mention a few.

The term *Monte Carlo* refers to a process used to randomly select sample values from a probability distribution. These sample values are then used as input or operational values for a simulation model. Monte Carlo sampling thus is not simulation, but rather is a procedure or method used in conjunction with probabilistic simulation models.

To demonstrate the process, assume that the probability distribution given in Table 21-3 represents the tons of trash collected per day by a city's department of sanitation. The objective is to simulate the tons of trash collected on a particular day.

To begin the process we need to develop a *cumulative probability distribution.* That is, we need to know the probability that the tons of trash collected on a given day is less than or equal to a given value. We can accomplish this by summing the probabilities beginning with the collection of 10 tons per day. Table 21-4 gives the original probability distribution and the associated cumulative probability distribution.

Since for any cumulative probability distribution the probabilities will fall in the range from 0 to 1, a random occurrence (variate) corresponding to a given probability distribution can be generated by selecting a number at random between 0 and 1, finding the range in the cumulative distribution within which the random number falls, and identifying the associated variate. To demonstrate how this is

**TABLE 21-3. Probability Distribution of Tons of Trash Collected per Day**

| Tons of Trash Collected per Day (d) | Probability p(d) |
| --- | --- |
| 10 | .10 |
| 20 | .22 |
| 30 | .25 |
| 40 | .20 |
| 50 | .12 |
| 60 | .07 |
| 70 | .04 |

| Tons of Trash Collected per Day (d) | Probability p(d) | Cumulative Probability P(d) = prob(collection ≤ d) |
|---|---|---|
| 10 | .10 | .10 |
| 20 | .22 | .32 |
| 30 | .25 | .57 |
| 40 | .20 | .77 |
| 50 | .12 | .89 |
| 60 | .07 | .96 |
| 70 | .04 | 1.00 |

**TABLE 21-4.**
**Cumulative Probability Distribution of Tons of Trash Collected per Day**

accomplished, we can develop a cumulative distribution curve for the data given in Table 21-4. Figure 21-2 is such a curve. Note that the length of the vertical line at each step corresponds with the probability value for each collection level. If a number between 0 and 1 is randomly generated (this can be read from a table or derived mathematically), then by determining the location of the randomly gener-

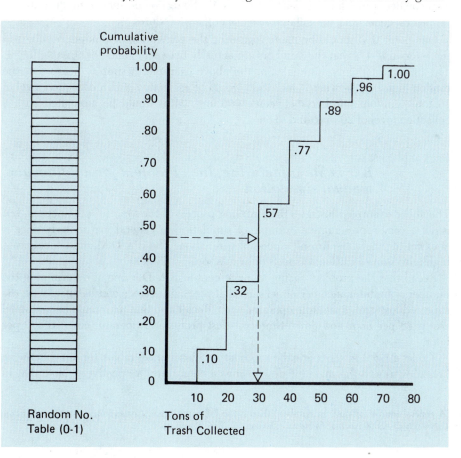

**FIGURE 21-2.**
**Cumulative Distribution Curve of Tons of Trash Collected per Day**

ated number along the vertical axis we obtain an associated sample value for the collection level. For example, assume we generate the random number .4764; the associated collection level would be 30. If we generate the random number .8416, the associated collection level would be 50 tons of trash. For the random number .9434, the associated collection level is 60. If we repeated this sampling process a large number of times (iterations), we would expect to obtain a value of 30 tons for the collection level 25% of the time, a collection value of 50 tons 12% of the time, a collection value of 60 tons 7% of the time, and so on. The simulated values over a large number of iterations thus would correspond to the original collection distribution.

Sampling from a probability distribution using the Monte Carlo method is fairly straightforward once the cumulative probability curve (distribution) is developed. To assume that the process is statistically correct however, one must be assured that the random numbers are indeed uniformly randomly distributed between 0 and 1. For a manual simulation, a random numbers table can be employed. The numbers generated in the above example were taken from the first column of digits in Table A-4 of Appendix A, at the end of the text. Similar random-number tables are available in most statistical texts and in other sources.[1] Computer-generated random numbers rely on mathematical procedures rather than tables. In the section on simulating distributions via process generators, we will examine one of the procedures.

One point that should be made regarding the generation of random numbers in the interval 0–1 is that the numbers are actually between 0 and .9999, excluding 1. The impact of this is minimal. For the above example, it simply means that the random numbers between 0 and .0999 would be associated with a collection level of 10 tons, random numbers between .1000 and .3199 would be associated with a collection level of 20 tons, and so on.

## *B & D Manufacturing, Inc.: Problem formulation and manual simulation*

The above example illustrates the sampling process of the Monte Carlo method, but is not a very representative example of simulation in general, particularly since it does not highlight the timing aspects of simulation. The B & D Manufacturing case highlights some additional aspects of simulation.

Recall that the problem facing management at B & D is one of determining the number of maintenance personnel such that the maintenance cost balances with the expected lost profits and idle operator costs. Recall also that maintenance personnel cost is $8 per hour and down-time cost (lost profits and operator costs) is $30 per hour.

Tables 21-5 and 21-6 are the cumulative distribution tables for time between breakdowns and the machine down-time (service time), respectively. Note that in

---

[1]A general source for random number tables is the following: Rand Corporation, *A Million Random Digits with 100,000 Normal Deviates* (Glencoe, Ill.: Free Press), 1955.

TABLE 21-5.
Cumulative
Probability
Distribution for
Time Between
Breakdowns

| Time Between Breakdowns (minutes) (b) | Probability of Occurrence p(b) | Cumulative Probability P(b) = prob.(time between breakdowns ≤ b) | Random-Number Interval |
|---|---|---|---|
| 15 | .0467 | .0467 | .0000–.0466 |
| 16 | .0933 | .1400 | .0467–.1399 |
| 17 | .1000 | .2400 | .1400–.2399 |
| 18 | .1867 | .4267 | .2400–.4266 |
| 19 | .2400 | .6667 | .4267–.6666 |
| 20 | .1800 | .8467 | .6667–.8466 |
| 21 | .1000 | .9467 | .8467–.9466 |
| 22 | .0533 | 1.0000 | .9467–.9999 |

developing Table 21-5 we had to compute the probability of the time between breakdowns before computing the cumulative probability. This was accomplished by dividing each frequency of occurrence by the total number of observations, 150. In each of the tables, an additional column labeled "Random-Number Interval" is also included. By including these columns we can avoid having to plot the cumulative distribution curves. The data in these columns, in essence, represent the vertical portions of the cumulative plots; therefore, we can generate random variates directly from the tables by generating a uniform random number, determining the interval within which it falls, and identifying the associated occurrences. (The cumulative plot was given in the previous example to highlight Monte Carlo sampling; plotting the curve is not mandatory.)

We start the simulation with the assumption that work begins at 8:00 A.M. The simulation will terminate at the end of an 8-hour work day. (We run the simulation until 4:00 P.M., under the assumption that no lunch break exists.) When a breakdown occurs, servicing will begin immediately if a maintenance person is available; otherwise the machine will go into a queue. Machines waiting in the queue will be serviced on a first-come–first-served basis. We collect data on the time that machines are in the queue, the number of machines in the queue, and the amount of time each maintenance person is idle. We will use these statistics to compute total cost.

TABLE 21-6.
Cumulative
Probability
Distribution for
Service Time for
Repair of
Machinery

| Service Time (minutes)° (t) | Probability of Occurrence p(t) | Cumulative Probability P(t) = prob.(service time ≤ t) | Random-Number Interval |
|---|---|---|---|
| 10 | .05 | .05 | .0000–.0499 |
| 20 | .25 | .30 | .0500–.2999 |
| 30 | .40 | .70 | .3000–.6999 |
| 40 | .25 | .95 | .7000–.9499 |
| 50 | .05 | 1.00 | .9500–.9999 |

°Note: Time is midpoint of the time shown in Table 21-2.

**TABLE 21-7.**
**Simulation of Partial Day of Breakdown–Service Activity for B & D Manufacturing: One-Maintenance-Person Case**

| Breakdown Number | Uniform Random Number (Breakdown) | Time Until Next Breakdown (minutes) | Time of Occurrence (A.M./P.M.) | Service Begins (A.M./P.M.) | Uniform Random Number (Service) | Service Time (minutes) | Ends (A.M./P.M.) | Waiting Time Maintenance Personnel (minutes) | Waiting Time Operators (minutes) | Number of Machines Waiting for Service |
|---|---|---|---|---|---|---|---|---|---|---|
| 1 | .6279 | 19 | 8:19 | 8:19 | .4446 | 30 | 8:49 | 19 | — | — |
| 2 | .8234 | 20 | 8:39 | 8:49 | .6427 | 30 | 9:19 | — | 10 | 1 |
| 3 | .5273 | 19 | 8:58 | 9:19 | .5902 | 30 | 9:49 | — | 21 | 1 |
| 4 | .1820 | 17 | 9:15 | 9:49 | .0318 | 10 | 9:59 | — | 34 | 2 |
| 5 | .6383 | 19 | 9:34 | 9:59 | .5901 | 30 | 10:29 | — | 25 | 2 |
| 6 | .1471 | 17 | 9:51 | 10:29 | .3044 | 30 | 10:59 | — | 38 | 2 |
| 7 | .3208 | 18 | 10:09 | 10:59 | .1699 | 20 | 11:19 | — | 50 | 2 |
| 8 | .8224 | 20 | 10:29 | 11:19 | .5783 | 30 | 11:49 | — | 50 | 2 |
| 9 | .6331 | 19 | 10:48 | 11:49 | .8764 | 40 | 12:29 | — | 61 | 3 |
| 10 | .5482 | 19 | 11:07 | 12:29 | .2162 | 20 | 12:49 | — | 82 | 3 |
|  |  | 187 |  |  |  | 270 |  | 19 | 371 | 19 |

Table 21-7 gives the simulation results when one maintenance person is available. The first random number for time until the first breakdown (drawn from the second column of Table A-4 in Appendix A), is .6279. Going to Table 21-5, the time until the first breakdown is 19 minutes; therefore, the first breakdown occurs at 8:19 A.M. Since the maintenance worker came to work at 8:00 A.M., he is immediately assigned to service the breakdown. To determine the length of time it will take to service the machine, we generate a service-time random number, .4446. (This number is taken from the third column of Table A-4 in Appendix A.) From Table 21-6, the associated service time for the random number .4446 is 30 minutes. The end of service for the first breakdown thus is 8:49 A.M. (8:19 A.M. + 30 minutes). Since the maintenance worker had to wait until 8:19 before the first breakdown occurred, the idle time for the worker is 19 minutes. Since the breakdown did not go into the queue before servicing, no idle time is incurred by the operator. (Lost time occurred because the machine was down, but this is a function of the outage, not the servicing function; the time we are interested in is the amount of time the operator loses because of waiting for service.)

Having processed the first breakdown, we are ready to examine the second breakdown. The random number .8234 associated with this breakdown results in a time between breakdowns (from Table 21-5) of 20 minutes. Since the first breakdown occurred at 8:19 A.M., the second breakdown occurs at 8:39 A.M. (8:19 + 20 minutes). The maintenance worker is still servicing the first breakdown (which had occurred at 8:19); therefore, the second machine must go into the queue. Service on the second machine begins at 8:49 A.M., when the maintenance worker completes service on machine number one. The operator on machine number two must wait 10 minutes in the queue since the machine broke down at 8:39 A.M. but service begins at 8:49 A.M. The queue length is 1.

Continuing in this fashion, the third breakdown occurs at 8:58 A.M. and must wait for service until 9:19 A.M., since the second breakdown takes 30 minutes of service time. The third operator waits for 21 minutes in the queue before being serviced; however, the queue length remains at 1 since the second machine service activity began at 8:49 A.M.

Examining the remaining portion of Table 21-7, we note that the queue length begins to increase with the fourth breakdown. The fourth breakdown occurs at 9:15 A.M., but service is not complete on the second breakdown until 9:19 A.M. Two machines are waiting for service in the time interval from 9:15 A.M. to 9:19 A.M. By the time the ninth breakdown occurs, the queue length has increased to three, and the ninth machine waits 61 minutes before service begins. Since it is obvious that the queue will continue to increase with only one maintenance worker, we terminated the calculations at the tenth breakdown.

Table 21-8 is the simulation of the breakdown-service activity for 8 hours of operation when two maintenance personnel are available. To differentiate between the maintenance workers and their respective assignments, we placed the worker number in parentheses where service begins and when service ends. Since the procedural process for this two-worker case is identical to the single-worker case, we will not repeat the computations. You are encouraged, however, to trace the first several breakdowns through the process in order to assure complete understanding.

# TABLE 21-8.
## Simulation of Full Day of Breakdown-Service Activity for B & D Manufacturing: Two-Maintenance-Personnel Case

| Breakdown Number | Uniform Random Number (Breakdown) | Time Until Next Breakdown (minutes) | Time of Occurrence (A.M./P.M.) | Service Begins (A.M./P.M.) | Uniform Random Number (Service) | Service Time (minutes) | Ends (A.M./P.M.) | Waiting Time — Maintenance Personnel (minutes) | Waiting Time — Operators (minutes) | Number of Machines Waiting for Service |
|---|---|---|---|---|---|---|---|---|---|---|
| 1 | .6279 | 19 | 8:19 | 8:19 (1) | .4446 | 30 | 8:49 (1) | 19 + 39 = 58 | — | — |
| 2 | .8234 | 20 | 8:39 | 8:39 (2) | .6427 | 30 | 9:09 (2) | 9 + 0 = 9 | — | — |
| 3 | .5273 | 19 | 8:58 | 8:58 (1) | .5902 | 30 | 9:28 (1) | 0 + 6 = 6 | — | — |
| 4 | .1820 | 17 | 9:15 | 9:15 (2) | .0318 | 10 | 9:25 (2) | 6 + 0 = 6 | — | — |
| 5 | .6383 | 19 | 9:34 | 9:34 (1) | .5901 | 30 | 10:04 (1) | 0 + 26 = 26 | — | — |
| 6 | .1471 | 17 | 9:51 | 9:51 (2) | .3044 | 30 | 10:21 (2) | 5 + 0 = 5 | — | — |
| 7 | .3208 | 18 | 10:09 | 10:09 (1) | .1699 | 20 | 10:29 (1) | 0 + 8 = 8 | — | — |
| 8 | .8224 | 20 | 10:29 | 10:29 (2) | .5783 | 30 | 10:59 (2) | 19 + 0 = 19 | — | — |
| 9 | .6331 | 19 | 10:48 | 10:48 (1) | .8764 | 40 | 11:28 (1) | 0 + 8 = 8 | — | — |
| 10 | .5482 | 19 | 11:07 | 11:07 (2) | .2161 | 20 | 11:27 (2) | 0 + 0 = 0 | — | — |
| 11 | .3445 | 18 | 11:25 | 11:27 (2) | .3694 | 30 | 11:57 (2) | 16 + 0 = 16 | 2 | 1 |
| 12 | .4611 | 19 | 11:44 | 11:44 (1) | .6072 | 30 | 12:14 (1) | 0 + 5 = 5 | — | — |
| 13 | .3193 | 18 | 12:02 | 12:02 (2) | .8224 | 40 | 12:42 (2) | 7 + 0 = 7 | — | — |
| 14 | .6273 | 19 | 12:21 | 12:21 (1) | .1455 | 20 | 12:41 (1) | 0 + 0 = 0 | — | — |
| 15 | .4841 | 19 | 12:40 | 12:41 (1) | .1443 | 20 | 1:01 (1) | 0 + 18 = 18 | 1 | 1 |
| 16 | .7303 | 20 | 1:00 | 1:00 (2) | .6255 | 30 | 1:30 (2) | 20 + 0 = 20 | — | — |
| 17 | .8875 | 21 | 1:21 | 1:21 (1) | .6251 | 30 | 1:51 (1) | 0 + 11 = 11 | — | — |
| 18 | .7051 | 20 | 1:41 | 1:41 (2) | .1108 | 20 | 2:01 (2) | 7 + 0 = 7 | — | — |
| 19 | .1989 | 17 | 1:58 | 1:58 (1) | .5595 | 30 | 2:28 (1) | 0 + 15 = 15 | — | — |
| 20 | .4071 | 18 | 2:16 | 2:16 (2) | .1456 | 20 | 2:36 (2) | 7 + 0 = 7 | — | — |
| 21 | .4762 | 19 | 2:35 | 2:35 (1) | .9509 | 50 | 3:25 (1) | 0 + 15 = 15 | — | — |
| 22 | .1322 | 16 | 2:51 | 2:51 (2) | .1347 | 20 | 3:11 (2) | 0 + 1 = 1 | — | — |
| 23 | .9223 | 21 | 3:12 | 3:12 (2) | .7707 | 40 | 3:52 (2) | 7 + 0 = 7 | — | — |
| 24 | .8123 | 20 | 3:32 | 3:32 (1) | .3172 | 30 | 4:02 (1) | 0 + 0 = 0 | — | — |
| 25 | .7273 | 20 | 3:42 | 3:52 (2) | .8263 | 40 | 4:32 (2) | 0 + 0 = 0 | — | — |
|  |  | 472 |  |  |  | 720 |  | 00 284 | 3 | 2 |

For the two-worker case, the maximum queue size for machines waiting to be serviced is 1. This occurs only twice in the entire 8 hours of operation. Total time lost by idle operators is only 3 minutes, while maintenance personnel are idle 284 minutes during the 8 hours.

In any simulation exercise, it is also mandatory that one develop a flowchart, particularly if a general model is sought. From the discussion of the one-worker and two-worker cases, one could easily conclude that two models are required; however, both problems can be analyzed with a single model. As a matter of fact, a general model that will accommodate $M$ workers can be developed. Figure 21-3 is the flowchart for B & D Manufacturing, where $M$ workers are employed. You should check the flowchart to verify that it can handle the one-worker and two-worker cases.

## B & D Manufacturing, Inc.: Analysis of the results

From the above results, one would conclude that B & D Manufacturing should employ two maintenance personnel to support the production operations. With one maintenance worker, the queue will build infinitely until the end of day; overtime operations would then be required to service machines waiting in the queue. For the two-worker case, an additional $64 ($8 per hour × 8 hours of work) is required to pay the second maintenance worker, but this is well justified when the savings in the cost of lost operator time is considered. For the first 10 breakdowns alone, 371 minutes of lost operator time results when a single maintenance worker is employed. When two workers are employed, there are zero minutes of lost time. A total of 371 minutes of lost time is saved by employing a second maintenance worker. In terms of cost,

$$(371 \text{ min} \times \$30 \text{ per hour} \div 60 \text{ min per hour}) - (\$8 \text{ per hour} \times 4 \text{ hour of work}) = \$153.50$$

So the two-worker case costs $153.50 less to service breakdowns over 4 hours than did the single-worker case.

One must be careful in drawing conclusions with only a single day of operation. A more statistically sound conclusion could be supported if we had simulated a much larger number of breakdowns (for example, 1000 breakdowns). This does not imply, however, that every simulation should be run an infinite number of iterations. A crude check of our simulation can be made by comparing the mean interarrival time (that is, the mean time between breakdowns) and the mean service time of the simulation with the empirical data. From Table 21-5, the expected time between breakdowns,

$$\bar{b} = \sum_{i=1}^{n} p_i b_i$$

**FIGURE 21-3.
Flowchart of Simu-
lation of B & D
Manufacturing
Case**

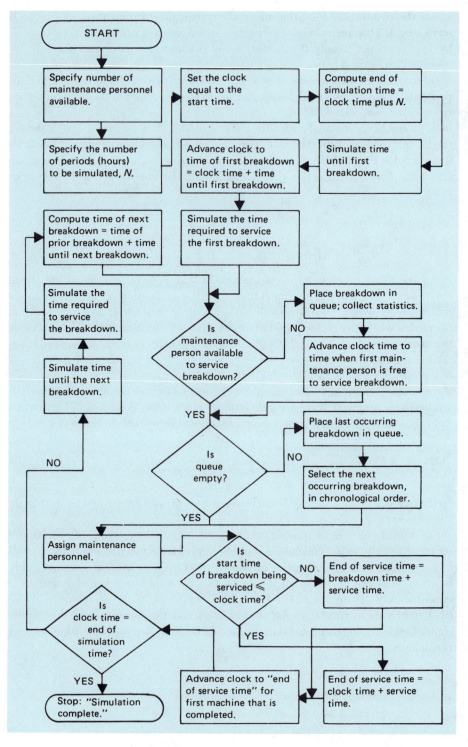

was 18.69 minutes; the simulated time between breakdowns for the 25 breakdowns was $\frac{472}{25}$ = 18.88 minutes. From Table 21-6, the expected service time,

$$\bar{t} = \sum_{i=1}^{n} p_i t_i$$

was 30.0 minutes, while the simulated service time was $\frac{720}{25}$ = 28.8 minutes. These data would tend to support the validity of our simulation and the use of a small sample ($n = 25$); however, this is not the general case. Most simulation experiments require a much larger number of samples. A detailed discussion of sample-size requirements is given later in the chapter.

## ■ Simulating distributions via process generators

From the manual simulation of B & D's machine maintenance problem, it should now be obvious that a manual approach to simulation is impractical, even for small-scale problems. To computerize the process, however, requires more than a one-to-one translation of the manual procedures described in the previous section, particularly if an efficient simulation model is to be developed. Two factors can help significantly in streamlining the development of a simulation model:

1. an automatic procedure for generating uniform random numbers.

2. a procedure for generating random variates that correspond to theoretical probability distributions.

Each of these points is covered in this section. Specifically, we will identify a procedure for generating uniform random numbers and a procedure for generating sampled variates that correspond to known theoretical probability distribution (such as the Poisson, binomial, exponential, normal, and others). We will also describe a procedure for testing whether a given set of empirical data can adequately be simulated via a given theoretical probability distribution.

The procedure for generating sampled variates from a specified probability distribution is referred to as a **process generator,** therefore, we have appropriately labeled the section "Simulating distributions via process generators."

*process generator*

### Generating random numbers

In simulating the B & D Manufacturing machine maintenance problem we indicated that tables of random numbers are readily available—as a matter of fact, we employed a set of random number tables. For computerized simulation, however, it is generally impractical, unnecessary, and undesirable to store random number tables, since such tables require a significant amount of storage.

A mathematical procedure is required if one is to generate random numbers without relying on a table. A variety of techniques exist, such as the mid-square method proposed by J. von Neumann in 1946 and the congruential method proposed by Lehmer in 1959.[2]

*pseudo-random numbers*

In practice, the numbers generated by these, as well as other, mathematical methods are referred to as **pseudo-random numbers.** The numbers are random (as determined by various statistical tests, such as a frequency test, a serial test, a permutation test, or a runs test). However, since each number is developed from a recursive mathematical relationship, any given number in a sequence of random numbers can be reproduced given the mathematical method and the preceding random number.

From the standpoint of simulation, it is more desirable to employ pseudo-random numbers than "pure" random numbers. The simulation model is easier to validate using pseudo-random numbers, since a given random-number sequence can be repeated. Likewise, multiple experiments can be performed under controlled conditions by employing a set of pseudo-random numbers.

*mid-square method*

To get a feel for how one goes about generating pseudo-random numbers, let us examine the **mid-square method.** This method operates by using as the next random number the middle digits of the square of the preceding random number; thus the label mid-square method. Specifically, the method operates as follows:

**1.** Select a random number of $n$ digits. (In computer terminology this is generally referred to as the *seed* for the generator.)

**2.** Square the number in the preceding step and add zero to the right-hand portion of the number, where needed, so as to produce a number of $2n$ digits.

**3.** The new random number is determined by selecting the middle $n$ digits from the number in step 2.

**4.** Repeat steps 2 and 3 in order to obtain additional random numbers.

To demonstrate the mid-square method, assume we wish to generate four-digit random numbers and the seed number is 2173. Squaring 2173 we have $(2173)^2 =$ 4721929; adding a zero, the resulting eight-digit number is 4721929[0]. The new random number then is 2192. Because $(2192)^2 = 4804864[0]$, the next random number is 0486. Using this same procedure, the fourth random number is 3619.

As noted in our manual simulation, random numbers are usually generated within the range between 0 and 1. To accomplish this using the mid-square method (or any of the other random number techniques) we simply place a decimal point in front of the first digit. For our example, the first four random numbers thus would be: .2173, .2192, .0486, and .3619.

In actual practice, it has been found that random numbers generated by the mid-square method tend to have a very short period before repetition occurs. Also, in many cases, it has been found that the numbers do not pass the statistical test for

[2]D. H. Lehmer, "Mathematical Methods in Large-scale Computing Units," *Proceedings of the Second Symposium on Large-scale Digital Computing Machinery* (Cambridge, Mass.: Harvard University Press), 1959, pp. 141–145.

randomness. Other techniques such as the congruential method are preferable for generating random numbers, since some of these methods can readily generate more than a billion statistically satisfactory pseudo-random numbers before repetition occurs.

Most computer manufacturers provide random-number subprogram packages that will automatically generate uniform random values, given a starting seed number. For example, the function subprogram RANDU(ISEED) (which is supplied by IBM and available on most of its machines) will generate uniformly distributed numbers between 0 and 1. Other function names for random-number generators commonly found on existing computer hardware include RAND($O$), RN($O$), and RND($X$).

Hereafter we will assume that a random-number generator is available, and that it will provide a random variate, $R$, which is uniformly distributed over the interval 0 to 1.

## Simulating continuous probability distributions

In simulating the B & D Manufacturing, Inc., case, we employed discrete values for time between breakdowns. In actuality, we were approximating these time values since in practice the times could take on any value, not just discrete values. A number of continuous variables of this nature exist in the real world—for example, the time between calls coming into a switchboard; the time between the beginning of service and the end of service at a bank teller's window; the time between flight departures at an airport. We can use an approximation approach to simulate these occurrences; however, since these, in essence, represent continuous random variables, we should use a continuous distribution in the analysis.

One of the advantages of employing continuous distributions is that a closed-form mathematical equation can be developed to serve as the process generator. To demonstrate how one goes about developing process generators for continuous distributions, we will examine the uniform, negative exponential, and normal distributions.

**Uniform process generator.**   Recall that in our discussion of the Monte Carlo method, data were given for a probability distribution, and from these we developed a cumulative probability distribution. To develop a process generator, we work with the same factors, but in mathematical form. Mathematically, these are referred to respectively as the *probability density function* (pdf) and the *cumulative density function* (cdf).

The probability density function for the uniform distribution is defined as follows:

$$p(x) = \frac{1}{b - a} \qquad \text{for } a \leq x \leq b \tag{21.1}$$

Graphically, this would appear as shown in Figure 21-4. Note that all the values between $a$ and $b$ have equal densities of $1/(b - a)$.

**FIGURE 21-4.**
**Uniform Probabil-**
**ity Distribution for**
**the Interval (*a, b*)**

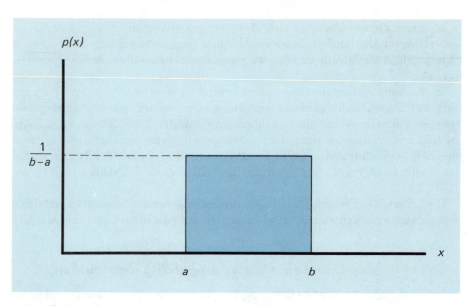

Recall that when we developed the cumulative distribution for the Monte Carlo example we summed the probabilities from the original probability distribution. This process is used to compute the cumulative density function, except we now need to use integral calculus since we are working with continuous data. The procedure involves integrating the probability density function over the range of values. Procedurally this is as follows:

$$P(x) = \int_a^x p(x)\, dx \tag{21.2}$$

Substituting $p(x) = 1/(b - a)$, then

$$P(x) = \int_a^x \frac{1}{b - a}\, dx$$

$$= \frac{1}{b - a} \int_a^x dx$$

$$= \frac{1}{b - a} [x]_a^x \tag{21.3}$$

$$= \frac{1}{b - a} [x - a]$$

Therefore,

$$\begin{aligned}
P(x) &= 0 && \text{for } x < a \\
P(x) &= \frac{x - a}{b - a} && \text{for } a \le x \le b \\
P(x) &= 1 && \text{for } x > b
\end{aligned} \tag{21.4}$$

Graphically, the cumulative density function appears as shown in Figure 21-5.

In the sampling procedure for the Monte Carlo method, we sampled from the cumulative probability distribution by generating a random number, identifying the associated cumulative probability, and selecting the corresponding value of the variable. Mathematically, the same procedure is used in developing a process generator. The technique is referred to as the **inverse transformation procedure.** *inverse transformation procedure* The procedure involves setting the uniform random variate $R$ (where $R$ is between zero and one) equal to $P(x)$ and solving for $x$.

For the uniform distribution this is as follows:

$$R = P(x) = \frac{x - a}{b - a} \tag{21.5}$$

Solving for $x$, we have

$$R(b - a) = x - a$$

or

$$x = a + R(b - a) \tag{21.6}$$

Given equation (21.6), which is the process generator for the uniform distribution, we can generate uniformly distributed variates between $a$ and $b$ by simply identifying $a$ and $b$, generating a random number ($R$), and substituting into the equation. For example, to generate (sample) a random variate between 10 and 20, the functional relationship would be

$$x = 10 + R(10)$$

For the random number .6134, the random variate would be 16.134.

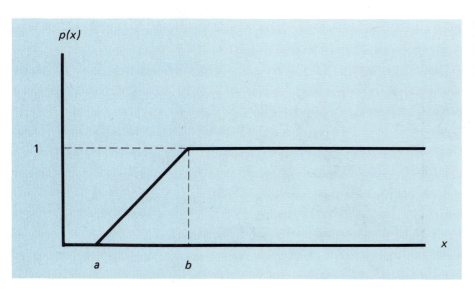

**FIGURE 21-5.**
**Cumulative Probability Distribution Uniform over the Interval (*a*, *b*)**

$p(x)$

1

$a$        $b$        $x$

Sampling from a uniform distribution is quite simple, once the process generator has been developed. This benefit, however, is not limited to the uniform distribution, but applies to all continuous distributions.

**Negative exponential distribution.**   In Chapter 20, in our discussion on queuing theory, we noted that the service-time distribution employed in many waiting-line situations is the negative exponential distribution. A process generator for this distribution can also be developed by using the inverse transformation technique.

The probability density function (pdf) for the negative exponential distribution is defined mathematically as follows.

$$p(x) = \mu e^{-\mu x} \qquad \text{for} \quad 0 \le x \le \infty \tag{21.7}$$

where $\mu$ is the average service rate, or the mean number of units serviced per time interval. Graphically, the density function appears as shown in Figure 21-6.

To develop the process generator, we first must compute the cumulative density function:

$$
\begin{aligned}
P(x) &= \int_0^x p(x)\, dx \\
&= \int_0^x \mu e^{-\mu x}\, dx \\
&= [-e^{-\mu x}]_0^x \\
&= [-e^{-\mu x}] - [-e^0] \\
&= -e^{-\mu x} + 1
\end{aligned}
\tag{21.8}
$$

$$P(x) = 1 - e^{-\mu x} \tag{21.9}$$

**FIGURE 21-6.**
**Negative Exponential Probability Distribution**

Next we set the uniform random variate, $R$, equal to $P(x)$, and solve for $x$.

$$R = P(x) = 1 - e^{-\mu x}$$

or

$$e^{-\mu x} = 1 - R$$

Taking the natural log of both sides of the equation we then have

$$\ln(e^{-\mu x}) = \ln(1 - R)$$

$$-\mu x = \ln(1 - R)$$

Therefore,

$$x = (-1/\mu) \ln(1 - R) \qquad (21.10)$$

Since the random variate $R$ is symmetrical and uniformly distributed between 0 and 1, the probability distribution for $(1 - R)$ is equivalent to that of $R$; therefore, we can replace $(1 - R)$ with $R$. Therefore, an equally valid process generator for the negative exponential distribution is

$$x = (-1/\mu) \ln R \qquad (21.11)$$

Given the average service rate, $\mu$, and a uniform random variate, $R$, we can now generate sample values for the length of time of service, $x$. For example, if the average service rate, $\mu$, for a given operation is 6 units per hour and the uniform random value of .5 is generated, then the sampled value would be

$$x = \frac{-1}{6 \text{ per hour}} \times \ln(.5)$$

$$= (-1/6)(-.693) \text{ hours}$$

$$= (-60/6)(-.693) \text{ minutes}$$

$$= 6.93 \text{ minutes}$$

## Simulating discrete probability distributions

A number of theoretical discrete probability distributions exist—the most frequently used discrete distributions for simulation modeling are the binomial and the Poisson. We will, therefore, limit our discussion to these two distributions.

Process generators can be developed for discrete probability distributions using the inverse transformation method. But a simpler approach is to employ a counting process known as the **composition method.** We will develop both the binomial and Poisson generators using this method.

*composition method*

**Binomial process generator.** The *probability mass function* (pmf), that is, the mathematical model for the binomial distribution, is expressed as follows:

$$p(x) = \frac{n!}{x!(n-x)!} p^x (1-p)^{n-x} \tag{21.12}$$

where       $n$ = the number of independent trials (sample size)

$p$ = the probability of success on any one trial

$x$ = the random variable that represents the number of successes in $n$ trials

Given the parameters $n$ and $p$, the binomial process generator simply involves sampling $n$ times and counting the number of successes, $x$. On each trial, a uniform random variate, $R$, is generated and compared with the probability of success, $p$. If the random variate $R$ is less than $p$, the trial is labeled a success and is counted; if $R \geq p$ the trial is a failure. After $n$ trials, the total number of successes is the value of the random binomial variate.

**Poisson process generator.** In Chapter 20, we discussed how the Poisson distribution is used in conjunction with waiting-line analysis. We noted that if data are collected in the form of *number of arrivals per time period,* then the data likely can be described by the Poisson distribution. Recall that we said the probability mass function for the Poisson distribution is defined as follows:

$$p(x) = \frac{(\lambda T)^x e^{-\lambda T}}{x!}, \qquad 0 \leq x \leq \infty \tag{21.13}$$

where       $\lambda T$ = the mean number of arrivals per time period $T$

$x$ = the number of arrivals in the time interval

To generate random variates for the Poisson we could use this relationship in conjunction with the inverse transformation process, but the composition method is more straightforward.

In Chapter 20, we noted the *dual* relationships between the negative exponential and the Poisson distribution. Specifically we noted that if the number of arrivals per time period can be described by the Poisson distribution, then the *time between arrivals* can be described by the negative exponential distribution. To develop a process generator for the Poisson distribution, we can take advantage of this relationship. One simply simulates the timing of arrivals using a negative exponential process generator and counts the number of arrivals that occur in the time period

$(T)$. The composition method for generating random Poisson variates is described as follows:

1. Identify the length of the time period, $T$. Initialize to zero a "number of arrivals counter," $n$, and an "interarrival time counter," $t$.

2. Generate the interarrival time for an arrival using the negative exponential process generator.

3. Add the interarrival time in step 2 to $t$; add 1 to the number of arrivals counter, $n$.

4. If $t > T$ in step 3, then discard the last arrival, subtract 1 from $n$, and go to step 5, otherwise go to step 2.

5. The value of $n$ is a random variate for the Poisson distribution.

## *Goodness-of-fit tests*

Before one can use a process generator in a simulation study, it first must be shown that the empirical data can be represented by a known theoretical probability distribution. (Recall the same is true with regard to the use of the queuing models in Chapter 20, where one must demonstrate that arrival rate is Poisson distributed and service time is exponentially distributed.) A number of statistical tests can be used to test the goodness of fit of a theoretical distribution to a given set of data. One of the most frequently used is the **chi-squared ($\chi^2$) test.**

*chi-squared test*

The $\chi^2$ test is a test to determine if there is any significant difference between expected frequencies (those based on the theoretical distribution) and the actual frequencies (those represented by the data). Steps used in the testing process are as follows:

1. State the test hypothesis, $H_0$, that the observed data are drawn from a population that is described by a known theoretical distribution.

2. State the alternate hypothesis, $H_1$, that the observed data are *not* drawn from the population in step 1.

3. Identify the level of significance, $\alpha$, at which the test will be performed. [Recall that $(1 - \alpha)$ is the level of confidence of a statistical test.]

4. Using the following mathematical relationship,

$$\chi_{cal}^2 = \sum \frac{(f_o - f_e)^2}{f_e} \tag{21.14}$$

$$\chi_{cal}^2 = \text{calculated } \chi^2 \text{ value}$$

where     $f_o$ = the observed frequencies

$f_e$ = the expected or theoretical frequencies

test the $\chi_{cal}^2$ with $\chi_{table}^2$. If $\chi_{cal}^2 > \chi_{table}^2$, then reject $H_0$ (accept $H_1$); if $\chi_{cal}^2 \leq \chi_{table}^2$, do not reject $H_0$. The $\chi_{table}^2$ value is found in a chi-squared table and is defined by the number of degrees of freedom (d.f.). Degrees of freedom, for most goodness-of-fit tests, is defined as follows:

$$\text{d.f.} = \begin{matrix} \text{number of} \\ \text{categories} \\ \text{(classes)} \end{matrix} - \begin{matrix} \text{number of} \\ \text{parameters} \end{matrix} - 1$$

where "number of parameters" is defined as the number of statistics ($\mu$, $\sigma$, $\lambda$, etc.) required to describe a given distribution.

To demonstrate use of the $\chi^2$ test, consider the following example. Assume that the data in the first two columns of Table 21-9 were collected on the number of customers who enter a bank each hour. These data were randomly collected over 204 one-hour periods. On the basis of these data, we could hypothesize ($H_0$) that the data can be represented by a Poisson distribution. The alternative hypothesis, $H_1$, is that the distribution cannot be represented by the Poisson distribution.

Before we can test hypothesis $H_0$, we need to calculate $\chi^2_{cal}$. We begin by first calculating the mean number of arrivals per hour, $\lambda$:

$$\lambda = \frac{\Sigma x f_o}{\Sigma f_o} = \frac{204}{204} = 1$$

Using $\lambda = 1$ and the Poisson density function (or a Poisson table), we can compute the probability that various numbers of customers enter the bank. These are expressed as follows:

$$p(x = 0) = \frac{(1)(e^{-1})}{0!} = .36788$$

$$p(x = 1) = \frac{(1)(e^{-1})}{1!} = .36788$$

$$p(x = 2) = \frac{(1)(e^{-1})}{2!} = .18394$$

$$p(x = 3) = \frac{(1)(e^{-1})}{3!} = .06131$$

$$p(x \geq 4) = \frac{(1)(e^{-1})}{4!} + \frac{(1)(e^{-1})}{5!} + \cdots + \frac{(1)(e^{-1})}{\infty} = .01899$$

**TABLE 21-9.**
**Calculations for $\chi^2$**
**Test for Customer**
**Arrivals at a Bank**

| Number of Arrivals per Hour $(x)$ | Observed Frequency $(f_o)$ | Expected Frequency $(f_e)$ | $\left[\dfrac{(f_o - f_e)^2}{f_e}\right]$ |
|---|---|---|---|
| 0 | 70 | 75.05 | .3398 |
| 1 | 84 | 75.05 | 1.0673 |
| 2 | 34 | 37.52 | .3302 |
| 3 | 12 } | 12.51 } | .0088 |
| 4 or more | 4 } | 3.87 } | |
| | 204 | | $\chi^2_{cal} = 1.7461$ |

Since $n$, the total number of observations, is 204, the expected or theoretical frequencies are determined by multiplying the above probabilities by 204. These data are shown in column 3 of Table 21-9. Applying equation (21.14), we can then compute column 4 for the table. The sum of column 4 yields $\chi^2_{cal}$. (In computing $\chi^2_{cal}$, it is assumed that each class of data has an $f_e$ of at least 5. Since our expected value for $x \geq 4$ is only 3.87 observations, we grouped the fourth and fifth classes.)

The number of degrees of freedom for this particular test is 2, since there are four classes of data in our modified set and the Poisson distribution has one parameter, $\lambda$. If we wish to test the hypothesis, $H_0$, at a 95% level of confidence, then $\alpha = .05$. Referring to the $\chi^2$ table in Table A-5 of Appendix A, we find that for $\alpha = .05$ and d.f. $= 2$, $\chi^2_{table} = 5.991$. Since $\chi^2_{cal}$ is less than $\chi^2_{table}$, we do not reject $H_0$, and conclude that our data can be simulated adequately with a Poisson process generator.

## ■ Simulation languages

One can develop a simulation model and perform simulation experiments without a special-purpose simulation language; however, it should be obvious from the previous application example that to do so requires a lot of time, effort, and detail work. A simulation language is not employed without a cost, however—one must become familiar with the language and the language must be available. In this section, we will look at some of the advantages and disadvantages of employing a simulation language. We hope this material will provide some insight into the use of simulation languages in general.

### *Advantages and disadvantages of special-purpose languages*

By employing a simulation language one usually can reduce program preparation time and cost. This occurs because most languages have such features as:

1.  a master scheduling routine that keeps track of events and schedules the events as they occur in simulated time

2.  random number generators

3.  process generators that can be used to generate random variates for different probability distributions

4.  automatic statistical data collection routines

5.  automatic statistical fixed-format reports and data plotting for output reporting

6.  flexible output report generators

7.  diagnostic capabilities within the language that check for language syntax errors and logic errors in the model

While most simulation languages provide most of these features, some languages have the added feature that the language is more *problem* oriented. Problem-oriented languages reduce the model-building time, but they have the limitation that they are applicable for only certain types of problems. For example, GPSS, an International Business Machines language, is designed specifically for queuing problems; and GERT, a language developed by Alan B. Pritsker and Associates, is applicable for network problems.[3]

Some problem-oriented languages have rapid execution times, but this is not generally the case. In most cases the processing–execution times are much longer for simulation languages, particularly problem-oriented languages, than would be the case had the model been developed on a more general-purpose language such as FORTRAN. Problem-oriented simulation languages thus are just the opposite of special-problem algorithms. Special-problem algorithms, such as a network code, have reduced processing time compared with a general-solution algorithm, such as SIMPLEX, whereas problem-oriented simulation languages have longer processing times compared with general-purpose languages. In problem-based simulation languages one thus has to weigh the advantages of the language against the cost of longer run times.

In addition to lengthy run times (in some cases) there are other disadvantages of simulation languages. Obviously the disadvantages will depend upon the particular language employed. The common disadvantages include (1) lengthy training in the use of languages may be required; (2) the language may not be available on a given computer—some languages are restricted to certain types or size of computers; (3) the language may not be suitable for the particular problem being modeled.

### *Languages*

A large number of special-purpose languages have been developed over the last two decades and are available on a number of different computers. We will not attempt to list these, since little would be gained from this exercise. A number of simulation texts provide reviews of languages and are a source for comparison of languages.

## ■ Activities (problems) associated with using simulation

Although simulation languages provide a variety of features and capabilities, very few of the problems associated with simulation can be resolved via a simulation language. A modeler should be aware of some of these problems.

As noted in the introduction, simulation involves an experimentation process. To

---

[3]A description of GPSS is found in Geoffrey Gordon, *The Application of GPSS V to Discrete System Simulation* (Englewood Cliffs, N.J.: Prentice-Hall), 1975. A description of GERT is found in A. A. B. Pritsker, *Graphical Evaluation and Review Technique*, RM-4973-NASA (Santa Monica, Calif.: Rand Corporation), April 1966.

obtain valid and useful results from a simulation study, one must be assured that the model is properly developed and the simulation experiment is properly conducted. This involves validating the simulation model, defining initial conditions, determining the number of iterations (samples) that should be drawn, and resolving transient effects that occur when each simulation experiment is conducted. We will not provide detailed procedures for each of these topics, but we can provide an overview of the topics and reflect on some of the key factors that should be considered in the simulation study.

## Validation

The validation of a simulation process is concerned with two factors: validation of the computer program with respect to logic and programming errors, and validation of the model with respect to the degree to which it represents the problem under study.

**Validation of the computer program.**     Several means are available for validating the computer program. First, the computer output can be compared with the results of manual simulations, using the same random variables used in a computer run. Second, one can compare the simulated results with analytical results (when available). This latter process may involve examining subsets of the overall model rather than the complete model, since in most cases analytical results will be difficult to produce.

**Validation of the model.**     Unfortunately, there is no clear-cut method that will assure that the model is a valid representation of the problem or system being studied. There are, however, several tests that will strengthen the probability of acceptance of the model. When there are historical data available, the ability of the model to reproduce prior results lends credibility to the model. Additionally, one can determine whether the results from the model are reasonable. For example, for a basic queuing model, one would expect to have minimum delays when the service rate is high compared with the arrival rate; conversely, when the arrival rate is large compared with the service rate, significant queues and delays should occur. If the model of such a system does not exhibit these characteristics, one could conclude that something is wrong with the model.

As noted earlier, there are statistical techniques available to assure (with some degree of confidence) that simulated data are valid. For example, a chi-squared test can be performed to test whether the simulated data and the actual data are from the same underlying probability distribution. Such tests, however, only test the validity of input data, not the overall model.

In the final analysis, the true validation of the model occurs only when the simulated results agree satisfactorily with the real-world results. It has been the authors' experience that running the simulation in parallel with the actual system being modeled can quite often convince management as to the soundness of the simulation, particularly if the model is used to predict (in advance) outcomes that ultimately occur regardless of whether the outcomes are desirable or undesirable.

## *Number of iterations (run size)*

Since simulation involves sampling, the output results from a simulation experiment are subject to sampling error, as is the case in any sampling experiment. The accuracy of the simulation output for a defined set of conditions is thus a function of the sample size, or the number of iterations, of the model. Since simulated time is related to the number of iterations (events) for a variable time-increment simulation, one could reason that sampling error can be minimized by running the simulation for a lengthy period of time. But, for many simulation models, this could result in needless computer costs. Simply running the simulation for a lengthy period of time is not a desirable alternative.

A more realistic approach to controlling the sampling error is to employ a basic statistical technique. Equation (21.15) is a suitable technique for this purpose.

$$n = \left(\frac{\sigma z_{\alpha/2}}{\text{error}}\right)^2 \tag{21.15}$$

where          $\sigma$ = standard deviation of the output being simulated
$z_{\alpha/2}$ = number of standard deviations associated with a given level of
confidence (for a 95% level of confidence, that is, for $\alpha = .05$, $z = 1.96$)
error = maximum error allowed in the simulated output

To employ equation (21.15) one simply specifies the acceptable sampling error; specifies the level of confidence (i.e., the desired level of statistical precision); utilizes the standard deviation, $\sigma$; and solves for the run size, $n$. As an example, assume that you have been asked by the production manager of a large manufacturing firm to simulate the demand during lead time for a stochastic inventory problem. It has been indicated that the standard deviation for the problem, $\sigma$, is 5000 units. Management would like to have 95% confidence in estimated demand during lead time. Management is interested in knowing the relationship between sample size, $n$, and the error size.

To analyze the problem, we can examine error sizes of 400, 2000, and 4000. Substituting into equation (21.15), we have the following results:

$$\text{for an error size of 400:} \quad n = \left(\frac{(1.96)(5000)}{400}\right)^2 = 600$$

$$\text{for an error size of 2000:} \quad n = \left(\frac{(1.96)(5000)}{2000}\right)^2 = 24$$

$$\text{for an error size of 4000:} \quad n = \left(\frac{(1.96)(5000)}{4000}\right)^2 = 6$$

From this basic example, it can quickly be noted that $n$ increases quadratically as the error size decreases. This clearly illustrates the price one must pay for greater accuracy in the simulation process: *the greater the degree of accuracy, the larger the number of samples that must be drawn, thus the greater the length of computer run time.*

One of the shortcomings of employing equation (21.15) to compute run size is that the standard deviation for the simulation, $\sigma$, must be available. Most likely, this is not readily available. One can, however, preprogram within the simulation structure a procedure that will compute the standard deviation of the output data based on all prior runs. Thus, given a starting estimate of $\sigma$, a new value for $\sigma$ is computed after each run, along with a new value of $n$. The simulation will terminate when the desired precision is achieved. (This will occur when the new value of $n$, computed at any given iteration, is smaller than the total number of runs that have been made.) A value of $\sigma$ is still required in this process, but only to get the process started.

## Steady-state condition

Equation (21.15) can be employed to assure a desired degree of accuracy in the simulation. However, the results from this are based on the sample data only and do not necessarily assure that the simulation will reach a steady-state condition. When the simulation reaches steady state, the output values will stabilize.

The relationship between sample size and steady-state conditions is illustrated in Table 21-10. These data were generated for an inventory problem, where the objective is to determine the economic order quantity, $Q°$, when demand and lead time are described by probability distributions. (Refer to Chapter 14.)

Note that as the run size, $n$, increases, the variability in $Q°$ decreases. (Compare the values for run sizes of 20, 100, and 2000.) These data appear to indicate that the steady-state value is approximately 113.2. To support the convergence of the data further, the simulation was replicated (repeated) four times by changing the seed of the random number generators and rerunning the simulation.

The above principle, referred to as **stochastic convergence,** can be employed to assure that the simulation reaches a steady state. The process, however, does not provide a straightforward means for computing the run size. In reality, the data suggest that large run sizes should be employed, but this is not always true. A significant amount of research, primarily *variance reduction techniques,* has been

*stochastic convergence*

| | Replication | | | | |
|---|---|---|---|---|---|
| $n$ | *1* | *2* | *3* | *4* | *Average ($\overline{Q}°$)* |
| 5 | 106.97 | 102.10 | 114.01 | 108.43 | 107.88 |
| 20 | 116.97 | 120.15 | 110.73 | 109.54 | 114.35 |
| 100 | 115.95 | 114.67 | 115.40 | 114.18 | 115.05 |
| 200 | 114.73 | 114.11 | 111.98 | 112.88 | 113.43 |
| 400 | 112.93 | 113.35 | 113.18 | 113.55 | 113.25 |
| 1000 | 113.56 | 113.05 | 113.87 | 113.26 | 113.44 |
| 2000 | 113.36 | 113.28 | 113.23 | 113.01 | 113.22 |

**TABLE 21-10.** Convergence (Steady State) of $Q*$ as a Function of Run Size ($n$)

**FIGURE** 21-7.
**Transient Versus
Steady-State
Conditions**

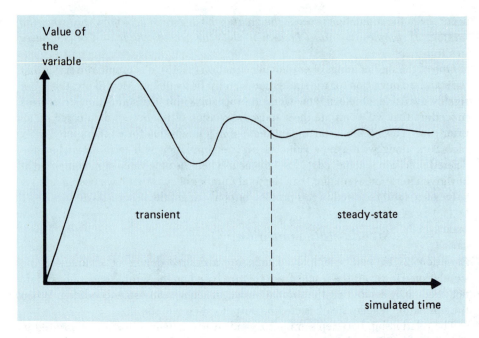

directed at more precise procedures.[4] These concepts are beyond the scope of this text; therefore, we will not review these materials. It should be obvious that achieving steady-state, whether by stochastic convergence or by some variance reduction technique, is an important segment of a simulation study.

## Resolving transient effects

In developing a simulation model, there is a general tendency to start the simulation "empty," particularly since the value of the variables under long-term running conditions is unknown. But starting the simulation empty means that many of the early runs in the simulation will not truly represent the simulated system.

To obtain useful output from the simulation, it is necessary to (1) run the simulation until the model results reach steady state (as noted above) and (2) discard all statistics collected during the transient phase (when a large degree of variability exists in output values compared from run to run).

Figure 21-7 depicts the relationship between transient and steady-state conditions in relationship to simulated time. As the model is moved through simulated time, the values of the model variable will approach steady-state levels.

The transient effects (the transient statistics), if not discarded when the final statistics are computed, can significantly affect the overall results. Although no given

[4]R. E. Shannon, *Systems Simulation* (Englewood Cliffs, N.J.: Prentice-Hall), 1975, pp. 197–205.

technique exists that can identify with 100% accuracy the end of the transient phase and the beginning of steady state, a number of statistical techniques exist that can aid in identifying when one should discard given data. One such technique is *correlated sampling*. To use this technique, one takes the first $k$ values for a given output variable, computes a correlation coefficient (correlated with time), and tests for significant correlation. If significant correlation exists, these output runs are assumed to be part of the transient phase, therefore, the data are discarded, the next $k$ runs are examined, and the output values are again tested. This process is continued until a block of $k$ observations (values) is formed in which no significant correlation exists. The remaining $(n - k)$ runs can then be used as an estimate of the steady-state value of the simulation.

In practice, it has been found the length of the transient period can be shortened by (1) starting the system empty (assuming this is the only viable place to begin), (2) making a series of short runs, and (3) employing the final steady-state values of the variables of each run as the initial conditions for the next run. One should recognize, however, that this will not entirely eliminate a transient period.

## ■ Summary

The intent of this chapter has been to provide an introductory exposure to the formulation and development of simulation models and the concepts and factors that must be considered in employing simulation. From the chapter it should be obvious that simulation is an extremely useful technique since it allows one to experiment with a model of a system rather than the actual system. It should also be obvious that, in many cases, particularly where complex relationships of a predictable and random nature occur, it is easier to utilize a simulation of the process than to develop an elaborate mathematical model.

As is the case with all MS/OR techniques, simulation has limitations. It is not an optimization technique; rather, each simulation run is like a single experiment conducted under a given set of conditions. A number of simulation runs thus are required in a simulation study. To ensure that the simulation output is valid and useful, one must be certain that

1. a sufficient number of runs have been made
2. all input distributions are accurately simulated
3. a sufficient number of replications of the model are made in order to minimize sampling errors
4. transient effects (resulting from the initial start conditions of the simulation) do not impact the final output

The Monte Carlo method is the basic element of any simulation experiment since, in essence, it is the sampling process associated with simulation. Fortunately, the sampling of random variates from continuous as well as discrete probability distributions can be accomplished via process generators as opposed to the table look-up procedure associated with the traditional Monte Carlo method. One must insure, however, that the empirical data can be simulated adequately by a given distribution prior to employing the associated process generator. The chi-squared test or some other suitable statistical test can be used to test the goodness of fit between the simulated data and the empirical data.

Collecting operating statistics and providing output reports are among the laborious aspects of simulation, as is keeping track of the time sequence of events. Fixed-time-increment as well as variable-time-increment methods can be used as the clocking mechanism of a simulation. But, regardless of the method, if one employs a general-purpose programming language (such as FORTRAN) a great deal of programming effort is required. Fortunately, simulation languages such as GPSS, provide timing mechanisms and embody many other features that greatly simplify simulation modeling. The use of a special simulation language allows one to concentrate on the simulation rather than on the programming. Employing a simulation language, however, does not mean one can ignore the operational aspects of simulation. Requirements such as validation of the model, initial conditions, number of simulation runs, and the like are still an integral part of the simulation study.

In the beginning of this chapter, we noted that simulation is one of the most widely used tools in the MS/OR field. Simulation will likely continue to be broadly employed in the future. Several reasons can be given to support this argument:

1. The cost of computing has and will continue to decrease in the future, making the cost of simulation studies more and more economically feasible.

2. As technological developments make on-line computing more widely available, simulation will become more widely employed for "what if" and decision-making studies, thus broadening the acceptability of simulation in general.

3. Special-purpose simulation languages tailored to specific problem structures have evolved, thus making the simulation process less time consuming (an example of this is GERT—Graphical Evaluation and Review Technique—designed for analyzing the network type of problems).

## ■ Glossary of terms

**chi-squared test:**   A goodness-of-fit test used to determine how well a theoretical distribution describes a given set of empirical data.

**composition method:**   A procedure used to develop a process generator for discrete probability distributions.

**fixed-time-increment simulation:**   A simulation experiment in which the system clock is advanced a fixed ($\Delta t$) time increment.

**inverse transformation procedure:**   A mathematical method used primarily in the development of process generators for continuous probability distributions.

**iterations:**   Refers to the run size or the number of samples that should be drawn in a simulation experiment.

**mid-square method:**   A mathematical procedure for generating pseudo-random numbers.

**Monte Carlo method:**   A sampling process used to select sample values randomly from a probability distribution.

**process generator:**   A mathematical function or procedure that will automatically generate random variates that correspond to the theoretical probability distribution for which the generator is designed.

**pseudo-random numbers:**   Mathematically generated, uniformly distributed numbers that occur randomly, as determined by various statistical tests.

**simulation:**   The process of developing a model of a problem and deriving measures of the problem's performance by performing sampling experiments on the model.

**simulation-modeling process:**   Steps and procedures involved in conducting a simulation study.

**stochastic convergence:**   When the output results of a simulation experiment reach a steady-state condition, i.e., the output results converge to a given value or level.

**transient effects:**   Variability that exists in the output of a simulation experiment as a result of initial starting conditions.

**validation:**   Refers to the process of assuming that a simulation program is properly written (validation of the program) and that the model adequately represents the problem being modeled (validation of the model).

**variable-time-increment simulation:**   A simulation experiment in which the system clock is advanced to the time of the next event, regardless of the size of the time step.

# ▪ Review questions

1. Define the term *simulation*.

2. Explain how the problem-solving process of simulation differs from the algorithm process associated with analytical models.

3. Identify and describe the simulation-modeling process employed in any simulation experiment. Give a brief description of each of the steps of the process.

4. Identify two methods for moving a simulation through time. Give a brief explanation of each.

5. Give a brief explanation of the Monte Carlo method of sampling. How is this concept employed in any simulation?

6. How are random number generators used in simulation?

7. What is a process generator? Give an example of how a process generator is used.

8. How is a chi-squared test used in simulation?

9. What is the advantage of using a special-purpose simulation language?

10. Identify some of the more common simulation languages.

11. Why is validation an important aspect in any simulation study? Explain what is meant by the term *validation*.

12. Explain what factor should be considered in determining the number of iterations (samples) that should be employed in a given simulation study. How does this problem relate to the steady-state condition of the simulation output?

13. What impact do transient effects have on the output of a simulation experiment? How does one go about resolving transient effects?

## ■ True/false questions

1. Monte Carlo sampling is employed in every simulation experiment.

2. Simulation is a descriptive problem-solving process, but an optimal solution can be derived.

3. Every problem that is applicable for solution via simulation must have a probabilistic base.

4. The mid-square method is a widely used technique for generating pseudo-random numbers.

5. The inverse transformation method can be used to develop a Poisson process generator.

6. The chi-squared $(\chi^2)$ test is used in simulation to determine whether a given set of data can be represented by a known theoretical probability distribution.

7. Program preparation time and cost can usually be reduced because most simulation languages have built-in capabilities such as random number generators, process generators, automatic data collection routines, or flexible output report generators.

8. By employing a simulation language, one can reduce not only preparation time and cost, but also run time and cost.

9. If one wishes to reduce by 50% the error that can exist in a simulation experiment, it simply requires that the number of runs be doubled.

10. Most simulation experiments are started "empty," but this problem can be resolved by discarding all statistics collected prior to the model reaching steady state.

## ■ Problems

1. The following data were collected on the number of emergency room arrivals that occur each hour at St. Mary's hospital, during the period from 8:00 P.M. to midnight. Using the Monte Carlo method, simulate 20 hours of emergency room activity. (Use the first column of random numbers in Table A-4 of Appendix A.)

| No. of Calls | Frequency |
|---|---|
| 0 | 2 |
| 1 | 3 |
| 2 | 5 |
| 3 | 8 |
| 4 | 15 |
| 5 | 21 |
| 6 | 28 |
| 7 | 17 |
| 8 | 10 |
| 9 | 3 |

2. Demand per day for a particular item is expressed by the following set of data. (Three hundred days of history were used in developing the data.) Simulate the demand for 10 days. (Use the second column of random numbers in Table A-4 of Appendix A.)

| Demand/Day | Frequency |
|---|---|
| 20 | 15 |
| 21 | 30 |
| 22 | 45 |
| 23 | 90 |
| 24 | 75 |
| 25 | 45 |

3. Using the data in Problem 2, assume that the item being demanded is the newspaper at the local convenience store. The manager at the store pays 10 cents per paper and sells the paper for 20 cents. Unsold papers are returned for a 3-cent credit. If a paper is demanded but unavailable, goodwill cost is 3 cents.

   The manager at the convenience store operates with the following ordering policy: the quantity ordered each day is equal to the quantity sold the previous day plus the number of lost sales the previous day. Simulate 20 days of operation in order to determine the average daily profit from the sale of newspapers. (Assume that demand for the previous day was 20 papers, and 3 lost sales occurred. Use the random numbers from the first column of Table A-4 in Appendix A.)

4. Jeff Adams, owner of the Mr. Haircut barbershop has three chairs in his shop but presently has only two barbers. He is contemplating hiring an additional barber. Jeff has observed that customers appear to arrive randomly; the data shown in Table P21-4 were collected on the time between arrivals. Jeff also made some estimates of the time it takes to give a haircut; these are shown in the right-hand part of Table P21-4. He has noticed that, if two customers are in the shop waiting for service, a new customer will not join the queue. To hire a new barber will cost $3.75 per hour plus $1.00 commission per haircut. Presently the price of a haircut is $4.50.

   a. Simulate 3 hours of operation to determine whether Adams should hire the additional barber. (Use the third and fourth columns of Table A-4 in Appendix A to generate arrival and service times, respectively.)

**TABLE 21-4. Mr. Haircut Barbershop**

| Time Between Arrivals | | Service Time | |
|---|---|---|---|
| Minutes | Frequency | Minutes | Probability |
| 2–4 | 10 | 5–15 | .10 |
| 4–6 | 15 | 15–25 | .35 |
| 6–8 | 20 | 25–35 | .30 |
| 8–10 | 35 | 35–45 | .15 |
| 10–12 | 50 | 45–55 | .10 |
| 12–14 | 40 | | |
| 14–16 | 20 | | |
| 16–18 | 5 | | |
| 18–20 | 5 | | |

**b.** Perform a rough check of the simulation to justify your conclusion. What additional comments can you make about the simulation, in terms of accuracy of results?

5. Use the mid-square method to generate a sequence of 15 pseudo-random numbers. Use the number 7239 as the seed for the generator.

6. The time required to wash an automobile at the Auto-Car Wash is uniformly distributed, with the minimal time being 8 minutes and the maximum being 12 minutes. Simulate the service time for processing 10 automobiles. Use the uniform process generator in your analysis. What is the expected time required to wash a single car? What is the average time for the 10 cars that you processed? (Use the random numbers from the first column of Table A-4 in Appendix A in employing the process generator.)

7. The time between arrivals for customers entering a convenience store can be described by a negative exponential distribution with a mean of 8 minutes. Simulate the arrival of 10 customers at the store. Use the negative exponential process generator in your analysis. (Use the random numbers from the second column of Table A-4 in Appendix A.)

8. The time between breakdowns for a particular manufacturing operation can be described by a negative exponential distribution with a mean of 100 hours. Simulate the timing of 5 breakdowns. Use the negative exponential process generator in your analysis. (Use the random numbers from the third column of Table A-4 in Appendix A.)

9. Given the following probability density functions:

$$p(x) = \begin{cases} 1/6, & 0 < x \le 2 \\ 1/3, & 2 < x \le 3 \\ 1/12, & 3 < x \le 7 \end{cases}$$

**a.** Sketch the function.
**b.** Identify the cumulative distribution function (cdf).
**c.** Using the inverse transformation method, develop the corresponding process generator.

10. Develop a process generator for the following probability density function.

$$p(x) = \begin{cases} (1/2)e^x, & -\infty < x < 0 \\ (1/2)e^{-x}, & 0 < x < \infty \end{cases}$$

11. The number of customers arriving at a drive-in bank can be described by a Poisson distribution with a mean of 4 arrivals per half-hour. Simulate the arrival of customers over a 1-hour period. (Recall the reciprocal relationship between the time between arrivals (negative exponential distribution) and the number of arrivals per time period (Poisson distribution). Use the random numbers from the fourth column of Table A-4 in Appendix A.)

12. The number of calls per hour coming into the crisis-line switchboard at the Bridgeport Hospital was monitored for 300 one-hour periods. The following data are a summary of

the results:

| Calls/Hour | Frequency $f_o$ |
|---|---|
| 4 or fewer | 120 |
| 5 | 105 |
| 6 | 45 |
| 7 | 21 |
| 8 | 6 |
| 9 or more | 3 |

Test the data to determine whether a Poisson distribution with $\lambda = 5$ can be used to describe the number of calls per hour coming into the switchboard. (Test the data using $\alpha = .05$.)

13. Ben Ellis is the dock-warehouse manager for a large grocery chain. Ben is in the process of studying the dock facilities in anticipation of adding an additional dock, and has collected data (shown in Table P21-13) for 50 truck arrivals (time between arrivals) and unloading times. Describe the steps Ben would have to go through to simulate the dock-warehouse operation.

**TABLE P21-13. Truck Arrival and Unloading Times**

| Time Between Arrivals (minutes) | | Unloading Time (minutes) | |
|---|---|---|---|
| 16.6 | 18.7 | 14.9 | 28.3 |
| 15.8 | 15.4 | 5.5 | 59.8 |
| 12.7 | 12.6 | 117.6 | 3.1 |
| 13.3 | 18.0 | 28.5 | 23.3 |
| 14.8 | 14.0 | 31.0 | 169.1 |
| 21.0 | 15.5 | 40.1 | 92.8 |
| 17.2 | 15.0 | 106.7 | 31.6 |
| 13.4 | 15.7 | 78.1 | 7.0 |
| 12.1 | 16.5 | 58.8 | 1.2 |
| 12.8 | 16.9 | 9.4 | 50.1 |
| 17.0 | 14.1 | 19.6 | .8 |
| 17.3 | 16.6 | 14.9 | 43.1 |
| 19.0 | 13.1 | 17.7 | 62.0 |
| 17.1 | 13.6 | 16.1 | 58.9 |
| 17.5 | 11.5 | 56.4 | 29.3 |
| 18.4 | 17.5 | 31.4 | 7.3 |
| 12.2 | 14.9 | 23.8 | 14.7 |
| 17.8 | 15.8 | 60.4 | 16.2 |
| 19.6 | 14.5 | 38.8 | 10.0 |
| 17.3 | 18.2 | 48.3 | 14.8 |
| 13.2 | 17.7 | 36.6 | 77.1 |
| 15.3 | 18.4 | 12.8 | 16.0 |
| 17.9 | 12.6 | 10.4 | 13.0 |
| 16.2 | 11.4 | 87.5 | 45.8 |
| 21.9 | 17.6 | 11.6 | 35.1 |

14. D. M. Blackmore is the manager of the East Avenue branch of the Guarantee Bank and Trust Company. Blackmore has gathered data on customers entering the bank and being serviced. He is of the opinion that the arrival pattern can be described by a Poisson distribution with an average arrival rate of 12 customers per hour (i.e., 1 customer per 5 minutes). He also feels that the service time can be described by a negative exponential distribution with an average service time of 4 minutes per customer. Use simulation to determine the average customer waiting time for this arrangement for 25 customers. (Use the random numbers from the fifth and sixth columns of Table A-4 in Appendix A.)

15. The banking service operation in Problem 14 consists of a single service desk. Assume the same 25 customers arrive (at the time indicated), but that two service desks are available. The average service time at each desk is now 6 minutes per customer. Customers are processed out of a single line by the first service desk that becomes available. Determine the average customer wait time for this service arrangement. (Use the first column of random numbers in Table A-4 in Appendix A for generating service times.)

16. An automobile license-tag station has been set up to handle the large number of customers that normally wait until April 1 to renew their licenses. Each customer passes through two operations: (1) inspection of old receipt/typing of new receipt and (2) payment of fees. Customers arrive at the station in a uniformly distributed manner with an arrival time of 4 ± 1 minutes. Service times at the two operations are uniformly distributed with parameters of 3 ± 1 and 2 ± .5 minutes, respectively. Simulate the arrival and processing of the first 25 customers. (Assume the office opens at 9:00 A.M.) What is the average waiting time per customer? (Use the first three columns of random numbers in Table A-4 in Appendix A.)

17. Trucks arrive at Long Island Shipping and Storage in a Poisson manner with an average of 2 arrivals per day. Three unloading docks are available for handling the trucks. On the average, a full day is required to unload a truck; prior data indicate that the service time can be described by a negative exponential distribution. Simulate 10 days of operation. Compute the average time that a truck spends waiting for a dock to become available. (Use the last two columns of random numbers in Table A-4 in Appendix A.)

18. The Freemore Clinic is in the process of evaluating waiting-room requirements for its incoming patients. It has been noted that patients arrive at the clinic in a random fashion (Poisson distributed) with a mean rate of 4 per hour. Patients are treated one at a time on a first-come–first-serve basis. The time a patient spends being treated is negative exponentially distributed with a mean time of 12 minutes. (a) Explain how you go about simulating the problem to determine the seating capacity of the waiting room such that the probability that an arriving patient will have to stand is less than or equal to .10. (b) Carry out such a simulation for 20 patients. (Use the random numbers from the third and fourth columns of Table A-4 in Appendix A.)

**22**

# Dynamic Programming

## ■ Introduction

In all of the previous chapters, except Chapter 18 on Markov processes, we studied static models—or models where the parameters remain the same during the period under consideration. For example, the use of linear programming assumes that all profits (or costs), supplies (and/or demands), and physical rates of substitution will remain the same during the entire period. Although we did consider some multiperiod models in both the linear and goal programming chapters, they were still static, since we assumed that all parameters remained constant. This allowed us to solve one problem for all time periods. In this chapter, we will consider a dynamic model that can accommodate a change of parameters over time. This model is called *dynamic programming*.

Dynamic programming (DP) is an approach to optimization that can be applied to numerous problems, some of which have been discussed in previous chapters. In general, DP seeks to find a solution to an optimization problem in a sequential manner. Unlike linear programming, DP is not a single-solution algorithm, but an approach to solving a single large problem by solving a sequence of small problems. This approach allows us to solve a time-dependent problem as a sequence of one-period problems, where the parameters of each period depend on the period being considered. In fact, the parameters of each period may not be known until the period arrives. Dynamic programming was first formalized in a book by Richard Bellman, who is considered the father of DP.[1]

The parameters in dynamic programming can be either deterministic or stochastic, but in this introductory text we will restrict ourselves to the simplest cases of dynamic programming, which involve solving problems with deterministic parameters. In some cases, we will use dynamic programming to solve problems that we have considered previously.

---

[1] Richard Bellman, *Dynamic Programming* (Princeton, N.J.: Princeton University Press), 1957.

## ■ Case

# Mi Tierra Tortilla Factory

The Mi Tierra Tortilla Factory is a small company located in San Antonio, Texas. It produces various corn and flour products for the growing Mexican food market. Primarily, these products are corn and flour tortillas. The corn tortillas are used for enchiladas, tacos, and tostadas; the flour tortillas normally go into burritos. The manager and primary owner of Mi Tierra is Juan Valdez.

Juan has been working very hard to land a contract with one of the new fast-food companies specializing in Mexican food. Just this week he heard that the Burrito Bell Company has decided to buy flour tortillas from Mi Tierra. Burrito Bell wants to buy 200 boxes of flour tortillas in each of the next seven months (with each box containing 1000 flour tortillas) at a fixed price.

Juan immediately started calculating Mi Tierra's profit figures and came to the conclusion that the company would make $1000 each month if Mi Tierra produced exactly the amount needed for that month. After a moment's thought, Juan also calculated the profit for producing more than the number of boxes needed for a single month. He did this because the flour tortillas can be produced and frozen for as long as four months. Mi Tierra could produce more tortillas in any single month by working overtime and by hiring extra help. This would not affect the production of other products that continued every month.

Juan's calculations of profits for production of various numbers of tortillas, or, as they are called, *batch sizes,* are shown in Table 22-1.

Due to a combination of economic and storage factors, there are economies of scale in producing a larger batch size, but there are also the costs of freezing the tortillas and the costs resulting from deterioration of some of the tortillas. Beyond a two-month period, the deterioration from freezing increases markedly.

Since Juan wanted to derive the greatest possible profit from Mi Tierra's seven-month contract with Burrito Bell, he wanted to produce batch sizes that would lead to the highest total profit. Juan realized that he might be able to work out this small problem by listing all possible combinations, but he couldn't do that if Burrito Bell decided to give Mi Tierra a longer contract in the future.

Juan had recently attended a conference for small-business owners on the application of financial and quantitative models to small-business problems. He quickly realized that his problem was a type of problem where one would seek to optimize a profit function. In this sense, it appeared to be somewhat like the linear programming models discussed by Professor Sandra Toney at the conference. However, there also appeared to be some crucial differences. For one, LP assumes fractional answers, but his problem involved exact batch sizes. Also, LP does not usually involve decisions over time whereas the tortilla production problem could be broken up into a sequence of decisions. Since he needed to solve this problem for the highest-profit batch size, Juan decided to ask Professor Toney to help Mi Tierra solve its batch-size problem.

When Sandra arrived, she first asked Juan to explain the tortilla production process. She then examined the profit–batch-size table (Table 22-1). She realized that Juan's problem involved a sequence of decisions to be made over time, and the parameters (profits, demands, etc.) were assumed to be known with certainty. She decided that the primary question facing Juan was how much to produce each month so as to maximize total profits for the entire seven-month planning period. Finally, she noted that Juan was constrained to produce at most four months' demand

**TABLE 22-1.**
**Profits for Various Batch Sizes**

| Batch Size | Profit |
|---|---|
| 200 boxes | $1000 |
| 400 boxes | $2500 |
| 600 boxes | $3750 |
| 800 boxes | $4750 |

at any one time because of spoilage after four months.

As Sandra explained to Juan, this batch-size problem can be formulated as a mathematical programming problem by letting

$w_1$ = number of times one months' demand (200 boxes) is produced

$w_2$ = number of times two month's demand (400 boxes) is produced

$w_3$ = number of times three months' demand (600 boxes) is produced

$w_4$ = number of times four months' demand (800 boxes) is produced

Using these variable definitions, Sandra then wrote the following formulation for the batch problem:

MAXIMIZE:

$$1000w_1 + 2500w_2 + 3750w_3 + 4750w_4 \qquad (22.1)$$

SUBJECT TO:

$$w_1 + 2w_2 + 3w_3 + 4w_4 = 7 \qquad (22.2)$$

$$w_i = 0, 1, 2, 3, \ldots \quad \text{for each } i \qquad (22.3)$$

Juan looked at the formulation and said, "That looks like the linear programming problems we discussed at the small-business conference. Can we solve it like the LP problem?"

"No, we can't use LP methods on this problem because of the requirement that the $w_i$ variables take on discrete values. We could use integer programming methods, but since this is a time-sequential problem, I suggest we use another method called dynamic programming, or DP for short.

"DP approaches a problem as a sequence of decisions and works to make a series of decisions that lead to the highest profit subject to whatever constraints exist for the problem."

"That sounds like the way to go!" exclaimed Juan. "How does that work?"

"DP requires that we change our perspective from trying to make a single decision to one of making a series of decisions. The usual way to do this is to start at the end of the planning period and work backward to the beginning of the planning period. In each case, we make sure that the sequence of decisions is optimal from that decision to the end. In your case, we will begin at the seventh month and make a decision of how much to manufacture."

"The contract ends after seven months so we wouldn't want to produce more than 200 boxes for that month if we are only considering the seventh month," Juan noted.

"That's right," replied Sandra, "and your profit for that decision would be $1000 for 200 boxes."

"There was no real decision there, but what about the sixth month?" asked Juan.

"For the sixth month we have two alternatives. First we could produce 200 boxes in the sixth month, then an additional 200 boxes in month 7 for a total profit of $1000 plus $1000 equals $2000. Or we could produce the entire remaining two months' demand, 400 boxes, in the sixth month and none in the seventh. In that case, the profit is $2500 from your batch size vs. profit table. Using these choices we can see that the batch size to use in the sixth month is to produce 400 boxes to supply the entire two-month demand."

"So far it appears that you are doing nothing except listing all of the choices. Is that all that DP does?" asked Juan.

Sandra smiled and said, "No, DP is more efficient than that. I think the difference will become clear in our third decision concerning the fifth month. In this month, we are faced with three choices, produce 200 boxes, 400 boxes, or 600 boxes. If we produce 200 boxes to meet the demand in the fifth month, we make an immediate profit of $1000, but we then have to make a decision about the sixth and seventh months."

"But we discovered before that the best policy for the sixth month was to produce all of the remaining demand in that month," noted Juan.

"Now you're catching on! The profit for the best decision that results from the decision in the fifth month is added to the immediate profit for that month. So if we produce 200 boxes in month 5 for a profit of $1000, the best policy for the remaining 400 boxes is to produce all of it in month 6 for a profit of $2500. The total of these two is $3500 profit. The second choice was to produce 400 boxes in month 5 for an immediate profit of $2500. This leaves only 200 boxes needed, and we saw earlier that this number should be produced in month 7 for a profit of $1000. Adding these two together, we get a total profit of $3500. Finally, if we produce the entire demand of 600 boxes in the fifth month, we realize a profit of $3750. Since this is the highest of the three, we would choose this policy whenever 600 boxes remain to be produced."

"Oh, I see," said Juan. "For a given decision, we sum the profit for a given production level and the highest profit for the amount that remains to be produced to achieve our total production

requirements. Does it always work out that Mi Tierra should produce the most possible?"

"I don't think it will, but let's check. We'll compute the highest profit for each month starting with the seventh. In each case I'll show the highest possible demand for that month, the various production choices, the profit for that choice, the amount that remains to be produced based on that choice, the highest profit for the remaining demand, and the total profit for each choice. I'll mark the highest profit with an asterisk (*)."

"What about the case where demand in some month is less than the maximum due to a previous production level? Don't we have to account for that case?" asked Juan.

"No. If you have less than the total possible demand, that means there is some inventory left over from a previous production period and no production is necessary in this period."

Sandra then wrote seven tables, one for each month. These tables are shown as Tables 22-2 through 22-8.

**TABLE 22-2. Seventh-Month Decision Table**

| Month | Demand | Production Choices | Immediate Profit | Remaining Demand | Best Profit on Remaining Demand | Total Profit |
|---|---|---|---|---|---|---|
| 7 | 200 | 200 | $1000 | 0 | 0 | $1000° |

**TABLE 22-3. Sixth-Month Decision Table**

| Month | Demand | Production Choices | Immediate Profit | Remaining Demand | Best Profit on Remaining Demand | Total Profit |
|---|---|---|---|---|---|---|
| 6 | 400 | 200 | $1000 | 200 | $1000 | $2000 |
|   |     | 400 | $2500 | 0   | 0     | $2500° |

**TABLE 22-4. Fifth-Month Decision Table**

| Month | Demand | Production Choices | Immediate Profit | Remaining Demand | Best Profit on Remaining Demand | Total Profit |
|---|---|---|---|---|---|---|
| 5 | 600 | 200 | $1000 | 400 | $2500 | $3500 |
|   |     | 400 | $2500 | 200 | $1000 | $3500 |
|   |     | 600 | $3750 | 0   | 0     | $3750° |

**TABLE 22-5. Fourth-Month Decision Table**

| Month | Demand | Production Choices | Immediate Profit | Remaining Demand | Best Profit on Remaining Demand | Total Profit |
|-------|--------|--------------------|------------------|------------------|---------------------------------|--------------|
| 4 | 800 | 200 | $1000 | 600 | $3750 | $4750 |
|   |     | 400 | $2500 | 400 | $2500 | $5000° |
|   |     | 600 | $3750 | 200 | $1000 | $4750 |
|   |     | 800 | $4750 | 0   | 0     | $4750 |

**TABLE 22-6. Third-Month Decision Table**

| Month | Demand | Production Choices | Immediate Profit | Remaining Demand | Best Profit on Remaining Demand | Total Profit |
|-------|--------|--------------------|------------------|------------------|---------------------------------|--------------|
| 3 | 1000 | 200 | $1000 | 800 | $5000 | $6000 |
|   |      | 400 | $2500 | 600 | $3750 | $6250° |
|   |      | 600 | $3750 | 400 | $2500 | $6250° |
|   |      | 800 | $4750 | 200 | $1000 | $5750 |

**TABLE 22-7. Second-Month Decision Table**

| Month | Demand | Production Choices | Immediate Profit | Remaining Demand | Best Profit on Remaining Demand | Total Profit |
|-------|--------|--------------------|------------------|------------------|---------------------------------|--------------|
| 2 | 1200 | 200 | $1000 | 1000 | $6250 | $7250 |
|   |      | 400 | $2500 | 800  | $5000 | $7500° |
|   |      | 600 | $3750 | 600  | $3750 | $7500° |
|   |      | 800 | $4750 | 400  | $2500 | $7250 |

**TABLE 22-8. First-Month Decision Table**

| Month | Demand | Production Choices | Immediate Profit | Remaining Demand | Best Profit on Remaining Demand | Total Profit |
|-------|--------|--------------------|------------------|------------------|---------------------------------|--------------|
| 1 | 1400 | 200 | $1000 | 1200 | $7500 | $8500 |
|   |      | 400 | $2500 | 1000 | $6250 | $8750° |
|   |      | 600 | $3750 | 800  | $5000 | $8750° |
|   |      | 800 | $4750 | 600  | $3750 | $8500 |

"Wait a minute!" interrupted Juan. "I followed the first three tables, but you lost me on the fourth month. Could you explain that table?"

"Okay. In the fourth month, we have a four-month demand to be met. So the total demand is 4 × 200 = 800 boxes. We have four production choices or batch sizes. Each choice comes from producing a one-, two-, three-, or four-month demand in the fourth month. We find the immediate profit value from your profit vs. batch size table (Table 22-1). We find the remaining demand for each production choice by subtracting the

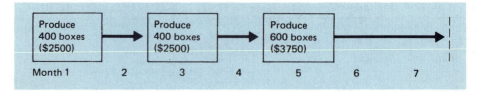

batch size from the total demand. The "best profit on remaining demand" values are found by finding a table whose total demand equals the remaining demand. The highest profit in that table is then used as the "best profit on remaining demand." For example, in the fourth-month table, if the production choice is 400 boxes, then the remaining demand is $800 - 400 = 400$ boxes. We then go to the table having a total demand of 400 boxes and find a highest profit of $2500. We sum the *immediate* profit and the *highest* profit on the remaining demand to find a *total* profit for this production choice."

After Juan nodded his understanding, Sandra proceeded with the remaining tables. After she had finished the tables, Sandra asked Juan, "Do you understand what this last table says?"

Juan thought for a moment and then said, "I think so. It appears that in month 1, which is the beginning of the contract, I will have 1400 boxes total demand to be produced. I can produce 200, 400, 600, or 800 boxes in that month. If 200 boxes are produced in month 1 for an immediate profit of $1000, 1200 boxes will remain to be produced. If the best policy on these 1200 boxes is followed, the profit will be $7500 on those boxes. Then my highest total profit from producing 200 boxes in month 1 is the sum of $1000 and $7500, or $8500. And, let's see, the total profit from producing either 400 or 600 boxes in month 1 is $8570. This is the highest so I'll produce either 400

or 600 boxes. But how do I know what to do after I produce, say, 400 boxes?"

"Well, if you produce 400 boxes, your remaining demand will be 1000 boxes. So go to the table with total demand of 1000 boxes and find the next production choice. In this case, we find this is the third-month table (Table 22-6), and the highest-profit production choice is to produce either 400 or 600 boxes. If we once again produce 400 boxes, the remaining demand is 600 boxes. Now we go to the table with total demand of 600 boxes for the next production choice. We find a total demand of 600 boxes in the fifth month table (Table 22-4) with a highest-profit production choice of 600 boxes. Since the remaining demand is zero we are finished. Let me diagram your production schedule."

Sandra then drew a diagram of Juan's highest-profit production schedule, which is shown in Figure 22-1.

"This looks very good," Juan said as he looked at the production schedule and profit values. "It's $1750 higher than just producing the Burrito Bell demand one month at a time. Can you use this procedure on bigger contracts?"

"Sure," replied Sandra. "The only difference is in the number of tables to be used, but a computer would have no trouble with such a problem. If you get a larger contract, give me a call and I'll put a graduate student on your problem as a field project."

## ■ Dynamic programming: Assumptions and terminology

The above case has attempted to explain the process used in solving problems through dynamic programming. As demonstrated, DP solves a large problem by solving numerous small problems. Before going on to other applications of DP, it is useful to look at the assumptions and terminology of DP.

Like any other approach to solving problems, dynamic programming has its own set of assumptions and terminology. We will first discuss the assumptions followed by terminology and then relate both to the Mi Tierra Case.

### Decomposition

The primary assumption of DP is that a single large problem may be decomposed or segmented into a sequence of smaller easy-to-solve subproblems; problems involving addition or multiplication are classic examples of decomposable problems. Implicit in the assumption of decomposition are the assumptions that (a) the larger problem can be solved through a sequence of decisions; and (b) the smaller problems can themselves be solved "easily."

Also implicit in the use of decomposition in dynamic programming is the concept known as **Bellman's Principle of Optimality:**

*Bellman's Principle of Optimality*

> An optimal set of decisions (a policy) has the property that if a given decision is optimal, then all subsequent decisions depending on the given decision must also be optimal.

This principle, together with the decomposition of a single large problem into a sequence of small problems, suggests the **backward approach** used in the Mi Tierra case. Essentially, we begin at the end of the process and work backward, always using the optimal decision from an earlier decision. In so doing, we are assured of finding the optimal set of decisions.

*backward approach*

### Stages, state variables, returns, decisions, and recursive relationships

In discussing DP, the key terms are *stages, state variables, returns, decisions,* and the *recursive relation*. Each of these terms and its meaning in DP will be discussed separately. The discussion will be more meaningful if we refer to Figure 22-2.

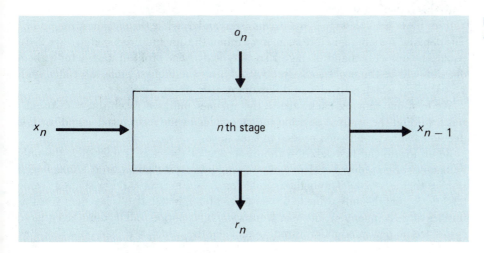

**FIGURE 22-2.
A Single Stage**

*stage*
*state variable*
*decision*

*return*

*recursive*
*relationship*

In Figure 22-2, we have shown the inputs and outputs at any point in the problem-solving sequence used in dynamic programming. This is the $n$th **stage** of the problem, and there exist two inputs. These are the **state variable** $x_n$ and the **decision** $d_n$. The state variable relates the present stage back to the previous stage. The state variable allows us to compute the remaining amount of scarce resource or demand; it is also used in conjunction with the decision to determine the outputs from the stage. The outputs from this stage are the **return** at stage $n$, which is denoted $r_n$ and the state variable $(x_{n-1})$ for stage $(n - 1)$. The return at any stage is the contribution to profit (or increase in cost) that occurs at *that* stage due to the decision and the state variable $x_n$. The decision at any stage is how much to allocate to each of the competing demands, and usually is made by solving an easy problem at each stage. The state variables in successive stages, $x_n$ and $x_{n-1}$, are tied together through the **recursive relationship** that computes the value of $x_{n-1}$, using the value of $x_n$ and the decision at this stage, $d_n$.

To relate this back to the Mi Tierra case, each stage is a month, and the state variable at each stage represents the total unmet demand in a previous stage, that is, a later month. The decision in Mi Tierra is how much to produce in the month (stage) being considered, and the return is the profit associated with each decision and state variable. The main difference that exists between this notation of $x_n$, $x_{n-1}$, $d_n$, and $r_n$ and the Mi Tierra case is the numbering system. In DP, we let stage 1 be the last decision and stage $n$ be the first. So in the Mi Tierra case, stage 1 is month 7, stage 2 is month 6, and so on until stage 7 is month 1 of the planning horizon. This is done to simplify the backward aspect of the dynamic programming approach to solutions.

In terms of state variables, stages, decisions, and returns, stage 1 of the Mi Tierra problem corresponds to month 7. At this stage, the inputs are the state variable $x_1$, and the decision $d_1$. The outputs for stage 1 are the profit resulting from the values of $x_1$, and $d_1$—this is $r_1$—and the next state variable, $x_0$. Obviously we want no output after the contract period, so $x_0 = 0$. The value of $x_0$ is also found by the relationship $x_0 = x_1 - d_1$, which says that the demand remaining *after* stage 1 must equal the demand remaining *before*, minus the amount produced in stage 1. Since $x_0 = 0$, then $x_1 = d_1$, and in stage 1 we will always produce an amount equal to the demand remaining. The profit in this month is equal to the profit on producing the amount $d_1$ since this is the first stage.

If we move back to stage 2, the inputs are $x_2$ and $d_2$ while the outputs are $x_1$ and $r_2$. The demand remaining before stage 2, $x_2$, minus the amount produced in stage 2, $d_2$, equals the unmet demand in stage 1 $(x_1 = x_2 - d_2)$. The profit in stage 2 for a given decision will be the profit associated with $d_2$ *plus* the highest profit associated with $x_1 = x_2 - d_2$, which is the demand remaining after $d_2$ is produced.

We continue moving backward in this manner until we reach stage $n$. At each stage, we find the optimal decision for each value of the state variable and use this decision and its profit when needed in later stages.

Returning to the first table in the discussion of the case, Table 22-2, the only demand to be considered with one month remaining is 200 boxes. So $x_1 = 200$, which implies that $d_1 = 200$. The highest profit for $d_1 = 200$ is \$1000. For stage 2, Table 22-3 shows that the only value to be considered for $x_1$ is 400. If $x_1$ is less than 400, this implies there is inventory left over from a previous period and $d_2$ must be equal to zero since no new production is required. Then the values of $d_2$ can be 200 or 400.

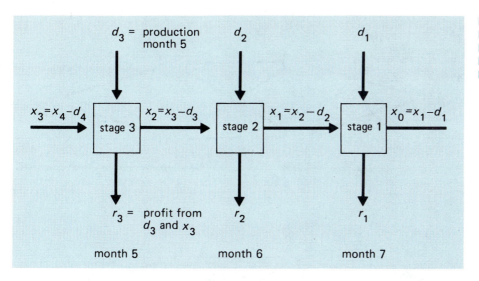

FIGURE 22-3.
Diagrammatic
Presentation of
Dynamic
Programming

The value of $d_2$ cannot be less than 200 because the demand could not be met in the remaining months. For each decision where $d_2 = 200$ or $400$, we calculate the sum of the profit for the decision value and the optimal profit for $x_2 - d_2$. We then maximize over these decisions to find the best decision for each value of the state variable. Since we are not interested in maximizing the profit for any period other than that which begins in month 1, we wait until we reach stage 7 to find the optimal solution over the entire period.

In Figure 22-3, we have a diagrammatic portrayal of this process. In each stage $x_{n-1} = x_n - d_n$ and $r_n = $ profit from $d_n$ *plus* optimal profit from $x_{n-1}$.

We will use this terminology and notation to discuss additional problems where dynamic programming is used.

# ▪ Applications of dynamic programming

## *Shortest path problem revisited*

Recall that in Chapter 11 we discussed the shortest path problem and formulated it as a network problem. We further said that this network formulation could be solved via a specialized version of the simplex method, but that there also existed other procedures for solving shortest path problems. One such procedure is a direct application of dynamic programming.

To demonstrate how DP can be used to solve shortest path problems, we have redrawn as Figure 22-4 the problem of going from New Orleans to Atlanta, originally shown as Figure 11-10 (distances in minutes).

To apply DP, we need to divide the problem into stages and decide upon state variables. In Figure 22-5, the New Orleans-to-Atlanta problem is redrawn again and divided into three stages. These stages are analogous to the three decision-making points in the trip. Note that the stages begin with stage 1 in Montgomery and Birmingham, since we are going to use the backward approach to solve this problem.

**FIGURE 22-4.
Driving Routes
from New Orleans
to Atlanta**

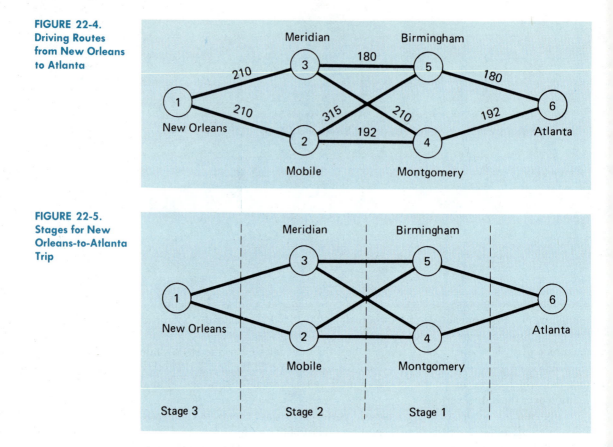

**FIGURE 22-5.
Stages for New
Orleans-to-Atlanta
Trip**

The state variables are the cities that a traveler is in whenever a decision must be made. For example, in stage 1, the state variable $x_1$ is Birmingham or Montgomery. The decision at each stage is which city to visit. For example, in stage 1 the decision is easy since we must go to Atlanta regardless of where we are. The reward associated with each state variable and each decision in a given stage is the driving time in minutes. For example, in stage 1 with $x_1 =$ Birmingham and the decision is to go to Atlanta (only decision possible), the return is 180. Remember that we wish to minimize in this problem rather than maximize.

For the first stage, we assume we have arrived in Atlanta. The question then becomes: how did we get there in the shortest time? Obviously we came from either Birmingham or Montgomery. This reasoning is shown in Table 22-9.

**TABLE 22-9.
Stage 1 Decision
Tableau**

| State $(x_1)$ Variable | Decision | Optimal Decision | Optimal Return |
|---|---|---|---|
| 4 | go to 6 | go to 6 | 192 |
| 5 | go to 6 | go to 6 | 180 |

**TABLE 22-10.**
**Stage 2 Decision**
**Tableau**

| State $(x_2)$ Variable | Decisions | | Optimal Decision | Optimal Return |
|---|---|---|---|---|
| | 4 | 5 | | |
| 2 | 192 + 192 | 315 + 180 | go to 4 | 384 |
| 3 | 210 + 192 | 180 + 180 | go to 5 | 360 |

We now use these optimal decisions in the next stage, where $x_2$ = Meridian or Mobile. We do this since Bellman's Principle of Optimality as applied to network problems may be stated as follows:

> If the optimal path includes a node, then the shortest path from that node to the end is a part of the optimal path.

For stage 2, the table used to make the decision is similar to Table 22-9 except that now there is more than one city to visit next. The possible cities to visit next (often referred to as decision variables) are listed across the top. The return associated with each decision is the sum of the distance from the state variable to the decision variable plus the optimal distance from the decision variable to the end.

In Table 22-10, for example, if we are in Mobile (2), the optimal decision is to go to Montgomery (4), with a total time of 384 minutes. And if we are in Meridian (3), the optimal decision is to go to Birmingham (5), with a total time of 360 minutes.

We now continue backward to New Orleans (1) and make the decision as to which city to visit next. This is done in Table 22-11.

Here, as in stage 2 decisions, the return for a given decision is the time from the state variable to the decision variable plus the optimal time from the decision variable to the end. For example, for a decision to go to Mobile (2), the shortest time is the sum of the shortest time to Mobile plus the shortest time from Mobile to Atlanta. This second value is found by looking in the previous stage's decision tableau (Table 22-10) with Mobile (2) as a state variable, to find 570 as the optimal return.

We have now found that the shortest driving time from New Orleans to Atlanta is 570 minutes, but how do we find the route that has this driving time? To determine the optimal path, we now do a *forward pass* through the decision tableaus from New Orleans to Atlanta. If we are in New Orleans (1), the optimal decision from Table 22-11 is to go to Meridian (3). So the first leg of the journey is to go to Meridian. To find where to go from Meridian, we treat Meridian as the state variable and look in the stage 2 decision tableau (Table 22-10). If this is done, we find that the optimal decision from Meridian (3) is to go to Birmingham (5). Once we are in Birmingham,

**TABLE 22-11.**
**Stage 3 Decision**
**Tableau**

| State $(x_2)$ Variable | Decisions | | Optimal Decision | Optimal Return |
|---|---|---|---|---|
| | 2 | 3 | | |
| 1 | 210 + 384 | 210 + 360 | go to 3 | 570 |

we then look in the stage 1 decision tableau to determine where to go next. In this case, the decision is to go to Atlanta (6).

The result of this forward pass through the decision tableaus is the shortest path from New Orleans to Atlanta. This path is

New Orleans → Meridian → Birmingham → Atlanta

## High Shoals School District

The High Shoals School District is an urban school district in which a sizeable proportion of the students have severe reading problems. Jane Smith, Curriculum Coordinator for the elementary schools in the district, has been successful in obtaining a grant from the Education Department to hire five special teachers. She wants to place these teachers in the three schools that have had the worst reading test scores in order to improve the overall reading ability of the students in the schools. However, she does not know how many teachers to place in each school so as to maximize the effectiveness of the reading program. In consultation with the principals and teachers in the schools, she has developed a table that shows the average increase in reading grade level (in school months) each school would experience when various numbers of teachers are placed there. This table is shown as Table 22-12.

In studying this table, Jane realized that an integer number of teachers is required in each case. She realizes this integer requirement precludes the use of any math models that have the assumption of divisibility. She also realizes that while she could enumerate all possible combinations for this small problem, such an approach would not be useful for any larger problems. Since she is considering applying for a grant to use the same instructional approach to the entire school district, she feels it is necessary to develop an analytical approach to the allocation of reading teachers.

Initially, the High Shoals School District problem does not appear to be one to which dynamic programming may be applied. There is not an evident sequence of decisions to be made and there is no timing of the assignment of teachers. However, if we view the problem as one of assigning teachers to School A, then to School B, and finally to School C, we have introduced a sequence of decisions. This sequence of

**TABLE 22-12.**
**Average Increase in Grade Level (School Months)**

|                    | School |     |     |
| ------------------ | ------ | --- | --- |
| Number of Teachers | A      | B   | C   |
| 0                  | 0      | 0   | 0   |
| 1                  | 6      | 9   | 12  |
| 2                  | 10     | 14  | 18  |
| 3                  | 15     | 18  | 21  |
| 4                  | 18     | 20  | 21  |
| 5                  | 20     | 20  | 21  |

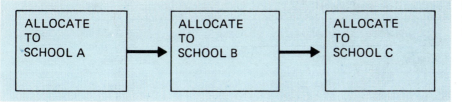

FIGURE 22-6.
Sequential Alloca-
tion

decisions allows us to approach the problem from a DP framework. This sequence is shown in Figure 22-6, where the order of the schools is unimportant as long as some sequence is followed.

Now if we use a backward approach, we will let stage 1 be the allocation to School C, stage 2 be the allocation to School B, and stage 3 be the allocation to School A. Then the decision at each stage is the number of teachers to assign to the school. The state variable is the number of teachers available to be assigned to the school. If $x_n$ is the state variable and $d_n$ is the decision at stage $n$, then

$$x_n = \text{number of teachers available for assignment}$$

$$d_n = \text{number of teachers assigned}$$

$$x_{n-1} = x_n - d_n \text{ (recursive relationship)}$$

At any stage, the return will be the sum of the immediate return associated with $d_n$ and $x_n$ plus the optimal return associated with $x_{n-1} = x_n - d_n$ from a previous tableau.

Using this approach, in stage 1 we will use a decision tableau like those used in the discussion of the shortest path problem (see Table 22-13). Then, using the results of this initial decision tableau, we go on to stage 2 (see Table 22-14).

This tableau is different from the stage 1 tableau since the decisions are listed across the top. In the body of the tableau, the sum of immediate return and the optimal return associated with $x_2 - d_2$ is shown at the intersection of the $x_2$ row and the $d_2$ column. For example, if $x_2 = 3$ and $d_2 = 2$, then $x_2 - d_2 = 1$, and we find the value of $14 + 12 = 26$ in this cell of the tableau. The 14 comes from Table 22-12 and is the immediate reward; the 12 comes from Table 22-13 and is the optimal reward for $x_1 = 1$.

TABLE 22-13.
Stage 1 Decision
Tableau (School C)

| State Variable $(x_1)$ | Immediate Return | Optimal Decision $(d_1^*)$ | Optimal Return |
|---|---|---|---|
| 0 | 0 | 0 | 0 |
| 1 | 12 | 1 | 12 |
| 2 | 18 | 2 | 18 |
| 3 | 21 | 3 | 21 |
| 4 | 21 | 3 or 4 | 21 |
| 5 | 21 | 3, 4, or 5 | 21 |

**TABLE 22-14. Stage 2 Decision Tableau (School B)**

| State Variable $(x_2)$ | Decisions $(d_2)$ | | | | | | Optimal Reward | Optimal Decision $(d_2^*)$ |
|---|---|---|---|---|---|---|---|---|
| | 0 | 1 | 2 | 3 | 4 | 5 | | |
| 0 | 0 | | | | | | 0 | 0 |
| 1 | 12 | 9 + 0 | | | | | 12 | 0 |
| 2 | 18 | 9 + 12 | 14 + 0 | | | | 21 | 1 |
| 3 | 21 | 9 + 18 | 14 + 12 | 18 + 0 | | | 27 | 1 |
| 4 | 21 | 9 + 21 | 14 + 18 | 18 + 12 | 20 + 0 | | 32 | 2 |
| 5 | 21 | 9 + 21 | 14 + 21 | 18 + 18 | 20 + 12 | 20 + 0 | 36 | 3 |

We now go to stage 3 (School A). At this school, which is at the beginning of the assignment process, there are five teachers to assign (Table 22-15). Therefore, the only value of $x_3$ is $x_3 = 5$. There are still the same decisions to be made here as in the stage 2 tableau, and the returns are calculated in the same way.

On the basis of the stage 3 decision tableau, the maximum average reading grade level increase is 38 school months. This maximum value is associated with assigning one teacher to School A. We now do a forward pass to find the assignments to Schools B and C. To do this, we note that $x_3 = 5$ and $d_3^* = 1$, so $x_2 = 5 - 1 = 4$ teachers are available for assignment to School B. We now go to the stage 2 decision tableau with $x_2 = 4$. In Table 22-14, we find that for $x_2 = 4$ the optimal decision is to assign two teachers to School B $(d_2^* = 2)$. Now if $x_2 = 4$ and $d_2^* = 2$, then $x_1 = 4 - 2 = 2$ teachers available for assignment to School C. We now go to the stage 1 decision tableau (Table 22-13) with $x_1 = 2$ to find that $d_1^* = 2$ teachers are assigned to School C.

To summarize, we assign 1 teacher to School A, 2 teachers to School B, and 2 teachers to School C to achieve an average grade level increase of 38 school months.

## JCL, Inc., revisited

In our chapter on integer programming, we discussed the formulation of the JCL, Inc., case as follows:

MAXIMIZE:    $Z = 12y_1 + 15y_2 + 8y_3 + 5y_4 + 11y_5$    (22.4)

SUBJECT TO:    $2y_1 + 5y_2 + 4y_3 + 1y_4 + 6y_5 \leq 9$    (22.5)

$$y_1, y_2, y_3, y_4, y_5 = 0 \text{ or } 1$$    (22.6)

This is obviously a *knapsack* problem like the one we solved using branch and bound in Chapter 13. Another approach to solving knapsack problems is to use

**TABLE 22-15. Stage 3 Decision Tableau (School A)**

| State Variable $(x_3)$ | 0 | 1 | 2 | 3 | 4 | 5 | Optimal Return | Optimal Decision $(d_3^*)$ |
|---|---|---|---|---|---|---|---|---|
| 5 | 0 + 36 | 6 + 32 | 10 + 27 | 15 + 21 | 18 + 12 | 20 + 0 | 38 | 1 |

dynamic programming. The solution will be much like that used to solve the High Shoals School District problem, in that, since there is no time dependency, we can begin with any variable and work our way through the remainder of the variables. The key difference is that the state variables must take on all possible values up to the total amount available for allocation. The state variable is the amount of the resource remaining to be allocated and the decision variable whether $y_j$ is 0 or 1.

In terms of our notation, if, at stage $n$, $x_n$ is the state variable, $d_n$ is the decision, $r_n( )$ is the return, $a_n$ is the constraint coefficient, and $c_n$ is the objective function coefficient, then:

$$x_n = \text{amount of resource left to be allocated}$$

$$d_n = 0 \text{ or } 1 = \text{the value of the decision variable}$$

$$x_{n-1} = x_n - a_n d_n = \text{the value of the previous state variable}$$

$$r_n(d_n) = c_n d_n + r_{n-1}(x_n - d_n) = \text{the return for the state and decision variables}$$

To use a tabular approach, we list the state variable values down the first column of the table. Then the returns corresponding to values of the decision variable—that is, 0 or 1—are shown in the next two columns. Remember, if the amount of resource available (the state variable) is less than the amount required by the decision variable, the decision variable must be zero and the return is the sum of the immediate return and the return corresponding to the amount of resource remaining after the resource needed for the decision variable is subtracted from the original resource level. The return on the amount remaining comes from the previous stage table using the amount remaining as the state variable. For example, if in stage 2 the state variable equals 8 and the decision variable, $d_2$ is equal to 1, then the amount of resource remaining is equal to $8 - 5 = 3$, where 5 units are required for the decision variable. We would then go to the stage 1 table to find the optimal return for 3 units and add this to the immediate return for $d_2 = 1$, which is 15. The next column gives the maximum of the two return columns. This is the optimal return for each state variable. The corresponding values of the optimal decision variable are given in the last column.

Using the tabular approach, we begin with Table 22-16 for stage 1 calculations.

The stage 1 tableau is fairly straightforward since there is no previous stage. The stage 2 tableau, shown in Table 22-17, is the first to use the result of a previous tableau.

Before going on, let's look at the stage 2 tableau. Note that for state variable values of 2 or less, the only return is zero since both of the first decision variables require more than 2 units or resource. For state variable values of 2 to 4 units, a decision variable of zero yields a return of 12, which corresponds to the return from the previous tableau. For state variable values of 5 to 7, the decision variable value of 1 yields a return of 15 corresponding to the immediate return for this variable. Finally, for state variable values of 7 through 9, the return for the decision variable value of 1 is equal to the immediate return of 15 *plus* the return from the stage 1 tableau for a state variable value equal to the stage 2 state variable value minus 5 (the resource required by the decision variable).

**TABLE 22-16.**
**Stage 1 Tableau**

| State Variable $(S_1)$ | Return on Decision | | Optimal Return, $r_1(d_1^*)$ | Optimal Decision, $d_1^*$ |
|---|---|---|---|---|
| | $d_1 = 0$ | $d_1 = 1$ | | |
| 0 | 0 | — | 0 | 0 |
| 1 | 0 | — | 0 | 0 |
| 2 | 0 | 12 | 12 | 1 |
| 3 | 0 | 12 | 12 | 1 |
| 4 | 0 | 12 | 12 | 1 |
| 5 | 0 | 12 | 12 | 1 |
| 6 | 0 | 12 | 12 | 1 |
| 7 | 0 | 12 | 12 | 1 |
| 8 | 0 | 12 | 12 | 1 |
| 9 | 0 | 12 | 12 | 1 |

**TABLE 22-17.**
**Stage 2 Tableau**

| State Variable $(S_2)$ | Return on Decision | | Optimal Return, $r_2(d_2^*)$ | Optimal Decision, $d_2^*$ |
|---|---|---|---|---|
| | $d_2 = 0$ | $d_2 = 1$ | | |
| 0 | 0 | — | 0 | 0 |
| 1 | 0 | — | 0 | 0 |
| 2 | 12 | — | 12 | 0 |
| 3 | 12 | — | 12 | 0 |
| 4 | 12 | — | 12 | 0 |
| 5 | 12 | 15 | 15 | 1 |
| 6 | 12 | 15 | 15 | 1 |
| 7 | 12 | 12 + 15 | 27 | 1 |
| 8 | 12 | 12 + 15 | 27 | 1 |
| 9 | 12 | 12 + 15 | 27 | 1 |

**TABLE 22-18.**
**Stage 3 Tableau**

| State Variable $(S_3)$ | Return on Decision | | Optimal Return, $r_3(d_3^*)$ | Optimal Decision, $d_3^*$ |
|---|---|---|---|---|
| | $d_3 = 0$ | $d_3 = 1$ | | |
| 0 | 0 | — | 0 | 0 |
| 1 | 0 | — | 0 | 0 |
| 2 | 12 | — | 12 | 0 |
| 3 | 12 | — | 12 | 0 |
| 4 | 12 | 8 | 12 | 0 |
| 5 | 15 | 8 | 15 | 0 |
| 6 | 15 | 8 + 12 | 20 | 1 |
| 7 | 27 | 8 + 12 | 27 | 0 |
| 8 | 27 | 8 + 12 | 27 | 0 |
| 9 | 27 | 8 + 15 | 27 | 0 |

**TABLE 22-19.**
**Stage 4 Tableau**

| State Variable $(S_4)$ | Return on Decision | | Optimal Return, $r_4(d_4^*)$ | Optimal Decision, $d_4^*$ |
|---|---|---|---|---|
| | $d_4 = 0$ | $d_4 = 1$ | | |
| 0 | 0 | — | 0 | 0 |
| 1 | 0 | 5 | 5 | 1 |
| 2 | 12 | 5 | 12 | 0 |
| 3 | 12 | 5 + 12 | 17 | 1 |
| 4 | 12 | 5 + 12 | 17 | 1 |
| 5 | 15 | 5 + 12 | 17 | 1 |
| 6 | 15 | 5 + 15 | 20 | 1 |
| 7 | 27 | 5 + 15 | 27 | 0 |
| 8 | 27 | 5 + 27 | 32 | 1 |
| 9 | 27 | 5 + 27 | 32 | 1 |

**TABLE 22-20.**
**Stage 5 Tableau**

| State Variable $(S_5)$ | Return on Decision | | Optimal Return, $r_5(d_5^*)$ | Optimal Decision, $d_5^*$ |
|---|---|---|---|---|
| | $d_5 = 0$ | $d_5 = 1$ | | |
| 9 | 32 | 11 + 17 | 32 | 0 |

The remaining tableaus for this problem are shown in Tables 22-18 through 22-20.

Now, starting with the stage 5 tableau, we can work our way back to determine the optimal solution. In the stage 5 tableau, we find that the optimal return is 32, which corresponds to $d_5 = 0$, so no resource is used here. We then go to the stage 4 tableau to find that the optimal return of 32 corresponds to a decision variable value of 1, that is, $d_4 = 1$. This uses 1 unit of resource so we go to the stage 3 tableau and with a state variable value of $9 - 1 = 8$. For this state variable value, we find that the optimal return corresponds to a decision variable value of zero. We then go to the stage 2 tableau for a state variable value of 8 and find that the optimal return corresponds to the decision variable being equal to 1. This uses 5 units of resource, so we go to the first tableau with a state variable value of 3. For this value, we find the optimal return corresponds to $d_1 = 1$. The results of this forward pass are summarized in Table 22-21.

**TABLE 22-21.**
**Determination of Optimal Decisions**

| Decision Variable | Decision | Next State |
|---|---|---|
| $d_5$ | 0 | 9 |
| $d_4$ | 1 | 8 |
| $d_3$ | 0 | 8 |
| $d_2$ | 1 | 2 |
| $d_1$ | 1 | 0 |

## ■ Other applications of dynamic programming

Besides the four examples presented in this chapter, there exist numerous other problems to which dynamic programming has been applied. Some of these problems have been formulated in previous chapters. One of the first solution methods proposed for the traveling salesman problems was DP.

Another integer programming problem to which DP has been applied is the integer knapsack problem (where more than one of each item may be placed in the knapsack). DP has also been successfully applied to inventory problems such as those discussed in Chapter 14, where the problems do not necessarily meet the assumptions of the inventory models discussed in that chapter. DP can be used in these inventory problems as long as the optimization problems for each period can be solved.

The Mi Tierra Tortilla Factory problem is an example of an inventory problem where the inventory costs have been already included in the profit costs. This same problem can also be shown to be a longest path problem. To see how this is accomplished, consider Figure 22-7 for a smaller example having a four-month planning horizon with production being possible for only three months. The profits are the same as those in Mi Tierra.

For this version of Mi Tierra, we will work in terms of months' demand to be produced instead of boxes of tortillas. This choice of units fits the network structure better. Doing this and letting month 4 be stage 1, we have the first row of Table 22-22. This table shows all of the tableaus for this problem at one time. In this case, going from $M4$ to $M5$ is equivalent to producing 200 boxes of tortillas since that is one month's demand.

We now use this optimal decision in stage 2 where $x_2 = M3$. In the section of Table 22-22 for stage 2, the optimal decision is to go to $M5$ from $M3$. This is equivalent to producing all of the demand necessary for this period (400 boxes).

We continue this approach at stage 3 where $x_3 = M2$ and use the stage 3 section of Table 22-22. Note that for our previous cases, the return for each decision was the sum of the immediate return for that decision plus the optimal return found for that decision in a previous section of Table 22-22. For example, if the decision was $M3$, we go to the previous section where $M3$ was a state variable to find the optimal return from $M3$ to $M5$.

Finally, we arrive at stage 4 with $x_4 = M1$ and use the stage 4 section of Table 22-22. The optimal return for stage 4 is $5000, which is generated by the decision to go to $M3$ from $M1$. This is equivalent to producing a two-month demand in month 1.

**FIGURE 22-7.**
**Longest Path**
**Formulation**

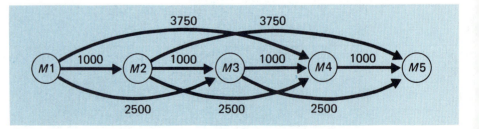

| Stage | State Variable | Possible Decisions | Return | Optimal Decision | Optimal Return |
|-------|----------------|--------------------|--------|------------------|----------------|
| 1 | $x_1 = M4$ | go to $M5$ | 1000 | go to $M5$ | 1000 |
| 2 | $x_2 = M3$ | go to $M4$<br>go to $M5$ | 1000 + 1000<br>2500 | go to $M5$ | 2500 |
| 3 | $x_3 = M2$ | go to $M3$<br>go to $M4$<br>go to $M5$ | 1000 + 2500<br>2500 + 1000<br>3750 | go to $M5$ | 3750 |
| 4 | $x_4 = M1$ | go to $M2$<br>go to $M3$<br>go to $M4$ | 1000 + 3750<br>2500 + 2500<br>3750 + 1000 | go to $M3$ | 5000 |

**TABLE 22-22.**
**Stage 1–4 Mi Tierra Tableaus**

This carries us forward to month 3. If we then go to the section having $M3$ as a state variable, we find that the optimal decision is to go to month 5. This, once again, is equivalent to producing a two-month demand in month 3. The optimal production plan then is to produce a two-month demand (400 boxes) in month 1 and another two-month demand (400 boxes) in month 3 for a total profit of $5000.

Dynamic programming can be used to solve many resource allocation problems. Linear programming problems can be solved via an approach somewhat like that used to solve the High Shoals School District problem. However, using DP is less efficient than using the simplex algorithm. DP has also been applied to stochastic problems by using expected values at each stage to compute rewards.

These and numerous more sophisticated applications are discussed in the references listed at the end of the chapter.

## ■ Summary

Dynamic programming is a quantitative model with wide and varying applications to managerial decision making. It is essentially a sequential model in that it looks at decisions on a one-at-a-time basis. It can also be classified as a normative model that seeks to optimize an objective function by determining the best—that is, lowest cost or highest profit—series of decisions. Dynamic programming, as discussed in this chapter, is strictly deterministic, but this is not necessarily the case in more sophisticated applications.

In terms of assumptions, dynamic programming only requires separability of a large problem into a series of small problems. Bellman's Principle of Optimality is then applied to arrive at an optimal solution. The important characteristic to remember about dynamic programming is that DP does not use a single algorithm as in the simplex method, but rather uses many different solution methods to solve the sequence of small problems.

In this discussion of dynamic programming, we solved batch-size problems, allocation-of-effort problems, shortest path problems, and knapsack problems using the DP approach.

## ▪ Glossary of terms

**backward approach:**   The dynamic programming approach to problems that works backward from a desired goal to find the means to reach the goal.

**Bellman's Principle of Optimality:**   If a series of decisions is optimal, then any of the series must be optimal regardless of which decision point it begins with.

**decision:**   The action that optimizes the small problem at each stage.

**recursive relationship:**   The relationship that allows for the calculation of the value of a state variable at a given state from the value of the state variable at a previous state.

**return:**   The optimal value of the optimization problem at each stage; a function of the state variable and the decision at the stage being considered.

**separability:**   The condition in which a single large optimization problem can be broken up into a series of small problems.

**stage:**   One of the small optimization problems into which a dynamic programming problem is separated.

**state variable:**   The variable that ties the stages or small optimization problems together.

## ▪ Review questions

1. Why are dynamic programming and Markov processes referred to as sequential models?
2. Discuss why dynamic programming cannot be applied to a problem that is not separable.
3. Discuss why Bellman's Principle of Optimality is essential to the use of dynamic programming.
4. Explain the difference between "stages" and "states."
5. Discuss the recursive relationship between state variables.
6. Why is the return at any stage a function of the value of the initial state variable and the decisions up to that stage?
7. For the Mi Tierra case, state the recursive relationship between state variables.
8. Why do we not need to assume linearity in order to solve problems using dynamic programming?

## ▪ True/false questions

1. Dynamic programming assumes that all relationships between variables are linear.
2. Dynamic programming can be compared to the branch-and-bound method for integer programming problems since both divide the problem up into small pieces.
3. Problems whose parameter values depend on the time period cannot be solved using dynamic programming.

4. Bellman's Principle of Optimality is the basis for the backward approach used in dynamic programming.

5. The state variable at any stage is determined from the next state variable via the recursive relationship.

6. At any stage, the values of the decision variable and the return are the outputs.

7. In a shortest path problem, the decision at any stage is which city to visit next.

8. In a allocation of effort problem, the order the sequence of decisions follows is crucial to the ultimate success of dynamic programming in solving the problem.

9. In the knapsack problem, the decision variables correspond to the 0–1 integer variables when we make the forward pass through the problem.

10. The procedure commonly used to find the critical path through an activity network is in no way associated with dynamic programming.

## ■ Problems

1. The Otto Apple Company has a constant demand for 500 bushels of apples per month over the next four months. It has found that the most its employees can pick in a month is 1000 bushels. The profit from picking 500 bushels is $500 while the profit on 1000 bushels is $1100.

   a. Determine an optimal picking schedule for the next four months *without* resorting to a network representation.

   b. Solve the same problem using a network representation.

2. For the network of Figure P22-2, determine the shortest path from point A to point G using dynamic programming.

FIGURE P22-2.

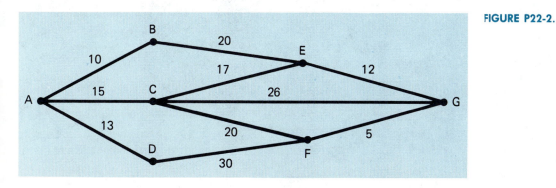

3. George P. Burdell, a recent graduate of a well-known eastern engineering school, is planning a trip to the West Coast before he begins work. He is not interested in visiting the intermediate spots on his route west but is interested only in getting to Los Angeles in the shortest possible driving time. Using an atlas, he has drawn the map in Figure P22-3, where the distances are in driving hours. As a friend of George's suggest the fastest route for George to use to travel from Atlanta to Los Angeles.

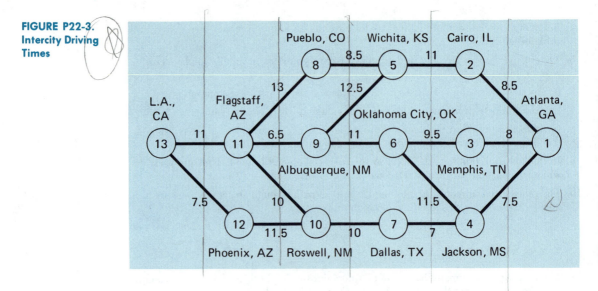

4. In Chapter 7, we presented a network representation of the PERT problem involving the setting up of a conference. That network is shown in Figure P22-4. Compute the longest path via dynamic programming.

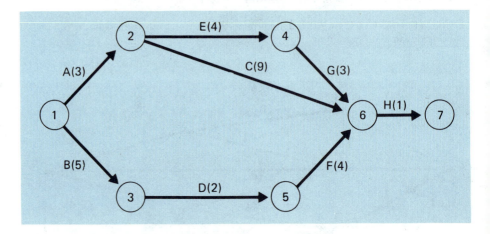

5. Susan Doright has decided to run for the city council of Gotham City. Being a newcomer to politics, she does not have experience in using the resources available to her to seek votes. Since her district of the city is naturally divided into four residential areas, one question facing her is how many workers should be assigned in each area to a door-to-door campaign. A public relations specialist has helped her to determine the number of votes she would receive in each area. She has only six workers available for the door-to-door campaign; the number of votes for each number of workers is shown in Table P22-5. Suggest to Susan an assignment of campaign workers that will maximize the number of votes she could receive as a result of the door-to-door campaign.

**TABLE P22-5. Number of Votes**

| Number of Workers | District | | | |
|---|---|---|---|---|
| | A | B | C | D |
| 0 | 500 | 1000 | 800 | 1100 |
| 1 | 900 | 1700 | 1500 | 1500 |
| 2 | 1300 | 2500 | 2100 | 1900 |
| 3 | 1500 | 3000 | 2800 | 2300 |
| 4 | 1600 | 3300 | 3400 | 2500 |
| 5 | 1600 | 3500 | 3900 | 2500 |
| 6 | 1600 | 3600 | 4100 | 2500 |

6. Yeehaw Tech, a private engineering school, has recently received a donation from an old alum, G. B. "Skeeter" Barnard, for the amount of $100,000. The financial vice president of Yeehaw Tech, Tom Cochran, plans to invest the money in order to fund a series of scholarships. He has three ways in which to invest this money, with differing returns. The three investment schemes and their returns (including principal) after three years are shown in Table P22-6 for differing investment levels. Suggest an investment portfolio to Tom that will produce the greatest yield for scholarships and reinvestment.

**TABLE P22-6. Investment Returns**

| Investment (000's) | Plan X | Plan Y | Plan Z |
|---|---|---|---|
| 0 | 0 | 0 | 0 |
| 25 | 50 | 60 | 40 |
| 50 | 110 | 90 | 100 |
| 100 | 150 | 130 | 175 |

7. The Gator Company produces a very popular variety of shirts for the college-age market. Because of increased demand, Joe Preppie, president of Gator, has decided to increase the company's production facilities. The company has $10 million available to increase production facilities. The increases in revenue resulting from various levels of investment in each of the company's four plants are shown in Table P22-7 (all values in millions).

**TABLE P22-7. Revenue Increases**

| Investment | Plant | | | |
|---|---|---|---|---|
| | Seattle | Denver | Chicago | New York |
| 0 | 0 | 0 | 0 | 0 |
| 1 | 5 | 3 | 6 | 4 |
| 2 | 6 | 6 | 7 | 6 |
| 3 | 7 | 8 | 8 | 8 |
| 4 | 7 | 8 | 9 | 9 |

Determine the maximum revenue method of investing the $10 million.

8. Grace Miller travels to college campuses in the northwestern part of the United States selling clothes to students. She visits dorms and sorority houses to display her items and make sales to the students. Due to the increase in the cost of gasoline, she recently purchased a smaller automobile and can no longer carry all of the items she would like. All of the items she sells come in boxes with 12 units to a box, and she does not wish to carry less than a full box of any one item. She is constrained to carry only those items that will fit into her car, which has only 8 cubic feet of storage. The four items she wishes to consider carrying are listed here, along with the number of cubic feet per box and the profit per box. Suggest what mix of clothing items she should carry in her car to maximize her profit while remaining within her capacity constraint. (*Hint:* Let stages be items and states be the number of boxes. Set up a table at all possible values of the state variable.)

| Item | Cubic Feet | Profit |
|------|------------|--------|
| Blouses | 1 | $50 |
| Jeans | 2 | $75 |
| Dresses | 2 | $100 |
| Shorts | 1 | $35 |

9. Dr. Kathy Hall, a new Ph.D. in psychology, has just accepted a job at Hays State University and must move there quickly. She will be using only her car as her husband, Tom, will be bringing the remainder of their household goods later. Kathy has determined that she has 9 cubic feet available for transporting needed items to Hays. The items that she is considering taking are shown in Table P22-9, along with their volume in cubic feet and the priority on a scale of 1 to 10 that Kathy places on each item.

**TABLE P22-9.**

| Item | Volume | Priority |
|------|--------|----------|
| Clothes | 2 | 8 |
| TV | 6 | 3 |
| Microwave | 6 | 5 |
| Books | 3 | 9 |
| Personal gear | 1 | 9 |

Determine what items Kathy should take to maximize her priorities.

10. Lenny Myers is a freshman at the University of Greater Albany (UGA) and has just received $10 from his Uncle Pat. Lenny is considering how best to spend this money. His alternatives, their cost, and the value Lenny places on each alternative are shown in Table P22-10.

**TABLE P22-10.**

| Alternative | Cost | Value |
|-------------|------|-------|
| Movie with date | $6 | 5 |
| Six pack | $3 | 6 |
| Dry cleaning | $2 | 4 |
| School supplies | $7 | 2 |
| Dinner with date | $8 | 8 |

Help Lenny decide how to spend his $10.

11. The Ozella Marina rents outboard motors and boats to fishermen on a daily basis. The life of these motors has been found to be at most four years. The new motors cost $1000 and can be resold at any point during the four-year period. Dale Myers, manager of the marina, wants to determine the best policy of buying, operating, and reselling the motors over the next five years. He has computed the repair and resale costs for a motor over a four-year period. The cost of a new motor is expected to remain constant at $1000. If purchase and resale decisions are made only once a year and Dale has just bought a supply of motors, suggest an optimal replacement policy to Dale. He expects to retire in five years, so no motors will be needed after five years. (*Hint:* You want to minimize the *total* cost of operating a motor.)

| Age of Motor | Repair Costs | Resale Value | | Operating cost |
|---|---|---|---|---|
| 1 | $ 50 | $500 | −600 | 50 |
| 2 | 125 | 450 | −550 | 125 + 50 + 50 |
| 3 | 150 | 400 | −600 | 150 + 125 + 50 + 100 |
| 4 | 250 | 350 | −650 | 250 + 150 + 125 + 50 + 150 |

*(handwritten annotation: 1000 above Resale Value column)*

12. Consider the following nonlinear integer programming problem:

MAXIMIZE:     $3x_1^2 + 4x_2^2 + 5x_3^2$

SUBJECT TO:     $x_1 + x_2 + x_3 \leq 4$

$x_1, x_2, x_3 \geq 0$ and integer

Use dynamic programming to solve this problem. Let the current variables $x_1, x_2, x_3$ be the stages and the state variables be the amount allocated.

# 23

# Differential Calculus Review

## ■ Introduction

Most of our modeling efforts thus far have involved situations characterized by linear relationships. In the next chapter we will look at the basic methodologies available for optimizing nonlinear models, but first we must review the concepts of differential calculus upon which these methodologies are based. The reader who is already comfortable with the concepts and mechanics of differentiation may wish to skip this chapter and proceed to the next.

## ■ The limit of a function

If we can find a value that a function $f(x)$ approaches as $x$ approaches some constant, this value is referred to as the **limit of the function.** More precisely, if the value of the function $f(x)$ gets closer and closer to $L$ as $x$ is chosen closer and closer to a constant $a$, then $L$ is said to be the limit as $x$ approaches $a$. This is expressed as

*limit of the function*

$$\lim_{x \to a} f(x) = L$$

The implication is that it is possible to make the absolute value of $f(x) - L$ infinitely small by choosing some value of $x$ sufficiently close to $a$. Limits may also be defined as a right-hand limit or a left-hand limit of a function, depending on whether the value of $a$ is approached from above or below. If the value of $a$ is approached through decreasing values of $x$, the resulting limit is referred to as the right-hand limit of the function. If the function is approached through increasing values of $x$, it is referred to as the left-hand limit. The limit of a function exists if and only if the left-hand and right-hand limits exist and are identical. We will use the notation $L^+$ and $L^-$ to represent right-hand and left-hand limits, respectively. As an example of finding the limit of a function, consider $f(x) = 3x + 2$. Suppose that we would like to find the limit of $f(x)$ as $x$ approaches 1. Table 23-1 details the values of $f(x)$ for values of $x$ chosen close to 1. We see that for the values 1.1, 1.01, and 1.001 (the decreasing values of $x$), the right-hand limit approaches the constant 5. Likewise for the values .9, .99, and .999, $x$ increases toward 1 from below and we approach the left-hand limit of 5. Since both the right-hand and left-hand limits are approaching the value 5, 5 is said to be the limit of the function.

A note of caution is appropriate at this point. For this particular function, the value of $f(a)$ or $f(1)$ is 5, which is also the limit of the function. We cannot assume,

TABLE 23-1.

| $x$ | .9 | .99 | .999 | 1.001 | 1.01 | 1.1 |
|------|-----|------|-------|-------|------|-----|
| $f(x)$ | 4.7 | 4.97 | 4.997 | 5.003 | 5.03 | 5.3 |

however, that $f(a)$ will be equal to $L$ in general. In many cases, $f(a)$ may not exist, while the limit $L$ as $x$ approaches $a$ may exist. As an example of a function that has a limit but where the limit is not equal to $f(a)$, consider the function

$$f(x) = \frac{1}{x^2}$$

Suppose that we want to find the limit of this function as $x$ approaches 0. Clearly, $f(0)$ is undefined, because division by 0 is undefined. However, as we approach $x = 0$ from below or above, $f(x)$ converges to infinity as the values of $x^2$ get smaller and smaller. Thus, $f(0)$ is not defined, but

$$\lim_{x \to 0} \frac{1}{x^2} = \infty$$

This concept of the existence of a limit in spite of the fact that $f(a)$ does not exist is an important concept, as the evaluation of a limit generally assumes that we are interested only in the behavior of the function as $x$ approaches some level and not in the actual value of the function at that level.

We have seen two examples of functions where the limit exists. As an example of a function where the limit does not exist, consider the function

$$f(x) = \frac{2}{x - 5}$$

where we are interested in the limit as $x$ approaches 5. The left-hand limit of this function is $-\infty$, but the right-hand limit is $+\infty$. Because the right- and left-hand limits are not the same, this function does not have a limit as $x$ approaches 5.

In some cases it is easier to evaluate the limit of a function by first simplifying the function by applying certain properties of limits. There are six properties that may be of help in evaluating a function:

1. The limit of a constant is that constant.

2. The limit of the sum or difference of two functions is equal to the sum or difference of their limits.

3. The limit of the product of two functions is equal to the product of their limits.

4. The limit of the quotient of two functions is equal to the quotient of their limits, provided that the limit of the divisor is not zero.

5. The limit of the *n*th power of any function is equal to the *n*th power of the limit of that function.

6. The limit of the principal *n*th root of a positive function is equal to the principal *n*th root of the limit of that function.

The application of these rules (especially those dealing with quotients of limits) may lead to certain indeterminate forms such as $0/0$ or $\infty/\infty$. It is usually possible through algebraic manipulation to change these indeterminate forms into determinate forms. Consider, for instance,

$$f(x) = \frac{3x^2 + 1}{x^2 + 3x + 2}$$

As *x* approaches infinity, the limit of this function is $\infty/\infty$, a meaningless form. However, suppose that we divide both the numerator and denominator of this function by $x^2$. The resulting function is

$$f(x) = \frac{3 + 1/x^2}{1 + 3/x + 2/x^2}$$

As *x* approaches infinity, the limit of this function is $3/1$ or 3.

Before we conclude our discussion of limits, let us take the opportunity to define the concept of **continuity**. A function $f(x)$ is continuous at the point $x = a$ if and only if:

*continuity*

1. $\lim\limits_{x \to a} f(x)$ exists
2. $f(a)$ exists
3. $\lim\limits_{x \to a} f(x) = f(a)$

If these conditions are met, it means that there is a smooth transition of the curve as the curve approaches *a* from below and above. In other words, a continuous function can be drawn without lifting the pencil from the paper at every point. More will be said about continuous functions a little later.

## ■ The derivative

In Chapter 2, we discussed the geometry and algebra of straight lines and defined the slope of a straight line to be the change in *y*, or $f(x)$, for a given change in *x*. For straight lines the slope is a constant value, because all along the line *y* changes at the same rate for any given change in *x*. This may not be true, however, for all curves representing various functions. For any function that plots in a nonlinear fashion, the slope will be different for each point along the function. Referring to Figure 23-1, suppose that we identify two points on the curve, where the first point is designated by $(x, y)$ and the second point by $(x + \Delta x, y + \Delta y)$. Now suppose that a line, called a

**FIGURE 23-1.**
**Nonlinear Curve**
**with Secants for**
**Decreasing Values**
**of** $\Delta x$

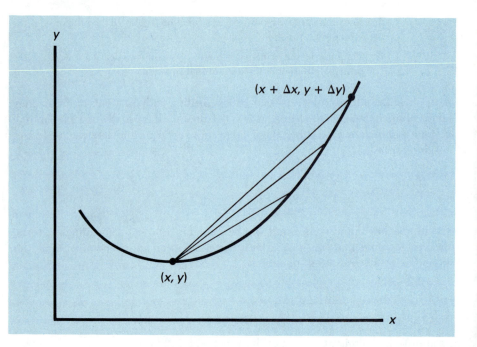

*secant*

**secant,** is drawn between these two points. The slope of this line, obviously, is $\Delta y / \Delta x$, the change in $y$ over the change in $x$. Now suppose that we decrease $\Delta x$ and consequently $\Delta y$, resulting in a second secant, located in Figure 23-1 just underneath the first. Because of new values for $\Delta x$ and $\Delta y$, the slope of this second secant is different than the slope of the first secant. If we continue to decrease $\Delta x$ toward 0, and examine each slope resulting from the corresponding changes in $\Delta y$, we find that the slopes of the corresponding secant lines are different each time but vary by smaller and smaller amounts, finally approaching a constant limiting value. This limiting value is, in fact, the slope of the line drawn tangent to the curve at the point $(x, y)$ or, more simply, the slope of the curve at $(x, y)$. This slope of the tangent line is

*derivative*

called the first **derivative** of the function at the point $(x, y)$. Because this slope indicates the change in $y$ for a unit change in $x$ at some point on the curve, the derivative actually represents the rate of change of the function at that point.

In providing a mathematical definition of the first derivative, note that the limiting secant is defined by $\Delta x$ approaching 0, and that $y + \Delta y$ is the same as $f(x + \Delta x)$ and $y$ is the same as $f(x)$. Letting $dy/dx$ be our notation for the first derivative, our mathematical representation of the first derivative is

$$\frac{dy}{dx} = \lim_{\Delta x \to 0} \frac{\Delta y}{\Delta x} = \lim_{\Delta x \to 0} \frac{(y + \Delta y) - y}{(x + \Delta x) - x} = \lim_{\Delta x \to 0} \frac{f(x + \Delta x) - f(x)}{\Delta x}$$

Note that because of the curvature of functions such as the one in Figure 23-1, the tangent line for each point along the curve will have a different slope. In other words, the first derivative itself will normally be a function that must be evaluated for any given point of interest. Also note that the derivative may not exist at every point, as the limit function may not be defined for certain points along the curve.

As an example of finding the derivative, consider the function $f(x) = x^2 + 1$. Inserting this function into our definition of the derivative results in the following steps:

$$\frac{dy}{dx} = \lim_{\Delta x \to 0} \frac{f(x + \Delta x) - f(x)}{\Delta x}$$

$$\frac{dy}{dx} = \lim_{\Delta x \to 0} \frac{[(x + \Delta x)^2 + 1] - (x^2 + 1)}{\Delta x}$$

$$= \lim_{\Delta x \to 0} \frac{x^2 + 2x\,\Delta x + (\Delta x)^2 + 1 - x^2 - 1}{\Delta x}$$

$$= \lim_{\Delta x \to 0} \frac{2x\,\Delta x + (\Delta x)^2}{\Delta x}$$

$$= \lim_{\Delta x \to 0} 2x + \Delta x = 2x$$

Thus, we have identified the derivative of $f(x) = x^2 + 1$, or $y = x^2 + 1$, to be $2x$. At the point $x = 2$, the first derivative or slope of the tangent line is 4. At the point $x = 3$, the first derivative is 6, and so on.

We now know how to find the derivative, if it exists, for any function by finding the equation of the slope of the tangency line. While this limit method always works, it may become difficult to find the limit for very complicated functions. In the next four sections we will look at some rules that provide shortcuts to finding derivatives for functional forms that are likely to be encountered often in practice. Each of these rules can be verified by going back to the original definition of a derivative and performing a mathematical proof of the rule. As these rules may be found in any beginning calculus text, we will state them without mathematical proof, and concentrate on illustrating the use of each rule. For simplicity, we will use the notation $f'(x)$ interchangeably with $dy/dx$ to represent the derivative, as both of these notational forms are commonly found in texts on calculus.

## Derivatives of simple functions

The following rules may be used to find derivatives of functions or terms in a function that contain constants and variables raised to a power:

**1. Derivative of a constant.**   If $f(x) = c$, where $c$ is a real number, then $f'(x) = 0$. That is, the derivative of a constant is 0.

This rule is quite logical, as $f(x) = c$ is the function of a horizontal line whose slope is 0 at every point along the line.

**2. Derivative of a power term.**   If $f(x) = x^n$ for any real exponent $n$, then $f'(x) = nx^{n-1}$.

As an example of this power rule, suppose that $f(x) = x^4$. Applying the rule, we bring down the exponent as a multiplier and decrease the exponent by 1, resulting in a derivative of $f'(x) = 4x^3$. Likewise, if $f(x) = x^{-2}$, then $f'(x) = -2x^{-3}$. If $f(x) = x^{.5}$, then $f'(x) = .5x^{-.5}$. If $f(x) = x$, then $f'(x) = 1$ (the implied exponent on $x$ is 1, and anything except 0 to the 0 power is 1).

**3. Derivative of a constant times a function.** If $f(x) = c \times g(x)$ for any real constant $c$ and any function $g(x)$ having a derivative $g'(x)$, then $f'(x) = c \times g'(x)$. That is, the derivative of a constant times a function is the constant times the derivative of the function.

Suppose that $f(x) = 3x^2$. Using this rule, the derivative of this function is 3 times the derivative of $x^2$, or 3 times $2x$. Thus, for $f(x) = 3x^2$, $f'(x) = 6x$.

**4. Derivative of a sum or difference.** If $f(x) = g(x) + h(x)$, where the derivatives of both $g(x)$ and $h(x)$ exist, then $f'(x) = g'(x) + h'(x)$. That is, the derivative of the sum or difference of functions is equal to the sum or difference of their derivatives.

This rule extends to as many terms as may be contained in the function. As an example, suppose that $f(x) = 5x^3 - 2x + 1$. The derivative of $5x^3$ is $15x^2$ by rule 2, the derivative of $-2x$ is $-2$ by rules 2 and 3, and the derivative of 1 is 0 by rule 1. Therefore, $f'(x) = 15x^2 - 2$.

## Derivatives of products and quotients

These rules may be used when a function or term of a function is actually the product or quotient of two other functions.

**1. Derivative of a product.** If $f(x) = g(x) \times h(x)$ and both $g'(x)$ and $h'(x)$ exist, then $f'(x) = g(x) \times h'(x) + h(x) \times g'(x)$. That is, the derivative of the product of two functions is equal to the first function times the derivative of the second plus the second function times the derivative of the first.

To illustrate, suppose that $f(x) = (5x^3) \times (4x^2 - 2)$, so that $g(x) = 5x^3$ and $h(x) = 4x^2 - 2$. Using the product rule, $f'(x) = (5x^3)(8x) + (4x^2 - 2)(15x^2) = 40x^4 + 60x^4 - 30x^2 = 100x^4 - 30x^2$.

**2. Derivative of a quotient.** If $f(x) = g(x)/h(x)$, where $g'(x)$ and $h'(x)$ both exist and $h(x)$ is not 0, then

$$f'(x) = \frac{h(x) \times g'(x) - g(x) \times h'(x)}{[h(x)]^2}$$

That is, the derivative of a quotient is equal to the denominator times the derivative of the numerator minus the numerator times the derivative of the denominator, all over the denominator squared.

As an example, suppose that $f(x) = 4x^3/x^2$. The derivative is

$$f'(x) = \frac{x^2(12x^2) - 4x^3(2x)}{x^4}$$

$$= \frac{12x^4 - 8x^4}{x^4}$$

$$= \frac{4x^4}{x^4} = 4$$

While it would have been easier to simplify this function before taking the derivative, that was not done so that the rule could be illustrated fully.

### The chain rule

There are two final rules we will identify that pertain to powers of functions and functions of functions.

1. **Derivatives of functions raised to a power.** If $f(x) = [g(x)]^n$ and $g'(x)$ exists, then $f'(x) = n[g(x)]^{n-1} \times g'(x)$. This is sometimes referred to as the extended power rule, because it extends our earlier rule for variables raised to a power to include functions raised to a power.

To illustrate, suppose that $f(x) = (6x^2 + 2x)^3$. Then $f'(x) = 3(6x^2 + 2x)^2 \times (12x + 2)$.

2. **Derivatives of chains of functions.** If $f(x) = f(u)$ and $u = g(x)$, then $f(x) = f[g(x)]$ and $f'(x) = f'(u) \times g'(x)$, provided both derivatives exist. This rule is often called the chain rule, and is a generalization of the extended power rule.

Suppose that $f(x) = 10(6x - 1)^3$. If we treat $6x - 1$ as a separate function $u = g(x) = 6x - 1$, then our original function is $f(x) = 10u^3$. Applying the chain rule, $f'(x) = 30u^2 \times 6$. Substituting back in for $u$, we get $f'(x) = 30(6x - 1)^2 \times 6 = 180(6x - 1)^2$. This procedure allows us to break down a complex function into a chain of simplier functions, and perhaps find derivatives that could not be found otherwise.

The preceding rules are designed to facilitate the differentitation of complex expressions while avoiding taking limits of functions. Other rules also exist, such as rules for exponential and logarithmic functions (where the exponents are not constants but are themselves functions). However, we will not go any deeper into these special rules. The interested reader will find these additional rules in any basic text on calculus.

## ■ Maxima and minima

Now that we know how to find derivatives, let us take a few moments to discuss an important application of the derivative. There are many applications, such as the use of derivatives for finding marginal costs and marginal revenues (since the slope found through the derivative is actually the rate of change of a function at some point, taking the derivative of a cost or revenue function will yield the marginal cost or revenue from that point). Economists employ differentation to determine marginal propensities to consume and to save by taking derivatives of consumption functions. The list goes on and on.

The application that we will cover in this section is one that is of prime importance in the area of management science, and that will lead into our more detailed discussion in the next chapter. It is the use of derivatives for the optimization of nonlinear functions. That is, differentiation can be used to identify all points for which a function reaches a maximum or minimum value. While the techniques of linear programming allow us to optimize models consisting only of linear functions, calculus and differentiation allow us to do the same thing for models with nonlinear functions.

*local maximum*
*local minimum*

A function $f(x)$ has a **local maximum** at the point $x = a$ if $f(a)$ is greater than $f(x)$ for all values of $x$ in a close interval around $a$. Likewise, a function has a **local minimum** at $x = a$ if $f(a) < f(x)$ for all $x$ in a close interval around $a$. These are very intuitive definitions. A point is a local maximum if it is the highest point over an interval of the function, and it is a local minimum if it is the lowest point over an interval. Figure 23-2 illustrates a function with several local maxima and minima.

While the concept is simple, identifying these high and low points requires that several rules and concepts be understood. Going back to our definition of the derivative, remember that the derivative at a point is the slope of a line drawn

**FIGURE 23-2.**
**A Function with Several Local Maxima and Minima**

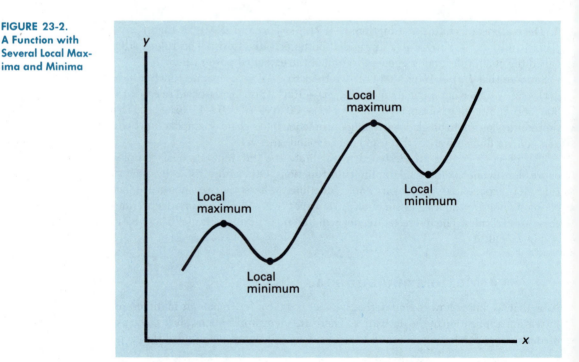

tangent to that point. For each of the local maxima and minima in Figure 23-2, note that the tangency lines at those points are horizontal lines with a slope of 0. Therefore, if a function $f(x)$ has a local maximum or minimum at $x = a$, then $f'(a) = 0$ if the derivative is continuous. We will talk about discontinuous $f'(x)$ in a moment.

Note that in presenting this rule, we said that a local maximum or minimum implies $f'(a) = 0$ for continuous $f'(x)$. We did *not* say that $f'(a) = 0$ implies a local maximum or minimum. While it is a necessary condition for continuous $f'(x)$ that $f'(a) = 0$ for $x = a$ to be a local maximum or minimum, that condition alone is not sufficient. As an example, consider $f(x) = x^3$. Figure 23-3 is a graph of this function. Certainly $f(x)$ and $f'(x)$ are continuous, and at $x = 0$ the derivative $f'(x) = 3x^2$ takes on the value 0. However, this point is neither a maximum nor a minimum. In simple terms, if $f'(a)$ is continuous, a maximum or minimum always means that $f'(a) = 0$, but $f'(a) = 0$ does not always guarantee a maximum or minimum.

Given a maximum or minimum, this necessary condition tells us that $f'(a) = 0$. However, we need to go in the other direction and be able to find a maximum or minimum given that $f'(a) = 0$, since the whole purpose of optimization is to locate these maxima and minima. What sufficient condition can we add to the rule above that will guarantee that a point is a maximum or minimum? This additional condition can be developed by noting that an increasing function has a positive slope

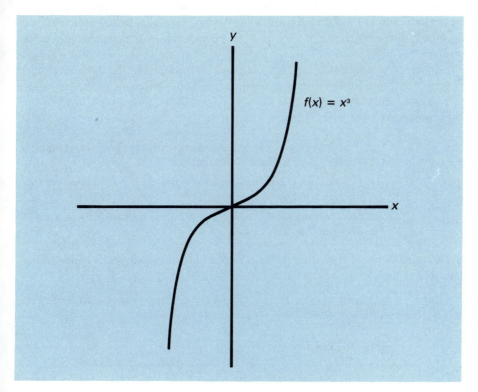

FIGURE 23-3.
Graph of the Function $f(x) = x^3$

**FIGURE 23-4.**
**Slope Behavior as**
**X Passes a Local**
**Minimum or Maxi-**
**mum**

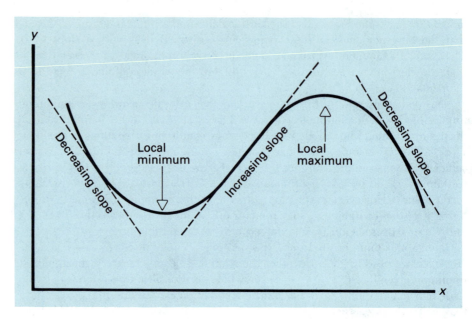

and a decreasing function has a negative slope, as shown in Figure 23-4. As $x$ is increased toward a local minimum, the slope is first negative, then zero, and as we pass the local minimum becomes positive. As $x$ is increased toward a local maximum, the slope is first positive, then zero, and as we pass the local maximum becomes negative.

Based on this understanding, we can now provide both the necessary and sufficient conditions for locating local maxima and minima for functions where $f(x)$ and $f'(x)$ are continuous.

For each point $x = a$ where $f'(a) = 0$:

1.  If $f'(x)$ changes in sign from positive to negative as $x$ is increased through $x = a$, then $x = a$ is a local maximum.

2.  If $f'(x)$ changes in sign from negative to positive as $x$ is increased through $x = a$, then $x = a$ is a local minimum.

3.  If $f'(x)$ does not change in sign as $x$ is increased through $x = a$, there is neither a maximum nor a minimum at $x = a$.

To illustrate the use of these necessary and sufficient conditions, let us look at some examples:

**Example 1.**   Suppose that $f(x) = 4x - x^2$. The derivative is $f'(x) = 4 - 2x$. Both $f(x)$ and $f'(x)$ are continuous. The point $x = a$ at which $f'(x) = 0$ is

$$f'(x) = 4 - 2x = 0$$

$$-2x = -4$$

$$x = 2$$

Checking this point $f'(2) = 0$ using the sufficient conditions, when $x$ is 1.5, $f'(1.5) = 4 - 2(1.5) = 1$. When $x$ is 2.5, $f'(2.5) = 4 - 2(2.5) = -1$. Therefore, since the sign of $f'(x)$ changes from positive to negative as $x$ is increased through $x = 2$, a maximum occurs at $x = 2$. The value of that maximum is $f(2) = 4(2) - (2)^2 = 8 - 4 = 4$.

**Example 2.** Suppose that $f(x) = 2x^2 - 6x$. The derivative is $4x - 6$, and both $f(x)$ and $f'(x)$ are continuous. The point $x = a$ at which $f'(x) = 0$ is

$$f'(x) = 4x - 6 = 0$$

$$4x = 6$$

$$x = \frac{6}{4} = \frac{3}{2}$$

Choosing values on both sides of $x = \frac{3}{2}$, $f'(1) = -2$ and $f'(2) = 2$. Because the sign of $f'(x)$ changes from negative to positive as $x$ is increased through $x = \frac{3}{2}$, there is a minimum at $x = \frac{3}{2}$.

**Example 3.** Consider our previous example, $f(x) = x^3$, from Figure 23-3. The derivative is $3x^2$ and is continuous. Obviously, $f'(x)$ can only equal 0 at $x = 0$. Choosing values on either side of $x = 0$, such as $x = -1$ and $x = 1$, we see that the sign of $f'(x)$ is positive in both cases. Thus, at $x = 0$ there is neither a maximum nor a minimum.

**Example 4.** For the function $f(x) = 5x^3 + 4x^2 - 12x$, the derivative is $f'(x) = 15x^2 + 8x - 12$, and $f'(x)$ is continuous. Solving this function for points at which $f'(x) = 0$:

$$f'(x) = 15x^2 + 8x - 12 = 0$$

$$(3x - 2)(5x + 6) = 0$$

$$(3x - 2) = 0 \quad \text{or} \quad (5x + 6) = 0$$

$$3x = 2 \qquad\qquad 5x = -6$$

$$x = \frac{2}{3} \qquad\qquad x = \frac{-6}{5}$$

Thus, there are two points at which this function may have a maximum or minimum. For the first point $x = \frac{2}{3}$, the sign of $f'(x)$ switches from negative to positive as we pass $x = \frac{2}{3}$, so the point is a minimum. For the second point, $x = -\frac{6}{5}$, the sign of $f'(x)$ switches from positive to negative as we pass the point, and a maximum occurs at that point. The reader might benefit from graphing this example and noting the presence of the local minimum and maximum.

As we noted earlier, the case of discontinuous $f'(x)$ deserves separate mention. If $f'(x)$ is discontinuous, it is possible for a maximum or minimum to occur at a point where $f'(x)$ does *not* equal 0. The same sufficient conditions still apply concerning the change in sign of the slope. As an example, consider $f(x) = (x - 2)^{-2}$. The derivative is $f'(x) = 1/[-2(x - 2)^{-3}]$. At the point $x = 2$, $f'(x)$ is infinitely discontinuous, as we are dividing 1 by 0. This point of discontinuity may be either a maximum or a minimum. If we insert values for $x$ on either side of 2 into $f'(x)$, we find that the sign of $f'(x)$ switches from positive to negative as we pass the point of discontinuity $x = 2$. Therefore, a maximum exists at $x = 2$ for the function $f(x)$, and that maximum is infinity. The bottom line is that points of discontinuity for $f'(x)$ must be evaluated by the sufficiency condition along with any points where $f'(x)$ equals 0 in order to identify all local maxima or minima.

Before we conclude our discussion of maxima and minima, we should point out another possible test for local maxima and minima. This test is sometimes used in place of the previous test if it is deemed to be more convenient. It is based on the *second* *derivative* **second derivative** of the function, denoted as $f''(x)$, which is simply the derivative of the first derivative that we have been working with (the third derivative is the derivative of the second derivative, and so on). Where the first derivative provided the slope of the tangent line, the second derivative gives the rate of change of that slope as $x$ is increased. Thus, a positive second derivative indicates an increasing slope in the neighborhood of $x = a$, and as we saw earlier, slope increases as we pass a local minimum. A negative second derivative indicates a decreasing slope and the presence of a local maximum. If the second derivative is 0, then the point could be a maximum, a minimum, or neither one. Formalizing this, for $f(x)$ and $f'(x)$ continuous and $f'(a) = 0$:

1.  If $f''(a) > 0$, there is a local minimum at $x = a$.

2.  If $f''(a) < 0$, there is a local maximum at $x = a$.

3.  If $f''(a) = 0$, the test is inconclusive and does not apply.

If we encounter the third case, where $f''(a) = 0$, then we have to return to the rules based on the first derivative to determine maximum or minimum status.

*convex* *concave* When the second derivative is positive, the bowl shape of the function is called a **convex** shape. When the second derivative is negative, the rainbow shape of the function is called a **concave** shape. Therefore, the second derivative is often used as a quick check on the concavity or convexity of a function. When the second derivative is equal to 0 as in rule 3, it may be due to a function changing from convex to concave *point of* *inflection* or vice versa at some point (Figure 23-3 is an example of this). This is called a **point of inflection,** and occurs when $f''(x)$ is either discontinuous or zero at a point and the sign of $f''(x)$ changes at that point.

## ■ Partial derivatives

Thus far in this chapter, we have been working strictly with functions containing a single variable. As we saw back in Chapter 2, many if not most functions encountered in practice contain more than one variable. Examples might be the expression of inventory cost as a function of the two variables "order quantity" and "backorder quantity," or the expression of total revenue as the product of individual product revenues times the variables representing the production level of each product. When a dependent variable $y$ depends on the values of several different independent variables, we can use the notation

$$y = f(x_1, x_2, \ldots, x_n)$$

to represent the situation.

When the methods of differentiation are applied to functions of more than one variable, it is referred to as *partial differentiation*, and the resulting derivatives are called **partial derivatives.** The basic concept of partial derivatives is that when we take the derivative of a multivariable function with respect to a certain variable, we treat all other variables as constants during that step. In other words, if we have a function $f(x, y)$ and we take the partial derivative of this function with respect to $x$, then $y$ will be treated as a constant. We will use the notation $f_x(x, y)$, or simply $f_x$, to represent this partial derivative. If we take the partial derivative of $f(x, y)$ with respect to $y$, $x$ is treated as a constant, and we denote the partial derivative as $f_y$.

*partial derivatives*

As an example, let $f(x, y) = 10x^3 + 5xy - 3y^2 + 2$. The partial derivative with respect to $x$ is $f_x = 30x^2 + 5y$. The derivatives of the last two terms that do not contain $x$ are zero, since the derivative of a constant is always zero. The partial derivative of the same function with respect to $y$ is $f_y = 5x - 6y$.

Second partial derivatives can be found in much the same way as ordinary second derivatives. In this case, we simply take the partial derivative of a partial derivative to obtain the second partial derivative. For a function of two variables $f(x, y)$ there are four second partial derivatives that may be developed. If we take the first partial derivative with respect to $x$ and then do partial differentiation again (find the second partial) with respect to $x$, this is referred to as $f_{xx}$. We could also find $f_{yy}$, $f_{xy}$, and $f_{yx}$ (the latter two will always be the same for continuous functions provided both partials exist). The order of variables in the subscript indicates which variable is used for partial differentiation at each step.

Using our same example, $f(x, y) = 10x^3 + 5xy - 3y^2 + 2$, where $f_x = 30x^2 + 5y$ and $f_y = 5x - 6y$, the four second partial derivatives are

$$f_{xx} = 60x$$

$$f_{yy} = -6$$

$$f_{xy} = 5$$

$$f_{yx} = 5$$

Partial derivatives and second partial derivatives can be used to find maxima and minima of multiple variable functions in a manner similar to the one we used in the previous section. First, identify all points $(a, b)$ for which both $f_x(a, b) = 0$ and $f_y(a, b) = 0$. Next, calculate the value

$$M = f_{xx}(a, b) \times f_{yy}(a, b) - [f_{xy}(a, b)]^2$$

for each of these points. The following rules will then allow us to determine whether each point $(a, b)$ is a local maximum, local minimum, or neither:

1. If $f_{xx}(a, b) > 0$ and $M > 0$, then the point is a local minimum.

2. If $f_{xx}(a, b) < 0$ and $M > 0$, then the point is a local maximum.

3. If $M < 0$, then the point is neither a maximum nor a minimum. Instead, it is a *saddle point* (a point that is a maximum over one variable and a minimum over the other).

4. If $M = 0$, these rules do not apply.

For functions of more than two variables, these rules can be generalized and a version of $M$ can be computed from the matrix of second partial derivatives. This is slightly beyond the scope of this text, but may be found in mid-level calculus texts.

As an example of applying the rules we have presented, consider the two-variable function $f(x, y) = 10x^2 + 6xy + 3y^2 + 2$. The first and second partial derivatives are

$$f_x = 20x + 6y \qquad f_y = 6x + 6y$$

$$f_{xx} = 20 \qquad f_{yy} = 6$$

$$f_{xy} = 6 \qquad f_{yx} = 6$$

Clearly, if we solve the two equations $f_x = 0$ and $f_y = 0$ simultaneously, the only point where both first partial derivatives are equal to zero is $(0, 0)$, and $f_{xx}(0, 0) = 20$. Calculating $M$ we get $M = 20 \times 6 - [6]^2 = 84$. Because $M$ is positive and $f_{xx}(0, 0)$ is positive, the point $(0, 0)$ is a local minimum for the function $f(x, y)$.

## ■ Summary

This chapter has reviewed the basics of differential calculus with particular emphasis on those concepts needed as background for the next chapter. While coverage has been superficial in some areas, the reader must remember that calculus is a complete subject in and of itself to which numerous texts have been devoted. The reader who wants more information about any of the topics presented in this chapter is once again urged to seek out one of those specialized texts.

## ■ Glossary of terms

**concave function:**  A function that is rainbow shaped.

**continuity:**  The characteristic where a function can be traced without lifting pencil from paper.

**convex function:**  A function that is bowl shaped.

**derivative:**  The slope of a line drawn tangent to a curve at some point of interest.

**inflection point:**   A point at which a curve changes from concave to convex, or vice versa.

**limit of a function:**   If the value of $f(x)$ converges to $L$ as $x$ approaches $a$, then $L$ is the limit of the function as $x$ approaches $a$.

**local maximum:**   $f(x)$ has a local maximum at $x = a$ if $f(a) > f(x)$ for all values of $x$ in a close neighborhood around $a$.

**local minimum:**   $f(x)$ has a local minimum at $x = a$ if $f(a) < f(x)$ for all values of $x$ in a close neighborhood around $a$.

**partial derivative:**   A derivative of a multiple variable function taken with respect to only one variable while the others are treated as constants.

**secant:**   A line drawn between two points on a curve.

**second derivative:**   The derivative of a first derivative.

## ■ Review questions

1. Construct at least three example functions for which the limit does not exist at some point.

2. List the six properties that are used to simplify functions when finding their limits.

3. Describe the concept of continuity. Construct at least one function that has a point of discontinuity.

4. What is a derivative? Explain the concept and what the derivative represents.

5. When would a derivative not exist for a function?

6. Eight rules were presented in the chapter for finding derivatives of special functional forms. List these eight rules along with a notational definition for each one.

7. Discuss the concept of local maxima and minima.

8. Explain the necessary and sufficient conditions for locating local maxima and minima.

9. Explain the usefulness of the second derivative of a function.

10. Briefly explain the methodology for finding the local maxima and minima of a multivariable function.

## ■ True/false questions

1. The limit of a function exists if both its left-hand and right-hand limits exist.

2. Given a function $f(x)$, if the limit as $x$ approaches $a$ exists, that limit will always equal $f(a)$.

3. The existence of a limit for the function $f(x)$ as $x$ approaches $a$ is a necessary condition for continuity at the point $x = a$.

4. The first derivative of a function represents the rate of change of the function at each point on its curve.

5. A strictly linear function has no first derivative.

6. The derivative of the sum or difference of two functions is equal to the sum or difference of their derivatives.

7. The derivative of a ratio of two functions is equal to the denominator times the derivative of the numerator minus the numerator times the derivative of the denominator.

8. All linear equations with the exception of a horizontal line have only one local maximum and one local minimum.

9. It is not possible for a maximum or minimum to occur at a point where $f'(x)$ does not equal zero.

10. Whereas the first derivative is the rate of change of a function, the second derivative is the rate of change of the first derivative.

11. The point where a function changes from being concave to convex is called a point of inflection.

12. Partial derivatives and second partial derivatives can be used to find local maxima and minima for multiple variable functions.

# ■ Problems

1. Find the limits (if they exist) for the following functions:

   a. $\lim_{x \to 0} (4x + 3)$

   b. $\lim_{x \to 0} (10 + 1/x)$

   c. $\lim_{x \to \infty} (10 + 1/x)$

   d. $\lim_{x \to 4} [1/(4 - x)]$

   e. $\lim_{x \to \infty} [(2x^3 + 5)/(x^3 + x^2)]$

2. Use the limit approach to find the first derivative of $f(x) = 2 - x^2$.

3. Use the limit approach to find the derivative of $f(x) = x^3 + 5x - 7$.

4. Use the limit approach to find the derivative of $f(x) = 1/x^2 - 6x$.

5. Use the rules of derivatives to find the derivatives of each of the following functions:

   a. $f(x) = 3$
   b. $f(x) = x^7$
   c. $f(x) = 5x^3$
   d. $f(x) = 6x^4 - 2x^3 + 12$
   e. $f(x) = 2x^2 + 4/x$

6. Use the product and quotient rules to find the derivatives of each of the following functions:

   a. $f(x) = (x^3 + 1)(2 - x^2)$
   b. $f(x) = (4 + 3/x^2)(x^2 - x)$
   c. $f(x) = (2x^2 + 3x + 8)/(x - 5)$
   d. $f(x) = x^3/(x^2 - x + 3)$

7. Use the rules of derivatives to find the derivatives of each of the following functions:

   a. $f(x) = (x^3 + 3x + 4)^2$
   b. $f(x) = (2x^2 + 3x)^{-4}$
   c. $f(x) = (x + 2)^3 \times (x^3 - 7)^{-2}$
   d. $f(x) = 5y^2$, where $y = 3x^3 - x^2 + 2$
   e. $f(x) = (2y^2 + 3y - 1)^3$, where $y = 6x^2 + 3x$

8. Identify the local maxima and/or minima for $f(x) = 6x^2 + 5x + 2$.

9. Identify the local maxima and/or minima for $f(x) = (x - 1)^2(2x + 5)$.

10. Identify the local maxima and/or minima for $f(x) = 2 + x^{4/3}$.

11. Southern Mills produces cloth by the thousands of yards. Southern realizes that their unit production cost will decrease with increasing volume per day as efficiencies are realized until they reach a point where machine capacities are taxed and the unit cost will begin to increase. Southern's production cost function has been derived as $f(x) = 5x^2 - 1000x + 30$, where $x$ is the daily production volume in thousands of yards. How many yards of cloth should Southern produce per day in order to keep their unit production cost at a minimum?

12. Maxcy's Department Store incurs two types of inventory-related costs. The cost of placing orders on an annual basis has been found to be ($50 \times D$)/$Q$, where $D$ is the annual demand and $Q$ is the number of units they order at a time. The cost of holding inventory on an annual basis is $3 \times Q/2$. Assuming an annual demand of 10,000 units, use differential calculus to find the optimal order quantity $Q°$ for Maxcy's.

13. Suppose that Maxcy's (see Problem 12) decides to allow backordering of units when they run out of stock. The cost of placing orders is the same as before. The cost of holding inventory is now $3(Q - S)^2/2Q$, where $S$ is the level of backorders allowed and $Q$ is as before. Finally, the annual cost associated with being out of stock (allowing shortages to occur) is $2S^2/2Q$. Determine the optimal order quantity and shortage level for Maxcy's [i.e., add the cost terms to get $f(Q, S)$ and identify the local minima].

14. Identify any maxima and/or minima associated with $f(x, y) = 5x^3 + 2x^2 + 9xy - 3y$.

# Nonlinear Models

## ■ Introduction

In Chapter 23 we learned how to use differential calculus to find the maxima or minima of nonlinear functions. Through the application of the derivative, we were able to identify all stationary points for functions with one variable and then test these points to find the maximum or minimum. For functions with more than one variable, we applied the concept of partial differentiation, and once again we were able to identify stationary points and the maximum or minimum. These procedures work so long as we have only the function to be maximized or minimized and do not have any side constraints that must be met—that is, an unconstrained optimization problem.

In reality, most business problems have these constraints that must be met, just as we discussed in Chapters 15 through 21. When a decision problem has a nonlinear relationship in the objective function, or in one or more of the side constraints, or both, it is referred to as a constrained nonlinear optimization problem. Because of the nonlinear aspects coupled with the existence of side constraints, these problems are more difficult to solve than any of the other mathematical programming structures we have examined thus far. There are, however, some basic approaches to the constrained nonlinear optimization problem that have proved to be useful in deriving solutions. We will examine some of these approaches in this chapter.

## ■ Case

### Timber King Incorporated

Timber King is a leading manufacturer of gasoline-powered chain saws. Their sales potential is in the millions of units annually, but the market is competitive and requires aggressive marketing of the product. Therefore Timber King is a frequent advertiser in several of the mass media. In an effort to get the maximum exposure for their advertising dollar, the advertising staff at Timber King has decided to consolidate their advertising and concentrate on only two media in the coming year: television and magazines.

Based on past history and some conceptual models that the corporate advertising staff has developed, they feel that they can accurately relate annual demand to the dollars expended on each of these two advertising media. They have come up with the equation

$$\text{demand} = 12x_1 - .03x_1^2 + 10x_2 - .02x_2^2 - .01x_1x_2$$

where $x_1$ is the advertising expenditure on television ads expressed in thousands of dollars and $x_2$ is the expenditure on magazine ads also in thousands of dollars. The resulting demand is in thousands of chain saws.

This is a typical type of function for demand reflecting the concept of diminishing returns. For each additional dollar spent on advertising, the nonlinear terms (the squared and cross-product terms that are subtracted) gain in magnitude in relation to the linear terms, until eventually the demand curve reaches a peak and either levels off or noses over with increased advertising expenditures. It is therefore a concave function with a single maximum or peak.

There is one constraint that also must be considered in deciding how much to spend on each advertising medium. The company has set an advertising budget of $350,000. Assuming that we will spend all of it, and remembering that our variables were expressed in thousands of dollars, the single constraint is

$$x_1 + x_2 = 350$$

Some of the advertising staff are aware of the use of differential calculus for solving unconstrained problems, but do not know how to incorporate constraints into their analysis.

Several questions need to be answered. How do we decide how to allocate the $350,000 advertising budget? How much larger could our demand be if the budget were unlimited? Is it possible that we do not need to spend all $350,000, and that in spending it we may be past the level of diminishing returns?

## ■ Constrained nonlinear optimization

The general form of the constrained nonlinear optimization problem is

MAXIMIZE
(or MINIMIZE):     $f(x_j)$                    $(j = 1, 2, \ldots, n)$

SUBJECT TO:     $\sum_{j=1}^{n} g_i(x_j) \begin{Bmatrix} \leq \\ = \\ \geq \end{Bmatrix} b_i$     $(i = 1, 2, \ldots, m)$

$$x_j \geq 0$$

where $f(x_j)$ and $g_i(x_j)$ are nonlinear functions of the $n$ different decision variables. In the next section we will look at how to solve this problem when the constraints are all equalities.

## The method of Lagrange multipliers

When all of the constraints in a constrained nonlinear optimization problem are equalities, we can solve the optimization using Lagrange multipliers. This method involves the formation of a single function called the **Lagrangean function** through the combination of the original objective function and the equality constraints, and the solution of this new single function using the method of partial derivatives for unconstrained functions that we discussed in the last chapter.

*Lagrangean function*

To construct the Lagrangean function, we introduce $m$ constants $\lambda_1, \lambda_2, \ldots, \lambda_m$ called Lagrange multipliers. After rewriting each equality constraint in the form $g_i(x_j) = 0$ such that the right-hand side constant has been taken to the left side and only 0 remains on the right-hand side, we use $\lambda_i$ as a multiplier times constraint $i$ and subtract the product from the objective function. Doing this for each constraint results in the composite function

$$h(x_j, \lambda_i) = f(x_j) - \sum_{i=1}^{m} \lambda_i g_i(x_j) \qquad (j = 1, 2, \ldots, n)$$

The optimal solution to $h(x_j, \lambda_i)$ is then obtained by taking the partial derivatives of $h$ with respect to each of the variables $x_j$ and $\lambda_i$, equating each partial derivative to zero, and solving the resulting set of simultaneous equations. (Because of the number of subscripts we are working with here, we will not use the subscript notation of the last chapter to represent partial derivatives, but will instead use the notation $\partial h/\partial x$ to represent the partial derivative with respect to $x$.) The simultaneous solution will be the solution to the original problem provided that the objective function is concave for a maximization problem (convex for a minimization problem). The values of the $\lambda_i$ are analogous to dual variables in the solution to linear programming problems. We will say more about their interpretation in a moment.

As an example of the Lagrangean method, consider the Timber King case. Timber King's sales function is concave, so that the solution using the Langrangean method will be the optimal solution. Putting the original formulation into the proper format for forming a Lagrangean function, we get

$$\text{demand} = 12x_1 - .03x_1^2 + 10x_2 - .02x_2^2 - .01x_1x_2$$

$$x_1 + x_2 - 350 = 0$$

Since we have only one constraint, we need a single multiplier $\lambda$, giving us a Lagrangean function:

$$h(x_1, x_2, \lambda) = 12x_1 - .03x_1^2 + 10x_2 - .02x_2^2 - .01x_1x_2 - \lambda(x_1 + x_2 - 350)$$

Taking the three partial derivatives of $h$ yields:

$$\frac{\partial h}{\partial x_1} = 12 - .06x_1 - .01x^2 - \lambda = 0 \qquad (24.1)$$

$$\frac{\partial h}{\partial x_2} = 10 - .04x_2 - .01x_1 - \lambda = 0 \tag{24.2}$$

$$\frac{\partial h}{\partial \lambda} = -(x_1 + x_2 - 350) = 0 \tag{24.3}$$

In order to solve the three simultaneous equations, let us apply the method of substitution. First, we will solve equation (24.3) for $x_1$:

$$-x_1 - x_2 + 350 = 0$$

$$-x_1 = x_2 - 350$$

$$x_1 = 350 - x_2$$

We will not substitute for $x_1$ in equations (24.1) and (24.2):

$$12 - .06(350 - x_2) - .01x_2 - \lambda = 0$$

$$10 - .04x_2 - .01(350 - x_2) - \lambda = 0$$

Equations (24.1) and (24.2) can now be rewritten as

$$12 - 21 + .06x_2 - .01x_2 = \lambda$$

$$10 - .04x_2 - 3.5 + .01x_2 = \lambda$$

Since both are equal to $\lambda$, they may be equated and solved:

$$-9 + .06x_2 - .01x_2 = 10 - .04x_2 - 3.5 + .01x_2$$

$$-9 + .05x_2 = 6.5 - .03x_2$$

$$.08x_2 = 14.5$$

$$x_2 = \frac{14.5}{.08} = 181.25$$

Substituting back into equation (24.3):

$$x_1 = 350 - x_2$$

$$= 350 - 181.25$$

$$= 168.75$$

Finally:

$$\lambda = -12 + .06x_2 - .01x_2$$

$$= -12 + .05(181.25)$$

$$= .0625$$

Therefore, our solution is $x_1 = 168.75$, $x_2 = 181.25$, and the Lagrange multiplier is $\lambda = .0625$. That is, Timber King should spend \$168,750 on television ads and \$181,250 on magazine ads. The resulting demand is

$$D = 12x_1 - 03x_1^2 + 10x_2 - .02x_2^2 - .01x_1x_2$$
$$= 12(168.75) - .03(168.75)^2 + 10(181.25) - .02(181.25)^2 - .01(168.75)(181.25)$$
$$= 2020.313$$

The annual demand for chain saws that would result from this advertising plan is 2,020,313.

We might ask at this point what effect the constraint had on Timber King's optimal plan. We know that the constraint has an effect, because the positive Lagrange multiplier, like a dual variable in linear programming, indicates the increase in the objective function that one more unit of the constraint right-hand side would cause. If we had solved the objective function as an unconstrained problem, the partial derivatives would have been

$$\frac{\partial D}{\partial x_1} = 12 - .06x_1 - .01x_2 = 0$$

$$\frac{\partial D}{\partial x_2} = 10 - .04x_2 - .01x_1 = 0$$

and their simultaneous solution would be

$$x_1 = 165.2$$

$$x_2 = 208.7$$

Putting these values back into the demand function, we get $D = 2034.783$, or a demand of 2,034,783 chain saws. In other words, if we let the budget increase to $x_1 + x_2 = 165.2 + 208.7 = 373.9$, or \$373,900, the demand would increase to 2,034,783. The extra \$23,900 in ad expenditures would increase demand by 14,470 chain saws. In answer to the questions posed in the case, we do need all of the ad budget, and, in fact, an extra \$23,900 would enhance demand even more. However, any ad expenditures beyond \$373,900 would be counterproductive and put us beyond the point of diminishing returns.

## Kuhn-Tucker conditions

When a constrained nonlinear optimization problem has one or more constraints that are inequalities, we must modify our Lagrangean approach slightly. As long as all equations were equalities, we knew that if a feasible solution existed, all of the constraints would be binding at that solution. In the case of inequalities, some of the constraints may be binding and some may not. Unlike linear programming, the optimal solution to a nonlinear problem may have none of the constraints binding.

*Kuhn-Tucker conditions*

While we can still use the Lagrangean multiplier approach and form a single composite function as we did before, the conditions necessary for an optimal solution are different because not all of the constraints have to be binding (as before, the sufficient condition that must also be met for a solution to be optimal is that the function must be concave or convex). These new conditions are called the **Kuhn-Tucker conditions,** and are as follows:

$$1. \ \frac{\partial f(x)}{\partial x_j} - \sum_{i=1}^{m} \lambda_i \frac{\partial g_i(x)}{\partial x_j} \leq 0$$

$$2. \ x_j^{\circ}\left[\frac{\partial f(x)}{\partial x_j} - \sum_{i=1}^{m} \lambda_i \frac{\partial g_i(x)}{\partial x_j}\right] = 0$$

at $x_j = x_j^{\circ}$
$j = 1, 2, \ldots, n$

$$3. \ g_i(x^{\circ}) - b_i \leq 0$$

$$4. \ \lambda_i[g_i(x^{\circ}) - b_i] = 0$$

$i = 1, 2, \ldots, m$

$$5. \ x_j^{\circ} \geq 0 \qquad\qquad j = 1, 2, \ldots, n$$

$$6. \ \lambda_i \geq 0 \qquad\qquad i = 1, 2, \ldots, m$$

While these conditions look similar to the previous Lagrange multiplier partial derivative conditions, there are differences. Conditions 1, 2, 3, and 5 are included to eliminate most of the feasible nonoptimal solutions from consideration. Because a constraint may be binding or nonbinding, condition 4 is added to ensure that either $\lambda_i$ or $g_i(x^{\circ}) - b_i$ is zero ($\lambda_i$ will be zero if the constraint is nonbinding, and $g_i(x^{\circ}) - b_i$ will be zero if the constraint is binding). Condition 6 is added for any maximization problem, as $\lambda_i$ must be strictly positive if the $i$th constraint is binding. For a minimization problem, the direction of the sign in condition 6 would be reversed.

To illustrate the use of the Kuhn-Tucker conditions, consider the following example.

MAXIMIZE:    $f(x_1, x_2) = 10x_1 - x_1^2 + 10x_2 - x_2^2$

SUBJECT TO:    $x_1 + x_2 \leq 20$

$x_1 - x_2 \leq 5$

Using $g_1 = x_1 + x_2$ and $g_2 = x_1 - x_2$, the Kuhn-Tucker conditions are

1a.  $10 - 2x_1 - (\lambda_1 + \lambda_2) \leq 0$

1b.  $10 - 2x_2 - (\lambda_1 - \lambda_2) \leq 0$

2a.  $x_1[10 - 2x_1 - (\lambda_1 + \lambda_2)] = 0$

2b.  $x_2[10 - 2x_2 - (\lambda_1 - \lambda_2)] = 0$

3a.  $x_1 + x_2 - 20 \leq 0$

3b.  $x_1 - x_2 - 5 \leq 0$

4a. $\lambda_1(x_1 + x_2 - 20) = 0$

4b. $\lambda_2(x_1 - x_2 - 5) = 0$

5a. $x_1 \geq 0$

5b. $x_2 \geq 0$

6a. $\lambda_1 \geq 0$

6b. $\lambda_2 \geq 0$

We must now devise a way to solve these 12 simultaneous equations. Figure 24-1, a graph of the feasibility region with objective function ellipses drawn in to indicate lines of equal value, gives us the hint we need to solve this problem. As these concentric ellipses collapse toward their center, the value of the objective function grows larger. It is clear from the graph that the center point, which will be the maximum for this particular function, is on the interior of the feasibility region defined by the two linear constraints, and that neither of the constraints will be

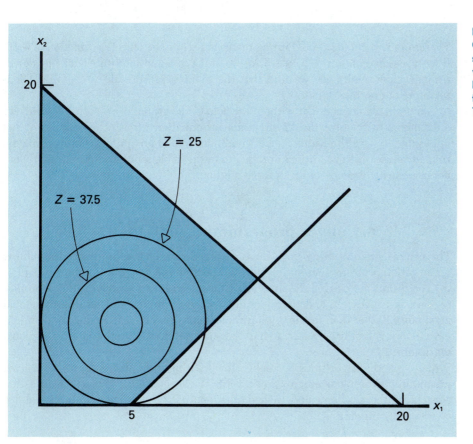

**FIGURE 24-1. Graph of the Feasibility Region with Objective Function Ellipses for the Kuhn-Tucker Example**

binding. This tells us that $x_1$ and $x_2$ will both be nonzero, and that $\lambda_1$ and $\lambda_2$ will both be zero since neither constraint is binding.

From conditions 2a and 2b above, if $x_1$ and $x_2$ are both nonzero, then

$$10 - 2x_1 - (\lambda_1 + \lambda_2) = 0$$

and

$$10 - 2x_2 - (\lambda_1 - \lambda_2) = 0$$

since the product of $x_j^\circ$ and its partial must be zero. Now, since $\lambda_1$ and $\lambda_2$ are both zero,

$$10 - 2x_1 = 0$$

and

$$10 - 2x_2 = 0$$

Therefore, $x_1 = 5$ and $x_2 = 5$. Putting these values into the objective function, $Z = 50$. If we take the solution $x_1 = 5$, $x_2 = 5$, $\lambda_1 = 0$, and $\lambda_2 = 0$ and substitute back into our 12 Kuhn-Tucker conditions, we find that the solution satisfies all of them, and it is therefore our optimal solution.

You probably noticed that without the help of the graph, it would have been very difficult for us to solve the 12 simultaneous equations. It is often difficult if not impossible to solve the Kuhn-Tucker conditions to find an optimal solution directly. In many cases, these conditions are used to test possible solutions for optimality, but not necessarily to generate the optimal solution.

## ■ Convex programming (optional)

*convex programming*

The **convex programming** problem is a special case of the constrained nonlinear optimization problem where the objective function is a concave function and all of the constraints are convex. Because all of the constraints are convex, the feasibility region is a convex set, and therefore any local maximum must also be the global maximum. Rather than test many local maxima as possible candidates as we might have before, it is only necessary to find the one local maximum that is also the global maximum.

Many of the algorithms available for locating the maximum in a convex programming problem employ some form of the *gradient*. We will look at the concept of the gradient, and then discuss one of the best-known algorithms for convex programming.

## *The gradient*

For any function $f(x)$ that is differentiable, its **gradient**, denoted by $\nabla f(x)$ at a point $x$, is the vector of partial derivatives of $f(x)$ evaluated at $x = x'$:

$$\nabla f(x') = \left(\frac{\partial f}{\partial x_1}, \frac{\partial f}{\partial x_2}, \ldots, \frac{\partial f}{\partial x_n}\right) \text{ at } x = x'$$

The importance of the gradient is that it points in the direction to move away from the starting point $x'$ in order to achieve the greatest immediate increase in $f(x)$, the so-called steepest ascent direction. Note that we said the gradient points in the direction of the greatest *immediate* increase in $f(x)$. The gradient does not point directly to the optimal solution. Therefore, the gradient must be applied in an iterative fashion, sometimes involving zigzag movement toward the optimum.

This zigzag movement at each iteration involves moving in the direction of the gradient until $f(x)$ stops increasing, then calculating the new gradient at the new departure point, and so on. Letting $t°$ represent the maximum distance in the direction of the gradient before $f(x)$ stops increasing, each iteration requires that we project the next point at the "end" of the gradient as follows:

Let $x = x' + t° \, \nabla f(x')$

where $t°$ is the positive value of $t$ that maximizes $f[x' + t \, \nabla f(x')]$; that is, where $t$ is the maximum distance we can travel along the gradient before $f(x)$ stops increasing.

The hardest part of applying the gradient method is usually the determination of $t°$. For simple problems, it may be possible to find $t°$ by applying classical optimization procedures to $f[x' + t° \, \nabla f(x')]$. For more complex problems, it may be necessary to select $t$ through trial and error. The following example illustrates application of the gradient for a simple problem.

Given the unconstrained function

MAXIMIZE:     $f(x) = 3x_1 + 3x_2 - x_1^2 - 2x_2^2$

the partial derivatives are

$$\frac{\partial f}{\partial x_1} = 3 - 2x_1$$

$$\frac{\partial f}{\partial x_2} = 3 - 4x_2$$

Starting our search at the arbitrary point $x = (0, 0)$, if we insert the values $x_1 = 0$ and $x_2 = 0$ into our partial derivatives, we get the gradient evaluated at $x = (0, 0)$ of

$\nabla f(0, 0) = (3, 3)$. Following our described procedure, the first iteration is

$$\text{Let } x = (0, 0) + t^\circ(3, 3) = (3t^\circ, 3t^\circ)$$

$$f(3t^\circ, 3t^\circ) = \max f(3t, 3t) = \max(9t + 9t - 9t^2 - 18t^2)$$

$$= \max(18t - 27t^2)$$

$$\frac{d(18t - 27t^2)}{dt} = 18 - 54t = 0$$

$$t^\circ = \frac{18}{54} = \frac{1}{3}$$

$$x = (3t^\circ, 3t^\circ) = \left(3\left(\tfrac{1}{3}\right), 3\left(\tfrac{1}{3}\right)\right) = (1, 1)$$

Thus, the gradient procedure directs that we move from $(0, 0)$ to $(1, 1)$. Now, using $(1, 1)$ as the new starting point, the text iteration is

$$\nabla f(1, 1) = (1, -1)$$

$$\text{Let } x = (1, 1) + t^\circ(1, -1) = (t^\circ + 1, 1 - t^\circ)$$

$$f(t^\circ + 1, 1 - t^\circ) = \max[f(t + 1, 1 - t)] = \max(3 + 2t - 3t^2)$$

$$\frac{d(3 + 2t - 3t^2)}{dt} = 2 - 6t = 0$$

$$t^\circ = \frac{1}{3}$$

$$x = (t^\circ + 1, 1 - t^\circ) = \left(\tfrac{1}{3} + 1, 1 - \tfrac{1}{3}\right) = \left(\tfrac{4}{3}, \tfrac{2}{3}\right)$$

Iteration 3 is

$$\nabla f\left(\tfrac{4}{3}, \tfrac{2}{3}\right) = \left(\tfrac{1}{3}, \tfrac{1}{3}\right)$$

$$\text{Let } x = \left(\tfrac{4}{3}, \tfrac{2}{3}\right) + t^\circ\left(\tfrac{1}{3}, \tfrac{1}{3}\right) = \left(\tfrac{4}{3} + \tfrac{1}{3}t^\circ, \tfrac{2}{3} + \tfrac{1}{3}t^\circ\right)$$

$$f\left(\tfrac{4}{3} + \tfrac{1}{3}t^\circ, \tfrac{2}{3} + \tfrac{1}{3}t^\circ\right) = \max f\left(\tfrac{4}{3} + \tfrac{1}{3}t, \tfrac{2}{3} + \tfrac{1}{3}t\right)$$

$$= \max\left(\tfrac{10}{3} + \tfrac{2}{9}t - \tfrac{1}{3}t^2\right)$$

$$\frac{d(10/3 + 2/9\,t - 1/3\,t^2)}{dt} = \frac{2}{9} - \frac{2}{3}t = 0$$

$$t^\circ = \frac{1}{3}$$

$$x = \left(\tfrac{4}{3} + \tfrac{1}{3}t^\circ, \tfrac{2}{3} + \tfrac{1}{3}t^\circ\right) = \left(\tfrac{13}{9}, \tfrac{7}{9}\right)$$

Iteration 4 is

$$\nabla f\left(\tfrac{13}{9}, \tfrac{7}{9}\right) = \left(\tfrac{1}{9}, -\tfrac{1}{9}\right)$$

$$\text{Let } x = \left(\tfrac{13}{9}, \tfrac{7}{9}\right) + t^\circ\left(\tfrac{1}{9}, -\tfrac{1}{9}\right) = \left(\tfrac{13}{9} + \tfrac{1}{9}t^\circ, \tfrac{7}{9} - \tfrac{1}{9}t^\circ\right)$$

$$f\left(\tfrac{13}{9} + \tfrac{1}{9}t^\circ, \tfrac{7}{9} - \tfrac{1}{9}t^\circ\right) = \max f\left(\tfrac{13}{9} + \tfrac{1}{9}t, \tfrac{7}{9} - \tfrac{1}{9}t\right)$$

$$= \max\left(\tfrac{91}{27} + \tfrac{2}{81}t - \tfrac{3}{81}t^2\right)$$

$$\frac{d(91/27 + 2/81\, t - 3/81\, t^2)}{dt} = \frac{2}{81} - \frac{6}{81}t = 0$$

$$t^\circ = \frac{1}{3}$$

$$x = \left(\tfrac{13}{9} + \tfrac{1}{9}t^\circ, \tfrac{7}{9} - \tfrac{1}{9}t^\circ\right) = \left(\tfrac{40}{27}, \tfrac{20}{27}\right)$$

Iteration 5 is

$$\nabla f\left(\tfrac{40}{27}, \tfrac{20}{27}\right) = (.037, .037)$$

$$\text{Let } x = \left(\tfrac{40}{27}, \tfrac{20}{27}\right) + t^\circ(.037, .037) = \left(\tfrac{40}{27} + .037t^\circ, \tfrac{20}{27} + .037t^\circ\right)$$

$$f\left(\tfrac{40}{27} + .037t^\circ, \tfrac{20}{27} + .037t^\circ\right) = \max f\left(\tfrac{40}{27} + .037t, \tfrac{20}{27} + .037t\right)$$

$$= \max(3.3743 + .0028t - .00411t^2)$$

$$\frac{d(3.3743 + .0028t - .00411t^2)}{dt} = .0028 - .00822t = 0$$

$$t^\circ = .3406$$

$$x = \left(\tfrac{40}{27} + .037t^\circ, \tfrac{20}{27} + .037t^\circ\right) = \quad (1.5, .75)$$

If we take the gradient at $x = (1.5, .75)$, we get $\nabla f(1.5, .75) = (0, 0)$. Since the gradient at this point is zero, there is no direction that will provide improvement, and this point is the optimal solution.

Figure 24-2 illustrates the zigzag search we conducted to arrive at the optimum. Three points need to be mentioned here. First, for the particular function we used in our example, the gradient search method is obviously not the easiest way to solve this problem. We used the gradient on this problem only to illustrate the method. Second, if we wish to minimize using the gradient approach, we move in the direction opposite the gradient; that is, we let $x = x - t^\circ \nabla f(x)$. Finally, the gradient approach as applied here is appropriate only for unconstrained problems like our example. Since our purpose in this chapter is to look at methods for solving constrained problems, we obviously intend to look at methods that employ the gradient but allow for side constraints. The next method does precisely that.

**FIGURE 24-2.**
**Search Paths for**
**the Gradient**
**Search Example**

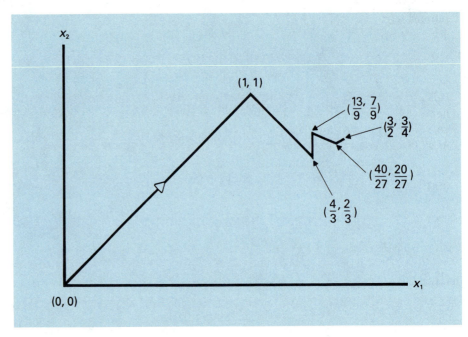

## The sequential unconstrained
## minimization technique

The sequential unconstrained minimization technique (SUMT) requires that the convex programming be reformulated as a minimization problem of the form:

MINIMIZE:      $f(x)$

SUBJECT TO:    $g_i(x) \geq 0$      $i = 1, 2, \ldots, m$

such that $f(x)$ is a convex objective function and the $g_i(x)$ are concave constraints. Any required nonnegativity conditions must be explicitly included as constraints, as the solution procedure does not implicitly enforce such conditions.

In much the same fashion as the earlier techniques, we combine the objective function and constraints into a single composite function of the form

$$P(x; r) = f(x) + r \sum_{i=1}^{m} \frac{1}{g_i(x)}$$

We then start with some arbitrary feasible solution and then use a gradient search technique or some comparable method to minimize $P(x; r)$ for smaller and smaller values of $r$. The resulting solutions from the iterations will converge to the optimal solution for the original problem if one exists. The optimal solution $x^\circ$ will satisfy the requirement

$$f(x) - r \sum_{i=1}^{m} \frac{1}{g_i(x)} \leq f(x^\circ) \leq f(x) + r \sum_{i=1}^{m} \frac{1}{g_i(x)}$$

for all values of the $x$ vector not equal to $x^\circ$. This means that we need only check either the lower limit or the upper limit in relation to $f(x)$; when they are sufficiently close, we will have the solution.

As an example of the SUMT, consider:

MINIMIZE: $\qquad f(x_1, x_2) = \dfrac{x_1 + 1}{x_2 + 2x_2}$

SUBJECT TO: $\qquad x_1 \geq 1$

$\qquad\qquad\qquad x_2 \geq 0$

Thus, $g_1(x) = x_1 - 1$ and $g_2(x) = x_2$. The composite function is

$$P(x; r) = x_1 + \frac{1}{x_2} + 2x_2 + r\left(\frac{1}{x_1 - 1} + \frac{1}{x_2}\right)$$

The partial derivatives of $P(x; r)$ are

$$\frac{\partial P}{\partial x_1} = 1 - \frac{r}{(x_1 - 1)^2}$$

$$\frac{\partial P}{\partial x_2} = -\frac{1}{x_2^2} + 2 - \frac{r}{x_2^2}$$

Because each of the two partial derivatives contain only a single variable and the constant $r$, it is not even necessary to apply the gradient (although we could). We can solve each equation that results from equating the partial derivatives to 0 directly for $x_1$ and $x_2$ as a function of $r$, and thereby find the minimum $P(x; r)$ for each smaller value of $r$ by plugging in that value.

Solving the first partial derivative equation gives

$$1 - \frac{r}{(x_1 - 1)^2} = 0$$

$$\frac{r}{(x_1 - 1)^2} = 1$$

$$r = (x_1 - 1)^2$$

$$\sqrt{r} = x_1 - 1$$

$$x_1 = \sqrt{r} + 1$$

**TABLE 24-1.**
**Results of the**
**SUMT for** $f(x) =$
$x_1 + 1/x_2 + 2x_2$

| Iteration | $r$ | $x_1$ | $x_2$ | $f(x) - r \Sigma 1/g_i(x)$ | $f(x)$ |
|---|---|---|---|---|---|
| 1 | 1 | 2 | 1 | 2.5 | 4.5 |
| 2 | $10^{-2}$ | 1.1 | .7106 | 3.814 | 3.928 |
| 3 | $10^{-4}$ | 1.01 | .707 | 3.828 | 3.838 |
| 4 | $10^{-6}$ | 1.001 | .7071 | 3.828 | 3.829 |

Solving the second gives

$$2 - \frac{r}{x_2^2} - \frac{1}{x_2^2} = 0$$

$$2 - \frac{(r+1)}{x_2^2} = 0$$

$$2 = \frac{r+1}{x_2^2}$$

$$x_2^2 = \frac{r+1}{2}$$

$$x_2 = \sqrt{\frac{r+1}{2}}$$

Using decreasing values of $r$ starting with $r = 1$, the first few iterations of this procedure are summarized in Table 24-1. From the table, it appears that the algorithm is converging to a solution of $x_1 = 1$, $x_2 = .7071$, and $f(x) = 3.828$. Advanced calculus texts can provide more depth on the theory and applications of the SUMT.

## ■ Quadratic programming (optional)

Certain structures of nonlinear programming problems may be solved without as much effort as the general nonlinear problems have been discussing. One such structure is the **quadratic programming** problem, where we have a quadratic objective function subject to linear constraints. We will discuss the approach for solving this class of problem without going into any of the theoretical details.

*quadratic*
*programming*

The quadratic programming problem involves solving

MAXIMIZE: $\quad \sum_{j=1}^{n} c_j x_j - \frac{1}{2} \sum_{j=1}^{n} \sum_{k=1}^{n} q_{jk} x_j x_k$

SUBJECT TO: $\quad \sum_{j=1}^{n} a_{ij} x_j \le b_i \quad \begin{array}{l} i = 1, 2, \dots, m \\ j = 1, 2, \dots, n \end{array}$

$$x_j \ge 0$$

where $q_{jk} = q_{kj}$ are constants. This structure may be solved through the equivalent linear programming formulation,

MINIMIZE:
$$\sum_{j=1}^{n} z_j$$

SUBJECT TO:
$$\sum_{k=1}^{n} q_{jk} x_k + \sum_{i=1}^{m} a_{ij} y_{n+i} - y_j + z_j = c_j \qquad j = 1, 2, \ldots, n$$

$$\sum_{j=1}^{n} a_{ij} x_j + x_{n+i} = b_i \qquad i = 1, 2, \ldots, m$$

$$z_j \geq 0 \qquad j = 1, 2, \ldots, n$$

$$x_j, y_j \geq 0 \quad \text{and} \quad x_j y_j = 0 \qquad j = 1, 2, \ldots, n + m$$

where the $y$'s are like the previous Lagrangean multipliers and the $z$'s are artificial variables necessary for the application of the simplex method. The only modification necessary to solve this problem with simplex is that we must ensure that $x_j y_j = 0$ for each value of $j$. We can do this by adding to simplex a restricted basis entry rule that says $x_j$ may not enter the basis if $y_j$ is already in the basis, and vice versa.

To illustrate putting a problem into this simplex-compatible format, consider the problem:

MAXIMIZE:      $2x_1 + 6x_2 - 4x_1^2 - 2x_1 x_2 - x_2^2$

SUBJECT TO:    $2x_1 - 3x_2 \leq 0$

$$x_1, x_2 \geq 0$$

The nonlinear part of the objective function is $-(4x_1^2 + 2x_1 x_2 + x_2^2)$, and must be put into the format $-\frac{1}{2}(q_{11}x_1^2 + q_{12}x_1 x_2 + q_{21}x_2 x_1 + q_{22}x_2^2)$ in order to fit the prescribed structure. If we rewrite it as $-\frac{1}{2}(8x_1^2 + 2x_1 x_2 + 2x_2 x_1 + 2x_2^2)$, it is equivalent to the original formulation for the nonlinear part, but is now in the required format. In other words, $q_{11} = 8$, $q_{12} = 2$, $q_{21} = 2$, and $q_{22} = 2$. Therefore, the equivalent linear programming formulation is

MINIMIZE:      $z_1 + z_2$

SUBJECT TO:
$$8x_1 + 2x_2 \quad + 2y_3 - y_1 \quad + z_1 \quad = 2$$

$$2x_1 + 2x_2 \quad - 3y_3 \quad - y_2 \quad + z_2 = 6$$

$$2x_1 - 3x_2 + x_3 \quad = 0$$

$$x_j, y_j, z_j \geq 0 \qquad \text{for all } j$$

This is now in the format to be solved using simplex with the restricted basis entry feature we discussed earlier.

# ■ Summary

In this chapter we have looked at several general approaches for tackling the constrained nonlinear optimization problem. We have discussed the Lagrangean method and Kuhn-Tucker conditions as two general approaches for these problems. We also found that for certain special structures, there are algorithms that make the task a little easier. We presented SUMT as an approach for problems with a concave objective function and convex constraints, generally as convex programming problems. We also looked at quadratic programming as an alternative when a quadratic objective function is to be maximized or minimized subject to linear constraints.

The important thing to note in this chapter is that most of the techniques we have discussed are just that. They are techniques or ways of approaching a problem as opposed to the definitive nature of simplex as a solution method for linear programming. The reader interested in knowing more about this area will find a wealth of information in the literature.

# ■ Glossary of terms

**convex programming:**   A special case of the constrained nonlinear optimization problem where the objective function is a concave function and all of the constraints are convex.

**gradient:**   The vector of partial derivatives for any function $f(x)$ that is differentiable. The gradient points in the direction of greatest immediate increase in $f(x)$ away from some selected starting point.

**Kuhn-Tucker conditions:**   The necessary conditions for optimality used when a constrained nonlinear optimization problem has one or more inequality constraints.

**Lagrangean function:**   A single function constructed by combining the objective function and one or more equality constraints, such that unconstrained optimization techniques may be used to solve the original constrained problem.

**quadratic programming:**   A special case of convex programming where the objective function is quadratic and all constraints are linear.

# ■ Review questions

1. Explain the Lagrangean approach to solving constrained nonlinear optimization problems with equality constraints.

2. Discuss the meaning of Lagrangean multipliers. What does the numerical value of the multiplier represent?

3. Why do we have to modify our approach to the constrained nonlinear optimization problem when one or more of the constraints are inequalities?

4. Explain the concept of the gradient. Why is the gradient particularly useful within the convex programming framework?

5. Could SUMT be used on a general nonlinear problem where the objective function (constraints) are nonconvex (concave)? Explain.

6. What is the primary advantage of being able to formulate a nonlinear problem as a quadratic programming problem?

## ▪ True/false questions

1. The Lagrangean method requires that all problem constraints be strict inequalities.

2. For a problem with $n$ constraints, it is necessary to create $n - 1$ Lagrange multipliers.

3. Lagrange multipliers have the same basic meaning as dual variables in linear programming.

4. The optimal solution to a nonlinear programming problem may have none of the constraints binding.

5. The Kuhn-Tucker conditions are identical to the necessary conditions for using Lagrange multipliers.

6. Kuhn-Tucker conditions may be used only for maximization problems.

7. Because of the large number of condition equations generated by the Kuhn-Tucker conditions, they are often used to test possible solutions for optimality rather than for direct generation of the optimal solution.

8. A convex programming problem may have several local maxima.

9. The gradient points toward the optimal solution, provided that the gradient exists.

10. We reach the optimal solution in a gradient search when the gradient assumes a value of zero.

11. SUMT employs the gradient or some similar technique to converge to the optimal when constraints are present.

12. Once a quadratic programming problem has been reformulated as a linear program, it can be solved using any existing simplex computer code.

## ▪ Problems

1. Given the following nonlinear programming problem, use the method of Lagrange multipliers to find the optimal solution:

MAXIMIZE:     $Z = 21x_1 - .02x_1^2 + 17x_2 - .01x_2^2 - .02x_1x_2$

SUBJECT TO:     $5x_1 + 4x_2 = 300$

2. Solve the following nonlinear programming problem using the method of Lagrange multipliers:

MAXIMIZE:     $Z = 15x_1 - .5x_1^2 + 6x_2 - .04x_2^2 - .03x_1x_2$

SUBJECT TO:     $2x_1 + x_2 = 100$

3. Use the method of Lagrange multipliers to solve the following nonlinear programming problem:

MAXIMIZE:     $Z = x_1^2 - 5x_1 + x_2^2 - 7x_2$

SUBJECT TO:     $x_1 + x_2 = 5$

4. Given the following nonlinear programming problem, use the method of Lagrange multipliers to find the optimal solution:

MAXIMIZE:          $Z = 2x_1^2 - 4x_1 + x_2^2 - 3x_2$

SUBJECT TO:          $2x_1^2 - 2x_1 + x_2 = 1.5$

5. Use the Kuhn-Tucker conditions to solve the following nonlinear programming problem:

MAXIMIZE:          $Z = x_1^2 + 2x_2^2 + 3x_1x_2$

SUBJECT TO:          $4x_1 + 3x_2 \le 48$

6. Solve the following nonlinear programming problem using the Kuhn-Tucker conditions:

MAXIMIZE:          $Z = -10x_1 - x_1^2 + 16x_2 - 2x_2^2$

SUBJECT TO:          $-x_1 + 2x_2 \le 8$

7. Given the following nonlinear programming problem, use the Kuhn-Tucker conditions to determine the optimal solution:

MAXIMIZE:          $Z = 30x_1 - 2x_1^2 + 50x_2 - x_2^2 + 2x_1x_2$

SUBJECT TO:          $x_1 + x_2 \le 90$

$5x_1 - 10x_2 \le 10$

8. Solve the following nonlinear programming problem using the Kuhn-Tucker conditions:

MINIMIZE:          $Z = -x_1^2 - x_2^2 + 3x_1x_2 - 4x_1$

SUBJECT TO:          $3x_1 + 2x_2 \ge 24$

$x_1, x_2 \ge 0$

9. Ignoring the constraints in Problem 7, use the gradient approach to find the optimal solution to the unconstrained maximization problem.

10. Ignoring the constraints in Problem 8, use the gradient approach to find the optimal solution to the unconstrained minimization problem.

11. Given the following convex programming problem, use SUMT to determine the optimal solution:

MINIMIZE:          $Z = 2x_1 + \dfrac{2}{x_1 - 1} + x_2 + \dfrac{3}{x_2 - 1}$

SUBJECT TO:          $x_1 \ge 1$

$x_2 \ge 1$

12. Given the nonlinear model in Problem 5 with a quadratic objective function and linear constraints, add nonnegativity constraints, write the problem as a quadratic programming problem, and construct the equivalent linear programming formulation.

13. Considering the nonlinear model in Problem 6, add nonnegativity constraints, write the problem as a quadratic programming problem, and construct the equivalent linear programming formulation.

14. For the nonlinear model in Problem 7, add nonnegativity constraints, write the problem as a quadratic programming problem, and construct the equivalent linear programming formulation.

# Implementation

## ■ Introduction

Throughout the text we have focused on models and techniques that can be employed in problem solving and decision making. We have stressed the importance of problem formulation and interpretation of the solution output from given algorithms. In a number of cases, we discussed in detail the structural base and solution procedure of the algorithms. Obviously a user of management science must be knowledgeable about these factors, but one should not conclude that management science is nothing more than a collection of mathematical models and that the use of MS/OR techniques and models simply requires the ability to formulate the problem, collect data, select the appropriate algorithm, generate a solution using the algorithm, and interpret the output. These activities are important, but alone, they will not assure the successful implementation of a given model. In this chapter we will examine a number of other factors related to implementation, such as the extent of top-level management support of a project, the organizational environment, and prior success (or failure) in using MS/OR techniques.

Unlike the discussion and examples in other chapters, the material in this chapter will not be mathematical. Rather, we will examine managerial, behavioral, and computer system factors that relate to the implementation and use of management science models. A considerable number of researchers have studied the problems associated with implementation and have identified a number of these factors. However, there is no universal process or guaranteed set of procedures that will assure successful use of a management science model or technique. The approach we will take in this chapter will be to: (1) identify and discuss the factors that researchers have found to be related to implementation; (2) identify a game-implementation process that has, on a limited basis, been successfully employed; and (3) present a case study that demonstrates application of the game-implementation process.

■ **Case**

# Roberts' Tool and Die, Inc.

Bill Houtchin, vice-president of manufacturing at Roberts' Tool and Die, Inc., was reviewing the production allocation output report generated by the management systems/sciences (MSS) department. Houtchin was extremely emphatic.

> This plant-product-allocation report is totally absurd. In all my years of experience I have never seen such an unrealistic allocation. With the thousands of dollars you guys have spent on developing your allocation system I would think you could produce something that is half-way sensible. I will not support the use of this system in any of our plants. We can do a better job than this by pulling numbers out of the air!

Bob Ellis, senior MS/OR analyst in the management systems/sciences department, was somewhat startled. Bob's department had spent more than two years developing the on-line product allocation system (OPASS). Now the manufacturing vice-president was unwilling to support the use of the system. Ellis remarked,

> We have double checked all the calculations in the system. I am certain they are correct. The allocations recommended by the system are correct; you simply have to have faith they will provide the proper results.
>
> We don't run on faith, replied Houtchin, we run on proven facts and operating procedures, and there is no proof that your system is anything other than another "blue-sky computer system." Until you can demonstrate that these results will meet customer demands in all product areas and markets and not constrain one plant while a second plant is running at less than capacity, I will not support the system.

Mr. Houtchin had been with the company more than 30 years. He had progressed up through the company from engineering design, to line supervisor, to manufacturing director, to plant manager.

For the past three years he had been vice-president of manufacturing for the entire firm, which now consisted of seven separate plants in three different locations. Bill always attempted to be innovative in terms of examining new ways to manage the manufacturing operations of the firm. However, he had concluded from his prior experience that cost control and knowledge of where the competition stood were key ingredients to success. Bill was convinced that most operations could be successfully managed through the use of a few basic principles. He was not convinced that computerization was the answer to all manufacturing control problems, which was the philosophy, in his opinion, under which the MSS department was operating.

Mr. Ellis had been with the company only a few years but had developed a strong working relationship with the vice-president of finance. Bob had developed an on-line financial planning system that allowed the vice-president to examine the financial portion of the company on a real-time basis. The system has helped tremendously in getting a handle on the financial operations of the firm.

Bob was convinced that manufacturing cost control and resource utilization could also be improved by employing a real-time, on-line system. However, he was not overwhelmingly received by Mr. Houtchin when he approached him two years ago and suggested the idea. Through the support of the vice-president of finance, Bob had convinced the president of the company that his idea was workable.

Bob was not disturbed with Houtchin's comments when he first began the development work on the product allocation system.

> I'm not convinced your idea will work, but I'll give you the support I can as long as you don't expect my people to get involved. We have to meet our monthly delivery commitments—they come first.

Bob got little support from any of the manufacturing areas or plant managers as he was developing the system. However, he was convinced that he had a sound idea; besides he had the support of top management.

Upon completing the development of the system, Bob prepared a formal educational seminar. In the seminar he described the theory and logic of the system and explained each of the calculations used in the system. He also described the output reports that the system produced and provided an on-line demonstration on how the system was used. Bob presented the seminar at each of the seven plants. Bob also went through the complete presentation with Houtchin, even though they were interrupted numerous times in order for Houtchin to respond to calls from plant managers and other operating people. After hanging up the phone for the fifth time Houtchin commented:

You may have proper calculations in your system, but until you can demonstrate to me that your system can duplicate the allocations and operations we used last year I will have a hard time accepting the system. I'm not convinced the system can help.

## Comments on the case

This case highlights some of the problems that management scientists have encountered in trying to sell MS/OR concepts and techniques. Though it may not be obvious from the dialogue in this case, several errors were made by the analyst in working with the manufacturing manager. We hope that after you have completed this chapter you will have a better understanding of some of the problems of implementation and how to address many of them.

# ■ Implementation: Prior studies

As noted in Chapter 1, over the past three decades MS/OR techniques have been successfully applied (1) to operational problems in industry (such as inventory control, resource utilization, transportation/logistics, and scheduling); (2) to political redistricting in the public sector; (3) to staffing of hospitals and emergency rooms in the medical field; and (4) to class scheduling and busing in the academic sector. The success cases, however, do not convey the total results; numerous implementation failures have occurred and still occur in the management science field.[1]

In its early development, management science was employed to solve small, specific operating problems within firms. As a result, implementation was viewed by the management science analyst as a mundane problem. Implementation was assumed to involve only the simple task of specifying the physical changes that were required in the organization in order to install a technique or system. In applying MS/OR techniques, a pattern thus evolved in which analysts either presented system alternatives to management for selection and implementation or concentrated on developing techniques to support existing operations. As the field developed and attempts were made to apply techniques and models to larger problems, this myopic attitude toward implementation resulted in a number of failures.

By the early 1960s, significant theoretical results had been produced in management science; but because of limited success in implementation, many managers and practitioners were expressing considerable doubt about the future viability of the field. As a result, researchers began to examine and study the implementation

[1]A. Harvey, "Factors Making for Implementation Success and Failure," *Management Science*, 16, No. 6 (February 1970), p. B312.

**TABLE 25-1. Factors Underlying Implementation Problems, As Described in 15 Literature Sources [Source: Adapted from Michael Radnor, Albert Rubenstein, and David A. Tansik, "Implementation in Operations Research and R & D Government and Business Organizations," *Operations Research*, 18 (November–December 1970), p. 972.]**

*Literature Source*

| Factor Number | Description | Ackoff (1) | Ackoff (2) | Churchman and Schainblatt (3) | Crane (4) | Hahn (5) | Heiman (6) | Hicks (7) | Hitch (8) | Hugsmans (9) | Malcolm (10) | Pennycuick (11) | Stillson (12) | Swager (13) | Swan (14) | Turban (15) | Number of Authors Mentioning the Factor |
|---|---|---|---|---|---|---|---|---|---|---|---|---|---|---|---|---|---|
| 1 | Need by OR to define results | | | | | X | X | | X | X | X | | | X | | X | 7 |
| 2 | Impact on users' goals | | | | | X | X | | | X | X | | | X | X | | 6 |
| 3 | Communications (understanding, timeliness, etc.) | | | | X | | | X | | | | X | | | X | X | 5 |
| 4 | Client involved (time, money, participation) | | X | | X | | X | | | | | X | | | | | 4 |
| 5 | Implementation costs and time | X | | | | | | | | | X | | X | | | | 3 |
| 6 | Low-level resistance to change (failure to participate) | X | | | | | | | | | | | X | | | | 2 |
| 7 | Client requests for help | | | | | | X | | | | | | | | X | | 2 |
| 8 | Urgency of results | | | | | | X | | | | | | | | | | 1 |
| 9 | Measurable savings | | | | | | X | | | | | | | | | | 1 |
| 10 | Improved information | | | | | | X | | | | | | | | | | 1 |
| 11 | Availability of trained people to implement | | | | | | | | | | | | X | | | | 1 |

| | | | | |
|---|---|---|---|---|
| 12 | Reporting level of OR/MS | X | | 1 |
| 13 | Availability of detailed implementation plan | X | | 1 |
| 14 | Complexity of computations needed to implement and use | X | | 1 |
| 15 | Changes in management structure | X | | 1 |
| 16 | "Mutual understanding" | | X | 1 |
| 17 | Cognitive style of managers | | X | 1 |

[1]Russell L. Ackoff, "Unsuccessful Case Studies and Why," *Operations Research*, 8 (March–April 1960), pp. 259–263.

[2]Russell L. Ackoff, "Some Unsolved Problems in Problem-Solving," *Operational Research Quarterly*, 13 (1962), pp. 1–11.

[3]C. West Churchman and A. H. Schainblatt, "The Researcher and the Manager: A Dialectic of Implementation," *Management Science*, 11, No. 4 (February 1965), pp. B69–B87.

[4]Roger R. Crane, "Building an OR Team Within Your Own Company," *Chemistry in Canada*, 8 (1956), pp. 38–47.

[5]Walter A. Hahn, Jr., "Applied Business Research," *IRE Transactions on Engineering Management*, EM-9 (1962), pp. 3–10.

[6]David R. Heiman, "A Procedure for Predicting the Potential Success or Failure of an OR/MS Activity," Master's Thesis, Northwestern University, Evanston, Illinois, May 1964.

[7]Harry T. Hicks, "An Analysis of Southern Pacific's Boxcar Information System and the Causes of Its Failure," Master's Thesis, University of California, Berkeley, December 1959.

[8]Charles J. Hitch, "Comments on 'Fallacies in OR,'" *Operations Research*, 4 (1956), pp. 426–430.

[9]Jan H. B. H. Huysmans, "The Implementation of Operations Research: A Study of Some Aspects Through Man-Machine Simulation," Internal Working Paper No. 78, Space Sciences Laboratory, Social Sciences Project, University of California, Berkeley, January 1968.

[10]D. G. Malcolm, "On the Need for Improvement in Implementation of OR," *Management Science*, 11, No. 4 (February 1965), pp. B48–B58.

[11]K. Pennycuick, "Presentation and Implementation of the Results of OR," in *OR for Management* (R. T. Eddison, K. Pennycuick, and B. H. P. Rivett, eds.), New York: Wiley, 1962, pp. 288–298.

[12]Paul Stillson, "Implementation of Problems in OR," *Operations Research*, 11, No. 1 (January–February 1963), pp. 140–147.

[13]William L. Swager, "Improving the Management of Research," *Business Horizons*, 2 (Winter 1959), pp. 47–49.

[14]A. W. Swan, "Running an OR Department in an Industrial Organization," *Journal of Industrial Engineering*, 8 (1957), pp. 269–274.

[15]E. Turban, "The Role of Information in the Implementation of Operations Research Techniques for Plant Maintenance Management," Working Paper No. 183, Center for Research in Management Science, University of California, Berkeley, August 1966.

process. By 1965, management scientists had recognized that implementation was truly a problem, and by 1970, management scientists had examined and documented the extent of the implementation problem. Table 25-1 is a summary of the findings of 15 studies reported in the literature.

Many of the problems associated with implementation have now been resolved, thanks to the studies made in the sixties and seventies and the fact that management and management scientists have come to realize that implementation involves more than providing financial support or specifying physical changes or procedures for installing a technique or system. To avoid some of the errors made in the past, it is important that a user of management science be aware of some of the factors that can have a bearing on the success (or failure) of implementation. In the section that follows we summarize many of these factors.

## Factors related to implementation success (failure)

In a study by Churchman and Schainblatt, the authors comment

> *Implementation* refers to the manner in which the manager may come to use the results of scientific effort. The *problem of implementation* is the problem of determining what activities of the scientist and the manager are most appropriate to bring about an effective relationship.[2]

This would appear to be a fairly logical definition of the implementation problem, since by the mid-sixties, management science analysts, as well as many managers of MS/OR groups, viewed implementation as "selling management on the use for a model or system," while operating managers viewed implementation as "producing timely results that make the business function more economically or effectively." A working relationship between the manager and the MS/OR analyst is important, but implementation involves more than this. Factors such as management characteristics, level of management support, exposure of management to management science and computer science, capabilities of the MS/OR analyst, understanding of organizational factors, urgency of results, communication, and cost of implementation must be considered.

**Management characteristics.**    Management characteristics can be correlated with the implementation of management science techniques. From an examination of 31 companies, Harvey identifies several factors that tend to be associated with management's decision to accept and use a given technique or system.[3] First, managers who have had previous success with developing and implementing sophisticated approaches to problem solving are receptive to applying management science techniques to problems. Conversely, it has been noted that in many cases where failure has occurred in implementing a new technique, the manager lacked

---

[2]C. W. Churchman and A. H. Schainblatt, "The Researcher and the Manager," *Management Science*, 11, No. 4 (February 1965), p. B69.
[3]A. Harvey, op. cit., p. B317.

conviction that management science would likely provide a solution to the problem.

A second factor, closely associated with the first, relates to management's attitude toward innovation. In cases where projects have been implemented, it has often been noted that management created, throughout the organization, a climate that encouraged innovation. In examining companies that failed in implementing particular projects, it has been generally noted that a negative attitude toward aggressive action existed.

Another important characteristic is management's ability to see trade-offs. Harvey concluded that the ability to see solutions in terms of trade-offs is critical to successful implementation:

> In examing those companies who failed to implement projects, a very low negative rating existed in management's ability to recognize the importance of interrelationships between activities as well as the significance of trade-offs.[4]

Another significant factor is management's confidence in the capabilities of its management science group. In many successful cases, there is a correlation between management's willingness to implement a project or activity and its confidence in the quantitative staff. In Harvey's study of implementation problems, such a high correlation existed that the decision was made to eliminate from the sample those companies that had an impressive history of successful implementation of management science solutions to problems.

In exploring some of the negative characteristics of management, Rader concluded that the unwillingness and inability of many managers to develop and communicate an explicit objective for the business is a major roadblock to implementing quantitative systems.[5] Management often fails to recognize that without a clear and concise objective, the ability of the quantitative staff is limited. On the other hand, with a clear identification of the business objective, aggressive and dynamic actions can be pursued.

Another factor that can be described as a negative characteristic of management is the tendency of some managers to use a performance ratio such as *net units per person*, or *output per man-hour* as a measure of an individual's level of contribution to the organization. Employing such measures gives the management scientist very little freedom in which to operate. Generally, most management science techniques require more time and effort to implement then less effective techniques; thus, a performance indicator may be meaningless as a measure of contribution. A manager who relies on some day-to-day measure as an indicator of the performance of the MS/OR staff may find that the group's actions are directed toward meeting this criterion rather than toward solving the desired problem.

---

[4]A. Harvey, op. cit., p. B318.
[5]L. T. Rader, "Roadblocks to Progress in the Management Sciences and Operations Research," *Management Science*, 11, No. 4 (February 1965), p. C4.

**Level of management support.**  Management's support appears to be a key variable affecting the success of a management science activity. A study by Radnor, Rubenstein, and Bean found that a strong relationship exists between the support of top management and the success of the management science/operations research group.[6] Loss of management support increased the probability that the activity, as well as the group, would not maintain its position in the organization. By contrast, activities that retain their sponsors are generally more stable and somewhat more successful.

**Exposure of management to the management science and computer science area.**  One of the most frequently discussed requirements for successful implementation of management science techniques is that of exposing management to the management science area. Without proper understanding of the concepts and techniques associated with the field, management cannot expect to comprehend the objectives of its MS/OR group. Also, with the increased utilization of computers within the quantitative environment, management should not only comprehend quantitative concepts, but should understand how these concepts integrate into a computerized system. Rader concluded in his study:

> . . . one of the major obstacles that retards progress within the quantitative area is management's education deficiency in management and computer sciences.[7]

**Attitudes and interests of the MS/OR group.**  In addition to organizational and management factors, implementation is also affected by the attitudes and interests of the management science/operations research group. Harvey, in his study, found that

> . . . a strong relationship exists between the extent to which implementation occurs and the willingness of the management science group to assume implementation responsibility.[8]

In general, most MS/OR groups are interested in developing theoretical solutions to problems and feel that operational implementation of the concept or technique should be the responsibility of the user group/department. For example, the following comments were made by a management science analyst in a large corporation:

> . . . my job is to develop mathematical techniques and models that provide answers or solutions to operational problems. It is *not* my job to get involved in the day to day problems of employing/using the models.

---

[6]M. Radnor, A. H. Rubenstein, and A. S. Bean, "Integration and Utilization of Management Science Activities in Organizations," *Operational Research Quarterly*, 9, No. 2 (June 1968), p. 134.
[7]L. T. Rader, op. cit., p. C3.
[8]A. Harvey, op. cit., p. B319.

Clearly, such attitudes must change. To support implementation successfully, the management science staff must develop a broader view of its responsibility for a project or system. Efforts must be extended to assure that the group gives continual support to the project or system throughout its life cycle.

**Capabilities and knowledge of the MS/OR group.** Technical knowledge and capability is required of any MS/OR group, but *organizational knowledge* is also necessary. Most management science groups have the technical knowledge required to develop a theoretical solution to a given problem, but are generally deficient in knowing organizational requirements associated with implementation.

The required knowledge of organizational needs and activities will vary with different types of projects. Developing a statistical forecast may require only a superficial knowledge of organizational requirements. In contrast, development of an inventory control system for a total corporation necessitates an in-depth knowledge of many organizational factors. In the latter case, the management scientist must be knowledgeable about the individual managerial responsibilities required, achievement possibilities with existing systems, system activities necessary at each level of operation, the personnel behavioral effect of changes in existing activities, and the sensitivity of the proposed system to the current organizational operations.

**Definition of project results.** Because of the highly technical nature of most quantitative projects or activities, there is a tendency on the part of the management scientist to use complex techniques and technical terminology. Often, this means that the manager and/or client is unable to comprehend the output results. In the study by Radnor, Rubenstein, and Tansik, a key factor underlying implementation problems was the need of the operations research group to identify and define explicitly the results or impact of a given project.[9]

**Urgency of results.** Most MS/OR techniques require more time to develop and implement than do less sophisticated and less efficient techniques. If management places too high an emphasis on "results," the management scientist may be forced to attempt to fit the problem into a prestructured technique. Similarly, if management has a preconceived solution to the problem, too strong an emphasis on quick results may force the management scientist into uncritically accepting the recommended solution. Such action may result only in alleviating the symptoms rather than solving the real problem.

**Communication.** Good communication is necessary in developing and implementing an MS/OR technique or system. This is particularly true at the beginning of a project. A common problem during the initial stages of a project concerns project scope and specifications. If the interaction between management and the management scientist is poor, the project may be improperly specified, which, in turn, leads

---

[9]M. Radnor, A. H. Rubenstein, and D. A. Tansik, "Implementation in Operations Research and R & D in Government and Business Organizations," *Operations Research*, 18, No. 6 (November–December 1970), p. 978.

to the development of inaccurate and inefficient techniques. A good communication feedback network is critical if a technique is to be developed and installed.

Poor communication can also lead to misunderstandings in the operations and use of a given project or system. In many cases, negative reactions on the part of management result from a lack of understanding of the structure and use of a system. This does not necessarily imply total rejection on the part of management, but this situation can easily lead to implementation failure. In one case, a large semiconductor firm developed a quality control system to limit production of low-quality devices. Eighteen months and thousands of dollars later, the system was declared a failure. In the initial stage of the project, management strongly supported the work and the clients were enthusiastic about the potential of the system. After the system was developed and placed in operation, the clients discovered that it failed to provide all the desired functions that had originally been envisioned; also there were some aspects of the system that did not appear to be consistent with normal operations. Analysis by the management science group indicated that management did not fully comprehend the system and that the lack of success was due to improper use. The management science group was unable to convince management that the system was being misused; and after a period of time, management support dwindled because system performance did not meet expectations. After 18 months the system was rejected, and the former system adopted. Lack of communication was a major problem throughout the project's life cycle.

**Cost of implementation.**    The cost of implementation is often either completely neglected or minimized. Malcolm made the following comment about the budget process:

> A tight budget impedes operations research/management science activities by delaying studies until a new fiscal period or by requiring that the proposed studies be placed in competition with other uses of the resources. This type action tends to force the proponents of a project to understate the expected cost in order for the project to be approved. In most cases the one area which is purposely minimized during this costing process is the cost of implementation of results.[10]

A policy of neglecting implementation cost can only result in problems. Management/management science relations are quickly placed in jeopardy when it becomes apparent that implementation and operating costs far exceed original estimates. Management confidence in its MS/OR staff is diminished when unforeseen implementation costs consume projected profits or savings. In evaluating a project, the anticipated cost must include the cost of implementation and operation. Project cost should include the cost for development and analysis, the estimated cost for implementation (including training), and the estimated operating cost (including both man-power and equipment).

---

[10]D. G. Malcolm, "On the Need for Improvement in Implementation of O.R.," *Management Science*, 11, No. 4 (February 1965), p. B50.

**The impact of change.** In addition to the specific ideas explored above, two remaining factors affect implementation. First, implementation must occur in a dynamic environment created by the changing demands of the organization. Second, the relevance of some factors is affected by changes that occur in the MS/OR group and in the project as the project moves through different stages of its development.

Time is a critical element within any systems activity, particularly with the design, development, and implementation of a quantitative system. The critical role of timing results from organizational changes. This is exemplified in the following comments by Stillson:

> ... in the development and implementation of a maintenance system for service station equipment, the time lapse between "selling" the system and obtaining a fully operational system was a critical factor. The enthusiasm which existed during the early stages of the study waned after several development problems occurred, and this extended the length of the development process. When the finalized system was complete, it was discovered that many of the basic factors of the system had changed and many of the initial operational personnel who supported the system were no longer associated with the operational area.[11]

A second example highlighting the impact of organizational change is included in the comments of a systems manager in a large industrial firm:

> One of the major problems that we have experienced in our implementation efforts has been organizational change. Before we can develop and implement a system, organizational changes have occurred that impact the operating priorities of the group and in most cases change the responsibilities of the operating managers. In one particular case, our operating group experienced five organizational changes (these changes affecting some of the key people associated with the systems effort in the area) within a period of thirteen months. With such an erratic environment it is very difficult to establish an operating base from which to implement a system.

**People problems.** One of the major sources of implementation problems is the lack of direction, motivation, and management of the people associated with a quantitative system, particularly during the latter stages of the project life cycle when the system is operationalized. Quite often implementation failure has been attributed to improper design, inappropriate use of a given MS/OR technique, or other system deficiencies when in reality the problem is related to the mismanagement of people.

People mismanagement can be illustrated by the example of a large industrial firm that experienced problems in implementing a resource allocation system.

---

[11]P. Stillson, "Implementation Problems in OR," *Operations Research*, 11, No. 1 (January–February 1963), p. 144.

Analysis of the case showed that, initially, management supported the project and agreed that the proposed approach appeared to be suitable for reducing production costs. In making the developed system operational, however, excessive time delays—resulting from an excessive load on the computer—caused output reports to be delayed. As a result, operating managers complained that the system could not be employed, primarily because the system's reports were so late. After a period of time, extra computer capacity was added to eliminate the excessive delays, and a backup computer was made available to increase the reliability of the system. Resolving these problems, however, failed to resolve the implementation problem. Operating managers then complained that the historical data carried within the system really could not be used as a valid data base for the system; it was claimed that a real-time updating capability was needed to support the data base.

Analysis of the data base problem and other problems by the MS/OR group revealed that the operating managers' lack of success in using the system was due to lack of direction, motivation, and control of the people who were directed to use the system. The department manager who initially endorsed the system had left the operating managers with the decision to use or reject the system. The department manager suggested adopting the system but gave no directive in this respect to the operating people. Also, no departmental controls were established for managing the total implementation effort. Many of the operating managers opposed the system because they did not understand how the system operated and thus were skeptical about using it. To avoid using the system, managers sought to discredit the data base. After eight months of unsuccessful use, the decision was made to drop the system. The failure was attributed to system weaknesses, but a more important reason was lack of direction, motivation, and control of the system users.

## Need for an integrated approach

In the previous section, we have shown that human and organizational factors, management needs and characteristics, the solution approach, characteristics of the MS/OR group, and characteristics of the problem are all elements that relate to the implementation of quantitative systems. Much of our discussion, however, focused on the problems in isolation. Successful implementation is dependent upon integrating these elements into the steps, procedures, and processes employed throughout a project's life cycle, that is, through conceptualization to full operation of the system.

*operations research and development process*

Malcolm proposed an **operations research and development process** for systematically developing and implementing an MS/OR system. The Malcolm process uses the following steps:[12]

1. Problem definition

2. Selection of the method of analysis (technique)

3. Presentation of alternatives

[12]D. G. Malcolm, op. cit., p. B49.

4. Selection of an alternative

5. Pilot implementation

6. Measurement of results against established criteria

7. Development of program for full-scale implementation

8. Execution of full-scale implementation

9. Review and update of the system, as required

These steps should appear familiar. If we group steps 5–8 into a single category and label this "implementation," then this operations research and development process could be adapted to the MS/OR problem-solving process that we identified in Chapter 1 (refer to Figure 1-1).

While either process provides a skeletal framework for implementation, neither provides enough detail for integrating all the implementation elements. This shortcoming can be overcome by overlaying a game-simulator on the operations research and development process. Historically, gaming has served as a training device for studying human behavior, as a means for evaluating strategies (war games), as a training device for management, and as a teaching aid. A computerized game, thus, logically should be a viable vehicle for integrating many of the implementation factors, particularly when the logic of the game incorporates the proposed MS/OR technique. The next section defines and describes such a game-implementation framework.

## ■ A game-implementation framework

### *Overview*

An important component of the game-implementation framework is the hypothesis that implementation is a special case or organizational change.[13] The framework is based upon the work of Radnor, Rubenstein, and Tansik, who contend that many potentially operational systems fail because organizational members are unable to adapt their behavior to a required change in operational procedures—implementation often necessitates system modifications, which in turn necessitate behavioral changes on the part of the manager/recipient.[14] The framework is supported by the research of Sorensen and Zand, who argue that a high level of implementation success results only when organizational constituents adapt to required change.[15] These researchers demonstrate that the organizational change process required for implementation follows the Lewin-Schein theory of change. Building upon the

---

[13]Much of the material in this section is drawn from K. R. Davis and B. W. Taylor, "Addressing the Implementation Problem: A Gaming Approach," *Decision Sciences*, 7, No. 4 (October 1976), pp. 677–687.

[14]M. Radnor, A. H. Rubenstein, and D. A. Tansik, op. cit.

[15]R. E. Sorenson and D. E. Zand, "Overcoming Problems of Decision Sciences Implementation," presented at the 1974 Southwestern AIDS Conference, March 30, Dallas, Texas.

**FIGURE 25-1.
The Change Pro-
cess**

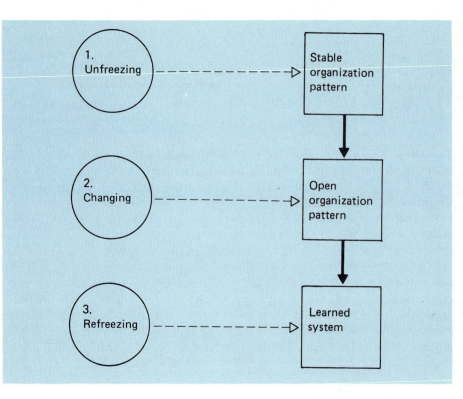

research of Sorensen and Zand, the game-implementation framework employs the methodology described in the Lewin-Schein theory.

*Lewin-Schein
theory*

Viewed in an implementation framework, the **Lewin-Schein theory** would define the implementation change process as a three-step procedure (see Figure 25-1): (1) *unfreezing* of the present system, (2) *changing*, and (3) *refreezing* of the new system.[16] Through empirical testing, Sorensen and Zand found that the degree of application of the Lewin-Schein theory explains the degree of success in implementation. Specifically, these researchers found that high levels of unfreezing, changing, and refreezing result in high levels of success, while low levels of the change process result in low levels of success.

An individual, a group of individuals, or some action-based activity must be incorporated in the Lewin-Schein process to unfreeze, change, and refreeze organizational behavior patterns. The game-implementation framework employs a "simulation game" as the change agent; that is, the item, circumstance, or individual that brings about change. A game insulator is employed to lead a manager, client, user, or any other individual involved with a given project or system systematically through the implementation process.

---

[16]E. H. Schein, "The Mechanism of Change," in *Interpersonal Dynamics*, W. G. Bennis, E. H. Schein, F. I. Steele, and D. E. Berlew, eds. (Homewood, Ill.: Dorsey, 1964), pp. 362–378.

## *The gaming approach*

Gaming is the use of a computerized simulation model to permit participants to make decisions and observe the behavior of the system as a result of those decisions. A gaming model consists of a simulated environment that mirrors some characteristics of the system under analysis.

Within the game-implementation framework, the initial step of introducing the game should occur in the form of a training session for management. The game is employed to demonstrate improved conditions that could result by use of the new technique. That is, the game demonstrates to the manager "what can be accomplished."

The second step, "game playing," involves employing the game model as a teaching device, with the game offering an alternative to a manager's previous behavior pattern. By playing the game, the manager begins to learn and use the new technique and becomes more receptive to it. In this step, the unfreezing process may continue and mesh with the "change" step. Old behavior patterns gradually change as new patterns are learned, and the manager becomes more aware of the need for a change.

As part of the change process, the manager may develop new objectives. If the goals and objectives of the overall project are successfully displayed as the manager becomes familiar with the game, new goals can easily be examined and evaluated.

The third step in the gaming procedure is the development of the new technique as an on-line computer system, where the system is similar to the game used to demonstrate the system. This step enables a manager to continue to use the familiar mode of implementation introduced in the learning process. In effect, the manager continues to "play the game." The value of the on-line system is that it allows the manager to progress through the Lewin-Schein steps via a single vehicle for learning and implementation. Continuity is generated, which contributes to the success of the implementation process.

A representative framework of the game-implementation methodology and its relationship to the three-step Lewin-Schein change process is depicted in Figure 25-2. The component parts of the framework may be defined in the following manner:

*Establish system objectives:* System objectives are the goals or desired results sought from the system to be implemented. By establishing objectives, which require output from the manager's area of responsibility, the *unfreezing* step in the change process begins.

*Abstract game development:* Development of an abstract game is the first part of a three-step phase that also requires identification of the present system and a comparative analysis between that system and the abstract game. The game is abstract in that it does not necessarily mirror the present system. Developing the game in this manner enables the management scientist to conceptualize a system without management input and bias.

*Identification of the system:* This activity provides a basis for comparative analysis (comparison of the abstract game and the current system). It further

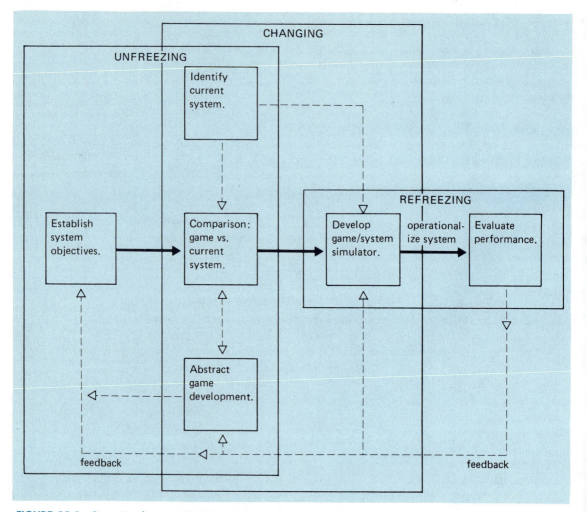

**FIGURE 25-2. Game-Implementation Framework**

provides both the management scientist and the manager a common point of departure (i.e., basis for discussion).

*Comparison—game vs. current system:* By comparing the abstract game with the present system, the manager is able to gain a new perspective. This further enhances the unfreezing step. By taking full advantage of the game environment, the unfreezing step can be finalized and the *change* step can be initiated. The structure of the gaming activity involves game play followed by critique sessions in which the manager participates via group discussion and/or private questionnaire. The critique sessions have a twofold effect. First, they enable the manager/participant to voice opinions and ask questions—actions that should promote the learning process. Second, the critique sessions offer feedback to the management scientist. This provides input that the management scientist can use to alter the abstract game to reflect a compromised system. By repeating the game-playing/critique session cycle several times, a participant begins to learn the fundamentals of the system, while the management scientist refines and develops the system. This process initiates the change step.

*Game/system simulation:* In this activity of the gaming framework, a simulation model of the actual system is developed. By employing the model as a game, the manager is in reality learning the actual system that will be operationalized. This activity will complete the change step by exposing the new system to the recipient and initiate the *refreezing* steps by demonstrating the system's effectiveness in achieving results.

*Evaluation of performance:* At this stage, the system is fully operational and the recipient is involved in its use. However, the management scientist must be careful to remain involved with the implementation process until the manager has completed the refreezing process. This involves evaluating the system to determine if it meets specifications and achieves desired results. Discrepancies must be corrected, through the feedback process, lest the manager revert to the previous system. When all problems are sufficiently resolved, the refreezing step will be complete.

The game-implementation approach, as defined, results in an on-line, game-model system that bears all the characteristics of the final system, but in actuality it is a miniversion of a fully operational system. To complete the project, one may need to develop an all-encompassing system.

Before concluding the discussion of the game-implementation framework, we should point out how the approach relates or compares with the traditional systems-development framework (Figure 25-3). In the traditional framework,

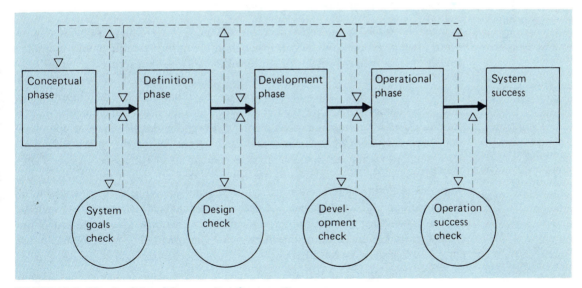

**FIGURE 25-3. The Traditional Systems Development Process**

implementation is attempted at the operational phase; thus, if gaming were employed, it would occur during the operational phase. In the game-implementation framework, however, gaming is employed throughout the systems-development process, not just at the final phase. Referring back to the Malcolm process, discussed earlier, the traditional approach would be to employ gaming during step 7 (development of a program for full-scale implementation). Using the game-implementation approach, we would employ a game through all nine steps.

## ■ A case example

The game-implementation framework was used in three different production systems in a major electronics corporation. One application involved the development and implementation of a production-line-balancing technique. It is particularly relevant to examine this application because a system existed prior to game development. On this basis, one could argue that the game was actually developed during the operational phase of the old system's development process (Figure 25-3). However, the game-implementation process actually resulted in the design and development of a new system; therefore, in actuality the game was developed during the conceptualization-definition phase.

In reviewing this case, we will examine the following activities: the problem and the existing system, the game and game activities, and the on-line system. You should bear in mind as each activity is presented how it relates to the unfreezing, changing, refreezing steps of the change process.

### The problem in brief

As noted, the problem addressed was the balancing of a production line. In simple terms, a balanced line is when all production operations are functioning simultaneously at a planned manufacturing rate with no change in in-process inventories.

There are numerous techniques available to achieve balanced conditions. Though these techniques differ somewhat in approach, each basically involves interrelating the same general factors. One must break down the operation into elements, specify the times required to perform each element, determine the efficiency of operators, identify the sequence of operations, and establish the required rate of production. Many solution techniques require physical changes in a production process. However, one can achieve a balance by specifying a desired output rate, back-tracing through the line to determine resource needs, and applying various heuristics to determine operator assignments.[17] It should be recognized, however, that such an approach, while not requiring physical changes, may require total acceptance of the change situation by production managers. The particular MS/OR technique employed in this case was heuristic.

[17]K. R. Davis and B. W. Taylor, op. cit.

## The current system

A large computerized, batch-mode balancing system had already been developed in the company. The system objective was to minimize process cycle time and control work-in-process inventories. The system was designed to furnish daily reports that specified machine and personnel utilization requirements necessary for meeting production output requirements. A data-collection system was designed to support the system. The data system provided an efficient means for on-line collection and entry of production data. Data were to be collected on-line in the production environment, transmitted to a control processor, and recorded on magnetic tape. The input tape could then be used on a daily basis for updating the data base of the balancing system.

Eighteen months after the balancing system was installed, division management noted that there had been little change in in-process inventories and that production cycle times were still extremely long. Upon discussing the problem with production managers, it was found that the majority of managers failed to implement the specified personnel utilization structure given in the daily production report. Several reasons were given for the lack of utilization; the most frequently mentioned factors were a lack of understanding of the system and an unwillingness to commit the production operation to a "black box" procedure. One manager expressed his views in the following manner:

> . . . Most production managers use planning and scheduling systems because these systems compliment the production process. They provide useful planning information. Most fellows do not understand the concepts associated with the production on-line balancing and allocation process. I find it difficult to visualize how the systems can help me.

The problem was basically viewed as a resistance to change on the part of line management. This resistance was personified in the lack of understanding and visualization of the system.

## The game

In an attempt to overcome the resistance to change associated with the balancing system and thus to increase its usage, the decision was made to develop a game to demonstrate the concepts employed in the system. The game was designed to parallel the logic employed in the system; however, it was not a simulation of the system. To maximize flexibility of the game, it was developed on a time-sharing computer utilizing portable terminals. This portable feature allowed the game to be conducted directly in the operating area.

## Gaming sessions—Comparative analysis

Gaming sessions were conducted within the production departments. The actual sessions involved a short lecture on the theory of line balancing, an explanation of the objectives of game play, actual game play, and finally a critique of the game and game sessions. Both production managers and operators were involved in the sessions.

Eleven game sessions involving 136 participants were sampled to gather data on the gaming activity. A game session questionnaire was completed by each participant at the conclusion of the game session. Some of the responses from the questionnaire were as follows:

> This is a good way to communicate systems to users. I would like to see more of this same sort of communication on other systems.
>
> The game gives you a chance to try different alternatives and study the effects.
>
> It helps you understand the problems in line-balancing and develop a better understanding of the role the system plays.

This activity acted to "unfreeze" the managers as well as initiate the "change" process.

## Game-system simulator

As managers began to play the game they began the changing phase of the Lewin-Schein process; that is, they began to note how the technique could aid in doing a better job, and they became less defensive and more receptive to the management scientists. However, after the game sessions were completed, there was a minimal increase in usage of the balancing system. Managers indicated the lack of usage was the result of two factors: (1) the transition to the large batch-mode system was difficult (because the system was much more sophisticated than the game); (2) the system forced a user to reduce in-process inventories to a minimum and to balance the line in a single time period. (This point was repeatedly voiced during the game session critiques.)

A system simulator (IBALS System: Interactive Balancing Through Simulation) was developed that provided a solution to the noted constraints. The simulator was designed so that the line could be balanced at existing in-process levels. To support the simulator, an on-line file-building, file-updating routine was developed.

With the update and solution alternative capabilities of the simulator, managers could test and explore different solution alternatives and line configurations. Also, a key advantage of the simulator was its capability to be employed as a game or as a test vehicle of past performances. By using prior personnel assignments and inventory levels, the validity of the simulator could be verified. Output of the simulator was tested and found to parallel the actual results from the line.

## Performance—Evaluation

The change–refreezing phase of the change process was noted when managers began to adopt the simulator and began to employ the operator assignments and flow rate as displayed by the simulator output. Increased usage was also noted in the large batch-mode system. To determine if a change had actually resulted, data on production operating indices of work-in-process inventories, production output, manpower employed, and cycle time were compared with prior data. (Data had been collected on the indices prior to development of the batch-mode system as well as after the introduction of the system.)

Data collected prior to introduction of the batch system and prior to and after introduction of the game concept were supplied to the respective production managers. Because the data changed in a positive manner, they reinforced usage of the system; that is, they supplied the force necessary for "refreezing the participants."

### Benefits of the game-implementation framework

Several benefits developed as a result of the application of the game-implementation approach. First, the game-system cycle tended to force the manager through the Lewin-Schein steps, thus minimizing the backsliding from step to step. In effect, the game meshed the unfreezing–changing–refreezing cycle, creating a smooth continuous change process.

Second, the on-line mode of implementation involved managers in the development of the model much more than expected. The on-line operation encouraged the exploration of "what if" questions and the use of soft information. Managers became aware of previously unknown computer capabilities, and the propensity to experiment was encouraged.

Another important benefit resulted in the form of positive and negative feedback to the management science group. When the game was used at the conceptualization stage of the system's process cycle, as opposed to the operational stage, managers were able to discover problems and inconsistencies that had gone unnoticed by the management scientist. Thus the game provided the analysts with an arena in which to test the technique and remove "bugs."

## ■ Evaluation of time/cost factors of implementation

In reviewing the factors associated with implementation, we noted that the timely provision of relevant reports and the cost of implementation are often overlooked or shortchanged in developing and implementing an MS/OR technique or system, particularly if there are budget constraints and/or pressure for results. In this section, we examine these two factors and present an approach for incorporating them into the initial phase of a project review. To complement the previous section we will focus the analysis on the game-implementation framework.

### Need for a time/cost evaluation

Game-implementation methodology has been found to greatly enhance the probability of successful implementation. However, such a methodology consumes resources (time and money). The process of game development, game playing, and operationalizing may encompass an extended period of time, which in retrospect may be undesirable or unwarranted by the firm. Time lags during implementation can result in decreased output and productivity, lost sales, and disrupted production schedules. Similarly, implementation costs may become extensive and may outweigh the cost savings expected from the new system.

Because of the possibility of cost and time overruns, some form of planning must be undertaken prior to implementation to ascertain whether the system warrants implementation. One approach to implementation planning is to estimate the resources (time and dollars) associated with implementation and simulate the implementation process. Specifically, if a series of time and cost factors can be projected for each step of an implementation process and if probabilities can be attached to the different estimates, then simulation can be employed to model the implementation activities. This simulation model will yield statistical data concerning expected time and cost of system development and implementation.

In the section that follows, we will employ a case example to describe and demonstrate the use of simulation for planning the implementation process. The case involves a computerized inventory-control system developed for use in a large manufacturing plant. The system was designed to provide operating decisions for maintaining proper inventories, minimizing inventory costs, and preventing unwarranted backlogs.

## Example of time/cost planning

**The simulation model.**  The inventory-control system had been developed a number of months prior to the project study. Problems had been encountered when the system was initially operationalized. Line managers argued that the system forced them to operate their lines with considerably lower inventories than were "operationally feasible." Marketing managers argued that they were losing sales because of stockouts. Top management was of the opinion that the system was theoretically sound but at least two problems existed: (1) managers probably did not understand the operation of the system, even though formal implementation classes and seminars had been conducted; and (2) the system forced managers to reduce inventories to theoretical minimums. The MS/OR group assured top management that slight changes could be made in the system such that individual managers could control the rate of reduction and thus avoid drastic inventory reductions that could result in missed customer deliveries.

Division management indicated it would "drop the system" if the problems could not be resolved and if the additional costs of "making the system operational" could not be justified. The game-implementation process was proposed for implementing the system, since it appeared to provide a means for both training and system modifications, if needed. The key questions raised were: What would be the cost of employing the process? What was the probability that the results would be the same as when the system was first implemented? And finally, what was the expected length of time for achieving full implementation?

**Monte Carlo sampling.**  Since Monte Carlo sampling could provide statistical data related to the questions raised, it was adopted as a suitable vehicle for studying the proposed implementation. To simulate the process, it was necessary to identify the time and cost associated with each activity of implementation and the probability of occurrence of each activity.

The first step in developing the simulation was to develop a network diagram of the game-implementation framework. This is shown in Figure 25-4. (This was developed from the game-implementation framework depicted in Figure 25-2.) The time associated with each activity was then defined. Three subjective estimates were made for each activity (optimistic, most likely, and pessimistic). These are shown in Figure 25-4 in parentheses. Fixed and variable costs were also subjectively determined for each activity, the fixed cost being realized when the activity was undertaken, and variable cost being determined by the duration of the activity. Finally, probability estimates were made for each of the activities. Table 25-2 is a complete description of all activities, branch probabilities, and time and cost estimates for the inventory system.

**Summary description of simulation development.**   For the inventory system, start up of the implementation process, indicated by activity 0–1, consisted of identifying the personnel and initial resources (space and equipment) necessary to begin the implementation process. The personnel group identified consisted of a systems analyst, a management scientist, and a computer support specialist. A fixed cost of $500 was assigned to the activity.

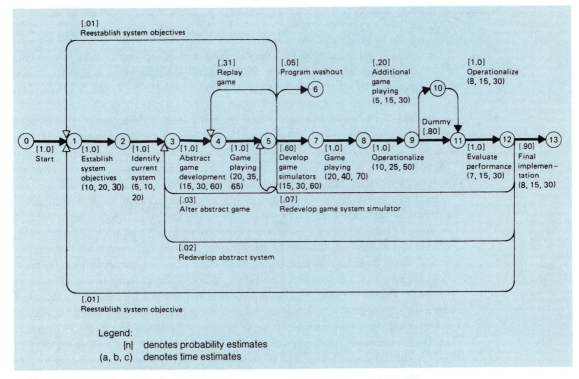

**FIGURE 25-4. A Simulation Network of the Game-Implementation Framework**

**TABLE 25-2. Activity Descriptions, with Associated Time and Cost Estimates: Inventory System**

| Activity (nodes) | Activity Description | Probability of Occurrence | Time Estimates (days) | | | Cost Estimates ($) | |
|---|---|---|---|---|---|---|---|
| | | | Min | Mode | Max | Setup | Variable |
| 0–1 | Start process | 1.00 | | 0 | | 500 | 0 |
| 1–2 | Establish system objectives | 1.00 | 10 | 20 | 30 | 0 | 100 |
| 2–3 | Identify current system | 1.00 | 5 | 10 | 20 | 0 | 75 |
| 3–4 | Abstract game development | 1.00 | 15 | 30 | 60 | 2500 | 100 |
| 4–5 | Game playing | 1.00 | 20 | 35 | 65 | 0 | 150 |
| 5–6 | System washout | .05 | | 0 | | 0 | 0 |
| 5–1 | Reestablish objectives | .01 | | 0 | | 0 | 0 |
| 5–3 | Alter abstract game | .03 | | 0 | | 0 | 0 |
| 5–4 | Replay game | .31 | | 0 | | 0 | 0 |
| 5–7 | Develop game simulator | .60 | 15 | 30 | 60 | 3000 | 100 |
| 7–8 | Game playing | 1.00 | 20 | 40 | 70 | 0 | 125 |
| 8–9 | Operationalize | 1.00 | 10 | 25 | 50 | 1000 | 100 |
| 9–10 | Additional game playing | .20 | 5 | 15 | 30 | 0 | 125 |
| 9–11 | Dummy | .80 | | 0 | | 0 | 0 |
| 10–11 | Operationalize | 1.00 | 8 | 15 | 30 | 0 | 100 |
| 11–12 | Evaluate performance | 1.00 | 7 | 15 | 30 | 0 | 75 |
| 12–13 | Final implementation | .90 | 8 | 15 | 30 | 0 | 100 |
| 12–5 | Redevelop game simulator | .07 | | 0 | | 0 | 0 |
| 12–3 | Redevelop abstract system | .02 | | 0 | | 0 | 0 |
| 12–1 | Reestablish system objective | .01 | | 0 | | 0 | 0 |

Activity 1–2 represents the first major phase of the implementation process. For implementing the inventory system this required assessing the time and cost that would be required (1) to meet with top management to ascertain objectives and (2) to disseminate the objectives to production and marketing managers who would use the system. The activity would involve working with each middle manager to identify the basis for the objectives of the proposed system. The activity was estimated to take between 10 and 30 days at a cost of $100 per day.

Activity 2–3, "identify current system," involved assessing the time and cost involved in working with middle managers to identify problems and weaknesses of the existing system and comparing the existing system output with management's established objectives. This activity would complete the unfreezing stage and initiate the change phase of the process. A time estimate of 5 to 20 days (with a most-likely estimate of 10 days) was established as the time that would be required to complete the activity; $75 per day was estimated to be the cost associated with the activity.

Development of a computerized abstract game is the activity involved between nodes 3–4. This is the stage of the implementation process where top management objectives are incorporated into the abstract computerized model (game) of the "to be developed/modified system." It was estimated that it would require between 15 and 60 days to develop the abstract model, with an initial cost of $2500 and a variable cost of $100 per day. The $2500 setup cost was the projected cost of capital equipment (on-line terminal) necessary to support development of the model.

Variable costs would be programming costs, cost of developing questionnaires, and costs of developing training-session transparencies.

Activity 4–5 is the point at which the abstract model is employed as a game. The game activity acts as a catalyst to complete the unfreezing phase of the implementation process—managers, through game playing, fully comprehend the defined objectives. The game playing involves managers making decisions in game playing sessions via an on-line terminal. Results of game play are discussed among the implementation staff and managers. It was estimated that this activity would consume between 20 and 65 days at a cost of $150 per day.

After the abstract game has been played for a reasonable period of time, decisions must be made at node 5 about the perceived future success of implementing the inventory system. If the entire approach appears to be futile and failure is imminent, the project is washed out (activity 5–6). This reduces the cost of completing the entire project and incurring system failure. Alternatively, at node 5 it may be decided that some activities should be repeated if implementation has not proceeded as expected. These alternatives are denoted by activities 5–1, 5–3, and 5–4. Neither time nor cost is associated with the rework activities, since these are nothing other than decision points. However, probabilities must be attached to each of the activities. The estimation of the probabilities associated with these activities is quite difficult since historical data are usually nonexistent or limited. However, since the model is quite sensitive to these probabilities, care should be exercised in the estimation process. For the case example, the estimated probabilities were .01, .03, and .31.

Unless it is necessary to alter the abstract game (5–3), participate in more gaming (activity 5–4), reestablish objectives (activity 5–1), or the system washes out (activity 5–6), the next activity in the implementation process is development of the game simulator that mirrors the actual inventory system (activity 5–7). As noted in our review of the game-implementation framework, this game is developed in the same manner as the abstract game but is in reality a simulation of the actual system. The time required for this activity was estimated to be between 15 and 60 days at a fixed cost of $3000 and variable costs of $100 per day.

After the game simulator has been developed, it is played (activity 7–8) in the same manner as the abstract game (via game sessions with production and marketing managers). It was estimated that this would be the longest activity in the implementation process since this is where managers experiment and learn the actual system to be operationalized. This activity is extremely important since it completes the change step and initiates the refreezing step in the implementation process.

Following the learning of the inventory system via game playing, the new system is operationalized (activity 8–9). Operationalizing the system requires modifying the simulator to reflect any problems or constraints noted during the gaming sessions. A period of 10 to 50 days, with an average of 25 days, was the time estimated as required to operationalize. A setup cost of $1000 was estimated for additional capital equipment.

After the system has been operationalized, it may be determined that the system has not been completely "learned"; additional game play may be required (activity 9–10). This problem should result only for a small portion of the managers. Following the operationalizing of the system, a period of time should be set aside to evaluate the performance of the system (activity 11–12). For the inventory system, a time estimation of between 7 and 30 days was established for system evaluation.

If the system, as a result of evaluation, is found to be successful (i.e., the objectives are accomplished), the system can be declared complete (activity 12–13). However, if it becomes apparent during system evaluation that the system is not meeting the established objectives, some or all prior stages of the implementation process must be repeated. These activities are denoted in Table 25-2 by activities 12–1, 12–3, and 12–5. As was the case at node 5, only probabilities of occurrence must be estimated for each rework activity leading from node 12. Note that in the case of node 12, the probabilities of rework should be smaller than those at node 5. For the inventory system, it was estimated that there was a 90% chance that rework would not be required. Again, as was the case at node 5, estimating the node probabilities is important in obtaining realistic cost and time results for the entire implementation process.

**Simulation results.**   The simulation network was iterated 1000 times in order to obtain operating statistics for time and cost. Table 25-3 gives the summary of time statistics for the project, while Table 25-4 gives the summary of cost statistics. Data in these tables show that the implementation process would on the average require 275 days for full implementation with an expected cost of $37,000.

However, recall that top management was interested in more than the expected cost and time for implementation. They also needed to know the probability that the new implementation process would result in failure, as was the case when the system was first implemented. Tables 25-3 and 25-4 indicate that there is an 8.6% chance of implementation failure at an expected cost of $17,000. Note that the expected cost of failure is almost half the expected cost of success. This results because a lengthy period of time elapses (on the average of 131 days) before the probability of failure is evaluated. Even though there was the possibility of large losses if failure occurred, the decision was made to employ the process.

**Operational results.**   The gaming process was employed to reimplement the inventory system, and the system was successfully implemented. Thirty-seven line managers were involved over a period of 218 days in 21 different manufacturing operations. Rework was required at two activities in the process. At the operationalizing activity, it was found that line workers who had not been involved in the early parts of the implementation process did not comprehend the system's operations. Game-playing exercises, using the game simulator (activity 9–10), were employed to familiarize the workers with the system. During the evaluation of the system

**TABLE 25-3.**
**Summary of Time Statistics for Implementation Process**

| Event | Prob. | Time (days) | | | |
| --- | --- | --- | --- | --- | --- |
| | | $E(t)$ | $\sigma_t$ | Min $t$ | Max $t$ |
| Process completion | .914 | 275 | 73 | 184 | 679 |
| Process washout | .086 | 131 | 56 | 78 | 319 |

| Cost | | Cost ($000's) | | | | TABLE 25-4. |
|------|------|------|------|------|------| |
| Cost | Prob. | $E(c)$ | $\sigma_c$ | Min $c$ | Max $c$ | |
| Process cost | .914 | 37 | 10 | 26 | 92 | |
| Washout cost | .086 | 17 | 8 | 10 | 45 | |

TABLE 25-4.
Summary of Cost
Statistics for
Implementation
Process

(activity 11–12) it was determined that additional flexibility was needed in the system; the simulator was modified (activity 12–5) to reflect the desired changes. Minigame playing sessions were conducted to reflect the changes in the system. The changes were then incorporated into the final system. Total cost of the implementation process was $38,200.

## General use of simulation for time/cost evaluation

The case example emphasizes the use of the game-implementation framework as the process suitable for implementation. The simulation-evaluation approach is not limited to this particular implementation process. Simulation can be adapted to any particular development/design/implementation framework. Activities related to any particular system of design/implementation framework can easily be incorporated into a simulation model.

A secondary benefit that can accrue from using the simulation is an increased understanding of the requirements of implementation. The simulation-evaluation approach forces management to identify the activities that will be used in developing and implementing a system. It also forces management to place time, cost, and probabilities on different activities, a factor that is generally ignored in developing most systems. Simulation is not a panacea for the often ignored questions of implementation time and cost, but it can provide some answers.

## ■ Summary

In the early years when management science was employed in solving small specific operating problems within firms, implementation was assumed to involve only the simple task of specifying the physical changes required in the organization in order to install the technique or system. But as the field evolved and techniques and models were applied to larger and more complex problems, it was recognized that a number of other factors have a bearing on the success (or failure) of implementation. A number of these factors were described in detail in the chapter; they include

> management characteristics
>
> level of management support
>
> exposure of management to the management science and computer area
>
> attitudes and interests of the MS/OR group

capabilities and knowledge of the MS/OR group

definition of project results

urgency of results

communication

cost of implementation (the impact of change)

people problems

In the second section of the chapter, a game-implementation framework was presented. The framework was described as a means for integrating the factors of implementation into a project life-cycle framework. The game-implementation framework was shown to be based upon the Lewin-Schein change theory and the research of Sorensen and Zand. Research by Sorensen and Zand indicates that a high incidence of unfreezing–change–refreezing results in a high level of implementation success. The game-implementation process acts as a change agent to guide managers/clients through the change process.

Often managers become overly concerned with "getting the system on line" and ignore the time and costs required for developing and implementing the system. Because of budget constraints or time demands, management scientists often understate time and cost requirements. In the latter section of the chapter, we demonstrated how simulation could be used to resolve these problems—it can be used to aid the planning function associated with developing (or redeveloping) and implementing a system. The data provided by simulation can aid management in evaluating the development/implementation process prior to beginning the development of the system.

It should not be concluded that the game-implementation framework is the only methodology that can be used in applying MS/OR to real-world problems. Likewise, it should not be concluded that every application of management science will require gaming; this would be a gross misapplication of the methodology.

It also should not be concluded that simulation is the only tool for evaluating the time and cost of implementation. The point that should be recognized is that a time and cost study must be made—the technique or tool for making this study is secondary.

There are still many situations in which management science is not being utilized to the fullest extent possible. In most cases, the problems are not technically based. Most have an operational, organizational, administrative, or behavioral basis. The material in this chapter, it is hoped, provides a means for addressing some of these problems. At the minimum, we have demonstrated that a successful management science practitioner must not only have a firm understanding of the MS/OR field, but must be able to manage behavioral and administrative problems.

## ■ Glossary of terms

**game-implementation framework:**   An implementation framework in which a computerized game is employed throughout the project life cycle to permit analysis, encourage behavioral interaction, and provide training.

**implementation:** In traditional terms, this referred to the procedures used to make operational a designed and developed system; in contemporary terms, it refers to all of the activities necessary to transform a conceptualized model or system into a fully operational system.

**Lewin-Schein change theory:** An organizational change theory built upon three steps: unfreezing, changing, and refreezing.

**operations research and development process:** A set of global steps designed for systematically developing and implementing an MS/OR system.

**simulation-implementation process:** Refers to the use of simulation to model the time and cost associated with employing the game-implementation framework.

## ■ Review questions

1. Describe the traditional view of implementation, i.e., the view held by management scientists in the early 1950s.

2. List the factors that researchers have found to be related to implementation success (failure).

3. Identify some of the management characteristics that have a bearing on implementation success (failure). Briefly describe these factors.

4. Briefly describe the implementation factors that are linked to the MS/OR group.

5. How does the cost of implementation relate to implementation success (failure)?

6. What does the term *people problems* refer to in relation to implementation?

7. Describe the operations research and development process. Show how this relates to the MS/OR problem-solving process as described in Chapter 1.

8. Briefly describe the game-implementation framework. How is the Lewin-Schein change theory related to this process?

9. Briefly describe how simulation can be used to evaluate the time and cost factors associated with developing and implementing a system in which an MS/OR model or technique is employed.

# ..Appendixes················································

# Appendix A
## *Tables*

| | s | | | | | | |
|---|---|---|---|---|---|---|---|
| $\rho$ | 1 | 2 | 3 | 4 | 5 | 6 | 7 |
| .100 | .9000 | .9048 | .9048 | .9048 | .9048 | .9048 | .9048 |
| .200 | .8000 | .8182 | .8187 | .8187 | .8187 | .8187 | .8187 |
| .300 | .7000 | .7391 | .7407 | .7408 | .7408 | .7408 | .7408 |
| .400 | .6000 | .6667 | .6701 | .6703 | .6703 | .6703 | .6703 |
| .500 | .5000 | .6000 | .6061 | .6065 | .6065 | .6065 | .6065 |
| .600 | .4000 | .5385 | .5479 | .5487 | .5488 | .5488 | .5488 |
| .700 | .3000 | .4815 | .4952 | .4965 | .4966 | .4966 | .4966 |
| .800 | .2000 | .4286 | .4472 | .4491 | .4493 | .4493 | .4493 |
| .900 | .1000 | .3793 | .4035 | .4062 | .4065 | .4066 | .4066 |
| 1.000 | | .3333 | .3636 | .3673 | .3678 | .3679 | .3679 |
| 1.100 | | .2903 | .3273 | .3321 | .3328 | .3329 | .3329 |
| 1.200 | | .2500 | .2941 | .3002 | .3011 | .3012 | .3012 |
| 1.300 | | .2121 | .2638 | .2712 | .2723 | .2725 | .2725 |
| 1.400 | | .1765 | .2360 | .2449 | .2463 | .2466 | .2466 |
| 1.500 | | .1429 | .2105 | .2210 | .2228 | .2231 | .2231 |
| 1.600 | | .1111 | .1872 | .1993 | .2014 | .2018 | .2019 |
| 1.700 | | .0811 | .1657 | .1796 | .1821 | .1826 | .1827 |
| 1.800 | | .0526 | .1460 | .1616 | .1646 | .1652 | .1653 |
| 1.900 | | .0256 | .1278 | .1453 | .1487 | .1494 | .1495 |
| 2.000 | | | .1111 | .1304 | .1343 | .1351 | .1353 |
| 2.100 | | | .0957 | .1169 | .1213 | .1222 | .1224 |
| 2.200 | | | .0815 | .1046 | .1094 | .1105 | .1107 |
| 2.300 | | | .0683 | .0933 | .0987 | .0999 | .1002 |
| 2.400 | | | .0562 | .0831 | .0889 | .0903 | .0906 |

**TABLE A-1.**
**Values of $P_0$**

| $\rho$ | $s$ | | | | | | |
| | 1 | 2 | 3 | 4 | 5 | 6 | 7 |
|---|---|---|---|---|---|---|---|
| 2.500 | | | .0449 | .0737 | .0801 | .0816 | .0820 |
| 2.600 | | | .0345 | .0651 | .0721 | .0737 | .0742 |
| 2.700 | | | .0249 | .0573 | .0648 | .0666 | .0671 |
| 2.800 | | | .0160 | .0502 | .0581 | .0601 | .0606 |
| 2.900 | | | .0077 | .0437 | .0521 | .0543 | .0548 |
| 3.000 | | | | .0377 | .0466 | .0490 | .0496 |
| 3.100 | | | | .0323 | .0417 | .0441 | .0448 |
| 3.200 | | | | .0273 | .0372 | .0398 | .0405 |
| 3.300 | | | | .0227 | .0330 | .0358 | .0366 |
| 3.400 | | | | .0186 | .0293 | .0322 | .0331 |
| 3.500 | | | | .0148 | .0259 | .0290 | .0298 |
| 3.600 | | | | .0113 | .0228 | .0260 | .0269 |
| 3.700 | | | | .0081 | .0200 | .0233 | .0243 |
| 3.800 | | | | .0051 | .0174 | .0209 | .0219 |
| 3.900 | | | | .0025 | .0151 | .0187 | .0198 |
| 4.000 | | | | | .0130 | .0167 | .0178 |
| 4.100 | | | | | .0111 | .0149 | .0160 |
| 4.200 | | | | | .0093 | .0132 | .0144 |
| 4.300 | | | | | .0077 | .0117 | .0130 |
| 4.400 | | | | | .0063 | .0104 | .0117 |
| 4.500 | | | | | .0050 | .0091 | .0105 |
| 4.600 | | | | | .0038 | .0080 | .0094 |
| 4.700 | | | | | .0027 | .0070 | .0084 |
| 4.800 | | | | | .0017 | .0061 | .0075 |
| 4.900 | | | | | .0008 | .0053 | .0067 |
| 5.000 | | | | | | .0045 | .0060 |

**TABLE A-1.**
**Values of $P_0$**
**(continued)**

| | n | | | | | | | | | |
|---|---|---|---|---|---|---|---|---|---|---|
| $\lambda$ | 0 | 1 | 2 | 3 | 4 | 5 | 6 | 7 | 8 | 9 |
| .100 | .905 | .090 | .005 | | | | | | | |
| .200 | .819 | .164 | .016 | .001 | | | | | | |
| .300 | .741 | .222 | .033 | .003 | | | | | | |
| .400 | .670 | .268 | .054 | .007 | | | | | | |
| .500 | .607 | .303 | .076 | .013 | .002 | | | | | |
| .600 | .549 | .329 | .099 | .020 | .003 | | | | | |
| .700 | .497 | .348 | .122 | .028 | .005 | | | | | |
| .800 | .449 | .359 | .144 | .038 | .008 | .001 | | | | |
| .900 | .407 | .366 | .165 | .049 | .011 | .002 | | | | |
| 1.000 | .368 | .368 | .184 | .061 | .015 | .003 | | | | |
| 1.100 | .333 | .366 | .201 | .074 | .020 | .004 | | | | |
| 1.200 | .301 | .361 | .217 | .087 | .026 | .006 | .001 | | | |
| 1.300 | .273 | .354 | .230 | .100 | .032 | .008 | .002 | | | |
| 1.400 | .247 | .345 | .242 | .113 | .039 | .011 | .003 | | | |
| 1.500 | .223 | .335 | .251 | .126 | .047 | .014 | .004 | | | |
| 1.600 | .202 | .323 | .258 | .138 | .055 | .018 | .005 | .001 | | |
| 1.700 | .183 | .311 | .264 | .150 | .064 | .022 | .006 | .001 | | |
| 1.800 | .165 | .298 | .268 | .161 | .072 | .026 | .008 | .002 | | |
| 1.900 | .150 | .284 | .270 | .171 | .081 | .031 | .010 | .003 | | |
| 2.000 | .135 | .271 | .271 | .180 | .090 | .036 | .012 | .003 | | |
| 2.100 | .122 | .257 | .270 | .189 | .099 | .042 | .015 | .004 | .001 | |
| 2.200 | .111 | .244 | .268 | .197 | .108 | .048 | .017 | .005 | .002 | |
| 2.300 | .100 | .231 | .265 | .203 | .117 | .054 | .021 | .007 | .002 | |
| 2.400 | .091 | .218 | .261 | .209 | .125 | .060 | .024 | .008 | .002 | |
| 2.500 | .082 | .205 | .257 | .214 | .134 | .067 | .028 | .010 | .003 | |
| 2.600 | .074 | .193 | .251 | .218 | .141 | .074 | .032 | .012 | .004 | .001 |
| 2.700 | .067 | .181 | .245 | .220 | .149 | .080 | .036 | .014 | .005 | .001 |
| 2.800 | .061 | .170 | .238 | .222 | .156 | .087 | .041 | .016 | .006 | .002 |
| 2.900 | .055 | .160 | .231 | .224 | .162 | .094 | .045 | .019 | .007 | .002 |
| 3.000 | .050 | .149 | .224 | .224 | .168 | .101 | .050 | .022 | .008 | .003 |
| 3.100 | .045 | .140 | .216 | .224 | .173 | .107 | .056 | .025 | .010 | .003 |
| 3.200 | .041 | .130 | .209 | .223 | .178 | .114 | .061 | .028 | .011 | .004 |
| 3.300 | .037 | .122 | .201 | .221 | .182 | .120 | .066 | .031 | .013 | .005 |
| 3.400 | .033 | .113 | .193 | .219 | .186 | .126 | .072 | .035 | .015 | .006 |
| 3.500 | .030 | .106 | .185 | .216 | .189 | .132 | .077 | .039 | .017 | .007 |
| 3.600 | .027 | .098 | .177 | .212 | .191 | .138 | .083 | .042 | .019 | .008 |
| 3.700 | .025 | .091 | .169 | .209 | .193 | .143 | .088 | .047 | .022 | .009 |
| 3.800 | .022 | .085 | .162 | .205 | .194 | .148 | .094 | .051 | .024 | .010 |
| 3.900 | .020 | .079 | .154 | .200 | .195 | .152 | .099 | .055 | .027 | .012 |
| 4.000 | .018 | .073 | .147 | .195 | .195 | .156 | .104 | .060 | .030 | .013 |
| 4.100 | .017 | .068 | .139 | .190 | .195 | .160 | .109 | .064 | .033 | .015 |
| 4.200 | .015 | .063 | .132 | .185 | .194 | .163 | .114 | .069 | .036 | .017 |
| 4.300 | .014 | .058 | .125 | .180 | .193 | .166 | .119 | .073 | .039 | .019 |
| 4.400 | .012 | .054 | .119 | .174 | .192 | .169 | .124 | .078 | .043 | .021 |
| 4.500 | .011 | .050 | .112 | .169 | .190 | .171 | .128 | .082 | .046 | .023 |
| 4.600 | .010 | .046 | .106 | .163 | .188 | .173 | .132 | .087 | .050 | .026 |
| 4.700 | .009 | .043 | .100 | .157 | .185 | .174 | .136 | .091 | .054 | .028 |
| 4.800 | .008 | .040 | .095 | .152 | .182 | .175 | .140 | .096 | .058 | .031 |
| 4.900 | .007 | .036 | .089 | .146 | .179 | .175 | .143 | .100 | .061 | .033 |
| 5.000 | .007 | .034 | .084 | .140 | .175 | .175 | .146 | .104 | .065 | .036 |

**TABLE A-2.**
**Values of**
$$P(n) = \frac{(\lambda)^n e^{-\lambda}}{n!}$$

| λ | n 0 | 1 | 2 | 3 | 4 | 5 | 6 | 7 | 8 | 9 |
|---|---|---|---|---|---|---|---|---|---|---|
| 5.100 | .006 | .031 | .079 | .135 | .172 | .175 | .149 | .109 | .069 | .039 |
| 5.200 | .006 | .029 | .075 | .129 | .168 | .175 | .151 | .113 | .073 | .042 |
| 5.300 | .005 | .026 | .070 | .124 | .164 | .174 | .154 | .116 | .077 | .045 |
| 5.400 | .005 | .024 | .066 | .119 | .160 | .173 | .156 | .120 | .081 | .049 |
| 5.500 | .004 | .022 | .062 | .113 | .156 | .171 | .157 | .123 | .085 | .052 |
| 5.600 | .004 | .021 | .058 | .108 | .152 | .170 | .158 | .127 | .089 | .055 |
| 5.700 | .003 | .019 | .054 | .103 | .147 | .168 | .159 | .130 | .092 | .059 |
| 5.800 | .003 | .018 | .051 | .098 | .143 | .166 | .160 | .133 | .096 | .062 |
| 5.900 | .003 | .016 | .048 | .094 | .138 | .163 | .160 | .135 | .100 | .065 |
| 6.000 | .002 | .015 | .045 | .089 | .134 | .161 | .161 | .138 | .103 | .069 |
| 6.100 | .002 | .014 | .042 | .085 | .129 | .158 | .160 | .140 | .107 | .072 |
| 6.200 | .002 | .013 | .039 | .081 | .125 | .155 | .160 | .142 | .110 | .076 |
| 6.300 | .002 | .012 | .036 | .077 | .121 | .152 | .159 | .144 | .113 | .079 |
| 6.400 | .002 | .011 | .034 | .073 | .116 | .149 | .159 | .145 | .116 | .082 |
| 6.500 | .002 | .010 | .032 | .069 | .112 | .145 | .157 | .146 | .119 | .086 |
| 6.600 | .001 | .009 | .030 | .065 | .108 | .142 | .156 | .147 | .121 | .089 |
| 6.700 | .001 | .008 | .028 | .062 | .103 | .138 | .155 | .148 | .124 | .092 |
| 6.800 | .001 | .008 | .026 | .058 | .099 | .135 | .153 | .149 | .126 | .095 |
| 6.900 | .001 | .007 | .024 | .055 | .095 | .131 | .151 | .149 | .128 | .098 |
| 7.000 | .001 | .006 | .022 | .052 | .091 | .128 | .149 | .149 | .130 | .101 |
| 7.100 | .001 | .006 | .021 | .049 | .087 | .124 | .147 | .149 | .132 | .104 |
| 7.200 | .001 | .005 | .019 | .046 | .084 | .120 | .144 | .149 | .134 | .107 |
| 7.300 | .001 | .005 | .018 | .044 | .080 | .117 | .142 | .148 | .135 | .110 |
| 7.400 | .001 | .005 | .017 | .041 | .076 | .113 | .139 | .147 | .136 | .112 |
| 7.500 | .001 | .004 | .016 | .039 | .073 | .109 | .137 | .146 | .137 | .114 |
| 7.600 | .001 | .004 | .014 | .037 | .070 | .106 | .134 | .145 | .138 | .117 |
| 7.700 | .000 | .003 | .013 | .034 | .066 | .102 | .131 | .144 | .139 | .119 |
| 7.800 | .000 | .003 | .012 | .032 | .063 | .099 | .128 | .143 | .139 | .121 |
| 7.900 | .000 | .003 | .012 | .030 | .060 | .095 | .125 | .141 | .139 | .122 |
| 8.000 | .000 | .003 | .011 | .029 | .057 | .092 | .122 | .140 | .140 | .124 |
| 8.100 | .000 | .002 | .010 | .027 | .054 | .088 | .119 | .138 | .139 | .126 |
| 8.200 | .000 | .002 | .009 | .025 | .052 | .085 | .116 | .136 | .139 | .127 |
| 8.300 | .000 | .002 | .009 | .024 | .049 | .082 | .113 | .134 | .139 | .128 |
| 8.400 | .000 | .002 | .008 | .022 | .047 | .078 | .110 | .132 | .138 | .129 |
| 8.500 | .000 | .002 | .007 | .021 | .044 | .075 | .107 | .129 | .138 | .130 |
| 8.600 | .000 | .002 | .007 | .020 | .042 | .072 | .103 | .127 | .137 | .131 |
| 8.700 | .000 | .001 | .006 | .018 | .040 | .069 | .100 | .125 | .136 | .131 |
| 8.800 | .000 | .001 | .006 | .017 | .038 | .066 | .097 | .122 | .134 | .131 |
| 8.900 | .000 | .001 | .005 | .016 | .036 | .063 | .094 | .120 | .133 | .132 |
| 9.000 | .000 | .001 | .005 | .015 | .034 | .061 | .091 | .117 | .132 | .132 |
| 9.100 | .000 | .001 | .005 | .014 | .032 | .058 | .088 | .114 | .130 | .132 |
| 9.200 | .000 | .001 | .004 | .013 | .030 | .055 | .085 | .112 | .129 | .131 |
| 9.300 | .000 | .001 | .004 | .012 | .028 | .053 | .082 | .109 | .127 | .131 |
| 9.400 | .000 | .001 | .004 | .011 | .027 | .051 | .079 | .106 | .125 | .131 |
| 9.500 | .000 | .001 | .003 | .011 | .025 | .048 | .076 | .104 | .123 | .130 |
| 9.600 | .000 | .001 | .003 | .010 | .024 | .046 | .074 | .101 | .121 | .129 |
| 9.700 | .000 | .001 | .003 | .009 | .023 | .044 | .071 | .098 | .119 | .128 |
| 9.800 | .000 | .001 | .003 | .009 | .021 | .042 | .068 | .096 | .117 | .127 |
| 9.900 | .000 | .000 | .002 | .008 | .020 | .040 | .066 | .093 | .115 | .126 |
| 10.000 | .000 | .000 | .002 | .008 | .019 | .038 | .063 | .090 | .113 | .125 |

**TABLE A-2.**
**Values of**
$$P(n) = \frac{(\lambda)^n e^{-\lambda}}{n!}$$
**(continued)**

| $x$ | $e^x$ | $e^{-x}$ |
|---|---|---|
| .100 | 1.105 | .905 |
| .200 | 1.221 | .819 |
| .300 | 1.350 | .741 |
| .400 | 1.492 | .670 |
| .500 | 1.649 | .607 |
| .600 | 1.822 | .549 |
| .700 | 2.014 | .497 |
| .800 | 2.226 | .449 |
| .900 | 2.460 | .407 |
| 1.000 | 2.718 | .368 |
| 1.100 | 3.004 | .333 |
| 1.200 | 3.320 | .301 |
| 1.300 | 3.669 | .273 |
| 1.400 | 4.055 | .247 |
| 1.500 | 4.482 | .223 |
| 1.600 | 4.953 | .202 |
| 1.700 | 5.474 | .183 |
| 1.800 | 6.050 | .165 |
| 1.900 | 6.686 | .150 |
| 2.000 | 7.389 | .135 |
| 2.100 | 8.166 | .122 |
| 2.200 | 9.025 | .111 |
| 2.300 | 9.974 | .100 |
| 2.400 | 11.023 | .091 |
| 2.500 | 12.182 | .082 |
| 2.600 | 13.464 | .074 |
| 2.700 | 14.880 | .067 |
| 2.800 | 16.445 | .061 |
| 2.900 | 18.174 | .055 |
| 3.000 | 20.086 | .050 |
| 3.100 | 22.198 | .045 |
| 3.200 | 24.533 | .041 |
| 3.300 | 27.113 | .037 |
| 3.400 | 29.964 | .033 |
| 3.500 | 33.115 | .030 |
| 3.600 | 36.598 | .027 |
| 3.700 | 40.447 | .025 |
| 3.800 | 44.701 | .022 |
| 3.900 | 49.402 | .020 |
| 4.000 | 54.598 | .018 |
| 4.100 | 60.340 | .017 |
| 4.200 | 66.686 | .015 |
| 4.300 | 73.700 | .014 |
| 4.400 | 81.451 | .012 |
| 4.500 | 90.017 | .011 |
| 4.600 | 99.484 | .010 |
| 4.700 | 109.947 | .009 |
| 4.800 | 121.510 | .008 |
| 4.900 | 134.290 | .007 |
| 5.000 | 148.413 | .007 |

**TABLE A-3.**
**Values of $e^x$ and $e^{-x}$**

| | | | | | | | | | |
|---|---|---|---|---|---|---|---|---|---|
| 4764 | 6279 | 4446 | 5582 | 1634 | 2396 | 7984 | 0892 | 6049 | 7488 |
| 8416 | 8234 | 6427 | 4959 | 7344 | 5582 | 8579 | 1652 | 8767 | 2934 |
| 9434 | 5273 | 5902 | 1824 | 2809 | 7556 | 2486 | 2963 | 2006 | 7914 |
| 3420 | 1820 | 0318 | 7041 | 0746 | 7468 | 0788 | 2913 | 5730 | 1305 |
| 6827 | 6383 | 5901 | 3555 | 3049 | 0858 | 8872 | 3181 | 0495 | 5501 |
| 8521 | 1471 | 3044 | 9717 | 6203 | 4840 | 8645 | 9348 | 3101 | 7983 |
| 1129 | 3208 | 1699 | 5571 | 2923 | 0382 | 0032 | 5459 | 4610 | 5684 |
| 5806 | 8224 | 5783 | 4674 | 6696 | 1011 | 6599 | 7695 | 4470 | 1598 |
| 9285 | 6331 | 8764 | 8461 | 4031 | 8934 | 7259 | 7712 | 8980 | 6963 |
| 6955 | 5482 | 2161 | 1838 | 2875 | 9525 | 9769 | 8136 | 9966 | 6852 |
| 5937 | 3445 | 3694 | 1834 | 3496 | 4466 | 4629 | 9659 | 5169 | 3131 |
| 8044 | 4611 | 6072 | 1084 | 8306 | 6117 | 8550 | 2526 | 3276 | 4537 |
| 2219 | 3193 | 8224 | 6791 | 4229 | 0579 | 8448 | 6988 | 7886 | 3739 |
| 5570 | 6273 | 1455 | 3007 | 9751 | 8758 | 8610 | 1781 | 8456 | 4518 |
| 5496 | 4841 | 1443 | 6085 | 8950 | 5867 | 1830 | 7652 | 3884 | 1657 |
| 5054 | 7303 | 6255 | 7005 | 2068 | 3442 | 8084 | 8559 | 1254 | 2478 |
| 0661 | 8875 | 6251 | 9846 | 7295 | 4338 | 5145 | 2204 | 3691 | 8096 |
| 7321 | 7051 | 1108 | 0625 | 3440 | 6284 | 4179 | 4339 | 3666 | 1786 |
| 1799 | 1989 | 5595 | 5457 | 5435 | 1938 | 4324 | 6299 | 9208 | 3997 |
| 4934 | 4071 | 1456 | 4076 | 3090 | 4586 | 2596 | 3397 | 3189 | 3251 |
| 8262 | 8374 | 4637 | 1581 | 2275 | 7185 | 8938 | 1194 | 1403 | 1840 |
| 9586 | 7055 | 6472 | 0928 | 4832 | 5912 | 2768 | 7070 | 3751 | 1718 |
| 1882 | 0684 | 0933 | 4112 | 7413 | 2027 | 4233 | 9662 | 6926 | 2455 |
| 9670 | 1291 | 4890 | 7457 | 7666 | 3246 | 4877 | 4168 | 1609 | 3896 |
| 2039 | 5973 | 9776 | 0099 | 0272 | 5058 | 7182 | 7786 | 5649 | 8697 |
| 8416 | 4676 | 2229 | 7245 | 0700 | 4369 | 0390 | 6289 | 2870 | 7244 |
| 5670 | 5432 | 2966 | 6749 | 6488 | 8453 | 1751 | 7768 | 4356 | 3516 |
| 1198 | 0414 | 0140 | 5503 | 9564 | 1048 | 8107 | 2043 | 0830 | 5920 |
| 5263 | 5133 | 4011 | 7164 | 2389 | 0693 | 8934 | 2723 | 1078 | 2653 |
| 0385 | 9999 | 7544 | 3593 | 9120 | 1661 | 7054 | 2791 | 1173 | 8148 |
| 5169 | 8408 | 1074 | 4192 | 4800 | 5589 | 8279 | 9855 | 7618 | 5088 |
| 4031 | 8123 | 0927 | 9697 | 5585 | 7698 | 1450 | 6706 | 3222 | 3469 |
| 3457 | 1531 | 7016 | 2007 | 9172 | 9358 | 0468 | 4212 | 2238 | 7065 |
| 3859 | 3643 | 4141 | 4584 | 4035 | 2295 | 9716 | 7871 | 1234 | 1723 |
| 7228 | 1267 | 4020 | 3840 | 9324 | 4281 | 9163 | 4899 | 2737 | 2626 |
| 1165 | 5407 | 3768 | 0190 | 0135 | 5534 | 7293 | 7472 | 0754 | 1557 |
| 5089 | 9780 | 2195 | 6766 | 8383 | 4123 | 3447 | 7244 | 1091 | 3490 |
| 5544 | 0016 | 3828 | 6315 | 6349 | 2892 | 6764 | 4509 | 0942 | 1833 |
| 0840 | 4942 | 1475 | 3908 | 4765 | 8715 | 0892 | 5274 | 9646 | 7686 |
| 1186 | 4425 | 3216 | 5570 | 5255 | 8678 | 8967 | 7269 | 4330 | 4904 |
| 7678 | 1351 | 6002 | 2999 | 4725 | 2305 | 6893 | 2079 | 0195 | 5658 |
| 1892 | 2323 | 3188 | 7864 | 3646 | 7732 | 7501 | 9132 | 3081 | 2445 |
| 3382 | 4579 | 1513 | 7065 | 5765 | 7341 | 3386 | 9137 | 4236 | 9718 |
| 8149 | 5468 | 6474 | 0654 | 0441 | 9946 | 2749 | 7297 | 5046 | 0704 |
| 3519 | 2481 | 8907 | 7830 | 7936 | 0624 | 6938 | 9750 | 7356 | 7141 |
| 9641 | 5049 | 7463 | 7626 | 5535 | 1056 | 2071 | 0890 | 7953 | 1190 |
| 8436 | 2928 | 9956 | 4785 | 1056 | 3446 | 6692 | 4251 | 7201 | 3454 |
| 8762 | 6185 | 6363 | 4627 | 1333 | 7703 | 4694 | 6380 | 1062 | 4247 |
| 8749 | 2282 | 5897 | 9376 | 5726 | 3922 | 9574 | 1451 | 4290 | 8413 |
| 9527 | 4711 | 8300 | 1127 | 0903 | 6653 | 6528 | 2003 | 7742 | 7629 |

**TABLE A-4.**
**Random Numbers**

| Degrees of Freedom | Probabilities | | | | | |
|---|---|---|---|---|---|---|
| | 0.99 | 0.98 | 0.95 | 0.90 | 0.80 | 0.70 |
| 1 | 0.000157 | 0.000628 | 0.00393 | 0.0158 | 0.0642 | 0.148 |
| 2 | 0.0201 | 0.0404 | 0.103 | 0.211 | 0.446 | 0.713 |
| 3 | 0.115 | 0.185 | 0.352 | 0.584 | 1.005 | 1.424 |
| 4 | 0.297 | 0.429 | 0.711 | 1.064 | 1.649 | 2.195 |
| 5 | 0.554 | 0.752 | 1.145 | 1.610 | 2.343 | 3.000 |
| 6 | 0.872 | 1.134 | 1.635 | 2.204 | 3.070 | 3.828 |
| 7 | 1.239 | 1.564 | 2.167 | 2.833 | 3.822 | 4.671 |
| 8 | 1.646 | 2.032 | 2.733 | 3.490 | 4.594 | 5.527 |
| 9 | 2.088 | 2.532 | 3.325 | 4.168 | 5.380 | 6.393 |
| 10 | 2.558 | 3.059 | 3.940 | 4.865 | 6.179 | 7.267 |
| 11 | 3.053 | 3.609 | 4.575 | 5.578 | 6.989 | 8.148 |
| 12 | 3.571 | 4.178 | 5.226 | 6.304 | 7.807 | 9.034 |
| 13 | 4.107 | 4.765 | 5.892 | 7.042 | 8.634 | 9.926 |
| 14 | 4.660 | 5.368 | 6.571 | 7.790 | 9.467 | 10.821 |
| 15 | 5.229 | 5.985 | 7.261 | 8.547 | 10.307 | 11.721 |
| 16 | 5.812 | 6.614 | 7.962 | 9.312 | 11.152 | 12.624 |
| 17 | 6.408 | 7.255 | 8.672 | 10.085 | 12.002 | 13.531 |
| 18 | 7.015 | 7.906 | 9.390 | 10.865 | 12.857 | 14.440 |
| 19 | 7.633 | 8.567 | 10.117 | 11.651 | 13.716 | 15.352 |
| 20 | 8.260 | 9.237 | 10.851 | 12.443 | 14.578 | 16.266 |
| 21 | 8.897 | 9.915 | 11.591 | 13.240 | 15.445 | 17.182 |
| 22 | 9.542 | 10.600 | 12.338 | 14.041 | 16.314 | 18.101 |
| 23 | 10.196 | 11.293 | 13.091 | 14.848 | 17.187 | 19.021 |
| 24 | 10.856 | 11.992 | 13.848 | 15.659 | 18.062 | 19.943 |
| 25 | 11.524 | 12.697 | 14.611 | 16.473 | 18.940 | 20.867 |
| 26 | 12.198 | 13.409 | 15.379 | 17.292 | 19.820 | 21.792 |
| 27 | 12.879 | 14.125 | 16.151 | 18.114 | 20.703 | 22.719 |
| 28 | 13.565 | 14.847 | 16.928 | 18.939 | 21.588 | 23.647 |
| 29 | 14.256 | 15.574 | 17.708 | 19.768 | 22.475 | 24.577 |
| 30 | 14.953 | 16.306 | 18.493 | 20.599 | 23.364 | 25.508 |

**TABLE A-5.
Values of Chi
Squared ($\chi^2$)**

*Probabilities*

| 0.50 | 0.30 | 0.20 | 0.10 | 0.05 | 0.02 | 0.01 |
|------|------|------|------|------|------|------|
| 0.455 | 1.074 | 1.642 | 2.706 | 3.841 | 5.412 | 6.635 |
| 1.386 | 2.408 | 3.219 | 4.605 | 5.991 | 7.824 | 9.210 |
| 2.366 | 3.665 | 4.642 | 6.251 | 7.815 | 9.837 | 11.345 |
| 3.357 | 4.878 | 5.989 | 7.779 | 9.488 | 11.668 | 13.277 |
| 4.351 | 6.064 | 7.289 | 9.236 | 11.070 | 13.388 | 15.086 |
| 5.348 | 7.231 | 8.558 | 10.645 | 12.592 | 15.033 | 16.812 |
| 6.346 | 8.383 | 9.803 | 12.017 | 14.067 | 16.622 | 18.475 |
| 7.344 | 9.524 | 11.030 | 13.362 | 15.507 | 18.168 | 20.090 |
| 8.343 | 10.656 | 12.242 | 14.684 | 16.919 | 19.679 | 21.666 |
| 9.342 | 11.781 | 13.442 | 15.987 | 18.307 | 21.161 | 23.209 |
| 10.341 | 12.899 | 14.631 | 17.275 | 19.675 | 22.618 | 24.725 |
| 11.340 | 14.011 | 15.812 | 18.549 | 21.026 | 24.054 | 26.217 |
| 12.340 | 15.119 | 16.985 | 19.812 | 22.362 | 25.472 | 27.688 |
| 13.339 | 16.222 | 18.151 | 21.064 | 23.685 | 26.873 | 29.141 |
| 14.339 | 17.322 | 19.311 | 22.307 | 24.996 | 28.259 | 30.578 |
| 15.338 | 18.418 | 20.645 | 23.542 | 26.296 | 29.633 | 32.000 |
| 16.338 | 19.511 | 21.615 | 24.769 | 27.587 | 30.995 | 33.409 |
| 17.338 | 20.601 | 22.760 | 25.989 | 28.869 | 32.346 | 34.805 |
| 18.338 | 21.689 | 23.900 | 27.204 | 30.144 | 33.687 | 36.191 |
| 19.337 | 22.775 | 25.038 | 28.412 | 31.410 | 35.020 | 37.566 |
| 20.337 | 23.858 | 26.171 | 29.615 | 32.671 | 36.343 | 38.932 |
| 21.337 | 24.939 | 27.301 | 30.813 | 33.924 | 27.659 | 40.289 |
| 22.337 | 26.018 | 28.429 | 32.007 | 35.172 | 38.968 | 41.638 |
| 23.337 | 27.096 | 29.553 | 33.196 | 36.415 | 40.270 | 42.980 |
| 24.337 | 28.172 | 30.675 | 34.382 | 37.652 | 41.566 | 44.314 |
| 25.336 | 29.246 | 31.795 | 35.563 | 38.885 | 42.856 | 45.642 |
| 26.336 | 30.319 | 32.912 | 36.741 | 40.113 | 44.140 | 46.963 |
| 27.336 | 31.391 | 34.027 | 37.916 | 41.337 | 45.419 | 48.278 |
| 28.336 | 32.461 | 35.139 | 39.087 | 42.557 | 46.693 | 49.588 |
| 29.336 | 33.530 | 36.250 | 40.256 | 43.773 | 47.962 | 50.892 |

**TABLE A-5.**
**Values of Chi**
**Squared ($\chi^2$)**
**(continued)**

| z | .00 | .01 | .02 | .03 | .04 | .05 | .06 | .07 | .08 | .09 |
|-----|-------|-------|-------|-------|-------|-------|-------|-------|-------|-------|
| 0.0 | .0000 | .0040 | .0080 | .0120 | .0160 | .0199 | .0239 | .0279 | .0319 | .0359 |
| 0.1 | .0398 | .0438 | .0478 | .0517 | .0557 | .0596 | .0636 | .0675 | .0714 | .0753 |
| 0.2 | .0793 | .0832 | .0871 | .0910 | .0948 | .0987 | .1026 | .1064 | .1103 | .1141 |
| 0.3 | .1179 | .1217 | .1255 | .1293 | .1331 | .1368 | .1406 | .1443 | .1480 | .1517 |
| 0.4 | .1554 | .1591 | .1628 | .1664 | .1700 | .1736 | .1772 | .1808 | .1844 | .1879 |
| 0.5 | .1915 | .1950 | .1985 | .2019 | .2054 | .2088 | .2123 | .2157 | .2190 | .2224 |
| 0.6 | .2257 | .2291 | .2324 | .2357 | .2389 | .2422 | .2454 | .2486 | .2517 | .2549 |
| 0.7 | .2580 | .2611 | .2642 | .2673 | .2704 | .2734 | .2764 | .2794 | .2823 | .2852 |
| 0.8 | .2881 | .2910 | .2939 | .2967 | .2995 | .3023 | .3051 | .3078 | .3106 | .3133 |
| 0.9 | .3159 | .3186 | .3212 | .3238 | .3264 | .3289 | .3315 | .3340 | .3365 | .3389 |
| 1.0 | .3413 | .3438 | .3461 | .3485 | .3508 | .3531 | .3554 | .3577 | .3599 | .3621 |
| 1.1 | .3643 | .3665 | .3686 | .3708 | .3729 | .3749 | .3770 | .3790 | .3810 | .3830 |
| 1.2 | .3849 | .3869 | .3888 | .3907 | .3925 | .3944 | .3962 | .3980 | .3997 | .4015 |
| 1.3 | .4032 | .4049 | .4066 | .4082 | .4099 | .4115 | .4131 | .4147 | .4162 | .4177 |
| 1.4 | .4192 | .4207 | .4222 | .4236 | .4251 | .4265 | .4279 | .4292 | .4306 | .4319 |
| 1.5 | .4332 | .4345 | .4357 | .4370 | .4382 | .4394 | .4406 | .4418 | .4429 | .4441 |
| 1.6 | .4452 | .4463 | .4474 | .4484 | .4495 | .4505 | .4515 | .4525 | .4535 | .4545 |
| 1.7 | .4554 | .4564 | .4573 | .4582 | .4591 | .4599 | .4608 | .4616 | .4625 | .4633 |
| 1.8 | .4641 | .4649 | .4656 | .4664 | .4671 | .4678 | .4686 | .4693 | .4699 | .4706 |
| 1.9 | .4713 | .4719 | .4726 | .4732 | .4738 | .4744 | .4750 | .4756 | .4761 | .4767 |
| 2.0 | .4772 | .4778 | .4783 | .4788 | .4793 | .4798 | .4803 | .4808 | .4812 | .4817 |
| 2.1 | .4821 | .4826 | .4830 | .4834 | .4838 | .4842 | .4846 | .4850 | .4854 | .4857 |
| 2.2 | .4861 | .4864 | .4868 | .4871 | .4875 | .4878 | .4881 | .4884 | .4887 | .4890 |
| 2.3 | .4893 | .4896 | .4898 | .4901 | .4904 | .4906 | .4909 | .4911 | .4913 | .4916 |
| 2.4 | .4918 | .4920 | .4922 | .4925 | .4927 | .4929 | .4931 | .4932 | .4934 | .4936 |
| 2.5 | .4938 | .4940 | .4941 | .4943 | .4945 | .4946 | .4948 | .4949 | .4951 | .4952 |
| 2.6 | .4953 | .4955 | .4956 | .4957 | .4959 | .4960 | .4961 | .4962 | .4963 | .4964 |
| 2.7 | .4965 | .4966 | .4967 | .4968 | .4969 | .4970 | .4971 | .4972 | .4973 | .4974 |
| 2.8 | .4974 | .4975 | .4976 | .4977 | .4977 | .4978 | .4979 | .4979 | .4980 | .4981 |
| 2.9 | .4981 | .4982 | .4982 | .4983 | .4984 | .4984 | .4985 | .4985 | .4986 | .4986 |
| 3.0 | .4987 | .4987 | .4987 | .4988 | .4988 | .4989 | .4989 | .4989 | .4990 | .4990 |

**TABLE A-6.
Standard Normal
Distribution**

**TABLE A-7. Binomial Distribution**

$$b(x|n, p) = \binom{n}{x} p^x (1 - p)^{n-x} = \frac{n!}{x!(n-x)!} p^x q^{n-x}$$

| n | x | 0.05 | 0.1 | 0.2 | 0.3 | 0.4 | 0.5 | 0.6 | 0.7 | 0.8 | 0.9 | 0.95 |
|---|---|------|-----|-----|-----|-----|-----|-----|-----|-----|-----|------|
| 2 | 0 | 0.902 | 0.810 | 0.640 | 0.490 | 0.360 | 0.250 | 0.160 | 0.090 | 0.040 | 0.010 | 0.002 |
|   | 1 | 0.095 | 0.180 | 0.320 | 0.420 | 0.480 | 0.500 | 0.480 | 0.420 | 0.320 | 0.180 | 0.095 |
|   | 2 | 0.002 | 0.010 | 0.040 | 0.090 | 0.160 | 0.250 | 0.360 | 0.490 | 0.640 | 0.810 | 0.902 |
| 3 | 0 | 0.857 | 0.729 | 0.512 | 0.343 | 0.216 | 0.125 | 0.064 | 0.027 | 0.008 | 0.001 |       |
|   | 1 | 0.135 | 0.243 | 0.384 | 0.441 | 0.432 | 0.375 | 0.288 | 0.189 | 0.096 | 0.027 | 0.007 |
|   | 2 | 0.007 | 0.027 | 0.096 | 0.189 | 0.288 | 0.375 | 0.432 | 0.441 | 0.384 | 0.243 | 0.135 |
|   | 3 |       | 0.001 | 0.008 | 0.027 | 0.064 | 0.125 | 0.216 | 0.343 | 0.512 | 0.729 | 0.857 |
| 4 | 0 | 0.815 | 0.656 | 0.410 | 0.240 | 0.130 | 0.062 | 0.026 | 0.008 | 0.002 |       |       |
|   | 1 | 0.171 | 0.292 | 0.410 | 0.412 | 0.346 | 0.250 | 0.154 | 0.076 | 0.026 | 0.004 |       |
|   | 2 | 0.014 | 0.049 | 0.154 | 0.265 | 0.346 | 0.375 | 0.346 | 0.265 | 0.154 | 0.049 | 0.014 |
|   | 3 |       | 0.004 | 0.026 | 0.076 | 0.154 | 0.250 | 0.346 | 0.412 | 0.410 | 0.292 | 0.171 |
|   | 4 |       |       | 0.002 | 0.008 | 0.026 | 0.062 | 0.130 | 0.240 | 0.410 | 0.656 | 0.815 |
| 5 | 0 | 0.774 | 0.590 | 0.328 | 0.168 | 0.078 | 0.031 | 0.010 | 0.002 |       |       |       |
|   | 1 | 0.204 | 0.328 | 0.410 | 0.360 | 0.259 | 0.156 | 0.077 | 0.028 | 0.006 |       |       |
|   | 2 | 0.021 | 0.073 | 0.205 | 0.309 | 0.346 | 0.312 | 0.230 | 0.132 | 0.051 | 0.008 | 0.001 |
|   | 3 | 0.001 | 0.008 | 0.051 | 0.132 | 0.230 | 0.312 | 0.346 | 0.309 | 0.205 | 0.073 | 0.021 |
|   | 4 |       |       | 0.006 | 0.028 | 0.077 | 0.156 | 0.259 | 0.360 | 0.410 | 0.328 | 0.204 |
|   | 5 |       |       |       | 0.002 | 0.010 | 0.031 | 0.078 | 0.168 | 0.328 | 0.590 | 0.774 |
| 6 | 0 | 0.735 | 0.531 | 0.262 | 0.118 | 0.047 | 0.016 | 0.004 | 0.001 |       |       |       |
|   | 1 | 0.232 | 0.354 | 0.393 | 0.303 | 0.187 | 0.094 | 0.037 | 0.010 | 0.002 |       |       |
|   | 2 | 0.031 | 0.098 | 0.246 | 0.324 | 0.311 | 0.234 | 0.138 | 0.060 | 0.015 | 0.001 |       |
|   | 3 | 0.002 | 0.015 | 0.082 | 0.185 | 0.276 | 0.312 | 0.276 | 0.185 | 0.082 | 0.015 | 0.002 |
|   | 4 |       | 0.001 | 0.015 | 0.060 | 0.138 | 0.234 | 0.311 | 0.324 | 0.246 | 0.098 | 0.031 |
|   | 5 |       |       | 0.002 | 0.010 | 0.037 | 0.094 | 0.187 | 0.303 | 0.393 | 0.354 | 0.232 |
|   | 6 |       |       |       | 0.001 | 0.004 | 0.016 | 0.047 | 0.118 | 0.262 | 0.531 | 0.735 |
| 7 | 0 | 0.698 | 0.478 | 0.210 | 0.082 | 0.028 | 0.008 | 0.002 |       |       |       |       |
|   | 1 | 0.257 | 0.372 | 0.367 | 0.247 | 0.131 | 0.055 | 0.017 | 0.004 |       |       |       |
|   | 2 | 0.041 | 0.124 | 0.275 | 0.318 | 0.261 | 0.164 | 0.077 | 0.025 | 0.004 |       |       |
|   | 3 | 0.004 | 0.023 | 0.115 | 0.227 | 0.290 | 0.273 | 0.194 | 0.097 | 0.029 | 0.003 |       |
|   | 4 |       | 0.003 | 0.029 | 0.097 | 0.194 | 0.273 | 0.290 | 0.227 | 0.115 | 0.023 | 0.004 |
|   | 5 |       |       | 0.004 | 0.025 | 0.077 | 0.164 | 0.261 | 0.318 | 0.275 | 0.124 | 0.041 |
|   | 6 |       |       |       | 0.004 | 0.017 | 0.055 | 0.131 | 0.247 | 0.367 | 0.372 | 0.257 |
|   | 7 |       |       |       |       | 0.002 | 0.008 | 0.028 | 0.082 | 0.210 | 0.478 | 0.698 |

**TABLE A-7. Binomial Distribution (continued)**

$$b(x|n, p) = \binom{n}{x} p^x (1 - p)^{n-x} = \frac{n!}{x!\,(n-x)!} p^x q^{n-x}$$

| | | | | | | | $p$ | | | | | |
|---|---|---|---|---|---|---|---|---|---|---|---|---|
| $n$ | $z$ | 0.05 | 0.1 | 0.2 | 0.3 | 0.4 | 0.5 | 0.6 | 0.7 | 0.8 | 0.9 | 0.95 |
| 8 | 0 | 0.663 | 0.430 | 0.168 | 0.058 | 0.017 | 0.004 | 0.001 | | | | |
| | 1 | 0.279 | 0.383 | 0.336 | 0.198 | 0.090 | 0.031 | 0.008 | 0.001 | | | |
| | 2 | 0.051 | 0.149 | 0.294 | 0.296 | 0.209 | 0.109 | 0.041 | 0.010 | 0.001 | | |
| | 3 | 0.005 | 0.033 | 0.147 | 0.254 | 0.279 | 0.219 | 0.124 | 0.047 | 0.009 | | |
| | 4 | | 0.005 | 0.046 | 0.136 | 0.232 | 0.273 | 0.232 | 0.136 | 0.046 | 0.005 | |
| | 5 | | | 0.009 | 0.047 | 0.124 | 0.219 | 0.279 | 0.254 | 0.147 | 0.033 | 0.005 |
| | 6 | | | 0.001 | 0.010 | 0.041 | 0.109 | 0.209 | 0.296 | 0.294 | 0.149 | 0.051 |
| | 7 | | | | 0.001 | 0.008 | 0.031 | 0.090 | 0.198 | 0.336 | 0.383 | 0.279 |
| | 8 | | | | | 0.001 | 0.004 | 0.017 | 0.058 | 0.168 | 0.430 | 0.663 |
| 9 | 0 | 0.630 | 0.387 | 0.134 | 0.040 | 0.010 | 0.002 | | | | | |
| | 1 | 0.299 | 0.387 | 0.302 | 0.156 | 0.060 | 0.018 | 0.004 | | | | |
| | 2 | 0.063 | 0.172 | 0.302 | 0.267 | 0.161 | 0.070 | 0.021 | 0.004 | | | |
| | 3 | 0.008 | 0.045 | 0.176 | 0.267 | 0.251 | 0.164 | 0.074 | 0.021 | 0.003 | | |
| | 4 | 0.001 | 0.007 | 0.066 | 0.172 | 0.251 | 0.246 | 0.167 | 0.074 | 0.017 | 0.001 | |
| | 5 | | 0.001 | 0.017 | 0.074 | 0.167 | 0.246 | 0.251 | 0.172 | 0.066 | 0.007 | 0.001 |
| | 6 | | | 0.003 | 0.021 | 0.074 | 0.164 | 0.251 | 0.267 | 0.176 | 0.045 | 0.008 |
| | 7 | | | | 0.004 | 0.021 | 0.070 | 0.161 | 0.267 | 0.302 | 0.172 | 0.063 |
| | 8 | | | | | 0.004 | 0.018 | 0.060 | 0.156 | 0.302 | 0.387 | 0.299 |
| | 9 | | | | | | 0.002 | 0.010 | 0.040 | 0.134 | 0.387 | 0.630 |
| 10 | 0 | 0.599 | 0.349 | 0.107 | 0.028 | 0.006 | 0.001 | | | | | |
| | 1 | 0.315 | 0.387 | 0.268 | 0.121 | 0.040 | 0.010 | 0.002 | | | | |
| | 2 | 0.075 | 0.194 | 0.302 | 0.233 | 0.121 | 0.044 | 0.011 | 0.001 | | | |
| | 3 | 0.010 | 0.057 | 0.201 | 0.267 | 0.215 | 0.117 | 0.042 | 0.009 | 0.001 | | |
| | 4 | 0.001 | 0.011 | 0.088 | 0.200 | 0.251 | 0.205 | 0.111 | 0.037 | 0.006 | | |
| | 5 | | 0.001 | 0.026 | 0.103 | 0.201 | 0.246 | 0.201 | 0.103 | 0.026 | 0.001 | |
| | 6 | | | 0.006 | 0.037 | 0.111 | 0.205 | 0.251 | 0.200 | 0.088 | 0.011 | 0.001 |
| | 7 | | | 0.001 | 0.009 | 0.042 | 0.117 | 0.215 | 0.267 | 0.201 | 0.057 | 0.010 |
| | 8 | | | | 0.001 | 0.011 | 0.044 | 0.121 | 0.233 | 0.302 | 0.194 | 0.075 |
| | 9 | | | | | 0.002 | 0.010 | 0.040 | 0.121 | 0.268 | 0.387 | 0.315 |
| | 10 | | | | | | 0.001 | 0.006 | 0.028 | 0.107 | 0.349 | 0.599 |
| 11 | 0 | 0.569 | 0.314 | 0.086 | 0.020 | 0.004 | | | | | | |
| | 1 | 0.329 | 0.384 | 0.236 | 0.093 | 0.027 | 0.005 | 0.001 | | | | |
| | 2 | 0.087 | 0.213 | 0.295 | 0.200 | 0.089 | 0.027 | 0.005 | 0.001 | | | |
| | 3 | 0.014 | 0.071 | 0.221 | 0.257 | 0.177 | 0.081 | 0.023 | 0.004 | | | |
| | 4 | 0.001 | 0.016 | 0.111 | 0.220 | 0.236 | 0.161 | 0.070 | 0.017 | 0.002 | | |
| | 5 | | 0.002 | 0.039 | 0.132 | 0.221 | 0.226 | 0.147 | 0.057 | 0.010 | | |
| | 6 | | | 0.010 | 0.057 | 0.147 | 0.226 | 0.221 | 0.132 | 0.039 | 0.002 | |
| | 7 | | | 0.002 | 0.017 | 0.070 | 0.161 | 0.236 | 0.220 | 0.111 | 0.016 | 0.001 |
| | 8 | | | | 0.004 | 0.023 | 0.081 | 0.177 | 0.257 | 0.221 | 0.071 | 0.014 |
| | 9 | | | | 0.001 | 0.005 | 0.027 | 0.089 | 0.200 | 0.295 | 0.213 | 0.087 |
| | 10 | | | | | 0.001 | 0.005 | 0.027 | 0.093 | 0.236 | 0.384 | 0.329 |
| | 11 | | | | | | | 0.004 | 0.020 | 0.086 | 0.314 | 0.569 |

**TABLE A-7. Binomial Distribution (continued)**

$$b(x|n, p) = \binom{n}{x} p^x(1 - p)^{n-x} = \frac{n!}{x!\,(n - x)!}\, p^x q^{n-x}$$

| | | | | | | | $p$ | | | | | |
|---|---|---|---|---|---|---|---|---|---|---|---|---|
| $n$ | $z$ | 0.05 | 0.1 | 0.2 | 0.3 | 0.4 | 0.5 | 0.6 | 0.7 | 0.8 | 0.9 | 0.95 |
| 12 | 0 | 0.540 | 0.282 | 0.069 | 0.014 | 0.002 | | | | | | |
| | 1 | 0.341 | 0.377 | 0.206 | 0.071 | 0.017 | 0.003 | | | | | |
| | 2 | 0.099 | 0.230 | 0.283 | 0.168 | 0.064 | 0.016 | 0.002 | | | | |
| | 3 | 0.017 | 0.085 | 0.236 | 0.240 | 0.142 | 0.054 | 0.012 | 0.001 | | | |
| | 4 | 0.002 | 0.021 | 0.133 | 0.231 | 0.213 | 0.121 | 0.042 | 0.008 | 0.001 | | |
| | 5 | | 0.004 | 0.053 | 0.158 | 0.227 | 0.193 | 0.101 | 0.029 | 0.003 | | |
| | 6 | | | 0.016 | 0.079 | 0.177 | 0.226 | 0.177 | 0.079 | 0.016 | | |
| | 7 | | | 0.003 | 0.029 | 0.101 | 0.193 | 0.227 | 0.158 | 0.053 | 0.004 | |
| | 8 | | | 0.001 | 0.008 | 0.042 | 0.121 | 0.213 | 0.231 | 0.133 | 0.021 | 0.002 |
| | 9 | | | | 0.001 | 0.012 | 0.054 | 0.142 | 0.240 | 0.236 | 0.085 | 0.017 |
| | 10 | | | | | 0.002 | 0.016 | 0.064 | 0.168 | 0.283 | 0.230 | 0.099 |
| | 11 | | | | | | 0.003 | 0.017 | 0.071 | 0.206 | 0.377 | 0.341 |
| | 12 | | | | | | | 0.002 | 0.014 | 0.069 | 0.282 | 0.540 |
| 13 | 0 | 0.513 | 0.254 | 0.055 | 0.010 | 0.001 | | | | | | |
| | 1 | 0.351 | 0.367 | 0.179 | 0.054 | 0.011 | 0.002 | | | | | |
| | 2 | 0.111 | 0.245 | 0.268 | 0.139 | 0.045 | 0.010 | 0.001 | | | | |
| | 3 | 0.021 | 0.100 | 0.246 | 0.218 | 0.111 | 0.035 | 0.006 | 0.001 | | | |
| | 4 | 0.003 | 0.028 | 0.154 | 0.234 | 0.184 | 0.087 | 0.024 | 0.003 | | | |
| | 5 | | 0.006 | 0.069 | 0.180 | 0.221 | 0.157 | 0.066 | 0.014 | 0.001 | | |
| | 6 | | 0.001 | 0.023 | 0.103 | 0.197 | 0.209 | 0.131 | 0.044 | 0.006 | | |
| | 7 | | | 0.006 | 0.044 | 0.131 | 0.209 | 0.197 | 0.103 | 0.023 | 0.001 | |
| | 8 | | | 0.001 | 0.014 | 0.066 | 0.157 | 0.221 | 0.180 | 0.069 | 0.006 | |
| | 9 | | | | 0.003 | 0.024 | 0.087 | 0.184 | 0.234 | 0.154 | 0.028 | 0.003 |
| | 10 | | | | 0.001 | 0.006 | 0.035 | 0.111 | 0.218 | 0.246 | 0.100 | 0.021 |
| | 11 | | | | | 0.001 | 0.010 | 0.045 | 0.139 | 0.268 | 0.245 | 0.111 |
| | 12 | | | | | | 0.002 | 0.011 | 0.054 | 0.179 | 0.367 | 0.351 |
| | 13 | | | | | | | 0.001 | 0.010 | 0.055 | 0.254 | 0.513 |
| 14 | 0 | 0.488 | 0.229 | 0.044 | 0.007 | 0.001 | | | | | | |
| | 1 | 0.359 | 0.356 | 0.154 | 0.041 | 0.007 | 0.001 | | | | | |
| | 2 | 0.123 | 0.257 | 0.250 | 0.113 | 0.032 | 0.006 | 0.001 | | | | |
| | 3 | 0.026 | 0.114 | 0.250 | 0.194 | 0.085 | 0.022 | 0.003 | | | | |
| | 4 | 0.004 | 0.035 | 0.172 | 0.229 | 0.155 | 0.061 | 0.014 | 0.001 | | | |
| | 5 | | 0.008 | 0.086 | 0.195 | 0.207 | 0.122 | 0.041 | 0.007 | | | |
| | 6 | | 0.001 | 0.032 | 0.126 | 0.207 | 0.183 | 0.092 | 0.023 | 0.002 | | |
| | 7 | | | 0.009 | 0.062 | 0.157 | 0.209 | 0.157 | 0.062 | 0.009 | | |
| | 8 | | | 0.002 | 0.023 | 0.092 | 0.183 | 0.207 | 0.126 | 0.032 | 0.001 | |
| | 9 | | | | 0.007 | 0.041 | 0.122 | 0.207 | 0.196 | 0.086 | 0.008 | |
| | 10 | | | | 0.001 | 0.014 | 0.061 | 0.155 | 0.229 | 0.172 | 0.035 | 0.004 |
| | 11 | | | | | 0.003 | 0.022 | 0.085 | 0.194 | 0.250 | 0.114 | 0.026 |
| | 12 | | | | | 0.001 | 0.006 | 0.032 | 0.113 | 0.250 | 0.257 | 0.123 |
| | 13 | | | | | | 0.001 | 0.007 | 0.041 | 0.154 | 0.356 | 0.359 |
| | 14 | | | | | | | 0.001 | 0.007 | 0.044 | 0.229 | 0.488 |

**TABLE A-7. Binomial Distribution (continued)**

$$b(x|n, p) = \binom{n}{x} p^x (1 - p)^{n-x} = \frac{n!}{x!\,(n - x)!} p^x q^{n-x}$$

| $n$ | $z$ | 0.05 | 0.1 | 0.2 | 0.3 | 0.4 | 0.5 | 0.6 | 0.7 | 0.8 | 0.9 | 0.95 |
|---|---|---|---|---|---|---|---|---|---|---|---|---|
| 15 | 0 | 0.463 | 0.206 | 0.035 | 0.005 | | | | | | | |
| | 1 | 0.366 | 0.343 | 0.132 | 0.031 | 0.005 | | | | | | |
| | 2 | 0.135 | 0.267 | 0.231 | 0.092 | 0.022 | 0.003 | | | | | |
| | 3 | 0.031 | 0.129 | 0.250 | 0.170 | 0.063 | 0.014 | 0.002 | | | | |
| | 4 | 0.005 | 0.043 | 0.188 | 0.219 | 0.127 | 0.042 | 0.007 | 0.001 | | | |
| | 5 | 0.001 | 0.010 | 0.103 | 0.206 | 0.186 | 0.092 | 0.024 | 0.003 | | | |
| | 6 | | 0.002 | 0.043 | 0.147 | 0.207 | 0.153 | 0.061 | 0.012 | 0.001 | | |
| | 7 | | | 0.014 | 0.081 | 0.177 | 0.196 | 0.118 | 0.035 | 0.003 | | |
| | 8 | | | 0.003 | 0.035 | 0.118 | 0.196 | 0.177 | 0.081 | 0.014 | | |
| | 9 | | | 0.001 | 0.012 | 0.061 | 0.153 | 0.207 | 0.147 | 0.043 | 0.002 | |
| | 10 | | | | 0.003 | 0.024 | 0.092 | 0.186 | 0.206 | 0.103 | 0.010 | 0.001 |
| | 11 | | | | 0.001 | 0.007 | 0.042 | 0.127 | 0.219 | 0.188 | 0.043 | 0.005 |
| | 12 | | | | | 0.002 | 0.014 | 0.063 | 0.170 | 0.250 | 0.129 | 0.031 |
| | 13 | | | | | | 0.003 | 0.022 | 0.092 | 0.231 | 0.267 | 0.135 |
| | 14 | | | | | | | 0.005 | 0.031 | 0.132 | 0.343 | 0.366 |
| | 15 | | | | | | | | 0.005 | 0.035 | 0.206 | 0.463 |

- ### Appendix B
  ### Derivation of economic order quantity models

  #### Derivation of the classic economic order quantity (EOQ) model

From Chapter 14, the general statement of the Classic EOQ model is

MINIMIZE:        Total Inventory Cost = Ordering Cost + Carrying Cost        (B.1.1)

Expressed mathematically, the model is

MINIMIZE:        $C_T = (C_O)(D/Q) + C_C)(Q/2)$        (B.1.2)

where        $C_T$ = total inventory carrying cost per time period
$C_O$ = ordering cost per order placed
$C_C$ = carrying cost per unit per time period
$Q$ = quantity ordered (order size)
$D$ = units demanded per time period

The value of $Q$ that minimizes $C_T$ is also the value of $Q$ where the slope of the total cost curve $(dC_1/dQ)$ is zero. Using differential calculus we thus take the derivative of equation (C.1.2), that is,

$$\frac{dC_T}{dQ} = -\frac{C_O D}{Q^2} + \frac{C_C}{2}$$        (B.1.3)

Setting equation (C.1.3) to zero and solving for $Q$, we have

$$\frac{-C_O D}{Q^2} + \frac{C_C}{2} = 0$$

$$\frac{Q^2}{C_O D} = \frac{2}{C_C}$$

$$Q^2 = \frac{2C_O D}{C_C}$$

therefore,

$$Q^\circ = \sqrt{\frac{2C_O D}{C_C}}$$        (B.1.4)

## *Derivation of the EOQ model with shortages (backorders allowed)*

From Chapter 14, the general statement of the EOQ model with shortages is

MINIMIZE:          Total Inventory Cost = Ordering Cost

          (B.2.1)

                            + Carrying Cost + Shortage Cost

Expressed mathematically, the model is

MINIMIZE:          $C_T = (C_O)(D/Q) + (C_C)(S^2/2Q) + (C_S)(Q - S)^2/2Q)$          (B.2.2)

where          $C_S$ = shortage cost per unit per time period

          $S$ = maximum inventory level

          $Q - S$ = number of units backordered per inventory cycle

    The value of $Q$ that minimizes $C_T$ is related to the value of $S$. However, we can reason that the optimal value for $S$ must fall in the interval $0 \leq S \leq Q$. We thus must take the partial derivatives of equation (C.2.2) with respect to $S$ and $Q$. This yields the following:

$$\frac{\partial C_T}{\partial Q} = \left[\frac{C_S(Q - S)}{Q}\right] - \left[\frac{C_C S^2 + C_S(Q - S)^2 + 2C_O D}{2Q^2}\right]$$          (B.2.3)

$$\frac{\partial C_T}{\partial S} = \left[\frac{C_C S}{Q}\right] - \left[\frac{(C_S)(Q - S)}{Q}\right]$$          (B.2.4)

    To find $Q°$ and $S°$ we set both these equations to zero and simultaneously solve the system of two equations in two unknowns. After a rather lengthy exercise in algebraic manipulation the following equations result:

$$Q° = \left(\sqrt{\frac{2C_O D}{C_C}}\right)\left(\sqrt{\frac{C_C + C_S}{C_S}}\right)$$          (B.2.5)

$$S° = \left(\sqrt{\frac{2C_O D}{C_C}}\right)\left(\sqrt{\frac{C_S}{C_C + C_S}}\right)$$          (B.2.6)

■ **Appendix C**
**Answers to selected problems**
*Chapter 2*

**2-5.**  C = cost
$x$ = bundles of shingles required
C = $800 + $7.80($x$)

**2-9.**  a. $x = \frac{3}{4}$ or $x = 1$

b. $x = -2.96115$ or $x = .86115$

c. This quadratic cannot be factored, and its solution is an imaginary number.

**2-11.**  $$\begin{bmatrix} 2 & 6 & -3 \\ 5 & -4 & -3 \\ 4 & 9 & 8 \end{bmatrix} \begin{bmatrix} x_1 \\ x_2 \\ x_3 \end{bmatrix} = \begin{bmatrix} 21 \\ 55 \\ 37 \end{bmatrix}$$

**2-13.**  $$\begin{bmatrix} 52.59 & 75.12 & 49.21 \\ 65.67 & 71.97 & 48.49 \\ 38.70 & 45.81 & 30.27 \end{bmatrix}$$

**2-15.**  $$\begin{bmatrix} \frac{5}{14} & -\frac{3}{14} \\ -\frac{1}{7} & \frac{2}{7} \end{bmatrix}$$

**2-17.**  The matrix is not square, and therefore has no inverse.

**2-19.**  $x_1 = 20\frac{70}{91}$, $x_2 = -3\frac{7}{91}$, $x_3 = -\frac{15}{13}$,

**2-21.**  rank of the coefficient matrix is 2
rank of the augmented matrix is 3
Because the ranks are different, there is no solution.

**2-23.**  basic solution 1: $x_1 = 0$, $x_2 = 6$,   $x_3 = 9$
basic solution 2: $x_1 = 5$, $x_2 = 0$,   $x_3 = \frac{3}{2}$
basic solution 3: $x_1 = 6$, $x_2 = -\frac{6}{5}$, $x_3 = 0$

Solution 3 is infeasible.

*Chapter 3*

**3-1.**  a. 1893.9393    b. 725

**3-3.**  breakeven = 610 rental nights
Assuming a 30 day month, Bob can only reach 600 rental nights even with full occupancy. He definitely has a problem.
new breakeven = 348.57
profit = $8,000

**3-5.**  116.67

**3-7.**  1637.04

## Chapter 4

**4-1.**

| Month | Sales | $F_t$ |
|-------|-------|-------|
| 1 | 52 | |
| 2 | 54 | |
| 3 | 63 | |
| 4 | 58 | 56.33 |
| 5 | 62 | 58.33 |
| 6 | 61 | 61 |
| 7 | 68 | 60.33 |
| 8 | 65 | 63.67 |
| 9 | 70 | 64.67 |
| 10 | 74 | 67.67 |
| 11 | — | 69.67 |

**4-3.**  **a.**

| Year | Quarter | Sales | $F_t$ (4 month MA) |
|------|---------|-------|--------------------|
| 1983 | 1 | 28 | — |
| | 2 | 32 | — |
| | 3 | 37 | — |
| | 4 | 35 | — |
| 1984 | 1 | 30 | 33 |
| | 2 | 33 | 33.5 |
| | 3 | 40 | 33.75 |
| | 4 | 38 | 34.5 |
| 1985 | 1 | 35 | 35.25 |
| | 2 | 39 | 36.5 |
| | 3 | 44 | 38 |
| | 4 | 41 | 39 |
| | — | — | 39.75 |

**b.** There is a definite seasonal component with a peak around the third quarter and a valley around the first quarter.

Smoothing removed this seasonal component, revealing a long term increasing trend.

**4-7.**  **a and b.**

| Week | Calls | $F_t (\alpha = .2)$ | $F_t (\alpha = .4)$ |
|------|-------|---------------------|---------------------|
| 1 | 44 | 44 | 44 |
| 2 | 40 | 44 | 44 |
| 3 | 36 | 43.2 | 42.4 |
| 4 | 43 | 41.76 | 39.84 |
| 5 | 41 | 42.01 | 41.1 |
| 6 | 47 | 41.81 | 41.06 |
| 7 | 45 | 42.85 | 43.44 |
| 8 | 42 | 43.26 | 44.06 |
| 9 | 44 | 43.01 | 43.24 |
| 10 | 48 | 43.21 | 43.54 |
| — | — | 44.17 | 45.32 |

**4-11.**  three-month (average):   MSE = 26.88 MAD = 4.50
three month (weighted): MSE = 30.48 MAD = 4.97

Unweighted seems to be better.

**4-13.**  *Residuals 1*          *Residuals 2*
$\quad$ −5 $\qquad\qquad\qquad$ 6.5
$\quad\ $ 3 $\qquad\qquad\qquad$ −1
$\quad$ $MSE_1 = 17$ $\qquad\quad$ $MSE_2 = 21.63$
$\quad$ $MAD_1 = \ 4$ $\qquad\quad$ $MAD_2 = \ 3.75$

$MSE_2$ is higher than $MSE_1$, but $MAD_1$ is higher than $MAD_2$
The same thing can happen in a real data set.

**4-15.**  **a.** $F_t = -.517 + 1.035Y_{t-2}$
**b.** $r^2 = .95$  Yes, it explains 95% of the variability.
**c.** $F_{11} = 82.283$

**4-17.**  **a.** $Y = 80.19 + .44\,x$
**b.** 83.49
**c.** $r^2 = .0705$  The relationship is very weak.

# *Chapter 5*

**5-2.**  **b.** (0,0), (0,10), (6,10), (10,6), (10,0)
**c.** $x_1 = 10$, $x_2 = 6$, $Z = 42$
**d.** $x_1 = 6$, $x_2 = 10$, $Z = 42$

**5-4.**  **a.** "to the left"
**b.** "directly on"
**c.** "to the left"
**d.** "above"
**e.** "to the left"

**5-6.**  $x_1 = 16$, $x_2 = 32$, $Z = 1,440$

**5-8.**  Vertices: (0,0), (0,100), (60,40), (80,0)

**5-12.**  Solutions: all points on line $6x_1 + 4x_2 = 48$ from (3.33,7) to (8,0) $z = 24$

**5-14.**  **b.** $x_1 = 300$, $x_2 = 300$, $Z = 6600$
**c.** A redundant constraint: $1x_1 + 1x_2 \le 600$

**5-16.**  **a.** B = (0,2); C = (6/5,16/5); D = (6,0) E = (−2,0)
**b.** Feasible vertices: A, B, C, D; Infeasible vertex: E
**c.** A: 0; B: −4; C: −2/5; D: 30
**d.** D

**5-18.**  **b.** Solutions: all points on the line $4x_1 + 2x_2 = 16$ from (0,8) to (2,4). $Z = 40$

**5-20.**  **b.** (2,4), (4,0)
**c.** no finite optimal solution; unbounded problem

## Chapter 6

**6-4.**   produce 0 diskettes
produce 0 cassettes
produce 20 cleaning kits
profit = $70

**6-6.**   produce 1.11 units of racket A
produce 0 units of racket B
produce 15.56 units of racket C
profit = $140

**6-8.**   use 1000 pounds of peanuts for the super mix
use 2000 pounds of raisins for the super mix
use 3000 pounds of carobs for the super mix
(all other values are 0)
total profit = $12,400

**6-10.**   load 40 tons of cargo on lower deck
load 13.33 tons of cargo on middle deck
load 16 tons of cargo on upper deck
profit = $645.33

**6-12.**   allocate 28.57 acres to soybeans
allocate 65 acres to wheat
allocate 36.43 acres to corn
profit = $47,774.35 − $14,500 = $33,274.35

**6-16.**   produce 150,000 pairs of shoes in month 1 to sell in month 1
produce 110,000 pairs of shoes in month 1 to sell in month 2
produce 180,000 pairs of shoes in month 1 to sell in month 3
produce 100,000 pairs of shoes in month 1 to sell in month 4
produce 200,000 pairs of shoes in month 5 to sell in month 5
produce 180,000 pairs of shoes in month 5 to sell in month 6
produce 110,000 pairs of shoes in month 5 to sell in month 7
(all other values are 0)
profit = $37,760,000
There are other solutions with the same objective value.

**6-20.**   assign operator number 1 to job number 2
assign operator number 2 to job number 3
assign operator number 3 to job number 1
assign operator number 4 to job number 4
assign operator number 5 to job number 5
maximum productivity rating: 88

**6-22.**   3 employees start at 12:00 midnight
6 employees start at 4:00 A.M.
4 employees start at 8:00 A.M.
2 employees start at 12:00 noon
8 employees start at 4:00 P.M.
0 employees start at 8:00 P.M.
total employees = 23

**6-24.**    1800 80″-width rolls
                  0 70″-width rolls
              600 60″-width rolls
              450 50″-width rolls
              500 70″- and 50″-width rolls
                  0 60″- and 50″-width rolls
             total rolls: 3350

# Chapter 7

**7-2.**    **b.** incoming variable is $x_1$

**c.** outgoing variable is $s_2$

**7-4.**    initial tableau: $s_1 = 24$, $s_2 = 20$
             second tableau: $x_1 = 10/3$, $s_1 = 4$
             third tableau: $x_1 = 2$, $x_2 = 8/3$
             fourth tableau: $x_1 = 6$, $s_2 = 8$, $Z = 60$

**7-6.**    $x_1 = 3$, $x_2 = 2$, $Z = 12$

**7-8.**    $x_1 = 3$, $x_2 = 1.5$, $Z = 4.5$

**7-10.**   **b.** outgoing variable is $s_3$

**7-12.**   produce 0 AM radios
             produce 16 AM-FM radios
             profit = $192

**7-13.**   **a.** $x_1 = 0$, $x_2 = 8.5$, $x_3 = 13$, $Z = 232$

**b.** alternate optimum: $x_1 = 13$, $x_2 = 5.25$, $x_3 = 6.5$

**c.** $(8.5 - .25x_1)\, 12 + (13 - .5x_1)\, 10 + 8x_1 = 232$ where $Q \leq x_1 \leq 13$

**7-16.**   **a.** 50

**b.** $1.2641 \times 10^{14}$

**c.** no

**d.** moves in such a way that each new vertex is an improvement over the previous vertex

# Chapter 8

**8-1.**    **a.** $x_1 = 4$, $x_2 = 0$, $Z = 8$

**b.** $x_1 = 4$, $x_2 = 0$, $Z = 40$

**c.** $x_1 = 4$, $x_2 = 0$, $Z = 8$

**8-3.**    **a.** $-\infty \leq c_1 \leq 3$

**b.** $0 \leq b_2 \leq \infty$

**c.** no change

**d.** $-\infty \leq c_2 \leq 6$

**8-5.**    **b.** current tableau optimal

**c.** 15 units $x_1$
         5 units $x_2$
         0 units $x_3$
         $Z = 25$
         10 units resource 1 left over
         0 units resource 2 left over
         0 units resource 3 left over

d. $1.50 premium on $x_2$
new values: $x_1 = 15.5$
$x_2 = 4.5$
$x_3 = 0$
$Z = 26.5$

e. increase by at least $1.50
availability of resource #3 could increase by 5 units or decrease by 10 units

8-7.   c. $y_1 = .86$    d. $Z = 128.57$
$y_2 = 2.43$    e. $x_2 = 30.7$
$y_3 = .71$        $x_3 = .3$
$Z = 131$         $x_4 = 2.7$
                          $Z = 134.55$

# Chapter 9

9-6.   b. 3-7-8-9-10

c. no, assuming there are no delays in the critical path activities and the delays in the noncritical path activities do not exceed the slack time

9-8.   c. d-3, f-0, j-7

d. critical path activities—a-c-f-i

e. It would not because b has a slack time of 3.

f. yes, b-3, d-3, e-8, g-7, h-3, j-7

9-10.   a. B–E–J

b. no impact on B or E but activity J would be started five periods earlier. The critical path would change to B–F–G–K

c. G-1, H-5

9-12.   b. expected project length: 17 weeks

c. A-7, B-0, C-9, D-7, E-0, F-9, G-0

9-14.   a. A-30, B-20, C-15, D-25, E-10, F-0

b. decrease expected time to complete project to 8 days and increase costs by $10 totaling $155

9-16.   a. A-0, B-40, C-0, D-50, E-100, F-175, G-0, H-150, I-0, J-0, K-40

b. normal completion time: 15 weeks, minimum completion time: 11 weeks

c. B–E–J and B–F–G–K

# Chapter 10

10-1.   a. $x_{11} = 35, x_{22} = 1, x_{23} = 29, x_{31} = 18, x_{32} = 27, Z = 601$

b. $x_{11} = 35, x_{21} = 2, x_{22} = 28, x_{31} = 16, x_{33} = 29, Z = 578$

c. $x_{11} = 35, x_{22} = 1, x_{23} = 29, x_{31} = 18, x_{32} = 27, Z = 601$

d. (b)

e. not optimal; optimal solution; $x_{11} = 8, x_{13} = 27, x_{22} = 28, x_{23} = 2, x_{31} = 45, Z = 547$

**10-3.**   **a.** (1,3), (2,3), (2,4)
      **b.** (1,3): $-1$, (2,3): $+1$, (2,4): $-1$
      **c.** (2,4)
      **d.** improvement cell: $\left(-2\right)$
      **e.** $x_{11}$:30, $x_{12}$:8, $x_{14}$:1, $x_{22}$:27, $x_{23}$:25, $x_{34}$:19

**10-5.**   $x_{11} = 200$, $x_{13} = 50$, $x_{22} = 225$, $x_{23} = 175$, $x_{32} = 300$, $Z = 18{,}575$; row minimum initial solution = optimal solution

**10-7.**   $x_{12} = 110$, $x_{22} = 80$, $x_{23} = 80$, $x_{31} = 140$, $x_{32} = 10$, $Z = 67{,}000$

**10-9.**   $x_{11} = 100$, $x_{12} = 150$, $x_{14} = 25$, $x_{15} = 25$, $x_{23} = 150$, $x_{25} = 250$, $x_{34} = 250$, $Z = 8200$

**10-13.**   One solution is A $\rightarrow$ 2, B $\rightarrow$ 1, C $\rightarrow$ 3 for total cost of 180

**10-15.**   One solution is W $\rightarrow$ 1, X $\rightarrow$ 2, Z $\rightarrow$ 3 and Y $\rightarrow$ 4 for a cost of 220

**10-17.**   One solution is I $\rightarrow$ 3, II $\rightarrow$ 2, III $\rightarrow$ 1, and IV $\rightarrow$ 4 for total profit of 380

# Chapter 11

**11-2.**   $x_{12} = 200$, $x_{13} = 200$, $x_{23} = 0$, $x_{24} = 0$, $x_{25} = 400$, $x_{34} = 0$, $x_{45} = 0$, $Z = 3100$

**11-4.**   Raleigh to Greensboro = 250
Columbia to Charlotte = 150
Greensboro to Charlotte = 25
Greensboro to Asheville = 100
Total Cost = 3675

**11-6.**   $x_{12} = 50$
$x_{14} = 50$
$Z = 400$

**11-8.**   Shortest path activities: C, D, E, G, I for total time of 18 days

**11-10.**   Maximum flow of 30: $x_{12} = 10$, $x_{13} = 10$, $x_{14} = 10$, $x_{43} = 5$, $x_{36} = 5$, $x_{46} = 5$, $x_{25} = 10$, $x_{35} = 10$, $x_{57} = 10$, $x_{67} = 10$

# Chapter 12

**12-2.**   produce 20 basic, 15 high precision, and 24 general purpose

**12-4.**   1235.29 first grade first blend
  564.71 first grade second blend
    0     first grade third blend
  938.82 second grade first blend
  790.59 second grade second blend
    0     second grade third blend
  296.47 third grade first blend
  903.53 third grade second blend

**12-6.**   intake: .29 gallons of milk, .01 pounds of beef, .07 dozen eggs

**12-10.**    50,000    in investment type 1 in year 1
             50,000    in investment type 1 in year 3
             50,000    in investment type 1 in year 4
          38,793.10   in investment type 2 in year 1
         506,206.90   in investment type 2 in year 2
          38,793.10   in investment type 2 in year 3
         526,413.79   in investment type 4 in year 4
             95,000    in investment type 4 in year 5
         511,206.90   in investment type 6 in year 1
              5,000    in investment type 6 in year 2
          11,206.90   in investment type 6 in year 3
              5,000    in investment type 6 in year 4
              5,000    in investment type 6 in year 5
         805,979.31   in investment type 6 in year 6

**12-13.**   $x_1 = 30$, $x_2 = 10$, $d_1^- = 0$, $d_1^+ = 0$, $d_2^- = 0$, $d_3^- = 20$, $d_4^+ = 0$, $d_4^- = 10$, $Z = 60p_3$

**12-15.**   $x_1 = 800$, $x_2 = 160$
All goals are achieved except the fourth which is underachieved by 240 units. The optimal solution is not affected by a change in the priorities of goal 1 and goal 3.

**12-17. a.** $x_1 = 1$, $x_2 = 7$, $d_1^- = 66$, $d_1^+ = 0$, $d_2^- = 1$, $d_2^+ = 0$, $d_3^- = 0$, $d_3^+ = 0$, $d_4^- = 16$, $d_4^+ = 0$, $d_5^+ = 0$. All goals achieved except third goal.

    **b.** The solution in part (a) is not optimal.
incoming variable: $d_3^+$
outgoing variable: $d_2^-$

**12-19.**   1235.29 fifths of Grade I used in Prairie High
             564.71 fifths of Grade I used in Lone Wolf
                0    fifths of Grade I used in Wild West
             938.82 fifths of Grade II used in Prairie High
             790.59 fifths of Grade II used in Lone Wolf
                0    fifths of Grade II used in Wild West
             296.47 fifths of Grade III used in Prairie High
             903.53 fifths of Grade III used in Lone Wolf

# Chapter 13

**13-2. a.** LP solution: $x_1 = \frac{3}{2}$, $x_2 = \frac{3}{2}$, $Z = 7\frac{1}{2}$
rounded solution: $x_1 = 1$, $x_2 = 2$, $Z = 5$ or
$x_1 = 2$, $x_2 = 1$, $Z = 7$

    **b.** IP optimal solution: $x_1 = 2$, $x_2 = 1$, $Z = 7$

**13-6.** Atlanta $\rightarrow$ Athens $\rightarrow$ Columbia $\rightarrow$ Chattanooga $\rightarrow$ Birmingham $\rightarrow$ Atlanta with total time of 13 hours

**13-8.** Committee: Cooper, Rainey, Rubin and Earey

**13-10.** Take the following players: Hanson, Stafford, Greve, Ellwanger, Ford, Davis, O'Koren, Sims, Scholle for average points of 11.1

# Chapter 14

**14-2.**  **a.** 80
       **b.** 40
       **c.** $3200
       **d.** 4.5 days
       **e.** 80

**14-6.**  **a.** $1333\frac{1}{3}$ units
       **b.** $666\frac{2}{3}$, $1333\frac{1}{3}$

**14-8.**  $625

**14-10.**  **a.** 17.888
        **b.** 1.174

**14-11.**  **a.** 866.025
        **b.** $\underline{\phantom{0}}$3464.10 setup
           $\dfrac{3464.10 \text{ in-process inventory}}{6928.20}$
        **c.** 10.83

**14-13.**  **a.** 1816.59
        **b.** 1200
        **c.** yes, an EOQ model with uncertain demand would be used

# Chapter 15

**15-1.**  **a.** (1,1)   (2,1)   (3,1)   (4,1)   (5,1)   (6,1)
           (1,2)   (2,2)   (3,2)   (4,2)   (5,2)   (6,2)
           (1,3)   (2,3)   (3,3)   (4,3)   (5,3)   (6,3)
           (1,4)   (2,4)   (3,4)   (4,4)   (5,4)   (6,4)
           (1,5)   (2,5)   (3,5)   (4,5)   (5,5)   (6,5)
           (1,6)   (2,6)   (3,6)   (4,6)   (5,6)   (6,6)
           $P(E_1) = P(E_2) = \cdots P(E_{36}) = 1/36$
           $P(\text{sample space}) = 1$
       **b.** $P(A) = P(1,5) + P(2,4) + P(3,3) + P(4,2) + P(5,1) = 5/36$
       **c.** $P(B) = P(2,1) + P(2,2) + \cdots + P(2,6) = 1/6$
       **d.** $P(C) = P(3,6) + P(6,3) = 1/18$
       **e.** $P(D) = P(1,1) + P(1,2) + P(2,1) = 1/12$

**15-3.**  **a.** 31/36      **b.** 5/18      **c.** 2/9      **d.** 1/36      **e.** 0

**15-5.**  $P(A/B) = .5$
       Since $P(A/B)$ is not equal to $P(A)$, the probability of receiving the contract is dependent on submitting the lowest bid.

**15-7.**  $P(\text{receive loan/have credit rating}) = .54$
       $P(\text{receive loan/no credit rating}) = .22$
       Although more applicants with credit ratings get loans, the percentage without a credit rating that eventually get a loan is large enough for the bank to still accept their applications.

**15-9.**   $P(L_1/W) = .246$      $P(L_2/W) = .3014$      $P(L_3/W) = .4526$
We might use this information to target negotiation proposals, etc.

**15-11.**  $P(x = 1) = .39516$
$P(x = 2) = .16082$
$P(x \leq 5) = .9999925$
Expected number of purchases = .84

**15-13.**  $P(x = 5) = .101$
$P(x = 0) = .0498$
$P(x \geq 2) = .8008$

**15-15.**  $E(y) = 45$
$\sigma_y^2 = 75$
$P(36 \leq y \leq 45) = 3/10$

**15-17.  a.** .6856    **b.** .2115    **c.** .9082    **d.** .2546

## Chapter 16

**16-1.**   **a.** Pessimist's Decision Model: Choose Alternative 2: payoff = 125
**b.** Optimist's Decision Model: Choose Alternative 1: payoff = 2000
**c.** Minimization of Regret Model: Choose Alternative 1: maximum regret = 680
**d.** Average Payoff Decision Model: Choose Alternative 1: average payoff = 737.50

**16-2.**   **a.** Pessimist's Decision Model: Choose Alternative 2: Payoff = 400
**b.** Optimist's Decision Model: Choose Alternative 1: Payoff = 700
**c.** Minimization of Regret Model: Choose Alternatives 1 or 2: maximum regret = 200
**d.** Average Payoff Decision Model: Choose Alternatives 1 or 2: average payoff = 466.67

**16-4.**   **a.** Pessimist's Decision Model: Choose Alternatives I or III with loss of 40
**b.** Optimist's Decision Model: Choose Alternative II with loss of 0
**c.** Minimization of Regret Model: Choose Alternatives I or II with maximum regret of 20
**d.** Average Loss Decision Model: Choose Alternatives I or II with average loss of 25

**16-7.**   Pessimist's Decision Model: Choose Pass with 0 gain
Optimist's Decision Model: Choose Pass with 15 yard gain
Minimization of Regret Model: Choose Pass with maximum regret of 10 yards
Average Payoff Decision Model: Choose Pass with average yards gained of 6.67 yards

**16-9.**   **c.** Pessimist's Decision Model: Choose bank investment with payoff of $5,000
Optimist's Decision Model: Choose invention with payoff of $15,000
Minimization of Regret Model: Choose bank investment with maximum regret of $10,000
Average Payoff Decision Model: Choose to buy property with average payoff of $8,500
**d.** Choose bank investment with EUV of $8,000 .

**16-12.  b.** Start on Cowee Road
**c.** Start on Cowee Road

# *Chapter 17*

**17-1.** $EMV_4 = 30.5$ is highest

**17-3.** **b.** Produce 30 units with EMV = 27
    **c.** $EMV_{PI} = 39$
        $V_{PI} = 39 - 27 = 12$

**17-5.** Buy 150 programs with EMV of $60

**17-9.** **b.** Plan II
    **c.** $50,000
    **d.** The survey should be used.

**17-10.** **a.** Bonds have highest EMV at $112,100
    **b.** $V_{PI} = $12,000$
    **c.** EMV (service) = $115,637
        Value of Test = $3,537 > $5,000 fee so do not use service.

**17-11.** EMV (without weather service) = $30
EMV (with service) = $31.375
Net value of test = $1.375 < $10 fee so do not use service.

**17-12.** EMV (without test) = $60
EMV (with test) = 70.75
Net value of test = 70.75 - 60 = $10.75

# *Chapter 18*

**18-2.** Steady-state probabilities for A = .4167, and B = .5833

**18-4.** $S_I = .3292$, $S_{II} = .31$, $S_{III} = .3608$

**18-6.**
$$\begin{bmatrix} .875 & .100 & .025 \\ .625 & .3125 & .0625 \\ .750 & .150 & .100 \end{bmatrix}$$

**18-8.** **a.**
$$\begin{bmatrix} .5 & .3 & .2 \\ .3 & .6 & .1 \\ .3 & .3 & .4 \end{bmatrix}$$
    **b.** $S_1 = .375$
        $S_2 = .43$
        $S_3 = .195$

**18-10.** **a.**
$$\begin{bmatrix} .1 & .8 & .1 \\ 0 & .5 & .5 \\ 1 & 0 & 0 \end{bmatrix}$$
    **b.** $S_1 = .24$
        $S_2 = .49$
        $S_3 = .27$

**18-12. a.**
$$\begin{bmatrix} 1 & 0 & 0 & 0 \\ .6 & .3 & .1 & 0 \\ .3 & .4 & .2 & .1 \\ 0 & 0 & 0 & 1 \end{bmatrix}$$

**b.**

|  | Paid Up | Bal. Due | Bal. Overdue | Bad Des. |
|---|---|---|---|---|
| next month | 136,000 | 23,000 | 9,000 | 7,000 |
| month after | 152,000 | 10,000 | 4,100 | 7,900 |

**c.** 98.1% of bal. due will become paid up
1.9% of bal. due will become bad debt
86.6% of bal. overdue will become paid up
13.4% of bal. overdue will become bad debt

**18-13.** Probability of going

| from | to | is |
|---|---|---|
| I | II | .5763 |
| I | III | .4237 |
| IV | II | .61 |
| IV | III | .39 |

**18-15. a.**

|  |  | # of Customer Waiting During Current Tanning Session | | | |
|---|---|---|---|---|---|
|  |  | 0 | 1 | 2 | ≥3 |
|  | 0 | .9 | .1 | 0 | 0 |
| # of Customers | 1 | .3 | .6 | .1 | 0 |
| Waiting During | 2 | 0 | .3 | .6 | .1 |
| Previous Session | ≥3 | 0 | 0 | .3 | .7 |

**b.** $S_1 = .675$, $S_2 = .225$, $S_3 = .075$, $S_4 = .025$
2.5% of the time there will be 3 or more people waiting

# Chapter 19

**19-1. a.** Player 1—Strategy 1, Player 2—Strategy A

**b.** Yes. Because the value of the game is the same for both players, neither would opt to change their choice.

**c.** Yes. For player 1, row 1 always yields higher payoffs than row 2.

**19-3. a.** American—Strategy 2, Consolidated—Strategy C

**b.** Pure Strategy. Same reason as problem 19-1.

**c.** Yes. Row 3 dominates row 1, row 2 dominates row 1, and column C dominates column B.

**19-5. a.** Player 1—Strategy 1, Player 2—Strategy A

**b.** Player 1, seeing that player 2 has chosen A, would switch to strategy 2, increasing his gain from 120 to 130. Player 2, seeing that player 1 has switched to strategy 2, would switch to strategy B, reducing his loss from 130 to 115. Player 1 would now switch to strategy 3, then player 2 back to A, then player 1 back to 2, and then the cycle would begin to repeat.

**19-7.**  **a.** Union—Strategy 1, Company—Strategy A

    **b.** Union:     $P(\text{strategy } 1) = .5$

                    $P(\text{strategy } 3) = .5$

                    value = 37.5

        Company: $P(\text{strategy A}) = .833$

                    $P(\text{strategy B}) = .167$

                    value = 37.5

**19-13.** Player 1's formulation:

$$\text{Min } Z = x_1 + x_2 + x_3$$
$$120x_1 + 130x_2 + 118x_3 \geq 1$$
$$145x_1 + 115x_2 + 160x_3 \geq 1$$
$$x_1, x_2, x_3 \geq 0$$

Player 2's formulation:

$$\text{Max } Z = y_1 + y_2$$
$$120y_1 + 145y_2 \leq 1$$
$$130y_1 + 115y_2 \leq 1$$
$$118y_1 + 160y_2 \leq 1$$
$$y_1, y_2 \geq 0$$

**19-17.** The subgame:

|   | A | B |
|---|---|---|
| 2 | 130 | 115 |
| 3 | 118 | 160 |

has the highest payoff. The solution is:

Player 1: $P(\text{strategy } 1) = 0$

            $P(\text{strategy } 2) = .7368$

            $P(\text{strategy } 3) = .2632$

            value = 126.84

Player 2: $P(\text{strategy A}) = .7895$

            $P(\text{strategy B}) = .2105$

            value = 126.84

# *Chapter 20*

**20-1.**  **a.** M/D/1

    **b.** D/M/4

    **c.** M/M/1

**20-3.**  **a.** $1/\mu = 6$ minutes

    **b.** $P(t > 1/6) = .1827$

    **c.** $P(t < 1/20) = 1 - e^{-\mu t} = 0.3935 \ (\approx 39\%)$

**20-5.**  **a.** does not fit, no steady state

    **b.** M/M/1

    **c.** M/M/1

    **d.** M/M/S

    **e.** M/M/1 in parallel

**20-7.**   **a.** $\lambda = 20/\text{hour}; \mu = 60/\text{hour}$

     **b.** $\rho = \lambda/\mu = 1/3$

     **c.** $W = \dfrac{1}{(\mu - \lambda)} = 1.5 \text{ minutes}$

     **d.** $Lq = \dfrac{\lambda^2}{\mu(\mu - \lambda)} = 1/6 \text{ student}$

     **e.** $p_0 = 1 - P_w = 1 - \lambda/\mu = 2/3$

**20-9.**   $\lambda = 10, \mu = 40$

     **a.** $W = \dfrac{1}{\mu - \lambda} = \dfrac{1}{40 - 10} = \dfrac{1}{30} \text{ month}$

     **b.** $Lq = \dfrac{\lambda^2}{\mu(\mu - \lambda)} = \dfrac{10^2}{40(40 - 10)} = 0.083 \text{ units}$

     **c.** $\lambda = 30 \qquad S = 3$

        $\mu = 40 \qquad \rho = 3/4$

        $P_0 = .4712$

        $P(\text{System busy}) = .0442$

        $W = .0255 \text{ month}$

        $Lq = .015 \text{ units}$

**20-11.** use 7 workmen at a total cost of $93.50

**20-13.** present system in 2 parallel lines: $W = 12$ minutes
proposed system (M/M/2): 6.86 minutes

**20-15.** Minimum cost for 2 docks uses 4 workers per dock for total cost of $127.65. So do not rent new dock.

**20-17.**   **a.** $W = 2$ minutes

     **b.** $L = 1, L_q = 1/2$

# Chapter 21

**21-2.**   23.2

**21-4.**   **a.** Mr. Adams should hire another barber.

**21-6.**   $\mu = 10 \text{ minutes}, \bar{x} = 10.5823$

**21-8.**

| Breakdown | Time Between Breakdowns |
|---|---|
| 1 | 80.6 |
| 2 | 44.2 |
| 3 | 52.7 |
| 4 | 344.8 |
| 5 | 52.7 |

**21-10.** $x = -\ln(1 - 2R), 1/2 \le R \le 1$

**21-12.** Poisson distribution cannot be used to describe the calls coming into the switchboard.

**21-15.** 10:03

**21-16.** 12 seconds

**21-18.** 1.6 hours

## Chapter 22

**22-2.** shortest path: A–C–F–G

**22-4.** longest path: 1–2–6–7 = 13 units

**22-7.** solution in millions:

| Seattle | 1 | 1 | 3 |
| Denver | 3 | 3 | 3 |
| Chicago | 2 | 3 | 1 |
| New York | 4 | 3 | 3 |

**22-9.** clothes, books and personal gear

**22-11.** optimal policy is to replace motors in years 2 or 3 and then hold to year 5 for a total cost of $1425.

## Chapter 23

**23-1.**  **a.** 3     **b.** does not exist     **c.** 10     **d.** does not exist     **e.** 2

**23-3.** $3x^2 + 5$

**23-5.**  **a.** 0
**b.** $.7x^{-.3}$
**c.** $15x^2$
**d.** $24x^3 - 6x^2$
**e.** $4x - 4/x^2$

**23-7.**  **a.** $2(x^3 + 3x + 4)(3x^2 + 3)$
**b.** $-4(2x^2 + 3x)^{-5}(4x + 3)$
**c.** $(x + 2)^3(-2)(x^3 - 7)^{-3}(3x^2) + (x^3 - 7)^{-2}(3)(x + 2)^2$
**d.** $(10)(3x^3 - x^2 + 2)(9x^2 - 2x)$
**e.** $(6(6x^2 + 3x)^2 + 9(6x^2 + 3x) - 3)^2(24x^2 + 12x + 3)(12x + 3)$

**23-9.** $x = -4/3$ local maximum.
$x = 1$ local minimum.

**23-11.** 100 yards.

**23-13.** $Q = 912.87$     $S = 547.72$

## Chapter 24

**24-1.**  $x_1 = 5.88$
$x_2 = 67.65$
$\lambda = 3.88$
$Z = 1219.1177$

**24-3.**  $x_1 = 2$
$x_2 = 3$
$\lambda = -1$
$Z = -18$

**24-5.** $x_1 = 0$
$x_2 = 16$
$\lambda = 21.33$

**24-7.** $x_1 = 34$
$x_2 = 56$
$\lambda_1 = 6$
$\lambda_2 = 0$

**24-9.** $x_1 = 40, x_2 = 65$

**24-11.** $x_1 = 2, x_2 = 2.73, Z = 10.46$

# Index